T0189729

Lecture Notes in Computer Science   12570

More information about this subseries at http://www.springer.com/series/7410

Mirosław Kutyłowski · Jun Zhang ·
Chao Chen (Eds.)

Network and System Security

14th International Conference, NSS 2020
Melbourne, VIC, Australia, November 25–27, 2020
Proceedings

Editors
Mirosław Kutyłowski (iD)
Wrocław University of Technology
Wroclaw, Poland

Jun Zhang (iD)
Swinburne University of Technology
Hawthorn, VIC, Australia

Chao Chen (iD)
James Cook University
Douglas, QLD, Australia

ISSN 0302-9743   ISSN 1611-3349   (electronic)
Lecture Notes in Computer Science
ISBN 978-3-030-65744-4   ISBN 978-3-030-65745-1   (eBook)
https://doi.org/10.1007/978-3-030-65745-1

LNCS Sublibrary: SL4 – Security and Cryptology

This Springer imprint is published by the registered company Springer Nature Switzerland AG
The registered company address is: Gewerbestrasse 11, 6330 Cham, Switzerland

Preface

This volume contains the papers selected for and presented at the 14th International Conference on Network and System Security (NSS 2020) held online in Melbourne, Australia, during November 25–27, 2020.

The mission of NSS is to provide a forum for presenting novel contributions related to all theoretical and practical aspects of network and system security, such as authentication, access control, availability, integrity, privacy, confidentiality, dependability, and sustainability of computer networks and systems. NSS aims to provide a leading-edge forum to foster interaction between researchers and developers with the network and system security communities, and to give attendees an opportunity to interact with experts in academia, industry, and governments.

There were 60 submissions. Each submission was reviewed by at least 3, and on average 4.2, Program Committee members. The evaluation process was based on significance, novelty, and technical quality of the submissions. After a rigorous review process and thorough discussion on each submission, the Program Committee selected 17 full papers and 9 short papers to be presented during the NSS conference and published in the LNCS 12570 proceedings. The submission and review process were conducted in the EasyChair system.

The selected papers are devoted to topics such as secure operating system architectures, applications programming and security testing, intrusion and attack detection, cybersecurity intelligence, access control, cryptographic techniques, cryptocurrencies, ransomware, anonymity, trust, recommendation systems, as well as machine learning problems.

In addition to the contributed papers, the following invited keynote speakers presented during NSS 2020: Professor Elisa Bertino, Professor Robert Deng, Professor Xun Yi, Professor Xiaofeng Wang, and Professor Jaideep Vaiday.

We would like to thank our general chairs Abderrahim Benslimane, Yong Xiang, and Javier Lopez-Munoz; our publication co-chairs Chao Chen and Yu Wang; the local chair Lei Pan; our publicity co-chairs Jianfeng Wang and Daniele Antonioli; our special issue co-chairs Weizhi Meng and Shigang Liu; the local organization team; and all the Program Committee members for their support to this conference. Despite the disruptions brought by COVID-19, we have made this conference so successful. We owe this success to all our Organization Committee.

Finally, we also thank Swinburne University of Technology, Australia, for their full support in organizing NSS 2020.

November 2020

Mirosław Kutyłowski
Jun Zhang
Chao Chen

Organization

Program Committee

Cristina Alcaraz	University of Malaga, Spain
Daniele Antonioli	EPFL, Switzerland
Joonsang Baek	University of Wollongong, Australia
Zubair Baig	Deakin University, Australia
Silvio Barra	University of Salerno, Italy
Rida Bazzi	Arizona State University, USA
Pino Caballero-Gil	DEIOC, University of La Laguna, Spain
Arcangelo Castiglione	University of Salerno, Italy
Luca Caviglione	CNR-IMATI, Italy
Chao Chen	James Cook University, Australia
Chia-Mei Chen	National Sun Yat-sen University, Taiwan
Fei Chen	Shenzhen University, China
Jiageng Chen	Central China Normal University, China
Songqing Chen	George Mason University, USA
Ting Chen	University of Electronic Science and Technology of China, China
Xiao Chen	Monash University, Australia
Xiaofeng Chen	Xidian University, China
Hung-Yu Chien	National Chi Nan University, Taiwan
Michal Choras	ITTI Ltd., Poland
K. P. Chow	The University of Hong Kong, Hong Kong
Cheng-Kang Chu	Institute for Infocomm Research, Singapore
Mauro Conti	University of Padua, Italy
Hui Cui	University of Wollongong, Australia
Jesús Díaz-Verdejo	University of Granada, Spain
Keita Emura	National Institute of Information and Communications Technology, Japan
Christian Esposito	University of Naples Federico II, Italy
Song Fang	The University of Oklahoma, USA
Yanick Fratantonio	University of California, Santa Barbara, USA
Alban Gabillon	Université de la Polynésie Française, French Polynesia
Xing Gao	The University of Memphis, USA
Stefanos Gritzalis	University of Piraeus, Greece
Shoichi Hirose	University of Fukui, Japan
Hongxin Hu	Clemson University, USA
Ren Junn Hwang	Tamkang University, Taiwan
Julian Jang-Jaccard	Massey University, New Zealand

Contents

Full Papers

Short Papers

Full Papers

Data Analytics of Crowdsourced Resources for Cybersecurity Intelligence

Nan Sun[1,3]([✉]), Jun Zhang[2], Shang Gao[1], Leo Yu Zhang[1], Seyit Camtepe[3], and Yang Xiang[2]

[1] School of Information Technology, Deakin University, Geelong, Australia
{nan.sun,shang.gao,leo.zhang}@deakin.edu.au
[2] School of Software and Electrical Engineering, Swinburne University of Technology, Melbourne, Australia
{junzhang,yxiang}@swin.edu.au
[3] Data61, CSIRO, Sydney, Australia
seyit.camtepe@data61.csiro.au

Abstract. Cybersecurity incidents are always enduring hazards to organizations and enterprises. The increasing number of high exposure makes cybersecurity-related data a valuable asset, offering chances to identify trends, to make decisions and address challenges for cybersecurity end-users. While facing a considerable amount of data, it is challenging to seek out an agile approach that directly points out the most severe risks and provides security recommendations. In this paper, we propose a novel methodology that begins with data collection, follows by representing information on the knowledge graph and finishes with offering security recommendations based on the systematic data analysis. It demonstrates the power of collective intelligence of social media community and cybersecurity experts and even hackers to monitor vulnerabilities, threats and security trends to further facilitate decision-making and future planning. Also, we develop a prototype to prove the effectiveness and deployability of the methodology. We applied Tweets containing the unique vulnerability identifiers to examine our tool. The analysis results indicate the tool enabling to point out the vulnerabilities with high priority and reflect the historical experiences on weaknesses. With the facilitation of public cybersecurity reports and databases, our tool can offer security recommendations for risk mitigation from various aspects that satisfy end-users' requirement within cybersecurity.

Keywords: Social network · Cybersecurity intelligence · Vulnerability · Weakness

1 Introduction

Cybersecurity attacks and related incidents are perceived as tremendous threats to network users, organizations and enterprises for long periods [35]. The typical impacts caused by cybersecurity incidents depend on the timing and duration,

© Springer Nature Switzerland AG 2020
M. Kutyłowski et al. (Eds.): NSS 2020, LNCS 12570, pp. 3–21, 2020.
https://doi.org/10.1007/978-3-030-65745-1_1

which may involve data breach, reputation damage and financial losses. In the face of overwhelming impact, security professionals spreading over worldwide are devoted to improving cyber resilience. Before attacks happening, comprehensive incident response planning, as well as relevant employee training, are fundamental for preparing and preventing cybersecurity incidents. In case the damage has already taken place, how to respond to the events and recover business to minimize impact are critical for the security team in terms of decision-making.

Moreover, it is worth mentioning that decision-making is continuously influenced by cybersecurity intelligence. Cybersecurity intelligence is what threat information becomes once it has been collected, evaluated, structured and eventually shared across various stakeholders in both academic and industry contexts [16]. However, it is challenging to harvest data and provide analysis for a massive amount of data collected from multiple data sources.

Driven by the community's needs, there is an increasing number of people who diffuse information and exchange ideas through the social network. Many existing researches apply data from social media to conduct analysis on meteorology [17,25], disaster [23,36], economics and politics [13], health [21,31] and other domains [15,30,34]. Also, in the cybersecurity area, there has been some work making use of social media data to predict vulnerability exploits [19], to discover indicator of compromise [29] and detect malware [28]. Social network data will be beneficial to many domains if well-analyzed [32].

If we solely rely on social media data, however, although its volume is enormous, its quality, including reliability, validity, relevancy etc. may be hard to guarantee [26]. Therefore, besides of information from social networks, several publicly available vulnerabilities and threats databases should not be taken lightly due to authority, such as the National Vulnerability Database (NVD) and Exploit Database (EDB). Aiming to bridge the gap between intelligence from security experts and common wisdom, we propose a system that harvests data from authoritative cybersecurity databases as well as social networks and provide efficient analysis for cybersecurity intelligence. Consequently, connecting authoritative security databases and social network data becomes another challenging task.

Generally speaking, launching cyber attacks does have to exploit one or more vulnerabilities. Vulnerabilities are firmly associated with cybersecurity threats, attacks and incidents, which are deemed as a good starting point to connect security databases and social network data. One characteristic among cybersecurity databases is that each record in NVD is directly or indirectly connected with a unique vulnerability identifier named Common Vulnerability Exposure (CVE) ID. If we collect streaming data from social networks according to CVE ID, massive data can be aggregated and then passed for processing and analysis. Combining the vast sea of vulnerability information from social media sites and public databases summarized by experts is the way to surfacing the most relevant information and target threats, as well as providing the holistic intelligence for security incident response.

In this work, we propose a novel data-driven methodology to conduct rapid analysis and measurement on vulnerabilities mentioned on Twitter through a process of incorporating the intelligence from security experts and social crowd. It is demonstrated that the cybersecurity intelligence derived from multi-angle analysis serves security end-users and satisfies their requirements in multiple use cases. We establish a prototype application[1] to illustrate the methodology. The output of the application can be utilized for prioritizing patching, inspecting threats and making proactive security recommendations for those under potential threats with respect to security demand considerations. With the rapid quantitative increase of vulnerabilities at present, the number of vulnerability related information rises unceasingly at the same time. The application can be customized by adding state-of-the-art data sources, which continually provides fresh, up-to-date threat alert and forward-looking suggestions to facilitate cyber intelligence and decision-making. To summarize, our main contributions are summed up as follows:

- Proposing a methodology, generating a bond between cybersecurity experts and Twitter users to drive for cybersecurity intelligence. It is proved to be effective to identify the most critical weaknesses during the specific period, supporting security decision-making and offering predictive suggestions.
- Implementing the data-driven system to demonstrate that the methodology can be deployed for target users, such as enterprises, organizations and individual users, to inspect threats and prepare incident response plans.
- Applying a set of recent Tweets that contain the unique vulnerability identifiers, to the proposed system. It shows that the cybersecurity intelligence derived from multi-angle analysis serves to cybersecurity end-users and satisfies their requirements.

2 Related Work

In this section, we respectively review the literature on vulnerability exploits prediction and cyber threat intelligence using social media data, which are highly related to our work.

2.1 Vulnerability Exploits Prediction

There has been some work on studying vulnerability exploits [14,18,19,22,33] using supervised machine learning methods. Bozorgi et al. [18] was the first to predict whether a vulnerability will be exploited or not by using Open Source Vulnerability (OSVDB) and Common Vulnerabilities and Exposures (CVE) [10] data. The accuracy of the prediction result can reach 90% according to their experiments which were conducted on the balanced positive and negative examples' dataset. Further, Sabott et al. [33] combined Tweets data for the first time to predict real-world and proof-of-concept exploits. However, recent work

---

[1] https://nansun.shinyapps.io/shiny/.

[19] replicated these previous work considering the practical settings, such as imbalance class on exploited and unexploited vulnerabilities. Bullough et al. [19] pointed out previous work seemed unable to predict exploits in practice. On the other hand, the prediction result of whether a vulnerability is likely to be exploited may be valuable to prioritize patching for security professionals, but hard to directly provide actionable security suggestion for enterprises, organizations and individual users.

2.2   Cyber Threat Intelligence Using Social Media Data

Cyber threat intelligence aims to provide highly performable, straightforward and technical-focused guides to deal with incoming specific incident [7,35]. There have been lots of work devoted to the evolution of cyber threat intelligence, involving vulnerability [19,22,33], indicators of compromise [29], malware [28], campaign [24] and so on. Also, among these, there is some work making use of social media data. Liao et al. [29] gathered articles from technical blogs to discover indicator of compromise relating to cyber attacks, which provides valuable guides and warnings on security defense and protection. Khandpur et al. [27] proposed a framework that was designed to detect cybersecurity attack using Tweets. Based on manually selected seed event triggers which target to specific cyberattack category, their approach can automatically identify events. In addition, Gupta et al. [24] collected Tweets data to identify spam campaigns on Twitter, and found phone numbers serve as action tokens in order to scam. As described above, considerable work contributed to cyber threat intelligence using social media data. However, to the best of our knowledge, we are the first to propose a methodology targeting for cyber threat intelligence that bridges the intelligence between security experts and social wisdom to pick up the most threatening weakness from the overload vulnerability related information.

3   Crowdsourced Resources Analytics Methodology

Driven by the huge number of high profile cybersecurity-related data, the insights and strategies for the cybersecurity recommendations should be derived from the most relevant information. Under the assumption that security risk is caused by the vulnerabilities existing, and real vulnerability exploit is the root of security attack and incident, the methodology begins with the data collection from Tweets with the vulnerability identifiers and aggregation with several publicly authoritative cybersecurity databases. Furthermore, we utilize the CWE (which is short for Common Weakness Enumeration) knowledge graph to cluster Tweets and related data into a hierarchical weakness category. Finally, we conduct analysis from multiple perspectives, including data distribution investigation, temporal characteristics analysis, and topic and sentiment exploration, to offer security recommendations. Below, we summarize an overview of the methodology, as shown in Fig. 1 and show how the methodology works after deployment.

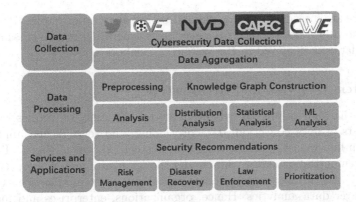

Fig. 1. Cybersecurity crowdsourced resources analytics methodology

Data Collection and Aggregation: The first step is data collection and aggregation. Data collected using Twitter API [6] and information crawled from vulnerability information databases, such as National Vulnerability database [5], together form the datasets used for this study. Should they reference the same Common Vulnerabilities and Exposures (CVE) ID that is a unique vulnerability identifier, the collected data can be aggregated and linked to each other to facilitate the following two steps.

Knowledge Graph Construction: Following the first step, we construct a knowledge graph to cluster, illustrate and visualize collected data. The knowledge graph bridges the gap between collected crowdsourcing data and security expert knowledge, and hierarchically presents data in the early stage of investigations. Also, the knowledge graph provides us with a general view of vulnerabilities as well as revealing fine-grained distribution on weaknesses, which aids in identifying high-risk threats.

Analysis, Evaluation and Deployment: Lastly, we conduct multiscale analysis on the vulnerability, weakness and exposure-related data collected from social media in the form of Twitter to answer the following two questions: "Does CVE related Twitter activities perceive cyber threats?" and "Can we provide effective and operable defense strategies for the threats thriving from crowdsourced intelligence analytic results?" Surrounding the two questions, we present the study on the relationship between CVE related data and cyber threats. By observing the temporal characteristics of Tweets activities, we find that Twitter message stream can directly reflect cyber threats. In addition, we show how we conduct multiscale analysis on nodes that should be on high alert in the knowledge graph, how to connect the nodes with potential threats and cyber attacks, and how to acquire actionable suggestions on proactive defense in Sect. 4.

4   Data-Driven System Architecture and Implementation

In this section, we describe the proposed system based on the cybersecurity crowdsourced resources analytics methodology. Firstly, system overview and architecture are introduced and explained with real-world examples. Besides, we illustrate how data flows, being processed, and generating results cross modules. Also, the datasets deployed in the system are elaborated.

4.1   System Overview and Architecture

Driven by the high volume of cybersecurity-related data, we propose a system that consists of data collection, data processing, and services and applications modules, in line with the methodology proposed as shown in Fig. 1. The data-driven system initially harvests data under the premise of high volume, reliability and quality and ultimately contributes to cybersecurity intelligence depending on multi-layer data analytics. Hence, organizations, enterprises and individual network users can make decisions and plans based on the current trend.

Tweet	CVE	Tweet content
T1	V1	Microsoft Windows iSCSI Packets Handling CVE-2014-0255 Remote Denial of Service Vulnerability
T2	V2	Vuln: Docker CVE-2014-9358 Multiple Directory Traversal Vulnerabilities
T3	V2	CVE-2014-9358 Docker before 1.3.3 does not properly validate image IDs, which allows remote attackers to conduct path traversal attacks
T4	V3	CVE-2014-8956 - Privilege Escalation In K7 Computing Multiple Products [K7Sentry.sys]
T5	V4	CVE-2014-9451 Multiple stack-based buffer overflows in the DIVA web service API (/webservice) in VDG Security SENSE (formerly DIVA) 2.
T6	V5	Vuln: Network Time Protocol CVE-2014-9295 Multiple Stack Based Buffer Overflow Vulnerabilities
T7	V6, V7	Security Notice on Shellshock / CVE-2014-6271 / CVE-2014-7169
T8	V6	More about Bash ShellShock CVE-2014-6271, including an explanation of the Qualys detection https://t.co/qakxcmrna8
T9	V6, V7	VMware investigating bash command injection vulnerability aka Shell Shock (CVE-2014-6271, CVE-2014-7169)

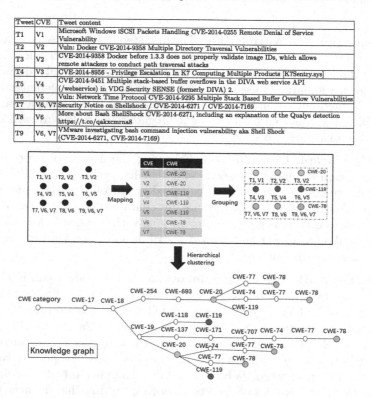

Fig. 2. Knowledge graph construction using sample Tweets

Data collection is one of the main challenging tasks for the system due to the consideration of quantity and quality of data. Throughout the top-down method, the first level is the data collection and aggregation module. There are totally three categories of data involved in this module: (1) social media data retrieved and filtered using cybersecurity keywords, which includes the sensor data codifying intelligence from everyday users, security professionals and even hackers; (2) publicly available cybersecurity databases; (3) other security posture data, which is uploaded by the system users for customization purposes. The unique vulnerability identifiers bridge the gap among various data sources, enabling information sharing and understandings between the authoritative and non-authoritative communities.

The data processing module is responsible for processing the collected and aggregated data, analyzing data and generating results. The prepossessing function filters the irrelevant metadata and extracts the unique vulnerabilities identified by CVE IDs. Before analyzing data, we construct the Common Weakness Enumeration (CWE) knowledge graph that maps the extracted CVE IDs from Tweets to a more general weakness category and visualizes the magnitude of related Tweets. As shown in Fig. 2, each cluster includes Tweets within the same weakness category that are organized in the form of hierarchy and displayed as a knowledge graph. There are two folds of function for the knowledge graph: (1) observing data before conducting analysis and visualizing the overall security trend at a high level; (2) inspecting social media data from the security experts' point of view. Distribution analysis, statistical analysis, and machine learning analysis, including sentiment analysis and opinion mining, are applied in the data processing module to accomplish results. The analytic tools seem straight-forward but can achieve feasible real-time results to deliver for multiple services and applications.

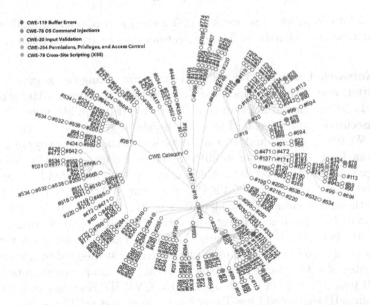

Fig. 3. Knowledge graph highlighting hot discussed weaknesses in 2014

In virtue of the CWE structure provided by NVD, we put the Tweets into the hierarchical structure in accordance with the corresponding CWEs. Each cluster includes Tweets with the same CWE ID and organized in the form of hierarchy, which is displayed as a knowledge graph. Due to the employed data aggregation, this knowledge graph not only gives information on weaknesses but also provides links to Tweets, vulnerabilities, attack patterns and threats. The hierarchical structure created by human intelligence gives us a precise way to cluster our data, which can be viewed as the bridge linking security expert knowledge and our collected data. On the one hand, the collected vulnerability related data is hierarchically grouped in a precise, professional and concise manner. On the other hand, the knowledge graph benefits people with limited cybersecurity knowledge, which helps them analyzing data and realizing forthcoming cyber threats. Figure 3 shows an example of the knowledge graph with the highlight of the top five heated discussion cybersecurity issues reflected in the knowledge graph nodes in 2014.

Finally, there is a services and applications module. Based on end-users' needs and requirements, the module offers security recommendations and facilitates decision-making processes. For example, the system provides analytic results, such as time, number of Tweets related to a threat, sentiment score, and critical points of the content, and mitigation approach to the threats, etc. The end-users can apply the results to assist with risk management, disaster recovery, law enforcement and threat prioritization.

4.2   Crowdsourced Dataset Description

We obtain data from social network (e.g. Twitter) and publicly available cybersecurity databases for analysis. The dataset details are given as follows:

Social Network Dataset. We collect Tweets containing the keyword "CVE" from Twitter, one of the most popular social networks, using Twitter streaming API [6]. Based on the assumption that if a user did not publish any Tweets in three consecutive months related to CVE, he/she may not be an active user in this area. We firstly gather and store all Tweets with the specific keyword "CVE" posted from June to September in 2018 as the seed dataset. Totally, we archive 2917 unique users in the seed dataset and crawl all Tweets posted by these users. We use the regular expression "CVE Prefix + Year + Arbitrary Digits" to filter Tweets with unique vulnerability identifiers posted between 2015–2018.

We also include historical Tweets data with CVE IDs from February 2014 to January 2015 collected by Sabottke et al. [33], in case Twitter users withdraw their contents due to longitudinal exposure control or suspended by Twitter. The key attributes of a Tweet object consist of: (1) id: the unique representation of a Tweet; (2) text: the text of status update; (3) CVE ID: common vulnerabilities and exposures ID extracted from Tweet text; (4) created_at: Tweet creation time represented as UTC; (5) screen_name: Twitter user screen name of a Tweet; (6) coordinates: geographic location of a Tweet. In summary, Tweets published in the past five years (2014–2018) with the keyword "CVE" are saved in a non-repeatable and sequential way.

Authoritative Cybersecurity Databases. Some cybersecurity reports and databases published and updated by organizations and governments are valuable to be crowdsourced with social network data for further analysis and information extraction. We obtain data on vulnerabilities, weaknesses, exposures, attacks and threats from the following authoritative security databases.

1. *Common Vulnerabilities and Exposures:* Common Vulnerabilities and Exposures (CVE) database provides a method of referencing vulnerabilities and exposures [10]. Each CVE ID is an identifier of a vulnerability, which makes it easy for people to share data and information about vulnerabilities across separate platforms, datasets and tools. CVE website documents details on the vulnerability that can be queried by CVE IDs. For example, the Common Vulnerability Scoring System (CVSS) score evaluates the impact of vulnerability by the scoring system, vulnerability type and other detailed information.

2. *Common Weakness Enumeration:* Common weakness enumeration (CWE) is a category of software vulnerabilities and weaknesses, which consists of more than 600 types, such as buffer overflows, cross-site scripting and race conditions. CWE serves as the universal standard for describing weaknesses and provides measuring sticks and baselines for security tools with respect to these weaknesses [11].

3. *Common Attack Pattern Enumeration and Classification:* Common Attack Pattern Enumeration and Classification (CAPEC) database provides a broad category of attack patterns, which are widely used by security analysts, developers and testers [8] Generally, attacks are caused by exploiting known weakness. CAPEC thus links the known vulnerabilities, weaknesses and attack patterns, contributing to advance the understanding of security attack and defences.

4. *The Web Application Security Consortium:* The members of Web Application Security Consortium (WASC) collect and organize the threats to the security of websites. By cooperative effort, industry-standard terminology is developed for describing security threats. WASC and CAPEC can be used together to understand the risks for security professionals, application developers and software vendors [12].

4.3   System Implementation and Deployment

We implement a prototype[2] to demonstrate the proposed system and present more results generated from data analytics using R Shiny framework [20]. The interrelated analysis activities are initially deployed in the prototype. It starts from collecting and aggregating data, constructing knowledge graph, conducting analytics, and ends with offering security recommendations based on assembled analysis methods.

Using a year as a unit of time, this tool provides an overview of social media posts on vulnerabilities. Research communities and industries can learn

---

[2] https://nansun.shinyapps.io/shiny/.

and summarize past experiences to avoid potential forthcoming incidents, and make plans for the future (e.g. next year) incident responses to improve cyber resilience. According to the posted Tweets in one month, the popularity of weakness/vulnerability discussed may provide suggestions on patching/upgrading priority and employee education, answering questions such as What's the new weakness/vulnerability appearing on social media today? Is there any brute increase in the number of specific weakness? Daily inspection can provide quick response on any unusual pattern and threat. Also, the corresponding attack patterns, threat classification and mitigation strategies can be found in virtue of public cybersecurity databases embedded in this tool. Each process can be customized according to the specific requirements and characteristics, such as loading data from external sources and conducting the analysis of any combination of existing knowledge.

5   Analysis, Applications and Evaluation

We conduct analysis on the collected 2014–2018 Tweets data, mainly focusing on distribution analysis, statistical analysis and machine learning analysis to evaluate the proposed system. In this section, we show the analytic results in the perspective of three use cases, illustrating how to apply the cybersecurity intelligence generated from the studies to real-world scenarios to satisfy cybersecurity end-user requirements.

5.1   Security Data Statistics and Distribution

The first step in data analysis is to understand the data. After collected Tweets with CVE IDs falling under CWE knowledge graph, we investigate the CWE category distribution to evaluate the reliability of data. When constructing the CWE tree, we try to map each CVE ID in a Tweet to corresponding CWE ID. Most of the Tweets can match the corresponding CWE IDs by querying the National Vulnerability Database (NVD), but there are some exceptional situations in reality. Totally, there are five categories of Tweets CWE labels. "NVD-CVE-CWE" stands for the category of Tweets can be labeled as CWE ID by matching CVE ID. "NVD-CWE-noinfo" is a weakness category in the NVD, which represents the CVE lacking sufficient information to classify it to a specific weakness type. Due to the fact that NVD is only using a subset of CWE for mapping instead of the entire CWE, and the weakness type is not covered by that subset, recorded as "NVD-CWE-other". "Reject" is the label representing the category of CVEs that are in NVD, but currently do not show up in NVD search results. "NA's" means that the CVE ID is not recorded in NVD.

According to the distribution result shown in Table 1, we find that the most significant proportion in the distribution is NVD-CVE-CWE, taking up 83.7%. It demonstrates the majority of vulnerabilities mentioned in the collected Tweets maps the corresponding weaknesses in the NVD.

Every month, hundreds of vulnerabilities emerge and provide attack surface for people with malicious intents. Looking into exploits distribution is essential to provide valuable information on defense because many attacks and incidents are achieved by exploiting known vulnerabilities. We further investigate the exploits distribution; here, we adopt Carl et al. method as [33] to find the groundtruth of vulnerability exploits.

As shown in Table 1, there are two types of exploits, namely real-world exploits and proof-of-concept (PoC) exploits. A real-world exploit is considered as an exploit used for real-world cyber attacks. The groundtruth of real-world exploit comes from Symantec's anti-virus (AV) signatures [1] and intrusion-protection (IPS) signatures [2]. Whereas, a PoC exploit does not cause harm, which is performed to prove that the hacker can exploit the vulnerability to attack. By querying ExploitDB [9] and Microsoft security advisories exploitability index, PoC exploits are identified.

Table 1. Distribution on the knowledge graph and exploits

Distribution	Category	Percentage
Knowledge graph	NVD-CVE-CWE	83.7%
	NVD-CVE-noinfo	8.0%
	NVD-CVE-other	3.0%
	Reject	2.9%
	NA's	2.4%
Exploits	Real-world Exploit	33.4%
	PoC Exploit	33.4%
	Other	33.2%

Looking over the exploits distribution on 2014 Tweets as an example, we find that vulnerabilities exploited by the real world, vulnerabilities exploited by PoC and unexploited vulnerabilities take up similar proportion (e.g. 33.4%, 33.4%, and 33.2% respectively) in our collected Tweets dataset. While, in the real world, very few vulnerabilities are exploited compared to the rapidly increasing number of these, but can cause tremendous damage. This distribution suggests that a large part of vulnerability-related Tweets are discussing the exploited vulnerabilities using which it is entirely possible to cause cyber attacks according to our dataset. It also demonstrates our dataset is capable of revealing to reveal potential cyber threats, attacks and security incidents.

5.2   System Implementation and Evaluation

Use Case 1: Identify Overall Trends Within Cybersecurity. Identifying the overall trends within cybersecurity directly singles out recurring issues, which can help the emergency managers address cybersecurity challenges and establish

	2014	2015	2016	2017	2018
CWE-119	0.21	0.19	0.16	0.16	0.08
CWE-78	0.09	0.00	0.00	0.01	0.01
NVD-CWE-noinfo	0.08	0.07	0.03	0.01	0.00
CWE-264	0.08	0.09	0.10	0.06	0.04
CWE-20	0.07	0.07	0.09	0.11	0.07
CWE-310	0.07	0.01	0.02	0.01	0.01
CWE-79	0.05	0.03	0.03	0.04	0.04
CWE-94	0.04	0.02	0.01	0.02	0.00
CWE-416	0.04	0.00	0.03	0.02	0.02
CWE-399	0.04	0.03	0.02	0.01	0.01
CWE-200	0.03	0.06	0.07	0.08	0.04

Fig. 4. Trend across five years on heated discussion weaknesses

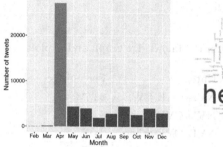 

(a) Tweets found with knowledge graph node CWE-119 in 2014

(b) Related Tweets text word cloud

Fig. 5. News reporting security incident - Heartbleed

a framework for further research into specific issues. Also, the trend facilitates law enforcement on the next potential targets that may be chosen by cybercriminals.

To observe the overall trend, we extract CVE IDs from each Tweet and map the vulnerability to a more general category. By ranking the number of the most frequently mentioned vulnerability category on Twitter, we visualize the top five heated discussed weaknesses based on the percentage of discussed on the CWE tree node through the year in Fig. 4. If vertically comparing the result, we can get the overall trends across five years. As shown in Fig. 4, CWE−119 buffer errors are always the most frequently mentioned weakness in the last five years. This kind of weakness usually happens under the condition that software can read or write the memory location outside the boundary of a buffer when performing a particular operation on memory. It is worth noting that CWE−310 Cryptographic Issues reached the peak in 2014 and then eased in the next four years, due to many vulnerabilities in Android applications related to SSL server certificates were discovered in 2014. Another feature is the CWE−200 information

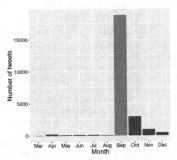 

(a) Tweets found with knowl-   (b) Related Tweets text word
edge graph node CWE-78 in   cloud
2014

Fig. 6. News reporting security incident - Shellshock (aka Bashdoor)

leak/disclosure, which should be highly prioritized due to the nearly doubled number since 2015.

According to the trend analysis of Annual Cybersecurity Report [3], in 2015, the top five critical risk weaknesses were buffer error (CWE-119), cross-site scripting (CWE-79), information leak/ disclosure (CWE-200), permissions, privileges and access control (CWE-264) and improper input validation (CWE-20), which precisely align with the trend plotted in Fig. 4. This result demonstrates that Twitter activities can indeed reflect the trends in vulnerabilities and related threats as a way of evaluation. Also, the analysis provides an approach to mirror the real world trend on highly regarded weaknesses, also facilitates the research community and industry to review and reflect on the past and future security threats.

Use Case 2: Risk Management. The multilevel analysis results can facilitate risk management effectively. The temporal characteristics identify, define, quantify the risks, threats and vulnerabilities, providing real-time monitoring in risk management for prioritization and risks rating. Also, the machine learning-based analysis contains sentiment analysis and opinion mining, helping seek out the viewpoints of cybersecurity-related Tweets and providing an in-depth description of the separation of concerns before making decisions.

We observe the fluctuation of Tweets changing over time and present the temporal characteristics of vulnerability related Tweets. Abnormal temporal features, such as a sudden increase in the number of specific weakness related Tweets or Tweets discussing a particular type of weakness take up the majority of traffic, would be taking further observation. To further investigate the text of Tweets, we generate a word cloud to inspect high-frequency words to show the content of responses on social media (see Fig. 5, 6 for examples). Besides, we apply sentiment analysis (see Fig. 7) to observe the opinions of reactions to the weakness nodes on the knowledge graph.

Table 2. News reporting security-related incidents

Date	April, 2014	June, 2014	Sep, 2014	Oct, 2014
Incident	The Heartbleed bug is a serious vulnerability, which allows stealing the information protected by the Secure Socket Layer (SSL) and Transport Layer Security (TLS) encryption used to secure the Internet	The Man-in-the-middle (MITM) attack affects the SSL and TLS protocols	Shellshock (aka Bashdoor) could enable an attacker to causeBash to execute arbitrary commands and gain unauthorized access	The POODLE attack (short for Padding Oracle On Downgraded Legacy Encryption) is an exploit that takes advantage of the way some browsers deal with encryption
Weakness	Buffer Errors	Cryptographic Issues	OS Command Injection	Cryptographic Issues
Knowledge Graph Node	CWE-119	CWE-310	CWE-78	CWE-310
CVE identifier	CVE-2014-0160	CVE-2014-0224	CVE-2014-6271	CVE-2014-3566
% of Tweets in the month	49.22%	27.71%	39.84%	8.6%
% of Tweets in the year	9.72%	2.38%	6.2%	1.51%
Average sentiment score	Pos: 0.26 Neg: 0.70	Pos: 0.20 Neg: 0.75	Pos: 0.19 Neg: 0.79	Pos: 0.23 Neg: 0.80
Keyword	HEARTBLEED	OpenSSL, MITM	SHELLSHOCK	POODLE

In Table 2, we summarize the news reporting cybersecurity incidents directly reflected in the discussion on Twitter, including analysis results generated from Tweets distribution, statistics and text. As a proof-of-concept, these security events that happened in 2014 validate that the temporal characteristics of online CVE discussion can straightly reflect the threats in the real world. For example, in April 2014, 49.22% of Tweets in this month are categorized into node CWE−119 buffer errors in the knowledge graph, which takes up almost half of the traffic in this month. If we visualize the number of Tweets related to CWE-119, there is explosive growth in April, as shown in Fig. 5(a), which raises the alarm to security professionals. Going further and looking at the contents of related Tweets, "heartbleed" and "OpenSSL" are the keywords that represent the topics of the incidents as shown in Fig. 5(b). Also, the 0.70 negative sentiment score calculated by using the National Research Council (NRC) emotional lexicon suggests Twitter users took a dim view of the events.

We adopt three layers of sentiment analysis. Firstly, we investigate users' attitude towards specific nodes in the knowledge graph. For example, as Fig. 7(a) illustrates, the attitudes of most online responses to CWE-119 buffer errors in April 2014 tend to fear and sadness. This layer sentiment analysis not only provides a general view on public opinion but also offers real-time trend of users responses to vulnerability and related threats. Moreover, the sentiment and emotion of people's reactions can reflect the damage of a specific node/period if compared with other nodes/periods. According to Table 2, the average

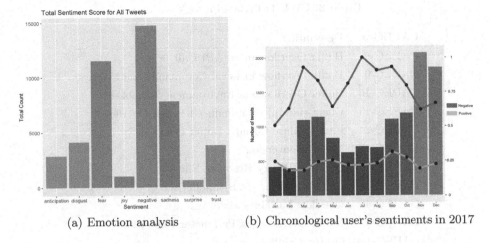

(a) Emotion analysis   (b) Chronological user's sentiments in 2017

Fig. 7. Emotion and sentiment analysis

sentiment scores of the three major cybersecurity incidents that have brought significant hazard in 2014 are listed. It is shown that the positive scores are all under 0.26, while the negative scores are above 0.7. While, when comparing with the average sentiment scores of 2017 displayed in Fig. 7(b), the positive scores in 2017 are generally higher than 0.26, while most of the negative scores given over the months are above 0.7, indicating that 2017 is indeed a challenging year for cybersecurity. Thirdly, sentiment scores can provide us with more information on vulnerabilities and related incidents that may be as supplements to the formerly discussed analysis approaches. As shown in Fig. 7(b), the negative sentiment score in July 2017 is abnormally high, although the number of Tweets posted in that month is relatively small, which is as the result of the Equifax data breach caused by exploiting the vulnerability CVE-2017-5638 and CWE-20 Improper Input Validation. Under the same node CWE-20 in the knowledge graph, another serve vulnerability indexed CVE-2017–9791 takes up the majority of the traffic of Twitter in that month. In summary, sentiment analysis provides a more in-depth insight on the text of vulnerability related Tweets, monitors users' opinions and facilitates plans strategically coping cyber attacks in the next step. The analysis results from multiple perspectives directly aid defenders monitor threats in real-time as well as knowing attackers in time, stopping or at least mitigating its impact and protecting most during risk management.

Use Case 3: Security Control and Business Continuity. Security recommendations corresponding to specific attack pattern and threat provide well-defined and mature processes that support information security, management obligations and end-user security awareness. Furthermore, following the standard practices and recommendations, security control should be applied at a high level of confidence. In the worst circumstances, organizations can maintain

Table 3. CWE-119 related attack patterns

CAPEC #	Description
CAPEC-8	Buffer Overflow in an API Call
CAPEC-9	Buffer Overflow in Local Command-Line Utilities
CAPEC-10	Buffer Overflow via Environment Variables
CAPEC-14	Client-side Injection-induced Buffer Overflow
CAPEC-24	Filter Failure through Buffer Overflow
CAPEC-42	MIME Conversion
CAPEC-44	Overflow Binary Resource File
CAPEC-45	Buffer Overflow via Symbolic Links
CAPEC-46	Overflow Variables and Tags
CAPEC-47	Buffer Overflow via Parameter Expansion
CAPEC-100	Overflow Buffers

business continuity and recover instantly after the disaster with offered recommendations.

When performing data aggregation, we link the collected Tweets to Common Attack Pattern Enumeration and Classification (CAPEC) database. As explained before, CAPEC is a public cybersecurity resource that provides us a comprehensive dictionary of attack patterns that can be employed by hackers and adversaries. It guides governments, organizations and individual users to prepare for the potential incidents in advance. For example, the prolonged critical node CWE−119 buffer errors related attack patterns are shown in Table 3. For security professionals, including security analysts, developers and testers, they can check the attack patterns to obtain information on the weakness related information and corresponding security recommendations on defences. Besides, WASC is made up of an international group of cybersecurity experts, organizational representatives and practitioners regularly share open-source on security for the World Wide Web. For people with limited knowledge of cybersecurity, WASC provides specific threat classification to advance community understanding. We take the node CWE-119 buffer errors as an example: its threat classification WASC-7 corresponds to the CAPEC attack patterns, which refers to buffer overflow attacks [4]. According to WASC threat classification, avoiding buffer overflows in the first place is the easiest way to address it. Also, runtime protection measures can be applied as defence-in-depth actions. Besides of buffer overflow attacks, WASC provides information on other attacks and threats classification, such as denial-of-service, information leakage and cross-site scripting, which also gives actionable suggestions on defences.

The attack pattern and threat classification aligning with weaknesses have been embedded and can be queried from our deployed system. Based on the analysis result, users can get useful information on attack patterns, threat classification and corresponding security suggestions on prevention, mitigation and defence. Once having obtained detailed security recommendations, the organizations can be protected if they follow the industry-standard best practices, conduct regular employee training and recover immediately after the exploits to ensure business continuity.

6 Conclusion

A vulnerability, known as an attack surface, belongs to a kind of weakness that can be exploited to cause threats to the system and steal data from the environment. Under the circumstance that a rapidly increasing number of security incidents damage lives and reputations, it is urgent and significant to improve cyber resilience. Individual users, hackers, or cybersecurity capable people would like to share, exchange, and discuss vulnerability related information and publish breaking news on social network platforms. Furthermore, security experts crowdsource collective knowledge to update and maintain vulnerability records and additional metadata on severity, categorization, and urgency of the threat. To combat information overload, we first proposed a methodology that begins with aggregating and structuring security relevant data combined with the intelligence of users active on Twitter and cybersecurity experts, then binds multiple data analysis strategies to support cybersecurity decision-making. It highlights the threatening factors and offers corresponding security recommendations by querying the integrated public cybersecurity databases. Besides, we applied 2014–2018 Twitter data combined with these public cybersecurity databases to the implemented prototype system. The use cases demonstrate that analysis results generated from the system are efficient to serve cybersecurity end-users for better planning, proper management, and recovery from disasters etc.

References

1. Symantec A-Z listing of threats & risks (2014). http://www.symantec.com/securityresponse/landing/azlisting.jsp. Accessed 26 Dec 2018
2. Symantec attack signatures (2014). http://www.symantec.com/security_response/attacksignatures/. Accessed 26 Dec 2019
3. Annual cybersecurity report (2016). http://www.ntt.co.jp/sc/media/NTTannual2016_e_web_lock.pdf. Accessed 11 Nov 2019
4. Buffer overflow (2018). http://projects.webappsec.org/w/page/13246916/Buffer%20Overflow/. Accessed 28 Dec 2019
5. National vulnerability dataset (2018). https://nvd.nist.gov/
6. Twitter APIs (2018). https://developer.twitter.com/en/docs
7. What is cyber threat intelligence? (2018). https://www.cisecurity.org/blog/what-is-cyber-threat-intelligence/. Accessed 11 Sept 2019
8. Common attack pattern enumeration and classification (2019). https://capec.mitre.org/. Accessed 20 Dec 2019
9. Exploits database by offensive security (2019). http://www.exploit-db.com/. Accessed 26 Dec 2019

10. Common vulnerabilities and exposures (2020). http://cve.mitre.org/. Accessed 11 Feb 2020
11. Common weakness enumeration (2020). http://cwe.mitre.org/index.html. Accessed 11 Feb 2020
12. Web application security consortium threat classification (2020). http://projects. webappsec.org/w/page/13246970/ThreatClassificationEnumerationView/. Accessed 20 Feb 2020
13. Allcott, H., Gentzkow, M.: Social media and fake news in the 2016 election. J. Econ. Perspect. **31**(2), 211–36 (2017)
14. Almukaynizi, M., Nunes, E., Dharaiya, K., Senguttuvan, M., Shakarian, J., Shakarian, P.: Proactive identification of exploits in the wild through vulnerability mentions online. In: International Conference on Cyber Conflict (CyCon US), pp. 82–88. IEEE (2017)
15. Atefeh, F., Khreich, W.: A survey of techniques for event detection in Twitter. Comput. Intell. **31**(1), 132–164 (2015)
16. Barnum, S.: Standardizing cyber threat intelligence information with the structured threat information expression (STIX). Mitre Corporation **11**, 1–22 (2012)
17. Bird, D., Ling, M., Haynes, K., et al.: Flooding Facebook-the use of social media during the Queensland and Victorian floods. Aust. J. Emerg. Manag. **27**(1), 27 (2012)
18. Bozorgi, M., Saul, L.K., Savage, S., Voelker, G.M.: Beyond heuristics: learning to classify vulnerabilities and predict exploits. In: Proceedings of the 16th ACM SIGKDD International Conference on Knowledge Discovery and Data Mining, pp. 105–114. ACM (2010)
19. Bullough, B.L., Yanchenko, A.K., Smith, C.L., Zipkin, J.R.: Predicting exploitation of disclosed software vulnerabilities using open-source data. In: Proceedings of the 3rd ACM on International Workshop on Security and Privacy Analytics, pp. 45–53. ACM (2017)
20. Chang, W., Cheng, J., Allaire, J., Xie, Y., McPherson, J., et al.: Shiny: web application framework for R. R package version **1**(5) (2017)
21. Chou, W.Y.S., Hunt, Y.M., Beckjord, E.B., Moser, R.P., Hesse, B.W.: Social media use in the united states: implications for health communication. J. Med. Internet Res. **11**(4), e48 (2009)
22. Edkrantz, M., Truvé, S., Said, A.: Predicting vulnerability exploits in the wild. In: 2015 IEEE 2nd International Conference on Cyber Security and Cloud Computing (CSCloud), pp. 513–514. IEEE (2015)
23. Gao, H., Barbier, G., Goolsby, R., Zeng, D.: Harnessing the crowdsourcing power of social media for disaster relief. Technical report, Arizona State Univ Tempe (2011)
24. Gupta, P., Perdisci, R., Ahamad, M.: Towards measuring the role of phone numbers in twitter-advertised spam. In: Proceedings of the 2018 on Asia Conference on Computer and Communications Security, pp. 285–296. ACM (2018)
25. Hyvärinen, O., Saltikoff, E.: Social media as a source of meteorological observations. Mon. Weather Rev. **138**(8), 3175–3184 (2010)
26. Immonen, A., Pääkkönen, P., Ovaska, E.: Evaluating the quality of social media data in big data architecture. IEEE Access **3**, 2028–2043 (2015)
27. Khandpur, R.P., Ji, T., Jan, S., Wang, G., Lu, C.T., Ramakrishnan, N.: Crowdsourcing cybersecurity: cyber attack detection using social media. In: Proceedings of the 2017 ACM on Conference on Information and Knowledge Management, pp. 1049–1057. ACM (2017)

28. Kwon, B.J., Mondal, J., Jang, J., Bilge, L., Dumitras, T.: The dropper effect: insights into malware distribution with downloader graph analytics. In: Proceedings of the 22nd ACM SIGSAC Conference on Computer and Communications Security, pp. 1118–1129. ACM (2015)

29. Liao, X., Yuan, K., Wang, X., Li, Z., Xing, L., Beyah, R.: Acing the IOC game: toward automatic discovery and analysis of open-source cyber threat intelligence. In: Proceedings of the 2016 ACM SIGSAC Conference on Computer and Communications Security, pp. 755–766. ACM (2016)

30. Mittal, S., Das, P.K., Mulwad, V., Joshi, A., Finin, T.: Cybertwitter: using twitter to generate alerts for cybersecurity threats and vulnerabilities. In: Proceedings of the 2016 IEEE/ACM International Conference on Advances in Social Networks Analysis and Mining, pp. 860–867. IEEE Press (2016)

31. Moorhead, S.A., Hazlett, D.E., Harrison, L., Carroll, J.K., Irwin, A., Hoving, C.: A new dimension of health care: systematic review of the uses, benefits, and limitations of social media for health communication. J. Med. Internet Res. 15(4), e85 (2013)

32. Rathore, M.M., Paul, A., Ahmad, A., Imran, M., Guizani, M.: Big data analytics of geosocial media for planning and real-time decisions. In: 2017 IEEE International Conference on Communications (ICC), pp. 1–6. IEEE (2017)

33. Sabottke, C., Suciu, O., Dumitras, T.: Vulnerability disclosure in the age of social media: exploiting twitter for predicting real-world exploits. In: USENIX Security Symposium, pp. 1041–1056 (2015)

34. Sun, N., Lin, G., Qiu, J., Rimba, P.: Near real-time twitter spam detection with machine learning techniques. Int. J. Comput. Appl. (2020). https://doi.org/10.1080/1206212X.2020.1751387

35. Sun, N., Zhang, J., Rimba, P., Gao, S., Zhang, L.Y., Xiang, Y.: Data-driven cybersecurity incident prediction: a survey. IEEE Commun. Surv. Tutor. 21(2), 1744–1772 (2019)

36. Yates, D., Paquette, S.: Emergency knowledge management and social media technologies: a case study of the 2010 haitian earthquake. In: Proceedings of the 73rd ASIS&T Annual Meeting on Navigating Streams in an Information Ecosystem-Volume 47, p. 42. American Society for Information Science (2010)

Security Evaluation of Smart Contract-Based On-chain Ethereum Wallets

Purathani Praitheeshan$^{(\boxtimes)}$ [ID], Lei Pan [ID], and Robin Doss [ID]

School of IT, Deakin University, Geelong, VIC 3220, Australia
{ppraithe,l.pan,robin.doss}@deakin.edu.au

Abstract. Ethereum is a leading blockchain platform that supports decentralised applications (Dapps) using smart contract programs. It executes cryptocurrency transactions between user accounts or smart contract accounts. Wallets are utilised to integrate with Dapps to manage and hold users' transactions and private keys securely and effectively. Ethereum wallets are available in different forms, and we especially examine on-chain smart contract wallets to measure their safeness property. We have conducted an exploratory study on 86 distinct bytecode versions of Ethereum smart contract wallets and analysed them using four popular security scanning tools. We have identified that, on average, 10.2% of on-chain wallets on the Ethereum platform are vulnerable to different problems. We propose a novel analysis framework to classify the security problems in smart contract wallets using the experimental data. Most of the vulnerabilities detected from smart contract wallets are related to security issues in programming code and interaction with external sources. Our experimental results and analysis data are available at https://github.com/ppraithe/on-chain-wallet-contracts.

Keywords: On-chain wallet · Security · Smart contract · Vulnerability

1 Introduction

Ethereum is a fast-evolving blockchain platform for cryptocurrency transactions with the support of wallets and decentralized applications [1,25]. The current market value of Ethereum is around 44.5 billion USD, according to the statistics provided by CoinMarketCap[1] in August, 2020. Ethereum's cryptocurrency denomination is called Ether or ETH for short. Losing an Ether is a significant financial loss as Ether's price varies between 150 and 350 USD during the past a few months[2]. Most Ethers are held in Ethereum wallets. These wallets are in different forms, including on-chain contract wallets, desktop wallets, mobile wallets, browser extensions, web-based wallets, hardware wallets, paper wallets,

---

[1] https://coinmarketcap.com/currencies/ethereum/.
[2] https://ethereumprice.org.

© Springer Nature Switzerland AG 2020
M. Kutyłowski et al. (Eds.): NSS 2020, LNCS 12570, pp. 22–41, 2020.
https://doi.org/10.1007/978-3-030-65745-1_2

and software wallets. On-chain wallets are implemented in smart contracts that are a script type of programming code running on the Ethereum platform [1,6]. Smart contract programs are used to implement wallet functions and business logic. Users need to deploy the smart contract wallet on Ethereum blockchain and process their cryptocurrency transactions with other user accounts or contract accounts. Contract types of wallets are more convenient and trustful since they run on Ethereum blockchain, and they are immutable once they deployed to the chain. However, security vulnerabilities in smart contract wallets have not been extensively analyzed.

This paper empirically studies the existing on-chain smart contract wallets on the Ethereum platform using popular security analysis tools. We choose the on-chain wallet contracts in our study to compute the security measures in smart contracts wallets running on Ethereum and identify reliable wallets to manage crypto assets safely. The Ethereum contract wallets interact with several components such as Dapps, contract libraries, third-party libraries, APIs, key management applications, smart contract accounts, and real user accounts on Ethereum [10]. Figure 3 in Appendix A, illustrates the inter-playing components with smart contract wallets on Ethereum. The wallet contracts call external libraries, accounts, and third-party web services through oracle interfaces. Decentralized applications utilize these contract wallets to govern their token/cryptocurrency transactions and private/public key management. These external linkages with the smart contract wallets cause security problems. Smart contract-based wallets rely on the program logic written in Solidity or Vyper languages [6,12]. Potential vulnerabilities in wallet contracts are identified related to imperfect coding practices and issues in programming language designs.

Due to the immutable feature in smart contract wallets, they are required to be implemented securely, and developers need to guarantee the reliability of the wallet contract source code. The wallet users do not know how these smart contract wallets are implemented and functioning on Ethereum. There is a research gap of finding state of the art on Ethereum on-chain wallet functions, existing vulnerabilities on wallet contracts, and available remedies or solutions to prevent on-chain wallets from attackers. To bridge these missing pieces of research, we investigated 86 distinct versions of smart contract wallets from the Ethereum platform[3] and scanned them using security analysis tools [9] to detect any critical vulnerabilities. Our contribution to this research are:

- Analyzing the state of the art security issues and attacks on Ethereum wallet contracts
- Proposing a new security analysis framework to classify the potential security issues existing in on-chain wallet contracts and how each element in the framework impacts
- Empirically evaluating the security vulnerabilities on collected data set of smart contract wallets using popular scanning tools.

The remainder of the paper is organized as follows. Section 2 is explaining background information about on-chain wallet contracts, major functionalities,

---
[3] https://www.ethereum.org/.

the literature of recent attacks on on-chain wallets, and proper analysis tools for scanning smart contract wallets. A new framework is presented in Sect. 3 to describe how we conducted the qualitative analysis of existing wallet contracts to identify potential security issues. Section 4 describes experiments, results, and discussion based on our evaluation data and solutions from GitHub smart contract developers, and Ethereum stack exchange communities. Section 5 concludes the paper.

2   Related Work

Ethereum wallets carry valuable assets, access credentials of user accounts, and transaction data. Therefore, adversaries are keen to attack, especially on-chain wallets that operate using the execution of smart contract programs. Smart contract programs are implemented using script-type languages [18], including Solidity, Vyper, and Bamboo. Solidity is the first language used to develop Ethereum smart contract wallets. Our analysis mainly focuses on the wallets implemented using solidity programming. The business rules in on-chain wallets are implemented on a smart contract program and compiled to an executable byte code using a solidity compiler (Solc). The compiled byte code is deployed to Ethereum Virtual Machine (EVM) by the owner of the wallet contract [6]. The EVM creates an abstraction to execute the smart contract bytecode on the Ethereum network. The smart contract functions are invoked by a user with his private signature or key to run the required operation. The deployed smart contract wallets cannot be modified, and they are immutable. They are required to be implemented using best practices and security measures on solidity programming [7]. Smart contract developers have to be aware of the issues on on-chain wallet contracts during their implementation phase.

2.1   On-chain Smart Contract Wallets on Ethereum

We collected 20 distinct smart contract wallets and their available versions from Etherescan explorer[4]. At least one version has both solidity source code and bytecode. Most of the deployed wallet instances have their compiled bytecode generated during their creation time on Ethereum blockchain. We classified them into four categories based on their behaviours and functionalities: Multisig wallets, Smart wallets, Retailer wallets, and Controller wallets, as listed in Table 1.

Multisig wallets use external Parity library functions to execute critical operations. Smart wallets call functions from SmartWalletLibrary contract. These wallet contracts can call an external function from another contract or library. This feature is facilitating to re-use the existing smart contract or library functions to fulfill any specific requirements. Retailer wallets deal with tokens and ether transactions for buying, selling, transferring, mining, trading, and withdrawing operations. Controller wallets are managing transaction logs, time-locked events, token balance updates, and proxy logic implementations. Further,

---

[4] https://etherscan.io/.

Table 1. Four on-chain smart contracts wallet categories

Multisig wallets	Smart wallets	Retailer wallets	Controller wallets
MultiSigWallet	SmartWallet	ConsumerWallet	Controller
BitgoMultisig	DapperSmart	SpendableWallet	TimeLocked
IvtMultiSig	ArgentSmart	BasicWallet	Intermediate
NiftyMultiSig	AutoWallet	Teambrella	EidooUpdate
CapitalMultisig	GenosisSafe	BitgoForwarder	LogicProxy

these wallets hold and control users' cryptographic keys [21]. Decentralized applications (Dapp) utilize these Ethereum wallets as an external service component to manage their users' private/public key pairs.

2.2 Security Attacks on On-chain Wallet Contracts

Smart contract wallets invoke external resources such as the existing library, other smart contract functions, API calls, and third-party services, they are vulnerable due to programming issues, human errors, and malicious hacks [5]. Several smart contract vulnerabilities are identified by researchers and ranked them according to critical issues. A few of them are most relevant to the wallet contracts, including unsecured fund, destroyable smart contracts, lock fund forever, non-restricted write operation, non-restricted fund transfer, integer overflow, integer underflow, re-entrance and external call problems [2,20]. These vulnerabilities caused real hacks on smart contract wallets in recent years, and attackers were benefited by stealing a massive amount of Ethers.

The first parity multi-sig wallet attack happened in July 2017, and attackers had stolen approximately 30M USD worth of Ethers from multi-sig wallet accounts [8,17]. The severe problem in the wallet contract code was allowing non-restricted to write and transfer operations. In solidity programming, there are pre-defined access modifiers that are public, private, external, and internal. If a function has not been specified to any access modifier, that would be considered the public function, and any external source can access the method without any restriction. In parity multi-sig attack, the wallet library contract had a method called *initWallet* that was not assigned to any access modifier [2,8,20]. That means the method had open access to call by any external accounts. The *initWallet* method is used to initialize the multi-sig wallet with the number of user addresses who need to sign and confirm a transaction. It also set the daily limit that allowed before confirmation of the transaction. When a multi-sig wallet contract calls the *initWallet* function from the library contract, it does not check any user accessibility since it is a public method. Thus, this was a critical attack vector in the parity multi-sig wallet problem. Hackers were able to set their account addresses to sign/confirm the transactions through *initWallet* method and freely transferred out all the money in the wallet contract. They have accessed the initialisation function with no restriction and easily acquired the ownership of the wallet contract.

The second attack occurred in November 2017, due to a critical vulnerability in the parity multi-sig wallet[5]. The multi-sig wallet calls library contract functions for essential operations such as withdraw funds, deposit funds, and assign ownership. The attacker was able to claim the ownership using the public function *initWallet* to his address. Once he received the library contract's ownership control, he had the right to kill the library contract instance. The parity library contract was killed, and all the multi-sig wallet contracts were unable to access the library functions. Since then, the multi-sig wallets were useless, and all the funds reserved in the contracts were frozen. Around 150M USD value of cryptocurrency was frozen, and account holders could not withdraw their funds.

2.3   Security Analysis Tools for Smart Contract Wallets

Since smart contracts are computerised programs developed by humans, considerable risks are caused by human errors and programming issues. The immutability nature in Ethereum blockchain prevents deployed smart contracts from malicious modification and manipulations. However, this feature restricts the smart contract owners or actual developers to change their code after the deployment. If they find any errors in their active smart contracts on Ethereum, they cannot correct them while running on the blockchain. Therefore, developers need to implement and test smart contracts carefully to make them accurate and error-free. Researchers are eager to study and proposed several security analysis frameworks and tools for evaluating smart contract programs. In [20], a comprehensive list of tools is reviewed and compared. We selected four relevant tools, including Oyente [14], Osiris [23], Mythril [15], and Maian [16].

The four tools that we chose to scan the on-chain wallet contracts based on their vulnerabilities detection. These tools mainly analyse the vulnerabilities in wallet contracts such as integer related operations, external function calls, call-stack depth limitation, miss-handled exceptions, arithmetic issues, and transaction ordering dependencies. Table 2 lists 15 critical vulnerabilities that exist in on-chain smart contract wallets and suitable tools to detect them with low false positives. We scanned all the versions of wallets' bytecode using four tools, including Oyente, Osiris, Mythril, and Maian. The analysis results from these tools on our collected wallet contracts, are provided and discussed in Sect. 4.

Many open-sourced tools are available to analyse either smart contract solidity source code or bytecode or contract address at Ethereum blockchain. Since all the smart contract wallets do not publish their verified solidity code at EtherScan, our experiments were conducted by feeding the bytecode of wallet contracts to the selected analysis tools. The compiled bytecode can be downloaded from the EtherScan explorer for all smart contract wallets. The wallet contracts with verified solidity source code in EtherScan, were required to correct many compilation errors before they can be scanned using any tools. Parity multi-sig wallet

---

[5] https://cointelegraph.com/news/parity-multisig-wallet-hacked-or-how-come.

Table 2. Key vulnerabilities and analysis tools

Key vulnerabilities	Security analysis tools
Parity multisig bug	Oyente
Call stack depth limitation	Oyente, Osiris
Integer underflow	Oyente, Osiris
Integer overflow	Oyente, Osiris
Transaction ordering dependency	Oyente, Osiris
Timestamp dependency	Oyente, Osiris
Re-entrancy bug	Oyente, Osiris
Arithmetic bugs	Osiris
Delegate call to a user-specified address	Mythril
Environment variable dependency	Mythril
External call to another contract	Mythril
Multiple external calls in same transaction	Mythril
Contract can be killed by any account	Mythril, Maian
Lock fund forever (greedy contracts)	Mythril, Maian
Leak fund or allow withdrawal by arbitrary user	Mythril, Maian

bug is detected by Oyente. Osiris especially detects a range of arithmetic bugs that is most important to check in all smart contract wallets. Mythril is one of the powerful tools that scans for 14 different vulnerabilities that are most relevant to solidity programming issues. Maian analyses the wallet contracts using the transaction tracing method and finding issues related to the parity multi-sig wallet attack such as leak fund, lock fund, and suicidal contract.

Smart contracts are implemented not only for on-chain wallets but also for several reasons such as the development of decentralised applications, intermediaries for retailing, banking and supply chain management, trustful storage element, and monitoring agent. Therefore, a range of security analysis tools, frameworks, and proposals are developed by research communities in recent years [11,13–16,22–24] for detecting and resolving existing vulnerabilities on smart contracts. A research study on Ethereum wallet contracts, focused on characteristics of on-chain wallets by grouping them into six types with regards to their functionalities [7]. They have analysed using wallet's transaction data to provide the temporal perspectives of smart contract wallets on Ethereum blockchain. The TokenScope tool [4] was implemented to detect inconsistent behaviors of cryptocurrency tokens in Ethereum. It inspects the transactions sent to the deployed tokens and triggers inconsistency in token contracts with regard to the ERC-20 token standard. However, no vulnerability analysis is conducted, especially on Ethereum wallet contracts. In this work, we have done security scanning and analysis using our new analysis framework to identify specific problems in smart contract wallets on Ethereum.

3   A Novel Analysis Framework

We propose our security analysis framework for qualitatively evaluate on-chain smart contract wallets. The framework has three major components that focus on security analysis, including solidity programming security, Ethereum Virtual Machine security, and External sources security, as shown in Fig. 1. The implementation and execution of wallet contracts are mostly dependent on three components and they are required to be controlled more securely. This section explains how each element in this framework impacts on smart contract wallets.

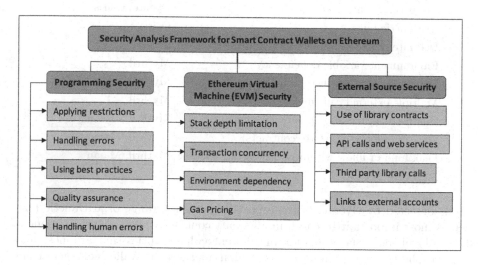

Fig. 1. Security analysis framework for on-chain contract wallets

3.1   Programming Security

In programming security, we have five factors to enhance the security level of solidity smart contract programming. Applying restrictions includes especially to apply proper access modifiers for variables and functions. The parity multisig attack occurred due to the use of public visibility for a critical method. The default function visibility level in contracts is `public`. If a function is implemented with an implicit visibility level, the compiler assumes that it has public accessibility. It is recommended to explicitly define the access modifier for all functions or variables in a smart contract. It would prevent unnecessary attacks from malicious users. In the sample code in the *AutoWallet.sol* contract, the `transfer` function is defined with implicit public visibility in line 3. The function is explicitly defined with internal access modifier in line 7.

```
1 // AutoWallet.sol
2 // Transfer function without access modifier
3 function transfer(address _to, uint _value) returns (bool) {
4 }
5 // Transfer function with internal access modifier
6 function transfer(address _to, uint _value) internal returns (bool) {
7 }
```

Before making a function call from a smart contract wallet, the user's privilege should be checked, whether he/she is an owner of the contract or authorized person to call the function. The user who sends the transaction to execute a wallet contract is set as an owner by the smart contract's constructor. When a smart contract instance is created as written in line 5 of the *Wallet.sol* file, the owner's address is assigned to the caller's address. The owner's address is verified before calling an external/internal functions by using the **require** keyword as specified in line 8 of the *Wallet.sol* file.

```
1 // Wallet.sol
2 contract Wallet {
3    address owner;
4    constructor() {
5       owner = msg.sender; // assign message sender as owner
6    }
7    function transfer(address _to, uint _value) external returns (bool) {
8       require(owner == msg.sender); // verify the message sender is owner
9       require(_value <= this.balance);
10      _to.transfer(_value);
11      return true;
12   }
```

Handling errors in smart contract development is vital to prevent errors from coding issues such as arithmetic bugs, out of bound problems in storage variables (array or list), access control problems, denial of services, and breaches from external resources. If an error is thrown from a statement, it should be handled properly using **try** and **catch** methods. The latest versions of solidity support try-catch functionality to get back the error message from an invalid code statement. In older versions of solidity, the errors are handled manually by checking the return value using if-else blocks. In the *SmartWallet.sol* file, it initiates the Wallet contract in line 2 and calls the transfer function of Wallet contract in line 3. It uses a **try** block when it calls the transfer function, and it returns the result inside the **try** block, if it is successfully executed. If it throws an error with the reasoning in a string message, it passes the error in the first catch block, as written in line 5–7. If the error is relevant to memory or cache, it goes to the second catch block and returns false with printing error message using a console statement (line 8–10).

```
1 // SmartWallet.sol
2 Wallet wallet; // initialise Wallet contract
3 try wallet.transfer(receiver_address, amount) returns (bool isTransfer) {
4    return (isTransfer, true);
```

```
5 } catch Error (string memory) { // throws a reason string of the error
6     console.error();
7     return(false, false);
8 } catch (bytes memory) { // throws low level data in the error
9     console.error();
10     return(false, false);
11 }
```

Using the best practices in smart contract implementation prevents compilation and run-time errors because developers lack understanding and mistakes in solidity coding. External calls to other contracts cause risks since the functions in the un-trusted contract can behave maliciously to get benefit from the caller contract. Smart contract developers have to bear in mind that such external calls are undesirable and would make serious security risks. They are required to follow coding recommendations and best practices to minimize or avoid the threats in solidity programming. In the code snippet of *SmartWallet.sol*, it calls an external function **transfer** from Wallet smart contract in line 3. If the Wallet contract is a malicious contract from an anonymous user, it can execute malefic calls inside the **transfer** function. It is better to use clear naming for the variables and methods when interacting with un-trusted external contracts.

```
1 LenderContract distrustLender; // initialise Wallet contract
2 distrustLender.borrow(borrwer_address, amount) returns (uint balance) {
3 }
```

This naming practice will give the developer a clear understanding that the specially named external call is unsafe, and it should have security measures when it is executing after making a function call to a distrusted smart contract. The re-entrancy problem in a smart contract occurs due to the external call to a malicious contract's function. The external contract from an attacker takes over the program's control flow and manipulates the victim contract. The malicious contract calls again to the caller contract recursively, before its first invocation completes. It is recommended to avoid state changes after a call to an external contract. The state variables should be updated before the external call to minimize the loss from the re-entrancy attack. Several best practices and advanced programming patterns are introduced by an upgraded solidity language. Since smart contracts are immutable after their deployment, developers need to follow secured coding standards[6] during their development phase.

Wallet contracts use **send()** or **tansfer()** operations without any condition or check on the return value. If the send or transfer operations fail to send the Ethers to a given recipient, the sender is unaware of the status of the execution. Their return value should be checked and continue the next program statement if it is a success. Otherwise, it should break the program from that line and notify the error message to the sender and receiver accounts.

---

[6] https://consensys.github.io/smart-contract-best-practices/.

Quality assurance testing is mandatory for wallet contracts after their development phase. Test cases can be written using the Truffle framework and run the test file to examine functionalities in each method in the smart contract. It is better to do quality assurance tests by professional testers rather doing by developers themselves. Several automation tools and test providers are available, especially for testing smart contracts. A few examples are SoftEQ, MagicBlockchainQA, LogiGeer, Populus, Corda Testing Tools, and EmbarkJS framework.

Human errors occur during the contract development phase. The latest versions of the solidity compiler warn most of the programming errors in compilation time. Coding mistakes are mostly relevant to making syntax errors, using costly gas patterns, assigning improper access modifiers, and not following best practices of programming standards.

3.2   Ethereum Virtual Machine (EVM) Security

Our framework qualitatively analyses the vulnerabilities of wallet contracts based on the nature of EVM security as well. The call-stack depth limitation problem was relevant to the maximum number of calls allowed for a smart contract on the Ethereum Virtual Machine. This issue is already fixed by increasing the operational cost for storage-related operations such as calling an internal function for input/output operation, invoke a function from another smart contract, and saving or retrieving data from storage variables. Hence, it is almost impossible to reach the maximum number of call-stack depth frames (1024) due to not having enough gas balance in a wallet contract.

Miners decide the order of transactions on Ethereum. Miners are the users who are having more computational power to create blocks and validate transactions on Ethereum. When a user sends a transaction to invoke a smart contract function, the transaction request is submitted to the EVM transaction pool. Then it is ordered according to the miners' decision based on the consensus protocol on Ethereum blockchain. Because of this feature, the users who send transactions to Ethereum are unaware of the execution state of their submitted transactions.

Ethereum Virtual Machine (EVM) does not handle many critical components of its execution model, but it leaves several features on programming language designers and depends on their manual implementation. The support of library contracts, compatibility for richer data types, and direct enforcement on APIs, external web services, and contract interfaces are given up to manage by Turing complete languages. This leads to EVM's execution environment to be expensive, insecure, and slow. EVM needed to upgrade with advanced features that are included in modern VMs such as java virtual machine. For example, EVM uses a top-down execution model that loads the entire smart contract body to execute a smart contract function. In contrast, the JVM loads only the particular namespace or method and execute it directly.

Ethereum implements a mechanism to get charged from account holders or transaction senders for executing costly EVM read/write operations [19], such as SSTORE and SLOAD. There are inconsistencies in EVM in allocating gas prices for different types of code instructions. It causes out of gas exceptions for simple execution. Sometimes, it executes costly operations with the cheapest gas usage [19]. The inconsistency in setting gas costs for EVM operations allows hackers to launch DoS attacks on Ethereum [3].

3.3   External Source Security

Smart contract wallets utilize external sources such as library contracts, external smart contract accounts, third-party libraries, and services. When they interact with these external elements, there are high possibilities for breaching the security of wallet contracts and hacks from malicious user accounts.

Wallet contracts use library contracts on Ethereum to access pre-defined functions to execute basic operations. Hackers exploit the library contracts, and the wallet contracts are becoming useless since they cannot invoke the library functions as emerged in parity multisig attack. The use of libraries in smart contract wallets reduces the deployment cost since the functions in the libraries are not implemented in the contracts. However, when on-chain wallet contracts make external calls to a library function, the execution cost is higher than compared to internal function calls. This gas cost can be reduced by using an internal modifier to the caller function that calls the external library function; it will pull the external function into the wallet contract during the deployment.

On-chain wallet contracts acquire services through API calls and third-party web services to complete advanced features. Many oracle interfaces are available like `oraclize` and `chainlink`; they act as an intermediary or connector between Ethereum smart contracts and third-party web services. Since the data from web services are not deterministic, smart contracts cannot directly invoke API calls[7] that would breach the consensus state changing mechanism on Ethereum. Because of blockchain's deterministic design, single contract-level oracle services are used to call API methods and external web services from wallet contracts.

Third-party libraries and interfaces that are used by smart contract wallets have to be more secure and reliable. They can initiate malicious activities or includes hacking codes when they return the data from their function. When a smart contract wallet invokes a third-party library, it is required to verify the external source's security level. Moreover, the returning value should be checked and handled the errors before executing the next line of code in the smart contract wallet.

3.4   Research Workflow Using Our Framework Components

We discussed the significant influences on security vulnerabilities of smart contract wallets through our framework components. To investigate the current state of safeness property in on-chain wallets, we scanned 86 bytecode versions of wallet contracts and detected an average of 10.22% of wallets are vulnerable on Ethereum platform. Figure 2 shows the workflow of how we analyze smart

---

[7] https://bit.ly/2SNQK3T.

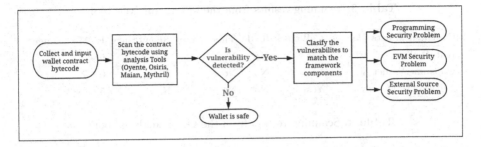

Fig. 2. The workflow diagram of our security analysis of on-chain wallets

contract wallets using scanning tools. If any vulnerabilities are detected from a wallet contract, we classify them into one of the security issues in our analysis framework and evaluate them based on their severity. When all four tools do not detect any vulnerabilities from a wallet contract bytecode, the wallet is regarded as safe.

4 Evaluation and Discussion

4.1 Experiment Setups and Results

We collected 20 different smart contract wallets and multiple versions of byte-code and verified solidity source code from the EtherScan explorer. Because the solidity source code of wallet contracts threw several compilation errors during their scanning process, we prioritised to bytecode analysis on smart contract wallets. In total, we collected 54 different versions of wallets' bytecode and 31 solidity source codes. All 20 smart contract wallets, their main contract names, and the number of contract versions in bytecode and solidity code are listed in Table 7 in Appendix B. Our whole set of data on wallet contracts and their scanning results using security analysis tools are available at our GitHub repository[8] for readers' reference.

We set up a docker environment to execute various tools. We pulled the latest docker images of Oyente, Osiris, Maian, and Mythril tools. Each docker container has configured with required dependencies, including Python, Solidity compiler Solc, Z3 theorem prover, Web3 library, Go Ethereum client Geth, and other external libraries to run the tools with accuracy and error-free.

During the bytecode analysis using the Oyente tool, it detected the call-stack depth issue in three wallets: AutoWallet, ConsumerWallet, and NiftyMultiSig-Wallet. Table 3 lists the scanning result from Oyente with wallet version number, scanned vulnerabilities, and the percentage of EVM coverage. EVM coverage means how much opcodes are executed by Oyente out of the total number of opcodes available in a contract. Oyente returned EVM coverage in the range

---

[8] https://github.com/ppraithe/on-chain-wallet-contracts.

Table 3. Scanning results from the Oyente analysis tool

On-chain-wallets	Version	Call-stack	TOD	Time-stamp	Re-entrancy	EVM coverage
AutoWallet	v1	Yes	No	No	No	9.9%
ConsumerWallet	v7	Yes	No	No	No	0.3%
NiftyMultiSig	v1	Yes	No	No	No	5%

Table 4. Scanning results from the Osiris analysis tool

On-chain-wallets	Version	Arith-metic	Call-stack	Con-currency	Time-stamp	EVM-coverage
AutoWallet	v1	No	Yes	No	No	10.2%
ConsumerWallet	v4	No	Yes	No	No	4.8%
ConsumerWallet	v5	No	Yes	No	No	4.8%
ConsumerWallet	v6	No	Yes	No	No	4.9%
ConsumerWallet	v7	No	Yes	No	No	0.3%
NiftyMultiSig	v1	No	Yes	No	No	6.6%
TeambrellaWallet	v1	No	Yes	No	No	2.9%
ControllerWallet	v1	No	Yes	No	No	9.2%

between 0% to 25% while analyzing smart contracts' bytecode. These vulnerabilities are classified into the EVM security issues' component of our analysis framework.

Osiris detected the call-stack depth vulnerability in five different wallet contracts, including AutoWallet, ConsumerWallet, NiftyMultiSigWallet, Teambrella-Wallet, and ControllerWallet. Four versions of ConsumerWallet are vulnerable to call-stack depth problem. EVM coverage from the Osiris tool is between 0% to 25%. The vulnerable contracts detected from the Osiris tool are presented in Table 4. In addition, the call-stack depth issue is under the category of EVM security issue in our qualitative framework.

Four wallet contracts are detected by Maian as greedy contracts that can lock Ether balance infinitely. The greedy contracts cannot release funds to anyone, and the Ethers would be frozen as occurred in the parity-multisig wallet attack [17]. AutoWallet, three versions of MultiSigWallet, three versions of BitgoMultiSigWallet, and TimbrellaWallet are detected as greedy contracts from the Maian tool. Maian returns their bytecode lengths. TeambrellaWallet has a lengthy contract code among these vulnerable wallets. Table 5 lists the security analysis results of vulnerable wallet contracts scanned from the Maian tool. Using improper access modifiers for functions in the library contracts causes to lock the fund in smart contract wallets. This vulnerability belongs to the programming security issues in our analysis model.

The Mythril tool detects 14 different types of smart contract programming bugs, including 1) Caller can redirect execution to arbitrary bytecode locations, 2) Caller can write to arbitrary storage locations, 3) Delegate call to a user-specified address, 4) Control flow depending on a predictable environment

Table 5. Scanning results from the Maian analysis tool

On-chain-wallets	Version	Suicidal contract	Prodegal contract	Greedy contract	Bytecode length
AutoWallet	v1	No	No	Yes	4542
MultiSigWallet	v1	No	No	Yes	6922
MultiSigWallet	v2	No	No	Yes	6922
MultiSigWallet	v3	No	No	Yes	6922
BitgoMultiSigWallet	v1	No	No	Yes	4106
BitgoMultiSigWallet	v2	No	No	Yes	7150
BitgoMultiSigWallet	v6	No	No	Yes	6988
TeambrellaWallet	v1	No	No	Yes	10644

variable, 5) Control flow depends on `Origin` of a transaction, 6) Any sender can withdraw ETH from the contract account, 7) Assertion violation, 8) External call to another contract, 9) Integer overflow or underflow, 10) Multiple external calls in the same transaction, 11) State change after an external call, 12) Contract can be accidentally killed by anyone, 13) Return value of an external call is not checked, and 14) A user-defined assertion has been triggered.

Mythril detected seven vulnerable on-chain wallet contracts—AutoWallet, SmartWallet, ConsumerWallet, TimeLockedWallet, BitgoMultiSigWallet, TeambrellaWallet, and IntermediateWallet. Six versions of BitgoMultiSig wallets are detected as vulnerable to assertion violations and arbitrary redirection. Table 6 lists the information about detected vulnerable wallet contracts by Mythril, contract versions, their existing vulnerabilities, and execution time. The vulnerability numbers are mapped to the numbering in the above list of bugs that are detecting by Mythril. Compared to other tools, Mythril's EVM coverage (between 30% and 99%) is better than other analysis tools.

4.2 Discussion

The major problems identified in our dataset of smart contract wallets are call-stack depth issue, lock fund infinitely (greedy contracts), delegate call problem, state change after an external call, assertion violation problem, and use of predictable environment variables. As discussed in our analysis framework, they can mitigate by taking proper security measures on smart contract wallet development. We have surveyed the questions and answers from Ethereum StackExchange[9] posts related to smart contracts' vulnerabilities. Possible fixes and solutions are proposed by experienced smart contract developers and by Ethereum GitHub developers.

The call-stack depth problem is related to Ethereum Virtual Machine implementation. EVM has configured the call stack depth limit to 1,024 frames [1,14]. If a smart contract calls another contract using `send()` method or `call()`

---

[9] https://ethereum.stackexchange.com/.

Table 6. Scanning results from Mythril analysis tool

On-chain-wallets	Version	Vulnerabilities (number)	EVM-coverage	Execution time (s)
AutoWallet	v1	3, 10, 11	51.62%	351.34
SmartWallet	v4	7	89.62%	21.13
TimeLockedWallet	v2	3, 4, 10	98.69%	33.33
BitgoMultiSig	v1	1	47.09%	1482.57
BitgoMultiSig	v2	7	29.33%	1143.70
BitgoMultiSig	v3	7	44.08%	163.67
BitgoMultiSig	v4	7	44.93%	439.14
BitgoMultiSig	v5	7	45.06%	452.85
BitgoMultiSig	v6	7	30.24%	86.15
TeambrellaWallet	v1	7	33.45%	572.32
ControllerWallet	v1	7	49.01%	8.59

method, the call-stack depth is increasing by one. Applying child gas restriction for external calls prevents them from reaching the maximal call-stack depth to 1,024.

Smart contract wallets are exploited by claiming ownership of the contract to lock the fund infinitely due to improper coding. The frozen contracts are identified by the Maian tool as *greedy contracts*. Since the smart contract wallets are backward-incompatible, they need to be developed cautiously and tested before their deployment on the Ethereum platform. This vulnerability can be prevented using restricted access modifiers for key functions, including state variable initialization and multiple ownerships assigned to users.

Mythril [15] detected the problem regarding `deligatecall` to a user-specified address in TimeLockedWallet contracts. The specified address can be an untrusted callee who may execute malicious functions to harm the caller contract. It is recommended to check whether the target address used in `delegatecall` is in the allow-list of trusted contracts [15].

External calls in smart contract wallets stimulate recursive calls from the `fallback` function of a callee contract. It is dangerous to update a state variable value immediately after an external call statement. If the external call re-entered the same function call and checked the value of a state variable, it will succeed in continuing the execution since the state variable has not been updated yet. Therefore, it is best practice to commit any value updates of state variables before invoking an external call.

Smart contract wallets use the `assert` function to evaluate if a statement is always true for given in-variants. If an assertion is reachable, then there is a bug in a wallet contract for allowing to enter an improper state. BitgoMultisig-Wallet, SmartWallet, TimbrellaWallet, and ControllerWallet are vulnerable to the assertion violation problem, as shown in Table 6 listing Mythril's detection results.

In our experiments, we discovered that the vulnerabilities detected in the older versions had been fixed in most latest versions of wallet contracts. For example, versions 1, 2, and 3 of MultisigWallet have detected as greedy contracts. But the latest versions of MultisigWallet have been resolved the greedy issue so that it was not reported by the Maian tool. The call-stack depth vulnerability no longer exists on Ethereum smart contracts since it has been resolved using gas cost changes for weighted input/output operations[10]. However, Oyente and Osiris detected the call-stack vulnerability in a few wallet contracts, as listed in Tables 3 and 4.

Moreover, the solidity compiler (Solc) can notify many possible errors during the contracts' compilation. Wallet contract developers can resolve the compiling errors using the compiler's auto recommendations or remedies advised by experienced GitHub developers or solutions from the stack overflow and the Ethereum stack exchange community. Through the wallet security analysis from four scanning tools, we investigated a considerable number of on-chain wallet contracts vulnerable to the Ethereum platform. Mythril discovered that 20.37% of wallet contracts bytecode are having different types of programming issues. Maian identified that 14.8% of wallet contracts are vulnerable to the greedy issue. Oyente detected that 5.5% of smart contract wallets are vulnerable to call-stack depth problem. Osiris detected that 14.8% of wallets contracts are erroneous to call stack depth limitation. Furthermore, our experiment results are manually verified to eliminate possible false positives.

5   Conclusion

As Ethereum on-chain wallets hold the crypto-asset, transaction data, and users' private keys, they are required to ensure well strong security to enhance the trustworthiness of the participants. These wallets are entirely based on immutable smart contract programs on the Ethereum platform. This paper empirically analyzed the security issues on existing smart contract wallets using detection tools such as Oyente, Osiris, Maian, and Mythril. We scanned 86 wallets with multiple versions, and 10.2% of them are identified as vulnerable for different issues. With the detection result, we have classified them into the components in our proposed framework. According to our analysis framework, we concluded that wallet contracts on Ethereum exist with several programming issues and improper interaction between external sources that breach the security of on-chain wallets. Further, we investigated the proposed solutions for the smart contract vulnerabilities from the discussions in *stack overflow* and *Ethereum exchange* communities. Our findings raise awareness of wallets' security among contract developers and users to ensure wallets' security level before the deployment.

---

[10] https://bit.ly/33PQeZo.

Appendix A Interactions of Smart Contract Wallets

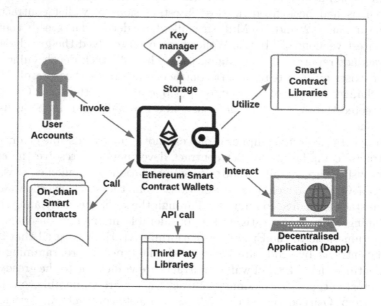

Fig. 3. Inter-playing components with Ethereum smart contract wallets

Appendix B Smart Contract Wallets Data

Table 7. On-chain wallets and source code versions

On-chain contract wallets	Main and sub contract names	ByteCode versions	SolidityCode versions
MultiSigWallet	MultiSigWallet	7 (v1-7)	4 (v4-7)
BitgoMultisig	WalletSimple	6 (v1-6)	1 (v1)
IvtMultiSig	IvtMultiSigWallet, ERC20Interface	1 (v1)	1 (v1)
NiftyMultiSig	NiftyWallet, MasterContract	1 (v1)	1 (v1)
CapitalMultisig	SmartWallet	1 (v1)	1 (v1)
SmartWallet	SmartWallet	6 (v1-6)	3 (v2,5,6)

(continued)

Table 7. (*continued*)

On-chain contract wallets	Main and sub contract names	ByteCode versions	SolidityCode versions
DapperSmart	FullWallet, CoreWallet	1 (v1)	1 (v1)
ArgentSmart	Proxy	1 (v1)	1 (v1)
AutoWallet	AutoWallet, Owned, ERC20, ERC721	1 (v1)	1 (v1)
GenosisSafe	GnosisSafe	1 (v1)	1 (v1)
ConsumerWallet	Wallet, Ownable, ResolverBase, Controller	7 (v1-7)	6 (v2-7)
SpendableWallet	SpendableWallet, Factory, ERC20, Ownable	6 (v1-6)	1 (v1)
BasicWallet	Wallet, ERC20Basic, BasicToken	2 (v1-2)	1 (v1)
Teambrella	TeambrellaWallet	1 (v1)	1 (v1)
BitgoForwarder	Forwarder, FixedSupplyToken, ForwarderTarget	1 (v1)	1 (v1)
Controller	Controller, AbstractSweeper, UserWallet, Token	1 (v1)	1 (v1)
TimeLocked	TimeLockedWallet, TimeLockedWallet-Factory, ERC20	7 (v1-7)	3 (v5-7))
Intermediate	IntermediateWallet, Ownable, ERC20Basic	1 (v1)	1 (v1)
EidooUpdate	Wallet, Connector, LoggingErrors, Token, Exchange	1 (v1)	1 (v1)
LogicProxy	UserWallet, AddressRecord, UserAuth, UserNote	1 (v1)	1 (v1)
Total		**54**	**32**

References

1. Antonopoulos, A.M., Wood, G.: Mastering Ethereum: Building Smart Contracts and DApps. O'Reilly Media, Sebastopol (2018)
2. Atzei, N., Bartoletti, M., Cimoli, T.: A survey of attacks on Ethereum smart contracts (SoK). In: Maffei, M., Ryan, M. (eds.) POST 2017. LNCS, vol. 10204, pp. 164–186. Springer, Heidelberg (2017). https://doi.org/10.1007/978-3-662-54455-6_8

3. Chen, T., et al.: An adaptive gas cost mechanism for Ethereum to defend against under-priced DoS attacks. In: Liu, J.K., Samarati, P. (eds.) ISPEC 2017. LNCS, vol. 10701, pp. 3–24. Springer, Cham (2017). https://doi.org/10.1007/978-3-319-72359-4_1

4. Chen, T., et al.: Tokenscope: automatically detecting inconsistent behaviors of cryptocurrency tokens in Ethereum. In: Proceedings of the 2019 ACM SIGSAC Conference on Computer and Communications Security, pp. 1503–1520 (2019)

5. Cheng, Z., et al.: Towards a first step to understand the cryptocurrency stealing attack on Ethereum. In: Proceedings of the 22nd international Symposium on research in Attacks, Intrusions and Defenses (RAID 2019), pp. 47–60 (2019)

6. Dannen, C.: Introducing Ethereum and Solidity. Apress, Berkeley (2017). https://doi.org/10.1007/978-1-4842-2535-6

7. Delmolino, K., Arnett, M., Kosba, A., Miller, A., Shi, E.: Step by step towards creating a safe smart contract: lessons and insights from a cryptocurrency lab. In: Clark, J., Meiklejohn, S., Ryan, P.Y.A., Wallach, D., Brenner, M., Rohloff, K. (eds.) FC 2016. LNCS, vol. 9604, pp. 79–94. Springer, Heidelberg (2016). https://doi.org/10.1007/978-3-662-53357-4_6

8. Destefanis, G., Marchesi, M., Ortu, M., Tonelli, R., Bracciali, A., Hierons, R.: Smart contracts vulnerabilities: a call for blockchain software engineering? In: Proceedings of the 2018 International Workshop on Blockchain Oriented Software Engineering (IWBOSE), pp. 19–25 (2018)

9. Di Angelo, M., Salzer, G.: A survey of tools for analyzing Ethereum smart contracts. In: Proceedings of the 2019 IEEE International Conference on Decentralized Applications and Infrastructures (DAPPCON), pp. 69–78. IEEE (2019)

10. Di Angelo, M., Salzer, G.: Characteristics of wallet contracts on Ethereum. In: Proceedings of the 2020 IEEE International Conference on Blockchain and Cryptocurrency (ICBC 2020), pp. 1–2. IEEE (2020)

11. Feist, J., Grieco, G., Groce, A.: Slither: a static analysis framework for smart contracts. In: Proceedings of the 2019 IEEE/ACM 2nd International Workshop on Emerging Trends in Software Engineering for Blockchain (WETSEB), pp. 8–15. IEEE (2019)

12. Harz, D., Knottenbelt, W.: Towards safer smart contracts: A survey of languages and verification methods. arXiv preprint arXiv:1809.09805 (2018)

13. Hildenbrandt, E., et al.: KEVM: a complete formal semantics of the Ethereum virtual machine. In: Proceedings of the 2018 IEEE 31st Computer Security Foundations Symposium (CSF), pp. 204–217. IEEE (2018)

14. Luu, L., Chu, D.H., Olickel, H., Saxena, P., Hobor, A.: Making smart contracts smarter. In: Proceedings of the 2016 ACM SIGSAC Conference on Computer and Communications Security, pp. 254–269 (2016)

15. Mueller, B.: Smashing ethereum smart contracts for fun and real profit. HITB SECCONF Amsterdam (2018)

16. Nikolić, I., Kolluri, A., Sergey, I., Saxena, P., Hobor, A.: Finding the greedy, prodigal, and suicidal contracts at scale. In: Proceedings of the 34th Annual Computer Security Applications Conference, pp. 653–663 (2018)

17. Palladino, S.: The parity wallet hack explained, July-2017. https://blog.zeppelin.solutions/on-the-parity-wallet-multisig-hack-405a8c12e8f7

18. Parizi, R.M., Dehghantanha, A., et al.: Smart contract programming languages on blockchains: an empirical evaluation of usability and security. In: Chen, S., Wang, H., Zhang, L.J. (eds.) Blockchain, pp. 75–91. Springer, Cham (2018). https://doi.org/10.1007/978-3-319-94478-4_6

19. Perez, D., Livshits, B.: Broken metre: attacking resource metering in EVM. arXiv preprint arXiv:1909.07220 (2019)
20. Praitheeshan, P., Pan, L., Yu, J., Liu, J., Doss, R.: Security analysis methods on Ethereum smart contract vulnerabilities: a survey. arXiv preprint arXiv:1908.08605 (2019)
21. Praitheeshan, P., Xin, Y.W., Pan, L., Doss, R.: Attainable hacks on Keystore files in Ethereum wallets—a systematic analysis. In: Doss, R., Piramuthu, S., Zhou, W. (eds.) FNSS 2019. CCIS, vol. 1113, pp. 99–117. Springer, Cham (2019). https://doi.org/10.1007/978-3-030-34353-8_7
22. Tikhomirov, S., Voskresenskaya, E., Ivanitskiy, I., Takhaviev, R., Marchenko, E., Alexandrov, Y.: Smartcheck: static analysis of Ethereum smart contracts. In: Proceedings of the 1st International Workshop on Emerging Trends in Software Engineering for Blockchain, pp. 9–16 (2018)
23. Torres, C.F., Schütte, J., State, R.: Osiris: hunting for integer bugs in Ethereum smart contracts. In: Proceedings of the 34th Annual Computer Security Applications Conference, pp. 664–676 (2018)
24. Tsankov, P., Dan, A., Drachsler-Cohen, D., Gervais, A., Buenzli, F., Vechev, M.: Securify: practical security analysis of smart contracts. In: Proceedings of the 2018 ACM SIGSAC Conference on Computer and Communications Security, pp. 67–82 (2018)
25. Wood, G.: Ethereum: a secure decentralised generalised transaction ledger. Ethereum Project Yellow Paper 151, 1–32 (2014)

ENCOD: Distinguishing Compressed and Encrypted File Fragments

Fabio De Gaspari[1], Dorjan Hitaj[1($\boxtimes$)], Giulio Pagnotta[1], Lorenzo De Carli[2], and Luigi V. Mancini[1]

[1] Dipartimento di Informatica, Sapienza Università di Roma, Rome, Italy
{degaspari,hitaj.d,pagnotta,mancini}@di.uniroma1.it
[2] Department of Computer Science, Worcester Polytechnic Institute, Worcester, MA, USA
ldecarli@wpi.edu

Abstract. Reliable identification of encrypted file fragments is a requirement for several security applications, including ransomware detection, digital forensics, and traffic analysis. A popular approach consists of estimating high entropy as a proxy for randomness. However, many modern content types (e.g. office documents, media files, etc.) are highly compressed for storage and transmission efficiency. Compression algorithms also output high-entropy data, thus reducing the accuracy of entropy-based encryption detectors.

Over the years, a variety of approaches have been proposed to distinguish encrypted file fragments from high-entropy compressed fragments. However, these approaches are typically only evaluated over a few, selected data types and fragment sizes, which makes a fair assessment of their practical applicability impossible. This paper aims to close this gap by comparing existing statistical tests on a large, standardized dataset. Our results show that current approaches cannot reliably tell apart encryption and compression, *even for large fragment sizes.* To address this issue, we design ENCOD, a learning-based classifier which can reliably distinguish compressed and encrypted data, starting with fragments as small as 512 bytes. We evaluate ENCOD against current approaches over a large dataset of different data types, showing that it outperforms current state-of-the-art for most considered fragment sizes and data types.

1 Introduction

Reliable detection of encrypted data fragments is an important primitive with many applications to security and digital forensics. For instance, ransomware detection algorithms use estimates of write-operations' data randomness to quickly identify evidence of malicious encryption processes [17,25,26,33]. When performing digital forensic analysis of hard drives and phones, it is oftentimes important to identify encrypted archives [16]. Finally, encryption detection is widely used in network protocol analysis [18,20].

© Springer Nature Switzerland AG 2020
M. Kutyłowski et al. (Eds.): NSS 2020, LNCS 12570, pp. 42–62, 2020.
https://doi.org/10.1007/978-3-030-65745-1_3

A popular approach to address this problem is to estimate the Shannon entropy of the sequence of interest using the Maximum Likelihood Estimator (MLE): $\hat{H}_{MLE}$. This approach leverages the observation that the distribution of byte values in an encrypted stream closely follows a uniform distribution; therefore, high entropy is used as a proxy for randomness. This estimator has the advantage of being simple and computationally efficient. As non-encrypted digital data is assumed to have low byte-level entropy, the estimator is expected to easily differentiate non-encrypted and encrypted content.

While this approach remains widely used (e.g., [17,25,26,33]), a number of works have highlighted its limitations. Modern applications tend to compress data prior to both storage and transmission. Popular examples include the zip compressed file format, and HTTP compression [21] (both using the DEFLATE algorithm). As compression removes recurring patterns in data, compressed streams tend to exhibit high Shannon entropy. As a result, compressed data exhibit values of $\hat{H}_{MLE}$ that are close and oftentimes overlapping with those obtained by encryption. In principle, compressed content can be identified by using appropriate parsers. However, many security-related applications, such as ransomware detection, traffic analysis and digital forensics, generally do not have access to whole-file information, but rather work at the level of *fragments* of data. In these settings, the metadata that is required by parsers is not present or is incomplete [35]. Given this issue, a number of works have been looking at alternative tests to distinguish between encrypted and compressed content [12,14,23,30,32,34,41]. While these works have the potential to be useful, there has been limited evaluation of their performance on a standardized dataset. Consequently, there is no clear understanding of how these approaches: (i) fare on a variety of compressed file formats and sizes, and (ii) compare to each other. The potential negative implications are significant: the use of ineffective techniques for identifying encrypted content can hinder the effectiveness of ransomware detectors [19], and significantly limit the capability of forensic tools.

Our work compares state-of-the-art approaches on a large dataset of different data types and fragment sizes. We find that, while more useful than entropy estimates, current approaches fail to achieve consistently high accuracy. To address this, we propose ENCOD (**En**cryption/**Co**mpression **D**istinguisher), a novel neural network-based approach. Our evaluation shows that ENCOD outperforms existing approaches for most considered file types, over all considered fragment sizes. ENCOD can classify data fragments as small as $512B$ with 86% accuracy, increasing to up to 94% for purely compressed data (i.e., zip, gzip) and up to 100% for compressed application data fragments (e.g., pdf, jpeg, mp3) for $8KB$ fragment sizes. Overall, this paper makes the following contributions:

- We review and categorize existing literature on the topic of distinguishing compressed and encrypted data fragments.
- We systematically evaluate and compare state-of-the-art approaches on a large, standardized dataset including a variety of fragment formats and sizes.

– We propose a new neural-network based approach, which outperforms current state-of-the-art tests in distinguishing encrypted from compressed content for most considered formats, over all considered fragment sizes.
– We propose a new multi-class classifier that can label a fragment with high accuracy as encrypted data, general-purpose compressed data (zip/gzip/rar), or one of multiple application-specific compressed data (png, jpeg, pdf, mp3).
– We thoroughly discuss the implications of our findings, in terms of the applicability of the evaluated approaches.

The rest of this paper is structured as follows: Section 2 provides background on entropy estimation and its applications. Section 3 reviews existing approaches to the problem. Section 4 presents and evaluates a novel approach to the problem, based on deep learning. Section 5 estimates the performance of the considered approaches, discussing their strengths and limitations. Section 6 discusses the implications of our findings. Section 7 discusses related work and Sect. 8 concludes the paper.

2   Background

Determining the format of a particular data object (e.g. a file in permanent storage, or an HTTP object) is an extremely common operation. Under normal circumstances, it can be accomplished by looking at content metadata or by parsing the object. Things get more complicated, however, when no metadata is available and the data object is corrupted or partly missing. In this paper, we focus on detection of *encrypted content* and, in particular, on distinguishing between encrypted and compressed data fragments. We begin by examining relevant applications of encryption detection primitives.

2.1   Ransomware Detection

Ransomware encrypts user files with the aim of making them unusable for the user. It then presents a prompt asking the user to pay a ransom in order to receive the decryption key. Ransomware attacks can cause significant financial damage to organizations [3,4,10].

Mitigating a ransomware infection requires rapid detection and termination of all ransomware processes. A number of approaches based on *behavioral process analysis* have been proposed for this purpose [17,25,26,33]. These approaches typically rely on a classifier trained on various process-related features to distinguish benign and ransomware processes. Virtually all proposed behavioral detectors use entropy of file write operations as one of the key features, based on the insight that frequently writing encrypted content is a characteristic behavioral fingerprint of ransomware. Entropy is typically estimated using $\hat{H}_{MLE}$. In several approaches entropy is estimated on the content of individual file writes [17,25,26], therefore the estimation procedure has only access to partial file fragments.

2.2 Forensics

Digital forensics oftentimes involves analysis of phone [39] or PC [35] storage that has been corrupted, or uses an unknown format. Therefore, forensic techniques attempt to recover data of interest (contacts, pictures, etc.) by searching for blocks with recognizable structure. These techniques typically only have access to data fragments, rather than whole files.

Encrypted and compressed data represent a corner case, as they exhibit a complete lack of structure. Still, detecting such content may be important in data recovery operations (e.g., if sensitive data is known to have been encrypted). Distinguishing between compressed and encrypted blocks is notoriously difficult, and some forensic approaches label data as *"compressed or encrypted"*, without attempting to pinpoint which one of the two it is [16].

2.3 Network Traffic Analysis

Network traffic analysis examines flows in/out of a network to identify security issues. Regulations (e.g. HIPAA in the U.S.) and best practices expect sensitive data to be encrypted in transit; therefore, entropy-based analyzers have been proposed to ensure that all traffic leaving a monitored network is encrypted [20]. Another application is reverse-engineering of network protocols used by malware. It has been observed [18] that malware protocols may mix encrypted and non-encrypted content within the same message. Encryption detection primitives can be applied to break messages into encrypted and non-encrypted fields.

In both cases above, encryption detectors have partial visibility on the data stream and can only access fragments of data (e.g., an encrypted stream broken into individual packets), rather than whole data objects.

2.4 Challenges

In the three domains above, the use of Shannon entropy has been proposed in order to identify encrypted content. Entropy is used to measure the *information content* of a byte sequence; highly structured data exhibit low entropy, while unstructured data—such as a randomly distributed sequence—have high entropy. Therefore, an entropy estimate can be used as a proxy for how close a sequence of bytes is to being randomly distributed. Most encryption algorithms output ciphertexts whose byte-value distributions tend to follow a uniform distribution. As a result, an encrypted bytestream will almost invariably exhibit high entropy.

One of the most common approaches to entropy estimation is the Maximum Likelihood Estimator $\hat{H}_{MLE} = -\sum_{i=0}^{255} f_i log_2(f_i)$, where f_i is the frequency of byte value i in the sequence. The entropy range is $[0-8]$. The frequency f_i of byte value i, which is measurable, is used in place of the probability $P(i)$ of that value occurring, which is unknown. This approach is commonly used in some of the applications above (e.g., [20,25]), due to its simplicity and efficiency.

This reasoning assumes that, while encrypted data has high entropy, non-encrypted data does not. This appears reasonable, as most relevant data types (e.g., text, images, audio) are information-rich and highly structured. However, this assumption does not hold true in modern computing. Modern CPUs can efficiently decompress data for processing, and compress it back for storage or transmission; this is oftentimes performed in real time and transparent to the user. As a result, most formats tend to apply compression [2,38]. Informally, a good compression algorithm works by identifying and removing recognizable structures from the data stream; as a result, compressed data tend to exhibit high entropy. In practice, this fact compromises the ability of entropy-based detectors to distinguish encrypted and non-encrypted, compressed content.

Entropy Estimates for Common Data Formats. In order to substantiate the claim above, we computed entropy estimates using a dataset consisting of **10,000** file fragments. The dataset covers various popular file formats and AES-256-encrypted data. We considered multiple fragment sizes, from 512B to 8 KB (details in Sect. 4). Figure 1 summarizes the distribution of estimated entropy values for eight different formats with block size 2048 (some ranges truncated for clarity). Results for other block sizes were qualitatively similar; full results are tabulated in Appendix A. As illustrated in Fig. 1, both general-purpose (zip, rar) and domain-specific (jpeg, mp3) compression algorithms result in data which exhibits entropy whose ranges are overlapping with that of encrypted content (enc). The only format that can be unambiguously distinguished is png. Even so, png still overlaps with various other formats. Interestingly, utilities that create and modify data in zip, gzip and png format internally all use the DEFLATE algorithm for compression: the differences in entropy are likely due to differences in file structure and algorithm implementation.

Due to the limits of entropy estimation, the attention of the community has been increasingly focusing on alternative measures that can more precisely estimate whether data follow a random distribution. However, no comprehensive review of such approaches exists. In the next section, we review state-of-art approaches, while we evaluate and compare them in Sect. 5.

3   Review of Existing Techniques

This section reviews three state-of-the-art approaches to distinguishing encrypted and compressed content: the NIST suite, χ^2 and HEDGE [12]. Strictly speaking, these approaches test the *randomness* of a string of bytes, and make no attempt to determine its type. However, due to their high precision they can be used to distinguish true pseudorandom (encrypted) sequences and compressed ones which, while approximating a randomly generated stream, maintain structure.

The NIST suite and χ^2 are standard statistical tests for identifying randomly-distributed data. HEDGE is a recently proposed statistical approach which shows promising results. HEDGE is a combination of a subset of the NIST tests and two forms of χ^2 tests. Note that, despite the inclusion of HEDGE, we decided

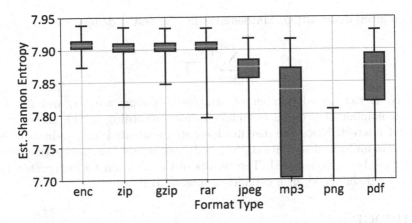

Fig. 1. Entropy ranges for common formats (2048B blocks)

to also report separate results for NIST and χ^2 due to the fact that those are designed to be, and oftentimes are, used as standalone tests.

3.1 NIST SP800-22

The NIST SP800-22 specification [36] describes a suite of tests whose intended use is to evaluate the quality of random number generators. The suite consists of 15 distinct tests, which analyze various structural aspects of a byte sequence. These tests are commonly employed as a benchmark for distinguishing compressed and encrypted content (e.g., [12,14]). Each test analyzes a particular property of the sequence, and subsequently applies a test-specific decision rule to determine whether the result of the analysis suggests randomness or not. When using the NIST suite for discriminating random and non-random sequences, an important question concerns aggregation of the results of individual tests. Analysis of the tests [36] suggests that they are largely independent. Given this observation, and the intrinsic complexity of *a priori* defining a ranking between the tests, we use a *majority voting* approach. In other words, we consider a fragment to be random (and therefore encrypted) when the majority of tests considers it so. Since some of the tests require a block length much bigger than the ones we use for our smaller fragment sizes, we did not consider in the voting the tests that cannot be executed.

3.2 χ^2 Test

The χ^2 test is a simple statistical test to measure goodness of fit. It has been widely applied to distinguish compressed and encrypted content [12,30,34]. Given a set of samples, it measures how well the distribution of such samples follows a given distribution. Mathematically, the test is defined as:

$$\chi^2 = \sum_{i=0}^{255} \frac{(N_i - E_i)^2}{E_i}$$

where N_i is the actual number of samples assuming value i, and E_i is the expected number of samples assuming value i according to the known distribution of interest. Since the distribution being evaluated for goodness of fit is the discrete uniform distribution, $\forall i E_i = L/256$, where L is the particular fragment length being considered. The results of the test can be interpreted using either a fixed threshold, or a confidence interval [12].

3.3 HEDGE

HEDGE [12] simultaneously incorporates three methods to distinguish between compressed and encrypted fragments: χ^2 test with absolute value, χ^2 with confidence interval and a subset of NIST SP800-22 test suite. Out of the NIST SP800-22 test suite HEDGE incorporates 3 tests: *frequency within block test, cumulative sums test*, and *approximate entropy test*. These tests were selected due to (i) their ability to operate on short byte sequences, and (ii) their reliable performance on a large and representative dataset. In the HEDGE detector the threshold of the number of the above-mentioned NIST SP800-22 tests failed is set to 0. For the χ^2 with absolute value test, the thresholds are pre-computed for each of the considered packet sizes, by considering the average and its standard deviation. For χ^2 with confidence interval, the $\chi\%$ interval is $(\chi\% > 99\% || \chi\% < 1\%)$. For classifying the content of a packet, HEDGE applies the three randomness tests to the input data. Data is considered random only if it passes all tests.

4 ENCOD: A Learning-Based Approach

Past work and our own evaluation suggest that tests based on byte-value distribution, such as χ^2, can distinguish some encrypted and compressed content, but have accuracy issues (ref. Sect. 5). Such tests, in a sense, "collapse" the entire distribution to a single scalar value, losing information concerning the shape of the distribution. It is therefore natural to ask if Deep Neural Networks (DNNs) can improve such results. DNNs can consider the entire discrete distribution (modeled as a feature vector), and can learn to recognize complex distributions [29].

In order to evaluate the potential of DNNs we designed ENCOD, a set of two distinct neural network-based approaches for distinguishing encryption and compression.

4.1 Model Architecture #1: Binary Classifiers

Our first model is a binary classifier trained to distinguish a single specific compressed format from encrypted content. It may be used in cases where only one compressed format is known to exist in the dataset (e.g., detecting writes of encrypted data performed by a potential ransomware on image files vs legitimate writes of JPEG-compressed data). We explored several alternative architectures for this application, and we found that the structure depicted in Fig. 2a provides the best performance. The binary-classifier architecture consists of 4 fully-connected layers with dimensions as shown in the figure. We initialize the model weights using Glorot uniform [22]. The activation function is ReLU for the first 3 layers, followed by a softmax on the output layer. We used a batch size of 64 for training our model. Each hyperparameter has been chosen using grid search. We used the same procedure also for the model described in Sect. 4.2.

4.2   Model Architecture #2: Content-Type Detector

In many applications, a classifier may encounter more than one type of compressed data. Furthermore, it may be important to determine the specific type being encountered. To support these use cases, we design a *content-type detector*: a multi-class classifier that can determine whether a given fragment is encrypted, or belongs to one of multiple known compressed formats. We explored several designs for the neural network, converging to the model depicted in Fig. 2b. Its architecture consists of 5 fully-connected layers with dimensions as shown in the figure. We initialize model weights using LeCun normal [28]. Differently from the binary models, this multi-class classifier seemed prone to the dying neuron problem associated with the ReLU activation function [37]. We therefore opted for the SelU activation function [27] for the first 4 layers, followed by a softmax on the output layer. We used a batch size of 64 instances for training.

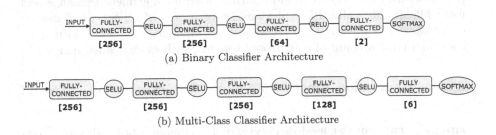

(a) Binary Classifier Architecture

(b) Multi-Class Classifier Architecture

Fig. 2. Neural network architectures

4.3   Fragment Dataset

We built a dataset of **200M encrypted and compressed fragments**. For the compressed data, we selected a set of formats covering common, popular content types. To generate the encrypted data fragments, we used the AES cipher in CBC mode implemented by the PyCryptodome library [1]. We chose AES because it is the most widely used and well known symmetric cipher, representative of modern ciphers which result in byte streams consistently close to random.

In constructing the dataset, we focused on ensuring a diversity of compressed formats, rather than compression algorithms. While algorithms such as DEFLATE are used in multiple compression formats, they are generally used with different parameters and/or embed compressed data in different ways within the compressed archive. Consequently, compressed archives created with different formats tend to differ considerably from each other even when using the same underlying compression algorithm. This observation is empirically confirmed by our evaluation in Sect. 5. Finally, our dataset does not include data which is both compressed and encrypted, and we ensured such data is not present in the dataset. The dataset is comprised of the following data types:

1. **AES encrypted data (enc).** We used the AES implementation provided by the Cryptodome Python library. AES was configured to use CBC mode with 256-bit keys, with a random IV generated before encrypting each file.
2. **DEFLATE- and rar-compressed data (zip/gzip and rar):** both DEFLATE and rar are de-facto standards for generic file compression. DEFLATE is also widely used for documents (such as in the MS OFFICE file formats), and network applications (e.g., HTTP header compression).
3. **png and jpeg images:** png is used for lossless image compression; it internally uses DEFLATE, but png files present a structure that is different from that of zip files. jpeg uses DCT-based lossy compression.
4. **mp3 audio files:** MP3 compressors use a psychoacoustic model to remove inaudible frequencies from audio data, and compress the resulting data using a lossy algorithm based on the modified-DCT transform.
5. **pdf documents:** PDF is an office format used for document exchange and form filling. Internally, PDF files consist of a tree of objects that can be compressed using a variety of techniques. In practice, most PDF documents contain a large amount of compressed content, such as embedded images.

Fragment Generation Process. We generate fragments from a dataset of files:

- **zip/gzip/rar/enc:** we used various textual documents obtained from a 2020 English Wikipedia dump [8]. We created four copies of each file, each of which was either compressed using one of zip, gzip, rar utilities (with default parameters), or encrypted using AES-256.
- **png:** we crawled 5000 png images from the web and various repositories [5].
- **jpeg:** we downloaded 10,000 images from the Open Images Dataset v5 [7].
- **mp3:** we used the FMA dataset [6], which contains 8000 mp3 files.
- **pdf:** we crawled 1,000 randomly-selected papers from arXiv [9].

We split each file into fragments of 512B, 1 KB, 2 KB, 4 KB, and 8 KB. We then selected 5M fragments for each fragment size/data type combination (this ensures that the dataset remains balanced).

4.4   Dataset Analysis Methodology

Statistical tests (NIST, χ^2, HEDGE): For each fragment size, we randomly selected 10,000 compressed fragments (evenly distributed across the different compressed data types) and 10,000 encrypted fragments. We then executed the tests directly on these fragments.

ENCOD/*Binary Classifiers:* We separately trained and evaluated classifiers for each fragment size. The features that are fed to our models for training/classification are derived from the histograms of the byte values for the observed fragment size. Each feature is the value of the probability density function at a given bin, normalized such that the integral over the range is 1.

We trained the binary classifiers by randomly selecting 3M vectors from the encrypted class and 3M vectors from the data type that we aim to distinguish. We partitioned this dataset into 85% training, 5% development and 10% test. Before fitting the data to the model for training, we applied a MinMax scaler to scale the dataset from the range $[0, 1]$ to the range $[0, 2]$ (range selected via grid search). Scaling helps the ML model to more easily capture minute differences in the inputs, allowing to better distinguish among the classes and converge faster.

ENCOD/*Content-Type Detector:* To train the content-type detectors, for each fragment size we randomly sampled 6M feature vectors consisting of a mix of the considered file types. This dataset was partitioned into training, development and test sets in the same ratios used for the binary classifiers. We also scaled the dataset using the MinMax scaler with the same parameters used above.

5   Evaluation

In this section, we comprehensively evaluate existing approaches discussed in Sect. 3, in addition to ENCOD, our novel neural network-based approach (see Sect. 4). We frame the evaluation in terms of the following comparisons:

1. **Binary classification: all formats.** In Sect. 5.2, we consider the ability of different detectors to discriminate encrypted and compressed data, regardless of the specific compressed format. Results show that our classifier heavily outperforms NIST, χ^2-test and HEDGE for all fragment sizes.
2. **Binary classification by format.** In Sect. 5.3, we break down the performance of χ^2, NIST and HEDGE by compressed format. We also report the performance of our per-format binary classifiers (see Sect. 4.1). The latter perform comparably or better than other tests on all formats but one.
3. **Format fingerprinting.** In Sect. 5.4, we evaluate the accuracy of our multiclass classifier in labeling unknown fragments as the correct compressed format (or as encrypted). Results show that our classifier is able to distinguish the file type with an overall accuracy of 90% for the 2048 byte chunk size. It also achieves high precision, especially on png, jpeg, mp3.

5.1   Implementation

We implemented the classifier described in Sect. 4 using the Keras Library [13] for machine learning. For the NIST tests, we used the official implementation [15]. In order to aggregate the NIST tests results, we use the majority voting approach described in Sect. 3.1. In order to label fragments as compressed or encrypted based on χ^2 results, we used the thresholds suggested in the HEDGE paper [12], as the analysis in HEDGE is specifically aimed at producing a dataset-independent threshold for general use. We implemented HEDGE according to the published description [12]. Finally, all experiments were conducted using the dataset described in Sect. 4.

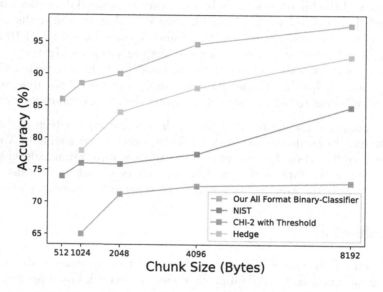

Fig. 3. Performance comparison (binary classification: all formats)

5.2   Binary Classification: All Formats

In the first part of our evaluation, we consider the binary classification problem of determining whether a given high-entropy data fragment is compressed or encrypted. Given a fragment, the χ^2 test, HEDGE, and the NIST test suite return whether the fragment's content appears random or not. Therefore, a binary classifier can be derived simply by labeling random content as encrypted. Our binary classifier used for this evaluation is based on our multi-class classifier. The multi-class classifier labels each fragment either as encrypted, or as one of the seven supported compressed formats. Since in this experiment we are only interested in distinguishing encryption and compression, regardless of the type, we combine all compressed type labels into one (we look at content fingerprinting accuracy in Sect. 5.4). Effectively, we consider classification in two labels: (1) a macro-label "compressed", which is comprised of the labels $\{zip, rar, gzip, png, jpeg, mp3, pdf\}$ and (2) the label "encrypted".

The results of this evaluation are depicted in Fig. 3. All classifiers tend to improve as fragment size increases; we discuss this phenomenon in Sect. 6. Our neural network-based approach heavily outperforms all the other approaches on all block sizes. The χ^2 accuracy remains consistently low across the range of block sizes. Results suggest that this test has an intrinsic difficulty in discriminating non-random content which closely approaches a uniform random distribution.

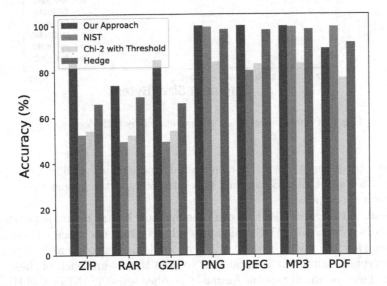

Fig. 4. Performance comparison between our binary-classifier approach, NIST, χ^2 with Threshold and HEDGE (2048B blocks)

5.3   Binary Classification by Format

In the second experiment, we consider the question of whether some compressed formats are harder than others to distinguish from encrypted content. Such phenomenon may arise due to (i) differences in effectiveness between compression algorithms in removing redundancy (and thus structure) from the uncompressed data; and (ii) presence (or absence) of metadata, or other structured information interleaved with compressed data.

In order to answer this question, we break down results for the χ^2-test, NIST suite, and HEDGE test by format. We do not evaluate our multi-class classifier in this experiment. This is due to the fact that this classifier can generate two different types of classification errors for compressed formats: (1) mislabeling a compressed fragment as an encrypted one; and (2) mislabeling a compressed

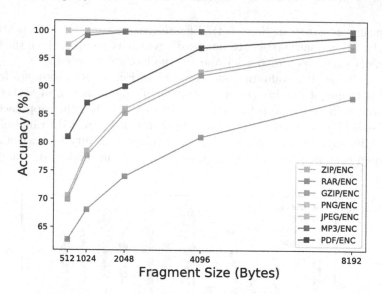

Fig. 5. Performance of our binary classifiers (all block sizes)

fragment of a given type for a compressed fragment of a different type. As χ^2-test, NIST and HEDGE can only generate errors of the former type, a direct comparison is not possible.

Instead, in this experiment we evaluate multiple binary neural network-based classifiers (see Sect. 4.1). With this approach, we train one binary classifier per compressed format. Each classifier is trained to distinguish content in that format from encrypted content. It is important to note that, while each of these classifiers is trained specifically on one format, the other tests (χ^2, NIST and HEDGE) work the same regardless of the format. Despite this limitation, we believe this to be an informative analysis of the potential of learning-based approaches.

Figure 4 shows the comparison between the three approaches on 2048-byte blocks. Overall, neural network-based classifiers tend to fare better than the other tests, particularly on challenging formats such as zip/gzip and rar. PDF is the only format on which the NIST and HEDGE tests outperform the neural network classifier. Interestingly, the χ^2 fares slightly better than NIST on most formats, but its accuracy is significantly worse on formats that are typically easy to distinguish, such as PNG. We believe this to be due to the fact that the NIST tests look at a richer set of properties beyond byte value distribution, such as a presence of runs and repeated sequences. HEDGE test outperform χ^2 on all file types, while outperforming NIST on most formats, beside PDF, and have similar performance on PNG and MP3 formats. Finally, Fig. 5 presents the performance of all our binary classifiers across the range of fragment sizes. These results again show that accuracy increases significantly as block size increases. For 8 KB-blocks, accuracy is above 85% for all types.

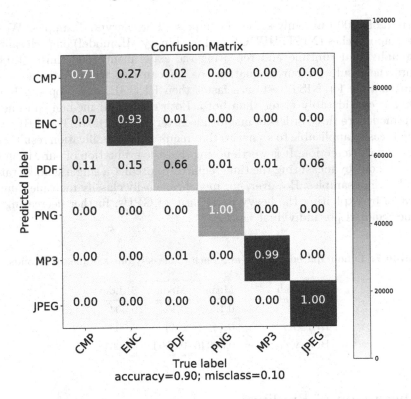

Fig. 6. Confusion matrix for the content-type classifier

5.4 Format Fingerprinting

Our multiclass classifier has the ability to (1) distinguish encrypted and compressed data, and (2) pinpoint the specific format compressed data belong to. This is a significant improvement over the functionality of existing tests, that can only distinguish encryption and compression. In this section, we evaluate the effectiveness of our multi-class classifier in fingerprinting the correct type of compressed content. Figure 6 shows the confusion matrix for the multi-class classifier. Results indicate that our classifier is able to pinpoint the file type with consistently high precision for most formats, especially png, mp3, and jpeg It performs fairly well on the other considered compressed formats such as cmp (which contains a mixture of zip, rar, and gzip feature vectors) but with a slightly higher rate of misclassified instances between enc and cmp. This can be explained by the fact that their distributions are very close, and intrinsically hard to distinguish.

5.5 Overhead

In the final part of our evaluation, we analyze the practical applicability of the three approaches, comparing their runtime in order to understand if they can be deployed in time-critical applications. For this test, we used a small dataset comprised of 1000 randomly-selected compressed or encrypted samples. We ran all three approaches (NIST, HEDGE and our binary ML model) on each sample, taking individual runtime and repeating the experiment 1000 times. Table 1 presents the results of our evaluation. As we can see, while both mean and median runtime for NIST tests are faster then HEDGE, our proposed binary classifier is considerably faster than both. Both mean and median runtime for the ML model are three orders of magnitude faster than both NIST and HEDGE, making it easily applicable to scenarios that require fast classification results such as ransomware detection. It is worth noting that the evaluation of our ML model was carried out by measuring the time required to predict a single sample, rather than a batch of samples. However, our model can easily classify multiple samples in parallel by exploiting the heavy parallelism of GPUs, further decreasing the runtime required per individual sample.

Table 1. Time required by each approach to classify one sample, in seconds.

Approach	Mean	Median	Std.dev
NIST	0.1	0.1	0.004
HEDGE	0.44	0.43	0.008
Binary classifier	0.00046	0.00044	0.00012

6   Discussion of Findings

Results shown in Sect. 5 highlight the difficulty of discriminating compressed and encrypted fragments. State-of-the-art statistical tests tend to fare better than entropy measures (ref. Sect. 2), but their performance varies significantly depending on the specifics of the compressed format and fragment size. Moreover, such approaches can only determine whether a given fragment is encrypted with a certain confidence, but cannot distinguish between different compressed formats. ENCOD, the learning-based approach introduced in Sect. 4, tackles both these limitations. Both per-format and multi-class classifiers outperform existing tests on all considered file types/block sizes. Moreover, our multi-class classifier can be used to determine the format of a given unknown fragment, even in the complete absence of any context or information on its type.

Results show that accuracy improves consistently with increasing fragment size. This is in a sense to be expected; all approaches considered in this paper leverage differences between the byte value distribution of random data (which is uniform) and that of compressed data. Perfectly estimating the byte value distribution of a short data stream is generally not possible. As sequences get shorter, the probability that the estimated distribution may not reflect the typical distribution for their content type increases. However, as the size of the sample increases, the estimated empirical distribution approaches the underlying data distribution, allowing us to capture any deviation from the uniform distribution.

For modern compression algorithms, these deviations are quite minor, and a 512-byte block gives even accurate tests very little data to work with. However, when enough data is available, it is possible to identify the class of data with high accuracy; our learning-based classifier exceeds 90% accuracy already for 2048-byte blocks. In general, we recommend against using any one approach as the sole guidance for automated security decisions (e.g. dropping/allowing flows, terminating processes, etc.). However, when integrated as part of a more complete set of features in a larger system, our proposed classifiers can provide an additional robust feature to use in the decision-making process.

Given the discussion above, we suspect an intrinsic bound on the accuracy reachable by any classifier which looks purely at byte value distributions. However, approaches attempting to parse fragments or identify recognizable structures are likely to incur an impractical computational cost. Moreover, it is not apparent that any such structure is preserved for very short fragment sizes.

7   Related Work

7.1   Entropy-Based Encryption Detection

Use of entropy estimation to detect encrypted content is common in ransomware detection. Proposals such as RWGuard [33], UNVEIL [26], Redemption [25] and ShieldFS [17] use entropy of written content either directly as a feature, or as part of feature calculation. It should be noted that none of these detectors use entropy as the sole feature for detection. However, evidence from Sect. 2 suggests that they may be better ignoring entropy altogether. In the realm of digital forensics, entropy estimation has been used to determine the type of unknown disk data fragments. One of the most complete approaches is that of Conti et al. [16]. However, the same authors found that such estimates have limited discerning power in distinguishing encrypted and compressed content, and aggregated the two types under a single label.

Entropy estimation has also been applied to the real-time analysis of network traffic. Dorfinger's Master thesis [20] proposes a system for discriminating encrypted and non-encrypted traffic, to ensure that all communications from a target network are encrypted. Similar approaches were also proposed by Mamun et al. [31] and Malhotra [30]. Zhang et al. proposed an entropy-based classifier for the identification of botnet traffic [42]. All these approaches also suffer from the limitations of using high entropy as a fingerprint of encryption. Wang et al. [41] report positive results in using an SVM classifier to discriminate between various data types using entropy estimates. Their application scenario is different from ours, as they consider both low-entropy (non-compressed) and high-entropy (compressed or encrypted) formats. We only consider high-entropy formats, which are difficult to distinguish using entropy alone.

Finally, MovieStealer [40] aims at identifying encrypted and decrypted-but-compressed media buffers in order to break DRM. It uses an entropy test to single out encrypted and compressed buffers from other data, and the χ^2-test to distinguish them. It requires 800 KB of data to reliably identify random data, which is far beyond the fragment size in the scenarios that we consider.

7.2   Non-entropy-based Approaches

HEDGE, by Casino et al. [12], evaluates a combination of χ^2-test and a sub-set of NIST SP800-22 [36] to discriminate encrypted and compressed traffic. They use a dataset which is significantly smaller than ours, and do not dis-cuss learning-based approaches. A limitation of this class of approaches is the fairly low accuracy, especially for small block sizes (ref. Sect. 5). Also, this and other similar approaches based on statistical randomness tests (e.g., [14,34]) can-not distinguish between different types of compressed archives. Mbol et al. [32] investigate the use of the Kullback-Leibler divergence (relative entropy) to dif-ferentiate encrypted files from JPEG images. Their analysis does not investigate other formats, and assumes the availability of blocks of significant size (128 to 512 KB) from the beginning of each file. Especially in forensic and networking applications, uninterrupted blocks of such size are difficult to obtain.

While the application of neural networks to the problem at hand is fairly new, there exist some preliminary work. Ameeno et al. [11] show promising preliminary results, however the analysis is limited in scope: it only attempts to distinguish zip archives from rc4-encrypted data, and considers whole files (not fragments). Hahn et al. [24] perform an exploratory analysis of machine learning models. Their dataset is order of magnitudes smaller than ours, and they lack a comparative analysis of statistical approaches.

8   Conclusions

Discriminating encrypted from non-encrypted content is important for a vari-ety of security applications, and oftentimes tackled via entropy estimation. We comprehensively highlighted the limits of this technique and reviewed the effec-tiveness of the leading alternative approaches: χ^2-test, NIST SP800-22 test suite, and HEDGE. In addition, we proposed ENCOD, a novel neural network classifier of our own design. In order to ensure generality of results, we created a dataset of 200M fragments covering 5 different sizes and 8 data formats.

Results show that previous state-of-the-art methods have blind spots which result in low accuracy for certain fragment sizes/data types. However, our neu-ral network-based approach appears promising. Besides being able to discrim-inate between compressed formats (which traditional statistical tests cannot), it exceeds 90% accuracy already on fragments of only 2 KB. This suggests that systems incorporating encrypted content detection (e.g., ransomware detectors) would be better served by learning-based, rather than hand-crafted statistical approaches. This finding also suggests that learning may have useful applications to other problems in content type inference. Overall, we believe this work is an important step forward towards reliable encryption detection.

Acknowledgments. We would like to thank Daniele Venturi and Guinevere Gilman for their useful insights and comments. This work was supported by Gen4olive, a project that has received funding from the European Union's Horizon 2020 research and inno-vation programme under grant agreement No. 101000427, and in part by the Italian

MIUR through the Dipartimento di Informatica, Sapienza University of Rome, under Grant Dipartimenti di eccellenza 2018–2022.

Appendix

A   Entropy Analysis Results

Full results for the entropy analysis discussed in Sect. 2.4:

Chunk size: 512B

Format	Min	Q1	Median	Q3	Max
enc	7.427	7.569	7.591	7.613	7.709
zip	7.163	7.560	7.584	7.607	7.695
gzip	7.154	7.560	7.585	7.607	7.703
rar	7.381	7.563	7.587	7.610	7.692
jpeg	3.820	7.512	7.548	7.576	7.676
mp3	0.000	7.451	7.527	7.565	7.680
png	0.000	1.070	2.605	4.549	7.572
pdf	0.000	7.453	7.534	7.574	7.676

Chunk size: 2048B

Format	Min	Q1	Median	Q3	Max
enc	7.873	7.903	7.908	7.914	7.938
zip	7.816	7.898	7.904	7.910	7.935
gzip	7.847	7.898	7.904	7.910	7.933
rar	7.795	7.900	7.905	7.911	7.933
jpeg	5.123	7.856	7.873	7.884	7.917
mp3	0.379	7.703	7.838	7.871	7.916
png	0.000	1.312	2.815	4.752	7.808
pdf	0.000	7.820	7.875	7.893	7.930

Chunk size: 8192B

Format	Min	Q1	Median	Q3	Max
enc	7.969	7.976	7.978	7.979	7.984
zip	7.955	7.973	7.975	7.976	7.983
gzip	7.955	7.973	7.975	7.976	7.983
rar	7.960	7.974	7.976	7.977	7.983
jpeg	5.646	7.930	7.945	7.952	7.967
mp3	0.497	7.789	7.918	7.942	7.971
png	0.014	1.451	2.963	4.852	7.914
pdf	0.010	7.903	7.953	7.968	7.981

References

1. Pycriptodome library. https://pycryptodome.readthedocs.io/en/latest/src/introduction.html
2. DOCX Transitional (Office Open XML), January 2017. https://www.loc.gov/preservation/digital/formats/fdd/fdd000397.shtml
3. Atlanta spent $2.6m to recover from a $52,000 ransomware scare (2018). https://www.wired.com/story/atlanta-spent-26m-recover-from-ransomware-scare/
4. Wannacry cyber attack cost the NHS £92m as 19,000 appointments cancelled (2018). https://www.telegraph.co.uk/technology/2018/10/11/wannacry-cyber-attack-cost-nhs-92m-19000-appointments-cancelled/
5. Evolvingai: Deep neural networks are easily fooled: High confidence predictions for unrecognizable images, December 2019. http://www.evolvingai.org/fooling
6. FMA: A dataset for music analysis, December 2019. https://github.com/mdeff/fma
7. Open images dataset v5, December 2019. https://www.figure-eight.com/dataset/open-images-annotated-with-bounding-boxes/
8. Wikipedia: database download, December 2019. https://dumps.wikimedia.org/enwiki/
9. arXiv.org e-Print archive, February 2020. https://arxiv.org/
10. Ransomware attacks grow, crippling cities and businesses (2020). https://www.nytimes.com/2020/02/09/technology/ransomware-attacks.html
11. Ameeno, N., Sherry, K., Gagneja, K.: Using machine learning to detect the file compression or encryption. Amity J. Comput. Sci. **3**(1), 6 (2019)
12. Casino, F., Choo, K.K.R., Patsakis, C.: HEDGE: efficient traffic classification of encrypted and compressed packets. IEEE Trans. Inf. Forensics Secur. **14**(11), 2916–2926 (2019)
13. Chollet, F., et al.: Keras (2015). https://keras.io
14. Choudhury, P., Kumar, K.R.P., Nandi, S., Athithan, G.: An empirical approach towards characterization of encrypted and unencrypted VoIP traffic. Multimedia Tools Appl. **79**(1–2), 603–631 (2020)
15. Computer Security Division, I.T.L.: NIST SP 800-22: Documentation and Software, May 2016. https://csrc.nist.gov/projects/random-bit-generation/documentation-and-software
16. Conti, G., et al.: Automated mapping of large binary objects using primitive fragment type classification. Digital Invest. **7**, S3–S12 (2010)
17. Continella, A., et al.: Shieldfs: a self-healing, ransomware-aware filesystem. In: ACSAC (2016)
18. De Carli, L., Torres, R., Modelo-Howard, G., Tongaonkar, A., Jha, S.: Botnet protocol inference in the presence of encrypted traffic. In: INFOCOM (2017)
19. De Gaspari, F., Hitaj, D., Pagnotta, G., De Carli, L., Mancini, L.V.: The naked sun: malicious cooperation between benign-looking processes. In: 18th International Conference on Applied Cryptography and Network Security. ACNS (2020)
20. Dorfinger, P., Panholzer, G., John, W.: Entropy estimation for real-time encrypted traffic identification. In: Traffic Monitoring and Analysis (2011)
21. Fielding, R., et al.: RFC 2616, hypertext transfer protocol - HTTP/1.1 (1999). http://www.rfc.net/rfc2616.html
22. Glorot, X., Bengio, Y.: Understanding the difficulty of training deep feedforward neural networks. In: AISTATS (2010)

23. Hahn, D., Apthorpe, N., Feamster, N.: Detecting compressed cleartext traffic from consumer internet of things devices (2018)
24. Hahn, D., Apthorpe, N., Feamster, N.: Detecting Compressed Cleartext Traffic from Consumer Internet of Things Devices. arXiv:1805.02722 [cs], May 2018. http://arxiv.org/abs/1805.02722
25. Kharraz, A., Kirda, E.: Redemption: real-time protection against ransomware at end-hosts. In: RAID (2017)
26. Kirda, E.: Unveil: a large-scale, automated approach to detecting ransomware (keynote). In: SANER (2017)
27. Klambauer, G., Unterthiner, T., Mayr, A., Hochreiter, S.: Self-normalizing neural networks. CoRR abs/1706.02515 (2017). http://arxiv.org/abs/1706.02515
28. LeCun, Y., Bottou, L., Orr, G.B., Müller, K.R.: Efficient backprop. In: Neural Networks: Tricks of the Trade (1998)
29. Lee, H., Ge, R., Ma, T., Risteski, A., Arora, S.: On the ability of neural nets to express distributions. In: Kale, S., Shamir, O. (eds.) Proceedings of the 30th Conference on Learning Theory, COLT 2017, Amsterdam, The Netherlands, 7–10 July 2017. Proceedings of Machine Learning Research, vol. 65, pp. 1271–1296. PMLR (2017). http://proceedings.mlr.press/v65/lee17a.html
30. Malhotra, P.: Detection of encrypted streams for egress monitoring. Master of Science, Iowa State University, Ames (2007). https://lib.dr.iastate.edu/rtd/14632/
31. Mamun, M.S.I., Ghorbani, A.A., Stakhanova, N.: An entropy based encrypted traffic classifier. In: Qing, S., Okamoto, E., Kim, K., Liu, D. (eds.) ICICS 2015. LNCS, vol. 9543, pp. 282–294. Springer, Cham (2016). https://doi.org/10.1007/978-3-319-29814-6_23
32. Mbol, F., Robert, J.-M., Sadighian, A.: An efficient approach to detect Torrent-Locker ransomware in computer systems. In: Foresti, S., Persiano, G. (eds.) CANS 2016. LNCS, vol. 10052, pp. 532–541. Springer, Cham (2016). https://doi.org/10.1007/978-3-319-48965-0_32
33. Mehnaz, S., Mudgerikar, A., Bertino, E.: Rwguard: a real-time detection system against cryptographic ransomware. In: Research in Attacks, Intrusions, and Defenses. RAID 2018 (2018)
34. Palisse, A., Durand, A., Le Bouder, H., Le Guernic, C., Lanet, J.-L.: Data aware defense (DaD): towards a generic and practical ransomware countermeasure. In: Lipmaa, H., Mitrokotsa, A., Matulevičius, R. (eds.) NordSec 2017. LNCS, vol. 10674, pp. 192–208. Springer, Cham (2017). https://doi.org/10.1007/978-3-319-70290-2_12
35. Park, B., Savoldi, A., Gubian, P., Park, J., Lee, S.H., Lee, S.: Data extraction from damage compressed file for computer forensic purposes. Int. J. Hybrid Inf. Technol. 1(4), 14 (2008)
36. Rukhin, A., et al.: A Statistical Test Suite for Random and Pseudorandom Number Generators for Cryptographic Applications. Special Publication 800-22r1a, NIST, April 2010
37. Trottier, L., Giguere, P., Chaib-draa, B.: Parametric exponential linear unit for deep convolutional neural networks. In: 2017 16th IEEE International Conference on Machine Learning and Applications (ICMLA) (2017)
38. Wallace, G.K.: The jpeg still picture compression standard. IEEE Trans. Consum. Electron. 38(1), xviii–xxxiv (1992)
39. Walls, R.J., Learned-Miller, E., Levine, B.N.: Forensic triage for mobile phones with DEC0DE. In: USENIX Security Symposium (2011)
40. Wang, R., Shoshitaishvili, Y., Kruegel, C., Vigna, G.: Steal this movie - automatically bypassing DRM protection in streaming media services. In: USENIX (2013)

41. Wang, Y., Zhang, Z., Guo, L., Li, S.: Using entropy to classify traffic more deeply. In: 2011 IEEE Sixth International Conference on Networking, Architecture, and Storage, pp. 45–52, July 2011
42. Zhang, H., Papadopoulos, C., Massey, D.: Detecting encrypted botnet traffic. In: 2013 Proceedings IEEE INFOCOM, pp. 3453–1358, April 2013

A Weighted Voting Framework for Android App's Vetting Based on Multiple Machine Learning Models

Honglei Hui, Yongbo Zhi$^{(\boxtimes)}$, Ning Xi, and Yuanqing Liu

School of Cyber Engineering, Xidian University, Xi'an, China
hlhui@stu.xidian.edu.cn, zhiyongbo51@163.com, nxi@xidian.edu.cn,
lyq@stu.xidian.edu.cn

Abstract. Android's openness and flexibility attract many cybercriminals to monitor user behavior or steal their personal information. To address these issues, different machine learning (ML) algorithms and models are proposed for classifying Android benign or malicious applications. Algorithms such as Random Forest (RF), SVM, and Naive Bayes (NB) can classify with high accuracy. Each model are trained on the specific data set with specific algorithms. And they play with different performance in different scenarios. Besides, if one training data set is polluted by attackers, it would be cause a high false alarm on benign apps or miss some malicious apps. In order to enhance the generality of classifications and improve the resistance on attacks to trained model, we propose a Weighted Voting Framework (WVF) for Android app's vetting based on multiple machine learning models. Instead of classifying based on a single ML model, WVF makes the final decision through a weighted voting mechanism conducted on multiple ML models. The experimental results show that the performance of the model is improved compared to the single model before the combination.

Keywords: Android applications · Machine learning · Malware detection · Weighted voting

1 Introduction

Usage of Android phones has increased significantly. However, due to the openness of Android, attackers have developed many malicious programs to perform malicious actions such as file theft and communication monitoring. According to the "Report on Mobile Phone Security in China in the First Quarter of 2020" [1] released by Qihoo 360 Technology Company. About 392,000 new malicious mobile programs has been detected by 360 Security Brain, which shows a continuous increase.

Android provides basic security mechanisms, particularly relying on a permission-based mechanism. The permission mechanism allows users to obtain the text description of the application's behavior and the list of permissions

© Springer Nature Switzerland AG 2020
M. Kutyłowski et al. (Eds.): NSS 2020, LNCS 12570, pp. 63–78, 2020.
https://doi.org/10.1007/978-3-030-65745-1_4

required for work [2]. For example, an application needs permissions to access location information. The users only know that the application uses the permissions but do not know how the data is used. There are a number of benign applications that require this permission, such as mapping applications that use location information for the navigation. But a few malicious applications may send it to a remote server, which may cause a leakage on user's privacy. In order to discover these malicious applications on time, a number of approaches have been researched and proposed by researchers. According to application's status, it can be categorized into static analysis and dynamic analysis.

The static analysis technology does not need to run an Android application, but relies on the extraction of the application's own characteristics. Enck et al. [3] analyzed the permissions applied by Android applications to determine whether there is malicious behavior. In recent years, machine learning (ML) algorithms have been widely used to detect malicious applications on smartphone platforms. Glodek et al. [4] use permissions, components, and native code as characteristics, and use random forest algorithm to identify malicious applications. Idrees et al. [5] analyzed the permission usage information and intentions of Android applications. They used ML algorithms to identify malicious applications and got a better classification effect. Arp et al. [6] extract permissions, intents, and suspicious APIS in the application, and use the SVM algorithm to classify the application. Santos et al. [7] used the opcode sequence frequency of executable files to train ML models to detect malicious applications. Dynamic analysis is to monitor the data flow in real time while the program is running. Tam et al. [8] capture dynamic information to reconstruct malware behavior. Burguera et al. [9] identififies malware by initiating and executing system calls in the client-server architecture.

The current technology of using machine learning to detect malware is relatively mature and can achieve good accuracy. But most of them use a single machine learning algorithm to build a classifier. But the single classifier model is vulnerable to targeted attacks. For example, Chen et al. [10] proposed to inject crafted adversarial examples into the training dataset so as to reduce detection accuracy. The joint working mode of multiple classifiers can widely resist many attacks on machine learning classifiers. In addition, this article also introduces the weighted voting method. This method assigns low weight values to classifiers with low accuracy. Even if a single classifier in the model is attacked, the impact can be minimized. We will describe the specific details later.

A single ML model is vulnerable to data poisoning attacks, resulting in a significant decrease in accuracy. Moreover, the generalization ability of a specific model is often poor and only suitable for special scenarios. The above reasons limit the accuracy of application review. To improve the performance of the malware's detection based on ML, this paper proposes a Weighted Voting Framework (WVF) for Android app's votting based on Multiple Machine Learning Models. This Framework collects a wide range of features extracted from application, mainly including, request permissions, activities, services, and the sensitive information flows. Then the integrated learning is performed to train different classifier models based on the same data set. Different classifier models work in parallel and get the final classification decision in a 'weighted voting' way.

In summary, this paper made the following contributions to vet applications on smartphones:

(1) We extracted permissions, activities, services and other information from the application. We also used FLOWDROID [16] to extract sensitive information flows from 1,555 benign and malicious applications, and used this information to construct the training data set for identifying malicious applications.
(2) Based on the idea of multiple classifiers working together and weighted voting, we proposed a Weighted Voting Framework for Android App's Vetting based on Multiple Machine Learning Models, which can identify malicious applications with high accuracy.
(3) We have carried out experiments on the framework and proved its effectiveness.

2   Preliminaries

2.1   Machine Learning Model

Simply put, ML is to convert disordered data into useful information [11]. This technology is widely used in today's network security and terminal security. There are different forms of ML, including supervised learning, unsupervised learning, reinforcement learning and semi-supervised learning. In this article, we use supervised learning to detect malicious Android applications.

Support Vector Machine (SVM). This is a supervised learning ML algorithm, which has a good performance on classification problems. In SVM, each data item can be represented as a point in n-dimensional space. Each specific coordinate is a characteristic value. Each specific coordinate is a feature value, where n represents the number of features contained in a data. SVM can also perform non-linear classification through the kernel method, which is also one of the common kernel learning methods [12].

Random Forest (RF). The Random Forest algorithm is an ensemble learning algorithm. This algorithm was proposed by Leo and Adele [13]. A random forest classifier contains multiple decision tree classifiers. The training sample set of each base classifier is obtained by sampling with replacement from the data set. The training of the base classifier uses a decision tree algorithm. The final result is obtained by comprehensive analysis of the results of multiple base classifiers.

Neural Network (NN). Neural Network, which simulates the nervous system of organisms, is composed of neurons with weights and biases. In the training process, by adjusting the weights and biases of neurons, a model whose output is close to or in line with the expected results according to the input information is finally obtained. A prominent and important property of neural network is "learning". In a broad sense, neural network learning can be divided into four types: supervised learning, unsupervised learning, reinforcement learning and semi-supervised learning [14].

Logistic Regression (LR). Logistic regression maps $wx + b$ to the hidden state p via the function L to obtain $p = L(wx + b)$. The values of p and 1-p affect the value of $wx + b$ and the form of $L()$. According to the form of the $L()$ function, it can be divided into logistic regression and polynomial regression. Logistic regression is usually used to deal with two classification problems and shows good results. It is also applicable to multi-classification problems under certain circumstances.

Naive Bayesian (NB). Bayesian classification is a statistical classification method and one of the most effective learning methods in machine learning and data mining [15]. Although Bayesian algorithm has a high accuracy rate, it is very complicated to apply. Naive Bayes algorithm is a simplified method based on Bayes algorithm. This method assumes that the attributes are conditionally independent of each other. This simplification measure reduces the complexity of the Bayesian method at the expense of partial accuracy.

For a clear description on our model, we select three main ML algorithms with better performance on app's vetting. Based on these basic ML models, we introduce a weighted voting procedure to reduce the false positive rate and improve accuracy. The detail of our framework and procedure is shown in Sect. 3.

2.2 Android Malware's Feature Set

As mentioned above, static analysis applications have achieved a lot. Through the analysis of existing work, the commonly used features are as follows:

(1) **Requested permissions.** Applications must request permission to access resources.
(2) **Applications components.** Components are an essential part of Android. *Activity*, *service*, and *contentprovider*, play an important role in applications.
(3) **Filtered intents.** Intents are the carriers of information, and malicious applications will monitor specific intents.
(4) **Used permissions.** Compared with the permissions requested by the application, the used permissions are more important.
(5) **Suspicious API calls.** Malicious applications use certain APIS to obtain sensitive data from smartphones.
    On the basis of inheriting these characteristics, we also added the description and extraction of information flow features:
(6) **Data flows.** Data flow can well describe the behavior of applications, and we can use the difference in data flow between benign and malicious applications to identify malicious programs.

3 A Weighted Voting Framework Based on Multiple Machine Learning Models

3.1 Android Malware Detection Methods

In order to improve the usability and accuracy of the model, we divide the model into three parts: **Feature Extraction**, **Weight Training** and **Weighted Voting**. Below we introduce these three parts in detail.

Feature Extraction. The framework first decompiled the input APK file, resulting in the *class.dex* file and *manifest.xml* file. Parses the manifest.xml file to obtain information about permissions, activities, and services requested by the application. By analyzing the Dalvik bytecode, the used permissions and the API calls information of the system can be obtained. FLOWDROID [16] was used to perform static taint analysis on the input APK to obtain sensitive data flow information and embed feature vectors together with the previously extracted information.

Weight Training. In the training phase, three classifier models are obtained using training data modeling. Use the test data set to test the three classifier models and get the results. The result is used as the feature value of the second round of RF training. After the second round of RF training, the weight coefficients of the three classifiers are obtained. So far, the training phase is over.

Weighted Voting. Three classifier models are read in the voting phase. Enter the data and get the judgment result. A score is obtained by weighted voting based on the judgment result and the weight coefficient. The APK is judged to be benign or malicious based on the score obtained by the weighted voting. The process architecture is shown in Fig. 1.

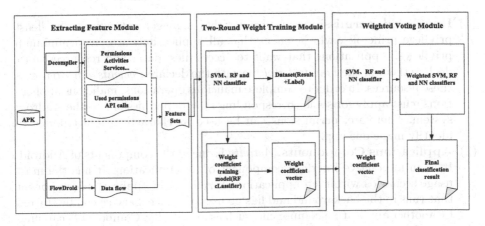

Fig. 1. Weighted voting framework based on multiple ML models for android

Table 1. Classification of sensitive sources of SUSI

Source	Examples
UNIQUE_IDENTIFIER	CDMAPhonegetDeviceId(), SipPhoneBasegetEsn()...
LOCATION_INFORMATION	Address.getFeatureName(), Address.getAdminArea()...
NETWORK_INFORMATION	SmsMessagegetNumOfVoicemails(), CdmaCall.getState()...
ACCOUNT_INFORMATION	AccountManagerServicegetAllAccounts(), Authorizer.getAuthToken()...
FILE_INFORMATION	ResponseHeaders.getUri(), PicasaFacadegetPostPhotosUri()...
BLUETOOTH_INFORMATION	BluetoothInputDevicegetConnectedDevices(), AdapterServicegetName()...
DATABASE_INFORMATION	CursorWrapper.getCount(), SQLiteConnection.getConnectionId()...
EMAIL	MessageListFragment.getMailboxId(), Controller.getSearchMailbox()...
SYNCHRONIZATION_DATA	ContentServicegetSyncStatus(), DataConnectionAc.getApnListSync()...
SMS_MMS	NotificationInd.getExpiry(), DeliveryInd.getDate()...
CONTACT_INFORMATION	Contact.getContentValues(), StreamItemEntry.getId()...
CALENDAR_INFORMATION	SimpleWeekView.getFirstJulianDay(), Event.getTitleAndLocation()...
SYSTEM_SETTINGS	CDMAPhonegetSmscAddress(), PhoneBasegetUnitTestMode()...
IMAGE	GLView.getVisibility(), ImageFilter.getMaxParameter()...
BROWSER_INFORMATION	BrowserSettings.getPageCacheCapacity(), Tab.getTitle()...
NFC	NfcV.transceive(), NdefRecord.getPayload()

3.2   Extracting Feature Set

This paper extracts the characteristic attributes described above from the Android application package (APK). An APK file contains the compiled code file (.dex), file resources, assets, Certificates, and manifest file [19]. We first used apkTool, a powerful third-party decompression tool, to decompile the input APK files, resulting in the class.dex file and the manifest.xml file, which declares the necessary information. By parsing the manifest.xml file, we obtain the permission, activities, services and contentproviders information requested by the application, such as accessing album, obtaining location information, reading SMS and other permission. The specific features are as follows:

(1) **Requested permissions.** Android rights management follows the 'least privilege principle', which means that all applications are given minimum privileges. Applications that want to access files, data, and resources must declare them in the *manifest.xml* file with the declared *permissions* to access these resources. In order to complete malicious operations, malicious applications must apply for some corresponding system permissions to the Android system. Therefore, permissions can be used as characteristic attributes to identify malicious app.

(2) **Applications Components.** *Activity* is one of the components of Android. It is an interactive interface component of an application. It has the most usage scenarios within an application. *Service* is an application component that runs in the background and has no user interface. Service can be started by another application component, such as an activity. Components can bind to and interact with services. For example, Service can handle things like file downloading and playing music. *Contentprovider* is primarily used to implement data sharing between different applications. Sensitive data may

be accessed when sharing content provider data with other applications. The three main components of Android can be extracted as feature properties to identify malicious applications.

(3) **Filtered intents.** *Intents* are designed to facilitate communication between applications, as well as interaction between components within an application. Intents are carriers of information that can be used to request a component to do something. Activities, services, and contentproviders in application are all related to intents. Malicious applications will listen for specific intents, and this paper will extract Intent information as the characteristic information.

DEBIN [6] implements a lightweight disassembler based on the dex libraries of the Android platform. We use DEBIN [6] to analysis the *Dalvik bytecode*, the API calls and the used permissions information of the system can be obtained. The specific features are as follows:

(4) **Used permissions.** The permissions characteristics of application applications have been mentioned above. But when it comes to identifying malicious Android malicious applications, analyzing used permissions is more important.Android applications are written in Java language and compiled into *Dalvik bytecode*, from which we can extract used permission information as feature attributes.

(5) **Suspicious API calls.** API, which encapsulates function functions with specific semantic information that can reflect the semantic and behavioral information of an application. Malicious applications use certain API to get sensitive data from the smartphone and send messages, such as *getDeviceId()* and *sendTextMessage()*. We extract these API calls as distinguishing features of malicious apps.

FLOWDROID [16] is a novel and highly accurate static taint analysis tool for Android applications. This paper uses FLOWDROID to extract the data flows.

(6) **Data flows.** Data flows can indicate how an application uses specific pieces of information and can be a good description of an application's behavior. For a malicious application, the data flow may come from unique sensitive sources and reach a few typical sensitive sinks. The data flow in a malicious application differs greatly from the flow of information in a benign application. We can use these differences to judge whether an application is benign or malicious.

We modified the source code of FLOWDROID allows the data flow information of each APK to be output in the corresponding JSON file in the form of key-value pairs. As SUSI [17] provides a list of APIS for accessing sensitive resources and the classification of these APIS, as shown in Tables 1 and 2. This paper considers non-classified sources and sinks insensitive. Therefore, We compare the data flow information extracted from APK with the API list. If the data flow information belongs to the SUSI list, the data flow will be regarded as a sensitive data flow and added to the feature set.

The combination of features can usually reflect the behavior of malicious applications. In this paper, six attribute sets are defined. Each attribute set

Table 2. Classification of sensitive sinks of SUSI

Sink	Examples
LOCATION_INFORMATION	ILocationManager.requestGeofence(), ILocationManager.addTestProvider()...
PHONE_CONNECTION	GSMPhone.sendBurstDtmf(), SipPhone.sendUssdResponse()...
VOIP	SIPTransactionStack.putDialog(), SipPhone.setOnPostDialCharacter()...
PHONE_STATE	SipPhoneBase.notifyDisconnect(), GSMPhone.notifyDataConnection()...
EMAIL	EmailServiceProxy.setLogging(), EmailServiceProxy.sendMail()...
BLUETOOTH	AdapterService.setScanMode(), setScanMode.openReceivedFile()...
ACCOUNT_SETTINGS	AccountManagerService.setUserData(), AccountManagerService.onBind()...
AUDIO	AudioEffect.setParameter(), AudioService.setSpeakerphoneOn()...
SYNCHRONIZATION_DATA	SyncManager.dumpSyncState(), Instrumentation.sendCharacterSync()...
NETWORK	NetworkState.writeToParcel(), ConnectivityManager.setUsbTethering()...
FILE	DatagramSocket.setNetworkInterface(), ParcelFileDescriptor.open()...
LOG	UserManager.setUserIcon(), Serializer.text()...
SMS_MMS	CDMAPhone.sendUssdResponse(), RetrieveConf.setMessageClass()...
CONTACT_INFORMATION	QuickContactBadge.setMode(), CallLogAdapter.bindGroupView...
CALENDAR_INFORMATION	CalendarController.sendEvent(), CalendarUtils.setSharedPreference()...
SYSTEM_SETTINGS	ITelephony.call(), GSMPhone.setSystemProperty()...
BROWSER_INFORMATION	Controller.setActiveTab(), Tab.setWebView()...
NFC	HandoverTransfer.onScanCompleted(), NfcService.handleMessage()

Table 3. Feature set

Features	Examples
Requested permission	WRITE_SMS, CALL_PHONE, SEND_SMS...
Applications Component	AboutAct, SHActivity, SHMenu...
Filtered intent	MESSAGE, PUSH_SERVICE, BOOT_COMPLETED...
Used permission	SEND_SMS, ACCESS_NETWORK_STATE, RECORD_AUDIO...
Suspicious API call	HttpPost, Context.getSystemService, PackageManager.getPackageInfo...
Data flow	TelephonyManager.getDeviceId()→Log.d()
	HttpEntity.getEntity()→Log.i()
	GsmCellLocation.getCid()→ByteArrayOutputStream.write()

represents a class of features extracted from APK, and a joint attribute set is defined, which contains all the features defined above. Table 3 shows the feature set and partially extracted features. After extracting the feature attributes, this paper builds a feature vector x for each application. If the application contains the attribute, the value of the corresponding position of the attribute is 1, otherwise it is 0.

3.3   A Weighted Voting for App's Vetting in Android

At present, machine learning (ML) has been widely used in the detection of malware and has shown good classification results. However, due to some factors such as the algorithm itself, there are always some restrictive factors in a single ML algorithm. For example, the data set of the SVM algorithm should not be too large and the SVM algorithm is not suitable for multi-classification problems, the Naive Bayes algorithm does not perform well when dealing with data with relatively large attributes, the Random Forest algorithm cannot handle data with fewer eigenvalues and is not suitable for regression problems. And people usually hope to use the ML model with smaller restrictions and high-precision results.

Therefore, this paper proposes a joint working mode of multiple classifiers. The main idea is to train different classifier models based on the same data set, the different classifier models work in parallel and get the final classification results in a weighted 'voting' way. On this basis, we no longer simply use the peer voting mode but use a weighted voting way to get the final result.

In order to obtain higher accuracy, we have introduced a weighting mechanism. Simply put, different classifiers have different influences on the final result. In this process, we combine the benign APP data set and the malicious APP data set into the initial data set D. Divide D into three parts randomly in proportion, training data set D_{train}, single classifier test data set D_{sct} and weighted voting test data set D_{wv}. First of all use D_{train} to train and model the ML algorithm described in Sect. 3. Then use the trained model to predict and classify the feature vectors in D_{sct}. Combine the classification result with the label L_{sct} in the weight training data set to obtain the weight coefficient training data set D_{weight}.

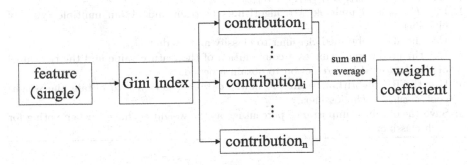

Fig. 2. The calculation process of the weight coefficient of the base classifier.

The second step use RF algorithm to model D_{weight}. Because the RF algorithm consists of a set of decision trees. This algorithm provides a function to calculate the contribution of eigenvalues in the process of constructing a RF. This function is based on the Gini index to calculate the contribution value of the characteristic value in the process of building a single decision tree. Use formula (1) to calculate the Gini index at node x. Where K indicates that there are K categories, and p_{xk} indicates the proportion of category k at node x. The importance of features at node x can be obtained by formula (2). $GINI_y$ and $GINI_z$ respectively represent the Gini index of two new nodes after branching. The contribution of the feature at all nodes on a single tree is summed to obtain the contribution value of the feature to a single decision tree. After that, the contribution of the eigenvalue to each decision tree is summed and averaged to obtain the contribution value of the eigenvalue in the modeling process. The process is shown in Fig. 2.

$$GINI_x = 1 - \sum_{K=1}^{K} p_{xk}^2 \tag{1}$$

$$IM_x = GINI_x - GINI_y - GINI_z \tag{2}$$

We use the contribution value of the corresponding feature as its weight coefficient. And the sum of the weight coefficients of all features is 1, as shown in formula (3). Because the results of different classifiers have different effects as features in the modeling process. We can obtain the weight coefficients of the three classifiers $[W_{SVM}, W_{RF}, W_{NN}]$. The specific steps of training to obtain weight coefficients are shown in Algorithm 1.

$$\sum_{i=1}^{n} WC_i = 1 \tag{3}$$

Algorithm 1 Train Classifiers And Get Weight Coefficient

INPUT: Data set D_{train} and D_{sct}

OUTPUT: $[W_{model1}, W_{model1}, ..., W_{modeln}]$

1: Use D_{train} and multiple ML algorithms to train and obtain multiple types of classifiers.
2: Use the above-obtained classifier to classify and predict D_{sct}.
3: Use the prediction result as a combination of the feature value and the true label of the data used for prediction to obtain a new data set.
4: Use the RF algorithm, train the newly obtained data set to obtain the weight coefficient of each classifier.
5: Save the obtained importance percentage as the weight coefficient when voting for each classifier.

Finally read the three classifier models previously saved. After we input the data set D_{wv}. The trained base classifier will read the feature data in D_{wv}. Each base classifier will get a set of results according to the classification rules of the respective algorithm. In this process, if the base classifier determines that an APP is malware, the score of the APP is -1. Otherwise, the APP score value is 1.

After the preliminary scoring, the result obtained by each basic classifier is multiplied with its weight coefficient to obtain multiple sets of weighted results. The weighted result is summed by the formula (4) to get the final score. MS_i represents the score value of the base classifier and WC_i represents the weight coefficient of the corresponding base classifier. The above process is shown in Fig. 3. Determine whether the APK is malicious based on the score. If $SCORE_f > 0$, the APK is judged to be malicious. Otherwise, the APK is determined to be benign. The specific weighted voting steps is shown in Algorithm 2.

$$SCORE_f = \sum_{i=1}^{n} MS_i * WC_i \tag{4}$$

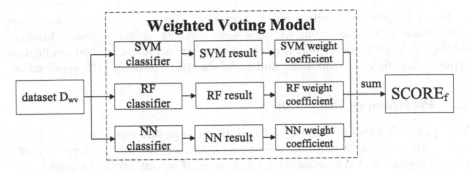

Fig. 3. Weighted voting mechanism process.

Algorithm 2 Weighted Voting
___
INPUT: Data set D_{wv}
OUTPUT: Judgement result
1: Obtain the saved multiple classifier models.
2: Obtain the classification results of the data set by the three classifier models.
3: Combine the respective results and weight coefficients of the three classifiers to perform weighted voting.
4: The result of voting will generate a score.
5: **if** *Source* > 0 **then**
6:     This APK is malicious.
7: **else**
8:     This APK is benign.
9: **end if**
10: Save the obtained importance percentage as the weight coefficient when voting for each classifier.

The above solution avoids some shortcomings of a single classifier through the weighted votting mode of multiple classifiers. If the results of individual classifiers are not very good, a lower weight will be obtained in the subsequent weight assignment. The final result is determined by the voting mechanism, even if an individual classifier gets a wrong result, it can be corrected by the correct result obtained by other classifiers. Therefore, compared with a single classifier, there would be a certain improvement in the accuracy of the results.

4   Experiment

4.1   Datasets

The implementation process is described in detail above, and the effectiveness will be demonstrated by experiments. We used the malicious and benign software dataset named CICAndMal2017 [18] with a total of 1555 samples, of which malware samples are divided into 4 categories: adware, ransomware, scareware and malware. The malicious samples were from 42 unique malware families, totaling 416 applications, and the benign data set included common application types such as life, entertainment, and social shopping, totaling 1139 applications.

4.2 Porformance Evaluation

This paper divides about 20% of the data set from the initial data set as the final verification data set, and uses these data to verify the performance of a single classifier and the performance indicators of a joint working classifier.

- **True Positive Ratio (TPR)/sensitivity**: The proportion of correctly classified malicious APKs to the number of all malicious APKs in the data set.

$$TPR = \frac{TP}{TP + FN}$$

- **True Negative Ratio (TNR)/Specificity**: The proportion of the number of correctly classified benign APKs to the number of all benign APKs in the data set.

$$TNR = \frac{TN}{FP + TN}$$

- **False Positive Ratio (FPR)**: The proportion of the number of misclassified benign APKs to the number of all benign APKs in the data set.

$$FPR = 1 - TNR = \frac{FP}{FP + TN}$$

- **False Negative Ratio (FNR)**: The number of misclassified malicious APKs is the proportion of all malicious APKs in the data set.

$$FNR = \frac{FN}{TP + FN}$$

- **Accuracy (Acc)**: The percentage of APKs that are correctly classified to the number of APKs that are classified in the data set.

$$Acc = \frac{TP + TN}{TP + FN + FP + TN}$$

- **Error rate (Err)**: The ratio of the number of misclassified APKs to the number of all classified APKs in the dataset.

$$Err = 1 - Acc$$

We randomly sort all APKs to form three data sets D_1, D_2, and D_3. We use these three data sets to perform the weight training process and weighted voting process described in Sect. 3.3, respectively. Here, we have chosen SVM, NN and RF, three better-performing ML algorithms for modeling. Use these three single classifiers to form a joint working model. The experimental environment is shown in Table 4. The following shows the accuracy and error rate of the WVF model on the three data sets. The accuracy and error rates of the data set D_1 are shown in Figs. 4 and 5. Figures 6 and 7 shows the accuracy and error rate of the model in D_2. Figures 8 and 9 shows the accuracy and error rate of the model in D_3.

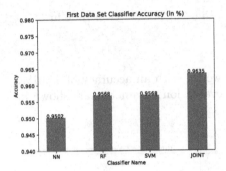

Fig. 4. Classifier accuracy in D_1 Fig. 5. Classifier error ratio in D_1

Table 4. System configuration.

Experimental host machine	
Processor	Intel(R) Core(TM) i7-4800MQ CPU @ 2.70 GHz(2701 MHz)
RAM	8.00 GB
System Type	64-bit Operating System
Operating System	Microsoft Windows 10
Processor	QEMU Virtual CPU version 2.5+ 2.09 GHz
RAM	16.00 GB
System Type	64-bit Operating System
Operating System	ubuntu16.04

The experiment uses three classifiers of SVM, RF and NN to test the results and accuracy separately. Then combine the three classifiers to get a joint model. Here we initiate three sets of data for experiments. We chose the third data set with the best effect for illustration. The results obtained by the three classifiers show that both SVM and RF have shown good classification results, reaching

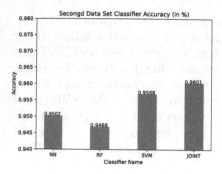

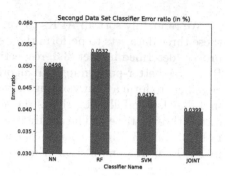

Fig. 6. Classifier accuracy in D_2 **Fig. 7.** Classifier error ratio in D_2

an accuracy of 95.68%, while NN is slightly worse, with an accuracy of 95.01%. The results are shown in Figs. 8 and 9. The evaluation parameters are shown in Table 5.

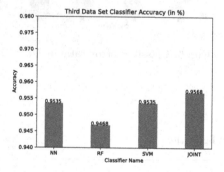

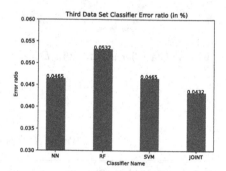

Fig. 8. Classifier accuracy in D_3 **Fig. 9.** Classifier error ratio in D_3

We follow the procedure in Sect. 3.3 to obtain the weight coefficients of the three classifiers as follows: [NN: 0.2799; RF: 0.3818; SVM: 0.3384]. Then use the same test data set as the test single classifier to test the joint working model and get the result. The result shows that the accuracy of the joint working model reaches 96.35%. Compared with the best-performing single classifier, the accuracy rate has been improved by 0.67%. Compared with a single classifier with poor performance, the accuracy rate has been improved by 1.34%. There are certain differences in the performance of the model on different data sets. However, the accuracy of the model is significantly improved compared to a single classifier.

Table 5. Performance evaluation index of each classifier in D_3 (in %).

Algorithm	TPR	TNR	FPR	FNR	Acc	Err
NN	96.43	94.47	5.53	3.57	95.02	4.98
RF	90.48	97.70	2.30	9.52	95.68	4.32
SVM	95.24	95.85	4.15	4.76	95.68	4.32
WVF	95.24	96.77	3.23	4.76	96.35	3.65

5 Conclusion and Future Work

Android is suffering from malwares due to its openness. Although many researchers have applied machine learning algorithms to malware detection. But the method is mostly to apply a single classifier. Moreover, this classifier is vulnerable to attacks from adversarial examples [20], and the single classifier model has poor anti-attack ability. And ensemble learning is a simple and effective way to deal with it. At present, many researchers have developed different ensemble learning models. However, these models mostly use average probability, maximum probability, probability product and majority vote mechanism in the decision stage. Because the weighted voting mechanism will give a larger weight coefficient to the base classifier with high accuracy. Therefore, the accuracy and resistance of this mechanism are better than the above-mentioned mechanisms. This article shows how to detect and classify malware in Android applications through a combination of multiple classifiers by weighted voting. The method proposed in this paper combines individual classifiers, namely NN, SVM and RF, and introduces a voting mechanism that assigns weights to a single classifier by a machine learning algorithm. From this we have obtained a model with better accuracy than a single classifier. This model can detect malware in Android with an accuracy of 96.35%, and it also overcomes the shortcomings and limitations of the single classifier algorithm. This method combines the advantages of each classifier and effectively reduces the impact of their limitations on the detection results. The whole method is more usable and accurate. In future work, We are going to introduce more classifiers to create new combinations and filter out better-performing combination models. We also aims to use more feature data sets to improve the robustness and accuracy of the detection model.

References

1. Report on Mobile Phone Security in China in the First Quarter of 2020. http://news.yesky.com/331/707089831.shtml
2. Avdiienko, V., et al.: Mining apps for abnormal usage of sensitive data. In: 2015 IEEE/ACM 37th IEEE International Conference on Software Engineering, Florence, pp. 426–436 (2015). https://doi.org/10.1109/ICSE.2015.61
3. Enck, W., Ongtang, M., McDaniel, P.: On lightweight mobile phone application certification. In: Proceedings of the 16th ACM Conference on Computer and Communications Security (CCS 2009), pp. 235–245. Association for Computing Machinery, New York (2009). https://doi.org/10.1145/1653662.1653691

4. Glodek, W., Harang, R.: Rapid permissions-based detection and analysis of mobile malware using random decision forests. In: MILCOM 2013 - 2013 IEEE Military Communications Conference, San Diego, CA, pp. 980–985 (2013). https://doi.org/10.1109/MILCOM.2013.170

5. Idrees, F., Rajarajan, M.: Investigating the android intents and permissions for malware detection. In: 2014 IEEE 10th International Conference on Wireless and Mobile Computing, Networking and Communications (WiMob), Larnaca, pp. 354–358 (2014). https://doi.org/10.1109/WiMOB.2014.6962194

6. Arp, D., Spreitzenbarth, M., Hubner, M., Gascon, H., Rieck, K., Siemens, C.E.R.T.: Drebin: effective and explainable detection of android malware in your pocket. In: NDSS, vol. 14, pp. 23–26, February 2014

7. Santos, I., Brezo, F., Ugarte-Pedrero, X., Bringas, P.G.: Opcode sequences as representation of executables for data-mining-based unknown malware detection. Inf. Sci. **231**, 64–82 (2013). https://doi.org/10.1016/j.ins.2011.08.020

8. Tam, K., Khan, S.J., Fattori, A., Cavallaro, L.: Copperdroid: automatic reconstruction of android malware behaviors. In: NDSS, February 2015

9. Burguera, I., Zurutuza, U., Nadjm-Tehrani, S.: Crowdroid: behavior-based malware detection system for android. In: Proceedings of the 1st ACM Workshop on Security and Privacy in Smartphones and Mobile Devices, pp. 15–26. ACM (2011). https://doi.org/10.1145/2046614.2046619

10. Chen, S., et al.: Automated poisoning attacks and defenses in malware detection systems: an adversarial machine learning approach. Comput. Secur. **73**, 326–344 (2018)

11. Richter, A.N., Khoshgoftaar, T.M.: A review of statistical and machine learning methods for modeling cancer risk using structured clinical data. Artif. Intell. Med. **90**, 1–14 (2018)

12. Hsieh, W.W.: Machine Learning Methods in the Environmental Sciences: Neural Networks and Kernels, chap. 7, pp. 157–169. Cambridge University Press, Cambridge (2009)

13. Alam, M.S., Vuong, S.T.: Random forest classification for detecting android malware. In: Green Computing and Communications, pp. 663–669 (2013)

14. Haykin, S.: Neural Networks and Learning Machines, 3rd edn. Prentice Hall, New Jersey (2008)

15. Zhang, H.: The optimality of Native Bayes. In: Proceedings of the Seventeenth International Florida Artificial Intelligence Research Society Conference (2004)

16. Arzt, S., et al.: FlowDroid: precise context, flow, field, object-sensitive and lifecycle-aware taint analysis for Android apps. SIGPLAN Not. **49**(6), 259–269 (2014). https://doi.org/10.1145/2666356.2594299

17. Rasthofer, S., Arzt, S., Bodden, E.: A machine-learning approach for classifying and categorizing android sources and sinks. In: NDSS, vol. 14 (2014)

18. Lashkari, A.H., Kadir, A.F.A., Taheri, L., Ghorbani, A.A.: Toward developing a systematic approach to generate benchmark android malware datasets and classification. In: The Proceedings of the 52nd IEEE International Carnahan Conference on Security Technology (ICCST), Montreal, Quebec, Canada (2018)

19. APK. https://zh.wikipedia.org/wiki/APK

20. Carlini, N., Wagner, D.: Towards evaluating the robustness of neural networks. In: Proceedings of IEEE Symposium on Security and Privacy (SP), pp. 39–57, May 2017

HyperWall: A Hypervisor for Detection and Prevention of Malicious Communication

Michael Kiperberg[1]([✉]), Raz Ben Yehuda[2], and Nezer J. Zaidenberg[3]

[1] Software Engineering Department, Shamoon College of Engineering,
Beer-Sheva, Israel
michaki1@sce.ac.il
[2] Department of Mathematical IT, University of Jyväskylä, Jyväskylä, Finland
raziebe@gmail.com
[3] School of Computer Science, The College of Management, Academic Studies,
Rishon LeZion, Israel
nzaidenberg@me.com

Abstract. Malicious programs vary widely in their functionality, from key-logging to disk encryption. However, most malicious programs communicate with their operators, thus revealing themselves to various security tools. The security tools incorporated within an operating system are vulnerable to attacks due to the large attack surface of the operating system kernel and modules. We present a kernel module that demonstrates how kernel-mode access can be used to bypass any security mechanism that is implemented in kernel-mode. External security tools, like firewalls, lack important information about the origin of the intercepted packets, thus their filtering policy is usually insufficient to prevent communication between the malicious program and its operator. We propose to use a thin hypervisor, which we call "HyperWall", to prevent malicious communication. The proposed system is effective against an attacker who has gained access to kernel-mode. Our performance evaluation shows that the system incurs insignificant ($\approx$1.64% on average) performance degradation in real-world applications.

Keywords: Virtual machine monitors · Hypervisors · Trusted computing base · Network security

1 Introduction

Malicious programs vary widely in their functionality, from key-logging to disk encryption. They utilize different vulnerabilities to achieve their goals: some attack applications [32] while others attack the kernel itself [17]. However, most malicious programs communicate with their operators, thus revealing themselves to various security tools. Specifically, firewalls attempt to detect and prevent such attacks by analyzing network packets that leave the network adapter. Unfortunately, firewalls must base their decision only on the content of the packets.

M. Kutyłowski et al. (Eds.): NSS 2020, LNCS 12570, pp. 79–93, 2020.
https://doi.org/10.1007/978-3-030-65745-1_5

The information about the origin of the packets, i.e., the name of the application that produced it, is lost. In practice, encryption is widely used for legitimate and malicious communication, thus firewalls have access only to the clear-text routing information, i.e., destination address and port. It is the responsibility of the system administrator to configure the list of allowed or the list of restricted destinations. These lists can be constructed automatically using machine learning techniques [2,8,13,26]. Similarly to traditional antiviruses, protection schemes based on black lists cannot withstand zero-day attacks, which are discovered weeks or months after infection [1].

On the other hand, software modules, like SELinux [31], can prevent the creation of sockets by unauthorized applications, regardless of their destination address. Unfortunately, these software modules, being part of the operating system, are vulnerable to attacks on the kernel and its modules [17].

Attacks on the kernel can be roughly divided into two categories: code attacks and data attacks. In code attacks [12], the goal of the attacker is to modify the instruction sequence. To achieve this goal, the attacker can replace the original code with their own or modify the control flow by manipulating the stack. Direct modification of the kernel code can be prevented using periodic verifications performed by the kernel itself, as done by Microsoft's Kernel Patch Protection [6], or by a more highly privileged software like a hypervisor [35].

Control flow integrity is a more challenging problem. It can be solved to some extent without recompilation of the kernel's code [22]. However better protection and performance can be achieved by analyzing the source code and recompiling the kernel [7].

Data attacks aim at altering the behavior of the kernel without modifying its code. The most common class of data attacks is Direct Kernel Object Modification (DKOM), in which kernel data structures are modified in order to achieve privilege escalation, process hiding [14], execution prevention [9], etc. Modern data attacks, called "data-oriented programming" achieve arbitrary computation (i.e., Turing complete) by assigning specially crafted values to the variables of a compromised program [11].

Due to the aforementioned security concerns, we see a migration of security modules from the kernel to an isolated environment. An isolated environment can be implemented using ARM's TrustZone [24], using a hypervisor that is available on most modern CPUs, or by introducing secure co-processor [21].

A hypervisor is a software component that has higher privileges than the operating system. Moreover, a hypervisor can configure interception of various events that occur in the operating system, thus making it an ideal candidate for security applications. For example, hypervisors can be used to protect the kernel code from modification [28], implement control flow integrity [22], provide additional security features like full disk encryption [29], etc.

The contribution of this paper is twofold. First, the paper describes a stealthy method by which malicious software can communicate with a remote operator. The communication cannot be detected by software modules executing inside the operating system because it is performed by direct manipulation of the network card registers. We demonstrate the viability of this method by implementing a kernel module for the Linux operating system. We note however that the same attack can be realized by employing random memory access vulnerability in the kernel. The method is not limited to the Linux operating system.

Then, the paper presents a design of a thin hypervisor we call "HyperWall" that detects and prevents malicious manipulation of network card registers. Because both legitimate and malicious accesses to the network card registers are performed from the kernel-mode, they are indistinguishable from the viewpoint of the hypervisor. Therefore, the hypervisor determines the legitimacy of access based on the content of the transmitted packets. Only packets that were previously transmitted by user-mode applications are considered legitimate.

Finally, we evaluate the security of the proposed solution and the impact of the hypervisor on the network and CPU performance. The results show insignificant ($\approx 1.64\%$ on average) performance degradation in real-world applications.

2 Background

In 2005, Intel introduced an extension to their CPUs [20] that enables the execution of multiple operating systems simultaneously. Each operating system executes in an isolated environment, called a "Virtual Machine" (VM), and the executing of all the virtual machines is governed by an isolated software, called a "Virtual Machine Monitor" (VMM) or "hypervisor". The hypervisor can configure interception of various events that occur in the VMs, e.g., execution of privileged instructions, access to IO ports, triggering of an exception, access to Model-Specific Registers (MSRs), etc. When an event configured for interception occurs, the CPU transfers the control from the VM to the hypervisor. This transition is called a "VM-exit". The information about the occurred event is stored in a special data structure for the hypervisor's inspection.

The hypervisor reacts to a VM-exit by inspecting the information about the occurred event. Instructions that were configured to be intercepted trigger a VM-exit before their actual execution. Therefore the hypervisor must emulate these instructions after a VM-exit. During the emulation, the hypervisor advances the instruction pointer of the VM to the next instruction. After completion of the event handling, the hypervisor transfers the control to the VM by executing a special instruction (VMRESUME). This transition is called a "VM-entry".

In early versions of the virtualization extension, memory management had a high overhead due to frequent events that had to be intercepted, e.g., page table switching, page faults, page invalidations. In order to solve this problem, Intel introduced a secondary-level Address Translation (SLAT) mechanism, called "Extended Page Tables" (EPT) [10]. The hypervisor can define a page table for each VM, which defines translation of the VMs physical addresses to real physical addresses. Each entry of EPT defines not only the mapping between addresses but also the access rights. Using EPT, the hypervisor can isolate itself and the VMs from each other.

A hypervisor can intercept a wide range of events. We will discuss only three of them, which we use in this paper. The first type of event is access to MSRs.

MSRs are used to report the features of a CPU and configure its state. They participate in the configuration of

- 64-bit environments via the EFER MSR,
- system call mechanism via the STAR family of MSRs and
- physical memory caching policies via the MTRR family of MSRs, etc.

Two special instructions, WRMSR and RDMSR, allow the software to write to and read from MSRs, which are identified by a number. The hypervisor can intercept read and write accesses to MSR separately of each MSR number and access type by setting an appropriate bit in the configuration of the VM (specifically in MSR bitmap field). Upon a VM-exit, the number of the MSR and its new value, in case of a write operation, are reported to the hypervisor.

Exceptions' delivery is another type of event. The hypervisor can intercept an exception before it is delivered to the VM by setting a bit that corresponds to the exception vector in the configuration of the VM (specifically in the exception bitmap field). Upon a VM-exit, the number of the exception as well as its error code is reported to the hypervisor.

The last type of event that has relevance to this paper is so-called "EPT-violations", i.e., access to the VMs physical addresses that cannot be translated to real physical addresses. In essence, EPT-violations are page faults in the secondary-level address translation. EPT-violations can occur either due to absent entries in the secondary level page table or due to inappropriate rights, e.g., write-access to a read-only page. Upon a VM-exit, the virtual and physical addresses are reported to the hypervisor. In addition the hypervisor receives a value that resembles an error-code. This value can be used to determine the reason for the EPT-violation.

2.1   Intel Network Cards

The attack that is presented in this paper targets the *i217* network card by Intel. The registers of this network card are memory-mapped, i.e., there is a set of physical addresses allocated for the network card, and values written to those addresses are transferred to the network card. Values read from those addresses are transferred from the network card. During its initialization, the operating system allocates two circular rings of descriptors TX and RX. The RX ring is used to transfer packets from the network card to the main memory. The TX ring is used to transfer packets from the main memory to the network card.

Each ring is defined by four registers whose purpose is depicted in Fig. 1. The TXDESCLO register holds the physical address of the base of the TX ring. The TXDESCLEN register holds the size of the TX ring. The TXDESCHEAD register holds the index of the first descriptor that is yet to be consumed by the network card. The TXDESCTAIL register holds the index of the first descriptor that is available for the operating system. Whenever possible, the network card consumes the descriptor indexed by TXDESCHEAD and advances the register to the next position. The network card stops when TXDESCHEAD reaches TXDESCTAIL.

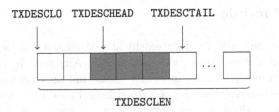

TXDESCLO TXDESCHEAD   TXDESCTAIL

TXDESCLEN

Fig. 1. Intel network card descriptor ring. The shaded descriptors are yet to be consumed by the network card.

Each descriptor points to a packet to be sent or provides some metadata (e.g., checksum offloading information) about the following packets. In order to send a packet, the operating system writes a descriptor to the TX ring at index TXDESCTAIL and advances the TXDESCTAIL register. In response, the network card consumes the descriptor and transmits the pointed packet or configures its internal state according to the metadata.

The network card provides checksum offloading functionality, i.e., it can automatically compute and insert checksums for the transmitted packets. Because the structures of headers vary between different protocols, before transmitting a serial of packets, the operating system prepares the network card for a specific protocol stack by inserting a metadata descriptor (or a context descriptor) with the relevant information. Metadata descriptors themselves do not transmit packets but rather affect the transmission of the following packets.

3 Threat Model

For this paper, we assume that the attacker has random access to the kernel memory, i.e., he can read from and write to arbitrary locations in the memory by exploiting a vulnerability [17]. However, this assumption is restricted as follows:

- We assume that the operating system is equipped with a code integrity verification mechanism [28] and a control flow integrity verification mechanism [22], thus preventing direct code modification or control flow alteration.
- We assume that attacks on data buffers in user-mode applications are not feasible. To justify this assumption, we note that user-mode buffers, unlike kernel-mode buffers, can be swapped out and their location is less predictable.
- We assume that the system is equipped with a system call filtering mechanism, e.g., [23] that prevents unauthorized socket opening by the vulnerable application.
- We assume the existence of a peripheral firewall that blocks packets whose headers specify unsupported protocols, see Sect. 5.3.

To conclude, we assume that the attacker can read and write data (but not code) in kernel-mode (but not in user-mode).

4   Attack Module

We demonstrate the viability of a stealthy attack using a tiny kernel module. The module performs the required reads and writes. Although in reality, the attack would be performed from user-mode by exploiting an existing vulnerability in kernel-mode, we believe that the described kernel module is an adequate model for this attack as it does not use any functions or data structures of the kernel.

Strictly speaking, communication with a network card varies between different vendors and models. Some network cards can be configured to communicate via Memory-Mapped Input/Output (MMIO), whereas others require legacy input/output or even a combination of both. Only network cards that communicate via MMIO are vulnerable to the described attack.

The attack begins by obtaining the physical address of the MMIO region allocated by the firmware for the network card. This information can be obtained by enumerating the PCI configuration space or by asking the operating system (*Device Manager* on Windows and *lspci* on Linux).

The MMIO region maps the registers of a network card. Values written to those registers are transferred to the network card. Values read from those registers are transferred from the network card. The driver uses the four TX-registers to send a single UDP packet containing the string "hello".

The sending procedure can be divided into four steps:

1. locating the buffer that will store the UDP packet;
2. filling the buffer with a UDP packet;
3. writing the metadata and the regular descriptors; and
4. advancing the TXDESCTAIL.

In order to locate the buffer, the driver first reads TXDESCLO and TXDESCLEN. Then, the driver traverses the circular ring searching for a descriptor that points to a packet and that was already consumed by the network card. The buffer containing the consumed packet will be used as storage for the "hello" UDP packet. The driver fills the buffer with the "hello" UDP packet, including the UDP, IP, and MAC headers. Then, the driver writes two descriptors: a metadata descriptor that corresponds to a UDP over IP packet, and a regular descriptor which points to the buffer containing the "hello" UDP packet. Finally, the driver advances the TXDESCTAIL by two.

We note that all the steps performed by the driver require only memory reads and writes. Therefore, they could be performed from user-mode by exploiting random access vulnerability in kernel-mode.

5   Hypervisor Design

5.1   Thin Hypervisors

HyperWall is a thin hypervisor that is capable of running only a single virtual machine. The hypervisor does not emulate any hardware devices and it allows the operating system to execute normally without any interruption with a few exceptions that will be described in this section.

In security applications, thin hypervisors are preferable over a full hypervisor, like Xen, KVM [5], Hyper-V [33], etc., due to their lower performance impact and smaller attack surface. Xen 3.3, for example, consists of ≈320 KLOC [27] while HyperWall has only ≈3 KLOCs.

5.2   Hypervisor Initialization

HyperWall runs on Intel processors. The hypervisor is implemented as an application for the EFI firmware interface [38]. The EFI application is configured to load before the bootloader of the operating system. The EFI application loads a configuration file to be used by the hypervisor. The configuration file contains information about the offsets of kernel functions and variables that are used during the interception process. The offsets can be copied from the *System.map* file deployed with a kernel image. Figure 2 provides an example of a configuration file.

```
ffffffff81c00010 T entry_SYSCALL_64
ffffffff81908b00 T sock_sendmsg
ffffffff82158380 R inet_dgram_ops
ffffffff82158480 R inet_stream_ops
```

Fig. 2. Configuration file obtained from a *System.map* file

The installation procedure is simple. The EFI application containing the HV and the configuration file are copied to an EFI partition that contains the operating system or to a USB disk. Then, the boot order is changed to load the EFI application before the bootloader of the operating system.

5.3   Interception of System Calls

The hypervisor intercepts an execution of a single function sock_sendmsg, which is responsible for sending data though sockets. This function is invoked by the three system calls that send data through sockets: sendto, sendmsg and sendmmsg. Therefore by intercepting sock_sendmsg, we intercept all the data sending system calls.

The interception is performed by replacing the first instruction of the intercepted function with a software breakpoint instruction. This instruction triggers an exception on vector 3, which triggers a VM-exit. The hypervisor emulates the instruction that was replaced and advances the instruction pointer to the next instruction.

Due to KASLR [4], the virtual addresses of kernel functions change on each boot. In order to determine the actual virtual address, the hypervisor intercepts a write to the **LSTAR** MSR. The kernel writes to this MSR, the address of the system call handler, specifically the address of the **entry_SYSCALL_64** function. The difference between the actual address of the **entry_SYSCALL_64** function to the address that appears in the *System.map* file is the random relocation of the kernel. By adding this difference to any other symbol that appears in the *System.map* file we obtain its actual address.

The prototype of the function **sock_sendmsg**, which sends a message over a socket, is given in Fig. 3. The function receives two parameters: **sock** and **msg**. The first parameter represents the socket over which the message is sent. The second parameter represents the message itself.

```
int sock_sendmsg(
    struct socket *sock,
    struct msghdr *msg)
```

Fig. 3. sock_sendmsg prototype

```
struct socket {
    ...
    const struct proto_ops *ops;
    ...
};
```

Fig. 4. socket structure

The first parameter points to a **socket** structure as shown in Fig. 4. The hypervisor uses the **ops** field of this structure in order to determine the protocol of the socket. The **ops** field points to a set of functions that are responsible to handle actions performed on the socket. Each protocol has a separate set of handling functions. These sets are stored in global variables of the kernel. By comparing the **ops** fields to the values of these variables, the hypervisor can determine the protocol of the socket. HyperWall handles only two protocols and, therefore, uses only two variables: **inet_dgram_ops** for UDP and **inet_stream_ops** for TCP.

Communication protocols can be divided into two sets: C—carrier protocols, such as TCP and UDP, A—auxiliary protocols, such as ARP. The set of protocols that are handled by HyperWall should include all the protocols that belong to C. Since protocols that belong to A cannot be used by an attacker, HyperWall does not handle these protocols. An external firewall should block all the packets belonging to C that are not handled by HyperWall.

The second parameter points to a **msghdr** structure as shown in Fig. 5. The **msg_iter** field of this structure contains an array of buffers to be transmitted;

```
struct iovec {
    void __user *iov_base;
    __kernel_size_t iov_len;
};

struct iov_iter {
    ...
    const struct iovec *iov;
    unsigned long nr_segs;
    ...
};
struct msghdr {
    ...
    struct iov_iter msg_iter;
    ...
};
```

Fig. 5. msghdr structure

specifically, the **nr_segs** fields represents the the number of buffers. The **iov** field is an array of buffers. Each buffer is described by an address (**iov_base**) and size ((**iov_len**)). The hypervisor computes a hash of each buffer and stores the hash in the hypervisor's internal data structure. The data structure is a balanced tree of a constant size. Initially, the tree is empty. When the tree reaches its maximal size, insertion of a new hash removes the eldest hash from the tree. This tree is used by the hypervisor for verification of packets that are transmitted by the network card. Because the operating system may attempt to retransmit a previously transmitted packet, it is incorrect to remove the hash upon a successful packet verification.

5.4   Interception of Network Card Accesses

The hypervisor uses an identity-mapping secondary-level page table. The hypervisor sets full access rights to all memory locations. There are only two exceptions for this setting. First, the region of physical memory containing the code and the data of the hypervisor is set to be inaccessible in the secondary level page table.

The second exception is the memory region containing the network card registers. The hypervisor configures the secondary-level page table such that any write attempt to the network card registers triggers a VM-exit. In response to the VM-exit, the hypervisor emulates the instruction that accesses the registers and advances the instruction pointer to the next instruction. If the emulated instruction attempted to modify the TXDESCTAIL register, then the hypervisor performs a verification procedure prior to emulation, thus guaranteeing that non-authentic packets will be dropped.

The verification procedure consists of a loop in which the hypervisor verifies each packet that was transmitted by the operating system to the network card. More precisely, on an attempt to change the value of the TXDESCTAIL register from X to Y, the hypervisor verifies the packets pointed by descriptors at positions $X+1, X+2, \ldots, Y$ (circularly). The verification itself consists of two steps. First, the hypervisor computes the packet's hash. Then, the hypervisor checks whether the hash exists in the balanced tree. If not, then the hypervisor fills the corresponding descriptor with zeroes, thus preventing transmission of the malicious packet.

6   Evaluation

6.1   Security Evaluation

We assess the security of the proposed system from two perspectives:

- We assess the ability of the hypervisor to protect its code and data.
- We assess the ability of the hypervisor to prevent malicious communication.

In order to protect its code and data, the hypervisor configures the secondary-level page table to prevent any access to its internal state. The hypervisor can also protect itself from DMA attacks by configuring the IOMMU page tables [18]. However, protection from DMA attacks was not implemented in our prototype. With an appropriate configuration, any attempt to access the physical pages containing hypervisor's internal state triggers an EPT-violation, allowing the hypervisor to respond. In our implementation, the hypervisor responds by entering an infinite loop.

HyperWall is implemented as an EFI application, which boots before the operating system. EFI firmware can verify the integrity of the EFI application via a feature called "Secure Boot" [38].

We assume that an attacker successfully compromised a user-mode application and the kernel. However, we assume that the compromised application does not have an open socket. We also assume that the attacker cannot manipulate the data sent to a socket that is open in another user-mode application. Therefore, the attacker can only manipulate kernel-mode buffers to achieve his goal. Examples of such buffers are *sk_buff*s, the address fields of the socket, and its state. By manipulating the buffer, the attacker can change the destination address and the content of a packet that was scheduled for transmission.

Alternatively, as described in Sect. 4, the attacker can write directly to the network card registers. This method is simpler because it does not depend on the existence of packets that were previously scheduled for transmissions. In addition, this method does not require the attacker to know the exact layout of various kernel data structures. With the introduction of data structure layout randomization [3], this problem becomes particularly relevant.

The hypervisor compares the packet fetched by the network card to the packet submitted to sock_sendmsg function, and rejects malicious packets.

The arguments of the sock_sendmsg function exist for a very short period of time and are pointed by local variables. Therefore, malicious modification of these arguments is unlikely.

We assume that the kernel is equipped with code and control flow integrity verification mechanisms. Therefore, the attacker will not be able to invoke the sock_sendmsg function directly and provide it with malicious arguments.

Our current implementation verifies only UDP and TCP packets; obviously, this can be extended to other protocols. Regardless of the set of implemented protocols, the peripheral firewall should be configured to block other protocols, thus preventing the attacker from using unverified protocols for communication. Auxiliary protocols, like ARP and ICMP should be allowed—but with care [30]—by the firewall.

6.2   Performance Evaluation

We evaluated the performance of HyperWall on a PC equipped with a 3.4 GHz Intel Core i5-7500 CPU and 8 GB of RAM running Ubuntu Desktop 18.04. We used the LM-Bench suite [19] for micro-benchmarking, and employed the Phoronix Test Suite (PTS) [15] to measure the performance impact on real-world applications.

To assess the performance impact of HyperWall on the kernel submodules, we used the LM-Bench. Table 1 compares latencies of various tests executed on a clean system and a system running HyperWall. The overhead of socket I/O is above 100% which can be explained by the additional interception of the involved system calls (which requires a context-switch) and hashing of the transmitted buffers.

To understand the performance of HyperWall in real-world applications, we used the Phoronix Test Suite. Table 2 compares the results of various tests executed on a clean system and a system running HyperWall. Different tests have different metrics: some measure latencies in seconds while others measure requests per second. The "Interpretation" column explains how the test metric should be interpreted in each case. The highest overhead is ≈7% while the average is ≈1.6%. In the SQLite test, the negative overhead is probably due to a measurement error.

7   Related Work

The idea to use hypervisors in security applications is not new. In many applications, researchers extended Xen to provide additional security for the underlying VMs. SBCFI [22] is a Xen-based hypervisor that provides control flow integrity verification for the underlying operating system. Because HyperWall depends on CFI mechanism for the kernel, SBCFI can complement our hypervisor. Nitro [23] is a Xen-based hypervisor for system call tracing. IntroVirt [37] is a stealthy Xen-based hypervisor that hooks system calls in Windows for introspection. We use a similar idea for hooking an inner function that is invoked by several system

Table 1. Performance results of vanilla Linux and HyperWall on the LMBench micro-benchmark.

Test name	Vanilla linux (μsec)	HyperWall (μsec)	Overhead
syscall	1.7996	1.8844	5%
read	0.4714	0.5892	25%
write	0.4340	0.5631	30%
fstat	0.4724	0.5838	24%
open/close	1.5462	2.4174	56%
select (10 fds)	0.5395	0.7116	32%
select (100 TCP fds)	5.2287	9.3992	80%
fork+exit	66.8446	80.2160	20%
fork+execve	210.5385	249.1556	18%
fork+/bin/sh	541.8947	1336.0000	147%
sigaction	0.4423	0.5148	16%
Signal delivery	1.0020	1.6766	67%
Protetcion fault	0.8230	1.1420	39%
Page fault	0.1495	0.3148	111%
Unix socket I/O	5.2694	7.8473	49%
TCP socket I/O	8.1917	18.4216	125%
UDP socket I/O	6.2157	16.4073	164%

calls. Another Xen-based hypervisor for ARM is described in [25]. The hypervisor is capable of performing stealthy instrumentation thus allowing for dynamic malware analysis. The mechanism of stealthy instrumentation can be introduced into HyperWall to make it suitable for malware analysis.

Thin hypervisors are not as prevalent as full hypervisors, probably due to the additional development effort compared with using an existing open-source full hypervisor. SecVisor [28] is a thin hypervisor that uses a secondary level address translation and IOMMU to prevent unauthorized code execution in kernel-mode. Functionality similar to SecVisor's must be added to our hypervisor to guarantee the kernel's code integrity. BitVisor [29] is a thin hypervisor that intercepts accesses to ATA hard disks and enforces storage encryption. HyperWall uses a similar method of IO interception. HyperSafe [34] is a CFI extension to BitVisor.

Secloack [16] is a security component that is able to reliably turn peripheral devices of a smartphone on and off. The component resides in ARM's TrustZone. Secloack prevents communication with peripheral devices completely, whereas HyperWall performs filtering on this communication.

HookMap [36] is a rootkit detector that is based on QEMU. Similarly to HyperWall, it uses the *System.map* file to obtain the locations of kernel functions.

Table 2. Performance results of vanilla Linux and HyperWall on the Phoronix Test Suite.

Test name	Interpretation	Vanilla Linux	HyperWall	Overhead
SQLite	Lower is better	55.00 s	53.64 s	−2.47%
GnuPG	Lower is better	11.56 s	11.58 s	0.00%
PyBench	Lower is better	1.121 s	1.198 s	6.87%
Dbench	Higher is better	80.57 MB/s	79.80 MB/s	0.96%
IOzone	Higher is better	1224.79 MB/s	1193.18 MB/s	2.58%
PostMark	Higher is better	5813 Req/s	5813 Req/s	0.00%
PHPBench	Higher is better	610,335 (Score)	588,940 (Score)	3.51%

8 Conclusions

Although it seems to be a difficult task to prevent the execution of malicious programs, it may be possible to detect and block their malicious behavior. In this paper, we presented a system that can detect and prevent malicious communication, which is essential for the operation of malicious programs. The system can withstand attacks from kernel-mode and incurs low overhead in real-world applications.

References

1. Bilge, L., Dumitraş, T.: Before we knew it: an empirical study of zero-day attacks in the real world. In: Proceedings of the 2012 ACM Conference on Computer and Communications Security, pp. 833–844 (2012)
2. Bilge, L., Sen, S., Balzarotti, D., Kirda, E., Kruegel, C.: Exposure: a passive DNS analysis service to detect and report malicious domains. ACM Trans. Inf. Syst. Secur. (TISSEC) 16(4), 1–28 (2014)
3. Chen, P., Xu, J., Lin, Z., Xu, D., Mao, B., Liu, P.: A practical approach for adaptive data structure layout randomization. In: Pernul, G., Ryan, P.Y.A., Weippl, E. (eds.) ESORICS 2015. LNCS, vol. 9326, pp. 69–89. Springer, Cham (2015). https://doi.org/10.1007/978-3-319-24174-6_4
4. Cook, K.: Kernel address space layout randomization. Linux Security Summit (2013)
5. Deshane, T., Shepherd, Z., Matthews, J., Ben-Yehuda, M., Shah, A., Rao, B.: Quantitative comparison of Xen and KVM, pp. 1–2. Xen Summit, Boston (2008)
6. Ermolov, M., Shishkin, A.: Microsoft windows 8.1 kernel patch protection analysis (2014)
7. Ge, X., Talele, N., Payer, M., Jaeger, T.: Fine-grained control-flow integrity for kernel software. In: 2016 IEEE European Symposium on Security and Privacy (EuroS&P), pp. 179–194. IEEE (2016)
8. Ghafir, I., Prenosil, V.: DNS traffic analysis for malicious domains detection. In: 2015 2nd International Conference on Signal Processing and Integrated Networks (SPIN), pp. 613–918. IEEE (2015)

9. Graziano, M., Flore, L., Lanzi, A., Balzarotti, D.: Subverting operating system properties through evolutionary DKOM attacks. In: Caballero, J., Zurutuza, U., Rodríguez, R.J. (eds.) DIMVA 2016. LNCS, vol. 9721, pp. 3–24. Springer, Cham (2016). https://doi.org/10.1007/978-3-319-40667-1_1

10. Guide, P.: Intel® 64 and IA-32 architectures software developer's manual. Volume 3B: System programming Guide, Part 2, 11 (2011)

11. Hu, H., Shinde, S., Adrian, S., Chua, Z.L., Saxena, P., Liang, Z.: Data-oriented programming: on the expressiveness of non-control data attacks. In: 2016 IEEE Symposium on Security and Privacy (SP), pp. 969–986. IEEE (2016)

12. Hund, R., Holz, T., Freiling, F.C.: Return-oriented rootkits: Bypassing kernel code integrity protection mechanisms. In: USENIX Security Symposium, pp. 383–398 (2009)

13. Kheir, N., Tran, F., Caron, P., Deschamps, N.: Mentor: positive DNS reputation to skim-off benign domains in botnet C&C blacklists. In: Cuppens-Boulahia, N., Cuppens, F., Jajodia, S., Abou El Kalam, A., Sans, T. (eds.) SEC 2014. IAICT, vol. 428, pp. 1–14. Springer, Heidelberg (2014). https://doi.org/10.1007/978-3-642-55415-5_1

14. Korkin, I.: Hypervisor-based active data protection for integrity and confidentiality of dynamically allocated memory in windows kernel. arXiv preprint arXiv:1805.11847 (2018)

15. Larabel, M., Tippett, M.: Phoronix test suite. Phoronix Media (2020). http://www.phoronix-test-suite.com/. Accessed June 2020

16. Lentz, M., Sen, R., Druschel, P., Bhattacharjee, B.: Secloak: arm trustzone-based mobile peripheral control. In: Proceedings of the 16th Annual International Conference on Mobile Systems, Applications, and Services, pp. 1–13 (2018)

17. Lu, S., Lin, Z., Zhang, M.: Kernel vulnerability analysis: a survey. In: 2019 IEEE Fourth International Conference on Data Science in Cyberspace (DSC), pp. 549–554. IEEE (2019)

18. Markuze, A., Morrison, A., Tsafrir, D.: True iommu protection from dma attacks: when copy is faster than zero copy. In: Proceedings of the Twenty-First International Conference on Architectural Support for Programming Languages and Operating Systems, pp. 249–262 (2016)

19. McVoy, L.W., Staelin, C., et al.: lmbench: portable tools for performance analysis. In: USENIX Annual Technical Conference, San Diego, CA, USA, pp. 279–294 (1996)

20. Neiger, G., Santoni, A., Leung, F., Rodgers, D., Uhlig, R.: Intel virtualization technology: hardware support for efficient processor virtualization. Intel Technol. J. **10**(3), 167–177 (2006)

21. Petroni Jr, N.L., Fraser, T., Molina, J., Arbaugh, W.A.: Copilot-a coprocessor-based kernel runtime integrity monitor. In: USENIX Security Symposium, San Diego, USA, pp. 179–194 (2004)

22. Petroni Jr, N.L., Hicks, M.: Automated detection of persistent kernel control-flow attacks. In: Proceedings of the 14th ACM Conference on Computer and Communications Security, pp. 103–115 (2007)

23. Pfoh, J., Schneider, C., Eckert, C.: Nitro: hardware-based system call tracing for virtual machines. In: Iwata, T., Nishigaki, M. (eds.) IWSEC 2011. LNCS, vol. 7038, pp. 96–112. Springer, Heidelberg (2011). https://doi.org/10.1007/978-3-642-25141-2_7

24. Pinto, S., Santos, N.: Demystifying ARM TrustZone: a comprehensive survey. ACM Comput. Surv. (CSUR) **51**(6), 1–36 (2019)

25. Proskurin, S., Lengyel, T., Momeu, M., Eckert, C., Zarras, A.: Hiding in the shadows: empowering arm for stealthy virtual machine introspection. In: Proceedings of the 34th Annual Computer Security Applications Conference, pp. 407–417 (2018)

26. Rahbarinia, B., Perdisci, R., Antonakakis, M.: Segugio: efficient behavior-based tracking of malware-control domains in large ISP networks. In: 2015 45th Annual IEEE/IFIP International Conference on Dependable Systems and Networks, pp. 403–414. IEEE (2015)

27. Rutkowska, J., Wojtczuk, R.: Preventing and detecting xen hypervisor subversions. Blackhat Briefings USA (2008)

28. Seshadri, A., Luk, M., Qu, N., Perrig, A.: SecVisor: a tiny hypervisor to provide lifetime kernel code integrity for commodity OSes. In: Proceedings of Twenty-First ACM SIGOPS Symposium on Operating Systems Principles, pp. 335–350 (2007)

29. Shinagawa, T., et al.: Bitvisor: a thin hypervisor for enforcing i/o device security. In: Proceedings of the 2009 ACM SIGPLAN/SIGOPS International Conference on Virtual Execution Environments, pp. 121–130 (2009)

30. Singh, A., Nordström, O., Lu, C., dos Santos, A.L.M.: Malicious ICMP tunneling: defense against the vulnerability. In: Safavi-Naini, R., Seberry, J. (eds.) ACISP 2003. LNCS, vol. 2727, pp. 226–236. Springer, Heidelberg (2003). https://doi.org/10.1007/3-540-45067-X_20

31. Smalley, S., Vance, C., Salamon, W.: Implementing selinux as a linux security module. NAI Labs Report 1(43), 139 (2001)

32. Szekeres, L., Payer, M., Wei, T., Song, D.: Sok: eternal war in memory. In: 2013 IEEE Symposium on Security and Privacy, pp. 48–62. IEEE (2013)

33. Velte, A., Velte, T.: Microsoft Virtualization with Hyper-V. McGraw-Hill Inc., New York (2009)

34. Wang, Z., Jiang, X.: Hypersafe: a lightweight approach to provide lifetime hypervisor control-flow integrity. In: 2010 IEEE Symposium on Security and Privacy, pp. 380–395. IEEE (2010)

35. Wang, Z., Jiang, X., Cui, W., Ning, P.: Countering kernel rootkits with lightweight hook protection. In: Proceedings of the 16th ACM Conference on Computer and Communications Security, pp. 545–554 (2009)

36. Wang, Z., Jiang, X., Cui, W., Wang, X.: Countering persistent kernel rootkits through systematic hook discovery. In: Lippmann, R., Kirda, E., Trachtenberg, A. (eds.) RAID 2008. LNCS, vol. 5230, pp. 21–38. Springer, Heidelberg (2008). https://doi.org/10.1007/978-3-540-87403-4_2

37. White, J.S., Pape, S.R., Meily, A.T., Gloo, R.M.: Dynamic malware analysis using introvirt: a modified hypervisor-based system. In: Cyber Sensing 2013, vol. 8757, p. 87570D. International Society for Optics and Photonics (2013)

38. Wilkins, R., Richardson, B.: Uefi secure boot in modern computer security solutions. In: UEFI Forum (2013)

Safety Analysis of High-Dimensional Anonymized Data from Multiple Perspectives

Takaya Yamazoe[1](✉) and Kazumasa Omote[1,2]

[1] Systems and Information Engineering, University of Tsukuba, Tsukuba, Japan
s1920600@s.tsukuba.ac.jp, omote@risk.tsukuba.ac.jp
[2] National Institute of Information and Communications Technology, Tokyo, Japan
http://www.risk.tsukuba.ac.jp
https://www.nict.go.jp

Abstract. Recently, large-scale data collection has driven data utilization in the medical, financial, advertising, and several other fields. This increasing use of data necessitates privacy risk considerations. K-anonymization and other anonymization methods have been used to minimize data privacy risks, but they are unsuitable for large and high-dimensional datasets required in machine learning and other data mining techniques. Although subsequent methods such as matrix decomposition anonymization can anonymize high-dimensional data while maintaining a high level of utility, they do not clarify anonymized data safety or adequately analyze privacy risks.

Therefore, in this study, we performed a multi-perspective analysis on the privacy risks of datasets anonymized with some anonymization methods using various safety metrics. In addition, we propose a new technique for evaluating privacy risk for each attribute of anonymized data. Experimental results showed that our method effectively analyzed privacy risks of high-dimensional anonymized data. Furthermore, our evaluation of the resistance to data re-identification using existing techniques showed that anonymization methods have their suitable attack types, and it is important to assess data safety using various metrics before publishing.

Keywords: Anonymaization · Privacy · Safety metrics

1 Introduction

Recently, data has become commonly utilized in all fields (e.g., medicine and finance), following the spread of web services and internet of things (IoT), as well as research developments in the machine learning and data mining fields. However, only a few institutions boast of both machine learning and data mining capabilities because the fields require advanced analytical techniques and huge amounts of data. For instance, assume a situation in which sensitive data has to be transferred to other institutions when a huge amount of data is required

© Springer Nature Switzerland AG 2020
M. Kutyłowski et al. (Eds.): NSS 2020, LNCS 12570, pp. 94–111, 2020.
https://doi.org/10.1007/978-3-030-65745-1_6

for machine learning or when a data analysis institution is asked to analyze the data. The transfer of data to other institutions may cause a violation of the sensitive information contained in the data. Examples of privacy violations from actual public data include the identification of a state legislator's personal information from the health care insurance data of a Massachusetts state legislator [1] and the unique identification of a user from the rating value of a user's movie released on Netflix [2]. These cases highlight the need for cautious processing and privacy protection when dealing with sensitive data. Anonymization is one of the techniques used to protect data privacy, and various data anonymization techniques have been proposed (e.g., k-anonymization [1] and noise addition). These methods have long been used to protect privacy when releasing datasets due to their use of intuitive data safety metrics [1,3,4].

However, conventional methods such as k-anonymization encounter difficulty in simultaneously maintaining a high level of utility and anonymizing large and high-dimensional datasets, which are used in techniques such as machine learning [7]. Thus, various techniques have been proposed to address this difficulty. One of the successful techniques combines matrix decomposition and k-anonymization or noise addition [5], but it does not sufficiently analyze the safety of the anonymized data. Although various evaluation metrics are required to analyze the safety of anonymized data [6], discussion is still lacking on evaluation metrics for the data anonymized by new techniques.

The aim of this study is to analyze the safety of high-dimensional datasets anonymized by matrix decomposition. Hence, we analyzed the safety of datasets anonymized by matrix decomposition, k-anonymization, and noise addition from multiple perspectives. To evaluate these risks, we propose a new technique to evaluate the vulnerability of each attribute of anonymized data, in addition to conventional techniques. Our proposed technique evaluates the vulnerability of each attribute, taking advantage of the fact that each attribute's distribution of values can only change slightly after anonymization. We futher discuss the safety of each anonymization method using various metrics. The major contributions of this study are as follows:

- We analyze anonymized data of comparable utility and provide some insight into the safety features of each anonymization method;
- We propose a new technique to evaluate the privacy risk of each attribute of anonymized data of using features that make the marginal distribution of each attribute unchanged after anonymization;
- We discuss the relationship between the safety features of each anonymization method and their resistance to malicious attacks on datasets, and the importance of using multiple metrics is demonstrated.

2   Related Works

2.1 K-anonymity

K-anonymization is a method that transforms data such that at least k records in the dataset have the same data within a quasi-identifier [1]. An intuitive metric whereby the number of data owners cannot be narrower than k is referred to as k-anonymity. When discussing k-anonymity, each attribute or combination is generally classified into attributes such as an identifier and a quasi-identifier. An identifier links the data owner to an individual (e.g., user id and username), whereas a quasi-identifier links the data owner to an individual by combining multiple data (e.g., age and gender). In the k-anonymization method based on k-anonymity, personal privacy is protected by deleting and processing quasi-identifiers such that the number of data owners cannot be narrowed down to k or fewer from a combination of quasi-identifiers. This metric is frequently used because it is intuitive and easy to understand. However, if the data to be handled is high-dimensional, the distance between the dataset records increase rapidly. Thus, k-anonymization does not efficiently anonymize high-dimensional data while retaining data utility [7]. Although l-diversity [3] and t-closeness [4] are other safety metrics that extend k-anonymity, neither can be used to evaluate data other than those anonymized by k-anonymization. The anonymization methods combined with matrix decomposition used in this study are not strict k-anonymization methods; thus, these metrics are unsuitable to ensure the safety of datasets anonymized by matrix decomposition anonymization.

2.2   Genome Privacy

Full sequencing of the human genome is now possible, and genomic data is rapidly being utilized in health care, research, and forensic science. Although genome data is invaluable in various fields, its use is highly likely to cause privacy invasion because genome sequences can uniquely identify individuals. Examples of privacy violations from genomic data range from patient disease condition leakage in the re-identification of anonymous participants in genome-wide association studies to genetic discrimination, such as using certain genetic predispositions to deny insurance. Consequently, privacy concerns necessitate considerable care when working with genomic data. Nevertheless, protection techniques and metrics for genomic privacy have not yet been established. Isabel proposed the use of various safety metrics to assess data privacy risks and investigated how an attacker can infer privacy information from genomic data [6]. Twenty-two metrics, including information entropy, mean-squared error, and Gini's coefficient, were used to analyze the potential risk of data privacy invasion. Analyzing the behavior of the 22 metrics showed that a single metric alone is insufficient to ensure data safety. This present study builds on the work of Isabel to analyze the safety of anonymized data from multiple perspectives using various metrics.

2.3   Maximum-Knowledge Attack

Record linkage is a method for re-identifying anonymized data. It is an attack that violates privacy by linking records in an anonymized dataset to those in an external dataset. Hence, it is important to consider record linkage risks when releasing anonymized data. However, in simulating record linkage, various items (e.g., the auxiliary information available to the attacker) are assumed. Furthermore, record linkage only focuses on record re-identification and does not include attacks where an attacker gains knowledge of specific sensitive attributes of an individual. Ferrer et al. [10] proposed a technique for evaluating the risk of anonymized data disclosure. The technique solves the problem of record linkage described above. Specifically, a record linkage attack can be simulated without considering the background knowledge of the attacker and possible disclosure of attributes by assuming a maximum-knowledge attacker (i.e., one who has both the original and anonymized data). This scenario is described thus. The attacker possesses both the original dataset X and anonymized dataset Y. The attacker generates a dataset Y' from the anonymized dataset Y by permuting each attribute to remove the dependencies between the attributes. The attacker then computes the distance between X and Y and between X and Y', and the distributions of the distances are defined as $dist$ and $dist'$, respectively. Finally, the attacker compares the distributions. If both distributions are equal, then there is no evidence that X contains any information that can be used to improve the linkage accuracy. This can be interpreted as X and Y being independent, indicating that the anonymization of Y is very strong. Thus, this method can be used to obtain the lower bound of achievable disclosure risk protection.

In addition to this method of evaluating the risk of record re-identification, they also propose a method for evaluating the vulnerability of each attribute of anonymized data. They divide the original dataset X with the number of m attributes into (x_b, x_m). Anonymized dataset Y is similarly divided into (y_b, y_m). x_b is a record that concatenates the attributes from x_1 to x_{m-1}. They then link the records using x_b and y_b and measure the distribution of distances x_m and y_m of the linked records. They evaluate the vulnerability of the attributes by comparing the distance distributions of the target attribute x_m and y_m, and the target attribute x_m and that of the permute dataset y'_m, in a similar way to the above assessment. Similar to the record re-identification risk described above, this assessment is also a technique to evaluate the lower bound of the vulnerability of each attribute.

2.4 Sensitive Attribute Disclosure

Recently, large-scale and high-dimensional data has been used for machine learning and data analysis. These data have many attributes, and it is difficult to identify the vulnerable attributes that should be protected among them. To solve these problems, Ito et al. [11] proposed an attacker model to assess the vulnerability of attributes. The attacker model quantifies the probability that an attacker will gain background knowledge about an attribute by accident, based on the information about the values contained in the attribute. Let the dataset be T, and let m and n be the numbers of records and users in the dataset, respectively. Let D_x be the set of values for attribute X of T. Let R_x and U_x be the sets of records containing a given $x \in D_x$ and users that have x in attribute X, respectively. Then, the joint probability $Pr(idf, x)$ is represented by the following equation, using the probabilities $Pr(x)$ and $Pr(idf|x)$ that an attacker will gain background knowledge of an attribute x and a user with an attribute x, respectively.

$$Pr(idf, x) = Pr(x)Pr(idf|x) = \frac{|R_x|}{m} \frac{1}{|U_x|} \tag{1}$$

Ito et al. showed that this risk model can be used to find the riskiest attributes in a dataset and guide the decision on which attributes to process or remove when anonymizing the data. As the risk model is intended to analyze the potential risk of attributes of the original dataset, it is not suitable for evaluating the privacy risk of anonymized datasets and cannot be used in this study.

3   Preliminary

In this section, we first describe the basis of our proposed method before detailing the method.

3.1   Matrix Decomposition as Anonymization

Matrix decomposition is a method of anonymizing high-dimensional data while maintaining a high level of utility. It decompose a matrix $M \in R^{n \times m}$ into two matrices, $U \in R^{n \times r}$ and $V \in R^{m \times r}$. Then, matrix $X = UV^T$ approximates M, and rank r is a parameter that specifies its accuracy. Mimoto et al. [8,9] showed that combining matrix decomposition and k-anonymization or noise addition can anonymize high-dimensional data while keeping the utility of the data. Therefore, data anonymized by this technique is expected to be used for machine learning. Additionally, Mimoto showed experimentally that data anonymized using matrix decomposition are more useful than those anonymized using only k-anonymization or noise addition in training machine learning models. However, although the utility of anonymized data is well-established, the assessment of data safety is inadequate. As the combination of matrix decomposition and k-anonymization does not guarantee strict k-anonymity of the anonymized data, a careful analysis of the risk of information leakage from anonymized data is necessary. However, only simple record-matching tests and record links between anonymized data have been tested [8]. In this study, we analyze the privacy risks of datasets anonymized using matrix decomposition from multiple perspectives. Specifically, starting with the analysis of basic metrics (e.g., information entropy and distribution distance), we analyze the re-identification risk of anonymized data and the privacy risk of each attribute of the anonymized data.

3.2   Evaluation of Utility

Various methods are used to evaluate the utility of anonymized data. For example, some methods use Hamming distance and cross-tabulation. In the Hamming distance methods, original datasets and anonymized ones are compared, and the ratio of different data records is calculated. In cross-tabulation methods, the tabulated values are obtained by the cross-tabulation of each original dataset and anonymized one, and the absolute error is calculated. Various methods can be used for the evaluation of utility, but it is necessary to consider the intended use of the dataset. In this study, we assumed that the anonymized data will be used for machine learning. Thus, we used the method proposed by Mimoto et al. [8] for evaluation of the utility. Precisely, the F measure of the models trained using the original and anonymized datasets are set to F_{ori} and F_{ano}, respectively, and the utility of the anonymized dataset is evaluated by the following formula. We used logistic regression and random forests as machine learning algorithms to predict the test data and measure the F-measure.

$$Utility = \frac{F_{ano}}{F_{ori}} \tag{2}$$

4 Our Method

In the following section, we introduce our proposed method for evaluating anonymized data.

4.1 Attacker Assumptions

In this study, we assumed that the attacker has the anonymized data. This situation corresponds to the case when the anonymized data are accessible to the public or when they are transferred to other institutions. In this case, the attacker may try to extract sensitive information about the original data from the anonymized data. Thus, we propose an attack method in which an attacker uses the anonymized data to estimate the original values of sensitive attributes. In addition, to assume an attacker with a vast background knowledge, we assumed an attacker in two levels.

Level1. Normal Attacker. The attacker has the anonymized data and has only background knowledge of the set of possible values for the target attributes.

Level2. Attacker with the Distribution. The attacker has the anonymized data. In addition to the set of possible values for the target attributes, the attacker also has background knowledge of the marginal distribution of target attributes in the original data.

4.2 Algorithm

We consider that when there is a high similarity between the distributions of identical attributes in the original and anonymized datasets, those attributes have a low level of anonymization. Therefore, we propose a method to evaluate the privacy risk of an attribute by using the distribution of that attribute in anonymized data. Let X be an attribute of the target dataset and D_x the set

---

Algorithm 1. Algorithm for attacker of level1

Input: values of target attribute $X_{ano} = (x_{ano_1}, x_{ano_2}, ..., x_{ano_n})$, set of possible values
   D_x
Output: estimated original value $X_{pred} = (x_{pred_1}, x_{pred_2}, ..., x_{pred_n})$
1: **for** $x \in D_x$ **do**
2:     Initialize d to $(d_1, d_2, ..., d_n)$
3:     Initialize p to $(p_1, p_2, ..., p_n)$
4:     Compute $d_i = \frac{1}{dist(x, x_{ano_i})}$ for each $x_{ano_i} \in X_{ano}$
5:     Compute $p_i = \frac{Rank(d_i)}{n}$ for each $d_i \in d$
6:     Set $Pr(x|x_{ano_i})$ to p_i for each $p_i \in p$
7: **end for**
8: **for** $i = 1$ to n **do**
9:     Set X_{pred_i} to x which has maximum value $Pr(x|x_{ano_i}) \in D_x$
10: **end for**
11: **return** $X_{pred} = (x_{pred_1}, x_{pred_2}, ..., x_{pred_n})$

Algorithm 2. Algorithm for attacker of level2

Input: In addition to Algorithm1, marginal distributions $(Pr(x_1), Pr(x_2), ..., Pr(x_m))$
Output: estimated original value $X_{pred} = (x_{pred_1}, x_{pred_2}, ..., x_{pred_n})$
1: **for** $x \in D_x$ **do**
2:     Compute p_i in the same way as Algorithm1
3:     Set $Pr(x|x_{ano_i}) \cdot Pr(x)$ to p_i for each $p_i \in p$
4: **end for**
5: **for** $i = 1$ to n **do**
6:     Set X_{pred_i} to x which has maximum value $Pr(x|x_{ano_i}) \in D_x$
7: **end for**
8: **return** $X_{pred} = (x_{pred_1}, x_{pred_2}, ..., x_{pred_n})$

---

of values that can be taken by attribute X of the original dataset. The attacker
calculates and ranks the distance of $x \in D_x$ from the value x_{ano} of the target
attribute X_{ano} in the anonymized data. Finally, we use the calculated ranks
to estimate the probability $Pr(x|x_{ano})$ that the original data is value x when
the anonymized data is x_{ano}. The proposed method is shown in Algorithm-1.
We also propose a second algorithm that assumes a level2 attacker who has
a marginal distribution of the target attributes of the original data in addition to the assumptions of the Algorithm1 attacker. When the attacker of this
assumption estimates the value of the original data from the anonymized data,
the attacker adds weights to the computation of $Pr(x|x_{ano})$ using the marginal
distribution $Pr(x)$. An attack by a level2 attacker is shown in Algorithm2.

5   Experiments

In this section, we describe the experiments performed to evaluate the utility
and safety of the anonymized data using the proposed method. The data used in
the experiments were processed by matrix-decomposition anonymization, using

k-anonymization or noise addition. As the aim of this study is to analyze the safety of anonymized data, we first evaluated the utility of the anonymized data before analyzing the safety of the anonymized data found to have the same level of utility. An adult [12] dataset and a diabetes dataset [13] were used in the experiments. The adult dataset contained personal information (e.g., age, occupation, and gender) from the 1994 Census database by Barry Becker and had more than 100 attributes when one-hot encoded. The diabetes dataset contained over 50 features representing patient and hospital outcomes. It also had more than 100 attributes from one-hot encoding.

5.1 Evaluation of Utility

It is important to keep anonymized data in such a way that they high utility. In this section, we describe the experiments conducted to evaluate the utility of anonymized data. We generated multiple matrix-decomposition anonymized datasets by adjusting the k values and noise levels. As we expected to use an anonymized dataset for machine learning, we trained a machine learning model with the generated anonymized dataset and obtained the F-measure. Furthermore, the utility of each anonymized dataset was calculated using the method introduced in Sect. 3.2. Tables 1 and 2 are the results of evaluating the utility of anonymized adult datasets, and Tables 3 and 4 are the results of evaluating the utility of anonymized diabetes datasets. The notations in the dataset columns are explained thus: k means using k-anonymization and its parameters, σ means using noise addition and its parameters, and d means using matrix decomposition and its parameters. The results in the tables show that k-anonymization is most useful when combined with matrix decomposition. More parameter tunings yield more useful results when the anonymization method is combined with matrix decomposition; however, we extracted a combination of parameters with similar utility in this experiment and included them in the table. Experimental results with the noise addition showed that the combination of matrix decomposition yields smaller σ values for anonymized data with the same utility than when noise addition is used alone. This shows that only a small amount of noise is needed to generate the anonymized datasets, which is a positive result considering the utility of the data. Therefore, we performed the safety analyses using anonymized data with the same level of utility.

5.2 Evaluation of Safety

In this section, we analyzed the safety of anonymized data using several safety metrics categorized as basic metrics such as entropy and distribution, robustness to record linkages, and attribute vulnerability.

Basic Analysis. First, we used techniques such as information entropy to perform simple analyses of anonymized data. The aim of this analysis was to consider the features and vulnerabilities of the anonymized data for each

Table 1. Utility evaluation of anonymized adult datasets using matrix factorization and k-anonymization.

Dataset	Score	
	F-measure	Utility
Ano(k = 3)	0.833	0.988
Ano(k = 20)	0.821	0.974
Ano(k = 50)	0.818	0.97
Ano(k = 70)	0.805	0.954
Ano(d = 50, k = 3)	0.841	0.998
Ano(d = 50, k = 20)	0.779	0.924
Ano(d = 50, k = 70)	0.775	0.919
Ano(d = 30, k = 30)	0.774	0.918
Ano(d = 30, k = 70)	0.778	0.922

Table 2. Utility evaluation of anonymized adult datasets using matrix factorization and noise addition.

Dataset	Score	
	F-measure	Utility
Ano($\sigma = 0.1$)	0.821	0.974
Ano($\sigma = 0.3$)	0.819	0.971
Ano($\sigma = 0.4$)	0.776	0.92
Ano($\sigma = 0.6$)	0.774	0.918
Ano(d = 80, $\sigma = 0.2$)	0.774	0.918
Ano(d = 50, $\sigma = 0.1$)	0.833	0.988
Ano(d = 50, $\sigma = 0.2$)	0.781	0.926
Ano(d = 30, $\sigma = 0.25$)	0.78	0.925
Ano(d = 30, $\sigma = 0.4$)	0.779	0.923

Table 3. Utility evaluation of anonymized diabetes datasets using matrix factorization and k-anonymization.

Dataset	Score	
	F-measure	Utility
Ano(k = 3)	0.566	0.911
Ano(k = 7)	0.553	0.89
Ano(k = 10)	0.527	0.848
Ano(k = 20)	0.521	0.838
Ano(d = 80, k = 3)	0.535	0.861
Ano(d = 50, k = 3)	0.571	0.919
Ano(d = 50, k = 10)	0.52	0.837
Ano(d = 10, k = 20)	0.517	0.832
Ano(d = 10, k = 30)	0.514	0.827

Table 4. Utility evaluation of anonymized diabetes datasets using matrix factorization and noise addition.

Dataset	Score	
	F-measure	Utility
Ano($\sigma = 0.1$)	0.56	0.901
Ano($\sigma = 0.2$)	0.539	0.868
Ano($\sigma = 0.3$)	0.54	0.869
Ano($\sigma = 0.45$)	0.51	0.821
Ano(d = 70, $\sigma = 0.01$)	0.546	0.879
Ano(d = 70, $\sigma = 0.03$)	0.542	0.872
Ano(d = 30, $\sigma = 0.01$)	0.538	0.866
Ano(d = 10, $\sigma = 0.05$)	0.501	0.807
Ano(d = 5, $\sigma = 0.01$)	0.513	0.826

anonymization method. The metrics used were information entropy, distance between distributions measured by KL divergence, and the marginal distribution of each attribute's values.

The complexity of each attribute is measurable using information entropy. It can be considered safer when each attribute of the anonymized dataset is more

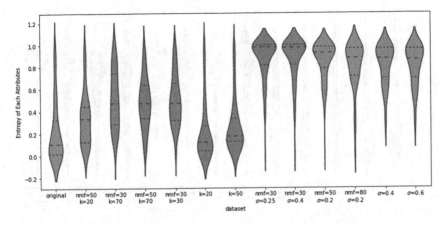

Fig. 1. Entropy details of each attribute in the adult dataset.

complex than that of the original dataset, because it is more difficult to infer the original value from the anonymized value. Figures 1 and 2 are plots of the information entropy of each attribute of the original and anonymized datasets on a violin graph. In the data using noise addition, the noise increased the complexity of the values. In the adult dataset, it can be seen that a combination with matrix decomposition has the same level of complexity as using noise addition alone. This positive result allows the same level of complexity to be achieved a smaller amount of noise. Noise is not added to anonymized datasets using k-anonymization; hence, the complexity of the values is at the same level as that of the original dataset. However, combining matrix decomposition tends to increase the complexity of the values. Thus, matrix decomposition apparently increases the complexity of the values and improves the anonymity of the data. However, as in the diabetes dataset, anonymizing a dataset using matrix decomposition docs not increase the complexity of the values. Therefore parameters should be carefully chosen. When the complexity of the values of each attribute in the anonymized data is not high, there is likely a risk of a higher success rate of attacks against the vulnerability of the attribute.

Figures 3 and 4 illustrate the distances between the distributions of each attribute of the anonymized and original datasets, measured by KL divergence. A larger distribution distance from the original data generally means a stronger level of privacy protection. When only k-anonymization is used and the value of k is small, we can confirm that there are many attributes with small distribution distances between the original and anonymized data. The anonymized data combined with matrix decomposition has attributes with larger distribution distances, which indicates stronger anonymization. This tendency can also be seen in the anonymized dataset of noise addition. When there are many attributes with small distribution distances between the original and anonymized data, we can predict that the risk is higher for attacks that take advantage of attribute vulnerability and record linkage.

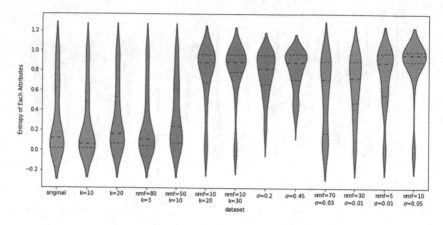

Fig. 2. Entropy details of each attribute in the diabetes dataset.

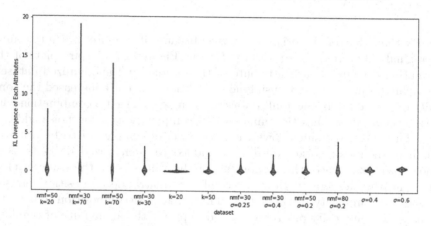

Fig. 3. KL divergence of each attribute in the adult dataset.

Figure 5 illustrates plots of the distribution of some adult dataset attributes. Each graph represents the original data and some anonymized data. The title of the graph indicates the attributes of the target, and the legend indicates the target dataset. The attributes of the graphs are as follows: "husband" means having a husband, "never-married" means, "some-college" means having attended college, and "private" means having a private occupation. From the figure, it can be seen that the distribution of k-anonymized data is similar to that of the original data, even when combined with matrix decomposition. When noise addition is used for anonymization, the distribution is far from the original data. Matrix decomposition did not seem to affect the distribution of attribute values, but noise addition affected the distribution of attribute values. This tendency was also observed for other attributes and parameters. If the distribution of attribute values is not different from that of the original data, the original values are more likely to be inferred even if the unusual values are anonymized. In other words,

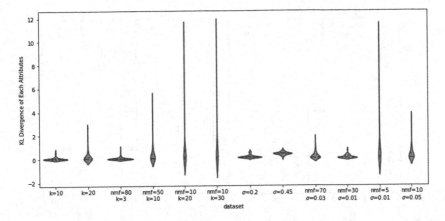

Fig. 4. KL divergence of each attribute in the diabetes dataset.

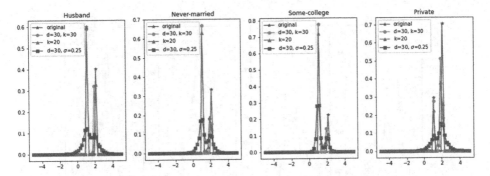

Fig. 5. Distribution of some attributes of the adult dataset.

it is easy to infer the original values of the anonymized data by simply ranking the attribute values by size.

Based on the results of the above basic metric analyses, we evaluated the actual risk of information leakage in attacks on anonymized data by the following attacks.

Maximum Knowledge Attack. We evaluated the resistance of the anonymized dataset to record linkage. For the evaluation method, we used the maximum knowledge attack of Ferrer et al. [10]. This technique makes it is possible to evaluate the lower bound of the information leakage risk of the original data from the anonymized data. Following Ferrer's method, we generated a permuted dataset Y' based on the anonymized data Y by removing the dependency between attributes. The distances between X and Y, and between X and Y' were then calculated before comparing the two distributions of distance. KL divergence was used to compute the distance between the two distributions. The closer the two distributions are, the less the information in X that an attacker

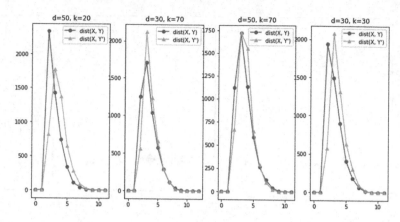

Fig. 6. Experimental results of maximum knowledge attack on an adult dataset using k-anonymization.

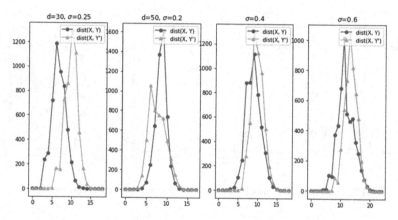

Fig. 7. Experimental results of maximum knowledge attack on an adult dataset using noise addition.

can use to improve the accuracy of the record linkage, meaning the anonymized dataset Y shows that strong anonymization is applied.

Evaluation results of the maximum knowledge attack for adult datasets are shown in Figs. 6 and 7. The title of each graph indicates the parameters of the anonymization method used. Each graph illustrates the distribution of the distance between the original data X and the anonymized data Y, and the distance between the original data X and the permuted data Y'. In Tables 5 and 6, the distance between the two distributions is calculated by KL divergence. In the evaluation of the maximum knowledge attack of the k-anonymized dataset, it can be seen that the distribution distance between $dist(X,Y)$ and $dist(X,Y')$ is small when the parameter is $(d = 30, k = 70)$ or $(d = 50, k = 70)$ and large when the parameter is $(d = 50, k = 20)$ or $(d = 30, k = 30)$. In comparison with the results of the basic analysis, the risk of record linkage tends to increase as the

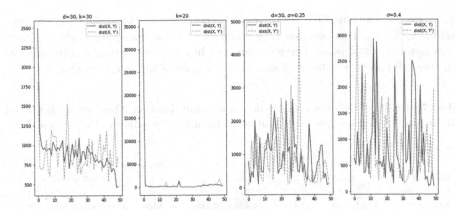

Fig. 8. Experimental results of maximum knowledge attack on an adult dataset attribute "Workclass".

Table 5. Distribution distance between $dist(X,Y)$ and $dist(X,Y')$ of anonymized datasets by k-anonymization.

Datasets	KL Divergence
Ano(d = 50, k = 20)	0.265
Ano(d = 30, k = 70)	0.079
Ano(d = 50, k = 70)	0.043
Ano(d − 30, k − 30)	0.248

Table 6. Distribution distance between $dist(X,Y)$ and $dist(X,Y')$ of anonymized datasets by noise addition.

Datasets	KL Divergence
Ano(d = 30, σ = 0.25)	2.535
Ano(d = 50, σ = 0.2)	0.323
Ano(σ = 0.4)	0.653
Ano(σ − 0.6)	0.731

number of attributes with KL divergence close to 0 increases. In other words, anonymized data with parameters $(d = 30, k = 70)$ or $(d = 50, k = 70)$, which have attributes with high KL divergence, have a lower risk of being affected by record linkage. Similarly, in the case of anonymization using noise summation, the risk of being affected by record linkage tends to be higher because the KL divergence between attributes is smaller for all parameters. When using noise addition for anonymization, the risk of record linkage will not be reduced if the noise is not increased, as stated in Ferrer et al.

In addition to the risk of record re-identification, we evaluated the vulnerability of each attribute of the anonymized data using the method of maximum knowledge attack. As introduced in Sect. 2.5, we linked X and Y using records other than the target's attribute x_b and y_b and compared the distance distributions of x_m and y_m with the distance distributions of x_m and y'_m for a record. The results of evaluating the vulnerability of attribute "Workclass" of the adult dataset are shown in Fig. 8. From the figure, it can be seen that the two distributions of k-anonymized data are similar, and that the attributes of the anonymized data are difficult to identify. On the contrary, the two distributions are far apart in the anonymized data with noise addition, but this can be mitigated using matrix decomposition. This trend was also observed in the evaluation of other attributes. Thus, it is possible to evaluate the vulnerability of each attribute of anonymized data using Ferrer's method, but the evaluation results are not intuitive. Moreover, the level of anonymization to be achieved is unclear.

Table 7. Results of the data invasion attack on adult datasets. The attacker is Level-1 and does not have a marginal distribution of the attribute values of the original data.

Dataset	Attribute							
	Workclass	Education	Marital	Occupation	Relationship	Race	Sex	Native
BaseLine	0.704	0.325	0.456	0.129	0.401	0.853	0.666	0.900
Ano(k = 20)	0.543	0.476	0.715	0.696	0.805	0.429	0.985	0.311
Ano(k = 50)	0.443	0.434	0.659	0.548	0.769	0.401	0.981	0.092
Ano(d = 30, k = 30)	0.290	0.409	0.550	0.586	0.772	0.385	0.856	0.104
Ano(σ = 0.4)	0.286	0.284	0.454	0.420	0.604	0.352	0.857	0.023
Ano(d = 30, σ = 0.25)	0.222	0.289	0.368	0.289	0.500	0.245	0.671	0.046

Table 8. Results of the data invasion attack on adult datasets. The attacker is Level-2 and has a marginal distribution of the attribute values of the original data.

Dataset	Attribute							
	Workclass	Education	Marital	Occupation	Relationship	Race	Sex	Native
BaseLine	0.704	0.325	0.456	0.129	0.401	0.853	0.666	0.900
Ano(k = 20)	0.841	0.740	0.846	0.766	0.936	0.891	0.994	0.902
Ano(k = 50)	0.842	0.600	0.826	0.596	0.916	0.888	0.992	0.900
Ano(d = 30, k = 30)	0.704	0.538	0.737	0.652	0.720	0.853	0.965	0.900
Ano(σ = 0.4)	0.704	0.393	0.682	0.544	0.695	0.853	0.895	0.900
Ano(d = 30, σ = 0.25)	0.704	0.428	0.634	0.425	0.617	0.853	0.736	0.900

Data Invasion. Finally, we used our proposed data invasion attack to evaluate the privacy risk of anonymized data attributes. Our method estimates the original value from the attribute values of the anonymized dataset. Using this proposed method, we can evaluate the privacy risk of each anonymized data attribute rather than the risk of re-identification as in record linkage. The privacy risk per attribute was evaluated, and this can be used in use cases such as applying further anonymization to high-risk attributes only.

Algorithm-1 and Algorithm-2 were introduced for each assumed level of the attacker. The results of Algorithm 1 are shown in Table 7 and Algorithm 2 in Table 8. The baseline is the percentage of the most common value x in the target's attributes. This baseline refers to the highest accuracy when an attacker can guess the original value at random. If the guess accuracy of the data invasion attack is higher than this baseline, then some information has been leaked from the anonymized dataset. Conversely, if it is smaller than the baseline, it indicates a higher level of anonymization. From Table 7, it can be seen that when the attacker does not own the distribution of the original data (Algorithm1 case), they can still estimate the value of the original data with a higher accuracy than the baseline. Particularly, the k-anonymized data showed that the estimates were highly accurate. The reason for this is supported by the analysis of the distribution of values performed in the basic analyses (Fig. 5). As the distribution of the values after anonymization has not changed much, the original values could easily be estimated in this attack using value ordering. Previous experiments have shown that k-anonymization is resistant to record re-identification. Thus, the risk of being identified is low. Nevertheless, care is needed in combining it with matrix decomposition because the resistance is also weak. The data invasion attack was less accurate when noise-addition anonymization was used; this result is also consistent with the results of the basic analysis. However, looking at the results of Algorithm-2, it can be seen in Table 8 that the probability of the original value being estimated is high regardless of which anonymization method is used. That is, an attacker has a marginal distribution of the original data, they can easily infer the original data from the anonymized data. From this result, we consider that when publishing anonymized data, it is necessary to keep the marginal distribution of the original data as confidential information or distort the distribution of attribute values significantly.

6 Discussion

6.1 Comparison of Our Method with Conventional Methods

Our method shows that an attacker can infer an original value of target attribute from the anonymized data when the attacker knows anonymized dataset and the possible values of the original data. This technique is an attack based on the results of basic analysis, which shows that the distribution of each attribute value in the anonymized data is not so different from the original data. This attack gives an intuitive indication of the extent to which the value of the target attribute is likely to be inferred. Ferrer's method [10] can also evaluate the vulnerability of each attribute of anonymized data, but there are two problems: the assumption of attacker is too strong, and it is unclear how much of the data should be anonymized in practice. We have assumed a realistic attacker and can check the level of anonymization by comparing the baseline with the evaluation results. We show in Table 9 that our attack more strongly reflects the difference in distribution distance between the original data and the anonymized data. This table shows the correlation coefficient between distribution distance between the anonymized data and the original data for an attribute and each evaluation method. From the table, we can see that the accuracy of the proposed method increases as the distribution distance between the original data and the anonymized data gets closer, which confirms that our proposed method can provide intuitive indicators that the distribution of data is sensitive to privacy.

6.2   Matrix Decomposition and Privacy

For record re-identification attacks, when k-anonymization is insufficient, we may reduce the risk of record re-identification attacks by adjusting the parameters with matrix-decomposition anonymization. When adjusting parameters, the distribution distance between the original and anonymized data should be large to reduce the risk of record re-identification. When using noise addition, the noise should be increased rather than the parameters adjusted because risk reduction results were not observed from matrix decomposition.

While matrix decomposition may provide a small reduction in privacy risk for attacks that take advantage of attribute vulnerabilities, Table 7 shows that an attacker can estimate the original value with greater accuracy than the baseline even when matrix decomposition is used. Furthermore, no anonymization method can be effective if the attacker has a marginal distribution of the original data.

We confirmed that the risk of certain attacks can be reduced by using matrix decomposition as described above. However, matrix decomposition may still increase privacy risk; therefore, it is necessary to consider the scenario in which the data are attacked and to analyze them sufficiently in advance.

Table 9. Correlation coefficients between the evaluated value of anonymized data attributes and the distance distribution of attribute values of the original and anonymized data.

Attribute	Method		
	Ferrer's [10]	Proposed1	Proposed2
Workclass	0.503	−0.942	−0.991
Education	0.249	−0.509	−0.722
Marital	0.912	−0.962	−0.966
Occupation	0.323	−0.529	−0.655

7   Conclusion

In this study, we conducted a multifaceted safety analysis of anonymization techniques proposed to anonymize large-scale and high-dimensional data. Analyzing the anonymized data using basic metrics revealed that the distribution of the data for each attribute did not change significantly after anonymization, and we proposed a method for estimating the original data using this feature. Experimental results further showed that our attack can be used to estimate the value of the original data with high accuracy when the attacker knows the distribution of the original data. Our evaluation of the resistance to data re-identification using existing techniques established that each anonymization method has its own suitable attack and it is crucial to assess the safety of the data using various metrics before the data are published.

References

1. Latanya, S.: k-anonymity: a model for protecting privacy. Int. J. Uncertain. Fuzziness Knowl.-Based Syst. **10**(5), 557–570 (2002)
2. Narayanan, A., Shmatikov, V.: Robust de-anonymization of large sparse datasets. In: Proceedings of 2008 IEEE Symposium on Security and Privacy (SP) (2008)
3. Machanavajjhala, A., Kifer, D., Gehrke, J.: l-diversity: privacy beyond k-anonymity. ACM Trans. Knowl. Discov. Data (2007)
4. Ninghui, L., Tiancheng, L., Suresh, V.: t-closeness: privacy beyond k-anonymity and l-diversity. In: IEEE 23rd International Conference on Data Engineering (2007)
5. Mimoto, T., Kiyomoto, S., Hidano, S., Basu, A., Miyaji, A.: The possibility of matrix decomposition as anonymization and evaluation for time-sequence data. In: 16th Annual Conference on Privacy, Security and Trust (PST) (2018)
6. Isabel, W.: Genomic privacy metrics: a systematic comparison. In: IEEE Security and Privacy Workshops (SPW) (2015)
7. Aggawal, C.: On k-anonymity and the curse of dimensionality. In: Proceedings of the 31st International Conference on Very Large Data Bases, pp. 901–909 (2005)
8. Mimoto, T., Kiyomoto, S., Hidano, S., Basu, A., Miyaji, A.: The possibility of matrix decomposition as anonymization and evaluation for time sequence data. In: Annual Conference on Privacy, Security (2018)
9. Mimoto, T., Kiyomoto, S., Hidano, S., Miyaji, A.: Anonymization technique based on SGD matrix factorization. IEICE Trans. Inf. Syst. **103**(2), 299–308 (2020)
10. Ferrer, J., Ricci, S., Comas, J.: Disclosure risk assessment via record linkage by a maximum-knowledge attacker. In: Annual Conference on Privacy, Security and Trust (PST) (2015)
11. Ito, S., Kikuchi, H., Nakagawa, H.: Attacker models with a variety of background knowledge to de-identified data. J. Ambient Intell. Humanized Comput. (2019)
12. UCI machine learning repository (2018) Adult data set. https://archive.ics.uci.edu/ml/datasets/adult
13. UCI Machine Learning Repository (2018) Diabetes 130-US hospitals for years 1999–2008 Data Set. https://archive.ics.uci.edu/ml/datasets/diabetes+130-us+hospitals+for+years+1999-2008

Defending Against Package Typosquatting

Matthew Taylor[1], Ruturaj Vaidya[1], Drew Davidson[1], Lorenzo De Carli[2(✉)],
and Vaibhav Rastogi[3]

[1] University of Kansas, Lawrence, KS, USA
{mjt,ruturajkvaidya,drewdavidson}@ku.edu
[2] Worcester Polytechnic Institute, Worcester, MA, USA
ldecarli@wpi.edu
[3] University of Wisconsin-Madison, Madison, WI, USA
vrastogi@wisc.edu

Abstract. Software repositories based on a single programming language are common. Examples include npm (JavaScript) and PyPI (Python). They encourage code reuse, making it trivial for developers to import external packages. Unfortunately, the ease with which packages can be published also facilitates *typosquatting*: uploading a package with name similar to that of a highly popular package, with the aim of capturing some of the popular package's installs. Typosquatting frequently occurs in the wild, is difficult to detect manually, and has resulted in developers importing incorrect and sometimes malicious packages.

We present TypoGard, a tool for identifying and reporting potentially typosquatted imports to developers. TypoGard implements a novel detection technique, based on the analysis of npm and PyPI. It leverages a model of lexical similarity between names, and incorporates the notion of package popularity. It flags cases where unknown/scarcely used packages would be installed in place of popular ones with similar names, before installation occurs. We evaluated TypoGard on both npm, PyPI and RubyGems, with encouraging results: TypoGard flags up to 99.4% of known typosquatting cases while generating limited warnings (up to 0.5% of package installs), and low overhead (2.5% of package install time).

1   Introduction

Package managers automate the complex task of deploying 3rd-party dependencies into a codebase, by transitively resolving and installing all code upon which a given package—which the user wishes to install—depends. One of the most common uses of package managers is in the context of large repositories of code packages based on a single programming language. Package managers are undeniably useful, with open, free-for-all repositories like npm for Node.js, PyPI for Python, and RubyGems for Ruby, collectively serving billions of packages per week. However, they also come with problems.

The open, uncurated nature of these repositories means that any developer can upload a package with a name of their choosing. This circumstance gives rise to *typosquatting*, whereby a developer uploads a "perpetrator" package that

M. Kutyłowski et al. (Eds.): NSS 2020, LNCS 12570, pp. 112–131, 2020.
https://doi.org/10.1007/978-3-030-65745-1_7

is *confusable* with an existing "target" package due to name similarity. As a result the user, intending to install the target package, may accidentally request the confusable perpetrator package. Determining why perpetrator packages are created is a challenging and ill-defined problem, as solving it requires inferring the intent of the package author. The perpetrator may wish to confuse users into installing a malicious payload, seek to increase the visibility of their own benign code, or create a confusable name by happenstance. A perpetrator might even upload a placeholder package to prevent an attacker from leveraging the name. The result is the same: users are confused into importing the incorrect package.

As part of our work, we identified known typosquatting incidents by reviewing security advisories from npm, PyPI and RubyGems. Overall, this yielded 1,002 incidents in the last 3 years. While typosquatting campaigns routinely make the news [13, 14, 16, 24], discovering instances is a laborious process as no tools exist that can warn developers or ecosystem maintainers of potential occurrences. From the point of view of a human analyst, identifying typosquatted packages is difficult and time-consuming, as typosquatting confuses manual inspection by definition. The scope of typosquatting is also far-reaching, due to the inter-dependent nature of packages: not only are the developers that make a typo exposed to unintended code, so are package that *transitively* depend on it.

Undetected typosquatting has numerous detriments, both to developers who integrate a perpetrator package, and to the end-users. An overtly malicious perpetrator may include Trojan functionality that attacks the client [17, 34]. Additionally, many package managers invoke configuration hooks bundled with the package at install time, often manifested as shell scripts that run with the privileges of the user. Multiple packages that open reverse shells when installed have been removed from npm [4, 33, 35]. Even in cases where the perpetrator is not malicious, it can confuse the user and weaken the integrity of the system. Ironically, a well-intentioned perpetrator might clone a victim to keep it out of the hands of an attacker but allow the clone to fall behind as the target is updated.

In this work, we develop TypoGard, a novel typosquatting detection technique to discover and prevent incidents of typosquatting before they can damage the user. TypoGard can be used to detect typosquatting incidents before they happen, or to detect possible perpetrator packages within a package repository. TypoGard is designed to work client-side, and requires no special cooperation on the part of repositories. We also find that our detection techniques are highly generalizable, and show high recall across several repositories. TypoGard's core insight is to identify unpopular packages whose name is close, according to a notion of lexical similarity, to the name of a popular package. It this condition is met, TypoGard issues an alert before the package is fetched and suggests the likely-correct victim package name. During the course of our experiments, TypoGard also identified a popular and previously unknown instance of typosquatting: the npm package *loadsh*, which was typosquatting *lodash*, providing an outdated version of the code vulnerable to prototype pollution. After our report, the npm security team confirmed our finding and deprecated *loadsh*.

Our Work Makes the Following Contributions:

- We present TypoGard, an enhancement to the package manager front-end which protects users against typosquatting.
- We evaluate the performance and efficacy of TypoGard, showing that it has a high TPR of **88.1%**, while being non-intrusive.
- We show that, while our design is based on npm and PyPI, it generalizes well: TypoGard achieves **99.4%** TPR on RubyGems typosquatting attacks.

Table 1. Repository statistics for npm, PyPI, and RubyGems.

	npm	PyPI	RubyGems
Packages	1,221,705	221,041	157,410
Weekly downloads	17,872,179,641	997,624,343	154,954,144
Avg. Dep. Tree Size	57.27	4.58	9.61

2   Background

2.1   Package Repositories

Package repositories are very popular: they encourage code reuse, and allow well-vetted, expertly-written codebases to be deployed by more developers. For these reasons, successful repositories have grown to enormous size. The first two rows of Table 1 show the current size and weekly download counts for npm, PyPI, and RubyGems. As the table shows, they contain hundreds of thousands (PyPI, RubyGems) to millions (npm) of publicly available packages. The total number of weekly downloads ranges from hundreds of millions to many billions.

Much of the complexity of package management is due to the interdependence of packages. For example, the popular npm package *webpack-dev-server* (6.6M weekly downloads) declares 33 dependencies, each requiring further packages, for a total of 391 transitive dependencies. These packages span many development teams, each of which may update out of step with one another. This is in line with the general trend of code reuse in software development [32]. Given the bulk of code existing in dependencies, it is infeasible to expect developers to manually vet every package that they integrate into their project.

Package manager front-ends automate the complex and tedious task of fetching, configuring, and updating a package and its transitive dependencies. When a user issues a command like npm install webpack-dev-server, the front-end relies on the package's metadata to build a spanning tree of the package dependency graph (or *dependency tree*), and then installs each package. Similarly, the command npm update updates the package dependency tree for the current set of packages. The third row of Table 1 shows that there is significant interdependence among packages in the package managers we study.

While package managers save users a significant amount of time, they do not help with the herculean task of vetting imported code; if anything, they complicate it. By design, they tend to obscure the provenance of dependencies, complicating the task for developers to decide whether to assign trust to such dependencies.

Characterization of Package Downloads: Based on the self-reported repository download counts, we classified the popularity of packages across npm and PyPI. Figures 1 and 2 show the distribution and dramatic imbalance of downloads across npm and PyPI. A majority of the packages are downloaded relatively infrequently. The top 1% of packages in both repositories receive essentially all downloads, as shown in Fig. 2. Locating desired packages in this ocean of unpopular packages without assistance is challenging.

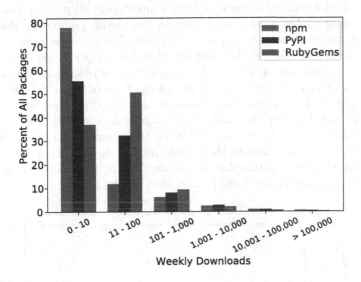

Fig. 1. Percentage of npm, PyPI, and RubyGems packages by weekly downloads.

2.2 Factors Contributing to Typosquatting

We propose that the following aspects of package repositories contribute to the threat of typosquatting:

- The open-source nature of repositories means that any user can upload a package, and it will be given equal trust to any other package.
- The provenance of a package is opaque to the user, and the interdependence between packages makes their behavior difficult to vet manually.
- The distribution of packages means there are a small number of "juicy" typosquatting targets, and a large number of packages from which a typosquatting attack could be launched.

We now review select cases of historical typosquatting.

2.3   Historical Package Typosquatting

More than one thousand historical typosquatting attacks have been documented [24,37,42]. However, the precise degree to which typosquatting has historically occurred is difficult to capture, due in part to the highly subjective nature of what constitutes typosquatting. In practice, most packages that are flagged by repository maintainers exhibit malicious functionality, and are retroactively deemed typosquatting perpetrators by qualitative manual analysis.

As an example of the complexities of determining typosquatting and its intent, consider the *js-sha3* typosquatting campaign. On October 25th, 2019, 25 packages were simultaneously identified by Microsoft Vulnerability Research and taken down by the npm security team. Upon close inspection, all those packages were determined to have malicious intent, and all package names were close, according to Levenshtein distance, to the victim package *js-sha3*. However, not all names were likely to confuse the user. For example, *js-sxa3* requires replacing the "h" with an "x". It is unlikely that a developer would misremember *js-sha3* (an implementation of the SHA-3 algorithm) as *js-sxa3*. A typo is equally unlikely on a QWERTY keyboard, given the distance between "h" and "x". As discussed in Sect. 3.3, we take the stance of only flagging cases where there is strong likelihood that name similarity may confuse the user. While this causes us to ignore some cases (as *js-sxa3* above), it has the advantage to avoid generating an excessive number of warnings that would ultimately stem from flagging pairs of packages with a Levenshtein distance of one. As discussed above, it is unlikely that the packages we ignore could be confused for the correct ones.

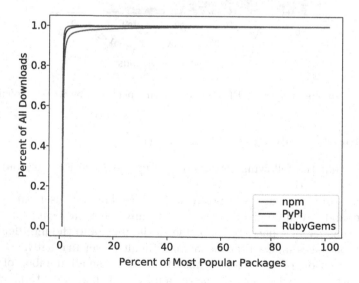

Fig. 2. Cumulative download distribution for npm, PyPI, and RubyGems.

One may also be tempted to always attempt to identify malicious intent, regardless of typosquatting. In practice, this is currently impossible to achieve reliably. JavaScript is a particularly difficult target to analyze, and malicious code can be automatically obfuscated to appear syntactically indistinguishable from benign code [18]. Furthermore, the highly dynamic nature of JavaScript means that malicious functionality may not appear until the code is deployed.

Currently, the standard technique for removing typosquatted packages is manual and reactive. Users who discover malicious typosquatting can file a report to the repository maintainers, who will then investigate the claim and remove the package. This approach does little to prevent the installation of malicious packages and fails to protect users from the consequences. Despite these short-comings, hundreds of package takedowns have been issued that involve package names similar to a popular target. We believe this number to be a lower bound on the total number of typosquatting attempts. The differential of effort favors the attacker, which can automatically generate and upload an arbitrary number of typosquatted variants (e.g., the 25 packages reported by Microsoft above). Many of the reported incidents were actives for months to years before take-down.

2.4 Consequences of Typosquatting

Attacks Against End-Users: The most subtle typosquatting attack is when an adversarial uploader delivers a malicious payload as part of the dependency code, which is subsequently used as part of a user-facing application. This impacts end-users of the application. Two highly-publicized examples involved a malicious payload that exfiltrated sensitive information such as credit card numbers [17] or cryptocurrency [35]. A stealthy adversary may attempt to obscure the payload by cloning the target package and adding the malicious functionality as a Trojan.

Attacks Against Developers Using a Package: An adversary may also target the developer who mistakenly requests the perpetrator package at install time. All three of the repositories analyzed here allow packages to invoke shell scripts—running with the privilege of the user—at install time. Since packages can be installed system-wide, the user may be the administrator, opening a vector for an adversary to take control of the developer's machine. A common choice for malicious package creators is to open a reverse shell on the victim machine [36].

Degradation of Functionality: Even when perpetrator does not deploy malicious code, they may still hinder operations by wasting developers' time in diagnosing and remediating package confusion.

Latent Vulnerabilities: If a perpetrator package is not detected immediately upon installation, it may remain latent in the victim's codebase for a significant time. For example, developers have typosquatted a target with a payload that is a clone of the current version of the package. While the victim experiences no initial consequences from using the wrong package, the perpetrator may become outdated as it does not receive the same updates as the right package.

An illustrative case is *loadsh*, mentioned in Sect. 1, which typosquats *lodash*. *loadsh* does not include any malicious functionality - the perpetrator package is an exact snapshot copy of *lodash* version 4.17.11 (*lodash* is currently at version 4.17.15). Nevertheless, the perpetrator still has a negative impact; because the perpetrator package has not been updated, its victims were effectively using an outdated version of *lodash*. We confirmed that *loadsh* was being used unintentionally by emailing the maintainers of packages that used *loadsh*. Three *loadsh*-dependent package maintainers responded to our email, all of whom acknowledged that they had intended to install *lodash* instead. Many of the packages using *loadsh*, including those maintained by our respondents, had been victims for over a year. In the case of this example, the older version contains known prototype pollution vulnerabilities [41], effectively leaving victims of *loadsh* open to attacks that have already been patched in *lodash*.

Misattribution: Even if a perpetrator replicates all of the target functionality, it nevertheless fragments the popularity of the target package. Thus, one minor consequence of typosquatting is that the target will not get as much credit as they would without the perpetrator. Misattribution can be found in packages like *asimplemde* on npm. In addition to typosquatting, this package contains identical functionality to *simplemde*. References attributing credit to the original author are the sole omissions from the duplicate package.

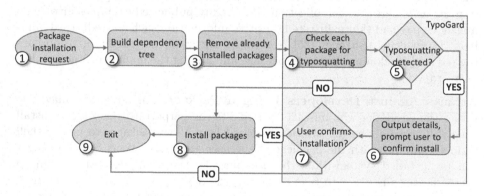

Fig. 3. Modified package installation process with typosquatting protection.

3   Detecting Typosquatting

Motivated by the number of historical instances, the ease of execution, and the severity of the consequences, we created TypoGard, a tool to detect typosquatting in package repositories. At a high level, TypoGard compares a given package name to a list of popular package names. If the given package name matches at least one of the popular packages after a set of allowed transformations, or *signals*, then it is considered to be a typosquatting suspect and the user is alerted.

3.1 TypoGard Workflow

The primary way in which we expect TypoGard to be deployed is as a user-facing utility that integrates with the package manager front-end. Figure 3 depicts the workflow of TypoGard. Algorithm 1 presents the typosquatting detection algorithm (steps 4 through 7 in the figure).

The user initiates the process by triggering a package's installation from the command line, e.g., npm install loadsh (**step 1**). The package manager computes the dependency tree of the package (**step 2**), discard from the tree the packages that are already installed (**step 3**), and begins installing the rest. At this point, the workflow triggers TypoGard's logic.

First, TypoGard considers each package queued to be installed (**steps 4–5**, lines 1–3 in Algorithm 1). A package is considered suspicious if its *popularity score* (Sect. 3.4) is below a tunable threshold T_p, and there exists a popular (popularity $\geq T_p$) package with a similar name (similarity is discussed in Sect. 3.3). If this is the case, TypoGard flags the package and warns the user (**step 5–6**, lines 4–6). If the user decides to ignore the warning, the package is installed (**step 8**, line 5), otherwise the process is terminated. Note that *AbortInstallation()* in line 6 terminates the process for all queued packages, not just the one which was the object of the warning. In line 7, any package which does not raise suspicion is directly installed without prompting the user.

3.2 TypoGard Batch Analysis

While we anticipate the workflow in Fig. 3 to be the most common application of TypoGard, we also envision repository maintainers may want to periodically apply the same analysis in batch fashion to the *entire package repository*. Our current implementation also supports this. In batch mode, TypoGard receives as input the list of all package names, and returns a list of candidate perpetrators, ranked by decreasing download count. Indeed, the *loadsh* package was identified in this way; TypoGard's batch analysis ranked it as the seventh most popular candidate matching a specific signal discussed in the next subsection.

3.3 Typosquatting Signals

At its core, TypoGard relies on string similarity; however, precisely defining the notion of similarity is challenging in this context. Initially we experimented with Levenshtein distance, a common measure of string similarity. However, we found that this approach is overly simplistic and fails to capture the elaborate typos used in past typosquatting attacks.

After extensively exploring alternative approaches, we devised a typosquatting detection scheme by analyzing and categorizing string transformation patterns that have been used in past typosquatting attacks. We refer to the presence of each of these patterns as a typosquatting *signal*. The insight behind our typosquatting detection scheme is that if a pair of packages exhibits one of these signals (i.e., one package name can be transformed in the other using one of the identified transformations), then one package in the pair is a potential typosquatting perpetrator. The signals are:

Repeated Characters: the presence of consecutive duplicate characters in a package name. For example, *reequest* is typosquatting *request*.

Omitted Characters: the omission of a single character. For example, *comander* is typosquatting *commander* and *require-port* is typosquatting *requires-port*.

Swapped Characters: the transposition of two consecutive characters. For example, *axois* is typosquatting *axios*.

Swapped Words: this signal depends on the presence of delimiters in a package name, where a delimiter is a period, hyphen, or underscore. It checks for any other ordering of delimiter-separated tokens in the package repository namespace. For example, *import-mysql* is typosquatting *mysql-import*.

Common Typos: character substitutions based on physical locality on a QWERTY keyboard and visual similarity. For example, *requeat* is typosquatting *request*, *1odash* (with the number one) is typosquatting *lodash* (with the letter L), and *uglify.js* is typosquatting *uglify-js*. Users may overlook visually-similar package names during manual analysis, especially in transitive dependencies.

Version Numbers: the presence of integers located at the end of package names. For example, *underscore.string-2* is typosquatting *underscore.string*. Note that *underscore.string-2* was previously undiscovered and TypoGard led us to find a latent vulnerability.

3.4   Package Popularity

In order to successfully implement TypoGard, we also necessitate a formal notion of *package popularity*. This requirement stems from a fundamental belief that we posit, which is that only unpopular packages can be typosquatting perpetrators and only popular packages can be typosquatting targets. Popular packages are, by our definition, incapable of perpetrating typosquatting attacks. Next,

---

Algorithm 1. TypoGard typosquatting detection.

Input: List I of packages to be installed
Input: Package graph G
Input: Popularity threshold T_P
 1: **for each** $p \in I$ **do**
 2:     **if** Popularity$(p) < T_P$ **then**
 3:         **if** $\exists p'$ s.t. Popularity$(p') \geq T_P$ **and** Similar(p, p') **then**
 4:             $R \leftarrow$ UserConfirm?(p, p');
 5:             **if** $R = True$ **then** Install(p);
 6:             **else** AbortInstallation();
 7:     **else** Install(p);

---

we believe that there exists no incentive for an adversary to typosquat a package which receives an insignificant amount of attention. If a negligible number of users download that package, then an even smaller number of people could potentially misspell the name of that package and fall victim to the attack. By this token, a package which is downloaded thousands, millions, or even tens of millions of times per week, is a far more rewarding target.

The two main possibilities for quantifying package popularity are the number of downloads and the number of dependents. We decided to use the number of downloads because we believe it is a more indicative measure of true package usage. The public number of dependents counts only the number of other packages that directly depend on a given package. Download count, on the other hand, counts the number of users who have downloaded that package either directly or indirectly through some arbitrarily long chain of dependencies.

Popularity based on download count requires the definition of a threshold to distinguish between popular and unpopular packages. This threshold is of crucial importance. An exceedingly low threshold results in many typosquatting packages being considered popular, thus making their detection impossible. Conversely, an exceedingly high threshold may miss packages which are frequently downloaded and are victims of typosquatting. We use a data-driven approach, discussed in Sect. 4, to determine the threshold.

4   Analysis and Evaluation

In this section, we perform an in-depth analysis of TypoGard's tunable parameter, the popularity threshold, and we evaluate TypoGard's effectiveness in flagging suspicious package installs. Our goal is to answer the following questions:

1. Is it possible to determine an optimal popularity threshold? What is the impact of varying this threshold? (Sect. 4.2).
2. What is the effectiveness of TypoGard's typosquatting signals in identifying suspicious packages? (Sect. 4.3).
3. How well does TypoGard generalize to ecosystems different from those for which it was designed? (Sect. 4.3).
4. Is the latency introduced by TypoGard acceptable? (Sect. 4.4).

Table 2. Database of typosquatting perpetrator packages.

Ecosystem	#packages	Source
npm	259	npm Security Advisories
PyPI	18	Snyk Vulnerability DB
RubyGems	725	ReversingLabs

4.1 Dataset

For package data, we consider the entire package graphs for npm, PyPI, and RubyGems. Copies of the exact datasets and download counts that were used have been made available for review[1]. A high-level quantitative summary of the repository snapshots is given in Table 1. Our dataset of known typosquatting perpetrator packages is summarized in Table 2 and was obtained from vetted public vulnerability report and—where possible—security advisories from ecosystem maintainers. Since some feeds do not explicitly distinguish typosquatting incidents from the rest, we reviewed such feeds and isolate entries which meet both the following conditions: (i) the word "typosquatting" is present in the advisory; and (ii) the language unambiguously identifies the incident as typosquatting.

4.2 Popularity Threshold

Download counts bear an obvious relationship to the popularity of a given package. Precisely understanding this relationship however requires careful analysis, due to the fact that download counts for a package represent more than the number of people who have installed a package. Packages are regularly downloaded by repository mirrors and bots which download all packages for analysis. Based on estimates made by the creators of npm, a package can be downloaded up to 50 times per day without ever being installed by an actual developer [25].

Therefore, we use 350 weekly downloads as lower bound for package popularity as packages with fewer than this number of downloads may have never been downloaded by an actual user. As seen in Fig. 1, a majority of packages across all three repositories receive fewer than 350 weekly downloads. This lower bound removes more than 90% of the packages in each repository from consideration. As an upper bound, we consider packages with more than 100,000 downloads per week to be unquestionably popular; packages above this upper bound make up less than 1% of each repository and account for a vast majority of all downloads. The analysis we describe in this section aims at finding an appropriate threshold to separate popular packages from unpopular ones between these two bounds. We emphasize that, in order to study generalizability, we conducted the analysis on npm and PyPI first, and designed TypoGard exclusively based on these ecosystems. We later incorporated RubyGems in order to determine whether our analysis, and therefore TypoGard, is effective beyond npm and PyPI.

Effect of Threshold on Number of Perpetrators: The first analysis aims to determine how the number of typosquatting targets influences the number of perpetrators. A package is considered to be a typosquatting perpetrator if it, or any package in its dependency tree, fits our definition of typosquatting. Doing this emulates real-world conditions, as users typically would not install a package without installing its dependencies. The results of this analysis is depicted in Fig. 4. Interestingly, the curve corresponding to PyPI is fundamentally different

---

[1] https://www.dropbox.com/sh/wrkz2l3njol0ecw/AAAqbv9hN83Cfdq2CGy6bBjma.

from the other two. As the popularity threshold increases, the number of popular packages decreases. With this decrease in typosquatting targets, one would initially expect the number of typosquatting perpetrators to decrease. The trend for PyPI is consistent with this behavior.

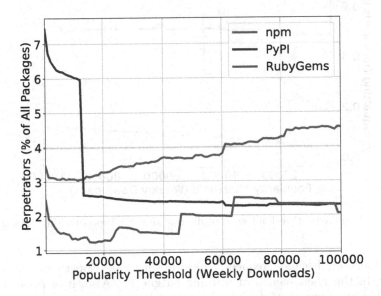

Fig. 4. Popularity threshold vs percent of repository typosquatting.

However, the curves corresponding to npm and RubyGems see gradual increases. The number of typosquatting perpetrators grows in spite of the fact that the number of targets shrinks. This highlights an interesting phenomenon: a significant amount of package name similarity between popular packages. This phenomenon causes the unintuitive increase in perpetrators seen in Fig. 4. As the threshold grows, it surpasses the weekly download count of the less popular package, allowing the package to be considered a perpetrator. Ultimately, this process increases the number of perpetrators as the number of targets decreases. We believe the threshold should be set low enough to avoid flagging reasonably popular packages as perpetrators, in order to reduce the false positive rate, and ultimately, the number of warnings that TypoGard users will experience.

Based on the analysis above, we have chosen to select a popularity threshold of 15,000 weekly downloads. A popularity threshold of 15,000 weekly downloads is the lowest threshold which keeps the number of flagged typosquatting packages reasonably low for both repositories. **We estimate that 3% of the packages on npm and PyPI, and 1.5% of the packages on RubyGems, are potential typosquatting perpetrators at this threshold.**

Effect of Threshold on Frequency of Warnings: We now examine the frequency with which TypoGard will intervene during the package installation process, by flagging a package as potential typosquatting. Keeping this frequency

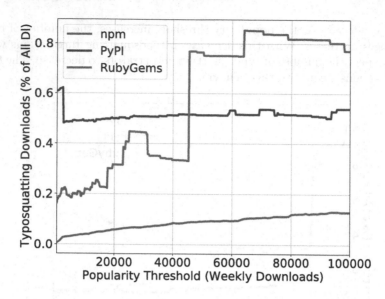

Fig. 5. Popularity threshold vs % of dls containing a typosquatting package.

low is important, because frequently interrupting a developer's workflow risks
incurring in the phenomenon of warning fatigue [8]. Also, it is reasonable to
expect that the number of packages imported by mistake is a relatively small
fraction of the overall number of packages imported by a developer. Therefore, a very high number of warning is likely to consist overwhelming of false
positives [3].

This analysis, like the first, is transitive. Results are shown in Fig. 5. With
the proposed popularity threshold of 15,000 weekly downloads, **the estimated
portion of package downloads which will result in a warning from
TypoGard is approximately 0.05% for npm, 0.5% for PyPI, and 0.25%
for RubyGems**. TypoGard generates on average a warning every 200 to 2000
package installs, which we consider an acceptable burden for the developer.

4.3   Typosquatting Signal Detection Rates

This section aims at estimating the true-positive rate (TPR), or sensitivity, of
TypoGard. We do so by measuring what fraction of past typosquatting perpetrators would have been detected by TypoGard. We use the set of attacks detailed
in Table 2, which includes more than 1,000 instances of typosquatting.

Meaningfully evaluating the performance of a typosquatting detector is complicated by the fact that typosquatting occurrences are inherently rare events
due to the sheer size of the ecosystem. For example, based on known occurrences
we can infer that there exist hundreds of perpetrators among more than one million packages on npm. Due to this, most packages flagged by even an extremely
accurate detector will be false positives (an instance of the well-known base-rate

fallacy [3]). Rather than false positives, we believe that a good typosquatting detector should attempt to minimize the rate at which alerts are generated (as discussed in Sect. 4.2), while maximizing the true-positive rate (TPR).

First, we measured TypoGard's TPR on our dataset of known perpetrators (Table 2). Each package name was passed to TypoGard to simulate installation, resulting in successful detection of **88.1%** of historical typosquatting perpetrators. We further note that the observed 11.9% of false negatives is inflated by two main factors: stochastic/exaggerated versions of our signals and combinations of multiple signals. For example, the npm Security Team technically specifies that `ruffer-xor`, `bufner-xor`, and `bwffer-xor` target `buffer-xor`. Furthermore, the malicious Python package `pwd` was accused of typosquatting `pwdhash`. These string modifications are not considered in our set of typosquatting signals, as confusion is unlikely. Extending our signals to capture these instances would essentially revert to a Levenshtein distance form of typosquatting detection, inevitably increasing false positives and presenting end users with frequent alerts. Likewise, checking for packages which utilize multiple signals simultaneously (like `cofee-script`, which targeted `coffeescript`) would exponentially increase the time required to determine if a given package name is typosquatting.

Interestingly, TypoGard confirmed **99.4%** of the typosquatting perpetrators discovered by security researchers on RubyGems, despite the fact that we did not consider any aspect of the RubyGems ecosystem while designing TypoGard. This encourages us to conclude that the underlying algorithm generalizes well beyond npm and PyPI (for which TypoGard was originally designed).

The analysis of the rate at which alerts are generated is likewise encouraging. As presented in Sect. 4.2, alerts can be expected on about 0.5% of PyPI package installations, 0.05% of npm package installations, and 0.25% of RubyGems package installation, which we believe to be sufficiently low not to disrupt developers' workflow, while providing protection against typosquatting.

4.4   TypoGard Overhead

The goal of our final analysis of TypoGard is to determine the temporal overhead it imposes on the package installation process. To quantify the performance of TypoGard, one thousand npm packages were selected at random, weighted by popularity (to simulate the downloading pattern of an actual user). Once selected, the contents of these packages were locally cached, and installation times for each package were measured using npm's official package manager and a version modified to incorporate TypoGard. The official npm package manager had an average installation time of 2.604 s, while TypoGard resulted in an average installation time of 2.669 s, meaning TypoGard imposes an **average temporal overhead of about 2.5%**. We believe this result is reasonable and the slowdown incurred by TypoGard is effectively unnoticeable.

Batch Mode Performance: TypoGard's batch mode (Sect. 3.2) can analyze the entire npm package set in **11 min**. This result suggests that TypoGard could be run frequently (e.g., once per day) allowing quick identification of unknown typosquatting cases.

5   Discussion

5.1   Extensions and Customizations to TypoGard

The goal of TypoGard is to decrease the chances of an incorrect package installation due to confusion. However, it is beyond the scope of this work to model all
of the ways in which a user might confuse package names. For example, confusion
may stem from misremembering a name, or hearing it incorrectly. Similarly, the
particular keyboard layout used by a developer influences typos that developer
is likely to make when typing in the package name. Collectively, these differences
may justify personalizing the typosquatting detection scheme.

TypoGard relies on the concept of popularity. It is possible to define alternative notions of popularity (e.g. using the number of dependent packages).
Exploring these is future work, but does not require major modifications.

5.2   Server-Side Protection Mechanisms

Our technique successfully detected typosquatting that was active in popular
package repositories for over a year, leading to effective remediation. Consequently, we feel that TypoGard could aid server-side security teams in scanning
their entire repository to discovered latent typosquatting instances. As discussed
in Sect. 3, repository maintainers can run TypoGard in batch mode to identify
suspicious packages that have already been uploaded. We also consider some
additional mechanisms that may help to combat the typosquatting problem.

Preemptive Takedown: TypoGard could be used to check every newly
uploaded package, effectively disallowing the existence of too-similar package
names. This approach is a natural extension to the case-insensitive and delimiter-
based naming restrictions currently in place on npm and PyPI [27,28,39]. It
further limits potential perpetrators from gaining traction and crossing the popularity threshold, thus achieving legitimacy through the confusion of users.

Variant-Insensitive Package Names: A repository could also map all variations of a package name to the canonical version of the package. This approach
means that the perpetrator would be unable to upload their package, since the
system would consider the name to be taken. Furthermore, it would address the
typo by suggesting the correct target. Some repositories already implement some
limited form of this behavior [39]. A potential concern with this approach is that
it crowds the set of possible names. We note that npm already incorporates a
typo-safe mechanism to allow similar package names, called *scoped packages* [26].
With this mechanism, package names can be declared to exist within a scope,
and will not conflict with packages with similar or identical names that exist outside the scope. For example, versions of many popular packages deployed using
TypeScript (a typed superset of JavaScript) are available under the @types/
namespace (e.g. @types/node). Scoped packages can be used to alleviate the
concern that a repository's names may become too crowded.

5.3 Defensive Typosquatting

One tactic currently used to prevent package typosquatting is to preemptively register confusable variants alongside the canonical package name, so that the variants cannot fall under the control of a typosquatter. We refer to this tactic as *defensive typosquatting*. We observed instances of defensive typosquatting in both npm and PyPI. The placeholder behaviors that we observed are as follows:

Transparent Inclusion of Target Package Functionality: One approach is to transparently provide the functionality of the target package to the user within the placeholder package. This can be accomplished by making the legitimate package a dependency of the placeholder. We observed this behavior in the npm package *buynan*, which (defensively) typosquats the legitimate package *bunyan*. One limitation of this defense is that it is indiscernible from a case of a malicious Trojan package; at any point a 3rd-party owner of a placeholder could change the redirect to a malicious payload. Furthermore, a less sophisticated method for transparently including target package functionality is to clone the code of the target. However, if the placeholder fails to stay up-to-date with the package it defends, it can actually expose the user to latent vulnerabilities (e.g., *loadsh*).

User Alerts: One possible option is to make the placeholder issue an informative alert with directions to change to the legitimate package. This approach has been extensively used within the PyPI repository [5,6]. In this case, placeholder packages utilize the install hook mechanism of PyPI to issue a message at install time that directs users to the packages they likely had in mind.

Package Deprecation: One mechanism used in practice to alert users is deprecation. This mechanism allows a package maintainer to indicate that the package should no longer be used. When a deprecated package is installed, the user is presented with an alert. One limitation of this technique is that deprecation is used for a variety of purposes, which may lead to confusion in the user.

Defensive typosquatting will continue to have a place as a stopgap mechanism to protect against package name confusion, to deal with context-dependent corner-cases that cannot be detected automatically. Nevertheless, tools like TypoGard can alleviate the limitations of placing placeholder packages.

6   Related Work

Typosquatting Defenses: Tschacher's Bachelor thesis [44] demonstrates a successful controlled typosquatting attack. It also briefly outlines defenses based on forbidding names similar to those of popular packages, but does not implement or evaluate them, and does not consider involving developers in the decision. The creators of npm and PyPI have taken basic countermeasures to combat typosquatting. Both platforms have incorporated restrictions on capitalization and punctuation-based differences [27,39]. User-led defense campaigns exist that aim to create placeholders for potential typosquatting names [5,7]. Limitations of these approaches are discussed in Sect. 5.

Domain Name Typosquatting: Domain name typosquatting has long been a popular attack vector, allowing cybercriminals to hijack web communications [38] and potentially emails [40] for financial gain. This is accomplished by registering a domain name similar to a popular one. In particularly serious cases, regulations allow ICANN to seize typosquatted domains [1]. Such legal framework does not exist for package typosquatting, and this approach may be difficult to apply due to the fast-evolving nature of software ecosystems. Furthermore, not all instances of package name typosquatting come from attacks.

Software Ecosystem Security: Most past efforts focused on vulnerabilities of package managers themselves [2,10], or potential attack strategies enacted by malicious packages [29]. Both analyses are orthogonal to ours, and none of these works reviewed actual incidents or measured the extent of the problem. Other works more specifically analyze security risks arising from the presence of malicious packages in highly interconnected software ecosystems [21,49]. [49] also identifies typosquatting as one of multiple possible avenues for attack, but it provides no in-depth analysis of the phenomenon, nor describes solutions.

General Characterization of Software Ecosystems: Literature presents many other analyses of software ecosystems. While these works present useful information for understanding these complex objects, they do not focus on typosquatting or other potential security-related issues. Examples include [19, 31,47].

Mobile Ecosystems: This work has direct parallels to the work done by Hu et al. [22] in the context of mobile applications. They search for typosquatting applications available on the Google Play store using techniques similar those we used in package repositories.

Another related line of work is the study of mobile application markets such as the Google Play store [11,12,45,46]. These works are primarily concerned with applications used by consumers, rather than packages that are specific to the language ecosystem and used by developers. As such, characterizations of app markets (and defenses proposed against malicious applications) are largely orthogonal to our work. The closest work is in the detection of *cloned* applications, which has typically been done via code similarity metrics [20] or behavior [15]. In contrast, our approach is based entirely on the package metadata and an analysis of the properties of the package repository.

Supply Chain Vulnerabilities: Others have looked at the related problem of *supply chain vulnerabilities*, i.e., vulnerabilities in the open-source applications on which a software package depends [9,23,30,43,48]. These works typically discuss identification or impact of potential upstream vulnerabilities. While an attacker could attempt to introduce such a vulnerability via typosquatting, analyzing this possibility is outside the scope of our work.

7   Conclusion

Typosquatting attacks in package repositories are frequent, and can have serious consequences—but have received little attention. In this paper, we have shown that defending against these attacks is both practical and efficient. By comparing the name in the requested package's dependency tree to a list of probable targets, our proposed solution can protect developers from typosquatting attacks. With an average overhead of 2.5%, a warning-to-install ratio of up to only 0.5%, and third-party confirmation of flagged packages, our solution imposes a negligible burden on developers while protecting package creators and end users alike.

References

1. Senate Report 106–140-THE ANTICYBERSQUATTING CONSUMER PROTECTION ACT, August 1999. https://www.govinfo.gov/content/pkg/CRPT-106srpt140/html/CRPT-106srpt140.html
2. Athalye, A., Hristov, R., Nguyen, T., Nguyen, Q.: Package Manager Security. Technical Report. https://pdfs.semanticscholar.org/d398/d240e916079e418b77ebb4-b3730d7e959b15.pdf
3. Axelsson, S.: The base-rate fallacy and its implications for the difficulty of intrusion detection. In: Proceedings of the 6th ACM Conference on Computer and Communications Security-CCS 1999, pp. 1–7. ACM Press (1999)
4. Baldwin, A.: Malicious package report: destroyer-of-worlds-snyk.io, May 2019. https://snyk.io/vuln/SNYK-JS-DESTROYEROFWORLDS-174777
5. Bengtson, W.: Defensive typosquatting packages created by PyPI user wbengtson, January 2018. https://pypi.org/user/wbengtson/
6. Bommarito, E., Bommarito, M.: An empirical analysis of the python package index (PyPI). arXiv preprint arXiv:1907.11073 (2019)
7. Bullock, M.: Python module: PyPI-parker, October 2017. https://pypi.org/project/pypi-parker/
8. Böhme, R., Grossklags, J.: The security cost of cheap user interaction. In: Proceedings of the 2011 Workshop on New Security Paradigms Workshop-NSPW 2011. ACM Press (2011)
9. Cadariu, M., Bouwers, E., Visser, J., van Deursen, A.: Tracking known security vulnerabilities in proprietary software systems. In: SANER (2015)
10. Cappos, J., Samuel, J., Baker, S., Hartman, J.H.: A look in the mirror: attacks on package managers. In: CCS (2008)
11. Chakradeo, S., Reaves, B., Traynor, P., Enck, W.: Mast: Triage for market-scale mobile malware analysis. In: Proceedings of the Sixth ACM Conference on Security and Privacy in Wireless and Mobile Networks. WiSec 2013, New York, NY, USA, pp. 13–24. ACM (2013). https://doi.org/10.1145/2462096.2462100, http://doi.acm.org/10.1145/2462096.2462100
12. Chatterjee, R., et al.: The spyware used in intimate partner violence. In: IEEE Symposium on Security and Privacy, pp. 441–458. IEEE Computer Society (2018)
13. Cimpanu, C.: Twelve malicious python libraries found and removed from PyPI, October 2018. https://www.zdnet.com/article/twelve-malicious-python-libraries-found-and-removed-from-pypi/
14. Claburn, T.: This typosquatting attack on npm went undetected for 2 weeks, August 2017. https://www.theregister.co.uk/2017/08/02/typosquatting_npm/

15. Crussell, J., Gibler, C., Chen, H.: Andarwin: scalable detection of android application clones based on semantics. IEEE Trans. Mob. Comput. **14**(10), 2007–2019 (2015)
16. Denvraver, H.: Malicious packages found to be typo-squatting in python package index, December 2019. https://snyk.io/blog/malicious-packages-found-to-be-typo-squatting-in-pypi/
17. Duan, R.: Malicious package report: device-mqtt - snyk.io, August 2019. https://snyk.io/vuln/SNYK-JS-DEVICEMQTT-458732
18. Fass, A., Backes, M., Stock, B.: HideNoSeek: camouflaging malicious JavaScript in Benign ASTs. In: CCS. ACM Press (2019)
19. German, D.M., Adams, B., Hassan, A.E.: The evolution of the r software ecosystem. In: CSMR (2013)
20. Gonzalez, H., Stakhanova, N., Ghorbani, A.A.: DroidKin: lightweight detection of android apps similarity. In: Tian, J., Jing, J., Srivatsa, M. (eds.) SecureComm 2014. LNICST, vol. 152, pp. 436–453. Springer, Cham (2015). https://doi.org/10.1007/978-3-319-23829-6_30
21. Hejderup, J.. In Dependencies We Trust: How vulnerable are dependencies in software modules? Master's thesis, Delft University of Technology, May 2015
22. Hu, Y., et al.: Mobile app squatting. In: Proceedings of the Web Conference, vol. 2020, pp. 1727–1738 (2020)
23. Kula, R.G., Roover, C.D., German, D., Ishio, T., Inoue, K.: Visualizing the evolution of systems and their library dependencies. In: IEEE VISSOFT (2014)
24. Lakshmanan, R.: Over 700 malicious typosquatted libraries found on rubygems repository, May 2020. https://thehackernews.com/2020/04/rubygem-typosquatting-malware.html
25. npm Maintainers: The npm blog - numeric precision matters: how npm download counts work, Jul y2014. https://blog.npmjs.org/post/92574016600/numeric-precision-matters-how-npm-download-counts
26. npm Maintainers: npm-scope—npm documentation, August 2015. https://docs.npmjs.com/using-npm/scope.html
27. npm Maintainers: New package moniker rules, December 2017. https://blog.npmjs.org/post/168978377570/new-package-moniker-rules
28. npm Maintainers: The npm blog-'crossenv' malware on the npm registry, August 2017. https://blog.npmjs.org/post/163723642530/crossenv-malware-on-the-npm-registry
29. Pfretzschner, B., ben Othmane, L.: Identification of dependency-based attacks on node.js. In: ARES (2017)
30. Plate, H., Ponta, S.E., Sabetta, A.: Impact assessment for vulnerabilities in opensource software libraries. In: ICSME (2015)
31. Raemaekers, S., van Deursen, A., Visser, J.: The maven repository dataset of metrics, changes, and dependencies. In: MSR (2013)
32. Security, C.: Contrast labs: Software libraries represent just seven percent of application vulnerabilities, July 2017. https://www.prnewswire.com/news-releases/contrast-labs-software-libraries-represent-just-seven-percent-of-applicationvulnerabilities-300492907.html
33. npm Security Team: Malicious package report: browserift - snyk.io, July 2019. https://snyk.io/vuln/SNYK-JS-BROWSERIFT-455282
34. npm Security Team: Malicious package report: comander - snyk.io, October 2019. https://snyk.io/vuln/SNYK-JS-COMANDER-471676
35. npm Security Team: npm security advisory: babel-laoder, November 2019. https://www.npmjs.com/advisories/1348

36. npm Security Team: npm security advisory: sj-tw-sec, November 2019. https://www.npmjs.com/advisories/1309
37. npm Security Team: npm security advisories, May 2020. https://www.npmjs.com/advisories
38. Spaulding, J., Upadhyaya, S., Mohaisen, A.: The landscape of domain name Typosquatting: techniques and countermeasures. In: 2016 11th International Conference on Availability, Reliability and Security (ARES), pp. 284–289, August 2016
39. Stufft, D.: Pep 503-simple repository API, September 2015. https://www.python.org/dev/peps/pep-0503/#normalized-names
40. Szurdi, J., Christin, N.: Email typosquatting. In: Proceedings of the 2017 Internet Measurement Conference, London, United Kingdom, pp. 419–431. IMC'2017, Association for Computing Machinery, November 2017
41. Team, S.S.: Prototype pollution in lodash—snyk, July 2019. https://snyk.io/vuln/SNYK-JS-LODASH-450202
42. Team, S.S.: Vulnerability db, May 2020. https://snyk.io/vuln
43. Tellnes, J.: Dependencies: No Software is an Island. Master's thesis, The University of Bergen, October 2013
44. Tschacher, N.P.: Typosquatting in Programming Language Package Managers. University of Hamburg, Hamburg (Bachelor), March 2016
45. Viennot, N., Garcia, E., Nieh, J.: A measurement study of google play. In: ACM SIGMETRICS Performance Evaluation Review, vol. 42, pp. 221–233. ACM (2014)
46. Wermke, D., Huaman, N., Acar, Y., Reaves, B., Traynor, P., Fahl, S.: A large scale investigation of obfuscation use in google play. In: Proceedings of the 34th Annual Computer Security Applications Conference, ACSAC 2018, San Juan, PR, USA, December 03–07, 2018, pp. 222–235. ACM (2018). https://doi.org/10.1145/3274694.3274726
47. Wittern, E., Suter, P., Rajagopalan, S.: A look at the dynamics of the javascript package ecosystem. In: MSR (2016)
48. Younis, A.A., Malaiya, Y.K., Ray, I.: Using attack surface entry points and reachability analysis to assess the risk of software vulnerability exploitability. In: HASE (2014)
49. Zimmermann, M., Staicu, C.A., Pradel, M.: Small world with high risks: a study of security threats in the npm ecosystem. In: USENIX, p. 17 (2019)

Graph Deep Learning Based Anomaly Detection in Ethereum Blockchain Network

Vatsal Patel⬤, Lei Pan$^{(\boxtimes)}$⬤, and Sutharshan Rajasegarar⬤

School of IT, Deakin University, Geelong, VIC 3220, Australia
{vspatel,l.pan,srajas}@deakin.edu.au

Abstract. Ethereum is one of the largest blockchain networks in the world. Its feature of smart contracts is unique among the other cryptocurrencies and gained wider attention. However, smart contracts are vulnerable to attacks and financial fraud within the network. Identifying anomalies in this massive network is challenging because of anonymity. Using traditional machine learning-based techniques, such as One-Class Support Vector Machine and Isolation Forest are ineffective in Identifying anomalies in the Ethereum transactions because of its limitations in terms of capturing the internode or account relationship information in the transactions. Ethereum transactions can be effectively represented using an attributed graph with nodes and edges capturing the inter-dependencies. Hence, in this paper, we propose to use a One-Class Graph Neural Network-based anomaly detection framework for detecting anomalies in the Ethereum blockchain network. Empirical evaluation demonstrates that the proposed method is able to achieve higher anomaly detection accuracy than traditional non-graph based machine learning algorithms.

Keywords: Ethereum blockchain · One-class methods · Graph neural networks

1 Introduction

Ethereum has become the largest blockchain supporting smart contracts and having mandatory programmable transactions that execute automatically with money transfer. Compared to the previous generations, Ethereum provides abundant data with the ability to analyze enhanced smart contracts. This setup empowers the user to send or receive money through direct money transfers or programmable smart contracts. Due to the popularity of blockchain, millions of transactions take place in the network, generating enormous amount of transaction data, which brings about challenges in terms of detecting anomalous activities in the network.

Three types of transaction activities occur in an Ethereum network, namely money transfer, smart contract creation, and smart contract invocation [2]. Blockchain has been known for its transparency and security, but the question

© Springer Nature Switzerland AG 2020
M. Kutyłowski et al. (Eds.): NSS 2020, LNCS 12570, pp. 132–148, 2020.
https://doi.org/10.1007/978-3-030-65745-1_8

remains: Is the blockchain genuinely secure? With the implementation of smart contracts, attempts have been made to manipulate smart contracts' execution in favor of the attacker [3]. Smart contracts are immutable and the attackers or developers cannot modify the contract. However, they can be terminated and new contracts can be created. The attacks on smart contracts through malfunctioning smart contract execution invoke a massive loss in the contract's virtual currencies. For example, in June 2016, the DAO (decentralized autonomous organization) attack caused a loss of more than 3.6 million Ethers [15]. The DAO attack was caused by the re-entrancy problem with the smart contracts [15,16]. The attackers could either call the function to invoke or terminate the contract, causing loss of currency from the contracts. For maintaining network integrity, it is essential to identify the malicious nodes and transactions that affect the network's security. Hence, in this paper, we propose a framework for detecting anomalies in the network, where the Ethereum transaction data are analyzed using graph representation [5] combined with neural networks and one-class processing.

Considering the Ethereum blockchain data's complexity, we have used a graph data structure to model the Ethereum blockchain network [10]. The basic unit in Ethereum is the accounts/addresses, which are considered as individual entities. These addresses are in the form of hex-decimal, unique for each account. Two major types of accounts are used in Ethereum, namely external owned accounts and smart contracts. The only significant difference between them is that the smart contracts are programmable transactions that are executed at a later stage [2]. To deploy a contract in Ethereum, the creator (*fromAddress*) sends a transaction, whose data field contains the bytecode, to the receiver's address (*toAddress*). With each transaction, several types of necessary information are stored. A graph can be constructed using the unique account addresses as a node set V, and the relationship or transaction between the node pairs as edges E. The edges between the data instances depict a relation, and performing graph analysis captures the long-range correlation. Hence, in this work, we use graph representation to capture the Ethereum transaction in the blockchain network.

In the recent past, graph based representation has been used for Ethereum transactions [1]. However, anomaly detection using graph data on Ethereum transactions have not been explored. This paper proposes a graph representation of the Ethereum data and an accurate anomaly detection model using a One-Class graph neural network-based framework. In summary, the contributions in this paper include 1) representing the Ethereum transactions using graphs, capturing the inter node/account relationships, 2) proposing an anomaly detection framework using OCGNN (one class graph neural network) [24] for Ethereum blockchain, and 3) evaluating on the publicly available Ethereum data to demonstrate the framework's capability to detect the attacks accurately compared to non-graph based methods.

The rest of this paper is organized as follows: Section 2 presents the related work. Section 3 proposes our framework. Section 4 provides the experimental results, followed by discussions in Sect. 5. Section 6 concludes the paper.

2   Related Works

Here, we briefly review the non-graph based and graph-based state-of-the-art techniques used for anomaly detection.

2.1   Traditional, Non-graph Based Techniques

Traditional non-graphical-based algorithms, such as K-means clustering and Mahalanobis distance-based algorithms, detect anomalies by partitioning the data into groups of similar patterns or clusters. These methods work well with data on which the euclidean distance measures can be used directly. However, for Ethereum transaction analysis, these methods are insufficient to extract the relationship between the accounts; the relationship can be accurately represented using a graph with accounts as nodes and the transactions between them as edges.

In the finance world, fraud transactions are relatively rare, and hence the cost of obtaining the ground truth anomalies is very high. Hence, unsupervised classification algorithms must effectively model the normal behavior and then identify the anomalies. The existing anomaly detection techniques used for such anomaly detection can be divided into three major categories as follows:

Distance-Based Technique: Methods including K-means clustering (K-Means), local anomaly factor (LOF), and isolation forest (IForest) [11] are some of the popular anomaly detection algorithms [13,14]. These methods assume that the normal data points are tightly clustered, and anomalous points are located far away from the nearest neighbors or cluster centroids. The relative distance is calculated based on how far a data point deviates from its neighbor or the centroid. The higher the anomaly score, the greater the chance of the point to be identified as an anomaly.

Boundary-Based Technique: Support Vector Data Description (SVDD) [12] is one of the boundary-based algorithms, which defines a hyper-sphere around the normal data points. The hypersphere is characterized by the center and the radius [19]. Any data point that falls outside the defined boundary is identified as an anomaly. This technique effectively solves classification problems where the anomalies are not previously known in a complex and big dataset. Another method in this category is the One-Class Support Vector Machine (OCSVM), where a plane, instead of the sphere, has been used to separate the normal and anomalous data in a higher dimensional feature space, to which the data are transformed using a kernel function. This method has been used to identify anomalies within the Bitcoin network [20].

Reconstruction-Based Techniques: Principal Component Analysis (PCA) and Autoencoders (AE) are some of the prominent methods in this category. PCA is a linear transformation and a feature extraction process, mainly used for dimensionality reduction before any anomaly detection tasks are performed [6].

Autoencoder is an unsupervised neural network technique that learns and reconstructs the data close to the original input. It comprises an encoder and a decoder. The reconstruction error is used as the anomaly score to detect anomalies.

One of the effective methods of detecting anomalies is through graph analysis, as in [2]. The first systematic study on Ethereum was conducted by leveraging graph analysis to characterize three major activities on Ethereum, including Money Transfer, Smart Contract Creation, and Smart Contract Invocation. Graph-based algorithms utilize these activities to detect accounts exhibiting abnormal behaviors. In this paper, we propose to use a Graph Neural Network based model that automatically process the network structure by aggregating neighborhood node features, and a hypersphere model based anomaly detection framework for detecting the anomalies in Blockchain.

2.2   Graph-Based Techniques

Graph Neural Network (GNN) is a graphical-based method that aggregates neighborhood node features to compute a new feature vector layer by layer [17]. With multiple iterations, the model learns the structural information of the adjacent nodes through the feature vector. Complex graph structures learned by the GNNs can be utilized to solve node classification, graph classification, and edge prediction [7, 28] problems. GNN can be categorized into two different forms based on how it aggregates the neighbor node information: isotropic model and anisotropic model [19]. Both of these models work on different assumptions on how each neighbor node contributes to updating the central node. The isotropic model assumes that each neighbor node contributes equally to the central node, while the anisotropic model uses different weights to aggregate the information of neighboring nodes. Some of the Isotropic models are Graph Convolutional Network (GCN), GraphSage, and Graph Isomorphism Network (GIN).

In contrast, anisotropic models work on an attention mechanism, for example, the Graph Attention Network (GAT). Autoencoder is a technique used to learn data in an unsupervised manner. The graph extension of the autoencoder, known as the Graph Autoencoder (GAE) [8], learns low dimensional node vector using the built-in encoder and reconstructs the node structure via a link prediction decoder. All the above neural network models aim to learn the graph's structural representation by breaking them down into each neighborhood node level to generate insights. However, only a few works use GNN for graph anomaly detection [4].

It can be observed from the above analysis that only a few efforts have been made to detect anomalies within the blockchain network, considering that it is the biggest unregulated network with anonymity features. For such a network, a better way to detect fraud/anomalies is by understanding the structural information of each neighbor node. This structural knowledge helps to detect trends in the data. Hence, we propose a one-class graph neural network-based framework for blockchain anomaly detection in this work.

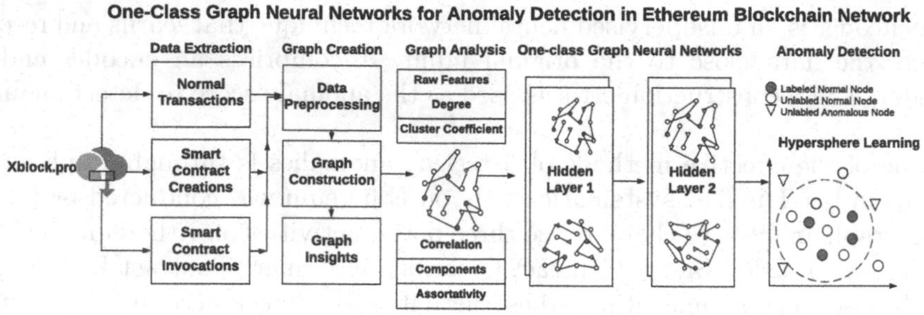

Fig. 1. The framework: Ethereum data extraction and graph creation prepare the data and creates an attributed graph for the transactions involved in the block chain. Features are computed for use in the processing. A hypersphere learning-based one class graph neural network is used to learn the normal model and to identify the anomalous transactions.

3   Methodology

Our proposed framework for Ethereum blockchain anomaly detection is shown in Fig. 1. The process comprises the following three steps:

- Data extraction: The Ethereum blockchain transaction data are processed, and three sets of data are extracted, namely the normal transactions, smart contract creations, and smart contract invocations. Twenty features are computed from the data, as shown in Table 2.
- Graph creation: An attributed graph is created using the data. The nodes of the graphs are the sender and the receiver addresses, i.e., accounts. The edges of the graphs are the set of unique pairs of sender and receiver. The edge demonstrates a relation between two nodes/accounts who entered into a transaction. Graph-based features are computed and used for processing. The last six rows of the Table 2 shows the features extracted from the graph.
- Deep learning-based anomaly detection: The obtained graph is presented to the one-class graph neural network to learn the normal behaviors and identify the anomalies.

Below, we explain each of the components of our proposed framework for anomaly detection in the Ethereum network in detail. We use similar notations used in [24] to describe the equations in these descriptions.

In our approach, the transaction data from the Ethereum Blockchain are first converted into an attributed graph. The graphs are used with the one-class graph neural network-based deep learning algorithm to learn the normal behaviors and then to identify anomalies. Here, we first define the graph as follows:

Definition 1. *Graph Construction: An attributed graph can be represented using $G = (V, E, X)$, where $V = \{V_1, V_2, \ldots, V_N\}$ is a set of nodes $N = |V|$, $E \subseteq V \times V$ is the set of $M = |E|$ edges between the nodes, and $X \in R^{N \times N}$ is the features of the N nodes. The adjacency matrix of the graph is represented using*

$A \in R^{N \times N}$, where $A_{i,j} = 1$ if a pair of nodes have an edge between them, i.e., if the sender and the receiver of the blockchain has a transaction between them.

Once the graph is obtained from the data, the aim is to learn the normal behavior using the attributed graph and detect the anomalies. It requires a hypersphere-based one class learning mechanism and a deep learning-based algorithm. We describe these algorithms in detail below.

3.1 Concept of Hypersphere Based Learning

The concept of hypersphere based learning has been widely used to detect anomalies in the literature [12,18,22]. Support Vector Data Description (SVDD) [22] is one of the algorithms used to detect anomalies in the real-world data, where the nature of anomalies is unknown.

The primary objective of SVDD is to find a compact hypersphere in the feature space F_k, with a center $c \in F_k$ and a radius $r > 0$ that captures the majority of the data points. The data space is denoted by $X \subseteq R^d$ and the mapping function from the data space X to a higher dimensional feature space F_k is denoted as $\phi_k : X \to F_k$. The positive definite kernel function that maps the data to the feature space is denoted as $k : X \times X \to [0, \infty]$. The SVDD solves the following optimization problem for a given data set $X_k = \{x_i \in X, i = 1, 2, \ldots, K\}$:

$$min_{r,c} \quad r^2 + \frac{1}{\beta K} \sum_{i=1}^{K} \xi_i$$
$$s.t. \ ||\phi_k(x_i) - c||^2_{F_k} \leq r^2 + \xi_i, \text{ and } \xi_i \geq 0, \forall i$$

The non-negative slack variable ξ_i allows tolerance for some of the anomalies to fall inside the normal region, hence, a generalized trained model can be obtained. The data points located far away from the hypersphere boundary are considered as anomalies. The hyperparameter $\beta \in (0, 1]$ controls the sphere volume and penalties for the anomalies. Solving the above optimization provides values for the center and radius, determining whether the data points fall inside the hypersphere or not. If a data point $\phi_k(x_i)$ satisfies the condition $||\phi_k(x_i) - c||^2_{F_k} > r^2$, then it is identified as an anomaly.

3.2 OCGNN: One Class Graph Neural Network

Hypersphere learning using SVDD helps build a hypersphere estimation of normal data points. Combining this with the graph neural network (GNN) forms the OCGNN framework [24]. OCGNN learns the structural information of the graph together with the hypersphere. GNN automatically learns the node embeddings by taking both node attributes and their interrelationships into consideration. GNN uses both adjacency matrix $A \in R^{N \times N}$, and the node attributes

$X \in R^{N \times D}$ as the input for the model for learning the node embedding vectors $Z \in R^{N \times F}$. Therefore, the input function for the model can be defined as $g(X, A; W)$, which represents a graph neural network with layer-wise set of weights $W = \{W1, \ldots, W^L\}$. $L \in N$ is the number of hidden layers. The forward propagation rule for the GNN's l^{th} layer can be formulated as follows:

$$H^{(l+1)} = g(H^{(l)}, A; W^{(l)}) \tag{1}$$

As per the above rule, $H^{(l)}$ serves as the input for the lth neural network layer, and $H^{(l+1)}$ is the output. For the first layer, the node attribute set X is the input, equal to $H^{(0)}$. The final output $H^{(L)}$ is the embedded matrix of nodes Z. The node embedding and structural learning capability of GNN help improve the performance for tasks, such as node or graph classification and link prediction. The primary objective of OCGNN is to learn the parameters W and take the smallest data description hypersphere, which is defined using radius $r \in R^+$ and center $c \in R^F$. Given the graph $G(X, A)$ and a set of K training nodes $V_{tr} \subseteq V$, where $K = |\{i : v_i \in V_{tr}\}|$, the loss function can be formulated as follows:

$$L(r, W) = \frac{1}{\beta K} \sum_{v_i \in V_{tr}} \{||g(X, A; W)_{vi} - c||^2 - r^2\}^+ + \frac{\lambda}{2} \sum_{l=1}^{L} ||W^{(l)}||^2 \tag{2}$$

The OGCNN model takes the nodes and edges as input information in the form of a graph structure and outputs a node embedded matrix $Z = g(X, A; W)$, $Z \in R^{N \times F}$. However, while computing the loss function, only K node embeddings are used $\{Z_{vi}, v_i \in V_{tr}\}$. In Eq. 2, the first term represents a penalty. If the distance between a data point and the center c is greater than the defined radius r, then the data point is considered as an anomaly since it is lying outside the hypersphere. The trade-off between the sphere's volume and the penalties are controlled by the hyperparameter $\beta \in (0, 1]$. Since the SVDD model aims to minimize the sphere's volume, the second term r^2 is introduced in the equation.

The model's objective helps the network map the data points close to the center c of the hypersphere. The training dataset used for the OCGNN will have only the normal data points. It defines the data description boundary of normal nodes, and the data points that fall outside this boundary are termed as anomalous nodes. We can obtain the anomaly score $S(v_i)$ by considering the location of the embedding in respect to the sphere: $S(v_i) = ||g(X, A; W^*)_{vi} - c||^2 - r^{*2}$. The output of the model is in binary form. If the $S(v_i) > 0$, then the node v_i is identified as anomalous. Otherwise, it is identified as a normal node. A trained OCGNN model can be completely characterized using the learned radius r^* and the network parameters W^*. OCGNN does not require the data to be stored, and hence the memory complexity is very low for this model.

The hyperparameter β allows some of the nodes to be mapped out of the hypersphere. Further, it has the property that it is an upper bound on the fraction of anomalous training nods and a lower bound on the fraction of nodes lying outside of the hypersphere [24].

3.3   Variants of OCGNN

Since OCGNN is a graph neural network-based anomaly detection framework, many varients can be formed using any suitable GNN layers, such as Graph Convolutional Network (GCN), Graph Attention Network (GAT), and Graph-SAGE. For illustration purposes, we use the GCN as an example to show how the One-Class Graph Neural Network learns the node representation. GCN is a graph neural network with a multi-layer structure, which can be represented using the following equation, extended from Eq. 2:

$$g(H^{(l)}, A; W^{(l)}) = \sigma(\tilde{D}^{-\frac{1}{2}} \tilde{A} \tilde{D}^{-\frac{1}{2}} H^{(l)} W^{(l)}) \tag{3}$$

Here, $\tilde{A} = A + I_N$ is a adjacency matrix of a graph whose nodes are added self-loop connections. $\tilde{A}$ has a diagonal matrix $\tilde{D}$, where $\tilde{D}_{ij} = \sum_j \tilde{A}_{ij}$. And $\tilde{D}^{-\frac{1}{2}} \tilde{A} \tilde{D}^{-\frac{1}{2}}$ is the symmetric normalized adjacency matrix $\hat{A}$, hence as a pre-processing step we can directly compute $\hat{A}$. For all the nodes in the graph, the weight matrix $W^{(l)}$ is shared. By aggregating its own features X_i and the neighbor feature X_j, GCN learns the node embedding Z_i, where $j \in N(v_i)$. Stacking multiple graph convolutional layers captures the kth order neighborhood. Next we describe the optimisation step.

3.4   Model Optimization

Three major parameters are involved in training the OCGNN model—weight matrix W, center c, and radius r. A stochastic gradient descent approach is used to optimize W of the GNN model with a one-class objective with backpropagation (BP). The radius r is difficult to be optimized since it is not an inner parameter of the OCGNN network. Hence, one-class processing and optimization of r and W are alternatively computed during the training phase using Algorithm 1 listed in the Appendix.

In the optimization algorithm, the weights W are trained for $\phi \in N$ epochs while keeping the value of radius r fixed. The value of radius can be solved with a simple linear percentile search with every epoch. For solving the radius, the distance set $d_{V_{tr}} \in R^K$ for the training node set V_{tr} are obtained. By sorting $d_{V_{tr}}$ in an ascending order, the radius can be found as the $(1 - \beta)$th percentile of distance $d_{V_{tr}}$. The value of center $c \in R^F$ is kept as constant value c_0 during the training phase computed as the mean of the training nodes embedding by an initial forward propagation. It is good to map the nodes around the target data center c_0 because most nodes are close to the center in the node embedding space.

4   Experiments

4.1   Raw Dataset

We collected all the external Ethereum transaction data from August 2nd, 2016 to January 15th, 2017 from *xblock.pro/Ethereum*. External transactions in Ethereum are initialized by external owned accounts (EOAs) and stored in the blockchain. For our research, we have used normal transactions from *xblock.pro/Ethereum*, where all the Ethereum transaction data are processed and stored [26]. In Ethereum, the first attack wave happened in mid-2016, and we have manually marked the anomalies for testing and validating the performance of our model based on the information given in a public blog[1]. The dataset contains *"blockNumber"*, *"timeStamp"*, *"transactionHash"*, *"fromAddress"*, *"toAddress"*, *"value"*, *"gasPrice"*, *"gasLimit"*, *"gasUsed"* and *"gas"* variables. A transaction has a sender and a receiver and is a signed data package containing useful information. For example, the *value* field in the transaction indicates the amount of money transferred. The sender and receiver addresses are unique hexadecimals, anonymous, and each pair can be repeated multiple times since they can be involved in more than one transaction. The attack related transactions are marked as 1 while the normal transactions as 0. For evaluating our model, we have sub-sampled our dataset to include 25,257 unique addresses out of the total 685,706 unique addresses, as shown in Table 1. From a total of 7.3 million transactions, we have chosen 50,422 transactions, making sure that each pair of sender/receiver is unique and calculated features for those pairs. Out of the total 25,257 nodes, 9185 are normal nodes, and 16,072 are anomalous nodes. The data set used in the model is further split into train, validation, and testing sets (train/val/test), which are shown in Table 1. The dataset used in the evaluation is available from GitHub[2].

Table 1. Data statistics

Statistics	Values
No. of Blocks	604,146
No. of Transactions	7,305,457
Total Unique Senders	348,726
Total Unique Receivers	336,980
Total Unique Addresses	685,706
Average Amount Transferred	5.43
Nodes	25,257
Edges	50,422
N-Classes	2
Features	34

Dataset%	Classes	Data Split
Train	Normal	5,511
	Abnormal	0
	Total	5,511
Val	Normal	1,378
	Abnormal	160
	Total	1,538
Test	Normal	2,297
	Abnormal	321
	Total	2,618

4.2 Feature Extraction

To gauge the total transactions executed by a given pair of sender and receiver, we first extracted the raw dataset features using all the 7.3 million transactions. We calculated various features, like counting the total incoming and outgoing transactions and the sum and the average amount transferred for each unique pair of sender and receiver. The features represent all of the total transactions and amount transferred for the unique pair of nodes between August 2nd, 2016 to January 15th, 2017. The raw and the calculated features were then compiled in a data frame to perform further data preprocessing. The computed features are listed in Table 2.

Table 2. Features extracted

Features	Explanation
Count by block	Total transaction count in each block
Amount by block	Total amount in each block
Unique in transaction block count	Total unique transaction from address in each block
Unique in transaction block count	Total Unique transaction to address in each block
From in transaction count	Total in transaction count all blocks
From in transaction block count	Total in transaction count by block
From out transaction count	Total out transaction count all blocks
From out transaction block count	Total out transaction count by block
To in transaction count	Total incoming amount from users for all blocks
To in transaction block count	Total incoming amount from users each block
To out transaction count	Total out transaction count all blocks
To out transaction block count	Total out transaction count by block
From in transaction value	Total in amount from users
From out transaction value	Total out amount from users
To in transaction value	Total in amount to users
To out transaction value	Total out amount to users
From Avg in transaction value	Total average in amount from user
From Avg out transaction value	Total average out amount from user
To Avg in transaction value	Total average in amount to user
To Avg out transaction value	Total average out amount to user
From in degree	Total number of incoming transaction from users
From out degree	Total number of outgoing transaction from users
To in degree	Total number of incoming transaction to users
To out degree	Total number of outgoing transaction to users
From cluster coefficient	Clustering Coefficient from users
To cluster coefficient	Clustering Coefficient to users

4.3   Ethereum Graph Data

The dataset is used to extract two sets of information to form the graph, namely edges and features. The edges contain a set of unique pairs of sender and receiver. The edge demonstrates a relation between two nodes which entered into a transaction. These edges are converted into a matrix and visualized in the form of a weighted directed graph. Several levels of processing are conducted to convert the hex-decimal addresses into numeric to form the graph network. Another set of data that contains features has been structured to have a list of unique receiver address and sender address in the first column and their features. All these features and the address (nodes) are also converted from hex values into decimal integer values for matrix conversion. The degree distribution of the graph network is shown in Fig. 2. The in-degree of a node in a directed graph is the number of edges whose heads end at that node, while the out-degree of a node in a directed graph is the number of edges whose tails end at that node.

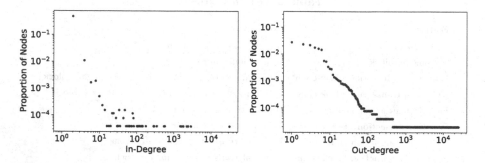

Fig. 2. Degree distribution of graph data. The left hand side diagram is for in-degree distribution, and the right hand side diagram is for out-degree distribution.

4.4   Influence of the Hyper-parameters

We used traditional non-graph-based algorithms (Euclidean Data-based algorithm), such as One class SVM (OCSVM) and Isolation Forest (IForest) [14,20,21,25] for anomaly detection, and compared them with the OCGNN model.

1. OCSVM is the traditional support vector machine-based algorithm, which forms the basis for OCGNN. We used the RBF kernel with γ and β parameters tuned for performance optimization. We select the ideal γ value between 0.01 and 0.4, and we set a range of 0.1 to 0.6 for the parameter β. We performed GridSearchCV using a cross-validation approach to identify the optimum hyper-parameter
2. Isolation Forest (IForest) is comparatively more straightforward to isolate anomalies from data based on random forest principle. A tree structure is used to partition the recursive presentation where the number of splittings isolates a sample, which is equivalent to the distance from the root node to the isolated node. This distance is averaged over the forest to serve as the measure of normality and decision function. The forest of random trees which produce shorter distance are likely to be anomalies. An important parameter of Iforest is the contamination, which determines the proportion of anomalies in the data set. It serves as a threshold on the scores of the sample. We optimized this parameter using the range of 0.1 to 0.5 for our model.

The One-Class Graph Neural Network model can be formed using any suitable layer (i.e., variants of GNN) to perform graph anomaly detection. For evaluating the performance of OCGNN, we used three best performing modules, namely GraphSAGE, GAT, and GCN. The model is initialized with Glorot uniform weight and optimized using the Stochastic Gradient Descent (SGD) with a learning rate of 0.001. While training the model, the weight decay has been used between 5×10^{-3} to 5×10^{-6} depending on the layers, β, and epochs. The model is designed for an early stopping strategy based on loss function and AUC score. For training the model, we used a different range of epochs, from 100 to 1000, using three different random seeds to validate the model's performance. For GAT, we applied 4 layers with 33 neurons in each layer, while for GraphSAGE and GCN, we have used 2 layers with 32 neurons in each layer. For each model, the output layer dimension is half of the hidden layer size, and the dropout parameter is used to move to the next layer. For GraphSAGE, the aggregate type is default and set as pooling, and for the GAT layer, the attention heads are set to 8. The threshold is determined by the distance of the data point from the center of the sphere.

Table 3. Average Performance Measures (Over 3 Random Seeds). Training % shows the percentage of normal training data (5,511) used, with no change in test/val dataset.

Training%	Method	Accuracy	F1
80%	IForest	50.22 ± 0.02	39.11 ± 0.03
	OCSVM	53.54 ± 0.03	60.27 ± 0.02
70%	IForest	52.63 ± 0.02	22.24 ± 0.01
	OCSVM	54.98 ± 0.03	36.94 ± 0.03
60%	IForest	40.32 ± 0.03	32.14 ± 0.01
	OCSVM	44.94 ± 0.05	36.78 ± 0.02
60%	OC-GAT	85.77 ± 0.05	82.21 ± 0.02
	OC-SAGE	84.83 ± 0.03	81.26 ± 0.04
	OC-GCN	66.34 ± 0.03	66.12 ± 0.01
30%	OC-GAT	86.97 ± 0.02	83.46 ± 0.01
	OC-SAGE	90.75 ± 0.03	74.61 ± 0.05
	OC-GCN	64.99 ± 0.02	65.26 ± 0.03
10%	OC-GAT	86.47 ± 0.02	82.93 ± 0.01
	OC-SAGE	85.65 ± 0.03	82.07 ± 0.03
	OC-GCN	66.04 ± 0.03	65.94 ± 0.02

5   Discussions

All the models' performance measures are recorded in Table 3 for a different level of training data set used to train the model. The first column of the table shows the percentage of normal data (training) used for learning the normal behavior. The purpose of reducing the training dataset in stages and performing the experiment is to gauge our model's performance even with the lowest data available to train, such as when using 10% training data. Note that the test and validation data set proportions are not changed when changing the training data size.

The results shown in the table reveal that the OCGNN outperforms the traditional anomaly detection algorithms in terms of accuracy and F1 score. It is further supported by the evidence from the loss curves and ROC curves, as shown in Fig. 3. Among the traditional algorithms, the OCSVM has shown better performance compared to the Isolation Forest. The accuracy and F1 Score for OCSVM and Isolation Forest reported are the average values of three random repetitions. The accuracy for OCSVM is the highest with 54.98%, using the data split of 70-30%, and the Isolation Forest is 52.63%. These results demonstrate that with lower training datasets, the traditional models struggle to detect anomalies. The accuracy goes down as the proportion of the data chosen for training the model becomes small.

On the other hand, the hypersphere learning-based GNN models' performance remains high even if we use 10% of the data for training the model. OC-GAT is the best performing model with an overall accuracy of 86%, followed by the OC-GraphSAGE with an average accuracy of 85%. The accuracy for both of the models is well supported by the F1 score with 83% and 82% for OC-GAT and OC-GraphSAGE, respectively. Looking at the loss curve, both the models show strong performance with no sign of over-fitting or under-fitting. When trained in the model with 10% of the training dataset, the loss curve shows variations for OC-GraphSAGE and OC-GCN model, but it remains smooth for the OC-GAT. This variation can further be optimized by tuning the parameters. When compared the OC-GraphSAGE with OC-GAT, the latter has shown better performance and a smooth loss curve. The AUC scores are averaged for three random repetitions, and are close to 98 ± 1.0 for both the models.

The OC-GCN is the weakest performing model among the OCGNN group. Optimizing the hyper-parameters of OC-GCN for a complex data structure is quite tricky. OC-GCN is a type of Laplacian smoothing [9], which requires the layers to be lowest, because this model is quite challenging to train with many layers. At the same time, repeatedly applying Laplacian smoothing may mix the features making them indistinguishable. We have used only two layers in this model to train the OC-GCN since it gives the best performance. The accuracy of OC-GCN is at the lowest among others at 66%, with a F1 score of 66.12%. If we train the model with 10% data, the accuracy remains the same; however, it negatively impacts the loss curve and AUC scores. For further optimization, using the concept of self-training and GraphMix might significantly improve the results [23, 27].

The hypersphere based learning approach's capability is demonstrated by training the model using varying amount of data, from 10% to 60% of training data, which consists of a set of normal transactions. The hypersphere learning based method works quite well even with minimal training data and still detects anomalies with high accuracy. As can be seen in Table 3, the performance of OCGNN remains consistent. When we train the model with only 10% of data, the loss curves are affected, but it can be further optimized.

6 Conclusion

Blockchain has become popular in the recent years due to its unique properties, such as being anonymous, decentralized, and using distributed public ledger principles. The same capabilities have also raised potential threats of attacks, and due to anonymity, it is quite challenging to identify the malicious transactions within the network. Ethereum has become the largest blockchain supporting smart contracts and having mandatory programmable transactions that execute automatically with money transfer. In this paper, an anomaly detection framework is proposed for Ethereum network that comprises graph representation, a neural network model and one-class processing. Evaluation on the publicly available Ethereum data reveals that the proposed one class graph neural network (OCGNN) based framework for ethereum is capable of detecting the anomalous activities in the network accurately, compared to other non-graph based methods. Further, its ability to learn the normal model from varying size of training data has been analysed, and shown that the framework is capable to work with smaller data to learn and perform accurate anomaly detection. In the future, in order to handle the challenge of real time detection of emerging anomalous activities in the Ethereum, incremental, multi-stage graph embedding process can be analysed, in addition to one class methods, for anomaly detection.

Acknowledgement. We would like to thank Mr. Xuhong Wang, one of the authors of [24], for sharing the source code and answering our queries promptly. We are also very grateful for the valuable comments provided by anonymous reviewers.

A   OCGNN Model Training Algorithm

Algorithm 1: OCGNN Model Training [24]

Input: Attributed Graph $G = (V, E, X)$, normal nodes set V_{tr}, Slack Parameter
$\beta \in (0, 1]$, weight decay $\gamma > 0$

Output: Weights W, center $c \in R^F$ and radius $r \in R^+$

1 Initialize W using Glorot uniform initialization;

2 Initialize $r = 0, c = \frac{1}{K} \sum_{v_i \in V_{tr}} g(X, A; W)_{vi}$;

3 **while** *epoch < max epoch budget* **do**

4 $\quad$ $d_{vtr} = ||g(X, A; W)_{vtr} - C||^2, d_{vtr} \in R^K$;

5 $\quad$ $L = \frac{1}{\beta K} \sum_{V_{tr}} [d_{vtr} - r^2]^+ + r^2 + \frac{\lambda}{2} \sum_{l=1}^{L} ||W^{(l)}||^2$;

6 $\quad$ Update W by its stochastic gradient $\Delta_w(L)$;

7 $\quad$ **if** *epoch mod ϕ = 0* **then**

8 $\quad\quad$ | Update r using $(1 - \beta) \times 100\%$ percentile of d_{vtr};

9 $\quad$ **end**

10 **end**

11 **return** W, c and r;

B   Loss Curves and AUROC Curves for Different Training Sample Sizes

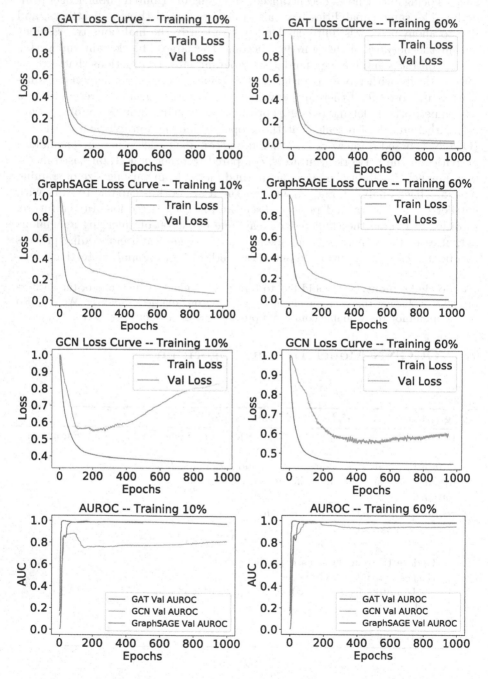

Fig. 3. Loss Curves and AUROC Curves for different training sample sizes

References

1. Bai, Q., Zhang, C., Xu, Y., Chen, X., Wang, X.: Evolution of ethereum: a temporal graph perspective. arXiv preprint arXiv:2001.05251 (2020)
2. Chen, T., et al.: Understanding ethereum via graph analysis. In: Proceedings of the IEEE Conference on Computer Communications (INFOCOM' 2018), pp. 1484–1492 (2018)
3. Cheng, Z., et al.: Towards a first step to understand the cryptocurrency stealing attack on ethereum. In: Proceedings of the 22nd International Symposium on Research in Attacks, Intrusions and Defenses (RAID' 2019), pp. 47–60 (2019)
4. Galke, L., Vagliano, I., Scherp, A.: Incremental training of graph neural networks on temporal graphs under distribution shift. arXiv preprint arXiv:2006.14422 (2020)
5. Guo, D., Dong, J., Wang, K.: Graph structure and statistical properties of ethereum transaction relationships. Inf. Sci., **492**, 58–71 (2019). https://doi.org/10.1016/j.ins.2019.04.013, http://www.sciencedirect.com/science/article/pii/S0020025519303159
6. Jablonski, J.A., Bihl, T.J., Bauer, K.W.: Principal component reconstruction error for hyperspectral anomaly detection. IEEE Geosci. Remote Sens. Lett. **12**(8), 1725–1729 (2015)
7. Kipf, T.N., Welling, M.: Semi-supervised classification with graph convolutional networks. arXiv preprint arXiv:1609.02907 (2016)
8. Kipf, T.N., Welling, M.: Variational graph auto-encoders. arXiv preprint arXiv:1611.07308 (2016)
9. Li, Q., Han, Z., Wu, X.M.: Deeper insights into graph convolutional networks for semi-supervised learning. arXiv preprint arXiv:1801.07606 (2018)
10. Lin, D., Wu, J., Yuan, Q., Zheng, Z.: Modeling and understanding ethereum transaction records via a complex network approach. Express Briefs, IEEE Trans. Circuits Syst. II (2020)
11. Lorenz, J., Silva, M.I., Aparício, D., Ascensão, J.T., Bizarro, P.: Machine learning methods to detect money laundering in the bitcoin blockchain in the presence of label scarcity (2020)
12. Pauwels, E.J., Ambekar, O.: One class classification for anomaly detection: support vector data description revisited. In: Perner, P. (ed.) ICDM 2011. LNCS (LNAI), vol. 6870, pp. 25–39. Springer, Heidelberg (2011). https://doi.org/10.1007/978-3-642-23184-1_3
13. Pham, T., Lee, S.: Anomaly detection in bitcoin network using unsupervised learning methods (2016)
14. Pham, T., Lee, S.: Anomaly detection in the bitcoin system – a network perspective. arXiv abs/1611.03942 (2016)
15. Praitheeshan, P., Pan, L., Yu, J., Liu, J., Doss, R.: Security analysis methods on ethereum smart contract vulnerabilities: a survey. arXiv preprint arXiv:1908.08605 (2019)
16. Praitheeshan, P., Xin, Y.W., Pan, L., Doss, R.: Attainable hacks on keystore files in ethereum wallets-a systematic analysis. In: Proceedings of the International Conference on Future Network Systems and Security (FNSS'2019), pp. 99–117. Springer (2019). https://doi.org/10.1007/978-3-030-34353-8_7
17. Puzyrev, V.: Deep convolutional autoencoder for cryptocurrency market analysis. arXiv preprint arXiv:1910.12281 (2019)
18. Rajasegarar, S., Leckie, C., Bezdek, J.C., Palaniswami, M.: Centered hyperspherical and hyperellipsoidal one-class support vector machines for anomaly detection in sensor networks. IEEE Trans. Inf. Forensics Secur. **5**(3), 518–533 (2010)

19. Ruff, L., et al.: Deep one-class classification. In: Proceedings of the International Conference on Machine Learning, pp. 4393–4402 (2018)
20. Sayadi, S., Rejeb, S.B., Choukair, Z.: Anomaly detection model over blockchain electronic transactions. In: Proceedings of the 2019 15th International Wireless Communications and Mobile Computing Conference (IWCMC' 2019), pp. 895–900. IEEE (2019)
21. Spagnuolo, M., Maggi, F., Zanero, S.: BitIodine: extracting intelligence from the bitcoin network. In: Christin, N., Safavi-Naini, R. (eds.) FC 2014. LNCS, vol. 8437, pp. 457–468. Springer, Heidelberg (2014). https://doi.org/10.1007/978-3-662-45472-5_29
22. Tax, D.M., Duin, R.P.: Support vector data description. Mach. Learn. 54(1), 45–66 (2004)
23. Verma, V., Qu, M., Lamb, A., Bengio, Y., Kannala, J., Tang, J.: Graphmix: Regularized training of graph neural networks for semi-supervised learning (2019)
24. Wang, X., Du, Y., Cui, P., Yang, Y.: OCGNN: One-class classification with graph neural networks. arXiv preprint arXiv:2002.09594 (2020)
25. Zarpelão, B.B., Miani, R.S., Rajarajan, M.: Detection of bitcoin-based botnets using a one-class classifier. In: Blazy, O., Yeun, C.Y. (eds.) WISTP 2018. LNCS, vol. 11469, pp. 174–189. Springer, Cham (2019). https://doi.org/10.1007/978-3-030-20074-9_13
26. Zheng, P., Zheng, Z., ning Dai, H.: Xblock-eth: Extracting and exploring blockchain data from ethereum (2019)
27. Zhou, Z., Zhang, S., Huang, Z.: Dynamic self-training framework for graph convolutional networks. arXiv preprint arXiv:1910.02684 (2019)
28. Zong, B., et al.: Deep autoencoding gaussian mixture model for unsupervised anomaly detection. In: Proceedings of the International Conference on Learning Representations (2018)

Game Theoretic Analysis of Reputation Approach on Block Withholding Attack

Lianyang Yu[1]([✉]), Jiangshan Yu[1], and Yevhen Zolotavkin[2,3]

[1] Faculty of Information Technology, Monash University, Clayton, Australia
lyuu0014@student.monash.edu, jiangshan.yu@monash.edu
[2] Centre for Cyber Security Research and Innovation, Deakin University,
Geelong, Australia
yevhen.zolotavkin@deakin.edu.au
[3] Cyber Security Cooperative Research Centre, Joondalup, Australia

Abstract. Bitcoin and the underlying technology blockchain introduced an open distributed system that incorporates Proof of Work and Nakamoto Consensus. Despite the broad adoption by enthusiasts, the consensus mechanism is vulnerable to certain issues, such as *block withholding attack*, *selfish mining*, and *51% attack*. Various solutions have been proposed to address these problems. *RepuCoin* is one successful example, which claims to solve the selfish mining and 51% attack by adopting a novel *reputation concept* and modified BFT protocol. We generalize the reputation concept introduced in RepuCoin, and implement it in traditional Bitcoin system to analyze whether it can prevent the *block withholding attack*. We propose a reputation-based reward mechanism for the Bitcoin blockchain and a reward sharing schema for the mining pools. We model the utility of honest mining and block withholding attack for pools, and find that the inclusion of reputation in Bitcoin's reward mechanism and pools' reward schema can prevent mining pools from launching block withholding attack.

Keywords: Blockchain · Game theory · Reputation · Block withholding attack

1 Introduction

Bitcoin [1] is the digital currency that implements blockchain as the technical foundation of the system. It has attracted substantial attention from both academia and industry. The estimated market capitalization of Bitcoin has reached over 110 billion US dollars. It is so far the most popular digital currency, and the underlying consensus mechanism has been widely adopted by other blockchain applications, such as Ethereum [19] and Monero [20]. Bitcoin system requires participants to submit certain proof that demonstrates the validity of effort they have made, which is called *Proof of Work* (PoW). The first one

---

The work has been partially supported by the Cyber Security Research Centre Limited whose activities are partially funded by the Australian Government's Cooperative Research Centres Programme.

© Springer Nature Switzerland AG 2020
M. Kutyłowski et al. (Eds.): NSS 2020, LNCS 12570, pp. 149–166, 2020.
https://doi.org/10.1007/978-3-030-65745-1_9

who submits the proof gains the opportunity to add a new block on top of the longest chain. This type of consensus is called *Nakamoto consensus*. However, the immutability of Bitcoin system are often questioned, due to non-trivial nature of incentives to participate in Proof of Work consensus. Many attacks have been proposed that allow the malicious participants to jeopardize the system, or earn disproportionate rewards with respect to their efforts. The most well-known attacks are selfish mining strategies [2], block withholding attack [3–5], and 51% attack. Our focus is the *block withholding attack*, which is a more practical problem and has happened in real life.

To address the security issues existing in Bitcoin, many new forms of blockchain have been proposed that modify the consensus protocol or blockchain structure. *RepuCoin* [6] adopts a novel concept of *reputation* and *reputation-based weighted voting mechanism*, which guarantees system security even in the presence of adversary holding more than 50% of the system's computational power. *RepuCoin* is proposed to solve the 51% attack and the selfish mining. The consensus and the blockchain structure vary significantly from the Bitcoin system settings. Whether the reputation concept can be applied to general blockchain mechanism to solve the *block withholding attack* is unknown. The advantage of *reputation* is that it can be implemented on the rewards distribution among and within *mining pools*, without changing the basic protocol of Bitcoin. Thus, we extract the reputation concept from RepuCoin and apply it to Bitcoin and mining pools to evaluate whether the reputation approach can provide adequate incentive for miners to follow the honest mining strategy.

We use game theoretic analysis to model the utility of honest strategy and block withholding attack in a two-pool scenario. In summary, our contributions are following:

1. Generalization of the reputation concept and definition of reputation mechanisms that are applicable to Bitcoin pool mining.
2. Definition of the generic utility function in a two-pool scenario.
3. Implementation of the One-Poisson-Mean-Test (OPMT) for pool members' honesty evaluation.
4. Conclusion that, in the two-pool scenario, the reputation mechanism prevents the block withholding attack.

2   Preliminaries

2.1   Bitcoin and the Underlying Blockchain

All blockchain systems can be deconstructed into three components, which are *membership selection*, *consensus mechanism*, and *structure* [7]. Following this framework, we evaluate the components of Bitcoin system.

Membership Selection
The Bitcoin system uses *Proof of Work (PoW)* as the membership selection algorithm. PoW requires nodes to prove their validity by performing some works

with certain cost, in order to propose the block. The work specified is the cryptographic puzzle, which involves heavy computation that consumes significant amount of electricity. In order to solve the puzzle, it is required to iterate through the computation of a double SHA-256 hash function to produce a block header. The first node that produces a result that is lower than the system's target can propose the new block and append it on the main chain. The process is called mining and the nodes performing such task are called miners.

Consensus Mechanism

The consensus of Bitcoin is called *Nakamoto Consensus*. The most crucial aspect of Nakamoto Consensus is the *longest chain rule*, which states that the nodes must choose the chain with the highest number of blocks as the single canonical chain. The longest chain is believed to have the most work performed. Following the assumption that the majority of the system computational power is owned by the honest nodes, the longest chain is supposed to be honest.

Structure

Bitcoin features a single canonical chain for all miners to work on. The chain contains homogeneous blocks, where every block has the same structure that stores a record of recent transactions, a reference to the previous block, the current time, etc.

Incentive Mechanism

Set by Nakamoto in the Bitcoin whitepaper [1], Bitcoin's reward consists of block mining reward and transaction fees. Miners add a transaction paid to them that creates new Bitcoins in their prospective blocks. Once a block is successfully appended on the chain, the miner will receive the reward (currently 6.25 BTC) plus transaction fees in that block. There are many attacks and mining strategies proposed since the inception of Bitcoin, which allows miners to earn disproportional gains [2,4,5].

Bitcoin Mining Pools

Miners may form the *mining pool*, which is controlled by the pool manager in the centralized manner. The pool members share the reward in accordance to the reward scheme established in the pool when a block is found. The main objective for miners to join mining pools is to receive regular income, in contrast to solo mining where miners receive infrequent rewards. The mining process for miners can be seen as a lottery, where the probability of individual miners with small computational power winning the next block proposition is extremely low. Thus, joining mining pools can reduce the uncertainty. Miners produce partial Proof of Work, which are called shares. The difficulty level of partial PoW set in the pool is lower than the system's specified difficulty level. When members find the puzzle solution that meets the system's target, called full Proof of Work, and send to the pool manager, the pool manager immediately broadcast the block to obtain corresponding mining rewards. The reward received by the pool will be distributed to the members according to the reward sharing schema.

There are many different reward functions for mining pools, as analysed by Schrijvers et al. [21]. It's important to use a reward schema that ensures incentive compatibility and optimize the pool's welfare. The most common approaches are *proportional reward*, *Pay-Per-Share (PPS)*, and *Pay-Per-Last-N-Shares (PPLNS)*. For the pool adopting *proportional reward*, the reward is divided according to the proportion of shares of a miner over all shares that were reported in the pool. Under the *PPS* schema, the pool members are paid a fixed amount for every share that is reported. *PPLNS* maintains a sliding window of length N, which allows each miner to get the reward that is proportional to the partial PoW exerted during the last N shares before a full solution. The aforementioned reward sharing schemas are susceptible to block withholding attack.

Currently, the majority of Bitcoin's mining power is controlled by mining pools. Individual miner's computational power is infinitesimal [22]. Thus, our analysis concentrates on the effect of reputation on mining pools.

2.2   RepuCoin

RepuCoin [6] is a blockchain system that guarantees system security. The system solves Bitcoin security issues by modifying membership selection approach, consensus mechanism, and the structure.

Membership Selection
RepuCoin introduces a novel membership selection approach called *Proof of Reputation*. It defines miner's integrated power by *reputation*, which is measured by the *total amount of valid work* and the *regularity of the work* over the entire period of the system running time. The work is the same as it is in Bitcoin. The top reputable miners will form the consensus committee to control the system.

Consensus Mechanism
RepuCoin adopts a modified *BFT protocol*, which can keep functioning even in the presence of a certain amount of Byzantine failures. The BFT protocol should satisfy the condition that $N \geq 3f + 1$, where f denotes the number of Byzantine nodes, and N is the total number of nodes [8]. RepuCoin adopts a *reputation-based weighted voting consensus*, which requires no less than $2f + 1$ votes from the committee to reach consensus agreement. Besides, the collective reputation from the nodes who have voted should be more than $\frac{2}{3}$ of the total reputation of the consensus committee. The novelty of the consensus is that it decouples the voting power and computational power, which prevents attacks from the adversaries with temporary high computational power.

Structure
RepuCoin implements a *parallel chain structure* with two types of blocks, namely keyblock and microblock. Keyblocks, which are created by all eligible miners solving cryptographic puzzles, are linked by referencing each predecessor and form one chain. Microblocks, which contains transactions, form a parallel chain

that is linked by referencing previous microblocks, and each microblock is referenced to the most recent keyblock. The consensus group decides which keyblock to be pinned. A leader is selected randomly from the consensus group to verify and gather transactions into microblocks. The transactions are decoupled from the block creation process.

Although the system can guarantee security from malicious majority miners, the system is too complex and specific. We extract a reputation concept from RepuCoin, and analyze its applicability to the general Bitcoin system.

2.3 Block Withholding Attack

Block withholding attack is a general type of strategic mining that causes detriments to mining pools. The attack is firstly proposed by Rosenfeld [3], which involves individual pool member attacking the pool. The attacking strategy includes sabotaging the pool by withholding the blocks, or lie in wait, which postpones the submission of the blocks. The attacker submits partial PoW regularly, but withholds the full PoW. This attack decreases victim pool's revenue, and the reward distributed to the attacker is in turn decreased. Thus, the attack is purely used to disrupt the pool, as there is no economic benefits to the attacker.

The idea is advanced to be used by mining pools [4]. The attacking pool deploys part of its mining power to infiltrate the victim pool. The infiltrated members in the victim pool submit partial PoW regularly to gain shares, but withhold the full PoW. The remaining miners in the attacking pool work honestly to propose blocks. This attack allows the attacking pool to earn more than honest mining. It leads to the tragedy of the commons, where pools choose to attack each other and each will earn less than honest mining.

Following the attack at pool level, Fork after Withholding Attack was proposed [5]. It specifies that if the attacker releases the withholding full PoW immediately after other honest non-infiltrated pools publish a valid block, the attacker can earn more. This will force a forked situation, and the attacker has the chance to win the longest chain and earn the reward.

For the reputation analysis, We focus on the *block withholding attack* at pool level, where the attacking pool infiltrates other pools with part of its mining power [4]. Assuming that the system's total mining power is m, and there are two pools in the system, where pool 1 is the block withholding attacker with m_1 mining power and pool 2 follows honest mining with m_2 mining power. Pool 1 deploys $x_{1,2}$ of its loyal members to pool 2. The revenue for pool 1 is $\frac{m_1-x_{1,2}}{m-x_{1,2}} + \frac{x_{1,2}}{m_2+x_{1,2}} \cdot \frac{m_2}{m-x_{1,2}}$, where $\frac{m_1-x_{1,2}}{m-x_{1,2}}$ is the revenue gained from honest mining in pool 1, and $\frac{x_{1,2}}{m_2+x_{1,2}} \cdot \frac{m_2}{m-x_{1,2}}$ is the block withholding attack revenue gained from pool 2. It's been proved that this attack can bring higher gains to the attacking pool [4,11,18], and honest mining is not an equilibrium point.

2.4   One-Poisson-Mean-Test as a Countermeasure to Block Withholding Attack

Let X be the Poisson random variable with parameter λ, which denotes the mean value of the Poisson process. The probability of $X = x$ ($x \in \mathbb{R}$) is defined as $Pr(X = x) = \frac{e^{-\lambda}\lambda^x}{x!}$. The cumulative probability function of $X \leq x$ follows gamma distribution that $F_X(x) = Pr(X \leq x) = \sum_{i=0}^{x} \frac{e^{-\lambda}\lambda^i}{i!} = 1 - F_{\Gamma\beta}(\lambda, x)$, with $\beta = 1$ as the rate parameter.

The One-Poisson-Mean Test (OPMT) [12,13] is useful to validate whether certain members in the pool are the block withholding attackers. Under block withholding attack, the infiltrated miners produce 0 full solution. The null hypothesis H_0 that the pool manager would like to reject is that "the member is a block withholding attacker", while the alternative hypothesis H_1 is that "the member is honest". The pool manager can test the hypothesis based on the number of shares received from each miner. On average, there is certain number of blocks on every K shares. The pool manager analyzes the number of full solutions each member produced within the K shares and tries to find the lowest significance level α under which hypothesis H_0 can be rejected. The lowest α is embedded in the reputation calculation of the pool member.

3   Reputation Mechanisms

There are two levels of reputation application in the mechanism. One reputation-based reward distribution among the pools, which enforces the pools to adopt consistent mining strategy; and one reputation-based reward sharing schema within the pools that punishes block withholding attack. We use Bitcoin as the baseline model. The *reputation mechanisms* only alter the system's reward distribution method and reward sharing schema in pools.

Every mining pool and pool member has a *reputation score* R assigned to them. The reputation is not transferable, as it relates to each's unique identity (i.e., public key). The reputation score is a ratio within $[0, 1]$. The block generation process is divided into *epochs*. As the average time taken to mine a new block is 10 min, each epoch contains 144 valid blocks, which is the number of blocks mined in 24 h. At the end of each epoch, the reputation score is updated, and the reward is distributed in accordance to the reputation score R. Instead of rewarding the miners each time the block is generated, the reward under the reputation mechanism is paid to eligible miners in lump sum at the end of each epoch. The reputation components are generalized from RepuCoin [6].

3.1   Reputation Generalization

Reputation is defined as "the perception that an agent creates through past actions about its intentions and norms" [9]. Applying this definition to Repu-Coin [6], the "past actions" of the RepuCoin miner is demonstrated by the total number of blocks the miner has generated in the system and the regularity of the block generation. The two components will form the reputation of the miner regarding his honesty. Only when the miner has produced as many valid blocks as possible in a constant pace for a long period of time can have a high reputation score to gain the voting power in RepuCoin system. Thus, the components of the reputation of a miner in RepuCoin are:

- Total amount of valid work done
- The regularity of the valid work

We generalize the above two components and apply them to Bitcoin system.

Table 1. Reputation mechanisms notation table

Notation	Explanation
t	The index of epochs
T	Total number of epochs
p	The index of pools
i	The index of pool members
N	Total number of blocks in each epoch ($N = 144$)
w_p	The number of valid works done by pool p
K	Total number of shares in a pool in one epoch
q_i	The number of valid works done by member i
W	The ratio of total amount of valid work done by a pool or a pool member
S	Regularity
R	Reputation score
M	Proportion of the pool's reward

3.2 Reputation-Based Reward Distribution for Pools

We propose a *reputation-based reward distribution* method for the system to allocate the total reward in one epoch, where every mining pool receives the reward based on its reputation. The *regularity of the valid work* captures the characteristic of the marginal productivity of mining, which represents the ratio of the additional gain for one more block generation. It follows the *law of diminishing marginal return*, where the mining pool will find a decrease in marginal gains after the number of blocks reaches certain point. The *total amount of valid work* represents the integration of the returns over all epochs. Thus, the *reputation* is the function of *regularity* and *total amount of valid work*. We use the reputation as the basis of the system's reward distribution.

Total amount of valid work is measured based on total number of blocks generated by the pool p and the total number of blocks in the system. The ratio represents the pool's average mining power throughout the system's running time. The function is as following:

$$W_{p,t} = \frac{\sum_{t=1}^{T} w_{p,t}}{N_t T} \tag{1}$$

Regularity of the work is measured by the standard deviation of the pool's block proposal ratio, as the standard deviation can reflect the fluctuations in the block proposal rate. Standard deviation, as the measure of variability, captures how every epoch varies from the mean. A low standard deviation indicates that the number of block generations in every epoch tend to be very close to the mean, which suggests that the pool's mining strategy tends to be consistent. The regularity function for pool p at epoch t is as following:

$$S_{p,t} = \frac{1}{1 + \sqrt{\frac{1}{T} \times \sum_{t=1}^{T}(\frac{w_{p,t}}{N_t} - \frac{\sum_{t=1}^{T} w_{p,t}}{N_t T})^2}} \tag{2}$$

The reputation score $R_{p,t}$ is calculated by multiplying the ratio of total amount of valid work $W_{p,t}$ and the regularity factor $S_{p,t}$.

$$R_{p,t} = W_{p,t} \times S_{p,t}, \quad R_{p,t} \in [0,1] \tag{3}$$

As $S_{p,t} < 1$, the pool will not receive the full reward for the blocks it has mined. In order to eliminate the reward residuals, the proportion of the reward pool p will receive is normalized:

$$M_{p,t} = \frac{R_{p,t}}{\sum_{p=1}^{j} R_{p,t}} \tag{4}$$

$M_{p,t}$ denotes the *reputation-based proportion* of the reward pool p will receive at the end of epoch t, assuming there are j pools in the system.

Reward Distribution
According to current Bitcoin reward, the total BTCs that will be distributed at the end of each epoch are $144 \times 6.25 = 900$. the number of BTCs is denoted as B. Under our reputation mechanism, miners will receive the reward according to the *reputation-based proportion*, so the gain $B_{p,t}$ the pool p will get at epoch t is:

$$B_{p,t} = B \times M_{p,t} \tag{5}$$

With the implementation of the reputation score, miners should try to generate as many blocks during each epoch, and maintain the regularity of the proposals as steady as possible to have a higher reputation score, and thus, receive higher reward.

3.3   Reputation-Based Reward Sharing Schema Within Pools

On top of the system's reward distribution mechanism, we propose a *reputation-based reward sharing schema* within the pools, where members receive reward according to their reputation. The reputation is calculated based on the *ratio of valid work done* by the member, and the *regularity of the work*.

The *ratio of valid work done* of a pool member is calculated based on the total number of shares she submitted during an epoch $(q_{i,t})$, over the total number of shares in the pool in that epoch $(K_{p,t})$. The ratio of valid work done represents the estimated mining power of the member. The formula is as following:

$$W_{i,t} = \frac{q_{i,t}}{K_{p,t}} \tag{6}$$

The *regularity* is measured using the *lowest* α (lowest significance level) calculated from the *One-Poisson-Mean-Test* (OPMT). The pool manager test the null hypothesis H_0 that "the pool member is a block withholding attacker" by comparing each member's estimated number of full solutions $(\hat{\lambda})$ with the actual number of full solutions she submitted. $\hat{\lambda}$ is obtained based on the estimated mining power observed from the actual partial solutions the member submitted. The alternative hypothesis H_1 is that "the pool member is honest". After computing the P-value $(Pr(X \geq x) = F_{\Gamma\beta}(\hat{\lambda}, x))$ from the actual blocks (x) each member submitted, the *lowest* α to reject the null hypothesis can be obtained $(\alpha = Pr(X \geq x))$. The value of the *lowest* α indicates the probability whether the member has submitted all full solutions. A high *alpha* value suggests that the member has a high probability of being a block withholding attacker. The null hypothesis H_0 and the alternative hypothesis H_1 are:

$$H_0 : \lambda_{i,t} < \hat{\lambda}$$
$$H_1 : \lambda_{i,t} \geq \hat{\lambda}$$

where $\lambda_{i,t}$ stands for the number of full solutions the member i submitted during the epoch t. The regularity S for member i at epoch t is calculated as:

$$S_{i,t} = \frac{1}{1 + c\alpha_{i,t}} \tag{7}$$

where c is the multiplier that adjusts the value of the $S_{i,t}$, which is determined by the pool manager. The *regularity* serves as the punishment factor in the reward sharing schema. If the member fails to produce enough full solutions as the pool manager expected, the reputation score will be lower.

The member's reputation $R_{i,t}$ is calculated as:

$$R_{i,t} = W_{i,t} \times S_{i,t} \tag{8}$$

The reward distributed to member i is thus:

$$B_{i,t} = B_{p,t} \times R_{i,t} \tag{9}$$

where $B_{p,t}$ denotes the reward the pool p gets at epoch t. Due to the regularity $S_{i,t} < 1$, pool members will not receive full rewards for all the shares they submitted. We set that the residuals of the reward are withheld by pool managers. We assume that the information to calculate the reputation is publicly available to all pool members. Therefore, all members can calculate and validate the reputation scores, which prevents the pool manager from cheating by maliciously setting certain members' reputation score lower.

The algorithms below summarize the reputation mechanism.

Algorithm 1: Pool's Reputation Calculation

Input : $\{N\}_{t=1}^{T}$, $\{w_p\}_{t=1}^{T}$
Output: Reputation score $R_{p,t}$.

1 **for** *each pool p* **do**

2    $\quad W_{p,t} = \frac{\sum_{t=1}^{T} w_{p,t}}{N_t T}$;

3    $\quad S_{p,t} = \dfrac{1}{1+\sqrt{\frac{1}{T} \times \sum_{t=1}^{T} (\frac{w_{p,t}}{N_t} - \frac{\sum_{t=1}^{T} w_{p,t}}{N_t T})^2}}$;

4    $\quad R_{p,t} = W_{p,t} \times S_{p,t}, \quad R_{p,t} \in [0,1]$

5 **end for**

Algorithm 2: Reputation-based Reward Distribution

Input : $\{R_t\}_{p=1}^{j}$, $K_{p,t}$, $q_{i,t}$, B, c, x, $\hat{\lambda}$
Output: Reward $B_{p,t}$ for pool p; and reward $B_{i,t}$ for pool member i.

1 **for** *each pool p* **do**

2    $\quad M_{p,t} = \frac{R_{p,t}}{\sum_{p=1}^{j} R_{p,t}}$;

3    $\quad B_{p,t} = B \times M_{p,t}$;

4    $\quad$ **for** *each member i in pool p* **do**

5    $\quad\quad W_{i,t} = \frac{q_{i,t}}{K_{p,t}}$;

6    $\quad\quad Pr(X \geq x) = F_{\Gamma\beta}(\hat{\lambda}, x)$, with $\beta = 1$;

7    $\quad\quad \alpha_{i,t} = Pr(X \geq x)$;

8    $\quad\quad S_{i,t} = \frac{1}{1+c\alpha_{i,t}}$;

9    $\quad\quad R_{i,t} = W_{i,t} \times S_{i,t}$;

10   $\quad\quad B_{i,t} = B_{p,t} \times R_{i,t}$

11   $\quad$ **end for**

12 **end for**

---

4 Game Theoretic Analysis

We adopt a non-cooperative game [10] to model the *honest strategy* and *block withholding attack* in a two-pool scenario under the reputation mechanism. Assuming that players are rational, do not form coalitions, and the information is not shared, players choose their best strategies to maximize payoff. A steady state, called *Nash Equilibrium*, might be reached, where no player can have higher payoff by changing strategies. The *Assumptions* are the following:

- There are two pools in the system.
- Mining pools' computational power remains constant over time.
- The normalized total system's hash power equals to 1.
- For a mining pool with constant mining power, the probability distribution of the number of valid blocks follows Poisson distribution, where mean value equals to the expected number of blocks mined within a fixed time frame (i.e. one epoch).

4.1   Honest Strategy Utility

Following honest mining strategy, the mining pools strictly obey the system protocol. It publishes the blocks immediately, and does not infiltrate others pools.

Honest Pools Reputation Calculation
Suppose both pools choose honest mining, The ratio of total amount of valid work done by pool 1 is:

$$W_1 = \frac{\sum_{t=1}^{T} w_t}{NT} \approx m_1 \tag{10}$$

If the mining power remains constant, the ratio of valid work done represents the approximation of the honest pool 1's mining power m_1. (Mining power cannot be directly measured; it can only be reflected by the ratio of blocks proposed.) As we assumed that the probability distribution of block generation is Poisson distribution, one property of Poisson distribution is $Variance = mean$. The mean of the number of pool 1's block proposal $\mu_1 = \frac{\sum_{t=1}^{T} w_t}{T}$. As $\sum_{t=1}^{T} w_t \approx m_1 \times T \times N$, we get $\mu_1 = \frac{m_1 \times T \times N}{T}$. Thus, the mean number of pool 1's block proposal μ_1 is

$$\mu_1 \approx m_1 N \tag{11}$$

The standard deviation of the honest mining is $\sqrt{\mu_1}$.

As $\frac{\sum_{t=1}^{T} w_t}{NT}$ is the mean of the pool's block generation ratio, and the total number of blocks N is fixed across all epochs, the standard deviation part in the regularity function can be rewrited as $\sqrt{\frac{1}{T} \times \sum_{t=1}^{T} (\frac{w_t - \mu_1}{N})^2}$. After extracting the N from the square root, we get $\frac{1}{N} \times \sqrt{\frac{1}{T} \times \sum_{t=1}^{T} (w_t - \mu_1)^2}$, which equals to $\frac{\sqrt{\mu_1}}{N}$. Thus, the regularity function S for pool 1 is:

$$S_1 = \frac{1}{1 + \frac{\sqrt{m_1 N}}{N}} \tag{12}$$

The *reputation of the honest mining pool 1* is

$$R_1 = W_1 \times S_1 = \frac{m_1}{1 + \frac{\sqrt{m_1 N}}{N}} = \frac{m_1 N}{N + \sqrt{m_1 N}} \tag{13}$$

Following the same calculation, *the honest pool 2's reputation* is:

$$R_2 = W_2 \times S_2 = \frac{m_2}{1 + \frac{\sqrt{m_2 N}}{N}} = \frac{m_2 N}{N + \sqrt{m_2 N}} \tag{14}$$

Honest Pools Reward Proportion
The *reputation-based reward proportion* for both pools are normalized among all pools according to Eq. (4). Thus, the reward proportion M_1 for pool 1 is

$$M_1 = \frac{R_1}{R_1 + R_2} \tag{15}$$

Honest Pools Utility Calculation

The utility for honest mining at each epoch is distributed according to reputation weighted reward proportion. The calculation is the following:

$$U_1 = B \times M_1 \tag{16}$$

The utility calculation for pool 2 is exactly the same as pool 1, as both pools adopt honest strategy.

4.2 Block Withholding Attack Utility

We assume that pool 2 strictly follows honest mining, while pool 1 launches block withholding attack since the inception of the system. The attacking pool distributes γ_1 portion ($\gamma_1 \leq m_1$) of the system's mining power to the honest pool. The attacking members submit partial PoW regularly but omit the full PoW in the victim pool, while the remaining members mine honestly in the attacking pool. The attacking pool will receive reward from honest mining of its $(m_1 - \gamma_1)$ members, and shares from the victim pool of its γ_1 members. We are going to examine whether our reputation mechanism can discourage such attack.

Attacking Pool Reputation

As the system normalizes the mining rate by the total number of miners who submit full PoW, the direct effective mining power of the attacking pool is reduced to $\frac{m_1 - \gamma_1}{1 - \gamma_1}$. Thus, the ratio of valid work done by the attacking pool W_1 is approximated to

$$W_1 \approx \frac{m_1 - \gamma_1}{1 - \gamma_1} \tag{17}$$

The mean number of block proposals is reduced proportionally to $\frac{m_1 - \gamma_1}{1 - \gamma_1} N$, and the standard deviation is thus, $\sqrt{\frac{m_1 - \gamma_1}{1 - \gamma_1} N}$. The regularity function is:

$$S_1 = \frac{1}{1 + \frac{\sqrt{\frac{m_1 - \gamma_1}{1 - \gamma_1} N}}{N}} \tag{18}$$

Multiplying W_1 and S_1, the reputation score R_1 for the attacking pool is

$$R_1 = \frac{\frac{m_1 - \gamma_1}{1 - \gamma_1} N}{N + \sqrt{\frac{m_1 - \gamma_1}{1 - \gamma_1} N}} \tag{19}$$

Victim Pool Reputation

Following the same logic, the victim pool's effective mining power is increased to $\frac{m_2}{1 - \gamma_1}$. We denote the ratio of valid work done, regularity, and reputation score as

W_2, S_2, and R_2 respectively. The Reputation components and Reputation score calculation is the following:

$$W_2 \approx \frac{m_2}{1 - \gamma_1} \tag{20}$$

$$S_2 = \frac{1}{1 + \frac{\sqrt{\frac{m_2}{1-\gamma_1}N}}{N}} \tag{21}$$

$$R_2 = \frac{\frac{m_2}{1-\gamma_1}N}{N + \sqrt{\frac{m_2}{1-\gamma_1}N}} \tag{22}$$

Reputation-Based Reward Proportion

The reward proportion for dishonest pool 1 and honest pool 2 is as following:

$$M_1 = \frac{R_1}{R_1 + R_2} \tag{23}$$

$$M_2 = \frac{R_2}{R_1 + R_2} \tag{24}$$

Attacking Pool Utility

The total utility of the attacking pool is from the shares in the victim pool and the honest mining in the own pool.

Utility from Victim Pool

The block withholding attackers omit all full solutions. Therefore, the number of full solutions the pool manager will observe at the end of each epoch is 0. Regardless of the mining power of each attacker, if the pool manager observes that the number of full solutions submitted by the member is 0, the P-value that $Pr(X \geq 0)$ is equal to 1. Therefore, the *lowest* α is 1, and the $S_{i,t}$ is $\frac{1}{2}$, assuming the multiplier $c = 1$.

The total gain of the victim pool in one epoch is $B \times M_2$. The total gain will be distributed to $m_2 + \gamma_1$ members. While the infiltrated members take γ_1 portion of the total shares, $\frac{\gamma_1}{m_2+\gamma_1}$ is the sum of the ratio of total work done by the attackers in pool 2 in one epoch. However, as analysed above, there is half of the reward withheld by the pool manager, which will not be gained by the attackers. Thus, the part of the utility $U_{1,2}$ of pool 1 gained from the victim pool 2 is

$$U_{1,2} = B \times M_2 \times \frac{\gamma_1}{m_2 + \gamma_1} \times \frac{1}{2} \tag{25}$$

Utility from Own Pool

the reward gained from the attacking pool $U_{1,1}$ is the honest block proposals made by the pool's own members, which is $B \times M_1$. The utility gained from the own pool is thus,

$$U_{1,1} = B \times M_1 \tag{26}$$

Total Utility
Summing up $U_{1,1}$ and $U_{1,2}$, the total utility of the malicious pool 1 is

$$U_1 = U_{1,2} + U_{1,1} = B \times (M_1 + M_2 \times \frac{\gamma_1}{m_2 + \gamma_1} \times \frac{1}{2}) \qquad (27)$$

4.3   Numerical Analysis

As discussed in Sect. 4.2, as long as the number of full solutions submitted by the attacker is 0, the reward received from the victim pool will be reduced by half due to the punishment factor *regularity*.

We compute the utilities for the attacking pool with mining power from 0.1 to 0.9. Both the honest strategy utilities and the average utilities of all possible infiltration rates of each distinct mining power are calculated. The utility curves are depicted below in Fig. 1.

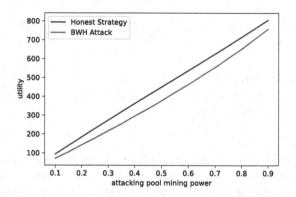

Fig. 1. Utility comparison for the attacking pool

It can be observed that the honest strategy always has a higher utility than block withholding attack. The pools have no incentive to launch block withholding attack, as the utility they gained from the attack is not optimal. Therefore, honest strategy is the *Nash Equilibrium*, as pools cannot have higher utility by deviating from the honest strategy.

5   Discussion

The *reputation-based reward distribution* among the pools allocates the total rewards in one epoch in lump sum to each eligible pools, based on their ratio of total valid work done and the regularity of the work over the entire system running time. This reward distribution method will incentivize mining pools to keep mining as many blocks as possible at a consistent rate to gain higher reputation score. If the pool switches mining strategies or adjusting the infiltration rate frequently, the reputation score will be lower, due to the increase in standard deviation and overall less total blocks generated. The pool will receive less reward. Therefore, the pools have to adopt a consistent mining strategy.

The *reputation-based reward sharing schema* within the pools is similar to *Pay-Per-Last-N-Shares*. Instead of keeping a sliding window of "N shares" every time a block is found by the pool, the "N shares" in our reputation-based schema is the total number of shares in one epoch, and there is no overlap between each epoch. On top of that, we introduce a *regularity* factor, which is calculated based on the *lowest* α from the OPMT that determines the probability of the member being a block withholding attacker. The member cannot receive full reward for the shares they submitted due to the *regularity* punishment. The members are incentivized to mine honestly and submit full solutions immediately to reduce their α level.

In the game theoretic analysis, we demonstrated that the two reputation mechanisms will make the attacking pool's reward gained from the victim pool reduced by $\frac{1}{2}$. As long as the attackers omit all full solutions, the reward they received will always be reduced by half, which makes the attack unprofitable.

The main limitation of the proposed reputation mechanisms is that the pool manager withholds the residuals of the reward for every pool member. The block withholding attack can be prevented, but at the cost of honest members losing some portion of the reward. In the existing mining pools, pool managers normally collect a fee from miners. The withheld residuals can be considered as the fee for mining in the pool. Managers can adjust the multiplier c in pool member's regularity calculation to alter the residuals, in order to make the honest miners less disadvantageous.

6 Related Work

6.1 Reputation Concept in Blockchain

Apart from RepuCoin [6], there are other modifications of blockchain using reputation concepts. Nojoumian et al. [14] proposed a reputation-based paradigm for pool member selection. each miner's past performance is evaluated based on certain criteria, which are vaguely defined, and an extra input value "lifetime", which determines the active time for a nodes in the reputation-based scheme. Miners' reputation defines the probability of them being selected in the pool. The paper only gives a brief explanation of how to measure the miner's performance, which lacks applicable fixed standards. Tang et al. [15] proposed a reputation mechanism that also serves for pool member selection. The miner's behaviour in the pool is represented by a vector of satisfaction scores, which are evaluated by the pool manager. The reputation is calculated based on the confidence interval estimation of the satisfaction scores. The randomly selected pool manager sets the thresholds for eligible miners entering the pool. The satisfaction scores are subject to the pool manager's perception, which cannot guarantee the objectiveness and fairness. Biryukov and Feher [16] proposed a system called ReCon. The reputation of the nodes is measured by nodes' participation in the consensus.

ReCon is only suitable for BFT protocols. Zhuang et al. [17] also determines reputation by the degree of consensus participation, but the system follows Proof of Stake. The aforementioned two papers are not directly related to this work.

6.2 Block Withholding Attack Mitigation

There are some literature that proposed block withholding attack mitigation methods. Bag and Sakurai [23] proposed a new notion of rewarding a miner called "special reward", which is disbursed to a miner who actually finds a full solution. Thus, any miner who launches block withholding attack will be unable to receive the "special reward". Bag et al. [24] proposed a generalized cryptographic commitment protocol and a variant that adopts hash function to countermeasure block withholding attack. The two schemes prevent the attack by making the partial PoW and full PoW indistinguishable by the miners. Chen et al. [25] defined a game theoretical model called DPBW game by allowing pool managers to directly deduct part of their total mining rewards before the reward distribution. They show that honest mining is always the Nash equilibrium for most reasonable deductions.

7 Conclusion and Future Work

Conclusion

We generalized the novel reputation concept from RepuCoin [6] and applied it to Bitcoin as the system's reward distribution method and pool's reward sharing schema. Every mining pool and pool member has a reputation score that determines the reward they will receive. We defined the generic utility functions for honest strategy and block withholding attack under two-pool scenario. We modelled the collective effect of the reputation mechanisms on preventing the block withholding attack by analysing the utilities of the pools, and concluded that the reputation mechanisms successfully disincentivizes the attack.

Future Work

As the limitation of the reputation mechanisms is that the pool manager withholds a portion of members' rewards, the future work will be to distribute the residuals in an appropriate way. For example, the reward residuals can be allocated to the loyal honest members who have stayed in the pool for a long time. In addition, the game theoretic analysis only focused on the two-pool scenario. The implementation of the mechanism in current dynamic Bitcoin settings needs to be conducted and evaluated. Furthermore, we only demonstrated that the combination of the two reputation mechanisms is effective to prevent Block Withholding attack. The effect of the individual mechanism can be analyzed separately.

References

1. Nakamoto, S.: Bitcoin: A peer-to-peer electronic cash system (2008)
2. Eyal, I., Sirer, E.G.: Majority is not enough: bitcoin mining is vulnerable. In: Christin, N., Safavi-Naini, R. (eds.) FC 2014. LNCS, vol. 8437, pp. 436–454. Springer, Heidelberg (2014). https://doi.org/10.1007/978-3-662-45472-5_28
3. Rosenfeld, M.: Analysis of bitcoin pooled mining reward systems. arXiv preprint arXiv:1112.4980. (2011)
4. Eyal, I.: The miner's dilemma. In: 2015 IEEE Symposium on Security and Privacy, pp. 89–103. IEEE (2015)
5. Kwon, Y., Kim, D., Son, Y., Vasserman, E., Kim, Y.: Be selfish and avoid dilemmas: fork after withholding (faw) attacks on bitcoin. In: Proceedings of the 2017 ACM SIGSAC Conference on Computer and Communications Security, Dallas, USA, pp. 195–209. ACM (2017)
6. Yu, J., Kozhaya, D., Decouchant, J., Esteves-Verissimo, P.: RepuCoin: your reputation is your power. IEEE Trans. Comput. 68(8), 1225–1237 (2019)
7. Natoli, C., Yu, J., Gramoli, V., Esteves-Verissimo, P.: Deconstructing blockchains: A comprehensive survey on consensus, membership and structure. arXiv preprint arXiv:1908.08316. (2019)
8. Pease, M., Shostak, R., Lamport, L.: Reaching agreement in the presence of faults. J. ACM (JACM) 27(2), 228–234 (1980)
9. Mui, L., Mohtashemi, M., Halberstadt, A.: Computational model of trust and reputation. In: Proceedings of the 35th Annual Hawaii International Conference on System Sciences, pp. 2431–2439. IEEE (2002)
10. Nash, J.: Non-cooperative games. Ann. Math., 286–295 (1951)
11. Courtois, N.T., Bahack, L.: On subversive miner strategies and block withholding attack in bitcoin digital currency. arXiv preprint arXiv:1402.1718. (2014)
12. Kuchta, V., Zolotavkin, Y.: Detection constraint for harvesting attack in proof of work mining pools (2019)
13. Weerahandi, S.: Exact Statistical Methods for Data Analysis. Springer Science and Business Media, New York, USA (2003)
14. Nojoumian, M., Golchubian, A., Njilla, L., Kwiat, K., Kamhoua, C.: Incentivizing blockchain miners to avoid dishonest mining strategies by a reputation-based paradigm. In: Arai, K., Kapoor, S., Bhatia, R. (eds.) SAI 2018. AISC, vol. 857, pp. 1118–1134. Springer, Cham (2019). https://doi.org/10.1007/978-3-030-01177-2_81
15. Tang, C., Wu, L., Wen, G., Zheng, Z.: Incentivizing honest mining in blockchain networks: a reputation approach. IEEE Trans. Circuits Syst. II: Express Briefs 67(1), 117–121 (2019)
16. Biryukov, A., Feher, D.: ReCon: sybil-resistant consensus from reputation. Pervasive Mobile Comput. 61, 101109 (2020)
17. Zhuang, Q., Liu, Y., Chen, L., Ai, Z.: Proof of reputation: a reputation-based consensus protocol for blockchain based systems. In: Proceedings of the 2019 International Electronics Communication Conference, pp. 131–138 (2019)
18. Luu, L., Saha, R., Parameshwaran, I., Saxena, P., Hobor, A.: On power splitting games in distributed computation: The case of bitcoin pooled mining. In: 2015 IEEE 28th Computer Security Foundations Symposium, Verona, Italy, pp. 397–411. IEEE (2015)
19. Wood, G.: Ethereum: a secure decentralised generalised transaction ledger. Ethereum Project Yellow Paper 151(2014), 1–32 (2014)

20. Monero.: Moneropedia. https://web.getmonero.org/resources/moneropedia/
21. Schrijvers, O., Bonneau, J., Boneh, D., Roughgarden, T.: Incentive compatibility of bitcoin mining pool reward functions. In: Grossklags, J., Preneel, B. (eds.) FC 2016. LNCS, vol. 9603, pp. 477–498. Springer, Heidelberg (2017). https://doi.org/10.1007/978-3-662-54970-4_28
22. Leonardos, N., Leonardos, S., Piliouras, G.: Oceanic games: centralization risks and incentives in blockchain mining. In: Pardalos, P., Kotsireas, I., Guo, Y., Knottenbelt, W. (eds.) Mathematical Research for Blockchain Economy. SPBE, pp. 183–199. Springer, Cham (2020). https://doi.org/10.1007/978-3-030-37110-4_13
23. Bag, S., Sakurai, K.: Yet another note on block withholding attack on bitcoin mining pools. In: Bishop, M., Nascimento, A.C.A. (eds.) ISC 2016. LNCS, vol. 9866, pp. 167–180. Springer, Cham (2016). https://doi.org/10.1007/978-3-319-45871-7_11
24. Bag, S., Ruj, S., Sakurai, K.: Bitcoin block withholding attack: analysis and mitigation. IEEE Trans. Inf. Forensics Secur. **12**(8), 1967–1978 (2016)
25. Chen, Z., Li, B., Shan, X., Sun, X., Zhang, J.: Discouraging Pool Block Withholding Attacks in Bitcoins. arXiv preprint arXiv:2008.06923 (2020)

Identity-Based Outsider Anonymous Broadcast Encryption with Simultaneous Individual Messaging

Mriganka Mandal[1(✉)] and Koji Nuida[1,2]

[1] Graduate School of Information Science and Technology, The University of Tokyo,
Tokyo, Japan
mriganka-mandal@g.ecc.u-tokyo.ac.jp, nuida@mist.i.u-tokyo.ac.jp
[2] National Institute of Advanced Industrial Science and Technology, Tokyo, Japan

Abstract. *Broadcast encryption* (BE) is an effective method to broadcast encrypted confidential content, although it does not support the transmission of personalized messages to individuals. *Broadcast encryption with personalized messages* (BEPM) simultaneously transmits not only the common encrypted message to a group of users but also encrypted personalized messages to individual users. Currently available BEPM schemes fail to provide the recipient's anonymity that means the information of the subscriber set is available to the enemies. This paper first introduces a new BEPM paradigm, called *identity-based outsider anonymous broadcast encryption with personalized messages* (IB-OAnoBEPM), by tweaking the identity-based framework over the most advanced and secure asymmetric Type-3 variant of the bilinear maps. In addition to being adaptively secure, our construction withstands *indistinguishable chosen-plaintext attack* under the standard asymmetric *decisional bilinear Diffie-Hellman exponent* assumption without using the *random oracle model*. More positively, the proposed scheme is the first BEPM system that achieves security without any non-standard q-type assumptions. In particular, our design is very efficient both in terms of communication and computation costs, as the ciphertext size is constant, and the decryption algorithm requires only three asymmetric bilinear pairings to recover the correct message and the personalized messages, which are highly desirable for light-weight devices.

Keywords: Broadcast encryption with personalized messages ·
Identity-based encryption · Privacy and anonymity

1 Introduction

Broadcast Encryption (BE), proposed by Fiat and Naor [10], benefits a data sender to cost-effectively transmit encrypted confidential data, aka ciphertext, to a subscribed group of customers over a vulnerable channel in such a method that only the approved customers can decrypt to retrieve the original information. In contrast, attackers can gather negligible information about the transmitted

© Springer Nature Switzerland AG 2020
M. Kutyłowski et al. (Eds.): NSS 2020, LNCS 12570, pp. 167–186, 2020.
https://doi.org/10.1007/978-3-030-65745-1_10

data, even if they conspire. An **I**dentity-**B**ased **B**roadcast **E**ncryption (IBBE), first described by Delerablée [8], is an advancement of BE in which the traditional **P**ublic-**K**ey **I**nfrastructure (PKI) is excluded. In an IBBE, the customer's public-key is generated utilizing a sole identifier correlated with its system index (e.g., a customer's Internet Protocol address or employment ID). Nonetheless, traditional BE [4,10] and IBBE do not endorse the data sender to concurrently convey both encrypted broadcast data to a subscriber's group and personalized encrypted session-key to each distinct subscriber of the group.

Broadcast **E**ncryption with **P**ersonalized **M**essages (BEPM), designed by Ohtake et al. [19], grants data sender to convey not only encrypted common data simultaneously but also personalized encrypted session-keys to subscribed customers. More particularly, BEPM favors a data sender to transfer a ciphertext produced under a common session-key and individualized ciphertexts generated under individual keys of customers in such a mode that the approved customers can rescue the original broadcast data. In contrast, only the designated customers can decrypt the individualized ciphertexts. Although the BEPM is an exceptionally cost-effective alternative of the usual BE, it is not safe against the physical attack anticipating that the present BEPM designs carry information of the subscribed customers as a part of the encrypted data to assure that approved consumers can redeem both original broadcast data and personalized session-keys correctly. Consequently, adversaries are capable of identifying who are the subscribed customers. It attempts to seize confidential information by compromising or even by endangering some of the subscribed customers. This can collapse the complete broadcast network system, and the common transmitted data and the personalized session-keys of all the customers might be unveiled. Therefore, it is expected that the BEPM networks must have the strength to guard its customer's anonymity against adversaries.

Anonymous **B**roadcast **E**ncryption (AnoBE) can effectively hibernate knowledge of subscribed customers. The AnoBE systems have been split into two primary classes: **O**utsider **An**onymous **B**roadcast **E**ncryption (OAnoBE) [9,16,23] and **F**ully **An**onymous **B**roadcast **E**ncryption (FAnoBE) [13,15,17,20]. In OAnoBE (including our proposed scheme in this paper), information of subscribed customers is entirely omitted from outside adversaries, whereas customers (belonging to the subscribed customer's group) know each other. Nevertheless, information about subscribed customers is totally secreted from both outside and inside adversaries in any FAnoBE. Kiayias et al. [14] have explicated a tight lower bound for communication bandwidth of a FAnoBE and proved that no farther advancement is possible. They have pointed that an AnoBE with customer's full anonymity must have a communication bandwidth of $\Omega(N \cdot \eta)$. Here, N denotes the size of subscribed customers, and η is the system's security parameter. Therefore, the ciphertext-size must be linear to N in any FAnoBE, and the AnoBE with constant-size ciphertext is only OAnoBE [16]. Furthermore, in the IBBE environment where **I**nternet-**o**f-**T**hings (IoT) enabled devices are accepted to access the transmitted data, they have ordinarily cheap computational ability, and are resource-constrained (e.g., low processing power, restricted battery backup). The FAnoBE protocols may not be fit-for-purpose as communication bandwidth increases with the size of subscribed customers, which may vastly enhance for a system with a large number of customers. Thus, to integrate customer's anonymity in any identity-based BEPM, the OAnoBE with fast computation and constant-size communication are acceptable for IoT enabled appliances. **Identity-Based Outsider Anonymous Broadcast Encryption with Personalized Messages**, denoted by IB-OAnoBEPM, can simultaneously transfer common encrypted data to a subscribed customer's group and personalized session-keys for individuals, in which customers are acknowledged with their identifiers instead of the system assigned indices. The number of subscribed customers in an IB-OAnoBEPM can exponentially expand with the system's security parameter, whereas it is only polynomial with the security parameter in the present BEPM scenarios. However, customer's outsider anonymity is at prime solicitude for any privacy-preserving IB-OAnoBEPM.

Over the last several years, insufficient advancements have been made in building secure and cost-effective BEPM [1,7,11,12,19,22], heading to a delimited class of constructions, which accomplish multiple trade-offs amidst performance, security, and underlying assumptions. In our work, we exhibit the *first* identity-based outsider anonymous BEPM, in which the subscribed customer set is entirely hibernated from the outside enemies. Furthermore, we expect the further deployment of BEPM that concurrently: (a) relishes constant-size communication, and fast decryption cost, which are incredibly desirable for IoT enabled devices, (b) effectuates adaptive security, (c) relies on non q-type assumptions in the standard security model, and (d) can be built with asymmetric prime-order bilinear systems. In any BEPM, prior mentioned four properties are profoundly seductive from both a realistic and technical perspective and defying to perform together [1]. Moreover, developments (a), (b), and (d) are indispensable for many real-world utilization, such as computerized medical records system, social messaging systems, online business networks, etc. Besides, properties (b), (c), and (d) are by presently approved cryptographic needs about speed and performance, robust security guarantees beneath practical and physical attack models, and least hardness assumptions. There are now too few types of protocols on BEPM [1,7,19] demonstrating how to fulfill various combinations of (a)-(d), culminating in diverse unifying structures that supply a firm understanding of the study and investigation of these systems. Although, before our protocol, it was unknown how to even concurrently effectuate (a)-(d) with customer's outsider anonymity in the identity-based framework; admittedly, this is broadly viewed as one of the leading open problems in pairing-based BEPM.

1.1 Motivating Application Scenarios

Due to the cost-efficient union of identity-based BEPM with the orthogonal characteristic of BE, namely the recipient's outsider anonymity, the IB-OAnoBEPM system has been found as an object of paramount concern for various practical scenarios where confidentiality of the message receiver's information along with the characteristic of BEPM are a primary concern. For example, consider the following practical example where IB-OAnoBEPM is an appropriate option.

(a) Soldiers want to transmit an encrypted message, along with the personalized messages, in the air so that attackers cannot retrieve the original message, the personalized messages, and the intended message receivers' physical identities. If attackers can learn who the opponents are, they can compromise with some of the opponents and get important information. Soldiers can use our IB-OAnoBEPM system, where the subscribers set is entirely anonymous from the outside attackers.

(b) Suppose the Prime Minister (PM) of a powerful nation wants to discuss a secret project with some of the Chief Ministers (CM) urgently. The project's primary intention is to investigate the terrorist activities inside the nation. The PM can apply any BEPM to transmit the upcoming strategies, soldier's activities, and state police's activities as a common broadcast data while account login identification, password to individual CMs as personalized session-keys. In this situation, the personal knowledge of the involved CMs requires to be protected from the terrorists. Assume that the terrorists anyhow able to know that the local state government has notified the information related to their terror movement. They will attempt to patch this by frightening the involved CMs or even by shooting them. This will fail the whole project, and the assembled data will be compromised. The PM can apply the IB-OAnoBEPM to guarantee the anonymity of the involved CMs.

1.2   Related Work

The notion of BEPM was proposed by Ohtake et al. [19]. The scheme is a selective **I**ndistinguishable **C**hosen-**P**laintext **A**ttack (IND-CPA) secure. Later, Fujii et al. [11] proposed advancement of [19] under a similar security framework along with the same size parameters. A selective IND-CPA secure BEPM with low transmission bandwidth has been exhibited by Han et al. [12] in which decryptors necessitates public-keys of all legitimate customers to successfully perform the decryption process. The works [11,12,19] have ciphertext size linear to the total number of subscribed customers, constant size customers secret-key, and public-parameter size grows linearly with the maximal customers of the system. An identity-based BEPM, adopting asymmetric multilinear maps, has been introduced by Xu et al. [22] in which the public-parameter size grows logarithmically with the total number of customers. A major drawback in the work of [22] is presented by Acharya et al. [1] by constructing three schemes. One of their constructions is an adaptive secure, while for another one, they have employed highly cost-expensive symmetric multilinear pairings. However, existing BEPM systems are proven to be secure under the non-standard q-type security assumption, which is highly non-desirable. Recently, Chen et al. [7] proposed an outsider anonymous certificate-based BEPM which has ciphertext size linear to the total number of subscribed customers. Their construction is secure under a nonstandard q-type security assumption in the **R**andom **O**racle **M**odel (ROM).

1.3   Our Contribution

The anonymity of the subscribed customers and the simultaneous personalized messaging to each customer individually are essential in any BE paradigm. It is not straightforward to obtain secure identity-based outsider anonymous BEPM protocols by simply coupling outsider anonymous BE [9] with the BEPM [1,7,11,12,19,22] as this might drive to high inefficiency, especially in terms of strong security guarantees, ciphertext, computation, and storage. In this paper, we alleviate the prior mentioned inefficiencies to develop the first explicit construction of an identity-based outsider anonymous BEPM scheme with order-of-magnitude advancements in the size of ciphertext, customer's secret-key, and decryption time without any security rupture. More specifically, we can summarize our main findings as follows.

- In offense to the present BEPM schemes [1,7,11,12,19,22], our proposed IB-OAnoBEPM is the first BEPM to achieve outsider anonymity of the message recipient's set in a cost-efficient manner without any security flaw. More specifically, the resulting scheme has constant-size communication bandwidth, which is desirable for lightweight devices. More positively, our proposed scheme is the first BEPM with the exponential number of users, where the PKI is not required, and the public key of each user is represented using a unique identifier string.
- At a technical level, contrasted to the existing BEPMs [1,7,11,12,19,22], our IB-OAnoBEPM is the first to achieve adaptive security without any q-type security assumption. The non-standard q-type assumptions are complex assumptions of the size that grows with some large parameter q, and such dynamic assumptions are not well-understood. The proposed construction is proven to be an IND-CPA secure under the standard asymmetric **D**ecisional **B**ilinear **D**iffie-**H**ellman **E**xponent (DBDHE) assumption without using non-standard ROM. In a ROM, all the parties are given black-box access to a truly random function. From the practical point of view, there does not exist such random-looking functions, and consequently, the proofs in ROM can be treated as heuristic arguments. At a technical level, hash functions are considered as a random oracle, which is a theoretical black-box that responds random reply to every query. However, there is a debate on the acceptance of a security proof in ROM as many security models which are secure in ROM may not be secure in the standard security model. The security against adaptive **I**ndistinguishable **C**hosen-**C**iphertext **A**ttacks (IND-CCA) is a strong and very useful notion of security for any **P**ublic-**K**ey **E**ncryption (PKE) schemes. Although the adaptive IND-CPA security has been proved, we discuss how our proposed design can be enhanced to achieve adaptive IND-CCA security.
- As pointed out in the works [6,21], various security assumptions on the symmetric elliptic curve based bilinear pairing groups have broken. While we inflicted new technological approaches to build our IB-OAnoBEPM atop the highly secure and most advanced asymmetric elliptic curve pairing groups, we emphasize that the construction can withstand those attacks. Therefore,

much more secure and efficient compared to the Type-1 pairing-based BEPM [1,7,11,12,19,22].

- The broadcast data encryption and decryption times in any BE are arguably the most important one. Those are the functions that broadcaster and recipients of the system invoke most of the time, often on computationally weak devices. In the current BEPM scenarios, decryption and encryption are reasonably expensive, particularly for symmetric setting, because pairing operation in Type-1 groups is almost two times slower and the multiplication is eight times slower opposed to the Type-3 groups [18]. More positively, our scheme requires only 1 pairing for encryption and 3 pairings for decryption in Type-3 setting, regardless of the few cost-efficient sum operations involved. This leads to significant savings in computation costs and makes our design even more practical.

Organization. We arrange the rest of the manuscript as follows. In subsequent Sect. 2, some cryptographic preliminaries are discussed, and we present the precise definition and security framework of our IB-OAnoBEPM. In Sect. 3, our $\Pi_{\text{IB-OAnoBEPM}}$ construction and its security proof are provided. We present the concrete comparison of our proposed protocol with the existing BEPM schemes in Sect. 4. In Sect. 5, we discuss the practical implementation features of $\Pi_{\text{IB-OAnoBEPM}}$ and the evaluation concerning the present literature. Lastly, we conclude the manuscript in Sect. 6.

2   Preliminary Background

Notations. We denote $[b]$ as the set of all positive integers from 1 to b that is $[1, b]$, where for all integers $0 < 1 < b$, $[1, b]$ signifies the set $\{x \in \mathbb{Z} | 1 \leq x \leq b\}$. Here, $y \leftarrow \mathsf{RandA}(z)$ represents that y is the output of algorithm RandA on input z, PPT means probabilistic polynomial time and $x \in_R S$ indicates that x chosen uniformly at random from S. Also, η represents security parameter of the system and $\mathsf{poly}(\eta)$ is a polynomial in η.

2.1   Asymmetric Bilinear Pairings and Hardness Assumptions

Definition 1 (Asymmetric bilinear map [16,20]). *Let $\mathbb{G}^\times$ and $\widetilde{\mathbb{G}}^\times$ be two multiplicative source groups and $\mathbb{G}_T^\times$ be a multiplicative target group. Assume that all the groups have same large prime order p ($> 2^\eta$). Let P, $\widetilde{P}$ be generators of $\mathbb{G}^\times$ and $\widetilde{\mathbb{G}}^\times$ respectively. A function $e : \mathbb{G}^\times \times \widetilde{\mathbb{G}}^\times \to \mathbb{G}_T^\times$ is said to be asymmetric bilinear mapping if it has the following properties.*

1. **Bilinearity:** $e(U^a, \widetilde{V}^b) = e(U, \widetilde{V})^{ab}$, $\forall\, U \in \mathbb{G}^\times$, $\widetilde{V} \in \widetilde{\mathbb{G}}^\times$ and $\forall\, a, b \in \mathbb{Z}_p$.
2. **Non-degeneracy:** *The function is non-degenerated, i.e., $e(P, \widetilde{P})$ is a generator of $\mathbb{G}_T^\times$.*
3. **Computability:** *The function e is efficiently computable.*

The tuple $\mathbb{BG} = (p, \mathbb{G}^\times, \widetilde{\mathbb{G}}^\times, \mathbb{G}_T^\times, e)$ is called a prime order asymmetric bilinear group system.

*Remark 1 (**Classification**).* Depending on some practical concerns, such as compact representation of the group elements, collision-resistant hashing to a group element, testing membership in the second source group, computationally efficient isomorphism, etc., the bilinear pairings have been classified into three main categories which are described below.

1. **Type-1(T1)**: In Type-1 setting, which is also known as *symmetric bilinear maps*, there is no compact representations for elements of the bilinear groups, where $\mathbb{G}^+ = \widetilde{\mathbb{G}}^+$. In the work of Chatterjee et al. [6], they have shown that several recent attacks have broken many security assumptions on T1 pairings.
2. **Type-2(T2)**: A less efficient alternative is when $\mathbb{G}^+ \neq \widetilde{\mathbb{G}}^+$ with an efficiently computable isomorphism from $\widetilde{\mathbb{G}}^+$ to $\mathbb{G}^+$ and vice versa are known. In T2 setting, there does not exists any efficient collision-resistant hashing method to the elements in $\widetilde{\mathbb{G}}^+$ and $\widetilde{\mathbb{G}}^+$.
3. **Type-3(T3)**: Here, $\mathbb{G}^+ \neq \widetilde{\mathbb{G}}^+$ and no such efficiently computable isomorphism between $\widetilde{\mathbb{G}}^+$ and $\mathbb{G}^+$ and vice versa exists. In T3 pairings, there exists an efficient collision-resistant hashing method to the group elements.

Note that the T3 parings outperforms T1, T2 pairings from practical implementation and security point of view [6,21].

■ **Decisional bilinear Diffie-Hellman exponent (DBDHE) assumption.**

The DBDHE assumption is due to Li et al. [16], which can be described as follows.

- **Input:** $\langle Z = (\mathbb{BG}, \widetilde{P}, \widetilde{P}^\alpha, \ldots, \widetilde{P}^{\alpha^m}, \widetilde{P}^{\alpha^{m+2}}, \ldots, \widetilde{P}^{\alpha^{2m}}, P, P^\alpha, \ldots, P^{\alpha^m},$ $P^c), K\rangle$, where α, c randomly chosen from $\mathbb{Z}_p^*$, i.e., $\alpha, c \in_R \mathbb{Z}_p^*$ and K is either $e(P, \widetilde{P})^{\alpha^{m+1} \cdot c}$ or a random element $X \in_R \mathbb{G}_T^\times$.
- **Output:** 0 if $K = e(P, \widetilde{P})^{\alpha^{m+1} \cdot c}$; 1 otherwise.

Definition 2 (DBDHE assumption). *The asymmetric DBDHE assumption holds with (t', ϵ') if for every PPT adversary $\mathcal{A}$ with runtime at most t', the advantage of $\mathcal{A}$ in solving the above problem is at most ϵ', i.e.,*

$$Adv_{\mathcal{A}}^{\text{DBDHE}}(\eta) = \left| Pr[\mathcal{A}(Z, K = e(P, \widetilde{P})^{\alpha^{m+1} \cdot c}) = 0] - Pr[\mathcal{A}(Z, K = X) = 0] \right| \leq \epsilon'$$

2.2 Identity-Based Outsider Anonymous Broadcast Encryption with Personalized Messages

An **Identity-Based Outsider Anonymous Broadcast Encryption** with **Personalized Messages** (IB-OAnoBEPM) protocol, denoted by $\Pi_{\text{IB-OAnoBEPM}} :=$ (Setup, KeyGen, Encrypt, Decrypt), consists of three randomize algorithms - (Setup, KeyGen, Encrypt) and a deterministic algorithm - Decrypt (cf. Fig. 1). Formally, IB-OAnoBEPM is

$$\Pi_{\text{IB-OAnoBEPM}} := \begin{bmatrix} (\text{OAnoMPK}, \text{OAnoMSK}) \leftarrow \text{Setup}(1^\eta, N), \\ (\text{OAnoSK}_u) \leftarrow \text{KeyGen}(\text{OAnoMPK}, \text{OAnoMSK}, ID_u), \\ (\text{CT}, \{K_u\}_{ID_u \in \mathcal{S}}) \leftarrow \text{Encrypt}(\text{OAnoMPK}, \mathcal{S}, M), \\ ((M, K_u) \vee \perp) = \text{Decrypt}(\text{OAnoMPK}, \text{OAnoSK}_u, \text{CT}) \end{bmatrix}$$

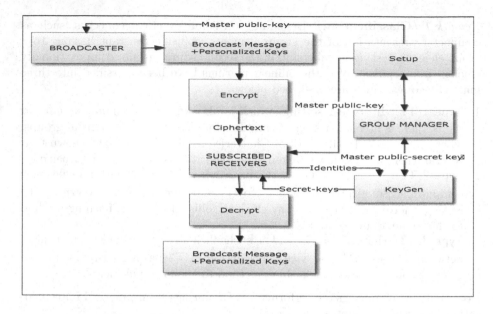

Fig. 1. System model of $\Pi_{\text{IB-OAnoBEPM}}$

specified by the following four algorithms.

- Setup($1^\eta, N$): Taking as input the security parameter η along with a positive integer $N = \text{poly}(\eta)$, a trusted third party, called **Private-Key Generation Center** (PKGC), runs this algorithm and outputs a master public-key OAnoMPK and a master secret-key OAnoMSK. The master public-key OAnoTPK is made publicly available and the master secret-key OAnoTMK is kept secret to itself.
- KeyGen(OAnoMPK, OAnoMSK, ID_u): On input master public-secret key pair (OAnoMPK, OAnoMSK) and an identity ID_u from a user $u \in [N]$, the PKGC generates a secret-key OAnoSK$_u$ and sends it securely to the user u.
- Encrypt(OAnoMPK, S, M): On input, the master public-key OAnoMPK, a set S of subscribed users identities and a message M from the message space $\mathcal{M}$, the broadcaster outputs a ciphertext CT and personalized keys K_u for each subscribed user $u \in [N]$ with identity $ID_u \in S$. It makes CT publicly available, while keeps $\{K_u\}_{ID_u \in S}$ secret to itself.
- Decrypt(OAnoMPK, OAnoSK$_u$, CT): Getting the OAnoMPK and the CT as inputs, a decryptor u with its secret-key OAnoSK$_u$ either recovers the correct message M and its personalized key K_u or gets a designated symbol $\perp$ indicating the decryption failure.

*Remark 2 (**Outsider anonymity** [9,23]).* The $\Pi_{\text{IB-OAnoBEPM}}$ is only outsider anonymous, whereas insider anonymity does not hold. Thus, the decryption algorithm does not require the information of subscribed users set S as an additional input. Therefore, the set S is completely anonymous from any outsider adversary. However, each subscribed user belonging to S (i.e., insider) knows the information of all other subscribers.

Definition 3 (Correctness). *We say that the $\Pi_{\text{IB-OAnoBEPM}}$ is correct if for all security parameter η, message $M \in \mathcal{M}$ and user identity $ID_u \in \mathcal{S}$ the following holds.*

$$(M, K_u) \leftarrow \textsf{Decrypt}(\textsf{OAnoMPK}, \textsf{OAnoSK}_u, \textsf{CT}),$$

where $(\textsf{CT}, \{K_u\}_{ID_u \in \mathcal{S}})) \leftarrow \textsf{Encrypt} \ (\textsf{OAnoMPK}, \ \mathcal{S}, M), \ (\textsf{OAnoSK}_u) \leftarrow \textsf{KeyGen}$ $(\textsf{OAnoMPK}, \textsf{OAnoMSK}, ID_u)$ *and* $(\textsf{OAnoMPK}, \textsf{OAnoMSK}) \leftarrow \textsf{Setup} \ (1^\eta, N).$

■ **Security notion of $\Pi_{\text{IB-OAnoBEPM}}$.** The ciphertext indistinguishability with receiver anonymity under adaptive IND-CPA security model [9,16] is the security attribute of $\Pi_{\text{IB-OAnoBEPM}}$ scheme. This security game is played between a PPT adversary $\mathcal{A}$ and a challenger $\mathcal{C}$. The advantage of $\mathcal{A}$ in winning the game is defined as

$$\textsf{Adv}^{\textsf{IND-CPA}}_{\mathcal{A}, \text{IB-OAnoBEPM}}(\eta) = \left| \textsf{CIAdvc}(\eta) - \frac{1}{4} \right|,$$

where $\textsf{CIAdvc}(\eta)$ is given by the following quantity.

$$\Pr \left[(\zeta = \zeta') \wedge (\varkappa = \varkappa') : \begin{array}{l} (\textsf{OAnoMPK}, \textsf{OAnoMSK}) \leftarrow \textsf{Setup}(1^\eta, N); \\ ((M_0, M_1), (\mathcal{S}_0, \mathcal{S}_1)) \leftarrow [\mathcal{A}(1^\eta)]^{\mathcal{O}\textsf{KeyGen}(\textsf{OAnoMPK}, \textsf{OAnoMSK}, \cdot)}; \\ \zeta \in_R \{0, 1\} \text{ and } \varkappa \in_R \{0, 1\}; \\ (\textsf{CT}, \{K_u^{(\zeta, \varkappa)}\}_{ID_u \in \mathcal{S}_\varkappa}) \leftarrow \textsf{Encrypt}(\textsf{OAnoMPK}, \mathcal{S}_\varkappa, M_\zeta); \\ (\zeta', \varkappa') \leftarrow \mathcal{A}\left(\textsf{CT}, \{\textsf{OAnoSK}_u : ID_u \in \mathcal{S}_0 \cap \mathcal{S}_1\}_{u=1}^q\right) \end{array} \right]$$

Here, $\mathcal{O}\textsf{KeyGen}(\textsf{OAnoMPK}, \textsf{OAnoMSK}, \cdot)$ denotes the key generation oracle access that allows $\mathcal{A}$ to query on a set of identities $\{ID_{u_i} : i \in \mathbb{I}\}$, where $\mathbb{I} \subseteq [N]$ with $|\mathbb{I}| \leq q \leq N$. It returns $(\textsf{OAnoSK}_{u_i}) \leftarrow \textsf{KeyGen} \ (\textsf{OAnoMPK}, \textsf{OAnoMSK}, ID_{u_i})$ for all $i \in \mathbb{I}$.

Definition 4 (Ciphertext indistinguishability with receiver anonymity). *The $\Pi_{\text{IB-OAnoBEPM}}$ is (t, ϵ, q) adaptive IND-CPA secure if $\textsf{Adv}^{\textsf{IND-CPA}}_{\mathcal{A}, \text{IB-OAnoBEPM}}(\eta)$ is negligible function of η for all PPT adversary $\mathcal{A}$ with run time at most t and making at most $q = \textsf{poly}(\eta)$ customer's secret-key queries.*

3 Proposed IB-OAnoBEPM construction

The description and the security analysis of our proposed IB-OAnoBEPM protocol are presented in this section.

3.1 Protocol Description

The communication model of our protocol $\Pi_{\text{IB-OAnoBEPM}} := (\textsf{Setup}, \textsf{KeyGen}, \textsf{Encrypt}, \textsf{Decrypt})$ involves a PKGC, a broadcaster and several customers (aka users). The algorithms work as follows.

- $\textsf{Setup}(1^\eta, N)$: The PKGC, on input the security parameter η and the total number of users $N = 2^l$ $(l > 0)$ of the system, proceeds as follows.
  - (i) It first generates a prime order Type-3 bilinear group system $\mathbb{BG} = (p, \mathbb{G}^\times, \widetilde{\mathbb{G}}^\times, \mathbb{G}_T^\times, e)$ (cf. Sect. 2.1). Let $P, \widetilde{P}$ be random generators of $\mathbb{G}^\times$ and $\widetilde{\mathbb{G}}^\times$ respectively.

(ii) It chooses random exponents α, β, $\{\delta_j\}_{j=1}^N$, $\{a_j\}_{j=1}^N \in \mathbb{Z}_p^*$ and computes $\{U_i = P^{a_i},\ \widetilde{U}_i = \widetilde{P}^{a_i},\ f_i = P^{\delta_i},\ \widetilde{f}_i = \widetilde{P}^{\delta_i}\}_{i=1}^N$, $P_2 = P^\beta$, $\widetilde{P}_1 = \widetilde{P}^\alpha$, $\widetilde{P}_2 = \widetilde{P}^\beta$, $\Omega = e(P_2, \widetilde{P}_1)$.

(iii) It chooses a collision-resistant cryptographic hash function $H : \{0,1\}^l \to \mathbb{Z}_p^*$ and sets master public-key and the master secret-key as follows.

$$\mathsf{OAnoMPK} = (P, \widetilde{P}, \widetilde{P}_1, \widetilde{P}_2, P_2, \{f_j\}_{j=1}^N, \{U_j\}_{j=1}^N, \Omega, H)$$

$$\mathsf{OAnoMSK} = (\widetilde{P}_2^\alpha, \{\widetilde{f}_j\}_{j=1}^N, \{\widetilde{U}_j\}_{j=1}^N)$$

(iv) The PKGC publishes OAnoMPK and keeps OAnoMSK secret to itself.

- KeyGen(OAnoMPK, OAnoMSK, id_u): On receiving a user identity $id_u \in \{0,1\}^l$ from the user $u \in [N]$, the PKGC executes the following steps.

  (i) It extracts the hash function H from OAnoMPK to compute the exponents $ID_i = H(id_i) \in \mathbb{Z}_p^*$, for $1 \le i \le N$.

  (ii) It chooses a random exponent $r_u \in \mathbb{Z}_p^*$ to compute the following.

$$d_{u,0} = (\widetilde{P})^{r_u},\ d_{u,u} = (\widetilde{P}_2)^\alpha \cdot (\widetilde{f}_u \cdot \widetilde{U}_u^{ID_u})^{r_u},\ d_{u,N+1} = (\widetilde{P}_2)^{ID_u},$$

$$d_{u,j} = (\widetilde{f}_j \cdot \widetilde{U}_j^{ID_u})^{r_u} \text{ for } 1 \le j \ne u \le N.$$

  (iii) The PKGC sets the secret-key as $\mathsf{OAnoSK}_u = (d_{u,0}, d_{u,u}, d_{u,N+1}, \{d_{u,j} : 1 \le j \ne u \le N\})$ and sends it to the user u through a secure communication channel between them.

- Encrypt(OAnoMPK, $\mathcal{S}$, M): The broadcaster takes as input OAnoMPK, a polynomial size set $\mathcal{S}$ of subscribed users' identities (i.e., the size of $\mathcal{S}$ is a polynomial in the security parameter η of the system) and a message M from $\mathbb{G}_T^\times$. For notational convenient, let us assume that the set is of the form $\mathcal{S} = \{ID_u : u \in I_\mathcal{S}\}$, where $ID_u = H(id_u) \in \mathbb{Z}_p^*$ corresponds to some identity id_u of user $u \in I_\mathcal{S}$ and $I_\mathcal{S}$ is the index set of $\mathcal{S}$ with $|I_\mathcal{S}| = L \le N$. It performs the following steps to produce an encrypted content, known as ciphertext, corresponding to the message M and the set $\mathcal{S}$.

  (i) It randomly selects an exponent $s \in \mathbb{Z}_p^*$ and computes the following ciphertext components.

$$C_0 = (P)^s,\ C_1 = \Big(\prod_{j \in I_\mathcal{S}} f_j \cdot (U_j)^{ID_j}\Big)^s,\ C_2 = M \cdot \Omega^s$$

  (ii) It sets the personalized keys $K_u = e(P_2, \widetilde{P}^{ID_u})^s \cdot \Omega^s$ for each user $u \in \mathcal{S}$.

  (iii) Finally, broadcaster publishes $\mathsf{CT} = (C_0, C_1, C_2)$ as the ciphertext and keeps $\{K_u\}_{u \in \mathcal{S}}$ secret to itself.

- Decrypt(OAnoMPK, OAnoSK$_u$, CT): The system is outsider anonymous. Consequently, this decryption algorithm does not require any information of subscribed users' set $\mathcal{S}$ as an input and the set $\mathcal{S}$ is completely anonymous from any outsider adversary. However, each subscribed user (i.e., any insider) knows the information of all other subscribers. An insider user u with its secret-key OAnoSK_u and the master public-key $\mathsf{OAnoMPK}$ first recovers correct message M from the ciphertext CT by executing the following computations.

$$C_2 \times \frac{e(C_1, d_{u,0})}{e(C_0, d_{u,u} \cdot \prod\limits_{j \in I_S \setminus \{u\}} d_{u,j})}$$

$$= M \times e(P, \widetilde{P})^{\alpha\beta s} \times \frac{e(\prod\limits_{j \in I_S \setminus \{u\}} f_j \cdot U_j^{ID_j}, \widetilde{P}^{r_u})^s}{e(P^s, \widetilde{P}_2^\alpha (\widetilde{f}_u \cdot \widetilde{U}_u^{ID_u})^{r_u} \cdot \prod\limits_{j \in I_S \setminus \{u\}} (\widetilde{f}_j \cdot \widetilde{U}_j^{ID_j})^{r_u})}$$

$$= M \times e(P, \widetilde{P})^{\alpha\beta s} \times \frac{e(\prod\limits_{j \in I_S \setminus \{u\}} f_j \cdot U_j^{ID_j}, \widetilde{P})^{sr_u}}{e(P, \widetilde{P})^{\alpha\beta s} e(P^s, \prod\limits_{j \in I_S \setminus \{u\}} (\widetilde{f}_j \cdot \widetilde{U}_j^{ID_j})^{r_u})}$$

$$= M \times \frac{e(\prod\limits_{j \in I_S \setminus \{u\}} P^{\delta_j} \cdot P^{a_j ID_j}, \widetilde{P})^{sr_u}}{e(P^s, \prod\limits_{j \in I_S \setminus \{u\}} (\widetilde{f}_j \cdot \widetilde{U}_j^{ID_j})^{r_u})} = M \times \frac{e(P, \widetilde{P}^{\sum\limits_{j \in I_S \setminus \{u\}} (\delta_j + a_j ID_j)})^{sr_u}}{e(P^s, \prod\limits_{j \in I_S \setminus \{u\}} (\widetilde{f}_j \cdot \widetilde{U}_j^{ID_j})^{r_u})}$$

$$= M$$

Finally, it recovers the personalized key by computing

$$K_u = e(C_0, d_{u,N+1}) \times \frac{C_2}{M} = e(P^s, \widetilde{P}^{\beta \cdot ID_u}) \times \frac{M \cdot \Omega^s}{M}$$

$$= e(P^\beta, \widetilde{P}^{\cdot ID_u})^s \cdot \Omega^s = e(P_2, \widetilde{P}^{\cdot ID_u})^s \cdot \Omega^s$$

Remark 3 (**DDH test for T1 and T3 pairings***).* Our IB-OAnoBEPM uses asymmetric T3 bilinear pairings. If instead, we use symmetric T1 bilinear pairing, then any outsider can run the *Decisional Diffie-Hellman* (DDH) test

$$e(P^s, \prod\limits_{ID_j \in S'} f_j \cdot U_j^{ID_j}) = e(P, (\prod\limits_{ID_j \in S} f_j \cdot U_j^{ID_j})^s),$$

and verify the subscribers set as f_j, U_j are publicly available in this setting. On the other hand, the DDH test

$$e(P^s, \prod\limits_{ID_j \in S'} \widetilde{f}_j \cdot \widetilde{U}_j^{ID_j}) = e(\widetilde{P}, (\prod\limits_{ID_j \in S} f_j \cdot U_j^{ID_j})^s)$$

is computationally hard in asymmetric T3 bilinear as $\widetilde{f}_j$ and $\widetilde{U}_j$ are kept secret.

Table 1. Comparative summaries of communication bandwidth and storage overhead

Scheme	Communication	Storage	
	Ciphertext	Public-parameter	Secret-key
Ohtake et al. [19]	$2|B_s| + 1|B_t|$	$(3N + 2)|B_s| + 1|B_t|$	$2|B_s|$
Acharya et al. [1]-I	$2|B_s| + 1|B_t|$	$(2N + 1)|B_s|$	$1|B_s|$
Acharya et al. [1]-II	$2|B_s| + 1|B_t|$	$(3N + 1)|B_s| + 1|B_t|$	$2|B_s|$
Acharya et al. [1]-III	$2|M_i| + 1|M_t|$	$1|M_i| + (l + 1)|M_s|$	$1|M_i|$
Chen et al. [7]	$2|B_s| + (2L + 1)|B_t|$	$5|B_s| + 3|B_t|$	$2|B_s| + 4|\mathbb{Z}_p|$
$\Pi_{\text{IB-OAnoBEPM}}$	$2|A_s| + 1|A_t|$	$(2N + 4)|A_s| + 1|A_t|$	$(N + 2)|A_s|$

N = total number of users, L = maximal receivers for one encryption, l = length of the user identity, $|B_s|$ = size of symmetric bilinear source group, $|B_t|$ = size of symmetric bilinear target group, $|A_s|$ = size of asymmetric bilinear source group, $|\mathbb{Z}_p|$ = size of cyclic group $\mathbb{Z}_p$, $|A_t|$ = size of asymmetric bilinear target group, $|M_s|$ = size of multilinear source group, $|M_t|$ = size of multilinear target group, $|M_i|$ = size of multilinear intermediate group.

3.2 Security Analysis

The security analysis of the scheme follows from the following theorem.

Theorem 1 (Ciphertext indistinguishability with receiver anonymity). *Our proposed $\Pi_{\text{IB-OAnoBEPM}}$ achieves $(t, \epsilon, poly(\eta))$ adaptive IND-CPA security (cf. Definition 4) under the standard asymmetric (t', ϵ')-DBDHE assumption (cf. Definition 2), where η is the security parameter of the system and $poly(\eta)$ represents a polynomial in η.*

Due to the page limit, the proof of the Theorem 1 is given in Appendix A.

*Remark 4 (**IND-CCA** security).* The security against adaptive IND-CCA adversary is a strong and very useful notion of security for any PKE schemes. Although we have proved the adaptive IND-CPA security, our $\Pi_{\text{IB-OAnoBEPM}}$ can be enhanced to achieve adaptive IND-CCA security. In the work of Canetti et al. [5], later improved by Boneh et al. [3], they have shown a technique to build a IND-CCA secure Identity-Based Encryption (IBE) scheme from a 2-level Hierarchical IBE (HIBE) scheme. Our proposed $\Pi_{\text{IB-OAnoBEPM}}$ is built under the IBE framework. We can transform the underlying IBE framework into a 2-level HIBE following [2], and then get the IND-CCA secure IB-OAnoBEPM scheme.

4   Efficiency

In this section, we explain comparative studies of our $\Pi_{\text{IB-OAnoBEPM}}$ scheme with the existing BEPM schemes [1,7,19] in Table 1, 2 and 3. More precisely, what we have achieved is summarized as follows.

- Our $\Pi_{\text{IB-OAnoBEPM}}$ protocol has constant communication bandwidth, which are similar to [1,19] (cf. Table 1). The work [1]-III is designed over the highly inefficient multilinear maps, whose secure and practical implementation are yet to be instantiated. Moreover, the designs of [19], [1]-II have public-parameter size somewhat high as argued to ours. Our design has secret-key size linear to the total number of users N of the system, which is significantly high as opposed to [1,19]. However, Kiayias et al. [14] have proved that an outsider anonymous system, like our proposed $\Pi_{\text{IB-OAnoBEPM}}$, must have secret-key size linear to N, and also no further improvement is possible. Compared to the work of [7], the storage overhead of our $\Pi_{\text{IB-OAnoBEPM}}$ is significantly high. However, we emphasize that the communication bandwidth of [7] is linear to the maximal receivers L for one encryption, which is highly inefficient as compared to our scheme.

- Compared to [1,19], our work is the first to satisfy receiver's outsider anonymity beneath the *identity-based* framework (cf. Table 2). Moreover, [19], [1]-I and [1]-III are selectively IND-CPA secure and [7] is adaptively IND-CCA secure under the non-standard q-type security assumptions, and [7], [1]-II are constructed using the insecure symmetric Type-1 bilinear maps. In contrast, our design is adaptive IND-CPA secure under the standard DBDHE assumption over the most advanced and secure asymmetric Type-3 bilinear maps. Moreover, identity-based design of [7] is secure under the ROM, which is non-standard compared to our work.

- The computation cost of the proposed protocol is more efficient than [1]-III, which is constructed under multilinear maps (cf. Table 3). Compared to [19], [1]-I, [1]-II and [7] our encryption algorithm is more efficient and faster, since we required less number of bilinear pairing operations, which is highly cost-effective. Moreover, [19], [1]-I, [1]-II and [7] are based on Type-1 maps, where the pairing operation is almost two times slower than that of Type-3 maps. The existing works [1,19] and our design have decryption time linear to L. However, our decryption algorithm requires significantly less running time, because it require only three asymmetric pairings to recover the correct message.

Table 2. Comparative summaries of security and other functionalities

Scheme	Traceable	Anonymity	ROM	Group type	Security		IBE
					Model	Assumption	
Ohtake et al. [19]	✗	✗	✗	Prime Order, T1	SEL-CPA	q-DBDHE	✗
Acharya et al. [1]-I	✗	✗	✗	Prime Order, T1	SEL-CPA	q-DBDHE	✗
Acharya et al. [1]-II	✗	✗	✗	Prime Order, T1	ADAP-CPA	mDBDHE	✗
Acharya et al. [1]-III	✗	✗	✗	Prime Order, ML	SEL-CPA	q-DHDHE	✗
Chen et al. [7]	✗	✓	✓	Prime Order, T1	ADAP-CCA	q-ABDHE	✓
$\Pi_{\text{IB-OAnoBEPM}}$	✓	✓	✗	Prime Order, T3	ADAP-CPA	DBDHE	✓

IBE = identity-based encryption, ROM = random oracle model, ADAP-CPA = adaptive chosen-plaintext attack, ADAP-CCA = adaptive chosen-ciphertext attack, SEL-CPA = selective chosen-plaintext attack, ML = multilinear map, T1 = Type-1 map, T3 = Type-3 map, DHDHE = decisional hybrid Diffie-Hellman exponent, DBDH = decisional bilinear Diffie-Hellman, DBDHE = decisional bilinear Diffie-Hellman exponent, mBDH = modified bilinear Diffie-Hellman, mDBDHE = modified decisional bilinear Diffie-Hellman exponent, ABDHE = augmented bilinear Diffie-Hellman exponent,

Table 3. Comparative summaries of computation cost

Scheme	Encryption Time	Decryption Time
Ohtake et al. [19]	$(L+1)P + E_1 + (L+2)E_2 + (L+1)M_1$	$3P + (L)M_1$
Acharya et al. [1]-I	$(L+1)P + 2E_1 + (L+1)E_2 + (L+1)M_1$	$3P + (L)M_1$
Acharya et al. [1]-II	$(L+1)P + E_1 + (L+1)E_2 + (L+1)M_1 + (L)M_2$	$3P + (L)M_1 + M_2$
Acharya et al. [1]-III	$P_{n'} + (L+1)P_2 + E_{sg} + (L+2)E_{tg} + M_{sg} + (L)M_{tg}$	$3P_2 + (L)M_{tg}$
Chen et al. [7]	$(2L)P + (2L+1)E_1 + (2L)M_2 + (L)\mathcal{H}$	$1P + 2E_1 + 2E_2 + 1M_1 + 1M_2 + 4\mathcal{H}$
$\Pi_{\text{IB-OAnoBEPM}}$	$1P + 3E_1 + 1E_2 + (L+1)M_1 + 2M_2$	$3P + (L)M_1 + 2M_2$

$n' = \log_2(N)$, $E_1 =$ exponentiation in bilinear source group, $E_2 =$ exponentiation in bilinear target group, $P =$ bilinear pairing operation, $M_1 =$ multiplication in bilinear source group, $M_2 =$ multiplication in bilinear target group, $P_{n'} =$ multilinear pairing operation with $n' = \log_2(N)$ elements, $P_2 =$ multilinear pairing operation with 2 elements, $E_{sg} =$ exponentiation in the multilinear source group, $E_{tg} =$ exponentiation in the multilinear target group, $M_{sg} =$ multiplication in the multilinear source group, $M_{tg} =$ multiplication in the multilinear target group, $\mathcal{H} =$ hash computation

Table 4. Runtime (milliseconds) of key operations in selected curves

Operation	P	E_1	E_2	M_1	M_2
Type D (d159.param)	6.661	0.005	0.010	1.191	2.118
Type E (e.param)	12.531	0.041	0.003	9.097	0.494

$P =$ bilinear pairing operation, $E_1 =$ exponentiation in bilinear source group, $E_2 =$ exponentiation in bilinear target group, $M_1 =$ multiplication in bilinear source group, $M_2 =$ multiplication in bilinear target group

5 Implementation and Evaluation

We have implemented the computation cost of our $\Pi_{\text{IB-OAnoBEPM}}$ design and the current BEPM [1, 19] on a laptop with the following specification: Dell with Intel i7-6500U 2.59GHz processor, 8GB memory, and 64-bit Windows10 operating system with assistance of Pairing-Based Cryptography (PBC) library [18]. Furthermore, virtual machine (version VMware10.0.1) is installed on the laptop for executing the program. Specifically, the configuration of the virtual machine is Ubuntukylin-15.10-desktop-i386 including 4GB RAM as well as one CPU. Note that we have excluded [1]-III, since this is constructed over the multilinear maps, whose secure instantiation and practical implementation are still unknown. We have also excluded the scheme [1]-I and [7], since [1]-I has all most same parameter sizes and the computation cost as that of [1]-II and [7] is secure under the nonstandard ROM. Moreover, [1]-I is selectively secure, whereas we have achieved adaptive security.

For the symmetric bilinear pairing, Type E (e.param) curve is the perfect choice for the implementation. On the other hand, Type D curve (d159.param) is considered for implementing the asymmetric bilinear pairings. The running time of the critical operations, such as pairing operation, exponentiation and multiplication, on the selected curves have been shown in Table 4. Based on this table, the implementation details of both the encryption and decryption time have been presented in Table 5.

Depending on the Table 5, we have shown the performance analysis of the encryption time and the decryption time in Fig. 2. We have considered the most simplistic case, where number of receivers L for one encryption varies from 10 to 100. From the performance analysis graph, we can easily conclude that our $\Pi_{\text{IB-OAnoBEPM}}$ scheme has the cost-efficient encryption time, as well as faster decryption time, opposed to the existing BEPM schemes [1, 19]-II.

Table 5. Implementation details of encryption and decryption time (seconds)

L	Ohtake et al. [19]		Acharya et al. [1]-II		$\Pi_{\text{IB-OAnoBEPM}}$	
	Encryption Time	Decryption Time	Encryption Time	Decryption Time	Encryption Time	Decryption Time
10	0.237982	0.128563	0.242922	0.12906	0.024023	0.036129
20	0.454292	0.219533	0.464172	0.22003	0.035933	0.048039
30	0.670602	0.310503	0.685422	0.31100	0.047843	0.059949
40	0.886912	0.401473	0.906672	0.40197	0.059753	0.071859
50	1.103222	0.492443	1.127922	0.49294	0.071663	0.083769
60	1.319532	0.583413	1.349172	0.58391	0.083573	0.095679
70	1.535842	0.674383	1.570422	0.67488	0.095483	0.107589
80	1.752152	0.765353	1.791672	0.76585	0.107393	0.119499
90	1.968462	0.856323	2.012922	0.85682	0.119303	0.131409
100	2.184772	0.947293	2.234172	0.94779	0.131213	0.143319

L = Number of receivers for one encryption

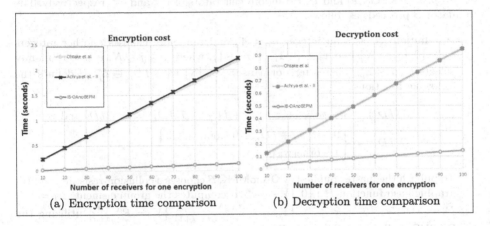

(a) Encryption time comparison   (b) Decryption time comparison

Fig. 2. The implementation of computation cost

6   Conclusion

We proposed the first identity-based outsider anonymous BEPM, which is proven to be adaptive IND-CPA secure beneath the standard DBDHE assumption over the asymmetric Type-3 bilinear maps. Our design has constant-size communication bandwidth and decryption requires only 3 pairings to recover the correct message, as well as the personalized keys. As a major contribution, we have eliminated the q-type non-standard security assumption without using the ROM.

Acknowledgements. This research was partially supported by the Ministry of Internal Affairs and Communications SCOPE (Grant Number 182103105) and by JST CREST (Grant Number JPMJCR14D6), Japan.

Appendix

A   Proof of Theorem 1

Proof. Assume that there exists a PPT adversary $\mathcal{A}$ in the ciphertext indistinguishability with receiver anonymity game that makes at most polynomial number of user secret-key queries, say $q = \mathsf{poly}(\eta)$, against our $\Pi_{\mathsf{IB\text{-}OAnoBEPM}}$ scheme. We can construct a simulator $\mathcal{B}$ that breaks the asymmetric DBDHE assumption (cf. Definition 2) using $\mathcal{A}$ as a subroutine. Here $\mathcal{B}$ works as the $\Pi_{\mathsf{IB\text{-}OAnoBEPM}}$ challenger in the adaptive IND-CPA secure ciphertext indistinguishability with receiver anonymity game. At the beginning of the game, $\mathcal{B}$ obtains the DBDHE challenge instance $\langle Z = (\mathbb{BG}, \widetilde{P},$ $\widetilde{P}^\alpha, \ldots, \widetilde{P}^{\alpha^m}, \widetilde{P}^{\alpha^{m+2}}, \ldots, \widetilde{P}^{\alpha^{2m}}, P, P^\alpha, \ldots, P^{\alpha^m}, P^c), K\rangle$ to decide whether K is $e(P, \widetilde{P})^{\alpha^{m+1} \cdot c}$ or a random element X from the target group $\mathbb{G}_T^\times$, where $\alpha, c \in_R \mathbb{Z}_p^*$, $\mathbb{BG} = (p, \mathbb{G}^\times, \widetilde{\mathbb{G}}^\times, \mathbb{G}_T^\times, e)$ and $P, \widetilde{P}$ random generators of $\mathbb{G}^\times$ and $\widetilde{\mathbb{G}}^\times$ respectively. The simulator $\mathcal{B}$ proceeds as follows.

Setup: Initially, $\mathcal{B}$ sets an integer $m = 4q$ and randomly chooses another integers $k_j \in \{0, 1, \ldots, N\}$ and $x_j \in \{0, 1, \ldots, m-1\}$, where $1 \leq j \leq N$. It also randomly selects $y', a \in \mathbb{Z}_p^*$. Thereafter, for a user $j \in [N]$ with $ID_j \in \mathbb{Z}_p^*$, $\mathcal{B}$ defines the following functions.

$$\mathcal{F}(ID_j) = (p - mk_j) + x' + x_j + ID_j, \quad \mathcal{J}(ID_j) = y' + ID_j \text{ and}$$

$$\mathcal{Q}(ID_j) = \left\{ \begin{array}{ll} 0, & \text{if } x_j + ID_j \equiv 0 \pmod{m} \\ 1, & \text{otherwise} \end{array} \right\}$$

To publish the master public-key OAnoMPK, $\mathcal{B}$ chooses a collision-resistant cryptographic hash function $H : \{0, 1\}^l \to \mathbb{Z}_p^*$. It computes the group elements $\widetilde{P}_1 = \widetilde{P}^\alpha$, $\widetilde{P}_2 = \widetilde{P}^{\alpha^N + a}$, $P_2 = P^{\alpha^N + a}$, $\{\widetilde{Y}_i = \widetilde{P}^{\alpha^i}\}_{i=1, i \neq N+1}^{2N}$, $\{Y_i = P^{\alpha^i}\}_{i=1}^{N}$ utilizing the DBDHE challenge instance $\langle Z, K\rangle$.

Finally, it sets the components $U_j = P \cdot Y_{N-j+1}$, $\widetilde{U}_j = \widetilde{P} \cdot \widetilde{Y}_{N-j+1}$, $\widetilde{f}_j = \widetilde{P}^{y'} \cdot \widetilde{Y}_{N-j+1}^{p - mk_j + x_j}$, $f_j = P^{y'} \cdot \widetilde{Y}_{N-j+1}^{p - mk_j + x_j}$, $\Omega = e(P_2, \widetilde{P}_1)$ and publishes the simulated master public-key OAnoMPK $= (P, \widetilde{P}, \widetilde{P}_1, \widetilde{P}_2, P_2, \{f_j\}_{j=1}^N, \{U_j\}_{j=1}^N, \Omega, H)$. It also sets the simulated master secret-key as OAnoMSK $= (\widetilde{P}_2^\alpha, \{\widetilde{f}_j\}_{j=1}^N, \{\widetilde{U}_j\}_{j=1}^N)$ and keeps secret to itself.

Phase 1: Now, $\mathcal{A}$ adaptively issues polynomially many, say $q = \mathsf{poly}(\eta)$, users secret-key queries. The adversary $\mathcal{A}$ sends an identity $id_u \in \{0, 1\}^l$ of user $u \in [N]$ to $\mathcal{B}$. To return a valid secret-key, $\mathcal{B}$ computes $ID_i = H(id_i) \in \mathbb{Z}_p^*$ for $1 \leq i \leq N$, and does the following.

- If $\mathcal{Q}(ID_u) = 0$, $\mathcal{B}$ aborts the game and randomly chooses a random bit from $\{0, 1\}$ to solve the asymmetric DBDHE problem.
- Otherwise, $\mathcal{B}$ randomly chooses an exponent $r \in \mathbb{Z}_p^*$ and sets $d_{u,0} = \widetilde{P}^r \cdot \widetilde{Y}_u^{-\frac{1}{\mathcal{F}(ID_u)}}$, $d_{u,u} = \widetilde{P}_1^a \cdot \widetilde{Y}_u^{-\frac{\mathcal{J}(ID_u)}{\mathcal{F}(ID_u)}} (\widetilde{f}_u \cdot \widetilde{U}_u^{ID_u})^r$, $d_{u,N} = (\widetilde{P}_2)^{ID_u}$ and $d_{u,j} = (\widetilde{f}_j \cdot \widetilde{U}_j^{ID_j})^r \cdot \widetilde{Y}_u^{-\frac{\mathcal{J}(ID_j)}{\mathcal{F}(ID_u)}} \cdot \widetilde{Y}_{N-j+1+u}^{-\frac{\mathcal{F}(ID_j)}{\mathcal{F}(ID_u)}}$, for $1 \leq j \neq u \leq N$.

- Finally, $\mathcal{B}$ returns the secret-key OAnoSK$_u$ = $(d_{u,0}, d_{u,u}, d_{u,N+1}, \{d_{u,j} : 1 \leq j \neq u \leq N\})$ to the adversary $\mathcal{A}$.

Observe that the components of OAnoSK_u are valid secret-key components as that of in the original protocol. Assume that $\hat{r} = r - \frac{\alpha^u}{\mathcal{F}(ID_u)}$, then

$$d_{u,0} = \widetilde{P}^r \cdot \widetilde{Y}_u^{-\frac{1}{\mathcal{F}(ID_u)}} = \widetilde{P}^{r - \frac{\alpha^u}{\mathcal{F}(ID_u)}} = (\widetilde{P})^{\hat{r}}, \quad d_{u,N} = (\widetilde{P}_2)^{ID_u}$$

$$d_{u,u} = \widetilde{P}_1^a \cdot \widetilde{Y}_u^{-\frac{\mathcal{J}(ID_u)}{\mathcal{F}(ID_u)}} (\widetilde{f}_u \cdot \widetilde{U}_u^{ID_u})^r = \widetilde{P}^{a\alpha - \frac{\alpha^u \mathcal{J}(ID_u)}{\mathcal{F}(ID_u)}} \cdot \widetilde{P}^{\alpha^{N+1} - \alpha^{N+1}} \cdot (\widetilde{f}_u \cdot \widetilde{U}_u^{ID_u})^r$$

$$= \widetilde{P}^{a\alpha} \cdot \widetilde{P}^{\alpha^{N+1}} \cdot \widetilde{P}^{-\frac{\alpha^u}{\mathcal{F}(ID_u)} - \alpha^{N+1}\frac{\mathcal{F}(ID_u)}{\mathcal{F}(ID_u)}} \cdot (\widetilde{f}_u \cdot \widetilde{U}_u^{ID_u})^r$$

$$= \widetilde{P}^{(a\alpha + \alpha^{N+1})} \big(\widetilde{P}^{\alpha^{N-u+1}\mathcal{F}(ID_u)} \cdot \widetilde{P}^{\mathcal{J}(ID_u)} \big)^{-\frac{\alpha^u}{\mathcal{F}(ID_u)}} \cdot (\widetilde{f}_u \cdot \widetilde{U}_u^{ID_u})^r$$

$$= \widetilde{P}_2^\alpha \big(\widetilde{P}^{\alpha^{N-u+1}(p - mk_u + x_u + ID_u) + y' + ID_u} \big)^{-\frac{\alpha^u}{\mathcal{F}(ID_u)}} \cdot (\widetilde{f}_u \cdot \widetilde{U}_u^{ID_u})^r$$

$$= \widetilde{P}_2^\alpha (\widetilde{f}_u \cdot \widetilde{U}_u^{ID_u})^{r - \frac{\alpha^u}{\mathcal{F}(ID_u)}} = \widetilde{P}_2^\alpha (\widetilde{f}_u \cdot \widetilde{U}_u^{ID_u})^{\hat{r}}$$

$$d_{u,j} = (\widetilde{f}_j \cdot \widetilde{U}_j^{ID_j})^r \cdot \widetilde{Y}_u^{-\frac{\mathcal{J}(ID_j)}{\mathcal{F}(ID_u)}} \cdot \widetilde{Y}_{N-j+1+u}^{\frac{\mathcal{F}(ID_j)}{\mathcal{F}(ID_u)}}$$

$$= (\widetilde{f}_j \cdot \widetilde{U}_j^{ID_j})^r \cdot \widetilde{P}^{-\frac{\alpha^u \mathcal{J}(ID_j)}{\mathcal{F}(ID_u)} - \frac{\alpha^{(N-j+1+u)}\mathcal{F}(ID_j)}{\mathcal{F}(ID_u)}}$$

$$= (\widetilde{f}_j \cdot \widetilde{U}_j^{ID_j})^r \cdot \big(\widetilde{P}^{y' + \alpha^{N-j+1}(p - mk_j + x_j) + ID_j + ID_j \alpha^{N-j+1}} \big)^{-\frac{\alpha^u}{\mathcal{F}(ID_u)}}$$

$$= (\widetilde{f}_j \cdot \widetilde{U}_j^{ID_j})^{r - \frac{\alpha^u}{\mathcal{F}(ID_u)}} = (\widetilde{f}_j \cdot \widetilde{U}_j^{ID_j})^{\hat{r}}$$

The simulator $\mathcal{B}$ can perform the above computations if and only if $\mathcal{F}(ID_u) \neq 0 \pmod{p}$. More precisely, only $\mathcal{Q}(ID_u) \neq 0$ is sufficient to continue the above computations, since $\mathcal{Q}(ID_u) \neq 0$ implies $\mathcal{F}(ID_u) \neq 0 \pmod{p}$.

Challenge: Now, $\mathcal{A}$ submits two equal length messages M_0, M_1 and two receiver's sets S_0, S_1 each contains $L = \text{poly}(\eta)$ users' identity subject to the restriction that for all id_u of secret key queries in Phase 1, $ID_u = H(id_u) \in S_0 \cap S_1$. Assume that the challenge set is of the form $S_\varkappa = \{ID_{\varkappa,i}\}_{i=1}^L$ for $\varkappa \in \{0,1\}$. Now, $\mathcal{B}$ aborts the game and chooses a random bit from $\{0,1\}$ if $\sum_{ID_{\varkappa,j} \in S_\varkappa} \alpha^{N-j+1}(p - mk_j + x_j + ID_{\varkappa,j}) \neq 0 \pmod{p}$ holds. Finally, $\mathcal{B}$ chooses $\zeta, \varkappa \in_R \{0,1\}$ and computes the cophertext components for the set $S_\varkappa = \{ID_{\varkappa,i}\}_{i=1}^L$ as follows.

$$C_{\varkappa,\zeta,0} = P^c, \quad C_{\varkappa,\zeta,1} = P^{c(\sum_{ID_{\varkappa,j} \in S_\varkappa} y' + ID_{\varkappa,j})}, \quad C_{\varkappa,\zeta,2} = M_\zeta e(P^c, \widetilde{P}_1^a) K$$

It sets the personalized keys as $K_u^{(\varkappa,\zeta)} = e(P^c, \widetilde{P}_2^{ID_u}) \cdot e(P^c, \widetilde{P}_1^a) K$ for each user identity $ID_u \in S_\varkappa$. Here, K is extracted from the DBDHE challenge instance. Finally, $\mathcal{B}$ passes $\mathcal{A}$ the challenge ciphertext $\mathsf{CT} = \big(C_{\varkappa,\zeta,0}, C_{\varkappa,\zeta,1}, C_{\varkappa,\zeta,2} \big)$ corresponding to the message M_ζ and $S_\varkappa$.

Note that CT is a valid ciphertext corresponding to the challenge message M_ζ

and the challenge set $\mathcal{S}_\varkappa$. Assume that $s = c$, $K = e(P, \widetilde{P})^{c \cdot \alpha^{N+1}}$, then

$$C_{\varkappa, \zeta, 0} = P^c = P^s$$

$$C_{\varkappa, \zeta, 1} = P^{c \left(\sum_{ID_{\varkappa, j} \in \mathcal{S}_\varkappa} \mathcal{J}(ID_{\varkappa, j}) \right)} = P^{c \left(\sum_{ID_{\varkappa, j} \in \mathcal{S}_\varkappa} y' + ID_{\varkappa, j} \right)}$$

$$= \left[\prod_{ID_{\varkappa, j} \in \mathcal{S}_\varkappa} P^{\alpha^{N-j+1} (p - mk_j + x_j)} \cdot P^{y'} \cdot P^{\alpha^{N-j+1} ID_{\varkappa, j}} \cdot P^{ID_{\varkappa, j}} \right]^c$$

$$= \left(\prod_{ID_{\varkappa, j} \in \mathcal{S}_\varkappa} f_j \cdot U_j^{ID_{\varkappa, j}} \right)^c = \left(\prod_{ID_{\varkappa, j} \in \mathcal{S}_\varkappa} f_j \cdot U_j^{ID_{\varkappa, j}} \right)^s$$

$$C_{\varkappa, \zeta, 2} = M_\zeta \cdot K \cdot e(P^c, \widetilde{P}_1^a) = M_\zeta e(P, \widetilde{P})^{c \cdot \alpha^{N+1}} e(P^c, \widetilde{P}_1^a) = M_\zeta e(P, \widetilde{P})^{(\alpha^N + a) c \alpha}$$

Since $(\alpha^N + a) c \alpha$ and s are uniformly distributed over $\mathbb{Z}_p^*$, CT is valid and uniformly distributed over the ciphertext space. Similarly, we can show that the personalized keys $K_u^{(\varkappa, \zeta)}$ are also the valid by the following computations.

$$K_u^{(\varkappa, \zeta)} = e(P^c, \widetilde{P}_2^{ID_u}) \cdot e(P^c, \widetilde{P}_1^a) K$$

$$= e(P^{\alpha^N + a}, \widetilde{P}^{ID_u})^c \cdot e(P, \widetilde{P})^{c \cdot \alpha^{N+1}} e(P^c, \widetilde{P}_1^a)$$

$$= e(P_2, \widetilde{P}^{ID_u})^c \cdot e(P, \widetilde{P})^{(\alpha^N + a) c \alpha}$$

Phase 2: The adversary $\mathcal{A}$ can adaptively issue additional user's secret-key generation queries as in Phase 1 with a restriction that queried identities lie in $\mathcal{S}_0 \cap \mathcal{S}_1$.

Guess: Finally, $\mathcal{A}$ returns a guess $(\zeta', \varkappa') \in \{0, 1\} \times \{0, 1\}$ of $(\zeta, \varkappa)$ to $\mathcal{B}$.

Probability analysis

If $(\zeta', \varkappa') = (\zeta, \varkappa)$, $\mathcal{B}$ outputs 0, indicating that $K = e(P, \widetilde{P})^{c \cdot \alpha^{N+1}}$; otherwise, it outputs 1, indicating that K is a random element of $\mathbb{G}_T^\times$. The simulation of $\mathcal{B}$ is perfect when $K = e(P, \widetilde{P})^{c \cdot \alpha^{N+1}}$. Therefore, we have

$$\Pr \left[\mathcal{B} \left(Z, K = e(P, \widetilde{P})^{c \cdot \alpha^{N+1}} \right) = 0 \right] = \frac{1}{4} + \mathsf{Adv}_{\mathcal{A}, \text{IB-OAnoBEPM}}^{\text{IND-CPA}}(\eta),$$

where $\mathsf{Adv}_{\mathcal{A}, \text{IB-OAnoBEPM}}^{\text{IND-CPA}}(\eta)$ is the advantage of $\mathcal{A}$ in the above game. However, the message is completely hidden from $\mathcal{A}$ when $K = X$, a random element from $\mathbb{G}_T^\times$. Therefore, we have the probability

$$\Pr \left[\mathcal{B} \left(Z, K = X \right) = 0 \right] = \frac{1}{4}$$

Hence, the advantage of $\mathcal{B}$ in breaking the DBDHE challenge is

$$Adv_{\mathcal{B}}^{\text{DBDHE}}(\eta) = \left| \Pr \left[\mathcal{B} \left(Z, K = e(P, \widetilde{P})^{c \cdot \alpha^{N+1}} \right) = 0 \right] - \Pr \left[\mathcal{B} \left(Z, K = X \right) = 0 \right] \right|$$

$$= \left| \frac{1}{4} + \mathsf{Adv}_{\mathcal{A}, \text{IB-OAnoBEPM}}^{\text{IND-CPA}}(\eta) - \frac{1}{4} \right| = \mathsf{Adv}_{\mathcal{A}, \text{IB-OAnoBEPM}}^{\text{IND-CPA}}(\eta)$$

Therefore, if $\mathcal{A}$ has non-negligible advantage in correctly guessing $(\zeta', \varkappa')$, then $\mathcal{B}$ predicts $K = e(P, \widetilde{P})^{c \cdot \alpha^{N+1}}$ or random element of $\mathbb{G}_T^\times$ (i.e., breaks the DBDHE challenge) with non-negligible advantage.

Hence, the proof.

References

1. Acharya, K., Dutta, R.: Provable secure constructions for broadcast encryption with personalized messages. In: Okamoto, T., Yu, Y., Au, M.H., Li, Y. (eds.) ProvSec 2017. LNCS, vol. 10592, pp. 329–348. Springer, Cham (2017). https://doi.org/10.1007/978-3-319-68637-0_20
2. Boneh, D., Boyen, X., Goh, E.-J.: Hierarchical identity based encryption with constant size ciphertext. In: Cramer, R. (ed.) EUROCRYPT 2005. LNCS, vol. 3494, pp. 440–456. Springer, Heidelberg (2005). https://doi.org/10.1007/11426639_26
3. Boneh, D., Katz, J.: Improved efficiency for CCA-Secure cryptosystems built using identity-based encryption. In: Menezes, A. (ed.) CT-RSA 2005. LNCS, vol. 3376, pp. 87–103. Springer, Heidelberg (2005). https://doi.org/10.1007/978-3-540-30574-3_8
4. Boneh, D., Waters, B.: A fully collusion resistant broadcast, trace, and revoke system. In: Proceedings of the 13th ACM Conference on Computer and Communications Security, pp. 211–220 (2006)
5. Canetti, R., Halevi, S., Katz, J.: Chosen-ciphertext security from identity-based encryption. In: Cachin, C., Camenisch, J.L. (eds.) EUROCRYPT 2004. LNCS, vol. 3027, pp. 207–222. Springer, Heidelberg (2004). https://doi.org/10.1007/978-3-540-24676-3_13
6. Chatterjee, S., Hankerson, D., Menezes, A.: On the efficiency and security of pairing-based protocols in the type 1 and type 4 settings. In: Hasan, M.A., Helleseth, T. (eds.) WAIFI 2010. LNCS, vol. 6087, pp. 114–134. Springer, Heidelberg (2010). https://doi.org/10.1007/978-3-642-13797-6_9
7. Chen, L., Li, J., Zhang, Y.: Anonymous certificate-based broadcast encryption with personalized messages. IEEE Trans. Broadcast. (2020)
8. Delerablée, C.: Identity-based broadcast encryption with constant size ciphertexts and private keys. In: Kurosawa, K. (ed.) ASIACRYPT 2007. LNCS, vol. 4833, pp. 200–215. Springer, Heidelberg (2007). https://doi.org/10.1007/978-3-540-76900-2_12
9. Fazio, N., Perera, I.M.: Outsider-anonymous broadcast encryption with sublinear ciphertexts. In: Fischlin, M., Buchmann, J., Manulis, M. (eds.) PKC 2012. LNCS, vol. 7293, pp. 225–242. Springer, Heidelberg (2012). https://doi.org/10.1007/978-3-642-30057-8_14
10. Fiat, A., Naor, M.: Broadcast encryption. In: Stinson, D.R. (ed.) CRYPTO 1993. LNCS, vol. 773, pp. 480–491. Springer, Heidelberg (1994). https://doi.org/10.1007/3-540-48329-2_40
11. Fujii, A., et al.: Secure broadcast system with simultaneous individual messaging. IEICE Trans. Fundam. Electron. Commun. Comput. Sci. 94(6), 1328–1337 (2011)
12. Han, J.H., Park, J.H., Lee, D.H.: Transmission-efficient broadcast encryption scheme with personalized messages. IEICE Trans. Fundam. Electron. Commun. Comput. Sci. 96(4), 796–806 (2013)
13. He, K., Weng, J., Liu, J.-N., Liu, J.K., Liu, W., Deng, R.H.: Anonymous identity-based broadcast encryption with chosen-ciphertext security. In: Proceedings of the 11th ACM on Asia Conference on Computer and Communications Security, pp. 247–255 (2016)
14. Kiayias, A., Samari, K.: Lower bounds for private broadcast encryption. In: Kirchner, M., Ghosal, D. (eds.) IH 2012. LNCS, vol. 7692, pp. 176–190. Springer, Heidelberg (2013). https://doi.org/10.1007/978-3-642-36373-3_12

15. Lai, J., Mu, Y., Guo, F., Susilo, W., Chen, R.: Anonymous identity-based broadcast encryption with revocation for file sharing. In: Liu, J.K., Steinfeld, R. (eds.) ACISP 2016. LNCS, vol. 9723, pp. 223–239. Springer, Cham (2016). https://doi.org/10.1007/978-3-319-40367-0_14

16. Li, X., Yanli, R.: Efficient anonymous identity-based broadcast encryption without random oracles. Int. J. Digit. Crime Forensics 6(2), 40–51 (2014)

17. Libert, B., Paterson, K.G., Quaglia, E.A.: Anonymous broadcast encryption: adaptive security and efficient constructions in the standard model. In: Fischlin, M., Buchmann, J., Manulis, M. (eds.) PKC 2012. LNCS, vol. 7293, pp. 206–224. Springer, Heidelberg (2012). https://doi.org/10.1007/978-3-642-30057-8_13

18. Lynn, B.: On the implementation of pairing-based cryptosystems. Stanford University (2007)

19. Ohtake, G., Hanaoka, G., Ogawa, K.: Efficient broadcast encryption with personalized messages. In: Heng, S.-H., Kurosawa, K. (eds.) ProvSec 2010. LNCS, vol. 6402, pp. 214–228. Springer, Heidelberg (2010). https://doi.org/10.1007/978-3-642-16280-0_15

20. Ren, Y., Niu, Z., Zhang, X.: Fully anonymous identity-based broadcast encryption without random oracles. IJ Network Secur. 16(4), 256–264 (2014)

21. Uzunkol, O., Kiraz, M.S.: Still wrong use of pairings in cryptography. Appl. Math. Comput. 333, 467–479 (2018)

22. Ke, X., Liao, Y., Qiao, L., Liu, Z., Yang, X.: An identity-based (IDB) broadcast encryption scheme with personalized messages (BEPM). PLoS ONE 10(12), e0143975 (2015)

23. Zhang, M., Takagi, T.: Efficient constructions of anonymous multireceiver encryption protocol and their deployment in group e-mail systems with privacy preservation. IEEE Syst. J. 7(3), 410–419 (2013)

Compactly Committing Authenticated Encryption Using Tweakable Block Cipher

Shoichi Hirose$^{(\boxtimes)}$ (iD)

University of Fukui, Fukui, Japan
`hrs_shch@u-fukui.ac.jp`

Abstract. Message franking is a cryptographic scheme introduced in the Facebook end-to-end encrypted messaging system. It enables users to report abusive messages to Facebook in a verifiable manner. Grubbs, Lu and Ristenpart initiated theoretical study of message franking. They formalized the notion and introduced a new primitive called compactly committing authenticated encryption with associated data (ccAEAD) in 2017. They also presented provably secure ccAEAD schemes. Dodis, Grubbs, Ristenpart and Woodage introduced a new primitive called encryptment as a core building block of ccAEAD in 2018. They presented a provably secure encryptment scheme using a Merkle-Damgård hash function and transformations to ccAEAD from it.

In this paper, we present a provably secure encryptment scheme using a tweakable block cipher (TBC). Then, we present a ccAEAD scheme using a TBC by showing a transformation from encryptment using a TBC. Similar to the previous schemes, our scheme requires a collision-resistant pseudorandom function. We adopt a double-block-length construction using TBC for it.

Keywords: Message franking · Authenticated encryption · Encryptment · Tweakable block cipher

1 Introduction

Background. With the spread of end-to-end encrypted messaging systems such as Facebook Messenger [10], Signal [20] and Whatsapp Messenger [22], new security problems arise other than those concerning confidentiality and integrity of the messages. One of the problems attracting interest recently is that malicious senders may send harassing messages, harmful contents such as malware, and so on. Facebook introduced a cryptographic scheme called message franking to its end-to-end encrypted messaging system [11]. It enables users to report abusive messages to their service provider in a verifiable manner.

Grubbs et al. [13] initiated formal study of message franking and introduced a new primitive of symmetric-key cryptography called compactly committing authenticated encryption with associated data (ccAEAD). Dodis et al. [9] introduced a core building block of ccAEAD called encryptment, which enables modular design and analysis of ccAEAD. They also presented a provably secure

© Springer Nature Switzerland AG 2020
M. Kutyłowski et al. (Eds.): NSS 2020, LNCS 12570, pp. 187–206, 2020.
https://doi.org/10.1007/978-3-030-65745-1_11

encryptment scheme using a Merkle-Damgård hash function and transformations to ccAEAD from it.

Our Contribution. We propose an encryption scheme using a tweakable block cipher (TBC). It follows the scheme by Dodis et al. [9] and uses a Merkle-Damgård hash function. Its compression function is constructed with a TBC and can be instantiated by TBCs such as Skinny [1] and Deoxys-BC [17].

The compression function is an instantiation of the double-block-length one [14] using a TBC. It is already used by Berti et al. [5] for leakage-resilient authenticated encryption to construct a collision-resistant hash function, which is conservative. The novelty of our proposal is that the compression function is used to construct a collision-resistant pseudorandom function, that is, a keyed pseudorandom hash function which is also collision-resistant simultaneously. Thus, our work is another step toward future wide deployment of TBCs.

A drawback of the encryption scheme by Dodis et al. [9] is that its underlying compression function should be a secure pseudorandom function against related key attacks [2]: For a secret key K, adversaries are allowed to choose X arbitrarily and ask on the key $K \oplus X$. Adversaries are also able to launch a kind of related-key attacks on a TBC adopting the tweakey framework such as Skinny and Deoxys-BC by changing the value of its tweak. However, our proposed scheme is expected to be more robust against related-key attacks than the scheme by Dodis et al. since the value of the tweak of the underlying TBC cannot be directly chosen by adversaries in our scheme.

We also present a transformation from encryption to ccAEAD using a TBC. Thus, a ccAEAD scheme can be constructed only with a TBC using our encryption scheme and transformation. Based on our security analysis, generic constructions by Grubbs et al. [13] can also be instantiated with the same TBC. However, the resultant ccAEAD schemes are not so efficient as ours.

Related Work. Grubbs et al. [13] presented two generic constructions of ccAEAD: Commit-then-Encrypt (CtE) and Committing Encrypt-and-PRF (CEP). CtE combines a commitment scheme and an AEAD scheme. CEP combines a pseudorandom generator, a pseudorandom function (PRF) and a collision-resistant PRF. HMAC [12] can be used as a collision-resistant PRF and other multi-property-preserving hash functions [4] may be other candidates.

Dodis et al. [9] showed an attack on the message franking protocol of Facebook. It enables a malicious sender to send an abusive message to a receiver and to prevent the receiver from reporting it to Facebook.

All the schemes in [9,13] as well as ours require receivers to reveal the entire message to the third party to report it as abusive. Message franking schemes requiring receivers to reveal only the abusive parts are proposed and discussed independently by Leontiadis and Vaudenay [19] and by Chen and Tang [8].

Huguenin-Dumittan and Leontiadis [15] formalized a message franking channel and presented a generic construction of a bidirectional message franking channel using a committing AEAD scheme and a MAC function.

ccAEAD is authenticated encryption with additional functionality that a small part of the ciphertext can be used as a commitment to the message [13].

Authenticated encryption was treated formally first by Katz and Yung [18] and by Bellare and Namprempre [3].

Tyagi et al. introduced and formalized asymmetric message franking [21]. They also constructed a scheme using an extended technique of designated verifier signatures [16].

Organization. Section 2 gives some notations and definitions of cryptographic primitives necessary for the discussion. Section 3 describes syntax and definitions of security requirements of encryptment. Section 4 presents an encryptment scheme using a TBC and shows its provable security. Section 5 first gives syntax and definitions of security requirements of ccAEAD. Then, it presents a transformation from encryptment to ccAEAD using a TBC and shows its provable security.

2 Preliminaries

2.1 Notations

Let $\Sigma = \{0,1\}$. For any integer $l \geq 0$, let Σ^l be identified with the set of all Σ-sequences of length l. The empty sequence is denoted by ε. $\Sigma^0 = \{\varepsilon\}$. Let $(\Sigma^l)^* = \bigcup_{i \geq 0} \Sigma^{li}$ and $(\Sigma^l)^+ = \bigcup_{i \geq 1} \Sigma^{li}$. For non-negative integers $k_1 \leq k_2$, let $(\Sigma^l)^{[k_1, k_2]} = \bigcup_{i=k_1}^{k_2} \Sigma^{li}$.

For $x \in \Sigma^*$, the length of x is denoted by $|x|$. For $x_1, x_2 \in \Sigma^*$, $x_1 \| x_2$ represents their concatenation. For $x \in \Sigma^*$ and an integer $l \geq 0$, $\mathsf{msb}_l(x)$ represents the most significant l bits of x, and $\mathsf{lsb}_l(x)$ represents the least significant l bits of x.

For integers n_1 and n_2 such that $n_1 \leq n_2$, let $[n_1, n_2]$ be the set of integers between n_1 and n_2 inclusive.

For integers a and b such that $b > 0$, let $a \bmod b$ be the remainder $r \in [0, b-1]$ such that $a = b \cdot q + r$ for some integer q.

Assignment of an element chosen uniformly at random from a set $\mathcal{S}$ to s is denoted by $s \leftarrow \mathcal{S}$.

Let $\mathcal{F}_{\mathcal{D}, \mathcal{R}}$ be the set of all functions with domain $\mathcal{D}$ and range $\mathcal{R}$.

2.2 Pseudorandom Functions

Let $f : \mathcal{K} \times \mathcal{D} \to \mathcal{R}$ be a keyed function with its key space $\mathcal{K}$. $f(K, \cdot)$ is often denoted by $f_K(\cdot)$. Let $\mathbf{A}$ be an adversary which has a function in $\mathcal{F}_{\mathcal{D}, \mathcal{R}}$ as an oracle and outputs 0 or 1. The advantage of $\mathbf{A}$ against f concerning a pseudorandom function (PRF) is given by

$$\mathrm{Adv}_f^{\mathrm{prf}}(\mathbf{A}) \triangleq \left| \Pr[\mathbf{A}^{f_K} = 1] - \Pr[\mathbf{A}^{\rho} = 1] \right| ,$$

where $K \leftarrow \mathcal{K}$ and $\rho \leftarrow \mathcal{F}_{\mathcal{D}, \mathcal{R}}$.

2.3   Tweakable Block Ciphers

A tweakable block cipher (TBC) is a function $e : \mathcal{K} \times \mathcal{J} \times \mathcal{X} \to \mathcal{Y}$ with its key space $\mathcal{K}$, tweak space $\mathcal{J}$, plaintext space $\mathcal{X}$ and ciphertext space $\mathcal{Y}$. It is common that $\mathcal{K} = \Sigma^{n_k}$, $\mathcal{J} = \Sigma^{n_t}$ and $\mathcal{X} = \mathcal{Y} = \Sigma^{n_s}$ for some positive integers n_k, n_t and n_s. For every $(K, T) \in \mathcal{K} \times \mathcal{J}$, $e(K, T, \cdot)$ is a permutation. $e(K, T, \cdot)$ is often denoted by $e_K^T(\cdot)$.

Let $\mathcal{P}_{\mathcal{J} \times \mathcal{X}}$ be the set of all tweakable permutations with their tweak space $\mathcal{J}$. Namely, for every $p \in \mathcal{P}_{\mathcal{J} \times \mathcal{X}}$ and $T \in \mathcal{J}$, $p(T, \cdot)$ is a permutation over $\mathcal{X}$.

The security of a TBC is formalized in terms of indistinguishability from a uniform random tweakable permutation. Let $\mathbf{A}$ be an adversary which has a tweakable permutation in $\mathcal{P}_{\mathcal{J} \times \mathcal{X}}$ as an oracle and outputs 0 or 1. The advantage of $\mathbf{A}$ against e concerning a tweakable pseudorandom permutation (TPRP) is given by

$$\mathrm{Adv}_e^{\mathrm{tprp}}(\mathbf{A}) \triangleq \left| \Pr[\mathbf{A}^{e_K} = 1] - \Pr[\mathbf{A}^{\varpi} = 1] \right| ,$$

where $K \leftarrow \mathcal{K}$ and $\varpi \leftarrow \mathcal{P}_{\mathcal{J} \times \mathcal{X}}$.

2.4   Cryptographic Hash Functions

A cryptographic hash function is a function mapping an input of arbitrary length to an output of fixed length. It is often called simply a hash function. It is required various kinds of security properties. Among them, collision resistance and preimage resistance are relevant to the discussion in this paper and they are discussed in the ideal model.

Let H^P be a hash function using a primitive P, which is a TBC in this paper. P is assumed to be ideal. Namely, P is chosen uniformly at random from the set of all TBCs with the same domain and range.

Let $\mathbf{A}$ be an adversary trying to find a collision pair for H^P. $\mathbf{A}$ can make encryption and decryption queries to its oracle P. A collision pair for H^P are a pair of distinct inputs to H^P mapped to the same output. The advantage of $\mathbf{A}$ against H^P concerning collision resistance is given by

$$\mathrm{Adv}_{H^P}^{\mathrm{col}}(\mathbf{A}) \triangleq \Pr[(X, X') \leftarrow \mathbf{A}^P : H^P(X) = H^P(X') \wedge X \neq X'] .$$

It is assumed that $\mathbf{A}$ makes all the queries to P necessary to compute both $H^P(X)$ and $H^P(X')$.

Let $\mathbf{A}$ be an adversary trying to find a preimage of an output for H^P. The advantage of $\mathbf{A}$ against H^P concerning everywhere preimage resistance is given by

$$\mathrm{Adv}_{H^P}^{\mathrm{epre}}(\mathbf{A}) \triangleq \max_Y \left\{ \Pr[X \leftarrow \mathbf{A}^P : H^P(X) = Y] \right\} .$$

It is also assumed that $\mathbf{A}$ makes all the queries to P necessary to compute $H^P(X)$.

3 Encryptment

3.1 Syntax

An encryptment scheme [9] is a symmetric-key cryptographic scheme defined to be a tuple of algorithms $\mathsf{EC} = (\mathsf{KGec}, \mathsf{ENec}, \mathsf{DEec}, \mathsf{VEec})$ specified below: Let $\mathcal{K}ec \triangleq \Sigma^n$ be a key space, $\mathcal{A}ec \subseteq \Sigma^*$ be an associated-data space, $\mathcal{M}ec \subseteq \Sigma^*$ be a message space, $\mathcal{C}ec \subseteq \Sigma^*$ be a ciphertext space, and $\mathcal{T}ec \triangleq \Sigma^\ell$ be a binding-tag space.

- KGec is a randomized key generation algorithm. It takes as input a security parameter n in the unary form of 1^n and returns a secret key $K_{ec} \in \mathcal{K}ec$ chosen uniformly at random.
- ENec is a deterministic encryption algorithm. It takes as input $(K_{ec}, A_{ec}, M_{ec}) \in \mathcal{K}ec \times \mathcal{A}ec \times \mathcal{M}ec$ and returns $(C_{ec}, B_{ec}) \in \mathcal{C}ec \times \mathcal{T}ec$.
- DEec is a deterministic decryption algorithm. It takes as input $(K_{ec}, A_{ec}, C_{ec}, B_{ec}) \in \mathcal{K}ec \times \mathcal{A}ec \times \mathcal{C}ec \times \mathcal{T}ec$ and returns $M_{ec} \in \mathcal{M}ec$ or $\perp \notin \mathcal{M}ec$.
- VEec is a deterministic verification algorithm. It takes as input $(A_{ec}, M_{ec}, K_{ec}, B_{ec}) \in \mathcal{A}ec \times \mathcal{M}ec \times \mathcal{K}ec \times \mathcal{T}ec$ and returns $b \in \Sigma$.

For $(C_{ec}, B_{ec}) \leftarrow \mathsf{ENec}(K_{ec}, A_{ec}, M_{ec})$, it is assumed that the length of C_{ec} depends only on that of M_{ec}.

EC is required to satisfy correctness: For any $(K_{ec}, A_{ec}, M_{ec}) \in \mathcal{K}ec \times \mathcal{A}ec \times \mathcal{M}ec$, if $(C_{ec}, B_{ec}) \leftarrow \mathsf{ENec}(K_{ec}, A_{ec}, M_{ec})$, then $\mathsf{DEec}(K_{ec}, A_{ec}, C_{ec}, B_{ec}) = M_{ec}$ and $\mathsf{VEec}(A_{ec}, M_{ec}, K_{ec}, B_{ec}) = 1$. A stronger notion of correctness called strong correctness is also introduced, which is defined as follows: For any $(K_{ec}, A_{ec}, C_{ec}, B_{ec}) \in \mathcal{K}ec \times \mathcal{A}ec \times \mathcal{C}ec \times \mathcal{T}ec$, if $M_{ec} \leftarrow \mathsf{DEec}(K_{ec}, A_{ec}, C_{ec}, B_{ec})$, then $\mathsf{ENec}(K_{ec}, A_{ec}, M_{ec}) = (C_{ec}, B_{ec})$.

3.2 Security Requirement

The security requirements of an encryptment scheme are confidentiality and second-ciphertext unforgeability. Binding properties with respect to a sender and a receiver are also introduced.

Confidentiality. Confidentiality of an encryptment scheme is defined in a real-or-random fashion. An adversary **A** is given access to either $\mathsf{ENec}_{K_{ec}}$ with $K_{ec} \leftarrow \mathsf{KGec}(1^n)$ or \$ as an oracle. **A** is allowed to ask only a single query $(A_{ec}, M_{ec}) \in \mathcal{A}ec \times \mathcal{M}ec$ to the oracle. Let $(C_{ec}, B_{ec}) \leftarrow \mathsf{ENec}_{K_{ec}}(A_{ec}, M_{ec})$. Then, \$ returns $(R_C, R_B) \leftarrow \Sigma^{|C_{ec}|} \times \Sigma^{|B_{ec}|}$ in response to the query (A_{ec}, M_{ec}). The advantage of **A** concerning confidentiality is defined as follows:

$$\mathrm{Adv}_{\mathsf{EC}}^{\mathrm{ot\text{-}ror}}(\mathbf{A}) \triangleq \left| \Pr[\mathbf{A}^{\mathsf{ENec}_{K_{ec}}} = 1] - \Pr[\mathbf{A}^{\$} = 1] \right| ,$$

where "ot-ror" stands for "one-time real-or-random."

Second-Ciphertext Unforgeability. An adversary $\mathbf{A}$ is given access to $\mathsf{ENec}_{K_{ec}}$ as an oracle, where $K_{ec} \leftarrow \mathsf{KGec}(1^n)$. $\mathbf{A}$ is allowed to ask only a single query $(A_{ec}, M_{ec}) \in \mathcal{A}ec \times \mathcal{M}ec$ to the oracle, which returns $(C_{ec}, B_{ec}) \leftarrow \mathsf{ENec}_{K_{ec}}(A_{ec}, M_{ec})$ and K_{ec}. Finally, $\mathbf{A}$ outputs $(A'_{ec}, C'_{ec}) \in \mathcal{A}ec \times \mathcal{C}ec$. The advantage of $\mathbf{A}$ concerning second-ciphertext unforgeability is defined as follows:

$$\mathrm{Adv}_{\mathsf{EC}}^{\mathrm{scu}}(\mathbf{A}) \triangleq \Pr[(A_{ec}, C_{ec}) \neq (A'_{ec}, C'_{ec}) \wedge \mathsf{DEec}_{K_{ec}}(A'_{ec}, C'_{ec}, B_{ec}) \neq \perp] \ .$$

Binding Properties. An encryptment scheme is also required binding properties for a receiver and a sender. Receiver binding captures the intuition that a malicious receiver should not be able to report a non-abusive sender for sending an abusive message. Sender binding captures the intuition that a malicious sender of an abusive message should not be able to prevent the receiver from reporting it.

For receiver binding, let $\mathbf{A}$ be an adversary producing a pair of elements in $\mathcal{K}ec \times \mathcal{A}ec \times \mathcal{M}ec$ and a binding tag in $\mathcal{T}ec$. The advantage of $\mathbf{A}$ concerning receiver binding is defined as follows:

$$\mathrm{Adv}_{\mathsf{EC}}^{\mathrm{r\text{-}bind}}(\mathbf{A}) \triangleq \Pr[((K_{ec}, A_{ec}, M_{ec}), (K'_{ec}, A'_{ec}, M'_{ec}), B_{ec}) \leftarrow \mathbf{A} :$$
$$(A_{ec}, M_{ec}) \neq (A'_{ec}, M'_{ec}) \wedge$$
$$\mathsf{VEec}(A_{ec}, M_{ec}, K_{ec}, B_{ec}) = \mathsf{VEec}(A'_{ec}, M'_{ec}, K'_{ec}, B_{ec}) = 1] \ .$$

The advantage of $\mathbf{A}$ concerning strong receiver binding is defined as follows:

$$\mathrm{Adv}_{\mathsf{EC}}^{\mathrm{sr\text{-}bind}}(\mathbf{A}) \triangleq \Pr[((K_{ec}, A_{ec}, M_{ec}), (K'_{ec}, A'_{ec}, M'_{ec}), B_{ec}) \leftarrow \mathbf{A} :$$
$$(K_{ec}, A_{ec}, M_{ec}) \neq (K'_{ec}, A'_{ec}, M'_{ec}) \wedge$$
$$\mathsf{VEec}(A_{ec}, M_{ec}, K_{ec}, B_{ec}) = \mathsf{VEec}(A'_{ec}, M'_{ec}, K'_{ec}, B_{ec}) = 1] \ .$$

It is easy to see that, for any adversary $\mathbf{A}$, $\mathrm{Adv}_{\mathsf{EC}}^{\mathrm{r\text{-}bind}}(\mathbf{A}) \leq \mathrm{Adv}_{\mathsf{EC}}^{\mathrm{sr\text{-}bind}}(\mathbf{A})$.

For sender binding, let $\mathbf{A}$ be an adversary producing an element in $\mathcal{K}ec \times \mathcal{A}ec \times \mathcal{C}ec \times \mathcal{T}ec$. The advantage of an adversary $\mathbf{A}$ concerning sender binding is defined as follows:

$$\mathrm{Adv}_{\mathsf{EC}}^{\mathrm{s\text{-}bind}}(\mathbf{A}) \triangleq \Pr[(K_{ec}, A_{ec}, C_{ec}, B_{ec}) \leftarrow \mathbf{A}, M_{ec} \leftarrow \mathsf{DEec}(K_{ec}, A_{ec}, C_{ec}, B_{ec}) :$$
$$M_{ec} \neq \perp \wedge \mathsf{VEec}(A_{ec}, M_{ec}, K_{ec}, B_{ec}) = 0] \ .$$

Lemma 1 ([9]). *Let EC be an encryptment scheme satisfying strong correctness. Then, for any adversary $\mathbf{A}$ against EC concerning second-ciphertext unforgeability, there exist adversaries $\mathbf{B}$ and $\mathbf{C}$ concerning sender binding and receiver binding, respectively, such that*

$$\mathrm{Adv}_{\mathsf{EC}}^{\mathrm{scu}}(\mathbf{A}) \leq \mathrm{Adv}_{\mathsf{EC}}^{\mathrm{s\text{-}bind}}(\mathbf{B}) + \mathrm{Adv}_{\mathsf{EC}}^{\mathrm{r\text{-}bind}}(\mathbf{C})$$

and both $\mathbf{B}$ and $\mathbf{C}$ run almost in the same time as $\mathbf{A}$.

4 Proposed Scheme

4.1 Scheme

The proposed scheme $\mathsf{ECtbc} = (\mathsf{KGtbc}, \mathsf{ENtbc}, \mathsf{DEtbc}, \mathsf{VEtbc})$ is described in this section. The building block is a TBC $E : \mathcal{K}\mathsf{tbc} \times \mathcal{T}\mathsf{tbc} \times \mathcal{P}\mathsf{tbc} \to \mathcal{C}\mathsf{tbc}$, where $\mathcal{K}\mathsf{tbc}$ is its key space, $\mathcal{T}\mathsf{tbc}$ is its tweak space, $\mathcal{P}\mathsf{tbc}$ is its plaintext space, $\mathcal{C}\mathsf{tbc}$ is its ciphertext space, and all of them are $\varSigma^n$. The compression function $F : \mathcal{V} \times \mathcal{W} \times \mathcal{X} \to \mathcal{V} \times \mathcal{W}$, where $\mathcal{V}, \mathcal{W}$ and $\mathcal{X}$ are $\varSigma^n$, is defined as follows: $(V_i, W_i) \leftarrow F(V_{i-1}, W_{i-1}, X_i)$ such that $V_i \triangleq E_{V_{i-1}}^{W_{i-1}}(X_i) \oplus X_i$ and $W_i \triangleq E_{V_{i-1}}^{W_{i-1}}(X_i \oplus c) \oplus X_i \oplus c$, where c is a constant in $\varSigma^n \setminus \{0^n\}$. F is also treated as a keyed function with its key space $\mathcal{V}$.

Let $\mathsf{pad} : \varSigma^* \to (\varSigma^n)^+$ be a padding function such that

$$\mathsf{pad}(X) = \begin{cases} 0^n & \text{if } X = \varepsilon, \\ X \| 0^{-|X| \bmod n} & \text{otherwise.} \end{cases}$$

The length of $\mathsf{pad}(X)$ is the least positive multiple of n greater than or equal to $|X|$. $\mathsf{pad}(X)$ is parsed as $X_1 \| X_2 \| \cdots \| X_x$, where $x = |\mathsf{pad}(X)|/n$ and $|X_i| = n$ for $i \in [1, x]$. For any integer $\alpha \in [0, 2^{n/2} - 1]$, let $\mathsf{bin}(\alpha)$ be the $(n/2)$-bit binary representation of α.

For $\mathsf{ECtbc} = (\mathsf{KGtbc}, \mathsf{ENtbc}, \mathsf{DEtbc}, \mathsf{VEtbc})$, $\mathsf{KGtbc}(1^n)$ simply outputs K chosen uniformly at random from $\varSigma^n$. The other algorithms are presented in Algorithm 1. ENtbc is also depicted in Fig. 1. From the definition of bin, $|M| \leq 2^{n/2} - 1$ and $|A| \leq 2^{n/2} - 1$. The initialization vector IV is a constant in $\varSigma^n$.

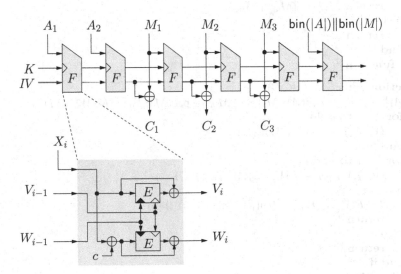

Fig. 1. The encryptment algorithm ENtbc of the proposed scheme. For the TBC E, the key input is V_{i-1} and the tweak input is W_{i-1}.

Algorithm 1. The proposed encryptment using a TBC

---

function ENtbc(K, A, M)
$\quad A_1 \| \cdots \| A_a \leftarrow \mathsf{pad}(A); \; M_1 \| \cdots \| M_m \leftarrow \mathsf{pad}(M); \; V_0 \leftarrow K; \; W_0 \leftarrow IV$
$\quad$**for** $i = 1$ **to** a **do**
$\quad\quad (V_i, W_i) \leftarrow F(V_{i-1}, W_{i-1}, A_i)$
$\quad$**end for**
$\quad$**for** $i = 1$ **to** m **do**
$\quad\quad C_i \leftarrow M_i \oplus W_{a+i-1}; \; (V_{a+i}, W_{a+i}) \leftarrow F(V_{a+i-1}, W_{a+i-1}, M_i)$
$\quad$**end for**
$\quad (B_\mathsf{f}, B_\mathsf{s}) \leftarrow F(V_{a+m}, W_{a+m}, \mathsf{bin}(|A|)\|\mathsf{bin}(|M|)); \; B \leftarrow B_\mathsf{f}\|B_\mathsf{s}$
$\quad$**return** $(\mathsf{msb}_{|M|}(C_1\|C_2\|\cdots\|C_m), B)$
end function

function DEtbc(K, A, C, B)
$\quad A_1 \| \cdots \| A_a \leftarrow \mathsf{pad}(A); \; C_1 \| \cdots \| C_m \leftarrow \mathsf{pad}(C); \; V_0 \leftarrow K; \; W_0 \leftarrow IV$
$\quad$**for** $i = 1$ **to** a **do**
$\quad\quad (V_i, W_i) \leftarrow F(V_{i-1}, W_{i-1}, A_i)$
$\quad$**end for**
$\quad$**for** $i = 1$ **to** $m - 1$ **do**
$\quad\quad M_i \leftarrow C_i \oplus W_{a+i-1}; \; (V_{a+i}, W_{a+i}) \leftarrow F(V_{a+i-1}, W_{a+i-1}, M_i)$
$\quad$**end for**
$\quad M'_m \leftarrow \mathsf{msb}_{|C|-(m-1)n}(C_m \oplus W_{a+m-1})$
$\quad (V_{a+m}, W_{a+m}) \leftarrow F(V_{a+m-1}, W_{a+m-1}, M'_m\|0^{mn-|C|})$
$\quad$**if** $B = F(V_{a+m}, W_{a+m}, \mathsf{bin}(|A|)\|\mathsf{bin}(|C|))$ **then**
$\quad\quad$**return** $M_1\|\cdots\|M_{m-1}\|M'_m$
$\quad$**else**
$\quad\quad$**return** $\perp$
$\quad$**end if**
end function

function VEtbc(A, M, K, B)
$\quad A_1 \| \cdots \| A_a \leftarrow \mathsf{pad}(A); \; M_1 \| \cdots \| M_m \leftarrow \mathsf{pad}(M); \; V_0 \leftarrow K; \; W_0 \leftarrow IV$
$\quad$**for** $i = 1$ **to** a **do**
$\quad\quad (V_i, W_i) \leftarrow F(V_{i-1}, W_{i-1}, A_i)$
$\quad$**end for**
$\quad$**for** $i = 1$ **to** m **do**
$\quad\quad (V_{a+i}, W_{a+i}) \leftarrow F(V_{a+i-1}, W_{a+i-1}, M_i)$
$\quad$**end for**
$\quad$**if** $B = F(V_{a+m}, W_{a+m}, \mathsf{bin}(|A|)\|\mathsf{bin}(|M|))$ **then**
$\quad\quad$**return** 1
$\quad$**else**
$\quad\quad$**return** 0
$\quad$**end if**
end function

4.2   Security

For ECtbc = (KGtbc, ENtbc, DEtbc, VEtbc), two keyed functions $I^E : \mathcal{V} \times \varSigma^* \to \mathcal{V} \times \mathcal{W}$ and $J^E : (\mathcal{V} \times \mathcal{W}) \times \varSigma^* \to \mathcal{W}^+ \times \mathcal{V} \times \mathcal{W}$ are introduced. The key spaces of I^E and J^E are $\mathcal{V}$ and $\mathcal{V} \times \mathcal{W}$, respectively. For $X \in \varSigma^*$, let $X_1 \| \cdots \| X_x \leftarrow \mathsf{pad}(X)$. I^E is defined as follows: $(V_x, W_x) \leftarrow I^E(K, X)$, where $(V_0, W_0) \leftarrow (K, IV)$ and $(V_i, W_i) \leftarrow F(V_{i-1}, W_{i-1}, X_i)$ for $i \in [1, x]$. J^E is defined as follows: $(W_0, \ldots, W_{x-1}, V_x, W_x) \leftarrow J^E(K, L, X)$, where $(V_0, W_0) \leftarrow (K, L)$ and $(V_i, W_i) \leftarrow F(V_{i-1}, W_{i-1}, X_i)$ for $i \in [1, x]$.

Let $\varPsi \triangleq \{\psi \mid \psi(X) \triangleq \psi_0(\varepsilon) \| \psi_0(X_1) \| \psi_0(X_{[1,2]}) \| \cdots \| \psi_1(X_{[1,x]}) \| \psi_0(X_{[1,x]}) \}$, where $X_1 \| \cdots \| X_x \leftarrow \mathsf{pad}(X)$, $X_{[1,i]} \triangleq X_1 \| \cdots \| X_i$ for $i \in [1, x]$, $\psi_0 \in \mathcal{F}_{(\varSigma^n)^*, \varSigma^n}$ and $\psi_1 \in \mathcal{F}_{(\varSigma^n)^+, \varSigma^n}$. Any function $\psi \in \varPsi$ has the same domain and range as $J^E(K, L, \cdot)$, and $|\psi(X)| = |J^E(K, L, X)|$ for any $X \in \varSigma^*$. Suppose that the length of inputs is bounded from above by ℓn for some positive integer ℓ. Then, the uniform random sampling from $\varPsi$ is the uniform random sampling from $\mathcal{F}_{(\varSigma^n)^{[0,\ell]}, \varSigma^n} \times \mathcal{F}_{(\varSigma^n)^{[1,\ell]}, \varSigma^n}$.

For an adversary $\mathbf{A}$, let $T_{\mathbf{A}}$ be the run time of $\mathbf{A}$. Let T_E be the time required to compute E.

Confidentiality. Confidentiality is evaluated in the standard model, that is, on the assumption that E is a TPRP.

Theorem 1. *Let $\mathbf{A}$ be an adversary against ECtbc concerning confidentiality. Suppose that the single query of $\mathbf{A}$ consists of associated data of length at most ℓ_a blocks and a message of length at most ℓ_m blocks after padding. Then, there exists some adversary $\mathbf{B}$ against E concerning TPRP such that*

$$\mathrm{Adv}^{\text{ot-ror}}_{\mathsf{ECtbc}}(\mathbf{A}) \le (\ell_a + \ell_m + 1)(\mathrm{Adv}^{\text{tprp}}_E(\mathbf{B}) + 1/2^n) \ .$$

$\mathbf{B}$ *makes at most two queries. $T_{\mathbf{B}}$ is at most about $T_{\mathbf{A}} + O((\ell_a + \ell_m)T_E)$.*

Theorem 1 follows from Lemmas 2, 3, 4 and 5 given below.

Lemma 2. *For any adversary $\mathbf{A}$ against ECtbc concerning confidentiality, there exist some adversaries $\mathbf{B}$ against I^E, $\mathbf{C}$ against J^E, and $\mathbf{D}$ against F such that*

$$\mathrm{Adv}^{\text{ot-ror}}_{\mathsf{ECtbc}}(\mathbf{A}) \le \mathrm{Adv}^{\text{prf}}_{I^E}(\mathbf{B}) + \mathrm{Adv}^{\text{prf}}_{J^E}(\mathbf{C}) + \mathrm{Adv}^{\text{prf}}_F(\mathbf{D}) \ .$$

Suppose that the single query of $\mathbf{A}$ consists of associated data of length at most ℓ_a blocks and a message of length at most ℓ_m blocks after padding. Then, $\mathbf{B}$ makes a single query to its oracle. $T_{\mathbf{B}}$ is at most about $T_{\mathbf{A}} + O(\ell_m T_E)$. $\mathbf{C}$ makes a single query to its oracle. $T_{\mathbf{C}}$ is at most about $T_{\mathbf{A}} + O(T_E)$. $\mathbf{D}$ makes a single query to its oracle. $T_{\mathbf{D}}$ is at most about $T_{\mathbf{A}}$.

The proof is given in Appendix A.

Lemmas 3 and 4 reduce the PRF security of I^E and J^E to that of the underlying compression function F, respectively. The proofs are omitted due to the page limit.

Lemma 3. *For any adversary* **B** *against* I^E *making only a single query whose length amounts to at most ℓ blocks after padding, there exists some adversary* **B′** *against F such that*

$$\mathrm{Adv}^{\mathrm{prf}}_{\mathsf{I}^E}(\mathbf{B}) \leq \ell \cdot \mathrm{Adv}^{\mathrm{prf}}_F(\mathbf{B'}) \ .$$

B′ *makes a single query and* $\mathrm{T_{B'}}$ *is at most about* $\mathrm{T_B} + O(\ell \cdot \mathrm{T}_E)$.

Lemma 4. *For any adversary* **C** *against* J^E *making only a single query whose length amounts to at most ℓ blocks after padding, there exists some adversary* **C′** *against F such that*

$$\mathrm{Adv}^{\mathrm{prf}}_{\mathsf{J}^E}(\mathbf{C}) \leq \ell \cdot \mathrm{Adv}^{\mathrm{prf}}_F(\mathbf{C'}) \ .$$

C′ *makes a single query and* $\mathrm{T_{C'}}$ *is at most about* $\mathrm{T_C} + O(\ell \cdot \mathrm{T}_E)$.

Lemma 5 reduces the PRF security of F to the TPRP security of the underlying TBC E. The proof is straightforward and omitted.

Lemma 5. *For any adversary* **X** *against F making only a single query, there exists some adversary* **X′** *against E such that*

$$\mathrm{Adv}^{\mathrm{prf}}_F(\mathbf{X}) \leq \mathrm{Adv}^{\mathrm{tprp}}_E(\mathbf{X'}) + 1/2^n \ .$$

X′ *makes at most two queries and* $\mathrm{T_{X'}}$ *is at most about* $\mathrm{T_X}$.

Binding Properties. For sender binding, $\mathsf{DEtbc}(K, A, C, B)$ returns $M \neq \bot$ only if $\mathsf{VEtbc}(A, M, K, B) = 1$:

Theorem 2. *For any adversary* **B** *against* ECtbc *concerning sender binding,* $\mathrm{Adv}^{\mathrm{s\text{-}bind}}_{\mathsf{ECtbc}}(\mathbf{B}) = 0$.

(Strong) receiver binding is evaluated in the ideal model, that is, E is an ideal TBC. The proof is omitted due to the page limit.

Theorem 3. *Let* **C** *be an adversary against* ECtbc *concerning strong receiver binding in the ideal TBC model. Suppose that* **C** *makes all queries to E necessary to compute its output and the number of them is at most $q(< 2^n/3)$. Then,*

$$\mathrm{Adv}^{\mathrm{sr\text{-}bind}}_{\mathsf{ECtbc}}(\mathbf{C}) \leq q/(2^{n-1} - q) \ .$$

Second-Ciphertext Unforgeability. Since ECtbc satisfies strong correctness, Corollary 1 follows from Theorem 2, Theorem 3 and Lemma 1.

Corollary 1. *For any adversary* **A** *against* ECtbc *concerning second-ciphertext unforgeability making at most $q(< 2^n/3)$ queries to E,*

$$\mathrm{Adv}^{\mathrm{scu}}_{\mathsf{ECtbc}}(\mathbf{A}) \leq q/(2^{n-1} - q)$$

in the ideal TBC model.

5   ccAEAD

5.1   Syntax

A scheme of compactly committing authenticated encryption with associated data (ccAEAD) [13] is a symmetric-key cryptographic scheme defined to be a tuple of algorithms $\mathsf{CAE} = (\mathsf{KGE}, \mathsf{ENC}, \mathsf{DEC}, \mathsf{VER})$ specified as follows: Let $\mathcal{K} \triangleq \Sigma^n$ be a key space, $\mathcal{A} \subseteq \Sigma^*$ be an associated-data space, $\mathcal{M} \subseteq \Sigma^*$ be a message space, $\mathcal{C} \subseteq \Sigma^*$ be a ciphertext space, $\mathcal{L} \subseteq \Sigma^*$ be an opening space and $\mathcal{T} \triangleq \Sigma^\ell$ be a binding-tag space.

- KGE is a randomized key generation algorithm. It takes as input a security parameter n in the unary form of 1^n and returns a secret key $K \in \mathcal{K}$ chosen uniformly at random.
- ENC is a randomized encryption algorithm. It takes as input $(K, A, M) \in \mathcal{K} \times \mathcal{A} \times \mathcal{M}$ and returns $(C, B) \in \mathcal{C} \times \mathcal{T}$.
- DEC is a deterministic decryption algorithm. It takes as input $(K, A, C, B) \in \mathcal{K} \times \mathcal{A} \times \mathcal{C} \times \mathcal{T}$ and returns $(M, L) \in \mathcal{M} \times \mathcal{L}$ or $\bot \notin \mathcal{M} \times \mathcal{L}$.
- VER is a deterministic verification algorithm. It takes as input $(A, M, L, B) \in \mathcal{A} \times \mathcal{M} \times \mathcal{L} \times \mathcal{T}$ and returns $b \in \Sigma$.

CAE is required to satisfy correctness: For any $(K, A, M) \in \mathcal{K} \times \mathcal{A} \times \mathcal{M}$, if $(C, B) \leftarrow \mathsf{ENC}(K, A, M)$, then $\mathsf{DEC}(K, A, C, B) = (M', L) \in \mathcal{M} \times \mathcal{L}$, $M' = M$ and $\mathsf{VER}(A, M, L, B) = 1$.

It is also required that $\Sigma^l \subseteq \mathcal{M}$ if there exists $M \in \mathcal{M}$ such that $|M| = l$. For any $(K, A, M) \in \mathcal{K} \times \mathcal{A} \times \mathcal{M}$, let $(C, B) \leftarrow \mathsf{ENC}(K, A, M)$. Then, $|C|$ depends only on $|M|$ and there exists a function $\mathsf{clen} : \mathbb{N} \to \mathbb{N}$ such that $|C| = \mathsf{clen}(|M|)$. B is compact, that is, ℓ is linear in n.

5.2   Security Requirement

The security requirements of a ccAEAD scheme are confidentiality, ciphertext integrity and binding properties.

Confidentiality. Confidentiality of a ccAEAD scheme is defined as real-or-random indistinguishability in the multiple-opening setting. The games MO-REAL and MO-RAND shown in Fig. 2 are introduced. An adversary $\mathbf{A}$ is given access to oracles **Enc**, **Dec** and **ChalEnc**. In both of the games, **Enc** returns $(C, B) \leftarrow \mathsf{ENC}(K, A, M)$ for each query (A, M). For each query (A, C, B), **Dec** returns $(M, L) \leftarrow \mathsf{DEC}(K, A, C, B)$ if the query is a previous answer from **Enc** and $\bot$ otherwise. For each query (A, M), **ChalEnc** returns $(C, B) \leftarrow \mathsf{ENC}(K, A, M)$ in MO-REAL, and $(C, B) \xleftarrow{} \Sigma^{\mathsf{clen}(|M|)} \times \Sigma^\ell$ in MO-RAND. $\mathbf{A}$ is not allowed to ask the same query both to **Enc** and to **ChalEnc**. The advantage of $\mathbf{A}$ concerning confidentiality is defined as follows:

$$\mathrm{Adv}_{\mathsf{CAE}}^{\mathrm{mo\text{-}ror}}(\mathbf{A}) \triangleq \left| \Pr[\mathrm{MO\text{-}REAL}_{\mathsf{CAE}}^{\mathbf{A}} = 1] - \Pr[\mathrm{MO\text{-}RAND}_{\mathsf{CAE}}^{\mathbf{A}} = 1] \right| .$$

$$K \leftarrow \mathsf{KGE}(1^n); \mathcal{Y} \leftarrow \emptyset$$
$$b \leftarrow \mathbf{A}^{\mathbf{Enc,Dec,ChalEnc}}$$
$$\mathbf{return}\ b$$

$\mathbf{Enc}(A, M)$
$(C, B) \leftarrow \mathsf{ENC}(K, A, M)$
$\mathcal{Y} \leftarrow \mathcal{Y} \cup \{(A, C, B)\}$
$\mathbf{return}\ (C, B)$

$\mathbf{Dec}(A, C, B)$
$\mathbf{if}\ (A, C, B) \notin \mathcal{Y}\ \mathbf{then}$
$\quad \mathbf{return}\ \bot$
$\mathbf{end\ if}$
$(M, L) \leftarrow \mathsf{DEC}(K, A, C, B)$
$\mathbf{return}\ (M, L)$

$\mathbf{ChalEnc}(A, M)$
$(C, B) \leftarrow \mathsf{ENC}(K, A, M)$
$\mathbf{return}\ (C, B)$

(a) MO-REAL$_{\mathsf{CAE}}^{\mathbf{A}}$

$$K \leftarrow \mathsf{KGE}(1^n); \mathcal{Y} \leftarrow \emptyset$$
$$b \leftarrow \mathbf{A}^{\mathbf{Enc,Dec,ChalEnc}}$$
$$\mathbf{return}\ b$$

$\mathbf{Enc}(A, M)$
$(C, B) \leftarrow \mathsf{ENC}(K, A, M)$
$\mathcal{Y} \leftarrow \mathcal{Y} \cup \{(A, C, B)\}$
$\mathbf{return}\ (C, B)$

$\mathbf{Dec}(A, C, B)$
$\mathbf{if}\ (A, C, B) \notin \mathcal{Y}\ \mathbf{then}$
$\quad \mathbf{return}\ \bot$
$\mathbf{end\ if}$
$(M, L) \leftarrow \mathsf{DEC}(K, A, C, B)$
$\mathbf{return}\ (M, L)$

$\mathbf{ChalEnc}(A, M)$
$(C, B) \xleftarrow{\ } \Sigma^{\mathsf{clen}(|M|)} \times \Sigma^{\ell}$
$\mathbf{return}\ (C, B)$

(b) MO-RAND$_{\mathsf{CAE}}^{\mathbf{A}}$

Fig. 2. The games for confidentiality of ccAEAD

Ciphertext Integrity. Ciphertext integrity is also defined in the multi-opening setting. The game MO-CTXT$_{\mathsf{CAE}}^{\mathbf{A}}$ shown in Fig. 3 is introduced. An adversary $\mathbf{A}$ is given access to oracles **Enc**, **Dec** and **ChalDec**. The game outputs true if $\mathbf{A}$ succeeds in asking a query (A, C, B) to **ChalDec** such that $\mathsf{DEC}(K, A, C, B) \neq \bot$ and (A, C, B) is not obtained by a previous query to **Enc**. The advantage of $\mathbf{A}$ concerning ciphertext integrity is defined as follows:

$$\mathrm{Adv}_{\mathsf{CAE}}^{\mathsf{mo\text{-}ctxt}}(\mathbf{A}) \triangleq \Pr[\text{MO-CTXT}_{\mathsf{CAE}}^{\mathbf{A}} = \mathbf{true}] .$$

Binding. The advantage of an adversary $\mathbf{A}$ concerning receiver binding is defined as follows:

$$\mathrm{Adv}_{\mathsf{CAE}}^{\mathsf{r\text{-}bind}}(\mathbf{A}) \triangleq \Pr[((A, M, L), (A', M', L'), B) \leftarrow \mathbf{A} :$$
$$(A, M) \neq (A', M') \wedge$$
$$\mathsf{VER}(A, M, L, B) = \mathsf{VER}(A', M', L', B) = 1] .$$

The advantage of an adversary $\mathbf{A}$ concerning strong receiver binding is defined as follows:

$$\mathrm{Adv}_{\mathsf{CAE}}^{\mathsf{sr\text{-}bind}}(\mathbf{A}) \triangleq \Pr[((A, M, L), (A', M', L'), B) \leftarrow \mathbf{A} :$$
$$(A, M, L) \neq (A', M', L') \wedge$$
$$\mathsf{VER}(A, M, L, B) = \mathsf{VER}(A', M', L', B) = 1] .$$

$K \leftarrow \mathsf{KGE}(1^n); \ win \leftarrow \texttt{false}$
$\mathbf{A}^{\mathbf{Enc,Dec,ChalDec}}$

return win

Enc(A, M)
$(C, B) \leftarrow \mathsf{ENC}(K, A, M)$
$\mathcal{Y} \leftarrow \mathcal{Y} \cup \{(A, C, B)\}$
return (C, B)

Dec(A, C, B)
return $\mathsf{DEC}(K, A, C, B)$

ChalDec(A, C, B)
if $(A, C, B) \in \mathcal{Y}$ **then**
   return $\bot$
end if
if $\mathsf{DEC}(K, A, C, B) \neq \bot$ **then**
   $win \leftarrow \texttt{true}$
end if
return $\mathsf{DEC}(K, A, C, B)$

Fig. 3. The Game MO-CTXT$^{\mathbf{A}}_{\mathsf{CAE}}$ for ciphertext integrity of ccAEAD

It is easy to see that, for any adversary $\mathbf{A}$, $\mathrm{Adv}^{\text{r-bind}}_{\mathsf{CAE}}(\mathbf{A}) \leq \mathrm{Adv}^{\text{sr-bind}}_{\mathsf{CAE}}(\mathbf{A})$.

The advantage of an adversary $\mathbf{A}$ concerning sender binding is defined as follows:

$$\mathrm{Adv}^{\text{s-bind}}_{\mathsf{CAE}}(\mathbf{A}) \triangleq \Pr[(K, A, C, B) \leftarrow \mathbf{A} : \mathsf{DEC}(K, A, C, B) \neq \bot$$
$$(M, L) \leftarrow \mathsf{DEC}(K, A, C, B) \wedge \mathsf{VER}(A, M, L, B) = 0] \ .$$

5.3 Scheme

A ccAEAD scheme CAEtbc $\triangleq$ (KGEtbc, ENCtbc, DECtbc, VERtbc) can be constructed with the encryptment scheme ECtbc and a TBC. Thus, CAEtbc is constructed only with a TBC. The algorithms of ENCtbc, DECtbc and VERtbc are presented in Algorithm 2. KGEtbc(1^n) simply outputs $K \xleftarrow{\$} \Sigma^n$.

5.4 Security

For an adversary $\mathbf{A}$, let $\mathrm{T}_{\mathbf{A}}$ be the run time of $\mathbf{A}$. Let T_E be the time required to compute E.

Confidentiality

Theorem 4. *Let $\mathbf{A}$ be an adversary against CAEtbc concerning confidentiality. Suppose that $\mathbf{A}$ makes at most q_e, q_d and q_c queries to the oracles **Enc**, **Dec** and **ChalEnc**, respectively. Suppose that each query to **Enc** or **ChalEnc** consists of associated data of length at most ℓ_a blocks and a message of length at most ℓ_m blocks after padding. Then, there exist some adversaries $\mathbf{D}$ against E concerning TPRP and $\mathbf{D}'$ against ECtbc concerning confidentiality such that*

$$\mathrm{Adv}^{\text{mo-ror}}_{\mathsf{CAEtbc}}(\mathbf{A}) \leq 2 \cdot \mathrm{Adv}^{\text{tprp}}_E(\mathbf{D}) + q_c \cdot \mathrm{Adv}^{\text{ot-ror}}_{\mathsf{ECtbc}}(\mathbf{D}') + 5(q_e + q_c)^2/2^n \ .$$

$\mathbf{D}$ makes at most $2(q_e + q_c)$ queries. $\mathrm{T}_{\mathbf{D}}$ is at most about $\mathrm{T}_{\mathbf{A}} + O((q_e + q_c)(\ell_a + \ell_m)\mathrm{T}_E)$. $\mathbf{D}'$ makes at most a single query consisting of associated data of length at most ℓ_a blocks and a message of length at most ℓ_m blocks after padding. $\mathrm{T}_{\mathbf{D}'}$ is at most about $\mathrm{T}_{\mathbf{A}} + O((q_e + q_c)(\ell_a + \ell_m)\mathrm{T}_E)$.

Algorithm 2. The proposed ccAEAD scheme using a TBC

---

function ENCtbc(K, A, M)
  $N \twoheadleftarrow \Sigma^n$; $L \leftarrow E_K^0(N)$
  $(C, B) \leftarrow$ ENtbc(L, A, M); $T \leftarrow E_K^{B_f}(B_s)$ $\triangleright$ $B = B_f \| B_s$ and $|B_f| = |B_s| = n$
  return $((N, C, T), B)$
end function

function DECtbc$(K, A, (N, C, T), B)$
  if $E_K^{B_f}(B_s) \neq T$ then
    return $\perp$
  end if
  $L \leftarrow E_K^0(N)$; $M \leftarrow$ DEtbc(L, A, C, B)
  if $M = \perp$ then
    return $\perp$
  end if
  return (M, L)
end function

function VERtbc(A, M, L, B)
  return VEtbc(A, M, L, B)
end function

Proof. First, two adversaries $\mathbf{D}_0$ and $\mathbf{D}_1$ against E concerning TPRP are considered. Both of them have oracle access to $E_{K'}$ or ϖ, where $K' \twoheadleftarrow \Sigma^n$ and $\varpi \twoheadleftarrow \mathcal{P}_{\Sigma^n \times \Sigma^n}$. $\mathbf{D}_0$ and $\mathbf{D}_1$ simulates MO-REAL$_{\mathsf{CAE}}^{\mathbf{A}}$ and MO-RAND$_{\mathsf{CAE}}^{\mathbf{A}}$, respectively. They run $\mathbf{A}$ and simulates its oracles $\mathbf{Enc}$, $\mathbf{Dec}$ and $\mathbf{ChalEnc}$ for $\mathbf{A}$ using their oracle instead of E_K, where $K \twoheadleftarrow \Sigma^n$. Then, $\mathbf{D}_0^{E_{K'}}$ and $\mathbf{D}_1^{E_{K'}}$ are equivalent to MO-REAL$_{\mathsf{CAE}}^{\mathbf{A}}$ and MO-RAND$_{\mathsf{CAE}}^{\mathbf{A}}$, respectively. Thus,

$$
\begin{aligned}
\mathrm{Adv}_{\mathsf{CAE}}^{\mathrm{mo\text{-}ror}}(\mathbf{A}) &= \left| \Pr[\text{MO-REAL}_{\mathsf{CAE}}^{\mathbf{A}} = 1] - \Pr[\text{MO-RAND}_{\mathsf{CAE}}^{\mathbf{A}} = 1] \right| \\
&= \left| \Pr[\mathbf{D}_0^{E_{K'}} = 1] - \Pr[\mathbf{D}_1^{E_{K'}} = 1] \right| \\
&\leq \left| \Pr[\mathbf{D}_0^{E_{K'}} = 1] - \Pr[\mathbf{D}_0^{\varpi} = 1] \right| + \left| \Pr[\mathbf{D}_1^{E_{K'}} = 1] - \Pr[\mathbf{D}_1^{\varpi} = 1] \right| \\
&\quad + \left| \Pr[\mathbf{D}_0^{\varpi} = 1] - \Pr[\mathbf{D}_1^{\varpi} = 1] \right| .
\end{aligned}
$$

$\mathbf{D}_0$ makes at most $2(q_e + q_c)$ queries to its oracle, and $\mathbf{D}_1$ makes at most $2q_e$ queries to its oracle. $\mathbf{T}_{\mathbf{D}_0}$ as well as $\mathbf{T}_{\mathbf{D}_1}$ is at most about $\mathbf{T}_{\mathbf{A}} + O((q_e + q_c)(\ell_a + \ell_m)\mathbf{T}_E)$. Notice that it is not necessary for $\mathbf{D}_0$ and $\mathbf{D}_1$ to make queries to their oracles to answer to the queries made by $\mathbf{A}$ to $\mathbf{Dec}$.

There exists some adversary $\mathbf{D}$ against E concerning TPRP such that

$$
\left| \Pr[\mathbf{D}_0^{E_{K'}} = 1] - \Pr[\mathbf{D}_0^{\varpi} = 1] \right| + \left| \Pr[\mathbf{D}_1^{E_{K'}} = 1] - \Pr[\mathbf{D}_1^{\varpi} = 1] \right| \leq 2 \cdot \mathrm{Adv}_E^{\mathrm{tprp}}(\mathbf{D}) ,
$$

$\mathbf{D}$ makes at most $2(q_e + q_c)$ queries. $\mathbf{T}_{\mathbf{D}}$ is at most about $\mathbf{T}_{\mathbf{A}} + O((q_e + q_c)(\ell_a + \ell_m)\mathbf{T}_E)$.

Suppose that $\rho \twoheadleftarrow \mathcal{F}_{\Sigma^n \times \Sigma^n, \Sigma^n}$. Then, since ρ is distinguishable from ϖ only if a collision is found for ρ among the outputs corresponding to a value of the tweak input,

$$\left|\Pr[\mathbf{D}_0^{\varpi} = 1] - \Pr[\mathbf{D}_1^{\varpi} = 1]\right|$$
$$\leq \left|\Pr[\mathbf{D}_0^{\varpi} = 1] - \Pr[\mathbf{D}_0^{\rho} = 1]\right| + \left|\Pr[\mathbf{D}_1^{\varpi} = 1] - \Pr[\mathbf{D}_1^{\rho} = 1]\right|$$
$$+ \left|\Pr[\mathbf{D}_0^{\rho} = 1] - \Pr[\mathbf{D}_1^{\rho} = 1]\right|$$
$$\leq (q_e + q_c)^2/2^{n-1} + q_e^2/2^{n-1} + \left|\Pr[\mathbf{D}_0^{\rho} = 1] - \Pr[\mathbf{D}_1^{\rho} = 1]\right| .$$

Let $\mathbf{D}_2$ be an adversary against ECtbc concerning confidentiality. $\mathbf{D}_2$ has q_c oracles which are either $(\mathsf{ENtbc}_{L_1}, \ldots, \mathsf{ENtbc}_{L_{q_c}})$ or $(\$_1, \ldots, \$_{q_c})$. $\mathbf{D}_2$ simulates $\mathbf{D}_0^{\rho}$. During the simulation, for the i-th query (A_i, M_i) to $\mathbf{ChalEnc}$ made by $\mathbf{A}$, where $1 \leq i \leq q_c$, $\mathbf{D}_2$ transfers it to its i-th oracle and gets an answer (C_i, B_i). $\mathbf{D}_2$ also generates $N_i \twoheadleftarrow \Sigma^n$ and computes $T_i \leftarrow \rho(B_{i,\mathrm{f}}, B_{i,\mathrm{s}})$, where $B_i = B_{i,\mathrm{f}} \| B_{i,\mathrm{s}}$. $\mathbf{D}_2$ returns $((N_i, C_i, T_i), B_i)$ to $\mathbf{A}$. Then,

$$\left|\Pr[\mathbf{D}_0^{\rho} = 1] - \Pr[\mathbf{D}_1^{\rho} = 1]\right| \leq \left|\Pr[\mathbf{D}_0^{\rho} = 1] - \Pr[\mathbf{D}_2^{\mathsf{ENtbc}_{L_1}, \ldots, \mathsf{ENtbc}_{L_{q_c}}} = 1]\right|$$
$$+ \left|\Pr[\mathbf{D}_2^{\mathsf{ENtbc}_{L_1}, \ldots, \mathsf{ENtbc}_{L_{q_c}}} = 1] - \Pr[\mathbf{D}_1^{\rho} = 1]\right|$$
$$\leq (q_e + q_c)^2/2^{n+1} + \left|\Pr[\mathbf{D}_2^{\mathsf{ENtbc}_{L_1}, \ldots, \mathsf{ENtbc}_{L_{q_c}}} = 1] - \Pr[\mathbf{D}_1^{\rho} = 1]\right|$$

since $\mathbf{D}_0^{\rho}$ and $\mathbf{D}_2^{\mathsf{ENtbc}_{L_1}, \ldots, \mathsf{ENtbc}_{L_{q_c}}}$ are identical to each other until a collision is found among the values of the nonce N. Furthermore,

$$\left|\Pr[\mathbf{D}_2^{\mathsf{ENtbc}_{L_1}, \ldots, \mathsf{ENtbc}_{L_{q_c}}} = 1] - \Pr[\mathbf{D}_1^{\rho} = 1]\right|$$
$$\leq \left|\Pr[\mathbf{D}_2^{\mathsf{ENtbc}_{L_1}, \ldots, \mathsf{ENtbc}_{L_{q_c}}} = 1] - \Pr[\mathbf{D}_2^{\$_1, \ldots, \$_{q_c}} = 1]\right|$$
$$+ \left|\Pr[\mathbf{D}_2^{\$_1, \ldots, \$_{q_c}} = 1] - \Pr[\mathbf{D}_1^{\rho} = 1]\right|$$
$$\leq \left|\Pr[\mathbf{D}_2^{\mathsf{ENtbc}_{L_1}, \ldots, \mathsf{ENtbc}_{L_{q_c}}} = 1] - \Pr[\mathbf{D}_2^{\$_1, \ldots, \$_{q_c}} = 1]\right| + q_c^2/2^{n+1}$$

since $\mathbf{D}_1^{\rho}$ and $\mathbf{D}_2^{\$_1, \ldots, \$_{q_c}}$ are identical to each other until a collision is found among the values of the binding tag B in the answers of $\mathbf{ChalEnc}$. $\mathbf{D}_2$ makes at most a single query to each of its oracles. $\mathbf{T}_{\mathbf{D}_2}$ is at most about $\mathbf{T}_{\mathbf{A}} + O((q_e + q_c)(\ell_a + \ell_m)\mathbf{T}_E)$.

From the hybrid argument, there exists some adversary $\mathbf{D}'$ such that

$$\left|\Pr[\mathbf{D}_2^{\mathsf{ENtbc}_{L_1}, \ldots, \mathsf{ENtbc}_{L_{q_c}}} = 1] - \Pr[\mathbf{D}_2^{\$_1, \ldots, \$_{q_c}} = 1]\right| \leq q_c \cdot \mathsf{Adv}_{\mathsf{ECtbc}}^{\mathsf{ot\text{-}ror}}(\mathbf{D}').$$

$\mathbf{D}'$ makes at most a single query to its oracle. $\mathbf{T}_{\mathbf{D}'}$ is at most about $\mathbf{T}_{\mathbf{A}} + O((q_e + q_c)(\ell_a + \ell_m)\mathbf{T}_E)$. $\square$

Corollary 2 follows from Theorems 1 and 4.

Corollary 2. *Let $\mathbf{A}$ be an adversary against CAEtbc concerning confidentiality. Suppose that $\mathbf{A}$ makes at most q_e, q_d and q_c queries to the oracles $\mathbf{Enc}$, $\mathbf{Dec}$ and $\mathbf{ChalEnc}$, respectively. Suppose that each query to $\mathbf{Enc}$ or $\mathbf{ChalEnc}$ consists of associated data of length at most ℓ_a blocks and a message of length at most ℓ_m blocks after padding. Then, there exist some adversaries $\mathbf{D}$ and $\mathbf{D}'$ against E*

concerning TPRP such that

$$\mathrm{Adv}^{\mathrm{mo\text{-}ror}}_{\mathsf{CAEtbc}}(\mathbf{A}) \leq 2 \cdot \mathrm{Adv}^{\mathrm{tprp}}_{E}(\mathbf{D}) + q_{\mathrm{c}}(\ell_{\mathrm{a}} + \ell_{\mathrm{m}} + 1) \cdot \mathrm{Adv}^{\mathrm{tprp}}_{E}(\mathbf{D}')$$
$$+ 5(q_{\mathrm{e}} + q_{\mathrm{c}})^2/2^n + q_{\mathrm{c}}(\ell_{\mathrm{a}} + \ell_{\mathrm{m}} + 1)/2^n.$$

$\mathbf{D}$ *makes at most* $2(q_{\mathrm{e}} + q_{\mathrm{c}})$ *queries and* $\mathbf{D}'$ *makes at most 2 queries.* $\mathrm{T_D}$ *as well as* $\mathrm{T_{D'}}$ *is at most about* $\mathrm{T_A} + O((q_{\mathrm{e}} + q_{\mathrm{c}})(\ell_{\mathrm{a}} + \ell_{\mathrm{m}})\mathrm{T}_E)$.

Ciphertext Integrity. Ciphertext integrity of CAEtbc is discussed in the ideal TBC model. Let $\mathsf{f}^E : (\Sigma^n)^3 \to \Sigma^n$ be a compression function such that $\mathsf{f}^E(V, W, X) \triangleq E^W_V(X) \oplus X$. Notice that $F(V, W, X) = (\mathsf{f}^E(V, W, X), \mathsf{f}^E(V, W, X \oplus c))$.

Theorem 5. *For any adversary* $\mathbf{A}$ *against* CAEtbc *concerning ciphertext integrity, there exist some adversaries* $\mathbf{B}$ *against* ECtbc *concerning strong receiver binding and* $\mathbf{C}$ *aganist* f^E *concerning everywhere preimage resistance such that*

$$\mathrm{Adv}^{\mathrm{mo\text{-}ctxt}}_{\mathsf{CAEtbc}}(\mathbf{A}) \leq \mathrm{Adv}^{\mathrm{sr\text{-}bind}}_{\mathsf{ECtbc}}(\mathbf{B}) + \mathrm{Adv}^{\mathrm{epre}}_{\mathsf{f}^E}(\mathbf{C}) + \frac{\sigma}{2^n} + \frac{1}{2^n - (q_{\mathrm{e}} + q_{\mathrm{d}} + q_{\mathrm{c}})},$$

where $\mathbf{A}$ *is assumed to make at most* q_{e}, q_{d} *and* q_{c} *queries to the oracles* **Enc**, **Dec** *and* **ChalDec**, *respectively, and* $\mathrm{MO\text{-}CTXT}^{\mathbf{A}}_{\mathsf{CAEtbc}}$ *is assumed to make at most* σ *queries in total to the ideal TBC* E. *Both* $\mathbf{B}$ *and* $\mathbf{C}$ *make at most* σ *queries to* E.

The proof is given in Appendix B.

Similar proofs to that of Lemma 6 are given to the Davies-Meyer compression function in [6,7].

Lemma 6. *For any adversary* $\mathbf{C}$ *making at most* σ *queries to* E,

$$\mathrm{Adv}^{\mathrm{epre}}_{\mathsf{f}^E}(\mathbf{C}) \leq \sigma/(2^n - \sigma)$$

in the ideal TBC model.

Corollary 3 follows from Theorem 3, Theorem 5 and Lemma 6.

Corollary 3. *Let* $\mathbf{A}$ *be an adversary against* CAEtbc *concerning ciphertext integrity. Suppose that* $\mathbf{A}$ *makes at most* q_{e}, q_{d} *and* q_{c} *queries to the oracles* **Enc**, **Dec** *and* **ChalDec**, *respectively, and that* $\mathrm{MO\text{-}CTXT}^{\mathbf{A}}_{\mathsf{CAEtbc}}$ *makes at most* $\sigma(< 2^{n-2})$ *queries in total to the ideal TBC* E. *Then,*

$$\mathrm{Adv}^{\mathrm{mo\text{-}ctxt}}_{\mathsf{CAEtbc}}(\mathbf{A}) \leq \frac{\sigma}{3 \cdot 2^{n-6}} + \frac{1}{2^n - (q_{\mathrm{e}} + q_{\mathrm{d}} + q_{\mathrm{c}})}.$$

Acknowledgements. The author was supported in part by JSPS KAKENHI Grant Number JP18H05289.

A   Proof of Lemma 2

From the definition of confidentiality,

$$\mathrm{Adv}^{\text{ot-ror}}_{\mathsf{ECtbc}}(\mathbf{A}) = \left| \Pr[\mathbf{A}^{\mathsf{ENtbc}_K} = 1] - \Pr[\mathbf{A}^{\$} = 1] \right|,$$

where $K \twoheadleftarrow \varSigma^n$. For a query (A, M), $\$$ returns an element chosen uniformly at random from $\varSigma^{|C|} \times \varSigma^{|B|}$, where $(C, B) \leftarrow \mathsf{ENtbc}_K(A, M)$. Notice that ENtbc_K is described with I^E and J^E as shown in Fig. 4. Let FJ_ρ be the function shown in Fig. 5. It is obtained by replacing I^E_K of ENtbc_K in Fig. 4 with ρ. If $\rho \twoheadleftarrow \mathcal{F}_{\varSigma^*, \mathcal{V} \times \mathcal{W}}$, then

$$\mathrm{Adv}^{\text{ot-ror}}_{\mathsf{ECtbc}}(\mathbf{A}) \le \left| \Pr[\mathbf{A}^{\mathsf{ENtbc}_K} = 1] - \Pr[\mathbf{A}^{\mathsf{FJ}_\rho} = 1] \right| + \left| \Pr[\mathbf{A}^{\mathsf{FJ}_\rho} = 1] - \Pr[\mathbf{A}^{\$} = 1] \right|$$

and there exists an adversary $\mathbf{B}$ against I^E such that

$$\left| \Pr[\mathbf{A}^{\mathsf{ENtbc}_K} = 1] - \Pr[\mathbf{A}^{\mathsf{FJ}_\rho} = 1] \right| = \mathrm{Adv}^{\text{prf}}_{\mathsf{I}^E}(\mathbf{B}).$$

$\mathbf{B}$ runs $\mathbf{A}$ and simulates the oracle of $\mathbf{A}$. If the oracle of $\mathbf{B}$ is I^E_K, then $\mathbf{A}$ is given access to ENtbc_K. If the oracle of $\mathbf{B}$ is ρ, then $\mathbf{A}$ is given access to FJ_ρ. $\mathbf{B}$ makes a single query to its oracle. $\mathbf{T_B}$ is at most about $\mathbf{T_A} + O(\ell_m \mathbf{T}_E)$.

Let F_ψ be the function shown in Fig. 6, where $\psi \in \varPsi$. Then, since $\mathbf{A}$ makes just a single query, FJ_ρ is equivalent to $\mathsf{F}_{\mathsf{J}^E_{(R,S)}}$ if $\rho \twoheadleftarrow \mathcal{F}_{\varSigma^*, \mathcal{V} \times \mathcal{W}}$ and $(R, S) \twoheadleftarrow \varSigma^n \times \varSigma^n$. Thus, if $\psi \twoheadleftarrow \varPsi$, then

$$\left| \Pr[\mathbf{A}^{\mathsf{FJ}_\rho} = 1] - \Pr[\mathbf{A}^{\$} = 1] \right|$$
$$\le \left| \Pr[\mathbf{A}^{\mathsf{F}_{\mathsf{J}^E_{(R,S)}}} = 1] - \Pr[\mathbf{A}^{\mathsf{F}_\psi} = 1] \right| + \left| \Pr[\mathbf{A}^{\mathsf{F}_\psi} = 1] - \Pr[\mathbf{A}^{\$} = 1] \right|.$$

There exists an adversary $\mathbf{C}$ against J^E such that

$$\left| \Pr[\mathbf{A}^{\mathsf{F}_{\mathsf{J}^E_{(R,S)}}} = 1] - \Pr[\mathbf{A}^{\mathsf{F}_\psi} = 1] \right| = \mathrm{Adv}^{\text{prf}}_{\mathsf{J}^E}(\mathbf{C}).$$

$\mathbf{C}$ runs $\mathbf{A}$ and simulates the oracle of $\mathbf{A}$ using its oracle which is either $\mathsf{J}^E_{(R,S)}$ or ψ. $\mathbf{C}$ makes a single query to its oracle. $\mathbf{T_C}$ is at most about $\mathbf{T_A} + O(\mathbf{T}_E)$.

There also exists an adversary $\mathbf{D}$ against F such that

$$\left| \Pr[\mathbf{A}^{\mathsf{F}_\psi} = 1] - \Pr[\mathbf{A}^{\$} = 1] \right| = \mathrm{Adv}^{\text{prf}}_F(\mathbf{D}).$$

$\mathbf{D}$ runs $\mathbf{A}$ and simulates the oracle of $\mathbf{A}$ using its oracle, which is either F_V or ν, where $V \twoheadleftarrow \varSigma^n$ and $\nu \twoheadleftarrow \mathcal{F}_{\mathcal{W} \times \mathcal{X}, \mathcal{V} \times \mathcal{W}}$. If the oracle of $\mathbf{D}$ is F_V, then $\mathbf{A}$ is given access to F_ψ. If the oracle of $\mathbf{D}$ is ν, then $\mathbf{A}$ is given access to $\$$. $\mathbf{D}$ makes a single query to its oracle. $\mathbf{T_D}$ is at most about $\mathbf{T_A}$.

```
function ENtbc_K(A, M)
    A_1‖···‖A_a ← pad(A); M_1‖···‖M_m ← pad(M)
    (R, S) ← I_K^E(A)
    (W_0, W_1, ..., W_{m-1}, V_m, W_m) ← J_{(R,S)}^E(M)
    (B_f, B_s) ← F(V_m, W_m, bin(|A|)‖bin(|M|))
    C ← M ⊕ msb_{|M|}(W_0‖W_1‖···‖W_{m-1}); B ← B_f‖B_s
    return (C, B)
end function
```

Fig. 4. Description of ENtbc using I^E and J^E

```
function FJ_ρ(A, M)
    A_1‖···‖A_a ← pad(A); M_1‖···‖M_m ← pad(M)
    (R, S) ← ρ(A)
    (W_0, W_1, ..., W_{m-1}, V_m, W_m) ← J_{(R,S)}^E(M)
    (B_f, B_s) ← F(V_m, W_m, bin(|A|)‖bin(|M|))
    C ← M ⊕ msb_{|M|}(W_0‖W_1‖···‖W_{m-1}); B ← B_f‖B_s
    return (C, B)
end function
```

Fig. 5. $FJ_ρ$

B   Proof of Theorem 5

Suppose that $\text{MO-CTXT}_{\text{CAEtbc}}^{\mathbf{A}} = \texttt{true}$. Let $Q^* \triangleq (A^*, (N^*, C^*, T^*), B^*)$ be the query to **ChalDec** by $\mathbf{A}$ which causes $win \leftarrow \texttt{true}$. Let $(M^*, L^*) \leftarrow \text{DECtbc}(K, A^*, (N^*, C^*, T^*), B^*)$.

First, suppose that $\mathbf{A}$ already obtains a tuple $(A, (N, C, T), B)$ by a query (A, M) to **Enc** such that $B = B^*$ before asking Q^*. Then, since $B = B^*$, $T = T^*$ and $(A, N, C) \neq (A^*, N^*, C^*)$. Let $L \leftarrow E_K^0(N)$. Then, $L = L^*$ if and only if $N = N^*$. Thus, $(A, L, C) \neq (A^*, L^*, C^*)$. If $(A, L, C) \neq (A^*, L^*, C^*)$ and $(A, L) = (A^*, L^*)$, then $C \neq C^*$ and $M \neq M^*$. Thus, $(A, L, C) \neq (A^*, L^*, C^*)$ implies $(A, L, M) \neq (A^*, L^*, M^*)$, which contradicts the strong receiver binding property of ECtbc.

```
function F_ψ(A, M)
    A_1‖···‖A_a ← pad(A); M_1‖···‖M_m ← pad(M)
    (W_0, W_1, ..., W_{m-1}, V_m, W_m) ← ψ(M)
    (B_f, B_s) ← F(V_m, W_m, bin(|A|)‖bin(|M|))
    C ← M ⊕ msb_{|M|}(W_0‖W_1‖···‖W_{m-1}); B ← B_f‖B_s
    return (C, B)
end function
```

Fig. 6. $F_ψ$

Let **B** be an adversary against ECtbc concerning the strong receiver binding. **B** simulates MO-CTXT$^{\mathbf{A}}_{\mathsf{CAEtbc}}$. If a query $(A^*, (N^*, C^*, T^*), B^*)$ to **ChalDec** by **A** causes $win \leftarrow$ **true** and **A** obtains $(A, (N, C, T), B^*)$ by a query (A, M) to **Enc** before the query $(A^*, (N^*, C^*, T^*), B^*)$, then **B** outputs a pair of (L, A, M) and (L^*, A^*, M^*), where $(M^*, L^*) \leftarrow \mathsf{DECtbc}(K, A^*, (N^*, C^*, T^*), B^*)$ and $L \leftarrow E^0_K(N)$. **B** aborts otherwise. **B** makes at most σ queries to E.

Second, suppose that B^* is new. Namely, **A** does not obtain a tuple $(A, (N, C, T), B)$ by a query (A, M) to **Enc** such that $B = B^*$ before asking Q^*. If $B^*_{\mathsf{f}} = \mathbf{0}$, then **A** finds (V, W, X) satisfying $E^W_V(X) \oplus X = \mathbf{0}$, which contradicts the everywhere preimage resistance of f^E. If $B^*_0 \neq \mathbf{0}$, then **A** finds (B^*, T^*) satisfying $T^* = E^{B^*_0}_K(B^*_1)$ with probability at most $\sigma/2^n + 1/(2^n - (q_{\mathsf{e}} + q_{\mathsf{d}} + q_{\mathsf{c}}))$.

Let **C** be an adversary against f^E concerning everywhere preimage resistance. **C** simulates MO-CTXT$^{\mathbf{A}}_{\mathsf{CAEtbc}}$. If a query $(A^*, (N^*, C^*, T^*), B^*)$ to **ChalDec** by **A** causes $win \leftarrow$ **true**, B^* is new and $B^*_{\mathsf{f}} = \mathbf{0}$, then **C** outputs the input to the last invocation of F in $\mathsf{ENtbc}(L^*, A^*, M^*)$, where $(M^*, L^*) \leftarrow \mathsf{DEtbc}(K, A^*, (N^*, C^*, T^*), B^*)$.

References

1. Beierle, C., et al.: The SKINNY family of block ciphers and its low-latency variant MANTIS. In: Robshaw, M., Katz, J. (eds.) CRYPTO 2016. LNCS, vol. 9815, pp. 123–153. Springer, Heidelberg (2016). https://doi.org/10.1007/978-3-662-53008-5_5

2. Bellare, M., Kohno, T.: A theoretical treatment of related-key attacks: RKA-PRPs, RKA-PRFs, and applications. In: Biham, E. (ed.) EUROCRYPT 2003. LNCS, vol. 2656, pp. 491–506. Springer, Heidelberg (2003). https://doi.org/10.1007/3-540-39200-9_31

3. Bellare, M., Namprempre, C.: Authenticated encryption: relations among notions and analysis of the generic composition paradigm. In: Okamoto, T. (ed.) ASIACRYPT 2000. LNCS, vol. 1976, pp. 531–545. Springer, Heidelberg (2000). https://doi.org/10.1007/3-540-44448-3_41

4. Bellare, M., Ristenpart, T.: Multi-property-preserving hash domain extension and the EMD transform. In: Lai, X., Chen, K. (eds.) ASIACRYPT 2006. LNCS, vol. 4284, pp. 299–314. Springer, Heidelberg (2006). https://doi.org/10.1007/11935230_20

5. Berti, F., Guo, C., Pereira, O., Peters, T., Standaert, F.X.: TEDT, a leakage-resilient AEAD mode for high (physical) security applications. Cryptology ePrint Archive, Report 2019/137 (2019). https://eprint.iacr.org/2019/137

6. Black, J., Rogaway, P., Shrimpton, T.: Black-box analysis of the block-cipher-based hash-function constructions from PGV. In: Yung, M. (ed.) CRYPTO 2002. LNCS, vol. 2442, pp. 320–335. Springer, Heidelberg (2002). https://doi.org/10.1007/3-540-45708-9_21

7. Black, J., Rogaway, P., Shrimpton, T., Stam, M.: An analysis of the blockcipher-based hash functions from PGV. J. Cryptol. **23**(4), 519–545 (2010)

8. Chen, L., Tang, Q.: People who live in glass houses should not throw stones: targeted opening message franking schemes. Cryptology ePrint Archive, Report 2018/994 (2018). https://eprint.iacr.org/2018/994

9. Dodis, Y., Grubbs, P., Ristenpart, T., Woodage, J.: Fast message franking: from invisible salamanders to encryptment. In: Shacham, H., Boldyreva, A. (eds.) CRYPTO 2018. LNCS, vol. 10991, pp. 155–186. Springer, Cham (2018). https://doi.org/10.1007/978-3-319-96884-1_6
10. Facebook: Facebook messenger. https://www.messenger.com. Accessed 16 Apr 2020
11. Facebook: Messenger secret conversations. Technical Whitepaper (2016)
12. FIPS PUB 198–1: The keyed-hash message authentication code (HMAC) (2008)
13. Grubbs, P., Lu, J., Ristenpart, T.: Message franking via committing authenticated encryption. In: Katz, J., Shacham, H. (eds.) CRYPTO 2017. LNCS, vol. 10403, pp. 66–97. Springer, Cham (2017). https://doi.org/10.1007/978-3-319-63697-9_3
14. Hirose, S.: Some plausible constructions of double-block-length Hash functions. In: Robshaw, M. (ed.) FSE 2006. LNCS, vol. 4047, pp. 210–225. Springer, Heidelberg (2006). https://doi.org/10.1007/11799313_14
15. Huguenin-Dumittan, L., Leontiadis, I.: A message franking channel. Cryptology ePrint Archive, Report 2018/920 (2018). https://eprint.iacr.org/2018/920
16. Jakobsson, M., Sako, K., Impagliazzo, R.: Designated verifier proofs and their applications. In: Maurer, U. (ed.) EUROCRYPT 1996. LNCS, vol. 1070, pp. 143–154. Springer, Heidelberg (1996). https://doi.org/10.1007/3-540-68339-9_13
17. Jean, J., Nikolić, I., Peyrin, T., Seurin, Y.: Deoxys v1.41 (2016)
18. Katz, J., Yung, M.: Complete characterization of security notions for probabilistic private-key encryption. In: Proceedings of the Thirty-Second Annual ACM Symposium on Theory of Computing, pp. 245–254 (2000)
19. Leontiadis, I., Vaudenay, S.: Private message franking with after opening privacy. Cryptology ePrint Archive, Report 2018/938 (2018). https://eprint.iacr.org/2018/938
20. Signal Foundation: Signal. https://signal.org/. Accessed 16 Apr 2020
21. Tyagi, N., Grubbs, P., Len, J., Miers, I., Ristenpart, T.: Asymmetric message franking: content moderation for metadata-private end-to-end encryption. In: Boldyreva, A., Micciancio, D. (eds.) CRYPTO 2019. LNCS, vol. 11694, pp. 222–250. Springer, Cham (2019). https://doi.org/10.1007/978-3-030-26954-8_8
22. WhatsApp: WhatsApp Messenger. https://www.whatsapp.com. Accessed 16 Apr 2020

Model Poisoning Defense on Federated Learning: A Validation Based Approach

Yuao Wang[1] , Tianqing Zhu[1](✉) , Wenhan Chang[1] , Sheng Shen[2] ,
and Wei Ren[1]

[1] China University of Geosciences, Wuhan, China
tianqing.e.zhu@gmail.com
[2] School of Computer Science, University of Technology Sydney, Sydney, Australia
Sheng.Shen-1@student.uts.edu.au

Abstract. Federated learning is an improved distributed machine learning approach for privacy preservation. All clients collaboratively train the model using on-device data, and the centralized server only aggregates clients' training results instead of collecting their data. However, there is a serious shortcoming for federated learning that the centralized server cannot detect the validity of clients' training data and correctness of training results due to its limitation on monitoring clients' training processes. Federated learning is vulnerable to some attacks when attackers maliciously manipulate training data or updates, such as model poisoning attacks. Attackers who execute model poisoning attacks can negatively affect the global models' performance on a targeted class by manipulating the label of this class at one or more clients. Currently, there is a gap in the defense methods against model poisoning attacks in federated learning. To address the above shortcoming, we propose an effective defense method against model poisoning attack in federated learning in this paper. We validate each client's local model with a validation set. The server will only receive updates from well-performing clients to protect against model poisoning attacks. We consider the following two cases: all clients have a very similar distribution of training data and all clients have a very different distribution of training data, and design our methods and experiments for both cases. The experimental results show that our defense method can significantly reduce the success rate of model poisoning attacks in both cases in a federated learning setting.

Keywords: Federated learning · Model poisoning attack · Defense

1 Introduction

Federated learning is an improved distributed machine learning approach that involves many clients collaboratively training a model under the orchestration of a server [12]. During every round of training, clients who are chosen and allocated the model by the server use on-device data to train the model and send model updates back to the server. And then, the central server averages all

© Springer Nature Switzerland AG 2020
M. Kutyłowski et al. (Eds.): NSS 2020, LNCS 12570, pp. 207–223, 2020.
https://doi.org/10.1007/978-3-030-65745-1_12

updates to update the global model as the result of training this round. Compared to traditional distributed machine learning, federated learning provides a substantial privacy preservation that clients' data keep on the device instead of being collected by others [5,16]. Each client is an isolated "data island", and data never leaves the island. Once used to train the model, the only 'ship' to leave is a model update to the central server [2,7]. Federated learning can also overcome the limitation of a data island on the size and characteristics. Therefore, federated learning ideally benefits both clients to protect their data being used securely, and the server to involve more clients [5,13].

Although federated learning made huge improvements in the privacy and security of distributed machine learning, federated learning is still attracting adversaries and malicious attacks. Recently, many attack methods are being proposed against federated learning. Poisoning attack is one of the powerful attacks in which adversaries inject crafted attack points into the training data or tamper with the model training process [3,6]. Poisoning attacks cause significant threats to federated learning.

Most of the proposed poisoning attacks fall into two broad categories, data poisoning attack, and model poisoning attack. Data poisoning attack focuses on the training data collection phase, injecting malicious data into the training dataset before the training process starts, while model poisoning attack targets on model training phase, directly manipulating the local model parameters [3]. Some researchers have studied how to defend against data poisoning attacks in federated learning setting. Cao et al. [2] defended data poisoning attacks by solving a maximum clique problem to ignore suspected local models during the global model aggregation.

However, few works focus on how to defense model poisoning attacks in federated learning due to some difficulties. Firstly, federated learning involves a huge amount of clients collaboratively training the model, and it is hard to guarantee none of them is malicious. Secondly, the central server cannot observe clients' since only updates will be uploaded to the server [1]. Clients may adversarially use poisoned data to train the model which can result in a negative impact on the model performance without the server's being aware. Therefore,the key point to solve the problem is how to find out the malicious participant without breaking the privacy of the participant, so that the central server will not receive the parameter updates submitted by the malicious participant. Thus defense against the model poisoning attacks.

In order to solve the challenge and problems mentioned above, we propose a new defense method against model poisoning attacks in federated learning. Our key contributions can be summarized as follows: 1. we propose a new defense method against model poisoning attacks which validates each client's local model with a validation set, and then gives each client a label based on the validation results, finally the central server receives only updates from the performing clients. 2. Our proposed method can hugely reduce the success rate of model poisoning attacks by validating each client in each round of federated learning training with the validation set. 3. Our method protects against model poisoning attacks by screening out malicious clients so that the central server does not aggregate updates from existing clients. We will introduce some background knowledge in Sect. 2, and our proposed method in Sect. 3. We demonstrate our experiment settings, results and analysis in Sect. 4.

2 Background

2.1 Federated Learning

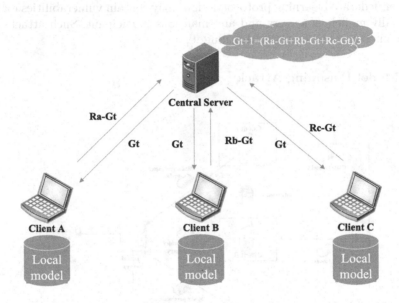

Fig. 1. Federal learning training process

Federated learning is an improved approach of distributed machine learning, which significantly reduces risks of privacy leakage [5,7]. Clients collaboratively train a model without their data being collected by others. Figure 1 shows the training process of federated learning: at each round t, the server announces a task and wait for all clients' responses for availability. The server then selects a sub-group of clients who are ready to train the model and sends the current global model parameter G_t to these clients. Then the chosen clients start training the received model using on-device data and update the local global R_i. When most clients finish training, they send model updates $R_i - G_t$ back to the central server, and the central server updates the global model for this round by averaging all updates from clients [2]. The process is repeated until the model converges.

That is, each client K runs a certain number of SGD steps locally and computes the average gradient on its local data at the current model G_t. Then the central server averages the updated local model to generate the updated global model $G_{t+1} \leftarrow \sum_{k=1}^{K} \frac{1}{K} G_{t+1}^{i}$. Each client sends an update to the central server as $G^k \leftarrow \sum G^k - \eta \bigtriangledown F_k(G^k)$. Among them, η is the learning rate [10].

Federated learning involves many policies to protect users' privacy and security [8]. The secure aggregation protocol, for example, protects data from other threats by ensuring that updates from clients remaining encrypted, thus a central server can only observe an encrypted update from clients instead of true value. Secure aggregation protocol includes a secret sharing scheme, differential privacy [18,19], secure multiparty computation and homomorphic encryption [7]. Through these strategies, federated learning is able to defense against many attacks, prevent information from being leaked, and reduce communication costs. However, federated learning protocol designs may contain vulnerabilities for both potentially malicious servers and any malicious participant. Such attacks pose significant threats to federated learning [9].

2.2   Model Poisoning Attack

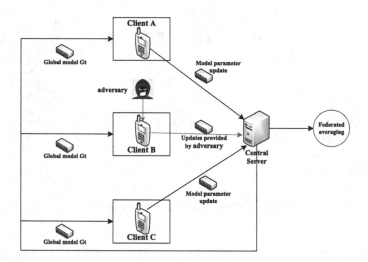

Fig. 2. Model Poisoning Attack. The attacker attacked client B and took control of all its local data. All updates sent by the attacked client B to the central server were specified by the attacker.

Poisoning attack mainly refers to the process of training data collection or model training in which the attacker attacks the model to achieve a malicious purpose.

Poisoning attacks have two categories: data poisoning attacks and model poisoning attacks [4]. For data poisoning attacks, the attacker contaminates the samples of the training dataset. On the other hand, the attacker can also execute model poisoning attacks by uploading malicious updates to the centralized server instead of modifying the training data directly [9], which results in a hugely negative impact on the model performance [14].

Model Poisoning Attack in Federated Learning. The target of model poisoning attack is to make the global model misclassify an attacker's expected class of things. Different from data poisoning attacks that aim at the integrity of training dataset collection, the adversary executing model poisoning attack in federated learning setting manipulates the label of a targeted class of data into a wrong label. The wrong label results in a wrong prediction result for the target class from the local model updates which will be sent to the central server for aggregation, and then negatively affect the global model's performance on this class of things [9]. Normally, model poisoning attack can lead the global model to reach a very high accuracy of prediction results on the manipulated class but keep performing well on other classes.

The attacker may have strong capabilities such as directly controlling the local training data of the client being attacked and modifying the value of the updates. This kind of attack can achieve high performance on both the main task of the model and the backdoor task as attacker's expectation. As we mentioned above, the centralized server cannot observe the clients' training data updates and be aware of malicious updates from the attacker, which causes a serious challenge to defend against such attacks. Currently, there is not too much effective work addressing the vulnerability of federated learning against model poisoning attacks.

3   Defenses Method for Model Poisoning

In order to solve the above problems, we propose a defense method. Our defense method successfully defended against the model poisoning attack.

3.1   Model Poisoning Defense Overview

Our basic idea is to identify the malicious participants so that the central server does not aggregate updates from the malicious participants, thus preventing model poisoning attacks. Therefore, we propose a defense strategy based on the verification set. At each round of training, after each client has trained the local model with the global model and the local training dataset, we use the validation set to verify the classification accuracy of the local model. If the local model has a much lower classification accuracy than other local models, we mark the client as a malicious client. The central server will not aggregate updates from that client. We take two scenarios into consideration, respectively each client is similar in composition and each client has only one type of data.

3.2   Scenario 1: The Client Is Similar in Composition

In this case, each client's local training dataset is composed similarly. In model poisoning attacks, the attacker's goal is to cause the federated learning model to misclassify a set of selected inputs. As mentioned in our defense policy, we need to screen out malicious participants. Therefore, we need to find out whether each client is "partial", in order to protect against backdoor attacks. "Partial" refers to misclassification of a certain type of numbers but accurate classification of other types of numbers.

Algorithm 1. Each client is similar in composition. M represents the number of clients participating in training in each round, T represents the total number of communication rounds, D represents the data set, A represents the classification accuracy of a model, and I represents the threshold.

1: initialize x_0
2: **for** each round $t = 1, 2, ..., T$ **do**
3:      $S_t \leftarrow (random\ set\ of\ M\ clients)$
4: **end for**
5: **for** each client $i \in S_t$ **do**
6:      $S_{t+1} \leftarrow ClientUpdate(i, x_t)$
7:      $A_{class}(x^i_{t+1}, D_v)$
8: **end for**
9: **for** each dataset j **do**
10:     **if** $A_{class}(x^i_{t+1}, D_j) < I$ **then**
11:         $x_i \leftarrow "Partial"$
12:     **end if**
13:     **if** $A_{class}(x^i_{t+1}, D_j) > I$ **then**
14:         $x_i \leftarrow "non - partial"$
15:     **end if**
16: **end for**
17: **if** $x_i = "non - partial"$ **then**
18:     $x_{t+1} \leftarrow \sum_{k=1}^{M} \frac{1}{M} x^i_{t+1}$
19: **end if**

In each round of training, the central server gives the current global model parameter G_t to each client. Each client performs local training on the local dataset based on the global model parameters. After training, we obtain the local model x^i_{t+1} . In the normal federated learning process, each client sends the updates $x^i_{t+1} - G_t$ back to the central server once the local model training is completed. But in our defense method, we validate the local model x^i_{t+1} with a validation set before committing the updates to central server. We need to verify the classification accuracy of the main tasks of the model and the accuracy of each type of number classification (verification of the accuracy of each type of number classification is to judge whether it is "partial"). The main task mentioned here is the main training task of the model, while the subtask is the target chosen by the attacker to control the behavior of the model.

The defense strategy has three steps. The first step is to verify the classification accuracy of the main tasks of the model. We have to note the classification success rate of the local model for each client on the validation set for reference. The second step is to verify the classification accuracy of each type of number. First of all, we divide the validation dataset in this round of training into 10 new validation datasets according to the label. Each new validation dataset contains only one class of data in order to verify the local model's classification accuracy for each class of Numbers. Then we validate the local model with each of the previously mentioned validation sets and record the results. If the classification accuracy rate of each type of the number of a client is higher than 65% (Experimental results show that the classification success rate of the client is more than 80% without attack while in the case of poisoning attack, the classification success rate of the client is about 50%. Based on the experimental results, we selected the median value of 65% as the threshold.), the client will be labeled "non-partial". The server will aggregate the updates from the client in this round of training. On the other hand, if the classification accuracy rate of a certain type of number is less than 65%, the client is labeled "partial", and the server is in this round of training does not aggregate updates on the client-side. The third step is to verify the label. If a client has a label "non-partial", it is judged as a normal client. However, if a client has a label "partial", it is judged as a malicious client.

3.3   Scenario 2: Client Has only One Type of Data

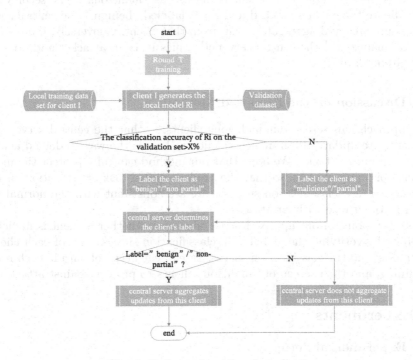

Fig. 3. Defense algorithm flow chart.

In this case, each client's local dataset has only one class of numbers. The attacker attacks one or more clients, modifies the parameter update of the attacked client, and causes the model to predict a certain class of numbers as the target label set by the attacker. Therefore, we need to find out which client is malicious and then screen out the malicious clients. This situation is different from the previous one, because each client's local training data set has only one class of numbers, so we don't need to judge "partial" issues.

Similarly, after each client has trained the local model, we validate the local model x_{t+1}^i with a validation set. Unlike the other scenario, we do not need to classify validation datasets by label, but use validation datasets directly. We need to verify the classification accuracy of the model. Similarly, after each client has trained the local model, we validate the local model with a validation set. There are two steps. The first step is to verify the classification accuracy of the model. If a local model has a higher classification accuracy than 12% on the validation set, the client is marked as "benign". On the other hand, if its classification accuracy on the validation set is less than 12%, (Experimental results show that the classification success rate of the client is more than 15% without attack while in the case of poisoning attack, the classification success rate of the client is about 9%. Based on the experimental results, we selected the median value of 12% as the threshold.) the client is marked as "malicious". The second step is to validate the client's label. If a client is labeled "benign," the central server receives updates and aggregates them from that client. Conversely, if a client is labeled "malicious," the central server identifies it as an attacker and does not aggregate updates from it.

3.4   Discussion on the Proposed Method

Our approach can screen out malicious clients so that the central server does not aggregate updates from malicious clients. This is the way to defend against model poisoning attacks. We hope that our method can fully protect the model against poisoning attacks, so that the model's global task classification success rate and subtask classification success rate are consistent with the normal federated learning rate without attacks.

The key point of our approach is to determine whether a client is malicious or benign by verifying the global task classification success rate of each client's local model and the classification success rate of each type of data in each round of training, and then screen out malicious clients to protect against attacks.

4   Experiments

4.1   Experimental Setup

We used a three-layer neural network with an input layer of 28×28, a hidden layer of 12 neurons, and an output layer of 10 neurons. We evaluate our attack strategies and defense strategies using MNIST dataset. The MNIST dataset

Algorithm 2. Each client has only one type of data. M represents the number of clients participating in training in each round, T represents the total number of communication rounds, D represents the data set, A represents the classification accuracy of a model, and H represents the threshold.

1: initialize x_0
2: **for** each round $t = 1, 2, ..., T$ **do**
3:    $S_t \leftarrow (random\ set\ of\ M\ clients)$
4: **end for**
5: **for** each client $i \in S_t$ **do**
6:    $S_{t+1} \leftarrow ClientUpdate(i, x_t)$
7:    $A_{class}(x_{t+1}^i, D_v)$
8: **end for**
9: **if** $A_{class}(x_{t+1}^i, D_v) < H$ **then**
10:    $x_i \leftarrow "malicious"$
11: **end if**
12: **if** $A_{class}(x_{t+1}^i, D_v) < H$ **then**
13:    $x_i \leftarrow "benign"$
14: **end if**
15: **if** $x_i = "benign"$ **then**
16:    $x_{t+1} \leftarrow \sum_{k=1}^{M} \frac{1}{M} x_{t+1}^i$
17: **end if**

is mainly composed of some pictures of handwritten digits and corresponding labels. There are 10 types of pictures, which correspond to 10 Arabic numerals from 0 to 9 respectively.

A. Each Client Is Similar in Composition

We mainly consider the case where the purpose of the malicious agent is to misclassify a single example in the desired target class (r = 1) while classifying other inputs correctly. For the MNIST dataset, the example belongs to class "4" (sandal), and its purpose is to misclassify it as the class "0".

We select 5,000 images from the 60,000 training images of the MNIST dataset as the training set for our experiment, and select 20,000 as the validation set. In each validation round, we randomly select one-tenth of the data from the validation set as the validation set for the round. That is, 2000 digital images are used as the verification set each time, so that each verification set is different. We first validate the classification accuracy of each client's local model with the selected validation set. Then, we divide the validation set into ten new validation sets according to the label of the digital image. The data label in the first new validation set is all "0", the data label in the second new validation set is all "1", and so on. The filtered validation set is used to verify the classification accuracy of the local model for each type of data.

We set the number of agents K to 10, that is, select all agents in each iteration. We run federated learning until the pre-specified test accuracy is reached.

B. Each Client Has only One Type of Data

Same as case A, we mainly consider the case where the purpose of the malicious agent is to misclassify a single example in the desired target class ($r = 1$) while classifying other inputs correctly. For the MNIST dataset, the example belongs to class "4" (sandal), and its purpose is to misclassify it as class "0".

We selected 30,000 training images from 60000 training images of MNIST dataset, and our experimental training data set was screened from these 30,000 digital images. We divided 30,000 digital images by label into 10 categories to form 10 new datasets. There is only one class of data in each dataset. For the data set labeled as '4', we divided it into three new datasets, which will be used as training data to participate in the experiment. For the other nine datasets, 1000 data are randomly selected from each dataset to form nine new datasets respectively. These nine datasets will be used as training data to participate in the experiment.

We set the number of agents K to 12, that is, select all agents in each iteration. The twelve datasets that we have previously partitioned will be divided into local training datasets as twelve clients. We run federated learning until the pre-specified test accuracy is reached.

4.2   Model Poisoning Attack Results

In this section, we use the adversarial goals laid out in the previous section3.1 to formulate the adversarial optimization problem. We then show how to achieve targeted model poisoning.

A. Each Client Is Similar in Composition

We first implemented federated learning for ten clients without an attacker, and the results are shown in Fig. 4.

In the experiment, the attacker attacked client A and controlled all the local data of Client A. After poisoning client A, the attacker tampered with the updates that Client A was going to send to the central server with malicious updates, expanded the weight of malicious updates, and made the global model deviate from the direction the attacker wanted.

The results (the results are shown in Fig. 5) show that after the attack, the classification accuracy of the benign client and the malicious client to the global main task is significantly reduced, and finally when the model converges, the classification accuracy is reduced to 50%. Compared with the non-attack condition, the model poisoning attack significantly reduces the classification accuracy of the model. For backdoor missions, that is, classify the number '4' as '0', the results show that backdoor missions have a high attack success rate in both malicious and benign models. Finally, when the model converges, the attack success rate of the backdoor mission reaches 80%. These results demonstrate the magnitude of the impact of model poisoning attacks on federated learning.

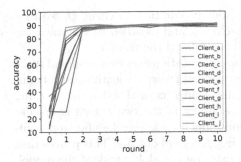 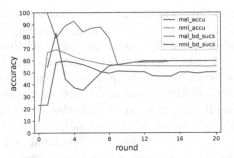

Fig. 4. Classification accuracy of five clients in normal federated learning training.

Fig. 5. Backdoor accuracy and Global task accuracy.

B. Each Client Has only One Type of Data

We first implemented the normal federated learning training without an attacker and we recorded the results, with which we will then compare the results of the model poisoning attack. We then implemented a model poisoning attack. The attacker poisons client D (the local data set label for client D is all '4') and takes control of all its local data. The attacker tampered with the update parameters of the client, sending malicious updates to the central server and increasing the weight of the malicious updates, which made the global model deviate from the direction the attacker wanted.

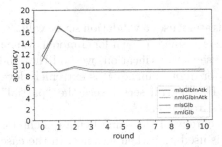 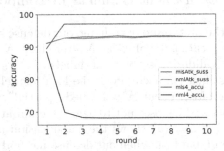

(a) Comparison of global task classification accuracy.

(b) Comparison of subtask classification success rate and attack success rate.

Fig. 6. Comparison of the classification accuracy of global and subtasks between benign and poisoned clients under normal federated learning training and attack.

We compared the classification success rate of benign and poisoned clients for global and subtasks in the case of normal federated learning training and model poisoning attacks. We selected the client D which was attacked in the attack situation and recorded the classification accuracy of the client in the normal training situation and the attacked situation. In addition to client D, we randomly selected a client from other benign clients, and recorded its classification accuracy in the two cases, and statistically compared the results.

Figure 6(a) shows the comparison of the classification accuracy of global tasks between benign and poisoned clients under normal federated learning and training conditions and under attack conditions. Under normal federated learning conditions, the global task classification accuracy of the two clients is around 15%. However, in the case of the model poisoning attack, the classification accuracy of the two clients on the global task dropped to about 9%. This proves that the model poisoning attack has a great impact on the global task of the model, which will lead to the reduction of the classification accuracy of the global task of the model.

Figure 6(b) shows the classification accuracy of benign clients and poisoned clients on subtasks under normal federated learning and training conditions and the attack success rate of benign clients and poisoned clients on subtasks under attack conditions. Under normal federated learning conditions, the benign client's classification accuracy for subtasks is around 70%. Client D, which is the client that was poisoned in the attack case, had a classification accuracy of about 96% for subtasks. However, in the case of model poisoning attack, the attack success rate of the two clients on subtasks reached about 92%. This proves that the attack success rate of model poisoning attacks against model subtasks is very high, and also proves that model poisoning attacks are powerful.

4.3   The Performance of Our Defenses Method

A. Each Client Is Similar in Composition

In the first round of training, our defense strategy uses a validation set to validate the local model of client A after client A has trained its own local model. When the validation set with all labels of '4' is used for verification, we find that the classification accuracy of the local model for digital image '4' is extremely low. Therefore, client A is labeled "partial". The central server sees the "partial" label and chooses not to aggregate updates from client A.

Figure 7 (a) shows the classification accuracy of the same benign client for the global task when our defense method is used and when it is not. In the case of no defense, the model poisoning attack reduces the classification accuracy of global tasks to 50%. After using our method for defense, the success rate of global task classification increased to 90%. Figure 7 (b) shows the classification accuracy of subtasks for the same benign client when our defense method is used and when it is not. In the case of no defense, the model poisoning attack reduces the classification accuracy of subtasks to 20%. After using our method for defense, the model's classification success rate for global tasks increased to 90%. The experimental results show that the defense method is effective and successful.

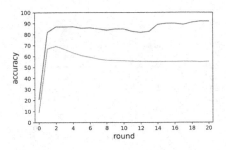 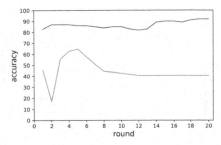

(a) The accuracy of main missions.   (b) The accuracy of backdoor missions.

Fig. 7. The model compares the accuracy of main missions and backdoor missions with and without defense.

B. Each Client Has only One Type of Data

In the first round of training, our defense strategy uses a validation set to validate the local model of client D after client D has trained its own local model. We find that the classification accuracy of the local model of client D is extremely low. Therefore, client D is labeled "malicious". The central server sees the "malicious" label and chooses not to aggregate updates from client D.

We compared the model's classification success rates for global and subtasks under three conditions: normal federated learning training, model poison attack, and defense. Use the experimental results to verify the effectiveness of our defense methods.

Figure 8(a) shows a comparison of the model's classification success rate for global tasks under three conditions: normal federated learning training, model poison attack, and defense. Under the condition of normal federated learning training, the classification accuracy of the model for global tasks is about 15%. In the case of model poisoning attack, the model's classification accuracy of global tasks is about 10%. In the case of using our defense strategy, the classification accuracy of the model for global tasks is about 13%.The results show that compared with the case of no defense, our defense method improves the accuracy of the model on the global task, although it is not as high as the normal federation learning and training, but it is close. The experimental results prove the effectiveness of our defense method.

Figure 8(b) shows the comparison of the model's classification success rate for subtasks under three conditions: normal federated learning training, model poison attack, and defense. Under normal federated learning and training conditions, the classification success rate of subtasks reached 70%. In the case of model poisoning attack, the model's classification success rate of subtasks was reduced to 10%. With our defense approach, the model's classification success rate for subtasks went back up to 50%. Compared with the non-defense case, our defense method improves the classification success rate of subtasks by 40%, which proves the effectiveness of our method.

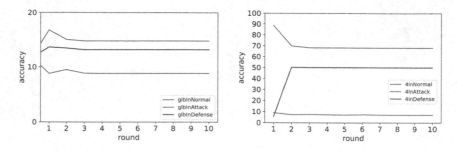

(a) Comparison of global task classifica-   (b)Comparison of subtask classification
tion accuracy.   accuracy.

Fig. 8. Comparison of the classification accuracy of the global task and the classification success rate of the subtask under federated normal learning training, model
poisoning attack and defense.

5   Related Work

In order to make federated learning more robust and practical, some researchers
have come up with some defense strategies against poisoning attacks. For
instance, Zhao et al. use client-side cross-validation to protect against poison
attacks [17]. They randomly selected a small group of clients that participate in
federated learning and asked them to evaluate each model update with their own
local data, which was used to detect abnormal updates. Specifically, the server
randomly divides K updates into D parts. Each part is then aggregated into
sub-models, and each sub-model is randomly assigned to the selected client, and
each client evaluates the sub-model. Next, the server adopts a majority voting
strategy, and the client participating in the evaluation needs to submit a binary
matrix to declare whether the corresponding category of data samples has been
properly classified. Although both this paper and ours detect abnormal updates
to prevent poisoning attacks, the strategy of this paper is quite different from
ours. Firstly, our defense strategy is to validate each model update with a validation set. And the data in our validation set is brand new data rather than local
private data from the client participating in federated learning. Our settings
reduce the risk of user privacy disclosure. Secondly, in order to defend against
backdoor attacks, we have verified the classification accuracy of each update on
the validation set for the main tasks of the model, as well as the classification
accuracy of each update for each type of data. In this way, the attacker can be
detected even if he performs well on the model's main task. After validating the
model updates, we label each client and the server determines whether or not to
aggregate the updates from a particular client. Our defenses are effective against
poisoning attacks and are low in computing and communication costs and easy
to deploy.

Tolpegin et al. propose an automated defense strategy that identifies the relevant parameter subset and study participant updates using dimensionality reduction (PCA) against label ipping attacks [15]. Because updates from malicious participants belong to a distinct cluster from those from benign participants. Based on this, they use gradient clustering to identify malicious actors before the servers aggregating updates from various clients. After the aggregator identifies the malicious actors, it will ignore their updates and eventually converge to a high-utility model. This defense strategy is completely different from our defense strategy. First of all, their defense strategy is against label ipping attacks in data poisoning attacks, while ours is against backdoor attacks in model poisoning attacks. Secondly, their strategy is to identify malicious actors through gradient clustering, while our defense strategy is to identify malicious actors by validating each client's model update through validation sets.

Also, to protect against backdoor attacks, Ozdayi et al. proposed a lightweight defense [11], which does not change the federated learning structure. Their defense strategy adjusts the learning rate during each round of training and move the model towards a particular direction to maximizes the loss of the attacker. The core idea behind their defense was to adjust the learning rate according to the sign information of updates from the agents. Compared to their defense strategy, our defense strategy changed the structure of federated learning, and we validated each model update with a validation set before the server aggregated. We were equally effective in defending against a backdoor attack.

In addition, there are many studies on the defense of deep learning. Such as Cretu et al. extend the training phase of anomaly sensors with a new sanitization phase that uses the novel micromodels in a voting scheme to eliminate attacks and anomalies from training data [4]. While not all of these methods of defense are intended for federal learning, they will help us continue to study the defense of federal learning in the future.

6   Conclusions and Future Work

In summary, federated learning is vulnerable to model poisoning attack. The challenge is caused by the fact that the centralized server cannot observe clients' training data and is difficult to perform the validation of clients' updates. To address the above challenges, we have presented a new defense method against model poisoning attack in federated learning in this paper. Our method validates every client's training results using a validation dataset, to evaluate if these client's updates are valid for aggregation. We have considered two cases in federated learning settings: all clients' training data have the similar distribution and all clients' training data have the different distribution. The experiment results demonstrate that our method can hugely reduce model poisoning attacks' success rate in both cases, and prevent misclassification on the poisoned class.

There is still much work we have to do in the future. We will continue to study how to defend against attacks in federated learning, such as data poisoning attacks, inference attacks, and so on. We know that there are obvious vulnerabilities in federated learning protocol designs, and these vulnerabilities pose significant threats to federated learning. In the future we may be able to improve the federated learning design to protect against attacks, making federated learning safer and more practical.

References

1. Bagdasaryan, E., Veit, A., Hua, Y., Estrin, D., Shmatikov, V.: How to backdoor federated learning. CoRR abs/1807.00459 (2018). http://arxiv.org/abs/1807.00459
2. Cao, D., Chang, S., Lin, Z., Liu, G., Sun, D.: Understanding distributed poisoning attack in federated learning. In: 25th IEEE International Conference on Parallel and Distributed Systems, ICPADS 2019, Tianjin, China, 4–6 December 2019, pp. 233–239. IEEE (2019). https://doi.org/10.1109/ICPADS47876.2019.00042
3. Fang, M., Cao, X., Jia, J., Gong, N.Z.: Local model poisoning attacks to byzantine-robust federated learning. CoRR abs/1911.11815 (2019). http://arxiv.org/abs/1911.11815
4. Kairouz, P., et al.: Advances and open problems in federated learning. CoRR abs/1912.04977 (2019). http://arxiv.org/abs/1912.04977
5. Konecný, J., McMahan, H.B., Ramage, D., Richtárik, P.: Federated optimization: Distributed machine learning for on-device intelligence. CoRR abs/1610.02527 (2016). http://arxiv.org/abs/1610.02527
6. Konecný, J., McMahan, H.B., Yu, F.X., Richtárik, P., Suresh, A.T., Bacon, D.: Federated learning: Strategies for improving communication efficiency. CoRR abs/1610.05492 (2016). http://arxiv.org/abs/1610.05492
7. Li, T., Sahu, A.K., Talwalkar, A., Smith, V.: Federated learning: Challenges, methods, and future directions. IEEE Sign. Process. Mag. 37(3), 50–60 (2020). https://doi.org/10.1109/MSP.2020.2975749
8. Lim, W.Y.B., et al.: Federated learning in mobile edge networks: a comprehensive survey. IEEE Commun. Surv. Tutorials 22(3), 2031–2063 (2020). https://doi.org/10.1109/COMST.2020.2986024
9. Lyu, L., Yu, H., Yang, Q.: Threats to federated learning: A survey. CoRR abs/2003.02133 (2020). https://arxiv.org/abs/2003.02133
10. McMahan, B., Moore, E., Ramage, D., Hampson, S., y Arcas, B.A.: Communication-efficient learning of deep networks from decentralized data. In: Singh, A., Zhu, X.J. (eds.) Proceedings of the 20th International Conference on Artificial Intelligence and Statistics, AISTATS 2017, 20–22 April 2017, Fort Lauderdale, FL, USA. Proceedings of Machine Learning Research, vol. 54, pp. 1273–1282. PMLR (2017). http://proceedings.mlr.press/v54/mcmahan17a.html
11. Özdayi, M.S., Kantarcioglu, M., Gel, Y.R.: Defending against backdoors in federated learning with robust learning rate. CoRR abs/2007.03767 (2020). https://arxiv.org/abs/2007.03767
12. Pillutla, V.K., Kakade, S.M., Harchaoui, Z.: Robust aggregation for federated learning. CoRR abs/1912.13445 (2019). http://arxiv.org/abs/1912.13445
13. Shen, S., Zhu, T., Wu, D., Wang, W., Zhou, W.: From distributed machine learning to federated learning: In the view of data privacy and security. CoRR abs/2010.09258 (2020). https://arxiv.org/abs/2010.09258
14. Suya, F., Mahloujifar, S., Evans, D., Tian, Y.: Model-targeted poisoning attacks: Provable convergence and certified bounds. CoRR abs/2006.16469 (2020). https://arxiv.org/abs/2006.16469

15. Tolpegin, V., Truex, S., Gursoy, M.E., Liu, L.: Data poisoning attacks against federated learning systems. CoRR abs/2007.08432 (2020). https://arxiv.org/abs/2007.08432
16. Yang, Q., Liu, Y., Chen, T., Tong, Y.: Federated machine learning: concept and applications. ACM Trans. Intell. Syst. Technol. **10**(2), 12:1–12:19 (2019). https://doi.org/10.1145/3298981
17. Zhao, L., Hu, S., Wang, Q., Jiang, J., Shen, C., Luo, X.: Shielding collaborative learning: Mitigating poisoning attacks through client-side detection. CoRR abs/1910.13111 (2019). http://arxiv.org/abs/1910.13111
18. Zhu, T., Li, G., Zhou, W., Yu, P.S.: Differentially private data publishing and analysis: a survey. IEEE Trans. Knowl. Data Eng. **29**(8), 1619–1638 (2017). https://doi.org/10.1109/TKDE.2017.2697856
19. Zhu, T., Ye, D., Wang, W., Zhou, W., Yu, P.S.: More than privacy: Applying differential privacy in key areas of artificial intelligence. CoRR abs/2008.01916 (2020). https://arxiv.org/abs/2008.01916

Fixing Vulnerabilities
Automatically with Linters

Willard Rafnsson$^{(\boxtimes)}$, Rosario Giustolisi, Mark Kragerup, and Mathias Høyrup

IT University of Copenhagen, Copenhagen, Denmark
{wilr,rosg,mabk,mahn}@itu.dk

Abstract. Static analysis is a tried-and-tested approach to eliminate vulnerabilities in software. However, despite decades of successful use by experts, mainstream programmers often deem static analysis too costly to use. Mainstream programmers do routinely use linters, which are static analysis tools geared towards identifying simple bugs and stylistic issues in software. Can linters serve as a medium for delivering vulnerability detection to mainstream programmers?

We investigate the extent of which linters can be leveraged to help programmers write secure software. We present new rules for ESLint that detect—and automatically fix—certain classes of cross-site scripting, SQL injection, and misconfiguration vulnerabilities in JavaScript. Evaluating our experience, we find that there is enormous potential in using linters to eliminate vulnerabilities in software, due to the relative ease with which linter rules can be implemented and shared to the community. We identify several open challenges, including third-party library dependencies and linter configuration, and propose ways to address them.

1 Introduction

Motivation. JavaScript is the most commonly used programming language today [36]. Popularized by the Web, JavaScript is now ubiquitous, used for implementing all kinds of software, including Web apps and services, desktop apps, mobile apps, and even embedded software. Its appeal is that it is dynamically and weakly typed, and that it is, at its core, quite simple. However, this is a double-edged sword; the type system and full semantics of JavaScript are infamous for their quirks [18] that frequently befuddle programmers, even experienced ones. As a result, bugs routinely make their way to deployed JavaScript code. These can lead to vulnerabilities that get exploited in privacy attacks, such as injection attacks, serialization attacks, and cross-site scripting attacks [30].

Static analysis is a tried-and-tested approach to eliminate bugs prior to deployment [13]. It involves reasoning about the behavior of a program without executing it, to see if it possesses an undesired property, e.g. "has certain bugs". Since a static analysis tool cannot be both free of false-positives and false-negatives (unless the property is trivial [32]), correctness proofs for tools typically focus on no-false-negatives, so e.g. "code deemed bug-free really is

© Springer Nature Switzerland AG 2020
M. Kutyłowski et al. (Eds.): NSS 2020, LNCS 12570, pp. 224–244, 2020.
https://doi.org/10.1007/978-3-030-65745-1_13

bug-free". Static analysis is successfully used by specialists at large companies, in situations where bugs are deemed too costly, e.g. SLAM at Microsoft [7], Infer at Facebook [10], Spark Ada at Boeing [15], and PolySpace at NASA [9]. Tools for enforcing security policies in JavaScript code, e.g. access control [28], information-flow [17], and others [16], have long existed. However, despite the use of such tools being long advocated [11], mainstream programmers seem reluctant to use static analysis tools in general [22], due to the poor manner in which they present issues, and the overwhelming number of false positives they generate [8,33,43].

Enter linters. A linter is a static analysis tool that scans (i.e. lints) code for a wide range of issues, including bugs, programming errors, suspicious constructs, stylistic errors, and code smells [40]. Linters have been used extensively since the 70s for all major programming languages, famous examples being Lint [24], FindBugs [6] and ESLint [46] for C, Java, and JavaScript respectively. Strikingly, mainstream linters have no correctness proofs. Rather, the focus of linters is on providing usable improvement suggestions and on reducing false positives [6,40]. This is indeed their appeal; for JavaScript, an overwhelming majority of developers use linters, and they do so to catch errors and produce maintainable code by reducing complexity and enforcing style [40]. Linters are even used together with unit tests as a second line of defense against bugs [40]. Finally, modern linters are fully configurable; linter rules can be toggled for different parts of the code base, and new linter rules can be developed in-house or downloaded from a community-maintained repository [46]. As new bugs, guidelines, and libraries arise, linters can immediately be configured to adapt.

With the lack of mainstream success of advanced static analysis tools for security, and with the popularity of linters, perhaps the most impactful way to deliver vulnerability checking to programmers is through a linter.

Contribution. We investigate the extent of which linters can be leveraged to help programmers write secure code. We focus on ESLint, as it is the most commonly used linter for the most commonly used programming language.

First, we present new rules for ESLint for eliminating vulnerabilities. These rules detect—and automatically *fix*—certain classes of cross-site scripting, SQL injection, and misconfiguration vulnerabilities, all of which are on the OWASP Top Ten list of Web application security risks [30]. Some of these rules are library-dependent, checking for vulnerabilities in the use of React [21] and Express [37], the two JavaScript frameworks that make up the popular MERN stack [26]. We demonstrate the practicality of these rules, notably that they have few false-positives, with examples and unit tests.

Next, supported by our experience, we critically evaluate the state-of-the-art in the use of linters to eliminate vulnerabilities. We evaluate the strengths and limitations of ESLint for eliminating vulnerabilities and find that, while ESLint provides useful facilities for analyzing code, there are shortcomings, notably that it only scans one file at a time. This has consequences when considering library dependencies. We survey existing ESLint plugins, and find only a few rules that check for vulnerabilities. The handful of those that see notable use identify only a few vulnerabilities, and focus on reducing false *negatives*, to the point that (we argue) the rule becomes too much of a hassle to use, and thus gets disabled by programmers. We analyze the ESLint guidelines for creating new rules [39], and find that most of the guidelines run counter to the needs of a rule that eliminates vulnerabilities. We also find that configuring ESLint is nontrivial, which is a well-known barrier to using linters effectively [40], and propose outsourcing the maintenance of linter configuration to community experts.

Finally, we make observations as well as recommendations with regards to using linters to eliminate vulnerabilities. We find that there is a great, and unexplored, potential in using linters to eliminate vulnerabilities. This is based on the popularity of ESLint, the rich features that ESLint provides for analyzing code, the scarcity and inadequacy of existing rules for security, and the relative ease with which we successfully implemented rules that are more practical. We find it crucial that linters are fully configurable. Community-maintained linter rules made ESLint successful, and are a necessary feature if programmers are to keep up with the rapidly-evolving security landscape. For the same reason, it is important that linter configuration can be outsourced to experts. For rules to be useful, we find it important that it be clear what kind of vulnerabilities the rule intends to detect. The rule should also detect vulnerabilities as precisely as possible, i.e. few false alarms. Together, this saves time, instills confidence, and reduces frustration, in the programmer. Finally, linters must provide more comprehensive means of scanning source code. Crucially, linters must analyze dependencies on third-party libraries. This is because 93% of the code of a modern Web application is open-source library code [42], 70.5% of Web apps have vulnerabilities from a library, and the vast majority of those vulnerabilities are known or have been patched [41]. A linter could detect these vulnerabilities.

Outline. We describe what we advocate in Sect. 2. We summarize ESLint in Sect. 3. We present our linter rules that find and eliminate vulnerabilities in Sect. 4. We evaluate the state-of-the-art against our experience in Sect. 5, and provide our recommendations in Sect. 6. Finally, we contrast our findings with related work in Sect. 7, and conclude in Sect. 8.

2   In a Nutshell

Mainstream programmers routinely use linters to eliminate bugs and improve the quality of their code. This is illustrated in Fig. 1. This JavaScript code sends a request to `myapi.com` and assigns the data in the response to the `href` on the page. The programmer has integrated ESLint, a linter for JavaScript, into her integrated development environment (IDE). ESLint reports, in Fig. 1a, that this code may be vulnerable to a cross-site scripting attack, since the data received from `myapi.com`, and thus the URL in the `href`, could be controlled by an attacker (e.g. if the API reads from a database that the attacker can inject code into). Any JavaScript in the response would be executed on the client upon pressing the URL. More importantly, ESLint also presents the option to *automatically fix* the vulnerability. Picking this option yields the code in Fig. 1b, which fixes the vulnerability by sanitizing the response from `myapi.com`.

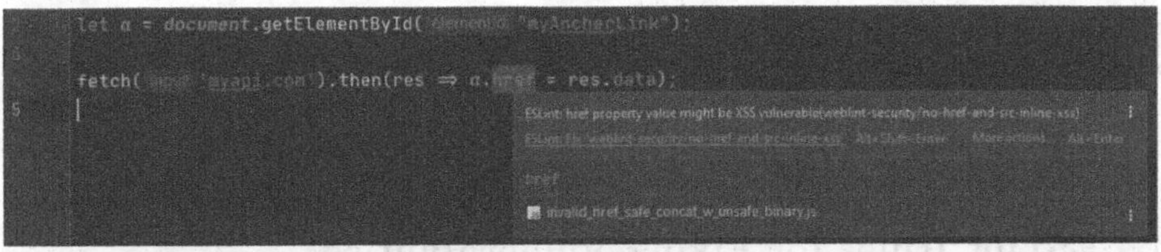

(a) finding a vulnerability

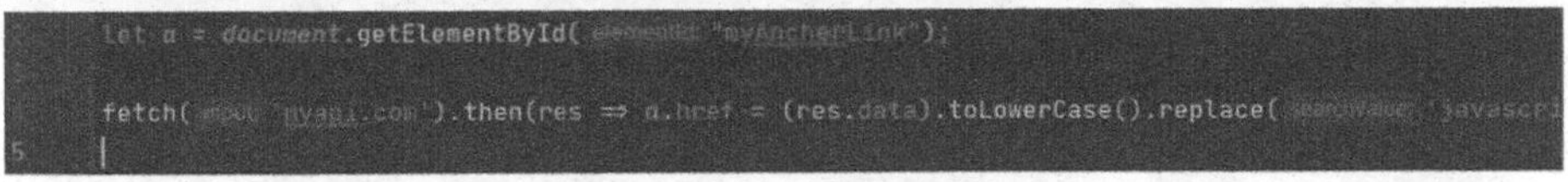

(b) fixing a vulnerability

Fig. 1. Using a linter in an IDE to find & fix a vulnerability.

This is `no-href-and-src-inline-xss`, one of the ESLint rules that we propose in this paper, at work. It is this kind of automatic finding and fixing of vulnerabilities that we desire and advocate. Automatic fixing of vulnerabilities is incredibly valuable to mainstream programmers, as some vulnerabilities are notoriously difficult to debug, requiring expertise and deep knowledge about the whole code base. Our goal in this paper is to investigate the extent of which linters can deliver on this. We do this in the context of JavaScript, and its most popular linter, ESLint.

3 ESLint

ESLint [46] is a linter for JavaScript. Initially released in 2013, ESLint has since become a *de facto* standard tool for JavaScript development, used by the vast majority of JavaScript developers [40]. ESLint is actively developed, supporting both current and upcoming standards of ECMAScript.

A description of how ESLint and its rules work can be found in the appendix. We now briefly list the defining features of ESLint.

3.1 Features

ESLint has several features that distinguish it from other linters.

Automatic. ESLint can fix problems automatically, thus freeing the developer from coming up with a fix.

Customization. ESLint rules can be turned on and off, new rules can be added by downloading plugins from a community-maintained repository, and developers can maintain their own custom rules in-house.

Integration. ESLint builds into mainstream text editors and IDEs and can be run as part of a continuous integration and deployment (CI/CD) pipeline.

ESLint is a community-effort; it is open-source (thus freely available), and actively scrutinized by its community. The ESLint developers emphasize the importance of clear documentation and communication; rules should be well documented, provide useful improvement suggestions, and have few false-positives.

4   ESLint Rules for Fixing Vulnerabilities

We implement four new ESLint rules for finding and fixing vulnerabilities. Our rules target well-defined instances of today's most critical Web security risks from the OWASP Top Ten [30]: cross-site scripting, server misconfiguration, and SQL injection. Three of our rules not only detect, but *automatically fix*, the vulnerabilities. We demonstrate that the rules have few false positives with unit tests. Together, this shows that linters can help programmers write secure code.

For each rule, we describe the vulnerability it targets, how existing ESLint rules fall short, our rule implementation, and automatic code fixing.

Testing. Our rules sections have multiple unit test files corresponding to the different use cases described for each rule. The tests utilize the built-in ESLint rule tester to validate code cases for the absence of false alarms, as well as for validating the automatic fixer functionality when applicable.

4.1   Cross-Site Scripting

Vulnerability. Cross-site scripting (XSS) is a code injection vulnerability where a victim, while navigating a benign (yet vulnerable) Web page, unwittingly executes attacker-controlled data in the browser. This lets an attacker obtain private information (e.g. access cookies and session tokens) from the victim's browser, redirect the victim to a malicious website, and more, all while the victims believe they are interacting with the original benign Web page. Our rule targets specific kinds of DOM XSS vulnerabilities, i.e. where a page calls a JavaScript API and uses the response to modify a DOM element in the victim's browser; an attacker can exploit a vulnerable API to ship code to the victim's browser. Concretely, we focus on modifications of `src` attributes, and of the `href` attribute of anchor tags. An example of such a vulnerability is the following.

```
1 fetch("myapi.com").then(res => a.href = res.data);
```

This is the scenario presented in Sect. 2. The result of the API call may contain unsanitized attacker-controlled data. Such data might contain a malicious script that will be executed in the victim's browser upon link activation.

Existing Rules. The most notable plugin which includes rules for detecting XSS is `eslint-plugin-no-unsanitized`. It includes rules that detect unsanitized data used for manipulating the HTML content of DOM elements. However, the plugin considers only the HTML content of elements, and is not capable of detecting vulnerabilities that occur when manipulating `href` and `src` attributes. Furthermore, the rules result in a lot of false positives; as existing user studies have pointed out [8,33,43], this would discourage programmers from activating the rule. Upon investigation, we found that the main issue is that the rule only considers explicit strings in the DOM assignments as safe, and raises a flag in any other case. We observe that there are, in fact, many valid and safe cases of DOM assignments, which could be ruled out as a possible vulnerability. One example of this would be the use of a variable holding an explicit string in the assignment. Additionally, the rules do not support web development frameworks that render HTML content dynamically, such as the popular framework React.

Our Approach. Our approach targets XSS attacks through modification of `href` and `src` attributes. This has not been addressed by ESLint plugins to date.

To achieve this, we maintain a set of variable identifiers that are in a safe state at any point while traversing the AST. We determine whether a variable is in a safe state by tracking and evaluating the values of all variable initializations and assignments in the code. We consider explicit strings as well as constructs that implicitly form string expressions from other explicit strings safe. This reduces false positives without affecting correctness. The benefit of this is clear when using template strings and string concatenations that involve variables that contain e.g. explicit strings.

When our `no-href-and-src-inline-xss` rule is run on the example above, it outputs the message *"href property value might be XSS vulnerable"*, and highlights the `".href ="` part of the code. Our rule documentation, accessible within ESLint, provides further information about the vulnerability to the programmer.

This approach generalizes to the use of libraries and frameworks. Our rule `no-href-and-src-inline-xss-react` shows this; it detects the same vulnerability in the use of Facebook's React [21] framework. Here, in addition to tracking the safety of variables, we need to track the safety of values held in special React states. React uses JSX (see React documentation) to dynamically render content and automatically modify the DOM in the user's browser. This syntax also applies to the `src` and `href` attributes, and the rule therefore considers this feature specifically. While the previous rule is part of the `"recommended"` rule set of the plugin, this rule is part of the `"react"` rule set. The two rules are specifically implemented in such a way that they do not conflict or overlap. The rule set of an ESLint configuration is normally extended first by recommended rules, and then by any additional rules, such as React-specific rules for full framework support.

Automatic Fix. We take advantage of the *fixer* functionality of the ESLint interface to enable the programmers to *automatically fix* the vulnerability identified by these rules. When selected by the programmer, the rule applies our suggested code change to the file directly.

When a value might contain malicious code, it is recommended to sanitize the value before using it. Unfortunately, while some libraries, such as Angular and React, sanitize some strings behind-the-scenes, their sanitization is not complete, and only focuses on `<script>` tags. Furthermore, SQL libraries have sanitization functions to protect against SQL injection attacks, which do not trivially port to our scenario. We propose a novel way of escaping executable code, using built-in Javascript string functions to sanitize the `javascript:` prefix.

```
1 val.toLowerCase().replace('javascript:','/javascript/:/'))
```

Applying the automatic fixer to the above example results in a replacement of the right-hand side of the assignment of the `href` attribute with escaping applied.

```
1 fetch("myapi.com").then( res => a.href = res.data
    .toLowerCase().replace('javascript:','/javascript/:/'));
```

Limitations. Our rules do have some false positives. Our rules flags any assignment of any function application regardless of its safety, due to the concern that the function calls an API which retrieves attacker-controlled data. For example, `"my".concat("string");` is safe, yet is flagged as unsafe. Furthermore, we have not tested the sanitization function in our fixer; it could potentially be circumvented through the use of filter evasion. There may also be tried-and-tested sanitizers that we can, and should use, such as the `xss-filters` package in npm.

4.2   Security Misconfiguration

Vulnerability. Security Misconfiguration is a broad security problem with equally broad ramifications. These can arise e.g. from default configurations, default credentials, unnecessary features being enabled (e.g. ports) or installed, and unpatched flaws in the server software/hardware stack. Our rule targets misconfiguration of HTTP response headers in Node.js backend applications, specifically ones built on the Express [37] Web application framework. The aim of the rule is to eliminate certain clickjacking, MIME-sniffing, and XSS attacks, by recommending the use of the Helmet [19] library for Express, which automatically configures some important HTTP headers in a safe manner. An example is

```
1 const myApp = require('express');
2 myApp.listen(8080);
```

This minimal Express application launches a Web server that accepts network traffic on port 8080. However, HTTP response headers have not been configured.

Existing Rules. The `eslint-plugin-security-node` plugin has a rule called `detect-helmet-without-nocache`. The rule flags code that uses Helmet for configuring HTTP response headers without the `noCache` setting enabled. However, we observe that there are much more impactful security settings available in Helmet; Helmet provides a set of default configurations for security [19] which can be enabled by invoking the Helmet object. No available ESLint rule encourages the use of these defaults. Furthermore, the existing rule encouraging the use of `noCache` is very limited in the cases that it covers. For example, it only considers programs where the variable holding the Express object is named `app`; if any other name is used, the rule would flag the concerned code, regardless of whether the code is vulnerable or not. Finally, `noCache` is deprecated. To the best of our knowledge, there are no other ESLint plugins that detect HTTPS response header vulnerabilities.

Our Approach. Our approach targets the use of Express without Helmet. It keeps track of the correct usage of Helmet with the recommended defaults and, if the recommended defaults are not correctly enabled, flags the line of code that launches the application.

To achieve this, we track whether Express and Helmet are enabled, and track identifier names holding the corresponding object instances. If the application uses Express but does not import Helmet at all, we flag the code as unsafe. If Helmet is imported, but the recommended defaults are not invoked, we also flag the code as unsafe. Since we cover all cases, our rule has few false alarms. Our rule is more general than the previous ones since it considers all uses of Express, and not just uses of Express, in an object named app, without noCache.

When our detect-missing-helmet rule is run on the example above, it outputs the message *"Use the Helmet.js module for enhanced security on HTTP response headers in your Express application."* with a link to the setup documentation. Our rule also suggests the use of the expectCT Helmet setting for information purposes (without enforcing it), which can help prevent certificate abuse.

Automatic fix. Again, we empower the programmer to fix this vulnerability, by implementing an ESLint fixer.

We utilize the stored identifier names to provide correct adaptations of the vulnerable code, which involves simply inserting lines that import Helmet and invoke it with its defaults. Applying our fixer on the above example thus yields the following modified code.

```
1 const myApp = require('express');
2 const helmet = require('helmet');
3 myApp.use(helmet());
4 myApp.listen(8080);
```

4.3 SQL Injection

Vulnerability. SQL Injection is a code injection vulnerability where an attacker can, by carefully crafting input data to the Web application frontend, inject his own SQL queries into the database in the backend. This can enable the attacker to bypass login authentication checks, read or modify database records, execute administrative operations on the database, and, in some cases, even issue commands to the underlying operating system. Our rule targets the occurrence of variables in the construction of SQL query strings in Node.js backend applications. An example of this follows.

```
1 let phone = readline.question("Your phone number?\n");
2 const sql = 'SELECT * FROM users WHERE tlf = ' + phone;
3 dbCon.query(sql, (err, result) => console.log(result));
```

This minimal command-line Node.js application queries a database of users for a record matching a phone number. However, the phone number is supplied as a variable; an attacker can obtain the whole table by providing the phone number "' OR 1=1" as input, or delete the users table by providing the phone number "'; DROP TABLE users".

Existing Rules. The previously mentioned plugin `eslint-plugin-security-node` has a rule for detecting SQL injection vulnerabilities: `detect-sql-injection`. This rule flags all queries that provide anything other than an explicit string as its first parameter. This leads to an explosion in the number of false positives. For example, the rule flags as vulnerable when an explicit string is stored in a variable, or when two explicit strings are concatenated into the parameter. Furthermore, the most common SQL queries for Web application depend in some way on user input, such as queries for login credentials. Alarmingly, the rule only considers cases where the database connection is stored in a variable named either `connection`, `connect`, or `conn`. Using a different name causes the rule to disregard the SQL queries, leading to potential false negatives. This limitation is not present in the plugin documentation.

Another plugin is `eslint-plugin-sql-injection`, which just includes a single rule for detecting SQL injections. The approach here is to check if a query call is using string concatenations where at least one value, in the concatenation, is not an explicit string. While this does reduce false positives (compared to the previous rule), it does dramatically increase false negatives. For instance, this rule does not flag a variable if it is not used in a concatenation or a template string. The rule also requires the programmer to manually specify the name of the function which queries the database in the ESLint configuration file. If the user does not provide such a configuration, the rule does not flag any vulnerabilities, leading to false negatives.

Our Approach. Our approach targets the occurrence of variables in queries, requiring instead the use of a prepared statement. A prepared statement fixes the structure of the query before values are inserted into the query, thus preventing such values from modifying the structure of the query.

To achieve this, we follow a similar approach as in our rules for XSS vulnerabilities. We maintain a set of safe variables throughout the analysis process. We flag only code that uses unsafe variables or unsafe values in the SQL query execution. This reduces false positives, as we do not impose restrictions on variable names. Furthermore, our approach considers any function call named `query` which takes parameters. As a result, our approach is not tailored to any specific database driver, which means that it can detect vulnerabilities in queries for e.g. MySQL, PostgreSQL, etc., since they all export a function named `query`.

When our `detect-sql-injection` rule is run on the example above, it outputs the message *"Parameterize the input for the query, to avoid SQL Injection vulnerabilities. See more at:* https://www.npmjs.com/\penalty\z@package/ \penalty\z@mysql#escaping-query-values". The warning highlights the query call for visual guidance in IDEs.

Fix. To fix the vulnerability, the programmer can, by looking at the information presented to him by the rule, turn the query into a prepared statement. For our example, the following fixed version is accepted by our rule.

```
1 let phone = readline.question("Your phone number?\n");
2 const sql = 'SELECT * FROM users WHERE tlf = ?';
3 dbCon.query(sql, [phone], (err, res) => console.log(res));
```

Neither of the existing rules would flag neither the original nor fixed version of this example, thus implying false negatives. However, if dbCon is renamed to a name that the rules recognize, then both rules would reject both examples, thus implying false positives.

For this rule, we do not include the automatic code fixing implementation as in the previously proposed rules. This is a highly desirable feature; we will experiment with this in the future. Implementing this is challenging because this requires changing the code on a previous line (`const sql`) while analyzing the node corresponding to the later line that performs the actual query. This also requires manipulating query strings and constructing arrays of parameters in a way which supports all possible ways of constructing such a string.

Limitations. Our rule does have some false positives, notably since it flags calls of functions named query. While this catches queries for all common SQL APIs, it at the same time catches same-named functions on any object.

5   Analysis

Supported by our experience with creating linter rules, we critically evaluate the state-of-the-art in the use of linters to eliminate vulnerabilities in software. We analyze ESLint as a tool, existing plugins for ESLint, existing guidelines for writing rules, and the challenge of maintaining a linter configuration. We make four important observations on the prospect of using linter rules for security.

5.1   ESLint Strengths and Limitations

Based on our experience, we evaluate the strengths and limitations of using ESLint to find and fix vulnerabilities.

Strengths. ESLint has several strengths which make it well-suited for helping programmers find and fix vulnerabilities.

First, and most important, is its *rules customization*. ESLint comes shipped with a host of rules, which can be turned on and off for different parts of the code base. More importantly, programmers can create their own custom rules in-house. ESLint provides a rich API for this; rules can maintain their own state, traverse the AST freely when invoked, and precisely assign blame to sections of the code that are at fault. Crucially, ESLint provides an API for automatically fixing a vulnerability. This is immensely beneficial to programmers, as debugging a vulnerability can be a complex, arduous, and time-consuming task. New rules can be shared with the community on npm, which already contains at least tens of thousands of linting rules. As soon as a new vulnerability and fix are discovered, they can be shared with everyone.

Second, ESLint provides advanced *linter customization* options. ESLint enables a programmer to use, or write, a custom parser, to provide additional capabilities to linter rules. This would prove useful for writing more advanced linter rules or for linting syntactic extensions to ESLint. In fact, this is done to enable linting of TypeScript [20]. Furthermore, a programmer can use, or write, a custom "processor", which pre-processes a non-JavaScript file before parsing it. This is done to enable linting of non-JavaScript files that contain JavaScript, e.g. HTML source files. In addition, a programmer can use, or write, a custom formatter, to change how ESLint displays linter results.

Third, and last, is *integration*. ESLint builds into mainstream text editors and IDEs, as we have seen in Sect. 2, making it easy to adopt by mainstream developers. Furthermore, as is clear from its customization options and since it can be run from the command-line, ESLint can be run as part of a CD/CI pipeline, as part of the building, testing, or deployment process.

Limitations. ESLint is not without its limitations, however.

First, like most linters, ESLint has *no correctness proof*. Not only need the programmer trust the claim of the maintainers of ESLint that ESLint does what it claims to do; the programmer also needs to trust the rule creators that their rules do what they specify. This is mitigated somewhat by the fact that ESLint, and the rules published on npm are publicly available, meaning that anyone can scrutinize them for correctness. However, the reason we have correctness proofs is that no amount of testing can guarantee the absence of bugs, and some bugs in open-source software are so subtle that they pass human scrutiny for decades [23]. Until we have formally-verified linters, this is the best we have got.

Second, and last, ESLint only scans *one file at a time*. This poses two problems for using ESLint for security. One is that ESLint will not scan dependencies. This is an issue since 93% of the code of modern Web apps is open-source library code [42], and 70.5% of Web apps have vulnerabilities from a library. This can be mitigated by making overapproximations on calls to libraries, although this would produce false positives. The other, more serious, problem is compositional reasoning. Even if all modules that make a modern Web app are scanned separately and found to be free of vulnerabilities, the way in which these modules interact may introduce vulnerabilities [29,45]. This can be mitigated by producing, from all JavaScript files that constitute a given Web app, one large JavaScript file, and then running ESLint on it. However, if ESLint finds a vulnerability in that composite file, assigning blame to the original source files would be difficult.

Evaluation. As demonstrated in Sect. 4, despite these limitations, we were quite successful in implementing practical rules that help programmers detect and eliminate vulnerabilities in software. Given how easy it is to share rules with the community, the potential impact of doing this is high. In fact, after being on npm for 1 week, our plugin has over 1.000 weekly downloads. This is without any promotion of the plugin. As awareness of this plugin increases, we imagine that its popularity will increase.

Observation 1. *Linters can (and should) be used to detect and eliminate vulnerabilities in software.*

Observation 2. *The potential impact of creating and sharing linter rules for security is high.*

5.2 ESLint Security Plugins

Given the above observations, the popularity of linters, our success with creating rules for vulnerabilities, and the prevalence of vulnerabilities in software, it stands to reason that ESLint would have rules for finding and fixing vulnerabilities in quantity and quality. Surprisingly, we find that this is not the case.

We surveyed the security relevance of more than 250 ESLint plugins in npm, in descending order of popularity, by briefly looking at their descriptions and then investigating the implementations of those that contain security-related rules. We also specifically investigated a handful of less popular security-specific plugins. We summarize our findings for the most relevant plugins in the following.

eslint-plugin-security (135.000 weekly downloads). This plugin informs programmers of a wide range of vulnerabilities in Node.js applications. It is the most popular ESLint security plugin. The popularity of the plugin is consistent over time. However, the maintenance of the code is not, with more than three years since the last update. Furthermore, as stated on the npm page of the plugin, the rules have a lot of false positives. Finally, the rules target narrow situations, none of which fall under the vulnerabilities that we target with our rules.

eslint-plugin-security-node (900 weekly downloads). This plugin also covers a wide range of vulnerabilities for Node.js applications. It has considerable overlap with the previous ones but does attempt to cover some different vulnerabilities. No documentation exists for many of the rules, and the quality of the rule implementations is very low. Some of the rules have considerable false *negatives*. This is illustrated in rules `detect-sql-injection` and `detect-helmet-without-nocache`, which we discussed in Sects. 4.2 and 4.3; if variables do not have the names that the rules expect, the rules completely disregard the code, thus possibly accepting vulnerable code. Despite the plugin being last updated 4 months ago, one of the rules throws an exception if the plugin is installed in projects using Node.js version 14 or above.

eslint-plugin-no-unsanitized (25.000 weekly downloads). This plugin discourages developers from using unsafe manipulation of the DOM with methods such as `document.write` and `.innerHTML`. The goal is to prevent XSS attacks. The plugin is consistently maintained by Mozilla. However, the rules have several shortcomings, discussed in detail in Sect. 4.1: The rules in the plugin generate many false positives; they only allow explicit strings in DOM assignments. Furthermore, the rules do not consider the manipulation of `href` and `src`. Finally, the rules do not support Web frameworks that render HTML dynamically, such as the popular React.

eslint-plugin-no-unsafe-innerhtml. (12.000 downloads per week). This plugin is the same as the previous one, except with a smaller scope of considering `.innerHTML` assignment. It was last updated 3 years ago.

eslint-plugin-no-secrets. (5.000 weekly downloads). This plugin discourages programmers from having different kinds of secrets in the source code. The rule uses regex to find patterns of potentially secret values in the code. However, the rule has false negatives, in the form of secrets that do not match any of the given patterns. The rule does include, as an option, to ignore specific secret identifiers, which can help decrease the number of false positives that the rule generates. The plugin was updated within the last 3 months.

eslint-plugin-sql-injection. (2 weekly downloads). This plugin discourages programmers from using string concatenation in SQL query execution. As discussed in detail in Sect. 4.3, this rule has a lot of false negatives, since it ignores all variables that are not specified in the rule configuration, and even then, does not consider e.g. template strings. It has not been updated in 2 years.

Evaluation. There are surprisingly few plugins that target vulnerabilities. The handful of security rules that see notable use identify only a few vulnerabilities in total. Alarmingly, they focus overwhelmingly on reducing false *negatives*, while still having considerably many false positives, to the point that the rules might be too inconvenient use, and thus gets disabled by programmers. Finally, the checks that the rules are making are rather simple. As demonstrated in Section 4, we were able to implement security rules as a proof-of-concept with relative ease.

Observation 3. *The effort needed to create & share linter rules is low.*

Observation 4. *Linting for vulnerabilities is underexplored.*

5.3   ESLint Rule Guidelines

Pondering the reason for the state of ESLint plugins for security, we analyze the ESLint guidelines for creating new core rules [39], to assess whether the guidelines are a good fit for writing rules for security. We find that most of the guidelines run counter to the needs of a rule for security. The following is a summary of the guidelines:

Widely applicable. The rule should be of importance to a large number of developers; no individual preferences.
Generic. The rule must not be so specific that it is hard to know when to use it; at most two "and"s.
Atomic. The rule must work on its own, and be oblivious to other rules.
Unique. The rule must not produce same warnings as existing rules (no overlap) as that confuses the programmer.
Library-agnostic. The rule must not be based on specific libraries or frameworks (except Node.js).
No conflicts. The rule must not conflict with other rules.

For a rule to be incorporated into the core rules set, the rule *had*[1] to follow these guidelines. However, "widely applicable" and "generic" runs counter to the

---

[1] ESLint no longer accepts new rules into the core rule set, as of 2020.

fact that vulnerabilities arise under highly specific circumstances, and "library-agnostic" runs counter to the fact that most vulnerabilities arise from libraries and their use, as explained under limitations in Sect. 5.1. While a rule author does not *have* to follow these guidelines, she might want to, in the hope that the rule makes its way to core, and thus has more impact. Finally, these are the only guidelines for writing rules; there are no guidelines for writing rules for security.

5.4   ESLint Configuration

Configuring ESLint is a nontrivial task, which is a well-known barrier to using linters effectively. A study conducted by Delft University of Technology in 2019, shows that 38,3% of the study participants (all JavaScript developers) agreed that *"creating or maintaining configurations was a challenging part of using a linter."* [40]. This validates our perception that the domain of linters contains problem areas and difficulties worth exploring and improving.

6   Recommendations

We formulate four recommendations on the use of linters for security.

Recommendation 1. *Linters should be configurable*

We find that there is no linter that comes with a set of fixed rules that addresses all critical security vulnerabilities. This observation is corroborated by our new rules on cross-site scripting, which demonstrate that the one-rule-fix-all approach is insufficient to tackle all facets of cross-site scripting attacks. Hence, linters should be configurable and pluggable so that users can extend them with either in-house rules or with community rules, which the users can enable as needed.

Recommendation 2. *Linters should scan code differently to enable the finding of more security vulnerabilities*

We have found that linters are precluded from finding some vulnerabilities because files are evaluated individually and in an arbitrary order. However, files often depend from other files, and vulnerabilities may arise by looking on how such files depend on each other (e.g. library dependencies). We observe that this can be potentially fixed by scanning multiple files, with the evaluation order provided by the user or automatically suggested. A linter could even report issues in libraries to the library authors, along with instructions on how to patch the vulnerability. With more general ways of scanning code in place, a linter can be viewed as a *framework* for implementing static analysis tools.

Recommendation 3. *Linter security rules should have proper descriptions*

We have found that existing rules do not precisely describe what kind of vulnerabilities they intend to detect. Rules should instead provide the user with a precise explanation of the potential issue flagged in a piece of code. Failing in doing so may affect the user understanding of the possible issues with their code and, even worse, may lead the user to ignore the output of the rule. We believe that providing proper descriptions is a key enabler to retain linter popularity also for finding security vulnerabilities.

Recommendation 4. *Linter security rules should maximize case coverage and reduce false positives*

A rule should detect as many instances of a vulnerability as possible, and it should do so as precisely as possible. The value that a rule provides to the programmer scales with its ability to correctly flag as many possible vulnerable code cases as possible. However, a rule should strive to eliminate false positives as these are a significant challenge when using linters [40]. Intuitively, maximizing case coverage and reducing false positive might be seen as two contrasting requirements: attempts at maximizing case coverage may introduce new false positives. Moreover, from a security perspective, much focus is put on avoiding missing vulnerabilities hence avoiding false negatives. However, we observe that the number of false positives affect considerably the development flow of the user, who has to investigate each flagged case to determine whether it is a false negative or not, which can lead the user to decide to disable the rule.

7   Related Work

A comprehensive list of open source and commercial static analysis tools is available in [31]. Here, we focus on prior works on linters and linter-like tools for JavaScript and other programming languages, putting emphasis on how they address security vulnerabilities.

JSLint [12] and JSHint [27] are two popular linters for JavaScript. The former being more dogmatic in linting, the latter being more flexible. None of them focuses on linting for security vulnerabilities nor allows for user-developed plugins. Sonarlint [35] is a linter that supports several programming languages, including JavaScript. It notably categorizes security-related rules in vulnerabilities and security hotspots. A vulnerability has a higher security impact than a security hotspot. For example, the use of a Web SQL database is considered a vulnerability, while hardcoding credentials is considered a security hotspot. Sonarlint cannot be extended via plugins and, at the time of writing this paper, it counts 3 non-deprecated vulnerability rules and 15 security hotspot rules for JavaScript. Similarly to our detect-sql-injection rule, Sonarlint has a rule that flags the execution of SQL queries that are built using formatting of strings. However, differently from our approach, Sonarlint has limited coverage on Node.js APIs and does not cover cross-site scripting attacks.

Several linters for other programming languages than JavaScript have considered vulnerability rules. Splint [14] is probably the first extensible linter for security vulnerabilities. It parses C code to find potential buffer overflows and provides a general language that enables users to define their own rules. However, to the best of our knowledge, there are no community-driven rules available today, hence, making a proper comparison against our proposed rules is impossible. Flawfinder [44] is a simpler tool that instead does a lexical analysis of C/C++ code in order to find security weaknesses. It has been recently found that Flawfinder detects more types of vulnerabilities than its competitors [25]. Cpplint [1] is an automated checker to make sure that a C++ program follows Google's style guide, which includes very few security tests. Neither Flawfinder nor Cpplint supports plugins.

Bandit [4] is a linter for finding security issues in Python code. Similarly to ESLint, Bandit allows one to write a plugin that can extend the tool with additional security tests. To the best of our knowledge, Bandit has not been as successful as ESLint in attracting new plugins. Differently from the rules proposed in our work, most of the preinstalled tests in Bandit concern hardcoded strings such as passwords, and command injections vulnerabilities such as attacks due to invoking external executables.

FindBugs [6] is a popular linter for Java with over 30 rules for security. It is not extensible. SpotBugs [2] is deemed as the successor or FindBugs and is extensible; Find Security Bugs [5] is the SpotBugs plugin for security vulnerabilities. However, SpotBugs does not provide a repository of plugins. Neither FindBugs nor SpotBugs facilitate automatic bug fixing.

GoCritic, Revive, and Ruleguard are linters for Go that allow external rules. A comparison of the tools is provided in [34]. Gosec [3] is a security linter for Go. It has a limited and not user-extensible number of available rules. It includes rules that raise issues in case of SQL query constructions using format string or string concatenation. However, it does not cover cross-site scripting attacks.

8 Conclusion

Linters are static analysis tools that have great potential to automatically detect and eliminate vulnerabilities in software. This topic is relatively unexplored, and in this work, we have investigated to which extent linters can help mainstream programmers to deliver vulnerability detection, with a specific focus on how a pluggable linter can help JavaScript programmers to write secure code.

We have found that the effort required to create ESLint rules for security vulnerabilities is rather low, while the impact of creating such rules is potentially high. This requires, however, the rules being well documented and being engineered to minimize false positives.

We also observe that linters should be easily configurable to adapt to the new security vulnerabilities facets that may arise in libraries, fostering the rapid development of rules that address such vulnerabilities. Similarly, linters should facilitate the scanning of dependencies since vulnerabilities are likely to come from invoked libraries [42].

We have demonstrated that automatic vulnerability fixing is effective, and believe that linters have the potential to enable detection and correction of vulnerabilities in libraries even before the library developers produce a patch for the vulnerable code: a library developer may add a rule for ESLint while working on a long-term fix for the vulnerability. We also note that library developers who do not use linters may introduce well-known vulnerabilities in their code. Linters that already have community-driven rules addressing such well-known vulnerabilities can thus facilitate the report of them to library developers.

Obviously, linters are not the sole tool for effective vulnerability detection and fixing. Other approaches might achieve a better balance in terms of security and tool popularity. With this work, we aim at broadening the view and at stimulating discussion within the program analysis community towards novel and practical ways to tackle vulnerability detection and fixing in software.

A   ESLint

A.1   How ESLint Works

ESLint builds on Node.js and can be installed through npm. After that a configuration file is created, ESLint can be run on source files, e.g. from the command line or within an IDE [46]. ESLint takes as parameters which source file to lint and a configuration which e.g. specifies which rules to use.

First, ESLint parses the source file to render an abstract syntax tree (AST) from it. Each node in the resulting AST is a record which contains, amongst others, the type of the syntactic element it represents (e.g. `VariableDeclaration`, `Identifier`, `FunctionDeclaration`, etc.), and information about where in the source file the syntactic element is located (for blame assignment). In case the information in this AST is insufficient (e.g. when writing advanced rules), ESLint lets one specify a different parser from the default one (i.e. Espree [38]), to construct an AST that stores additional information.

Next, ESLint traverses this AST to check that all rules are upheld. Each rule in ESLint is represented by an object. A rule object maintains its own state and exports methods which ESLint calls while traversing the AST. At each node, both while going down and up the AST, ESLint invokes, on each rule object, a method representing the type of the node (`VariableDeclaration`, etc.; see above) and code paths (`onCodePathStart`, `onCodePathSegmentLoop`, etc.). If a rule detects an issue, then the rule reports the issue to a `context`, which ESLint passes as a parameter when it creates the rule object.

A.2   Rules

Each rule in ESLint consists of three files(See footnote 3): a source file, a test file, and a documentation file.   Source files[2],(e.g. Fig. 2), are stored in `lib/rules`. They have the following format[3]. A source file exports an object with two properties.

```
1 module.exports = { meta:meta, create:create }
```

---

[2] This is a slightly simplified version of the original, from ESLint core.

[3] Rules are not strictly required to follow this format; some deviate from it.

```
1   module.exports = {
2     meta: {
3       docs: {
4         description: "no returning value from constructor",
5         url: "https://eslint[...]/no-constructor-return",
6         category: "Best Practices",
7         recommended: false
8       },
9       type: "problem"
10     },
11    create: function(context){
12      const message = "Unexpected return in constructor."
13      const stack = [];
14      return {
15        onCodePathStart: function(_,node){stack.push(node)},
16        onCodePathEnd:   function()     {stack.pop()},
17        ReturnStatement: function(node){
18          const last = stack[stack.length - 1]
19          if (!last.parent) { return }
20          if ( last.parent.type === "MethodDefinition" &&
21               last.parent.kind === "constructor" &&
22               node.parent.parent === last || node.argument
23          ){ context.report({ node, message }) } }}}}
```

Fig. 2. no-constructor-return source file.no-constructor-return source file.

The objects *meta* and *docs* have four properties.

```
1  meta = { docs : docs, type : string, fixable : boolean, schema :
      schema }
2  docs = { description : string, url : string, recommended : boolean
      , category : string }
```

In *docs*, `description` is a description of what the rule checks. `url` is the URL to the rule's documentation. `recommended` specifies whether this rule should be added to the list of recommended ESLint rules (which can all be turned on with a single option in the configuration). `category` specifies where this rule should appear in the rules index; valid values include `"Possible Errors"`, `"Best Practices"`, `"Strict Mode"`, & `"Stylistic Issues"`. In *meta*, `type` specifies the type of the rule; valid values are `"problem"` for a rule that identifies bad behavior, `"suggestion"` for a rule that provides improvement suggestions, and `"layout"` for a rule that provides stylistic tips. If a rule does not automatically fix an issue, then the `fixable` property should be omitted. Otherwise, `fixable` should be set to `"whitespace"` if it only affects whitespace, and `"code"` otherwise. *schema* specifies which configuration options the rule accepts and should be omitted if the rule accepts no such options. *create*, called when the rule object is created, returns an object which contains the functions that

ESLint calls while traversing the AST (see above). The rule in Figure 2 gives an example of how a rule can maintain state and traverse the AST. Its state is a stack of code paths, which it uses, upon encountering a `return` statement, to examine the AST to see if the statement is occurring within a constructor.

Test files are stored in `tests/lib/rules`. The test file contains sample inputs, along with the expected result of applying the rule on said input (valid, invalid). The unit test can then be run using the testing facility built in ESLint. Documentation files, stored in `docs/rules`, are written in Markdown syntax, and provide a description of what rules check, and how to configure them.

Plugins. Additional rules can be added to ESLint by downloading ESLint plugins. A plugin is a collection of ESLint rules. Plugins are routinely created by individuals and organizations, and shared as packages on npm. At present, npm contains thousands of ESLint plugins, each of which often contains tens of rules.

References

1. Cpplint (2009). https://github.com/cpplint/cpplint/
2. Spotbugs (2017). https://spotbugs.github.io/
3. Gosec - golang security checker (2018). https://github.com/securego/gosec
4. Bandit (2019). https://github.com/PyCQA/bandit
5. Arteau, P.: Find security bugs (2012). https://find-sec-bugs.github.io
6. Ayewah, N., Hovemeyer, D., Morgenthaler, J.D., Penix, J., Pugh, W.: Using static analysis to find bugs. IEEE Softw. **25**(5), 22–29 (2008)
7. Ball, T., et al.: Thorough static analysis of device drivers. In: Proceedings of the 2006 EuroSys Conference, Leuven, Belgium, 18–21 April 2006, pp. 73–85. ACM (2006)
8. Bessey, A., et al.: A few billion lines of code later: using static analysis to find bugs in the real world. Commun. ACM **53**(2), 66–75 (2010)
9. Brat, G., Klemm, R.: Static analysis of the mars exploration rover flight software. In: Proceedings of the First International Space Mission Challenges for Information Technology, pp. 321–326 (2003)
10. Calcagno, C., Distefano, D., O'Hearn, P.W., Yang, H.: Compositional shape analysis by means of bi-abduction. In: Proceedings of the 36th ACM SIGPLAN-SIGACT Symposium on Principles of Programming Languages, POPL 2009, Savannah, GA, USA, 21–23 January 2009, pp. 289–300. ACM (2009)
11. Chess, B., McGraw, G.: Static analysis for security. IEEE Secur. Priv. **2**(6), 76–79 (2004)
12. Crockford, D.: Jslint (2002). https://www.jslint.com/
13. Ernst, M.D.: Invited talk: static and dynamic analysis: synergy and duality. In: Proceedings of the 2004 ACM SIGPLAN-SIGSOFT Workshop on Program Analysis For Software Tools and Engineering, PASTE 2004, Washington, DC, USA, 7–8 June 2004, p. 35. ACM (2004)
14. Evans, D., Larochelle, D.: Improving security using extensible lightweight static analysis. IEEE Softw. **19**(1), 42–51 (2002)
15. Feldman, M.B.: Who's using ADA? real-world projects powered by the ADA programming language, November 2014 (2014). https://www2.seas.gwu.edu/~mfeldman/ada-project-summary.html

16. Guarnieri, S., Livshits, V.B.: GATEKEEPER: mostly static enforcement of security and reliability policies for JavaScript code. In: 18th USENIX Security Symposium, Montreal, Canada, 10–14 August 2009, Proceedings, pp. 151–168. USENIX Association (2009)
17. Guarnieri, S., Pistoia, M., Tripp, O., Dolby, J., Teilhet, S., Berg, R.: Saving the world wide web from vulnerable JavaScript. In: Proceedings of the 20th International Symposium on Software Testing and Analysis, ISSTA 2011, Toronto, ON, Canada, 17–21 July 2011, pp. 177–187. ACM (2011)
18. Guha, A., Saftoiu, C., Krishnamurthi, S.: The essence of JavaScript. In: D'Hondt T. (ed.) ECOOP 2010 - Object-Oriented Programming, 24th European Conference, Maribor, Slovenia, 21–25 June 2010. Proceedings. LNCS, vol. 6183, pp. 126–150. Springer, Heidelberg (2010). https://doi.org/10.1007/978-3-642-14107-2_7
19. Hahn, E.: Helmet (2012). https://helmetjs.github.io/
20. Henry, J.: Typescript eslint parser (2019). https://www.npmjs.com/package/@typescript-eslint/parser
21. Inc., F.: React (2013). https://reactjs.org/
22. Johnson, B., Song, Y., Murphy-Hill, E.R., Bowdidge, R.W.: Why don't software developers use static analysis tools to find bugs? In: 35th International Conference on Software Engineering, ICSE 2013, San Francisco, CA, USA, 18–26 May 2013, pp. 672–681. IEEE Computer Society (2013)
23. Johnson, P.: 11 software bugs that took way too long to meet their maker (2015). CSO, From IDG Communications. https://www.csoonline.com/article/3404334/11-software-bugs-that-took-way-too-long-to-meet-their-maker.html
24. Johnson, S.C.: Lint, A C Program Checker. Bell Telephone Laboratories, New Providence (1977)
25. Kaur, A., Nayyar, R.: A comparative study of static code analysis tools for vulnerability detection in C/C++ and Java source code. Proc. Comput. Sci. **171**, 2023–2029 (2020)
26. Keinänen, M.: Creation of a web service using the MERN stack (2018)
27. Kovalyov, A.: Jshint (2011). https://www.jshint.com/. Accessed 25 Jun 2020
28. Meyerovich, L.A., Livshits, V.B.: Conscript: specifying and enforcing fine-grained security policies for JavaScript in the browser. In: 31st IEEE Symposium on Security and Privacy, S&P 2010, 16–19 May 2010, Berleley/Oakland, California, USA, pp. 481–496. IEEE Computer Society (2010)
29. Mitchell, J.C.: Programming language methods in computer security. In: Proceedings of the 28th ACM SIGPLAN-SIGACT Symposium on Principles of Programming Languages, POPL 2001, London, UK, 17–19 January 2001. ACM (2001)
30. OWASP Foundation: OWASP Top Ten (2017)
31. OWASP Foundation: source code analysis tools (2020). https://owasp.org/www-community/Source_Code_Analysis_Tools
32. Rice, H.G.: Classes of recursively enumerable sets and their decision problems. Trans. Am. Math. Soc. **74**(2), 358–366 (1953)
33. Sadowski, C., Aftandilian, E., Eagle, A., Miller-Cushon, L., Jaspan, C.: Lessons from building static analysis tools at google. Commun. ACM **61**(4), 58–66 (2018)
34. Sharipov, I.: Ruleguard: dynamic inspection rules for Go (2020). https://quasilyte.dev/blog/post/ruleguard/
35. SonarSource: Sonarlint (2008). https://www.sonarlint.org/
36. Stack Exchange Inc.: Stack overflow developer survey (2020)
37. StrongLoop: Express (2010). https://expressjs.com/
38. Team, E.: Espree (2014). https://github.com/eslint/espree

39. Team, E.: Eslint: contributing new rules (2020). https://eslint.org/docs/developer-guide/contributing/new-rules
40. Tómasdóttir, K.F., Aniche, M., Van Deursen, A.: The adoption of JavaScript linters in practice: a case study on ESLint. IEEE Trans. Softw. Eng. **46**, 863 - 891 (2018)
41. VeraCode: State of software security: Open source edition (2020)
42. Voss, L.: NPM and the future of Javascript (2018). https://slides.com/seldo/npm-and-the-future-of-javascript/. invited talk at JSConf US 2018
43. Wedyan, F., Alrmuny, D., Bieman, J.M.: The effectiveness of automated static analysis tools for fault detection and refactoring prediction. In: Second International Conference on Software Testing Verification and Validation, ICST 2009, Denver, Colorado, USA, 1–4 April 2009, pp. 141–150. IEEE Computer Society (2009)
44. Wheeler, D.: Flawfinder (2001). https://dwheeler.com/flawfinder/
45. Wing, J.M.: A call to action: look beyond the horizon. IEEE Secur. Priv. **1**(6), 62–67 (2003)
46. Zakas, N.C.: Eslint (2013). https://eslint.org/

Sequential Anomaly Detection Using Feedback and Prioritized Experience Replay

Anish Reddy Ellore[1], Sanket Mishra[1,2]($\boxtimes$), and Chittaranjan Hota[1]

[1] BITS Pilani Hyderabad Campus, Hyderabad, Telangana, India
anishreddy.ellore@gmail.com, hota@hyderabad.bits-pilani.ac.in
[2] Vellore Institute of Technology, Amaravati, Andhra Pradesh, India
p20150408@hyderabad.bits-pilani.ac.in

Abstract. Time series anomaly detection is essential because it helps in identifying faulty sensors and malicious behaviour in real-time. Most of the research work on anomaly detection revolves around density-based unsupervised learning techniques for batch data and forecasting (threshold-based) techniques for streaming data. Typically in streaming data, we continuously encounter concept drifts due to which the forecasting approaches' threshold becomes insignificant with time. Also, forecasting techniques cannot identify sequential anomalies, as they try to forecast as per the ingested data. The reason behind less implementations using supervised learning for anomaly detection is because of the class imbalance problem in the dataset and unavailability of the labels. Most of the anomaly datasets contain 5% outliers due to which any learning model will overfit on normal data class and will not be able to learn about the anomalous class. In this work, we address these issues using Prioritized Experience Replay and introduce a novel state function which incorporates feedback to identify sequential anomalies. We evaluate our model on the Yahoo benchmark dataset, which contains 367 time-series datasets (each testing different aspects of anomaly detection), four smart home energy datasets and Numenta Anomaly benchmark datasets consisting of 58 time series data. The paper exhibits better performance of the proposed approach over the baseline approaches across different anomaly datasets.

Keywords: Anomaly detection · Internet of Things · Prioritized Experience Replay · Feedback mechanism · Long Short Term Memory Network

1 Introduction

Anomaly detection has been an active research area owing to its ubiquitous nature in various fields. It is a very important field of study and has proven useful in the field of intrusion detection [8], android malware analysis [15], fault diagnosis [29], energy [23] and fraud detection in financial transactions [9]. Internet of Things(IoT) witnessed an exponential growth in last half decade as its

© Springer Nature Switzerland AG 2020
M. Kutyłowski et al. (Eds.): NSS 2020, LNCS 12570, pp. 245–260, 2020.
https://doi.org/10.1007/978-3-030-65745-1_14

applications are becoming more complex in nature and estimated to reach 25 billion "things" by 2025 [4]. As IoT devices continuously capture data from various sensors, the collected data is heterogeneous in nature. As a result extraction of actionable knowledge from this raw data streams needs in-depth data analysis. Event Driven Applications (EDA) form complex events from these dynamic IoT streams and presence of anomalies can lead to increased false positives or false alarms. Also, sequential anomaly detection can help in identifying targeted slow attacks early.

An anomaly is an outlier that can be defined as an instance that deviates significantly from other data instances. Anomalies are synonymous with outliers in data mining in representing particular data points which follow a different distribution with respect to underlying distribution of the data [30]. Recent research has included supervised solutions and unsupervised solutions (forecasting) for addressing the issue of detection of anomalies. An underlying assumption in unsupervised anomaly detection approaches is that anomalies are rare instances that are prevalent in the low density regions of the feature space or points exhibiting significant deviations from the underlying data distribution. However, these characteristics are defied in real-world data and thus, leading to a supposedly drop in performance. A notable shortcoming in forecasting approaches is that these approaches try to minimize the difference between the actual value and predicted value, this difference is termed as an anomaly score. In order to identify anomalies in high-dimensional data, various deep learning approaches [17,33,35] have been proposed. Supervised learning methods [22] usually offer better performance in comparison to unsupervised techniques [18,19].

In this work, we undertake the problem of anomaly detection as a classification task. But we face two limitations in this respect.

- The imbalanced nature of anomaly datasets.
- The inability of existing algorithms to give progressive feedback for identification of sequential anomalies.

To address the above shortcomings, we propose a deep learning approach augmented with a feedback module and Prioritized Experience Replay (PER) [25]. PER effectively samples the data and prioritizes the anomalies so that the learning model can effectively train on these instances. This is in contrary to regression approaches or other classification approaches who train on normal data and then mark data as anomalies which are not aligned on their prediction. The proposed work uses a Long Short Term Memory (LSTM) model to classify instances as inliers or outliers[1]. The LSTM network is trained on a novel state function using PER.

---

[1] The terms outliers and anomalies have been used interchangeably in this work.

2   Motivation

In time-series anomaly detection, most of the research works revolves around forecasting techniques [18,19], where anomaly detection is implemented based on prediction error. One of the issues with using this method is that it requires a cumbersome process of hand modeling the static threshold. This static threshold will not be able to adapt to the concept drift in streams. In the forecasting method, every model tries to reduce the prediction error, which is an issue when the data streams contain anomalies and the model is trying to predict based on anomalies. Due to this inability, forecasting models are not successful in detecting sequential anomalies. To overcome these problems, we pose time-series anomaly detection as a sequence classification problem and introduce a feedback mechanism to detect sequential anomalies. The intuition behind using feedback is that for a model to detect sequential anomalies, it needs to know if the previous data point is an anomaly or not, so that it can use this context to take a decision in regard to the new data point. Similar feedback can be included for forecasting approaches to prevent the models from trying the reduce the difference between predicted values and the actual values once the anomalies begin to appear (discussed in Sect. 5.4). And, one of the problems of dealing anomaly detection as supervised sequence classification is the imbalance in data leading to over-fitting the normal class. To overcome this problem, we prioritize anomalous class using Prioritized Experience Replay.

3   Related Work

Anomaly detection approaches can be broadly classified into two categories, namely unsupervised and supervised anomaly detection approaches. Unsupervised approaches consist of distance based approaches [6,21] and deep learning approaches [17,33,35]. Authors [17] proposed an ensemble of LSTMs for detecting anomalies on time-series data. They trained on non-anomalous data in order to predict degree of outlierness on anomalous data. Zong et al. [35] implemented a Deep Autoencoder with Gaussian Mixture Model and formulated an objective function to obtain an optimized threshold that separates anomalous and non-anomalous instances. Rashid et al. [23] proposed Artificial Neural Network (ANN) regression approach to predict the data and found anomalous instances by finding the difference between actual data and predicted value. The authors depicted the importance of usage of context in anomaly detection by fusing weather and temporal information in the analysis. However, a CNN-LSTM (Convolutional-Long Short Term Memory) approach [22] proposed a classification approach to identify anomalies on cloud data. To balance the data in the anomaly datasets, the authors also suggested a novel Variational AutoEncoder data sampling strategy that improved the end predictions. Lopez-Martini et al. [14] presented their work for detection of anomalies on network traffic using a CNN-LSTM approach. Yamanaka et al. [34] proposed a supervised Autoencoder for binary classification on MNIST, KDD and CIFAR datasets. They modeled the data as a Bernoulli distribution and computed the conditional probability of the labels. The reconstruction error of the proposed autoencoder is formed from the negative logarithm of the likelihood calculated earlier. The model tries to minimize the negative log likelihood for inliers and maximize the reconstruction error to infer anomalous instances.

4   Proposed Methodology

In this section, we present our state function with feedback and the details of training and testing components of the framework. In this paper, we pose the time-series anomaly detection problem as a sequence classification problem and we solve the imbalanced class classification problem with the help of Prioritized Experience Replay. Furthermore, we introduce a feedback mechanism to detect sequential anomalies. The feedback represents the anomaly score of the previous state. This feedback helps in detecting sequential anomalies as we depict in the experimental section by comparing model performance with and without feedback.

4.1   Feedback

Feedback to the model is nothing but whether the previous data point in the time series setup is an anomaly or not, it is a message passed from previous state to the new state. In the proposed framework, we take the feedback as the model's decision on the previous data point, but this can also be extended and made foolproof by introducing other anomaly detection models to generate the feedback. Including external feedback from other anomaly detection models is left for future work but this component is shown in the testing framework for illustration purpose. The feedback is considered perfect if the feedback is always accurate. However this is only limited to training stage and for hypothetical scenarios as it is not possible to get perfect feedback in testing stage or a real setup.

4.2   State Function

Figure 1 shows the training and testing states used where each state is of length L, and each timestep has two features (datapoint and previous state feedback). During the training stage, we can get the perfect feedback regarding the previous state, so we consider the previous state's anomaly label as feedback. But in the testing stage, we do not have access to the anomaly labels. Thus, the feedback score can be taken from external sources (another model) or the existing model itself. We elaborately discuss on this aspect in the testing stage section. Even though all the figures represent univariate time-series data, the feedback mechanism can also be used with multivariate time-series data.

Table 1. Symbol table

Symbol	Description
X	Data point
Y	Anomaly label
A	Feedback
L	Lookback
Exp	Experience (Training state)
t	Time step

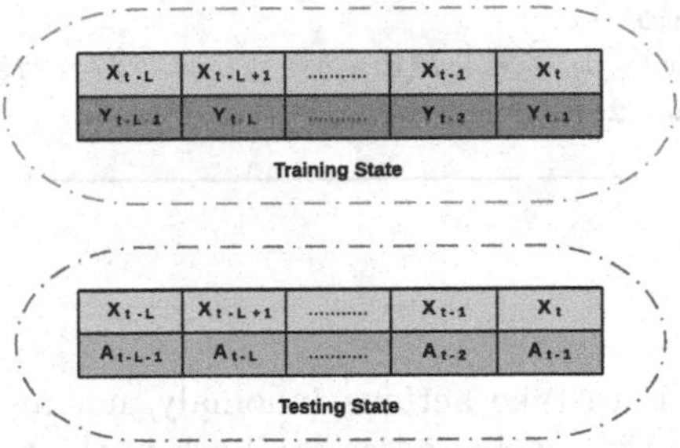

Fig. 1. Training and testing states where (X, Y, A, L) represent (Datapoint, Anomaly Label, Action, Look-back) and t represents timestamp.

4.3 Prioritized Experience Replay

PER helps in prioritizing the unlearnt experiences by giving them more priority and in this case such experiences are anomalies. PER contains a Replay Buffer which stores experiences along with their priorities. These priorities are calculated based on the prediction error of the model. Prioritized Batch sampling is used to sample micro batches instead of a random sampling. These techniques are discussed in a detailed manner in the Algorithm 1. The authors [25] conduct experiments on imbalanced image dataset and conclude that using the PER results in faster training and outperforms random batch sampling. This faster training helps with real-time scenarios where we can have less training time to deploy new model. Other implementation details are mentioned in Algorithm 1. In the algorithm, the prioritization constant α represents the priority given to the prediction error in calculating the probability. If the value of α is zero then the PER is nothing but random sampling, but with $\alpha > 0$ the algorithm will be prioritizing based on the prediction error. Also, ϵ is used as a smoothing constant to avoid zero probabilities for the experiences with zero prediction error.

Algorithm 1: Prioritized Experience Replay for supervised learning

   Input: budget T, mini batch size K, smoothing constant ϵ, prioritization
      constant α

1 Add all the experiences E (Training State) to replay buffer R with priority $p = \epsilon$
  for $t = 1$ to T **do**
    /* sampling batch based on priorities   */
2   **for** $j = 1$ to K **do**
3   Sample experience s_j with probability $P(j) = p_j^\alpha / \sum_i p_i^\alpha$
4   add s_j to mini batch M
5   Train the model on mini batch M
    /* update priorities based on training error   */
6   **for** $j = 1$ to K **do**
7   Update priority $p_j \leftarrow \epsilon + L(\theta; s_j)$ // ϵ is added for making
      priority non zero

4.4 Agent

The role of an agent is to take actions (anomaly, not anomaly) based on the given state. This action is considered as feedback in the testing framework. The learning model used here is a Long Short-Term Memory Network. We have used LSTM because of its ability to learn sequential data, remove or add information to the cell state and retain important information when the sequence becomes longer. In this work we have used stacked LSTM network as the model but one can use any learning model as long as it supports the state function.

4.5 Training Framework

In Fig. 2, the training state contains anomaly label as feedback and these training states are sampled using PER to train the agent. The prioritized sampling described in section PER is handled by update-priorities module and sample-batch-based-on-priorities module. The update priorities module is responsible for updating priorities of each experience (sample state) based on the prediction error. The sample-batch-based-on-priorities module handles sampling a micro batch based on the priority of each experience and prioritization constant α as discussed in section PER. If this prioritization constant α is zero then this module does nothing but random batch sampling resulting in no PER. PER helps in identifying and learning unlearned experiences (anomalies) faster. The agent is trained in a micro-batch fashion where each micro batch's errors are transmitted to update corresponding priorities. For the agent's learning model, Binary-Cross-Entropy is used as loss function and Adam optimizer is used with a batch size of 128. Our model consists of an LSTM layer with 64 LSTM units, dropout layer and a dense layer to predict the anomaly and the state function used has a lookback of '15'. This learning model is a sequence-to-one type of model. Here F-score is used instead of accuracy to identify the best model during the training stage because of a very low anomaly percentage in the datasets leading to high accuracy. Details about the anomalies in the training and the testing split are discussed in Sect. 5.

4.6 Testing Framework

The testing framework is shown in Fig. 3 where the feedback from agent's previous prediction is transmitted to the state function generator to create a new

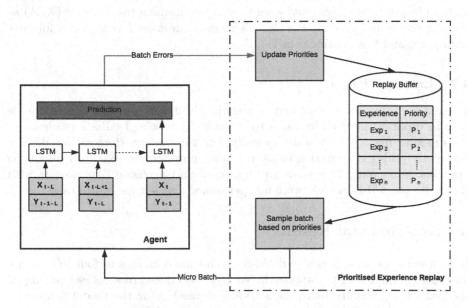

Fig. 2. Training Framework

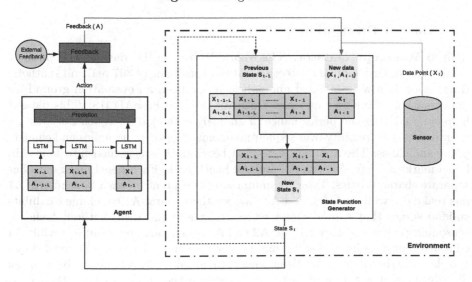

Fig. 3. Testing Framework

state. However instead of simply using agent's feedback we can merge it with external sources (other models) and send this combined feedback as the new feedback, experiments on this is left for future work. The feedback is considered perfect if the prediction about previous data point is accurate. The state function generator produces a new state S_t from the previous state S_{t-1}, new data point X_t and feedback A_{t-1}, it does this process by maintaining a fixed length in a rolling window fashion. This new state is sent to the agent to make a decision about it's anomalous nature.The LSTM model in the agent uses this state of length L(lookback) and each timestep containing two features (X, A) as a input vector and predicts it's class. This decision is used as feedback for next data point and this continues in loop.

4.7   External Sources

The external sources module can be seen in Fig. 3, the purpose of this module is to incorporate external feedback to the model's existing feedback mechanism. This module may contain other anomaly detection models (forecasting, density based etc.), this incorporation helps in getting more accurate feedback about the previous data point. This leads to high recall and precision.Experiments with the inclusion of this module were not performed and left for future work.

5   Experimental Results

In this work, we have considered Yahoo Webscope dataset and four IoT energy datasets for validating the approach. We have also done cross dataset testing on the Numenta Anomaly Benchmark (NAB) dataset using the model trained on A1 benchmark to check the generalization of the model on unseen datasets.

5.1   Dataset Description

Yahoo Webscope Dataset. The Yahoo Webscope [11] dataset is a publicly available standard anomaly detection dataset consisting of 367 real and synthetic time series data with labelled anomalies. It has been an evaluation ground for benchmarking the performance of DeepAnt [19] and FuseAD [18]. This dataset helps in analyzing the performance of anomaly detection approaches by testing their detection capability over sequential anomalies, point anomalies and change-point anomalies. The anomaly detection benchmark is classified into four sub-benchmarks namely, A1, A2, A3 and A4 benchmark. Each benchmark data has separate characteristics. Table 2 summarizes the contents of each benchmark. A1 has real data, while A2, A3, and A4 have synthetic data. A1 benchmark exhibits sudden surges that can be classified as anomalous instances without trend or seasonality characteristics in data. A2 and A3 benchmarks have outliers while A4 contains change-point anomalies making each benchmark unique. Figure 4 shows the class distributions of the Yahoo dataset and from A1, A3 and A4 benchmark distributions, it is tough to distinguish between the classes as both their class

Table 2. Yahoo dataset description

Benchmark	Type	Data characteristics	Number of time series	Data instances	Anomaly count
A1	Real	Contains Yahoo membership logins	67	94,866	1669
A2	Synthetic	Contain outliers only	100	142,100	466
A3	Synthetic	Contain outliers only	100	168,000	943
A4	Synthetic	Contains change point anomalies	100	168,000	837

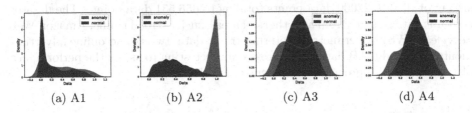

(a) A1   (b) A2   (c) A3   (d) A4

Fig. 4. Class distributions of Yahoo benchmark dataset using Kernel Density Estimation [11]

distributions are intertwined, whereas in the A2 benchmark there is a clear distinction between anomalies and normal class. From these class distribution plots, we can say that density-based approaches will fail to identify anomalies.

Energy Dataset. We reviewed four open-source datasets comprising of energy signatures of appliances from four different countries for assessing the performance of the proposed approach. The datasets considered in this work are Dataport [28], AMPds [16], ECO [5] and REFIT [20]. The characteristics of the datasets are enumerated in Table 3. Figure 5 depicts the class distributions of the energy datasets, namely dataport [28], AMPds [16], ECO [5] and REFIT [20]. In these distributions, both the means of class populations are closely leading to intertwined and inseparable distributions.

Table 3. Energy dataset characteristics

Dataset	Homes used	Number of appliances per home	Country	Training anomalies	Testing anomalies
Dataport [28]	24	9	USA	21668	8275
AMPds [16]	1	20	Canada	674	368
ECO [5]	6	8	Switzerland	2709	1134
REFIT [20]	20	9	UK	12145	6253

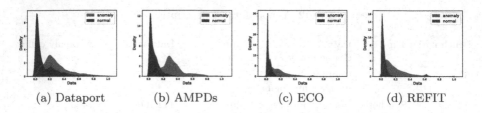

(a) Dataport   (b) AMPDs   (c) ECO   (d) REFIT

Fig. 5. Class distributions of energy datasets using Kernel Density Estimation

NAB Dataset. Numenta released NAB dataset for benchmarking anomaly detection approaches. The dataset comprises of 58 time-series data streams consisting of 1000 to 22000 data points totaling to 356,551 data points. The dataset contains data streams from a plethora of areas, such as, road traffic, Amazon Web Services (AWS) server metrics, internet traffic data, tweets and online advertisements. We used NAB dataset for cross-dataset testing to assess the performance of the proposed approach on this benchmark dataset.

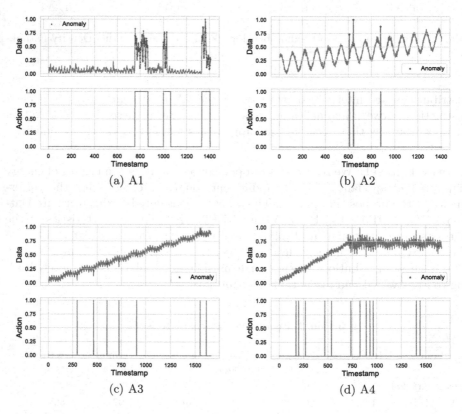

(a) A1   (b) A2

(c) A3   (d) A4

Fig. 6. Proposed model detecting anomalies in the Yahoo webscope dataset [11]

Table 4. Impact of feedback on proposed approach

Benchmark	Anomaly (Train, Test)	LSTM (No feedback)	LSTM (Feedback)	LSTM (Perfect feedback)
A1	621, 1030	0.26	0.63	0.94
A2	266, 288	0.98	0.98	0.98
A3	640, 295	0.98	0.97	0.97
A4	595, 234	0.95	0.96	0.96

5.2 Proposed Model and Variants

In this section, we compare the performance of our model with and without feedback. Table 4 shows the performance of the model in different settings on the Yahoo Webscope dataset, and anomalies in training and testing data-sets. The three experimental variants are:

1. **Model without feedback:** In this setting, we do not use feedback. So, the state function depicted in Fig. 1 contains no feedback feature at each timestep.
2. **Model with feedback (proposed model):** This is the proposed model that we discussed in Sect. 4, where the feedback is taken from the agent(model) itself without any external help.
3. **Model with perfect feedback (hypothetical scenario):** This setting is a hypothetical scenario designed to show the importance of feedback. Here the model gets perfect feedback regarding the previous data-point helping it to identify sequential anomalies. Although this is not possible in real life settings this opens possibilities for different type of anomaly detectors acting as a feedback module to each other.

In Table 4, the model with perfect feedback gets a very high score, which shows the importance of feedback in the sequential anomaly detection. Even though perfect feedback model is not possible, the proposed model is performing better than its counterpart with no feedback and other baselines which are discussed in later sections. Proposed model and model without feedback exhibit similar performance on A2, A3, A4 benchmarks but not on A1 benchmark. This is due to the lack of sequential anomalies in A2, A3 and A4 benchmarks. Figure 6 depicts the model's performance on a single dataset from A1, A2, A3 and A4 benchmarks respectively and these are some of the datasets where the model detected all the anomalies. In Fig. 6a, the model is detecting sequential anomalies where action = 1 represents an anomaly and action = 0 represents a normal datapoint. In Fig. 6b and Fig. 6c, the model is detecting anomalies on time-series data with random seasonality, trend and noise. Finally in 6d the model is detecting anomalies even when the data is changing its seasonality and trend. From these plots, we infer that the proposed approach detects various type of anomalies in different situations. The next section outlines the various baselines considered for comparison with our proposed work on the considered datasets.

5.3   Results

Table 5 depicts the results of the comparative approaches and their performance on the basis of F-score. It is noticed that the performance of DeepAnT [19] with LSTM approach is the worst on A1 benchmark with a score of 0.44 closely followed by its CNN variant with a score of 0.46. TAD with $\alpha = 0.2$ exhibits a similar performance with EGADS(Extensible Generic Anomaly Detection System) and marginally better than its variants which differ by a value of 0.01. The score of TAD is worst on A2 and A3 benchmark with α exhibiting minimal contribution to the overall detection of anomalies on streaming data. Yahoo EGADS and TAD (Twitter Anomaly Detection) record an average performance with F-measure scores of 0.29–0.30. KPI-TSAD exhibits the best performance with a score of 0.92 and exceeds the benchmark performance of both variants of DeepAnT on A1 and A4. In A2 benchmark, KPI-TSAD(Key Performance Indicators-Time Series Anomaly Detection) shows a comparative score with both variants of DeepAnT and similar performance to LSTM variant of DeepAnT in A3 benchmark. Our proposed approach exceeds the performance of all baselines in A2, A3 and A4 benchmarks. It is marginally better than KPI-TSAD in A2 benchmark but not in A1 because in KPI-TSAD whole dataset is used for oversampling and later divided into training and testing set, as a result there is high chance that model might encounter all types of anomalies in the training set leading to a better performance in the testing set.

Table 5. Performance evaluation of proposed approach against baseline approach

Approach	A1	A2	A3	A4
Yahoo EGADS [12]	0.47	0.58	0.48	0.29
TAD($\alpha = 0.05$) [24,31]	0.48	0	0.26	0.31
TAD($\alpha = 0.1$) [24,31]	0.48	0	0.27	0.33
TAD($\alpha = 0.2$) [24,31]	0.47	0	0.3	0.34
DeepAnT(CNN) [19]	0.46	0.94	0.87	0.68
DeepAnT(LSTM) [19]	0.44	0.97	0.72	0.59
KPI-TSAD [22]	**0.92**	0.97	0.72	0.76
Proposed approach	0.63	**0.98**	**0.97**	**0.96**

Table 6 depicts the performance of the proposed approach against the baseline approaches on energy dataset. The performance of LOF (Local Outlier Factor) is worst on REFIT and AMPds datasets, which is expected from the distributions of energy datset 5. LOF performs better than ARIMA on Dataport and ECO datasets but our proposed approach exceeds the performance of the baseline approaches on all datasets on the basis of F-score. Our F-scores on individual energy datasets are comparatively better than the performance of Rimor [23].

Table 7 shows the cross dataset validation of our model trained on A1 benchmark versus the state of the art techniques. Cross dataset validation is used to

Table 6. Performance evaluation of LOF and ARIMA against the proposed approach

Energy data	LOF	ARIMA	Proposed approach
AMPds	0.24	0.41	**0.88**
Dataport	0.28	0.22	**0.68**
ECO	0.26	0.24	**0.90**
REFIT	0.17	0.27	**0.82**

see if our anomaly detection model can generalize and detect anomalies from another unseen datasets. We have used anomaly detection model trained on A1 benchmark dataset for this analysis because A1 benchmark consists of real world data and so does NAB dataset. The F-measure of the proposed approach is quite good when compared with DeepAnt in 4 out of 6 of the datasets. This might be due to the presence of more sequential anomalies present in NAB dataset used for NAB scoring. But it is interesting to see our anomaly detection model performing exceptionally good on another benchmark dataset that has not been used in training. The probable reason behind this performance might be due to similarities in Yahoo Webscope data and Numenta's NAB data. This leads us to believe that anomalies might come from the same anomalous distribution after all.

The next section elaborates the limitations of the current work and enumerates the methodology to mitigate the issues.

Table 7. Performance comparison of proposed approach against state of the art approaches on the NAB dataset on the basis of F-measure

Approach	Artificial with anomaly	Real Ad exchange	Real AWS cloud watch	Real known cause	Real traffic	Real tweets
Bayes Changepoint [1]	0.009	0.018	0.006	0.007	0.012	0.003
Context OSE [7]	0.004	0.022	0.007	0.005	0.02	0.003
EXPoSE [26]	0.004	0.005	0.015	0.005	0.011	0.003
HTM JAVA [2]	0.017	0.034	0.018	0.013	0.032	0.01
KNN CAD	0.003	0.024	0.006	0.008	0.013	0.004
Numenta [13]	0.012	0.04	0.017	0.015	0.033	0.009
Numenta TM [3]	0.017	0.035	0.018	0.012	0.036	0.01
Relative Entropy [32]	0.021	0.024	0.018	0.013	0.033	0.006
Skyline [27]	0.043	0.005	0.053	0.008	0.091	0.035
Twitter ADVec [10]	0.017	0.018	0.013	0.017	0.02	0.018
Windowed Gaussian	0.013	0.026	0.06	0.006	0.045	0.026
DeepAnt [19]	0.156	**0.132**	0.146	**0.2**	0.233	0.075
Proposed Approach	**0.176**	0.114	**0.213**	0.175	**0.251**	**0.156**

5.4 Threats to Validity

There are some benefits of using unsupervised learning like not needing data labels and usage of less data but unsupervised learning in this context needs clean and fewer data to identify underlying patterns. Its performance does not increase much with data due to inherent disabilities. In Fig. 7 we are using a LSTM (forecasting) model to show how the forecasting approach tries to reduce the prediction error and here the model is trying to forecast according to anomalous data which results in low anomaly score making it difficult for the threshold to identify anomalies.

Supervised learning approaches get better with data but a noticeable issue with supervised learning is that we cannot expect it to detect unseen anomalies. It is because the job of a supervised approach is to generalize to data from the same distribution. Also, by considering feedback from the same model it might lead to a series of wrong predictions because of one wrong prediction. This issue can be resolved by taking feedback from another model, which increases its precision, but its recall might be affected.

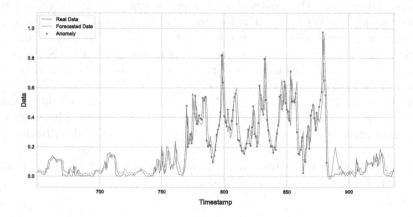

Fig. 7. Forecasting results on a dataset from A1 benchmark for the dataset depicted in Fig. 6 (zoomed view)

6   Conclusion and Future Work

In this work we have built a framework to incorporate feedback for sequential anomaly detection and incorporated Prioritized Experience Replay to solve the imbalance of data in anomaly detection approaches. Also, to verify the effectiveness of the approach we have tested on standard anomaly detection datasets and compared it with state of the art models. For the future work, we would like to experiment by incorporating external feedback on model stability and performance. Experimenting this approach with different machine learning models is another direction for future work. Another interesting direction for this work is to add feedback to forecasting approaches for sequential anomaly detection and compare their performance.

References

1. Adams, R.P., MacKay, D.J.: Bayesian online changepoint detection. arXiv preprint arXiv:0710.3742 (2007)

2. Ahmad, S., Hawkins, J.: Properties of sparse distributed representations and their application to hierarchical temporal memory. arXiv preprint arXiv:1503.07469 (2015)
3. Ahmad, S., Lavin, A., Purdy, S., Agha, Z.: Unsupervised real-time anomaly detection for streaming data. Neurocomputing **262**, 134–147 (2017)
4. Arshad, R., Zahoor, S., Shah, M.A., Wahid, A., Yu, H.: Green IoT An investigation on energy saving practices for 2020 and beyond. IEEE Access **5**, 15667–15681 (2017)
5. Beckel, C., Kleiminger, W., Cicchetti, R., Staake, T., Santini, S.: The eco data set and the performance of non-intrusive load monitoring algorithms. In: Proceedings of the 1st ACM Conference on Embedded Systems for Energy-Efficient Buildings, pp. 80–89 (2014)
6. Breunig, M.M., Kriegel, H.P., Ng, R.T., Sander, J.: Lof: identifying density-based local outliers. In: Proceedings of the 2000 ACM SIGMOD international conference on Management of data, pp. 93–104 (2000)
7. Detector, C.A.: Contextose (2015). https://github.com/smirmik/CAD
8. Faker, O., Dogdu, E.: Intrusion detection using big data and deep learning techniques. In: Proceedings of the 2019 ACM Southeast Conference, pp. 86–93 (2019)
9. Fiore, U., De Santis, A., Perla, F., Zanetti, P., Palmieri, F.: Using generative adversarial networks for improving classification effectiveness in credit card fraud detection. Inf. Sci. **479**, 448–455 (2019)
10. Kejariwal, A.: Twitter engineering: Introducing practical and robust anomaly detection in a time series (2015)
11. Laptev, N., Amizadeh, S.: Yahoo anomaly detection dataset s5 (2015). http://webscopesandbox.yahoo.com/catalog.php
12. Laptev, N., Amizadeh, S., Flint, I.: Generic and scalable framework for automated time-series anomaly detection. In: Proceedings of the 21th ACM SIGKDD International Conference on Knowledge Discovery and Data Mining, pp. 1939–1947 (2015)
13. Lavin, A., Ahmad, S.: Evaluating real-time anomaly detection algorithms-the numenta anomaly benchmark. In: 2015 IEEE 14th International Conference on Machine Learning and Applications (ICMLA), pp. 38–44. IEEE (2015)
14. Lopez-Martin, M., Carro, B., Sanchez-Esguevillas, A., Lloret, J.: Network traffic classifier with convolutional and recurrent neural networks for internet of things. IEEE Access **5**, 18042–18050 (2017)
15. Ma, Z., Ge, H., Liu, Y., Zhao, M., Ma, J.: A combination method for android malware detection based on control flow graphs and machine learning algorithms. IEEE Access **7**, 21235–21245 (2019)
16. Makonin, S., Ellert, B., Bajić, I.V., Popowich, F.: Electricity, water, and natural gas consumption of a residential house in Canada from 2012 to 2014. Sci. Data **3**, 160037 (2016)
17. Malhotra, P., Ramakrishnan, A., Anand, G., Vig, L., Agarwal, P., Shroff, G.: Lstm-based encoder-decoder for multi-sensor anomaly detection (2016). arXiv preprint arXiv:1607.00148
18. Munir, M., Siddiqui, S.A., Chattha, M.A., Dengel, A., Ahmed, S.: Fusead: unsupervised anomaly detection in streaming sensors data by fusing statistical and deep learning models. Sensors **19**(11), 2451 (2019)
19. Munir, M., Siddiqui, S.A., Dengel, A., Ahmed, S.: Deepant: a deep learning approach for unsupervised anomaly detection in time series. IEEE Access **7**, 1991–2005 (2018)

20. Murray, D., Stankovic, L., Stankovic, V.: An electrical load measurements dataset of united kingdom households from a two-year longitudinal study. Sci. Data **4**(1), 1–12 (2017)
21. Papadimitriou, S., Kitagawa, H., Gibbons, P.B., Faloutsos, C.: Loci: Fast outlier detection using the local correlation integral. In: Proceedings 19th International Conference on Data Engineering (Cat. No. 03CH37405), pp. 315–326. IEEE (2003)
22. Qiu, J., Du, Q., Qian, C.: KPI-TSAD: A time-series anomaly detector for KPI monitoring in cloud applications. Symmetry **11**(11), 1350 (2019)
23. Rashid, H., Batra, N., Singh, P.: Rimor: towards identifying anomalous appliances in buildings. In: Proceedings of the 5th Conference on Systems for Built Environments, pp. 33–42 (2018)
24. Rosner, B.: Percentage points for a generalized ESD many-outlier procedure. Technometrics **25**(2), 165–172 (1983)
25. Schaul, T., Quan, J., Antonoglou, I., Silver, D.: Prioritized experience replay. arXiv preprint arXiv:1511.05952 (2015)
26. Schneider, M., Ertel, W., Ramos, F.: Expected similarity estimation for large-scale batch and streaming anomaly detection. Mach. Learn. **105**(3), 305–333 (2016)
27. Stanway, A.: Etsy skyline. Online Code Repos (2013)
28. Street, P.: Dataport: the world's largest energy data resource. Pecan Street Inc (2015)
29. Sun, W., Paiva, A.R., Xu, P., Sundaram, A., Braatz, R.D.: Fault detection and identification using bayesian recurrent neural networks. arXiv preprint arXiv:1911.04386 (2019)
30. Tietjen, G.L., Moore, R.H.: Some grubbs-type statistics for the detection of several outliers. Technometrics **14**(3), 583–597 (1972)
31. Vallis, O., Hochenbaum, J., Kejariwal, A.: A novel technique for long-term anomaly detection in the cloud. In: 6th {USENIX} Workshop on Hot Topics in Cloud Computing (HotCloud 14) (2014)
32. Wang, C., Viswanathan, K., Choudur, L., Talwar, V., Satterfield, W., Schwan, K.: Statistical techniques for online anomaly detection in data centers. In: 12th IFIP/IEEE International Symposium on Integrated Network Management (IM 2011) and Workshops, pp. 385–392. IEEE (2011)
33. Xu, H., et al.: Unsupervised anomaly detection via variational auto-encoder for seasonal KPIS in web applications. In: Proceedings of the 2018 World Wide Web Conference, pp. 187–196 (2018)
34. Yamanaka, Y., Iwata, T., Takahashi, H., Yamada, M., Kanai, S.: Autoencoding binary cassifiers for supervised anomaly detection. In: Nayak, A.C., Sharma, A. (eds.) PRICAI 2019. LNCS (LNAI), vol. 11671, pp. 647–659. Springer, Cham (2019). https://doi.org/10.1007/978-3-030-29911-8_50
35. Zong, B., et al.: Deep autoencoding Gaussian mixture model for unsupervised anomaly detection. In: International Conference on Learning Representations (2018)

A Framework of Blockchain-Based Collaborative Intrusion Detection in Software Defined Networking

Wenjuan Li[1,2], Jiao Tan[3], and Yu Wang[1(✉)]

[1] Institute of Artificial Intelligence and Blockchain,
Guangzhou University, Guangzhou, China
yuwang@gzhu.edu.cn
[2] Department of Applied Mathematics and Computer Science,
Technical University of Denmark, Kongens Lyngby, Denmark
[3] KOTO Research Center, Macao, China

Abstract. To protect network assets from various cyber intrusions and fit the distributed environments like Internet of Things (IoTs), collaborative intrusion detection systems (CIDSs) are widely implemented allowing each detection node to exchange required data and information. This aims to improve the detection performance against some complicated attacks. In recent years, software defined networking (SDN) is developing rapidly, which can simplify the network complexity by separating the controller plane from the forwarding plane. In this way, the controller can manage the whole network without knowing the underlying structure and devices. To identify underlying malicious nodes or devices, CIDSs are still an important solution to secure SDN, but might be vulnerable to insider threats, in which an attacker can behave maliciously insider the network. In this work, we focus on this issue and advocate the merit on combining trust management and blockchain technology. Trust management can help evaluate the trustworthiness of each node, and blockchain technology can allow communication without a trusted party while ensuring the integrity of shared data. We then introduce a general framework of blockchain-based collaborative intrusion detection in SDN. In the study, we take challenge-based CIDS as a case, and evaluate our framework performance under both external and internal attacks. Our results indicate the viability and effectiveness of our framework.

Keywords: Collaborative intrusion detection · Blockchain technology · Software defined networking · Insider attack · Trust management

1 Introduction

Intrusion detection systems (IDSs) are a basic security solution that monitors a conventional system or network environment for malicious activities or policy violations [16,25]. For example, it can analyze a packet payload for malicious content, or examine an application's malicious behavior. According to the

© Springer Nature Switzerland AG 2020
M. Kutyłowski et al. (Eds.): NSS 2020, LNCS 12570, pp. 261–276, 2020.
https://doi.org/10.1007/978-3-030-65745-1_15

deployment, an IDS can be considered as either host-based or network-based, which can be further categorized into rule-based detection and anomaly-based detection [45]. The rule-based IDS is able to find an attack by performing signature matching [32], while the anomaly-based IDS can discover anomalies by utilizing data mining and artificial intelligence [50].

Currently, distributed or collaborative intrusion detection systems (DIDSs or CIDSs) have become common in order to fit the distributed network functionality. In an Internet of Things (IoT) environment, collaborative intrusion detection can enhance the detection performance by exchanging required information (e.g., alarms) with other nodes. As an example, Eskandari et al. [7] introduced an intelligent intrusion detection system (IDS) in IoT, called Passban. It can be deployed on cheap IoT gateways and communicated with edge computing devices against malicious traffic from Port Scanning, HTTP and SSH Brute Force. However, with the growth of IoT devices and the inclusion of cloud services, network management would become difficult and error-prone.

To address this problem, the concept of software defined networking (SDN) is developed, which relies on controllers or application programming interfaces (APIs) to manage the underlying infrastructure and network traffic [46]. That is, it can separate the network control from the data plane, achieving an increased control with greater speed and flexibility, i.e., network managers can configure network resources and update network infrastructure in real-time via one centralized controller. A report from IDC predicted that the data center SDN market would be worth more than $12 billion by the end of 2022 [47]. Followed this trend, research has investigated the deployment of CIDSs on SDN. Chen and Yu [3] presented a collaborative intrusion prevention architecture, which can disperse its lightweight computation power to the programmable switches of the substrate in SDN. Chin et al. [4] introduced a lightweight kernel-level intrusion detection and prevention framework by leveraging modular string searching and filtering mechanisms with SDN.

However, SDN-based CIDSs may be still vulnerable to some security threats, i.e., cyber-attackers can compromise one of the underlying devices or Virtual Machines (VMs) to launch an insider attack [22]. Also, manipulated information can degrade the detection effectiveness, i.e., faked flows can be used to deceive switches and controllers in the network [46]. In the literature, trust management is an important approach to build trust relationship among network nodes and components. For instance, Liu et al. [24] presented a detection scheme using the K-means classification algorithm and the routing path optimization to identify insider attacks in an IoT environment. While how to ensure the integrity of shared information still remains a challenge.

With the recent adoption of blockchain technology, it is a promising approach to combine blockchain with SDN. This is because blockchain can ensure the integrity of shared information and data, and allow mutually unknown parties to exchange data without the need of a trusted third party [23]. In this work, we advocate the merits of combining SDN-based CIDS with blockchain, and introduce a framework of blockchain-based collaborative intrusion detection in SDN. With the integration of blockchain, the framework can ensure the exchanged data among various nodes and enhance the robustness of trust management against insider attacks. The contributions can be summarized as below.

- We introduce a framework of blockchain-based collaborative intrusion detection in SDN. The blockchain can help ensure the data integrity and enable the communication among different nodes without a trusted third party. The shared data can be used to build trust management schemes for CIDSs and be added to the chain based on concrete requirements. A centralized control or action can be made by the SDN controller if malicious behavior is detected, i.e., based on the information on the chain.
- To test the framework, we take challenge-based CIDS as an example and evaluate the performance in a simulated environment. Under some adversarial scenarios (e.g., flooding attacks), our results indicate that our framework is viable and works well in our settings.

The paper is structured as follows. Section 2 introduces the background and related work regarding SDN, blockchain and collaborative intrusion detection. Section 3 introduces our proposed framework, and Sect. 4 shows an evaluation and analyzes the collected results. Section 5 concludes our work.

2   Background and Related Work

This section introduces the background on SDN and blockchain, and reviews the relevant research studies on the combination of SDN, collaborative intrusion detection and blockchain.

2.1   Software Defined Networking

With the rapid growth of network devices, network management may become tedious and complex, as dynamic configuration is difficult in conventional network environments [46]. The emergence of SDN can mitigate this issue by decoupling the network control from the data plane of the network device [2]. The separation allows implementing network applications according to the specific network requirements and conditions.

The idea of SDN is suitable to large networks like data center. It can help align the requirements of a data center network through automated provisioning, flexible network management, pervasive application-oriented visibility, and more. In addition, SDN can make distributed networks (e.g., IoT, cloud computing and edge computing devices) simpler and more cost efficient. The SDN environment can generally provide some benefits as follows [2, 46].

- *Logically centralized management.* The network manager only needs to control the devices in the data plane via the centralized controller. A global view of network status and flow statistics can be achieved.

- *Flexibility.* The network manager can have more flexibility in selecting and deciding networking devices (i.e., making a balance between cost and performance), as they can handle those devices via a centralized controller and a single protocol.
- *Programmability.* In SDN, the underlying devices in the data plane can be controlled by the applications in the controller. This makes it easier to add new network and security features via programming.

Thanks to the above features, SDN provides many ways to enhance security with global visibility, while the centralized controller needs a special protection to avoid the issue of single point of failure [23]. A typical SDN architecture often includes three layers: data plane, control plane and application plane.

- *The data plane.* The layer contains various devices including routers, switches and end-computers, which can receive information from the controller and forward traffic.
- *The control plane.* This layer aims to manage the whole network status, i.e., checking the information from applications and deciding how to route a data packet. One or more controllers can be deployed.
- *The application plane.* This layer provides a platform for various applications to communicate resource requests or information, i.e., business applications can retrieve data from external appliances based on the pre-defined policies.

For SDN implementation, OpenFlow [38] is considered as the first standard to define the communication protocol in SDN environments, and handle how the controller interacts with the forwarding plane of network devices such as switches and routers, in either physical or virtual ways. OpenFlow mainly contains three components [17]: OpenFlow switch, OpenFlow channel and OpenFlow controller. (1) OpenFlow channel can help connect switches and controllers. (2) OpenFlow switch often contains one or more flow tables to do packet lookup and forwarding by receiving the command from the controller. (3) OpenFlow controller manages the network operations, i.e., deciding how to process traffic and handle flow table.

2.2   Blockchain

The success of blockchain technology is motivated by digital currencies like bitcoin. A blockchain is a series of time-stamped and immutable data records distributed in the environment. In other words, blockchain is a distributed ledger technology, allowing data to be stored globally and distributed on different nodes and servers, which can be openly shared an unchangeable record of transactions [28]. Currently, blockchain has been investigated in may fields, such as intrusion detection [29,34], healthcare industry [43], transportation [35], Public Key Infrastructure [5], and more.

A blockchain (electronic ledger) mainly includes a list of digital records (blocks), ordered in a chronological manner by means of discrete timestamps [53]. A digital record contains several major items such as payload, timestamp and cryptographic value. Genesis block is the first record in a blockchain, and the following blocks can link to the previous one through cryptographic hashing, making it a verifiable and auditable record. In addition, a blockchain can only be updated via consensus algorithms among all parties in the network, and once new data is added, it cannot be changed. Figure 1 shows the high-level review of blockchain structure.

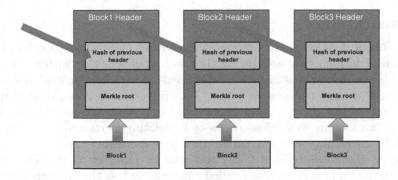

Fig. 1. The high-level review of blockchain structure.

Generally, there are two types of blockchains: public blockchain ledgers and private or permissioned blockchain. The former means that all participants can access to the data and the system, like Bitcoin [36] and Ethereum [52]. There is no need for an administrator, and the chain can be managed autonomously when sharing data between parties. By contrast, a private chain is controlled by only a group of authorized and only defined activities can be done like Hyperledger [11]. Then a consortium blockchain can be considered as a 'semi-private' chain, which has a controlled user group where the preliminarily assigned users may come across different organizations. To update the record or perform certain activities, a consensus algorithm needs to be agreed among all participants. A smart contract is a self-executing computer code to digitally facilitate, verify, or enforce the agreement between participants.

There are many studies focus on designing smart contracts and enhancing the blockchain scalability. For example, Kalodner et al. [12] presented a cryptocurrency system named Arbitrum, which supports smart contracts without the scalability and privacy limitations of previous systems such as Ethereum. On the one hand, Arbitrum allows parties to create smart contracts by using code to specify the behavior of a virtual machine (VM) that implements the contract's functionality, which is similar to Ethereum. On the other hand, it moves the verification of VMs' behavior off-chain by incentivizing parties to agree off-chain on what a VM would do so that miners of the system need only to verify digital signatures and confirm that parties have agreed on a VM's behavior. Specifically, if the parties cannot reach unanimous agreement off-chain, the scheme still allows honest parties to propose the VM state on-chain, and the dishonest party lying about a VM's behavior will be identified and penalized efficiently. Krupp et al. [14] investigated the problem of automatic vulnerability identification and exploit generation for smart contracts and developed a generic definition of vulnerable contracts. Based on this, they built a tool named TEETHER that allows creating an exploit for a contract given only its binary bytecode. Moreover, they performed an automatic large-scale analysis of 38,757 Ethereum contracts and found working exploits for 815 contracts via this tool.

2.3 Related Work

Trust-Based CIDS. Collaborative intrusion detection aims to enhance the detection performance by exchanging the required information within a network system, but a big threat is insider attack, where an attacker can exploit network vulnerabilities insider the environment. For protection, building trust management is one of the effective approaches. Duma et al. [6] introduced an overlay IDS that can identifies malicious nodes by correlating alerts and measuring reputation by developing several communication components.

A type of challenge-based CIDS was give by Fung et al. [8]. The behind idea is to send a kind of message called challenge to test the trustworthiness of other nodes. Li et al. [18,19] then introduced a sensitivity-based CIDS, which applies the notion of intrusion sensitivity for evaluating the detection sensitivity of a detector. To automatically assign the value of sensitivity, several machine learning classifiers can be used, like SVM and KNN [26]. By highlighting the importance of expert nodes, sensitivity-based CIDS can detect malicious nodes in a fast way, like pollution attack [20]. Veeraiah and Krishna [40] designed a Trust-aware fuzzy clustering and fuzzy Naive Bayes system, by using several trust factors to predict the trust value of a node, such as direct trust, indirect trust, and the recent trust.

Blockchain-Based CIDS. Due to the potential merits of blockchain, many studies have started exploring its usage in intrusion detection. An early CIDS framework [1] was proposed through considering a set of alarms as transactions in a blockchain. Then, CIDS nodes can communicate and perform activities via consensus protocols. A more detailed analysis was given by a review [29], which discusses how to combine blockchain with IDS/CIDS, and what are the main limitations. Blockchain was believed to be helpful in the aspects of data sharing, trust management and alarm exchange (ensuring integrity).

An anomaly-based CIDS was introduced by Golomb et al. [9], which used blockchains to help enhance anomaly detection. A blockchain- and rule-based CIDS [21,51] was then developed, which could use blockchain to help build a verifiable rule database. Meng et al. [33] focused on rule-based IDS, and designed a blockchain-enabled single character frequency-based matching scheme, which can build a verifiable database of malicious payloads via blockchains. Hu et al. [9] introduced a blockchain-based CIDS for multimicrogrid systems, while they only used the blockchain to store the final detection results. Kanth et al. [13] introduced an Ethereum blockchain-based CIDS by leveraging pluggable authentication modules.

SDN-Based Intrusion Detection. In SDN, Lamb and Heileman [15] presented a concept of trust-based CIDS that interacts among host, switches, controllers, repositories and applications. Yan et al. [54] introduced a trust framework for SDN, using a reputation management component to measure the trustworthiness of others. A system of TruSDn was introduced by Paladi and Gehrmann [42], which used Intel Software Guard Extensions (SGX) to enhance the trust in SDN. Meng et al. [27] introduced a trust-based security mechanism based on Bayesian inference to defeat insider attacks in a healthcare SDN environment. Their idea is to monitor the traffic status and identify malicious actions. Zhang et al. [55] explored the use of deep reinforcement learning to establish a trust relation for connected vehicles using SDN, i.e., the controller aims to communicate with vehicles at discrete time steps. Li et al. [22] studied the performance of challenge-based CIDS in SDN, and found its effectiveness against insider attacks.

Blockchain, SDN and CIDS. In the literature, there are not many relevant studies regarding the combination of blockchain, SDN and CIDS. Steichen *et al.* [49] presented an OpenFlow-based firewall named ChainGuard, which could secure blockchain-based SDN by detecting malicious events inside the network. A snort-based CIDS was introduced by Ujjan et al. [44], which used SDN to help enhance the detection performance.

The above studies combined SDN-based CIDS with blockchain, whereas none of them considered a trust-based CIDS. As aforementioned, trust management is an important solution to protect computer networks against insider attacks. In this work, we therefore aim to bridge this gap and introduce a framework for blockchain- and trust-based CIDS in SDN.

3   Our Framework

Since each of SDN, blockchain, CIDS and trust management can contribute to either network management or security, the combination of them should be able to complement each other. Figure 2 depicts the framework of blockchain-based CIDS in SDN.

- *CIDS*. Each CIDS node can connect with each other and exchange required data or information. A node can contain several major components such as connection component (for physical connection), collaboration component (for information exchange), blockchain component (for communicating with the chain), and trust management component (for measuring nodes' reputation). Based on the requirements, both rule-based and anomaly-based detection approach can be deployed in a node.
- *Blockchain*. A blockchain can be established and updated via consensus protocol and smart contract agreed among all CIDS nodes. The consensus can be extended to SDN controller and applications. Based on the concrete schemes and requirements, various information can be chained, e.g., alarms, rules, messages. Intuitively, the blockchain ensures the data integrity and facilitates the information to be visible to other parties. For example, all SDN planes

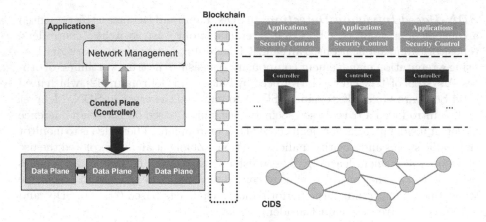

Fig. 2. The framework of blockchain-based CIDS in SDN.

can access the chain for retrieving expected information. In practical usage, privacy-preserving techniques can be used to protect privacy.

– *SDN*. As introduced earlier, SDN has three layers (or planes): application layer, control layer and data layer. The application layer can deploy customized applications and security mechanisms. For example, a trust management application can be deployed here to guide the controller how to retrieve the information from both the blockchain and CIDS, and then determine the network status and a node's reputation. The controller layer can enforce the security policies and react to malicious nodes and traffic. A CIDS often works at the data layer to detect various external or internal attacks, and share the information to both the chain and the controller.

Hence each of CIDS, blockchain and SDN can complement and work with each other, i.e., the trust management can be enhanced by retrieving information from the chain, and the SDN controller can enforce the policies. The framework can maintain the merits of SDN, blockchain and trust-based CIDS.

– *Data integrity*. This refers to the reliability and trustworthiness of data. Due to the nature design of blockchains, the chained data and information are inherently resistent to the modification (e.g., edition, deletion), as long as the data has been added.
– *Efficiency*. The framework can ensure the quality of information shared via consensus in the network and measure the reputation of each participant. The SDN controller can take actions immediately when malicious traffic or behavior are detected.
– *Dynamicity*. Participants (e.g., customers, users) can configure the software and applications on the controllers, and easily enforce their demands (e.g., on-demand services, access rules), without the need of understanding the underlying devices in the data plane.

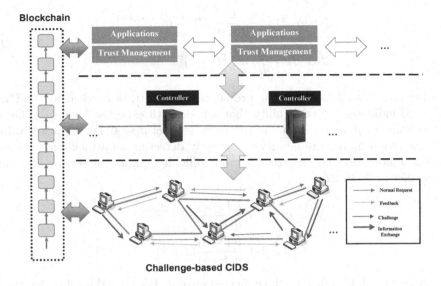

Fig. 3. Case study: challenge-based CIDS with blockchain in SDN.

- *Privacy.* To protect participants' privacy, the framework allow implementing privacy-preserving schemes and access control list. Hence the blockchain data can be visible to authorized parties, who need to have credentials to recover the data and information.
- *Scalability.* The framework can be scalable to a large computer network. This is because most CIDSs are scalable, and the SDN itself is developed to help handle a large amount of network nodes. For blockchains, scalability (e.g., a high transaction per second) can be achieved by changing its consensus mechanism or adjusting some system parameters.
- *Security.* As the blockchain enables the integrity and the trustworthiness of data, it is more difficult for cyber-attackers to intrude the network and compromise the in-between channel. With trust management, the framework can be robust against insider attacks. When a malicious node is identified, SDN controller can take a quick response to mitigate the risk.

Case Study. To implement the framework, an important step is to select a type of trust-based CIDS. As a study, we take challenge-based CIDS [8, 19] as a case, which evaluates the reputation of other nodes via challenges. The framework can be realized accordingly, as shown in Fig. 3.

Node Expertise. Similar to previous studies [8, 19, 22], this work describes an IDS with three expertise levels with low (0.1), medium (0.5) and high (0.95). A beta function can be used to model the expertise of an IDS node:

$$f(p'|\alpha, \beta) = \frac{1}{B(\alpha, \beta)} p'^{\alpha-1}(1-p')^{\beta-1}$$

$$B(\alpha, \beta) = \int_0^1 t^{\alpha-1}(1-t)^{\beta-1}dt \tag{1}$$

where $p'(\in [0,1])$ indicates the probability of an attack checked by the IDS. $f(p'|\alpha, \beta)$ indicates the probability that a node with expertise level l responses with a value of p' to an attack of difficulty level of $d(\in [0,1])$. A bigger value of l indicates a higher probability of correctly detecting an attack and a bigger value of d indicates that an attack is more difficult to find. The setting of α and β can refer to [8,19,22]:

$$\alpha = 1 + \frac{l(1-d)}{d(1-l)} r$$

$$\beta = 1 + \frac{l(1-d)}{d(1-l)}(1-r) \tag{2}$$

where $r \in \{0,1\}$ indicates the expected output. For a fixed level of detection difficulty, the node with a higher level of expertise can achieve higher probability of correctly detecting an attack.

Trust Evaluation at Nodes. To measure the trustworthiness of a node, a testing node can send a *challenge* to another node using a random generation process, and then check its satisfaction level by comparing the received feedback with the expected feedback. We can derive the reputation of a node i according to node j as follows:

$$T_i^j = (w_s \frac{\sum_{k=0}^n F_k^{j,i} \lambda^{tk}}{\sum_{k=0}^n \lambda^{tk}} - T_s)(1-x)^d + T_s \tag{3}$$

where $F_k^{j,i} \in [0,1]$ indicates the score of the received feedback k and n is the total number of feedback. λ is a *forgetting factor* that assigns less weight to older feedback. w_s means a *significant weight* relying on the total number of received feedback, if there is only a few feedback under a certain minimum m, then $w_s = \frac{\sum_{k=0}^n \lambda^{tk}}{m}$; otherwise $w_s = 1$. x is the percentage of "don't know" answers during a time period. d is a positive incentive parameter to control the severity of punishment to "don't know" replies.

Satisfaction Evaluation. The satisfaction level can be measured based on an expected feedback ($e \in [0,1]$) and an actual received feedback ($r \in [0,1]$). A function $F (\in [0,1])$ is built to reflect the satisfaction by measuring the difference between the received answer and the expected answer as follows.

$$F = 1 - (\frac{e-r}{max(c_1 e, 1-e)})^{c_2} \quad e > r \tag{4}$$

$$F = 1 - (\frac{c_1(r-e)}{max(c_1 e, 1-e)})^{c_2} \quad e \le r \tag{5}$$

where c_1 controls the degree of penalty for wrong estimates and c_2 controls the sensitivity of estimation. This work sets $c_1 = 1.5$ and $c_2 = 1$.

4 Evaluation

In this work, we first set up the SDN environment by means of Open vSwitch [39] and POX controller [41], and then constructed a challenge-based CIDS with 55 nodes (based on Snort [48]), which were randomly distributed in a 15×15 grid region. The challenge-based CIDS encourages nodes to connect and share information like alarms with each other. Each node maintains a *partner list* and the reputation of newcomers would be $T_s = 0.5$. To avoid performance bias, we repeat each experiment for five times.

To set up the strategy of sending challenges, we assume each node can send a challenge randomly to its partners with an average rate of ε, according to previous work [8,19,22]. In particular, two levels of request frequency are used: the request frequency of ε_l is low for a highly trusted or highly untrusted node, since their feedback should be very confident. By contrast, the request frequency of ε_h should be high for others with a trust value around the threshold. The consortium blockchain was deployed in a mid-end computer with Intel(R) Core (TM)i6, CPU 2.5 GHz with 500 GB storage. There is a need for 2/3 nodes in the network to sign a block to be appended to the blockchain. Table 1 summarizes the simulation parameters.

Table 1. Experimental setup with simulation parameters.

Parameters	Value	Description
λ	0.9	Forgetting factor
ε_l	10/day	Low request frequency
ε_h	20/day	High request frequency
r	0.8	Trust threshold
T_s	0.5	Trust value for newcomers
m	10	Lower limit of received feedback
d	0.3	Severity of punishment

External Attack. In this experiment, we aim to explore the performance of our framework against external attacks like flooding attack. We used NetScanTools [37] to generate packets and flood our network environment, through randomly manipulating the IP sources. Figure 4 presents the impact of flooding attacks on the bandwidth between our framework and OpenFlow (normal condition).

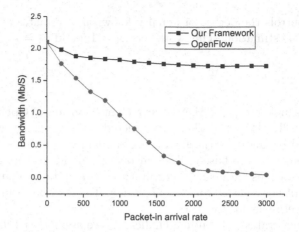

Fig. 4. The impact of flooding attacks on the bandwidth.

It is found that there was a fast decrease regarding the bandwidth under OpenFlow during the flooding period. When the packet-in arrival rate achieved at around 1400 packets/s, the bandwidth decreased to below 0.55, while the network function was compromised when the packet-in arrival rate reached 2800–3000 packets/s. In contrast, our framework could protect the environment and maintain the bandwidth after a small decrease to around 1.7. This is because our framework could identify malicious traffic and response rapidly, through SDN controllers and blockchains.

Insider Attack. To investigate the performance against insider attacks, we randomly selected three expert nodes to perform a betrayal attack (in which a trusted node becomes malicious), by either sending malicious packets or share untruthful alarms. During alarm aggregation, our framework can attach the received alarms to the chain, which should be examined by other nodes.

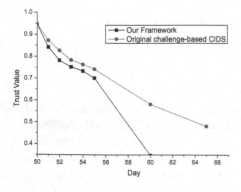

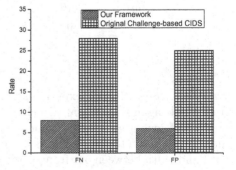

Fig. 5. The average trust value of malicious nodes.

Fig. 6. Alarm aggregation errors under insider attacks.

Figure 5 and Fig. 6 demonstrate the average trust value of malicious nodes and alarm aggregation errors under insider attack, respectively. It is found that our framework could decrease the trustworthiness of malicious nodes in a faster manner compared to the original challenge-based CIDS. This is because under SDN, the controller can quickly take actions to highlight the penalty on the malicious nodes. On the other hand, our framework could greatly reduce the alarm aggregation errors to below 10%, as compared with over 20% for the original scheme. The main reason is that our framework uses blockchain and it can help identify some malicious alarms if no consensus is made among nodes.

Discussion. Our experimental results indicate the viability and effectiveness of our framework in our settings against external and insider threats. While we acknowledge that our framework is developed at an early stage, some framework properties and features should be explored in our future work. (1) *Blockchain performance.* The current framework involves blockchain technology, but blockchain itself may bring some new issues like latency and energy consumption. How to mitigate these issues can be considered in our future plan. (2) *Communication workload.* To make all components and parties collaborated with each other, our framework may cause some additional communication load to each CIDS node and the whole network environment. This is an important topic in our future study. (3) *Advanced attack evaluation.* Our current work mainly studies some intuitive attacks aiming to evaluate the viability of our framework. One of our future directions is to explore the framework performance against advanced external and internal attacks. Furthermore, we plan to provide a large comparison with similar approaches and platforms.

5   Conclusion

To leverage the benefits of SDN, blockchain and CIDS, we introduce a general framework of blockchain-based collaborative intrusion detection in SDN. The framework can provide some properties such as data integrity, efficiency, dynamicity, privacy, scalability and security. As a case study, we consider challenge-based CIDS that measures the reputation of nodes by using a type of message called challenge. In our evaluation, we investigate the framework performance under both external attack (flooding attack) and internal attack (betrayal attack). Our results demonstrate the viability and effectiveness of our framework, i.e., can maintain the network bandwidth, decrease the trust values of malicious nodes quickly and reduce the alarm aggregation errors.

Acknowledgments. This work was partially supported by National Natural Science Foundation of China (No. 61802080 and 61802077).

References

1. Alexopoulos, N., Vasilomanolakis, E., Ivanko, N.R., Muhlhauser, M.: Towards blockchain-based collaborative intrusion detection systems. In: Proceedings of the 12th International Conference on Critical Information Infrastructures Security, pp. 1–12 (2017)
2. Alsmadi, I., Xu, D.: Security of software defined networks: a survey. Comput. Secur. **53**, 79–108 (2015)
3. Chen, X.F., Yu, S.Z.: CIPA: a collaborative intrusion prevention architecture for programmable network and SDN. Comput. Secur. **58**, 1–19 (2016)
4. Chin, T., Xiong, K., Rahouti, M.: SDN-based kernel modular countermeasure for intrusion detection. SecureComm **2017**, 270–290 (2017)
5. Chiu, W.-Y., Meng, W., Jensen, C.D.: NoPKI - a point-to-point trusted third party service based on bockchain consensus algorithm. In: Xu, G., Liang, K., Su, C. (eds.) FCS 2020. CCIS, vol. 1286, pp. 197–214. Springer, Singapore (2020). https://doi.org/10.1007/978-981-15-9739-8_16
6. Duma, C., Karresand, M., Shahmehri, N., Caronni, G.: A Trust-aware, P2P-based overlay for intrusion detection. In: DEXA Workshop, pp. 692–697 (2006)
7. Eskandari, M., Janjua, Z.H., Vecchio, M., Antonelli, F.: Passban IDS: an intelligent anomaly-based intrusion detection system for IoT edge devices. IEEE Internet Things J. **7**(8), 6882–6897 (2020)
8. Fung, C.J., Baysal, O., Zhang, J., Aib, I., Boutaba, R.: Trust management for host-based collaborative intrusion detection. In: De Turck, F., Kellerer, W. Kormentzas, G. (eds.): DSOM 2008, LNCS 5273, pp. 109–122 (2008)
9. Golomb, T., Mirsky, Y., Elovici, Y.: CIoTA: Collaborative IoT anomaly detection via blockchain. In: Proceedings of workshop on Decentralized IoT Security and Standards (DISS), pp. 1–6 (2018)
10. Hu, B., Zhou, C., Tian, Y.-C., Qin, Y., Junping, X.: A collaborative intrusion detection approach using blockchain for multimicrogrid systems. IEEE Trans. Syst. Man Cybern. Syst. **49**(8), 1720–1730 (2019)
11. Hyperledger C Open Source Blockchain Technologies. https://www.hyperledger.org/
12. Kalodner, H., Goldfeder, S., Chen, X., Weinberg, S., Felten, E.W.: Arbitrum: scalable, private smart contracts. In: Proceedings of 27th USENIX Security Symposium (USENIX Security), August 15C17 (2018)
13. Kanth, V., McAbee, A., Tummala, M., McEachen, J.C.: Collaborative Intrusion Detection leveraging Blockchain and Pluggable Authentication Modules. In: Proceedings of HICSS, pp. 1–7 (2020)
14. Krupp, J., Rossow, C.: teEther: gnawing at ethereum to automatically exploit smart contracts. In: Proceedings of 27th USENIX Security Symposium (USENIX Security), Baltimore, MD, USA, August 15C17 (2018)
15. Lamb, C.C., Heileman, G.L.: Towards robust trust in software defined networks. GLOBECOM Workshops, pp. 166–171 (2014)
16. Lee, W., Cabrera, J.B.D., Thomas, A., Balwalli, N., Saluja, S., Zhang, Y.: Performance Adaptation in Real-Time Intrusion Detection Systems. RAID **2002**, 252–273 (2002)
17. Li, W., Meng, W., Kwok, L.F.: A survey on openflow-based software defined networks: security challenges and countermeasures. J. Netw. Comput. Appl. **68**, 126–139 (2016)

18. Li, W., Meng, Y., Kwok, L.-F.: Enhancing trust evaluation using intrusion sensitivity in collaborative intrusion detection networks: feasibility and challenges. In: Proceedings of the 9th International Conference on Computational Intelligence and Security (CIS), pp. 518–522. IEEE (2013)
19. Li, W., Meng, W., Kwok, L.-F.: Design of intrusion sensitivity-based trust management model for collaborative intrusion detection networks. In: Zhou, J., Gal-Oz, N., Zhang, J., Gudes, E. (eds.) IFIPTM 2014. IAICT, vol. 430, pp. 61–76. Springer, Heidelberg (2014). https://doi.org/10.1007/978-3-662-43813-8_5
20. Li, W., Meng, W.: Enhancing collaborative intrusion detection networks using intrusion sensitivity in detecting pollution attacks. Inf. Comput. Secur. 24(3), 265–276 (2016)
21. Li, W., Tug, S., Meng, W., Wang, Y.: Designing collaborative blockchained signature-based intrusion detection in IoT environments. Future Gen. Comput. Syst. 96, 481–489 (2019)
22. Li, W., Wang, Y., Jin, Z., Yu, K., Li, J., Xiang, Y.: Challenge-based collaborative intrusion detection in software defined networking: an evaluation. Digit. Commun. Netw. In press, Elsevier
23. Li, W., Meng, W., Liu, Z., Au, M.H.: Towards blockchain-based software-defined networking: security challenges and solutions. IEICE Trans. Inf. Syst. 103(2), 196–203 (2020)
24. Liu, L., Yang, J., Meng, W.: Detecting malicious nodes via gradient descent and support vector machine in Internet of Things. Comput. Electr. Eng. 77, 339–353 (2019)
25. Meng, Y.: The practice on using machine learning for network anomaly intrusion detection. In: Proceedings of the 2011 International Conference on Machine Learning and Cybernetics (ICMLC 2011), pp. 576–581. IEEE (2011)
26. Meng, W., Li, W., Kwok, L.-F.: Design of intelligent KNN-based alarm filter using knowledge-based alert verification in intrusion detection. Secur. Commun. Netw. 8(18), 3883–3895 (2015)
27. Meng, W., Raymond Choo, K.K., Furnell, S., Vasilakos, A.V., Probst, C.W.: Towards bayesian-based trust management for insider attacks in healthcare software-defined networks. IEEE Trans. Netw. Serv. Manage. 15(2), 761–773 (2018)
28. Meng, W., et al.: Position paper on blockchain technology: smart contract and applications. The 12th International Conference on Network and System Security (NSS), pp. 474–483 (2018)
29. Meng, W., Tischhauser, E.W., Wang, Q., Wang, Y., Han, J.: When intrusion detection meets blockchain technology: a review. IEEE Access 6(1), 10179–10188 (2018)
30. Meng, W., Li, W., Yang, L.T., Li, P.: Enhancing challenge-based collaborative intrusion detection networks against insider attacks using blockchain. Int. J. Inf. Secur. 19(3), 279–290 (2019). https://doi.org/10.1007/s10207-019-00462-x
31. Meng, W., Li, W., Zhu, L.: Enhancing medical smartphone networks via blockchain-based trust management against insider attacks. IEEE Trans. Eng. Manage. 67(4), 1377–1386 (2020)
32. Meng, Y., Li, W.: Adaptive character frequency-based exclusive signature matching scheme in distributed intrusion detection environment. In: Proceedings of the 11th IEEE International Conference on Trust, Security and Privacy in Computing and Communications (TrustCom), pp. 223–230 (2012)
33. Meng, W., Li, W., Tug, S., Tan, J.: Towards blockchain-enabled single character frequency-based exclusive signature matching in IoT-assisted smart cities. J. Parallel Distrib. Comput. 144, 268–277 (2020)

34. Meng, W., Li, W., Yang, L.T., Li, P.: Enhancing challenge-based collaborative intrusion detection networks against insider attacks using blockchain. Int. J. Inf. Sec. **19**(3), 279–290 (2020)
35. Mu, Y., Rezaeibagha, F., Huang, K.: Policy-driven blockchain and its applications for transport systems. IEEE Trans. Serv. Comput. **13**(2), 230–240 (2020)
36. Nakamoto, S.: Bitcoin: A peer-to-peer electronic cash system (2008). http://bitcoin.org/bitcoin.pdf
37. NetScanTools. (access on July 2020) https://www.netscantools.com/nstpro_packet_generator.html
38. OpenFlow Switch Specification - Open Networking Foundation. https://www.opennetworking.org/wp-content/uploads/2014/10/openflow-switch-v1.5.1.pdf
39. Open vSwitch, an open virtual switch. http://openvswitch.org/. Accessed June 2020
40. Veeraiah, N., Krishna, B.T.: Trust-aware FuzzyClus-Fuzzy NB: intrusion detection scheme based on fuzzy clustering and Bayesian rule. Wirel. Netw. **25**(7), 4021–4035 (2019)
41. The POX Controller. https://github.com/noxrepo/pox/>. Accessed March 2020
42. Paladi, N., Gehrmann, C.: Bootstrapping trust in software defined networks. EAI Endorsed Trans. Secur. Safe. **4**(11), e5 (2017)
43. Pirtle, C., Ehrenfeld, J.M.: Blockchain for healthcare: the next generation of medical records? J. Medical Syst. **42**(9), 1–3 (2018)
44. Ujjan, R.M.A., Pervez, Z., Dahal, K.P.: Snort based collaborative intrusion detection system using Blockchain in SDN. In: Proceedings of SKIMA, pp. 1–8 (2019)
45. Scarfone, K., Mell, P.: Guide to Intrusion Detection and Prevention Systems (IDPS). NISTSpecial Publication, 800-894 (2007)
46. Sahay, R., Meng, W., Jensen, C.D.: The application of software defined networking on securing computer networks: a survey. J. Netw. Comput. Appl. **131**, 89–108 (2019)
47. What is SDN and where software-defined networking is going. https://www.networkworld.com/article/3209131/what-sdn-is-and-where-its-going.html. Accessed 1 Sept 2020
48. Snort: An an open source network intrusion prevention and detection system (IDS/IPS). Homepage: http://www.snort.org/
49. Steichen, M., Hommes, S., State, R.: ChainGuard - A firewall for blockchain applications using SDN with openflow. In: Proceedings of International Conference on Principles, Systems and Applications of IP Telecommunications (IPTComm), pp. 1–8 (2017)
50. Tan, K.M.C., Killourhy, K.S., Maxion, R.A.: Undermining an anomaly-based intrusion detection system using common exploits. Proc. RAID **2002**, 54–73 (2002)
51. Tug, S., Meng, W., Wang, Y.: CBSigIDS: towards collaborative blockchained signature-based intrusion detection. In: Proceedings of The 1st IEEE International Conference on Blockchain (Blockchain), pp. 1228–1235 (2018)
52. Wood, G.: Ethereum: A secure decentralised generalised transaction ledger. EIP-150 Revision (2016)
53. Wüst, K., Gervais, A.: Do you need a blockchain? In: CVCBT, pp. 45–54 (2018)
54. Yan, Z., Zhang, P., Vasilakos, A.V.: A security and trust framework for virtualized networks and software-defined networking. Secur. Commun. Netw. **9**(16), 3059–3069 (2016)
55. Zhang, D., Yu, F.R., Yang, R., Tang, H.: A deep reinforcement learning-based trust management scheme for software-defined vehicular networks. DIVANet@MSWiM, pp. 1–7 (2018)

Evaluation of Anomaly-Based Intrusion Detection with Combined Imbalance Correction and Feature Selection

Andreas Heidelbach Engly[1], Anton Ruby Larsen[1], and Weizhi Meng[1,2]([✉])

[1] Department of Applied Mathematics and Computer Science,
Technical University of Denmark, Kongens Lyngby, Denmark
weme@dtu.dk
[2] Institute of Artificial Intelligence and Blockchain, Guangzhou University,
Guangzhou, China

Abstract. Intrusion detection systems (IDSs) are an important security mechanism to protect computing resources under various environments. To detect malicious unknown events, machine learning is often used to support anomaly-based detection. However, such kind of detection often requires high quality data to ensure accuracy, which may face several issues like imbalanced data and ineffective features. In this work, we aim to evaluate a combined approach of both imbalance correction and feature selection, and explore how much it can mitigate the issues. As a study, we generate several feature-selected and imbalance-corrected datasets based on NSL-KDD data and conduct experiments on Random Forests, Neural Networks and Gradient-Boosting Machines. The results indicate that the combined approach can significantly improve the detection performance on the refined data as compared to being trained on the original data, by 10% in overall accuracy and 24% in overall F1-score.

Keywords: Intrusion detection · Feature selection · Imbalanced data · Machine learning · Anomaly detection

1 Introduction

With the rapid development of computer networks, many companies, organizations and individuals benefit from such increasing digitisation and interconnection. However, it also opens a hole for attackers, as it is difficult to maintain the high-security standards with the size and complexity of systems. Cybersecurity Ventures, a world leading researcher in global cyber economy, predicted the annual loss from cybercrime to exceed six trillion dollars by 2021 [14].

Nowadays with Hacking-as-a-Service (HaaS), the number of entities that pose a threat has increased significantly. It is no longer required to be an expert when one can acquire sophisticated tools online. The hackers have all sorts of motivations, including political, financial, or even intellectual, which makes detection even harder. To identify potential attacks, intrusion detection systems

© Springer Nature Switzerland AG 2020
M. Kutyłowski et al. (Eds.): NSS 2020, LNCS 12570, pp. 277–291, 2020.
https://doi.org/10.1007/978-3-030-65745-1_16

(IDSs) [12,15] are a basic and important security mechanism, which are widely adopted by various organizations. Generally, an IDS can be either rule-based or anomaly-based, where an anomaly-based IDS has the potential to identify zero-day vulnerabilities (or unknown threats). Machine learning is the main tool to help build a classification model for anomaly-based detection [2,13].

Anomaly-based detection is an important approach to complement rule-based detection in real scenarios. For instance, the difficulties have appeared during the COVID-19 outbreak. The unusual network traffic has made it hard for a rule-based IDS to distinguish unknown malicious traffic. Though COVID-19 is not an ordinary situation, it certainly cements the need for scalable, versatile, and intelligent solutions. By integrating with machine learning (or even artificial intelligence), anomaly-based detection can help identify malicious packets. For this purpose, there is a need for using high quality data to train machine learning classifiers before they can be applied for detection. However, two major issues are still remained like imbalanced data and ineffective features, which could greatly degrade the detection performance (i.e., resulting in low detection accuracy).

Related Work. To obtain high quality data is not easy in practice, which hinders the performance of anomaly-based detection [11]. In particular, imbalanced data and ineffective features are two major challenges. To mitigate these issues, imbalanced correction like [7,19] and feature selection like [8,9] are the main solutions. However, it is unclear to what degree these solutions can improve the detection performance. There are few studies focusing on this question in the research community.

Contributions. In this work, we aim to conduct an evaluation on how to solve the issues of imbalanced data and ineffective features, by using imbalance correction and feature selection. More specifically, we start by creating an imbalance-corrected dataset with an algorithm named SMOTE, and then perform feature selection on the original data with three different methods: correlation-based, fast-correlation-based and consistency-based selection. The refined datasets obtained from NSL-KDD are then used to train an ensemble of neural networks, a random forest, a gradient-boosting machine, and an ensemble of neural networks and a gradient-boosting machine. In the evaluation, our purpose is to compare the classifier performance between the refined data and the original data.

The remaining parts of this paper are structured as follows. Section 2 introduces the background and our motivation on the use of NSL-KDD. Section 3 describes the focused imbalanced correction and feature selection methods in this work. In Sect. 4, we introduce the performance metrics. Section 5 presents the algorithms and analyzes the obtained results. We conclude our work in Sect. 6.

2   Background on NSL-KDD Dataset

The NSL-KDD dataset [16] is an improvement to the KDD99 dataset. 1) They removed all redundant samples. 2) They selected seven of the most popular machine learning algorithms at that time and trained them with three randomly selected datasets from KDD99 training data with each containing 50,000 samples.

This results in 21 models they used to predict all data in the whole KDD99 dataset. All samples were then polled into groups describing how many of the models had gotten that sample right. The succeeding five groups were made, 0–5, 6–10, 11–15, 16–20 and 21 learners predicted the sample correct.

Each group constituted a percentage of the whole KDD99 dataset. To put emphasis on harder instances while also reducing the size of the space, the authors of NSL-KDD took the inverse of each group and sampled at random this amount from the given group. This results in a more even ratio between attack types, as well as an increased level of difficulty. Due to the increased difficulty, the performance of different machine learning algorithms can be also spread out on the new data. In consequence of the above actions, the dataset decreased to a manageable size. This makes it possible to train learning algorithms on the whole dataset, and hence possible to compare different projects.

The NSL-KDD dataset is far from robust and perfect, i.e., simulation of a military network can hardly represent a day-to-day public network. While it is a widely accepted dataset that has been used for comparison in many research studies. For our purpose, this work adopts it to compare the performance among different machine learning algorithms.

3   Imbalanced Correction and Feature Selection

3.1   Handling Imbalanced Data

When using imbalanced data for classification, it can lead to a large bias towards the majority class. This can be counteracted by applying what is known as sampling techniques.

Sampling techniques can be divided into two groups: under-sampling and over-sampling. When doing under-sampling, we remove samples of the majority class to balance the ratio between the classes. However, when having very imbalanced classes in a dataset, it is in general not a beneficial technique. For instance, to get a reasonable ratio between the minority and the majority class, we would need to remove a lot of information from the majority class, which could be used for better classification.

Therefore, we normally apply over-sampling where we upscale the minority class instead. The simplest way to do this is by sampling with replacement from the minority class until balance has been established between the classes. One problem with this method is when facing severe imbalances, the up-scaled minority class would consist of several replications of the same data leading to overfitting of the minority class.

In this work, we thus focus on Synthetic Minority Over-sampling Technique (SMOTE), which can create new synthetic samples of the minority class by using the K-nearest neighbours (KNN) algorithm. For every sample in the minority class, SMOTE finds the Euclidean distance between minority samples and chooses n of the neighbours at random, where n depends on how much the minority class needs to be up-scaled. Then a random point on the straight line segment between the sample in focus and the chosen neighbour is generated as a new synthetic sample.

3.2   Feature Selection

When predicting something by using machine learning, we require data to estimate a model. This is true for all different techniques, and we expect the data to represent what we want to predict as good as possible. Feature selection can be used for this goal, and this work focuses on correlation-based, fast correlation-based and consistency-based feature selection.

1. Correlation-Based Filter [CFS]. This method [6] aims to maximise the correlation between the class set and the feature set, meanwhile minimising the correlation within the features. Here the following equation is used to evaluate a subset of features.

$$M_S = \frac{k\bar{r}_{Yf}}{\sqrt{k + k(k-1)\bar{r}_{ff}}}$$

where M_s is the score for the subset of features S, and k is the number of features in S, i.e., $|S|$. $\bar{r}_{Yf}$ is the average correlation between the class set Y and the features in S, and $\bar{r}_{ff}$ is the average correlation within S.

We observe that the evaluation function is in-fact a modified version of Pearson's correlation coefficient where the predictiveness of S with respect to Y, which is normalised by the redundancy in S.

The correlation measure r is the symmetrical uncertainty and the minimum description length is used to discretise the feature space. More detail can refer to the previous work [5]. To find the optimal subset of all the features, we select the search technique of best-first search. For the best-first search, we can use the stopping criteria that when five consecutive fully expanded subsets show no improvement over the best found, the algorithm stops.

2. Fast Correlation-Based Filter [FCBF]. This method was introduced by Yu and Liu [18] with the goal of maximising the relevance of the input features with respect to the classes and minimising the redundancy between the input features. First, we can define F as a set of features, F_i as a specific feature and $S_i = F - F_i$ as the subset of the features F without F_i.

C and F Correlation: We can establish a correlation between features called F-correlation and a correlation between features and classes called C-correlation, as follows.

$$C - correlation: \ SU_{i,Y} = SU(F_i, Y)$$
$$F - correlation: \ SU_{i,j} = SU(F_i, F_j)$$

Approximate Markov Blanket: F_j forms an approximate Markov blanket for F_i if and only if

$$SU_{j,Y} \geq SU_{i,Y} \wedge SU_{i,j} \geq SU_{i,Y}$$

Relevance: A feature F_i is relevant if

$$SU_{i,Y} \geq \gamma \ \wedge \ P(Y|F_i, S_i) \neq P(Y|S_i)$$

Predominant Features: A relevant feature is predominant if and only if it does not have any approximate Markov blanket in the current set of features.

Based on the concept of relevance, redundancy by the approximate Markov blanket and a joint measure of both redundancy and relevance by the predominant feature, we can explain the steps of FCBF-algorithm as below.

1. Select a predominant feature.
2. Remove all features for which it forms an approximate Markov blanket.
3. Repeat the above steps until only predominant features are left in the input space.

3. Consistency Methods. Another way to determine a subset of the feature space is consistency. The term "consistency" in statistics refers to the situation when a population-sample grows, the estimator for the population distribution converges towards the true mean of the population. To translate this concept into an applicable method, this work uses the methods introduced by [1] and [3].

Inconsistency and consistency can be defined as below.

$$Inconsistency = \frac{number \ of \ inconsistent \ examples}{number \ of \ examples}$$

$$Consistency = 1 - Inconsistency$$

One advantage of our consistency measure is that it is monotonic. This means that if we have some subsets $\{S_0, S_1, ..., S_n\}$ in the feature space, we can denote the measure of consistency by U, it holds that:

$$if \ S_0 \subset S_1 \subset ... \subset S_n \implies U(S_0) \leq U(S_1) \leq ... \leq U(S_n)$$

This gives us the ability to apply the best-first search for the optimal subset among the 2^m subsets of features, where m is the cardinality of our feature set. If we did not apply such a technique, it would become an infeasible task to find the optimal subset.

4   Evaluation Metrics

In order to evaluate the performance of different classifiers, we need a way of quantifying their performance. However, as one is often faced with imbalanced datasets, we must carefully select the metrics so they are not misleading [17]. For this reason, a few important definitions are needed. These are usually used for binary classification, but the following is an attempt to generalise the terms.

- **True Positive [TP]:** The classifier correctly predicts the presence of class label.
- **True Negative [TN]:** The classifier correctly predicts the absence of class label.
- **False Positive [FP]:** The classifier predicts the presence of class label, when it is absent.
- **False Negative [FN]:** The classifier predicts the absence of class label, when it is present.

4.1   Performance Metrics

Confusion Matrix. A confusion matrix, which is also known as a contingency table, can predict classes and true classes placed in respectively columns and rows.

A good classifier will have most of its values placed in the diagonal, which corresponds to *true positives*. A confusion matrix is not sensitive to imbalanced data, since it is a raw presentation of predictions and true observations [17].

Recall [R]. It is a ratio between the number of correctly classified positive samples and the total number of positive samples.

$$R = \frac{TP}{TP + FN} \tag{1}$$

It can be interpreted as the classifier's ability to correctly detect the presence of a class label. It is used interchangeably with the terms of *true positive rate*, *sensitivity*, and *hit rate* [10].

False Positive Rate [FPR] and False Negative Rate [FNR]. These are two metrics of high importance to intrusion detection. The definitions are shown as follows.

$$FPR = \frac{FP}{FP + TN}, \quad FNR = \frac{FN}{FN + TP} \tag{2}$$

4.2 Sensitive Metrics

Accuracy [A]. A natural way of quantifying the performance is to look at the number of correct predictions. It is defined as follows.

$$A = \frac{TP + TN}{TP + TN + FP + FN} \tag{3}$$

Precision [P]. It is the ratio of correctly predicted positives to the total number of predicted positives. It can be interpreted as the extend to which a classifier can be trusted when it predicts the presence of a class label.

$$P = \frac{TP}{TP + FP} \tag{4}$$

F-Measure [F]. It is the harmonic mean of precision and recall. Since it depends on precision, it is sensitive to changes in the class distribution [17]. It can be defined as follows:

$$F = \frac{2 \cdot P \cdot R}{P + R} \tag{5}$$

A high F-measure (i.e., close to 1) can be seen as an indicator of good performance.

5 Evaluation and Results

Figure 1 shows the workflow in our evaluation. Before doing any preprocessing, we grouped the attack types into 5 major classes: Normal, DoS, Probe, R2L, and U2R. Preprocessing is a wide term for any manipulation done to the data prior to creating models. In this work, it involves three operations: Imbalance Correction, Feature Selection, and One-Hot-Encoding on nominal features.

Depending on types of preprocessing operations that has been made, Table 1 summarizes the refined datasets based on NSL-KDD.

The hyperparameter fitting was carried out by choosing a parameter space on which we performed a search technique to find the optimal set of features for a given model. We have used random search and grid search to find the optimal parameters for the earlier discussed models. The found optimal hyperparameters were then used in the training of models and then were evaluated on the test data.

Table 1. Names for different datasets

Imbalance-corrected	Feature-selection method	Dataset name
None	None	Original (raw) dataset
SMOTE	None	SMOTE dataset
None	CFS	CFS dataset
None	FCBF	FCBF dataset
None	Consistency	Consistency dataset
SMOTE	CFS	CFS SMOTE dataset

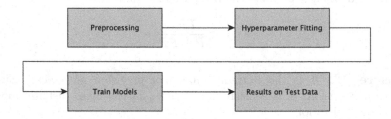

Fig. 1. Overview of workflow

5.1   Results from Imbalance Handling and Feature Selection

The imbalance correction was performed based on the SMOTE algorithm. We obtained an almost perfectly balanced dataset with 25194 instances of probe, and 25195 instances of respectively DoS, normal, U2R, and R2L. We then applied the feature selection methods of CFS, FCBF, and a consistency based method. The features selected by each method are shown in Table 2.

5.2   Specifications of Used Models

Gradient Boosting Machine. Four different hyperparameters were fitted for the gradient boosting machine model, including the number of trees, the maximum depth of each tree, the maximum number of leaves, and minimum data points of each leaf in a tree. We then applied grid search for each dataset to find the optimal set of hyperparameters. The found range for the grid search was:

$\text{trees} = \{465, 475, 490\}$
$\text{max depth} = \{23, 24, 25\}$
$\text{max leafs} = \{165, 170, 175\}$
$\text{min samples} = \{4, 5, 6\}$

The learning rate was set to 0.005 because it did not result in divergence. Therefore we found no reason for trying lower values as it would only result in a slower training process.

Table 2. Selected features for each method

	Selected features
CFS:	x3, x4, x5, x6, x12, x25, x29, x30, x37, x39
FCBF:	x5, x25
Consistency:	x1, x3, x5, x6, x12, x23, x32, x33, x35, x37, x38, x39, x40

Table 3. Confusion matrix for neural networks trained on CFS SMOTE dataset and evaluated on the test data.

	2 hidden layers, 200 units per layer					6 hidden layers, 275 units per layer				
	DoS	Normal	Probe	R2L	U2R	DoS	Normal	Probe	R2L	U2R
DoS	**5816**	1006	146	492	0	**5369**	647	76	25	1343
Normal	55	**9112**	193	272	79	36	**8643**	285	31	716
Probe	221	639	**1480**	63	18	153	250	**1997**	12	9
R2L	10	1765	14	**927**	169	3	2025	20	**209**	628
U2R	0	5	0	21	**41**	0	11	0	0	**56**

Random Forest. The random forest has two hyperparameters, which were fitted following the same approach as in the gradient boosting machine. The final range to apply grid search was found to be:

trees $= \{300, 350, 400\}$
split features $= \{22, 24, 26\}$

Neural Network. For neural networks, we used random search to find suitable hyperparameters for the networks. We tried 59 different configurations, which corresponds to a 95% certainty that at least one configuration is the top 5% best result in the chosen hyperparameter space. We chose the following space:

learning rates $= \{4\cdot10^{-3}, 1\cdot10^{-3}, 7\cdot10^{-4}, 4\cdot10^{-4}, 1\cdot10^{-4}, 7\cdot10^{-5}, 4\cdot10^{-5}, 1\cdot10^{-5}\}$
hidden layers $= \{2, 4, 6, 8, 10, 12, 14\}$
hidden units $= \{50, 75, 100, 125, 150, 175, 200, 225, 250, 275, 300, 325, 350\}$

The tuning is based on the assumption that the optimal configurations can be found in the chosen space. The learning rate was considered around the default value of ADAM optimiser [4], as this value was chosen by the developers to be versatile. For the hidden layers and the number of weights, computational feasible sizes were chosen.

At first glace, the results seemed to indicate that deeper networks with a large number of weights would lead to better performance, since they performed the best on the validation set taken from the training data. When performed on the test data, we can see a huge bias towards the U2R and normal class. Specifically, Table 3 presents the confusion matrix of a network with 6 hidden layers with 275 units in each, which was trained on the CFS SMOTE dataset, while the pattern was similar for all the datasets.

It is found that the large models may overfit the training data. To tackle this problem, we restricted us to only consider shallow networks with only two layers. This is a form of manual regularisation that could also have been implemented automatically in the selection procedure. The best performing network that satisfied this had 2 hidden layers and 200 units in each. It can be seen from Table 3 that the classification is much more uniform than for the one with 6 hidden layers and 275 units in each. With the model with 2 hidden layers and 200 units, we could reach good results for all the datasets.

5.3   Specification of Ensemble

The ratio between the gradient boosting machine and the neural networks can be considered as a "hyper-hyper"-parameter. Hence it should be also fitted before evaluating the model on an unseen test set. It is a problem however, that the training data is already used to train the models that constitute the ensemble.

We thus try to fit the models on the raw dataset and then fit the ensemble on the SMOTE dataset. The idea was to mimic new data by introducing all the synthetic points. Table 4 shows that the gradient boosting machine is either correct or normal. This could indicate that the gradient boosting machine is overfitting on the data.

It is also found that the ensemble of the neural network and the gradient boosting machine always had a lower accuracy rate than the pure neural network and a lower F1 score than the pure gradient boosting machine. We believe one of the main reasons for these problems was that some training data was already known to the models, so that they were trivially classified. Hence we concluded that fitting on the synthesized training data was infeasible. We therefore decided to split up the test data in a training part and a testing part. This has the risk of not generalising to other attack distributions, and some of the idea behind testing on another distribution may disappear. We found that the neural network exhibits a better performance regarding the R2L class in both the confusion matrix from Table 4 and Table 5. This provides us confidence that the ensemble would be able to generalise to other distributions.

Table 4. Confusion matrix for neural networks and gradient boosting machine trained on the Raw dataset and examined on the SMOTE dataset

	Neural networks					Gradient boosting				
	DoS	Normal	Probe	R2L	U2R	DoS	Normal	Probe	R2L	U2R
DoS	24415	547	233	0	0	23621	1574	0	0	10
Normal	152	24765	264	14	0	0	25192	3	0	0
Probe	152	1739	23280	23	0	0	9681	15513	0	0
R2L	3	18737	847	5608	0	5	21943	0	3240	7
U2R	20	24372	788	15	0	0	17323	0	0	7872

Table 5. Confusion matrix for neural networks and gradient boosting machine trained on the CFS SMOTE dataset and examined on the test data

	Neural networks					Gradient boosting				
	DoS	Normal	Probe	R2L	U2R	DoS	Normal	Probe	R2L	U2R
DoS	**5816**	1006	146	492	0	**5737**	1698	23	0	2
Normal	55	**9112**	193	272	79	67	**9401**	228	7	8
Probe	221	639	**1480**	63	18	165	170	**2080**	4	2
R2L	10	1765	14	**927**	169	0	2675	27	**162**	21
U2R	0	5	0	21	**41**	0	25	0	2	**40**

Table 6. Specifications for ensembles of neural networks and gradient boosting machines

Data	No. neural networks	Gradient boosting ratio	Neural network ratio
Raw	5	68%	32%
Smote	4	75%	25%
CFS	6	71%	29%
FCBF	5	69%	31%
Consistency	4	68%	32%
Smote and CFS	2	75%	25%

The test data was split into a training set consisting of 15780 samples and a test set consisting of the remaining 6764 samples. We then fitted all ensembles on the new training data and Table 6 shows the ratios for neural networks and gradient boosting machines.

5.4 Effect of Imbalance Correction

First, we compared the models trained on the Raw dataset and the SMOTE dataset. Table 7 and Table 8 show that the accuracy is not much different, but F1-score is significantly higher for the corrected dataset as seen in Table 8. The reason might be that the accuracy is not a robust metric. Hence, being good at DoS and normal class is sufficient to achieve a high accuracy since the test data is also imbalanced. On the other hand, every class has equal weights for F1 score, thus one will never be able to score high F1 measure by only being able to classify two classes. This is the main reason that SMOTE can achieve a higher F1-score than the Raw dataset.

5.5 Effect of Feature Selection

To assess the performance of each feature selection method we compare how well they can hold up against models trained on the Raw dataset. Table 9 shows that CFS has fewer features than the consistency method but could achieve better results. It also performs better than the Raw data in almost every aspect, especially for the low FNR.

Table 7. Metrics for training on the raw dataset

	Neural networks	Random forest	Gradient boost	Ensemble
Accuracy	0.72	0.70	0.69	0.71
F1-score	0.45	0.45	0.43	0.44
Precision	0.54	0.88	0.48	0.48
Recall	0.46	0.45	0.42	0.44
FPR	0.09	0.10	0.11	0.10
FNR	0.54	0.55	0.58	0.56

Table 8. Metrics for training on the SMOTE dataset

	Neural networks	Random forest	Gradient boost	Ensemble
Accuracy	0.75	0.75	0.78	0.77
F1-score	0.57	0.57	0.65	0.63
Precision	0.59	0.77	0.81	0.79
Recall	0.62	0.56	0.62	0.62
FPR	0.08	0.08	0.07	0.08
FNR	0.38	0.44	0.38	0.38

Table 9. Metrics for training on the CFS dataset

	Neural networks	Random forest	Gradient boost	Ensemble
Accuracy	0.73	0.77	0.75	0.76
F1-score	0.45	0.55	0.49	0.48
Precision	0.43	0.80	0.89	0.70
Recall	0.48	0.56	0.49	0.49
FPR	0.09	0.08	0.08	0.09
FNR	0.52	0.44	0.51	0.51

It is apparent from Table 10 that the FCBF method with only two features is not desired. It is worse in every aspect compared to the models trained on the Raw dataset. The consistency method is better than the FCBF method as shown in Table 11, whereas it is still worse than the Raw dataset in all aspects.

Table 10. Metrics for training on the FCBF dataset

	Neural networks	Random forest	Gradient boost	Ensemble
Accuracy	0.68	0.74	0.73	0.73
F1-score	0.34	0.45	0.43	0.43
Precision	0.33	0.56	0.44	0.45
Recall	0.37	0.45	0.44	0.44
FPR	0.10	0.09	0.09	0.09
FNR	0.63	0.55	0.56	0.56

Table 11. Metrics for training on the consistency dataset

	Neural networks	Random forest	Gradient boost	Ensemble
Accuracy	0.74	0.74	0.73	0.74
F1-score	0.47	0.48	0.46	0.47
Precision	0.62	0.74	0.69	0.49
Recall	0.47	0.48	0.46	0.47
FPR	0.09	0.09	0.09	0.09
FNR	0.53	0.52	0.54	0.53

5.6 Effect of Imbalance Correction Combined with Feature Selection

As CFS is the only method that performed better than raw data, we decided to combine it with SMOTE. We first performed SMOTE on the Raw dataset and then performed CFS.

Compared to the features in the CFS dataset (refer to Table 2), this results in discarding the features of x25 and x29, and adding the features of x1, x14, x17, x23, and x33. Table 12 shows that it could achieve superior performance compared to all the other datasets. More specifically, the ensemble of both gradient boosting machine and neural networks could stand out with an accuracy of 81% and an F1 score of 68%. This indicates that the ensemble can correctly label many of the samples, which belong to the minority classes.

Based on the above results, the ensemble of two neural networks and a gradient boosting machine could reach the best performance in our evaluation. In Table 13, we further present the confusion matrix, which validates our observation that it achieved good performance for all the classes. The only problem in classification is that the R2L and the DoS class may have a bias towards the normal class. This could be further enhanced through considering new machine learning classifiers or optimizing current settings.

Table 12. Metrics for training on the CFS SMOTE dataset

	Neural networks	Random forest	Gradient boost	Ensemble
Accuracy	0.77	0.78	0.77	0.81
F1-score	0.59	0.61	0.64	0.68
Precision	0.62	0.72	0.80	0.75
Recall	0.64	0.61	0.65	0.70
FPR	0.07	0.07	0.08	0.06
FNR	0.36	0.39	0.35	0.30

Table 13. Confusion matrix for the ensemble model trained on the CFS SMOTE dataset

		Predicted class				
		DoS	Normal	Probe	R2L	U2R
True class	DoS	**1852**	318	25	43	0
	Normal	13	**2829**	63	5	4
	Probe	53	98	**570**	3	2
	R2L	0	697	3	**202**	14
	U2R	0	6	0	0	**14**

6   Conclusion

Anomaly-based intrusion detection is an important approach for identifying unknown threats, but may face the issues of imbalanced data and ineffective features. This work focuses on conventional machine learning in anomaly-based intrusion detection, and conducts an evaluation to explore how a combined approach of imbalance correction and feature selection can mitigate these issues. In particular, we explore the following preprocessing techniques: SMOTE as a means for handling imbalance correction of data, and several feature selection methods such as CFS, FCBF and consistency-based selection.

As a study, we generate several feature-selected and imbalance-corrected datasets based on NSL-KDD data and conduct experiments on Random Forests, Neural Networks and Gradient-Boosting Machines. It is found that the best detection performance can be achieved by an ensemble with two neural networks and a gradient boosting machine, Specifically, we obtained an accuracy rate of 81% and an F1-score of 68%, which is an improvement by 10% and 24% respectively, as compared to training the model on the original dataset.

Acknowledgments. This work was partially supported by National Natural Science Foundation of China (No. 61802077).

References

1. Arauzo-Azofra, A., Benitez, J.M., Castro, J.L.: Consistency measures for feature selection J. Intell. Inf. Syst. 30, 273–292 (2007). https://doi.org/10.1007/s10844-007-0037-0
2. Buczak, A.L., Guven, E.: A survey of data mining and machine learning methods for cyber security intrusion detection. IEEE Commun. Surv. Tutorials 18(2), 1153–1176 (2016)
3. Dash, M., Liu, H.: Consistency-based search in feature selection. Artif. Intell. 151(1–2), 155–176 (2003)
4. Diederik P. Kingma, J.L.B.: Adam: a method for stochastic optimization (2015)
5. Grünwald, P.: A tutorial introduction to the minimum description length principle (2004)
6. Hall, M.A.: Correlation-based feature selection for machine learning. Ph.D. thesis, The University of Waikato, April 1999
7. Huang, S., Lei, K.: IGAN-IDS: an imbalanced generative adversarial network towards intrusion detection system in ad-hoc networks. Ad Hoc Netw. 105, 102177 (2020)
8. Li, X., Chen, W., Zhang, Q., Wu, L.: Building auto-encoder intrusion detection system based on random forest feature selection. Comput. Secur. 95, 101851 (2020)
9. Li, Y., Wang, J., Tian, Z., Lu, T., Young, C.: Building lightweight intrusion detection system using wrapper-based feature selection mechanisms. Comput. Secur. 28(6), 466–475 (2009)
10. Liu, H., Lang, B.: Machine learning and deep learning methods for intrusion detection systems: a survey. Appl. Sci. 9(20), 4396 (2019)
11. Meng, Y.: The practice on using machine learning for network anomaly intrusion detection. In: 2011 International Conference on Machine Learning and Cybernetics, vol. 2, pp. 576–581 (2011)
12. Meng, Y., Kwok, L.: Adaptive context-aware packet filter scheme using statistic-based blacklist generation in network intrusion detection. In: 7th International Conference on Information Assurance and Security, IAS, pp. 74–79. IEEE (2011)
13. Meng, Y., Kwok, L.-F.: Enhancing false alarm reduction using pool-based active learning in network intrusion detection. In: Deng, R.H., Feng, T. (eds.) ISPEC 2013. LNCS, vol. 7863, pp. 1–15. Springer, Heidelberg (2013). https://doi.org/10.1007/978-3-642-38033-4_1
14. Morgan, S.: Global cybercrime damages predicted to reach $6 trillion annually by 2021. Accessed 25 Apr 2020. https://cybersecurityventures.com/cybercrime-damages-6-trillion-by-2021/
15. Nisioti, A., Mylonas, A., Yoo, P.D., Katos, V.: From intrusion detection to attacker attribution: a comprehensive survey of unsupervised methods. IEEE Commun. Surv. Tutorials 20(4), 3369–3388 (2018)
16. Tavallaee, M., Bagheri, E., Lu, W., Ghorbani, A.A.: A detailed analysis of the KDD CUP 99 data set (2009)
17. Tharwat, A.: Classification assessment methods. Appl. Comput. Inform. 16, 1–25 (2018)
18. Yu, L., Liu, H.: Efficient feature selection via analysis of relevance and redundancy. J. Mach. Learn. Res. 5, 1205–1224 (2004)
19. Zhou, Q., Gu, L., Wang, C., Wang, J., Chen, S.: Using an improved C4.5 for imbalanced dataset of intrusion. In: Proceedings of the 2006 International Conference on Privacy, Security and Trust PST, vol. 380, p. 67. ACM (2006)

AC^0 Constructions of Secret Sharing Schemes – Accommodating New Parties

Shion Samadder Chaudhury[1]([✉]), Sabyasachi Dutta[2], and Kouichi Sakurai[3]

[1] Applied Statistics Unit, Indian Statistical Institute, Kolkata, India
chaudhury.shion@gmail.com
[2] University of Calgary, Calgary, Canada
saby.math@gmail.com
[3] Faculty of Information Science and Electrical Engineering,
Kyushu University, Fukuoka, Japan
sakurai@inf.kyushu-u.ac.jp

Abstract. The possibility of implementing secret sharing in the complexity class AC^0 was shown in a recent work by Bogdanov et al. (Crypto'16) who provided constructions of ramp schemes. Cheng-Ishai-Li (TCC'17) forwarded the work by achieving robustness for such schemes. In this paper we construct secret sharing schemes which can include new parties over time keeping the entire construction implementable by AC^0 circuits. We provide AC^0 constructions of a dynamic secret sharing scheme and an evolving secret sharing scheme. The constructions are more flexible than similar existing schemes, use less resources and have several notable advantages.

Keywords: Dynamic secret sharing · Evolving secret sharing · Share redistribution · AC^0 Circuits · Error-correcting codes.

1   Introduction

Secret sharing is a method to distribute a secret data or information among n many participants so that any predefined "qualified" sets of participants can recover the secret information, whereas every predefined "forbidden" sets of participants do not get any information about the secret. The *monotone* collection of qualified sets of participants is called an *access structure*. Secret sharing schemes have found applications in cryptography as well as in secure distributed computing. All the classical secret sharing schemes assume that the number of participants as well as the access structure are fixed from the very beginning.

S. S. Chaudhury is financially supported by Indian Statistical Institute, Kolkata, India under a research fellowship program. The work presented in this paper was carried out while the first author visited Kyushu University, Japan.
S. Dutta is grateful to the National Institute of Information and Communications Technology (NICT), Japan for financial support under the NICT International Exchange Program during 2018–19 when the preliminary draft was prepared.

© Springer Nature Switzerland AG 2020
M. Kutyłowski et al. (Eds.): NSS 2020, LNCS 12570, pp. 292–308, 2020.
https://doi.org/10.1007/978-3-030-65745-1_17

An access structure is called an *evolving* access structure if the number of participants can grow without any bound and be potentially infinite with the possibility that the access sets are also changing over time. Existing classical methodology fails to provide a secret sharing scheme when the access structure is evolving. Some recent works (*see* Sect. 1.1) have put forward secret sharing schemes for evolving access structures. In a recent development researchers have considered the problem of minimizing the computational complexity of cryptographic primitives and some recent positive results confirm the possibility of secret sharing with minimal computational complexity. More precisely, secret sharing with added randomness is possible with both share-generation algorithm and reconstruction algorithms are in the complexity class AC^0.

Hence the goal of this paper is to bring these two together to construct AC^0 implementable secret sharing schemes which can add new participants over time.

1.1 Related Work

Classical Secret Sharing. Secret sharing schemes were proposed independently by Shamir [22] and Blakley [7] in 1979. They proposed schemes where any k (or more) out of n participants are qualified to recover the secret with $1 < k \leq n$. The access structure is called a (k, n)-threshold access structure where a subset of size greater than or equal to the threshold value k is deemed to be qualified. Both schemes were fairly efficient in terms of the size of the shares and computational complexity. Later, Ito et al. [16] showed the possibility of constructing secret sharing schemes given any monotone (general) access structures. However, their generic constructions resulted in exponentially large share sizes.

Evolving Secret Sharing. Komargodski et al. [17] introduced evolving secret sharing schemes where the secret holder a.k.a *dealer* does not know the number (or any upper bound) of participants that would participate in the protocol. Theoretically speaking, number of participants could be potentially infinite and the definition of access sets may change as a function of time – a subset is declared to be qualified when the last participant who completes the set has arrived. The authors considered the scenario when players participate one at a time (in a sequential manner) and each player receives its share from the dealer. Main challenge in designing such a protocol is that the dealer cannot update the shares that he has already distributed. The authors [17] showed that for every evolving access structure there exists a generic secret sharing scheme with 2^{t-1} as the share size of the tth incoming participant. They also constructed (k, ∞)-threshold evolving secret sharing scheme for a fixed threshold value k with share size $(k - 1) \log t + \mathcal{O}(\log \log t)$ of the tth participant.

Komargodski and Paskin-Cherniavsky [18] constructed evolving dynamic threshold schemes such that share size of the tth participant is $\mathcal{O}(t^4 \log t)$ bits. Moreover, they used AMD codes to generically transform such evolving threshold schemes to *robust* schemes. Robustness of a secret sharing scheme means the correct secret is reconstructed even if some of the participants maliciously hand in tampered shares during the reconstruction process.

Later, Beimel and Othman [6] constructed evolving (a, b) ramp scheme with share size $\mathcal{O}(1)$.

Dynamic Secret Sharing. Many secret sharing schemes have been proposed where the access structure changes over time. *Dynamic* secret sharing scheme allows, without reconstructing the shared secret, to add or delete shareholders, to renew the shares, and to modify the conditions for accessing the secret. This important primitive of redistributing the secret was initially considered by Chen et al. [9], Frankel et al. [14] and Desmedt-Jajodia [12].

To describe a dynamic secret sharing scheme more formally, let us consider two sets of participants $\mathcal{P}$ and $\mathcal{P}'$ containing n and n' many participants respectively. Let us suppose that each participant P_j in $\mathcal{P}$ has received a share s_j of the secret value s. $\Gamma_\mathcal{P}$ denote the access structure that specifies which subsets of $\mathcal{P}$ are *authorized* to recover the secret s from their shares. The *goal* of redistribution is that *without* the help of the original dealer, the participants in $\mathcal{P}'$ will receive the shares of s in accordance with a possibly different access structure $\Gamma_{\mathcal{P}'}$. In the protocol, the participants in $\mathcal{P}$ act like virtual dealers, while participants in $\mathcal{P}'$ are the ones who receive shares. A *notable* difference between evolving secret sharing and dynamic secret sharing is – in the former, dealer is present through out and he distributes new shares to joining parties.

Nojoumian-Stinson [21] proposed unconditionally secure share re-distribution schemes, in absence of a dealer, based on a previously existing VSS protocol of Stinson-Wei [23]. In their construction, they have assumed less than one-fourth of participants behave dishonestly and also that the number of participants is fixed throughout. Their work was improved upon by the work of Desmedt-Morozov [13] who relaxed the proportion of dishonest participants to one-third of the total population and also allowed the number of participants to change.

Secret Sharing in AC^0. The motivation to study secret sharing schemes that can be implemented by constant-depth circuits comes from two different sources. First, most well-known secret sharing schemes require computations that can not be implemented by constant-depth circuits (i.e. AC^0 circuits). For example, Shamir's scheme in [22] requires linear algebraic computations over finite field and hence cannot be computed in AC^0. Secondly, the visual secret sharing schemes introduced by Naor and Shamir [20] require only computation of OR function which can be implemented by AC^0 circuit. Recent work by Bogdanov et al. [8] considers the question of whether there exists secret sharing scheme such that both share generation algorithm and secret reconstruction algorithm are computable in AC^0.

They considered a variant of threshold secret sharing scheme, known as *ramp* schemes where any k participants learn nothing about the secret but when all n participants collaborate together, they are able to reconstruct the secret. The scheme is called ramp because unlike classical secret sharing scheme there is a gap between the privacy threshold viz. k and reconstructability threshold viz. n. Their construction connects the idea of *approximate degree* of a function with the privacy threshold of a secret sharing scheme. Existing literature on the approximate degree lower bounds gives several secret sharing schemes in AC^0. Their schemes however achieve large privacy threshold $k = \Omega(n)$ when the alphabet size is $2^{poly(n)}$ and achieve $k = \Omega(\sqrt{n})$ for binary alphabets. The work of Bogdanov et al. [8] was followed up by a work of Cheng et al. [10] who achieved privacy threshold $k = \Omega(n)$ with binary alphabets by allowing negligible privacy error. They have also considered robustness of the schemes in presence of honest majority with privacy threshold $\Omega(n)$, privacy error $2^{-n^{\Omega(1)}}$ and reconstruction error $\frac{1}{poly(n)}$.

1.2 Our Contribution

In this paper we construct dynamic secret sharing schemes and evolving schemes keeping the secret sharing and the reconstruction procedures in the complexity class AC^0. Our main idea is to use new share redistribution schemes based on good error-correcting codes [10,11], and pseudorandom generators to give shares to the new nodes being added to a secret sharing scheme. The number of nodes is time-dependent and throughout the whole process (lifetime) of accommodating new nodes and share redistribution, secrecy of original data is maintained.

- Our first goal is to construct a dynamic AC^0 secret sharing scheme which can include new parties into the system even when the dealer is absent after generating shares of the old parties. To this end, using a secret redistribution scheme and by suitably modifying the scheme of [10], we construct a robust secret sharing scheme which can accommodate a bounded number of new parties. The advantage of redistribution here is that alphabet size need not be increased to accommodate new parties. The downside is, we can only add a bounded number of them.
- Next we construct a $(2, \infty)$ evolving secret sharing scheme in AC^0 where we can accommodate unbounded number of storage nodes but collective shares from any two nodes can reconstruct the secret. This theoretical result shows that threshold secret sharing with unbounded number of parties is possible with constant depth circuits and this can be of independent interest also. The generalization to an AC^0-implementable (k, ∞) evolving scheme is left as an open question.

2 Preliminaries

AC^0 **Complexity Class.** AC^0 is the complexity class which consists of all families of circuits having constant depth and polynomial size. The gates in those circuits are NOT, AND, OR, where AND gates and OR gates have unbounded fan-in. Integer addition and subtraction are computable in AC^0, but multiplication is not. It is also well known that calculating the parity of an input cannot be decided by any AC^0 circuits. For any circuit C, the size of C is denoted by size(C) and the depth of C is denoted by depth(C). Recently, a lot of research [1–4] have been done focusing on possibilities of obtaining cryptographic primitives in low complexity classes e.g. AC^0 or NC^1. We will later describe some primitives that are needed for our constructions.

Statistical Distance. The statistical distance between two random variables X and Y over Σ^n for some alphabet Σ, is $SD(X; Y)$ which is defined as follows,

$$SD(X; Y) = \frac{1}{2} \sum_{a \in \Sigma^n} |Pr[X = a] = Pr[Y = a]|.$$

2.1   Secret Sharing Scheme

In a secret sharing scheme there is a dealer who has a secret s, a set of participants $[n]$ and an access structure $\mathcal{A}$. The dealer shares the secret among the participants in such a way that any qualified set of participants can recover the secret but any forbidden set of participants has no information about the secret.

Definition 1 *(Secret Sharing Scheme [5]). A secret sharing scheme $\mathcal{S}$ for an access structure $\mathcal{A}$ consists of a pair of algorithms (Share, Rec). Share is a probabilistic algorithm that gets as input a secret s (from a domain of secrets S) and a number n, and generates n shares $\Pi_1^{(s)}, \Pi_2^{(s)}, \ldots, \Pi_n^{(s)}$. Rec is a deterministic algorithm that gets as input the shares of a subset B of participants and outputs a string. The requirements for defining a secret sharing scheme are as follow:*

1. *(Correctness) For every secret $s \in S$ and every qualified set $B \in \mathcal{A}$, it must hold that $Pr[Rec(\{\Pi_i^{(s)}\}_{i \in B}, B) = s] = 1$.*
2. *(Security) For every forbidden set $B \notin \mathcal{A}$ and for any two distinct secrets $s_1 \neq s_2$ in S, it must hold that the two distributions $\{\Pi_i^{(s_1)}\}_{i \in B}$ and $\{\Pi_i^{(s_2)}\}_{i \in B}$ are identical.*

The *share size* of a secret sharing scheme $\mathcal{S}$ is the maximum number of bits each participant has to hold in the worst case over all participants and all secrets.

Definition 2 *(Ramp Secret Sharing Scheme). A (k, l, n) ramp secret sharing scheme with $k < l \leq n$, on a set of n participants is such that any subset of participants of size greater than equal to l can recover the secret whereas, any subset of size less than k has no information about the secret.*

Definition 3 *(Evolving Secret Sharing Scheme [17]). Let $\mathcal{A} = \{\mathcal{A}_t\}_{t \in \mathbb{N}}$ be an evolving access structure. A secret sharing scheme $\mathcal{S}$ for $\mathcal{A}$ consists of a pair of algorithms (SHARE, REC). SHARE is a probabilistic algorithm and REC is a deterministic algorithm which satisfy the following:*

1. *$SHARE(s, \Pi_1^{(s)}, \Pi_2^{(s)}, \ldots, \Pi_{t-1}^{(s)})$ gets as input a secret s from the domain of secrets S and the secret shares of participants $1, 2, \ldots, t-1$ and outputs the share of the tth participant viz. $\Pi_t^{(s)}$.*
2. *(Correctness) For every secret $s \in S$, every $t \in \mathbb{N}$ and every qualified set $B \in \mathcal{A}_t$, it must hold that $Pr[Rec(\{\Pi_i^{(s)}\}_{i \in B}, B) = s] = 1$.*
3. *(Security) For every $t \in \mathbb{N}$ and every forbidden set $B \notin \mathcal{A}_t$ and for any two distinct secrets $s_1 \neq s_2$ in S, it must hold that the two distributions $\{\Pi_i^{(s_1)}\}_{i \in B}$ and $\{\Pi_i^{(s_2)}\}_{i \in B}$ are identical.*

Secret Sharing Scheme in AC^0 [8]. Let Σ denote set of alphabets. Two distributions μ and ν over Σ^n are called k-wise indistinguishable if for all subsets $S \subset [n]$ of size k, the projections $\mu|_S$ and $\nu|_S$ of μ and ν to the coordinates in S are identical. Thus, while sharing the secret bit 0 (resp. 1) if sampling is done using μ (resp. ν) then we see a direct connection to the fact that any k participants gain no information about the secret bit. However, if there is a function $f : \Sigma^n \to \{0,1\}$ which can tell apart the distributions then f can be thought of as a reconstruction function. Of course, the gap between the privacy threshold k and the reconstructability threshold n makes the scheme a ramp scheme. The definition is as follows.

Definition 4 *(AC^0 Secret Sharing [8]). An (n,k,r) bit secret sharing scheme with alphabet Σ, reconstruction function $f : \Sigma^r \longrightarrow \{0,1\}$ and reconstruction advantage α is a pair of k-wise indistinguishable distributions μ and ν over Σ^n such that for every subset S of size r we have $Pr[f(\mu|_S) = 1] - Pr[f(\nu|_S) = 1] \geq \alpha$.*

Minsky-Papert CNF Function. The sharing function, Share, used in AC^0 constructions in the literature is based on the CNF function given by Minsky-Papert [19]. This scheme can share one bit among n participants, with binary alphabet, privacy threshold $\Omega(n^{1/3})$ and perfect reconstruction.

Random Permutation. It is well known that random permutation is in AC^0. For any $n \in \mathbb{N}$, a permutation over $[n]$ is defined to be a bijective function $\pi : [n] \to [n]$.

K-wise Independent Generators. A construction of K-wise independent generators based on unique neighbour expander graphs were proposed by Guruswami-Smith [15]. A set of n random variables, $X_1, \ldots, X_n$, is said to be k-wise independent(and uniform) if any k of them are independent(and uniformly distributed). For any $r, n, k \in \mathbb{N}$, a function $g : \{0,1\}^r \to \Sigma^n$ is a k-wise (uniform) independent generator, if for the uniform distribution U on $\{0,1\}^r$, the random variables $g(U) = \{Y_1, \ldots, Y_n\}$ are k-wise independent (and uniform).

Expander Graphs. A bipartite graph G with N left vertices, M right vertices is a (K, A) vertex expander if for all sets $S \subseteq [N]$ of at most K vertices, the neighborhood $N(S) = \{u | \exists v \in S : (u, v) \in E\}$ is of size at least $A \cdot |S|$.

2.2 Error-Correcting Codes

In coding-theoretic terms, the goal of secret sharing is to encode a secret S into a sequence $Y_1, \ldots, Y_n$ such that S can be recovered from the encoding and moreover for any $i_1, \ldots, i_t \in [n]$, the sequence $Y_{i_1}, \ldots, Y_{i_t}$ has the same distribution. In this light Shamir's scheme can be seen as following: a secret S is appended with t uniformly random and independent elements from a suitable finite field and the result is encoded using a Reed Solomon code of length n and dimension $t + 1$. Using coding-theoretic properties one can prove that Shamir's scheme is in a sense robust. In this paper we consider the optimal robust error-correcting codes/secret sharing scheme Cheng et al. [10]. The scheme of [10] is described in Sect. 3.1 and is AC^0 implementable.

Definition 5 (Robust secret sharing in AC^0 [10]). *For a secret x, if Y denotes the share string $Share(x)$ then for any adversary observing d shares and arbitrarily changing those values to transform the sharing string from Y to Y', the probability of correctly reconstructing the original secret is $Pr[Rec(Y') = x] \geq 1 - \eta$.*

3   Main Results and Technical Details

In this section we present our main constructions with technical details. First we show how to construct a dynamic secret sharing scheme implementable in AC^0 where the existing shareholders accommodate new participant into the system and generate its share without the help of dealer. Our construction also achieves robustness thanks to the underlying basic scheme [10]. Second we give an AC^0 construction of evolving secret sharing scheme with reconstructability threshold 2 that can accommodate infinitely many parties. In this construction, we assume the dealer to be present to generate new shares. One of the basic differences between these constructions is that in dynamic secret sharing some or all of the old shares are modified whereas, in the evolving case no old shares are changed.

3.1   A Dynamic Robust Secret Sharing Scheme in AC^0

Our construction of a dynamic secret sharing scheme is based on that of Cheng et al. [10]. We modify their scheme to accommodate new parties. For the ease of understanding we first briefly describe their construction.

Overview of the Construction of Cheng et al. [10]. For a short random seed R, it is shared using the one-in-a-box function [19] to get n shares with privacy threshold k_0. R and a k-wise independent generator are used to generate an n-bit string Y. To share a secret X, $Y \oplus X$ is computed. To reconstruct the secret, all the n parties are used to reconstruct R, compute Y and then compute X. This whole procedure can be computed in AC^0. To boost the privacy threshold and make the scheme robust the authors took the following steps:

(a) The parties are divided into blocks of size $O(\log^2 n)$.
(b) For each block a secret sharing scheme based on asymptotically "good" error-correcting codes is applied to obtain $O(\log^2 n)$ shares.
(c) These shares are further divided into $O(\log n)$ smaller blocks of size $O(\log n)$ each and a random permutation of these smaller blocks is applied. By increasing the alphabet size we can store each block together with its index permutation as one share.

The security of the scheme is argued in the following manner – if the adversary sees a constant fraction of the shares, since a random permutation is applied, the adversary learns each block with some constant probability. By using a Chernoff type bound combined with the fact that there are two levels of blocks, it can be ensured that the number of shares the adversary learns is below the privacy threshold of the larger block and thus the adversary actually learns nothing.

In Fig. 1 we sketch the main steps of the share generation algorithm of [10]. The scheme uses random permutations, k-wise independent generators and asymptotically good error correcting codes. The notations that were used (and we also use the same) in [10] are described below.

Notations. For any $n, k, m \in \mathbb{N}$ with $k, m \leq n$, alphabets Σ_0, Σ, let $(Share, Rec)$ be a k-out-of-n secret sharing scheme with share alphabet Σ, message alphabet Σ, message length m. Let $(Share_C, Rec_C)$ be an (n_C, k_C) secret sharing scheme from Lemma 3.13 of [10] with alphabet Σ, message length m_C, where $m_C = \delta_0 n_C$, $k_C = \delta_1 n_C$, $n_C = O(\log n)$ for some constants δ_0 and δ_1. For any constant $a \geq 1$, $\gamma \in (0, 1]$, [10] constructs a $(n_1 = O(n^a), k_1 = \Omega(n_1))$ secret sharing scheme $(Share_1, Rec_1)$ with share alphabet $\Sigma \times [n_1]$, message alphabet Σ, message length $m_1 = \Omega(n_1)$.

---

1. The share generation algorithm is a function $Share_1 : \Sigma^{m_1} \to (\Sigma \times [n_1])^{n_1}$.
2. Let $\bar{n} = \Theta(n^{a-1})$ with large enough constant factor.
3. (*Independent generator step*) Let $g_\tau : \Sigma_0^{m\bar{n}} \to \Sigma^{m_1}$ be l-*wise independent generator* where $l = \Omega(\frac{m\bar{n} \log |\Sigma_0|}{\log |\Sigma|})^{1-\gamma}$.
4. For a secret $x \in \Sigma^{m_1}$, draw a string $r = (r_1, \ldots, r_{\bar{n}})$ *uniformly* from $\Sigma_0^{m\bar{n}}$.
5. Write $y = (y_s, y_g)$, where $y_s = (Share(r_1), \ldots, Share(r_n)) \in (\Sigma^n)^{\bar{n}}$ and $y_g = g_\tau(r) \oplus x \in \Sigma^{m_1}$.
6. Get $\hat{y}_s \in (\Sigma^{m_C})^{n_s}$ from y_s by parsing $y_{s,i}$ in blocks each having length m_C for every $i \in [\bar{n}]$, where $n_s = \lceil \frac{n}{m_C} \rceil \bar{n}$.
7. Get $\hat{y}_g \in (\Sigma^{m_C})^{n_g}$ from y_g by parsing y_g to blocks each having length m_C, where $n_g = \lceil \frac{m_1}{m_C} \rceil$.
8. Compute

   $$(Share_C(\hat{y}_{s,1}), ..., Share_C(\hat{y}_{s,n_s}), Share_C(\hat{y}_{g,1}), ..., Share_C(\hat{y}_{g,n_g}))$$

   and parse it as $y1 = (y1_1, \ldots, y1_{n_1})$, *where* $n_1 = (n_s + n_g)n_C$.
9. (*Generate a random permutation*) $\pi : [n_1] \to [n_1]$ and apply it on $y1$ to get the desired output $\pi(y1) = Y$.

Fig. 1. The share generation algorithm of Cheng et al. [10]

Dynamic Construction. When a new party arrives, we take the following steps

(1) Add it in any of the larger blocks. Adding a new party in the larger block keeps the size of the block $O(\log^2 n)$.
(2) Generate share for the new party.
(3) Store the additional information e.g. the generation of the new party and to which block it is added multiples times.
(4) Divide the share into $O(\log n)$ blocks of size $O(\log n)$ each and proceed by applying the random permutation as before.

The share generation and reconstruction algorithms for the basic dynamic scheme accommodating just one new party are described in Fig. 2 and Fig. 3 respectively. Notice that we assume "centralized passive adversary model" where the parties under adversarial control follow the protocol but are interested in gaining information that they are not supposed to.

- **Share generation of an arriving party**

1. Before the arrival of a new party, the old parties hold shares as generated in Fig. 1.
2. Generate a share $S(T)$ for the new participant T by the following algorithm
   - Select two random parties from the old set of parties, say A, B
   - *Parse* shares of A and B as (A_1, A_2) and (B_1, B_2) respectively.
   - *New share* of A is (B_1, A_2) and the old share is deleted.
   - Share of B remains (B_1, B_2).
   - *Share of* the new party T is (A_1, B_1).
3. This changes the shares string Y to Y_{temp} (due to the change to share of party A.)
4. Concatenate $S(T)$ to Y_{temp} to get Y'_{temp}
5. Store the relevant information multiple times.
6. Apply a random permutation σ_T on the elements of the string Y'_{temp} to get the output $Y_T (= \sigma_T(Y'_{temp}))$.

Fig. 2. Share generation algorithm for the basic dynamic scheme in the passive adversary model.

Discussions on the Correctness and Security. We sketch an overview of the correctness and security properties here. Full details can be found in the Appendix. From the above algorithms it is easy to see the correctness – that is, $n_1 + 1$ shares together can reconstruct the secret. However, if n_1 out of the $n_1 + 1$ parties are chosen, they do not have complete information about the secret since

---

● **Reconstruction algorithm**

1. *Compute the inverse permutation $\sigma_T^{-1}(Y)$ to get Y'_{temp}.*
2. *Remove $S(T)$ from Y'_{temp} to get Y_{temp}.*
3. *Using $S(T)$, restore the original shares of the corresponding old parties and recover the string Y.*
4. *Compute the inverse permutation $\pi^{-1}(Y)$ to get $y1$.*
5. *Compute Rec_C on all the elements of $y1$ to get y_s and y_g.*
6. *Apply Rec on every entry of y_s to get r.*
7. *Output $g_\tau(r) \oplus y_g$.*

Fig. 3. Reconstruction algorithm for the basic dynamic scheme.

the share of a party A has been changed. The dealer, at the beginning, can give an ordering to the parties and include the information multiple times $O(\log^2 n))$ in the shares. When a new party arrives the old shares are modified according to the order of the old parties. In the absence of dealer the parties modify their shares according to the order themselves. As a trade off we assume that a little storage is available to keep the information of the order of the shares. Combined with [10], all the remaining operations are AC^0 implementable and the scheme is robust. Hence we have constructed a robust dynamic AC^0 implementable secret sharing scheme. In this construction the share size is exponential. This robustness of this scheme follows from the usage of error-correcting codes. The size of the outer and the inner levels are $O(\log^2 n)$ and $O(\log n)$ respectively. To be AC^0 implementable, size of the outer block must be $O(\log^2 n)$. Hence our scheme can accommodate upto $O(\log^2 n)$ new parties for each block.

We have the following theorem. A discussion on proof can be found in the Appendix.

Theorem 1. *For any $n, m \in \mathbb{N}$, $m \leq n$, any $\epsilon, \eta \in [0; 1]$ and any constant $a \geq 1, \alpha \in (0; 1]$, if there exists an explicit $(n' = O(n^a \log n); (1 - \alpha)n' = k')$ secret sharing scheme in AC^0 with share alphabet $\Sigma \times [n']$, message alphabet Σ_0, message length $\Omega(mn^{a-1})$, adaptive privacy error $O(n^{a-1})(\epsilon + 2^{-\Omega(k)})$ and reconstruction error $O(n^{a-1}\eta)$, then, assuming a predefined order on the participants and a small storage to keep the information of the order of the participants, there exists an explicit $(n' + O(\log^3 n); (1 - \alpha)n')$ dynamic secret sharing scheme with adaptive privacy error $O(n^{a-1})(\epsilon + 2^{-\Omega(k)})$ and reconstruction error $O(n^{a-1}\eta)$. The share and message alphabet and the message length of the new participants remain the same.*

Accommodating More Parties. To accommodate more parties we may divide them into more equal sized blocks. $A = \{A_1, A_2, A_3, \ldots, A_f\}$ and $B = \{B_1, B_2, B_3, \ldots, B_f\}$. We can modify the shares of A as $\{B_1, A_2, A_3, B_4, \ldots\}$ and give the share of t as $\{A_1, B_2, B_3, \ldots\}$ or $\{A_1, B_2, A_3, \ldots\}$ and so on. Ours is a code based secret sharing scheme, so the number of blocks must be more than the distance of the code.

3.2   Evolving Secret Sharing in AC^0

We now give a construction which shows that an AC^0 secret sharing is possible for an evolving access structure where any two participants are qualified to reconstruct the secret whereas any one participant is unable to get any information about the secret bit. This result shows the possibility to include an unbounded number of participants in a secret sharing scheme where both the share generation algorithm and reconstruction algorithm are in AC^0.

Suppose the secret bit is $s \in \{0,1\}$. Let $(\texttt{Share}_+, \texttt{Rec}_+)$ be a 2-out-of-2 threshold secret sharing scheme which can be obtained using the techniques of [8]. Applying this $(\texttt{Share}_+, \texttt{Rec}_+)$ algorithm multiple times, we show how the dealer prepares the shares for the participants.

- **Share Generation**

  1. The dealer first applies $\texttt{Share}_+$ algorithm on s and outputs (s_1^1, s_1^2).
     - Participant 1 receives s_1^1 as its share.
  2. When participant 2 arrives, the dealer obtains $(s_2^2, s_2^3) \longleftarrow \texttt{Share}_+(\texttt{s})$ by an independent run.
     - Share of 2 is (s_1^2, s_2^2) and dealer stores s_2^3.
  3. In general, for $t \geq 3$, share of the t-th participant consists of
     - the first $t - 2$ entries of the share of $(t-1)^{th}$ participant
     - s_{t-1}^t [which is obtained as the second entry of the output of $\texttt{Share}_+(\texttt{s})$ (independently) run for the $(t-1)^{th}$ time to generate shares of participant $t - 1$]
     - the random string s_t^t which is the first entry of $(s_t^t, s_t^{t+1}) \longleftarrow \texttt{Share}_+(\texttt{s})$ run for the t-th time.

Fig. 4.   Share generation algorithm for $(2, \infty)$-evolving access structure.

Figure 5 gives a pictorial depiction of share generation process for $(2, \infty)$ access structure. Vertically shaded regions show the outputs of the basic (2-out-of-2) $\texttt{Share}_+$ algorithm run independently every time with the fixed secret bit s as input.

- The reconstruction algorithm is simple. When two participants come together they produce only the corresponding shares that connects them. Details are given in the following theorem.

Theorem 2. *There exists a $(2, \infty)$-secret sharing scheme implementable in AC^0 for which the share size of the t-th participant is linear in t.*

Proof. It is easy to see the share size of the tth participant is linear in t. The proposed scheme runs the basic (2-out-of-2) AC^0 secret sharing scheme (independently) multiple times. So both the sharing and reconstruction phases can be implemented by AC^0 circuits.

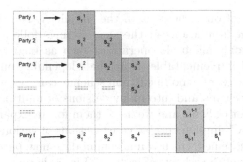

Fig. 5. Step-construction of $(2, \infty)$ secret sharing scheme in AC^0.

To prove that any two participants can recover the secret let us suppose that participants i and j collaborate with each other. Without loss of generality, let $i > j$. We observe that participant j has s_j^j and it can collaborate with participant $j+1$ (who has s_j^{j+1}) to recover the secret. Recall that, $(s_j^j, s_j^{j+1}) \longleftarrow$ Share$_+$(s) when run for the j-th time. Since share of participant i includes s_j^{j+1}, we have the proof.

The share generation algorithm ensures the secrecy of the scheme.

Remark 1. We observe that to improve the information rate of the scheme if we start with l bit secrets and assume the existence of a basic 2-out-of-2 AC^0 secret sharing scheme (for l bit secret) with negligible privacy error as in [10]. It is not very hard to see that the above construction gives a secret sharing scheme with the same privacy error as the basic one.

Example 1. (Yet another example)
Let us consider a star-graph based access structure where the internal vertex is fixed but the number of leaves changes/increases over time. A minimal qualified set is defined by two vertices which has an edge between them. More precisely, {fixed internal node, any leaf} constitutes a minimal qualified set. Let (Share$_+$, Rec$_+$) be a 2-out-of-2 AC^0 implementable threshold secret sharing scheme. The dealer runs Share$_+$(s) (one time) to output (s_1, s_2). Dealer assigns s_1 to the internal node and stores s_2. Whenever, a new leaf is added, the dealer assigns s_2 to the leaf.

Discussion. At this point, it is not clear to the authors whether it is possible to construct other evolving threshold secret sharing schemes implementable in AC^0. Any possibility (or, impossibility) results is worth pursuing in future.

4   Comparison with Existing Schemes

Upon drawing comparisons with existing schemes in the literature, we observe the following: none of the existing dynamic schemes are AC^0 implementable.

Another advantage of our scheme is in the simplicity. New shares can be generated by simple manipulations of the share strings followed by random permutations. This avoids algebraic operations such as Lagrange's interpolations which are not AC^0 implementable. Note that depending on the choice of participants whose shares are modified, our scheme can be modified to make it into a hierarchical scheme and into many versions of multipartite schemes. The constructions are not difficult and we leave them for an expanded future version where we present AC^0 implementable constructions of various cases of multipartite secret sharing schemes which can accommodate new participants over time. The main drawback of the scheme (Fig. 2 and Fig. 3) is that it can accommodate only a bounded number of new participants. We have attempted to overcome this drawback to construct an AC^0 implementable $(2, \infty)$ scheme. Ours is the first construction of an evolving secret sharing scheme which can accommodate potentially infinitely many participants over time. But our method cannot be generalized to construct AC^0 implementable scheme for general (k, ∞)-scheme for higher values k as there are more combinations of participants. Hence we leave that as an open problem.

5   Conclusion

In this work we proposed two AC^0 implementable secret sharing schemes which can accommodate new parties into the system. First construction is a dynamic scheme where the dealer shares the secret and goes offline after distributing the shares to the parties. Later the parties present in the system redistributes their shares to generate shares of new parties without reconstructing the secret. Second construction is an evolving scheme where the dealer is present throughout and generates shares for the incoming parties with the constraint that the old shares cannot be modified.

This work opens up numerous possibilities of implementing AC^0 secret sharing schemes e.g. for hierarchical access structures, evolving ramp schemes to name a few important ones. However we leave those for an expanded future work.

There can be scenarios where during the process the secret gets perturbed within a certain Hamming distance. A relevant question is can a scheme be constructed which can handle such a situation without making too many modifications to the shares and without leaking the secret. Another question is related to reproduction number. It is the average number of parties to which a share gets distributed from a single party. We know that when the reproduction number is less than 1, the system eventually ends. Can the share size be reduced in such scenarios is a problem for an expanded work.

Appendix A : Security Proof Outlines of Theorem 1

Theorem 3. *$Share_1$ and Rec_1 can be computed by AC^0 circuits.*

Proof. We know that construction 1 can be done in AC^0. The extra functions that we are computing during adding a new participant are :

1. Generating the share $S(T)$ of the new participant. This can be done in AC^0 since copying and concatenating string are AC^0-implementable operations.
2. Concatenating the share $S(T)$ to $y1$. This operation can be done in AC^0.
3. Applying a random permutation which is in AC^0.

For the reconstruction procedure, in our construction, the functions which we are computing other than those of [10] are

1. Inverse permutation σ_T^{-1}.
2. Restoring the original shares of the old participants.
3. Deleting the shares of some of the old participants.

Now the inverse permutation can be computed in AC^0. Restoring the share involves dividing a share into two halves and concatenating to the half of another share. Clearly this whole operation can be done in AC^0. The remaining deletion operation can be done in AC^0 too. Hence the $Share_1$ and Rec_1 functions can be computed in AC^0.

Theorem 4. *Let the error during reconstruction of (Share; Rec) be η, then the error during reconstruction of $(Share_1, Rec_1)$ is $n' = \bar{n}\eta$.*

Proof. The reconstruction is done in two phases. First the shares of the new participants are used to restore the shares of the old participants. Next the old participants are used to reconstruct the secret. Although we need all the participants to reconstruct the secret, in the second phase it is the old participants who actually recover the secret. Hence our reconstruction error is essentially same as that of [10]. The proof is a simple application of the union bound in probability.

Note: We stipulated that the adversary does not have any information regarding the order of the participants. So, from the adversary's point the old participants whose shares are modified when a new participant arrives is completely random and the share of the new participant is independent of the previous shares. Hence concatenating the share of the new participant does not affect the privacy of our scheme. Coupling this with the random permutation effectively results only in an increase in the length of the string. Hence our construction does not affect the privacy of the original scheme of Fig. 1.

The overall effect is that the adversary only sees an increase in the number of repeated alphabets. Since the adversary sees only a constant fraction of shares, due to the repetitions and random permutations, it cannot infer any information about the secret. The details are given next.

In order to show privacy, the following Chernoff Bound is needed.

Negative Correlation. Binary random variables $X_1, X_2, \ldots, X_n$ are said to be negatively correlated if for any subset I of $[n]$,

$$Pr[\wedge_{i \in I}(X_i = 1)] \leq \prod_{i \in I} Pr[X_i = 1]$$

and

$$Pr[\wedge_{i \in I}(X_i = 0)] \leq \prod_{i \in I} Pr[X_i = 0]$$

.

Theorem 5 *(Negative Correlation Chernoff Bound). Let $X_1, X_2, \ldots, X_n$ be random variables which are negatively correlated with $X = \sum_{i=1}^{n} X_i$, $\mu = \mathbb{E}(X)$. Then*

1. *for any $\delta \in (0,1)$, $Pr[X \leq (1-\delta)\mu] \leq e^{-\delta^2\mu/2}$ and $Pr[X \geq (1+\delta)\mu] \leq e^{-\delta^2\mu/3}$.*
2. *for any $d \geq 6\mu$, $Pr[X \geq d] \leq 2^{-d}$.*

Here we mention two lemmas regarding random permutations using which we can show the privacy of our scheme. For exact statements and proofs of these lemmas we refer the reader to Lemmas 3.7 and 3.8 of [10].

Lemma 1 [10]. *Given π a random permutation of $[n]$. For any pair of sets $S, W \subseteq [n]$, let $u = \frac{|W|}{n}|S|$. The following items hold.*

1. *for any $\delta \in (0,1)$, $Pr[|\pi(S) \cap W| \leq (1-\delta)\mu] \leq e^{-\delta^2\mu/2}$ and $Pr[|\pi(S) \cap W| \geq (1+\delta)\mu] \leq e^{-\delta^2\mu/3}$.*
2. *for any $d \geq 6\mu$, $Pr[|\pi(S) \cap W| \geq d] \leq 2^{-d}$.*

Lemma 2 [10]. *Let π be a random permutation of $[n]$. Let $W \subseteq [n]$ with $|W| = \gamma n$. Let δ be constant $\delta \in (0,1)$. Let $t, l \in \mathbb{N}^+$ such that $tl \leq \frac{0.96}{1+0.96}\gamma n$. Let S be a collection of subsets $\{S_1, \ldots, S_l\}$ such that for each $i \in [l]$, the sets $S_i \subseteq [n]$ are disjoint and $|S_i| = t$. Finally, let X_i be the indicator random variable such that $X_i = 1$ is the event $|\pi(S_i) \cap Wj| \geq (1+\delta)\gamma t$. Taking $X = \sum_{i \in [l]} X_i$, we have for any $d \geq 0$, $Pr[X \geq d] \leq e^{-2d+(e^2-1)e^{-\omega(\gamma t)l}}$.*

Using the above lemmas one can show privacy of the secret sharing scheme as follows.

Lemma 3 [10]. *Let Σ be a set of alphabets and let $n, k \in \mathbb{N}$ with $k \leq n$. Given a distribution $X = (X_1, \ldots, X_n)$ over Σ^n, let Y be the distribution obtained by the action of π^{-1} on X where $\pi : [n] \to [n]$ is a random permutation. If an adaptive adversary observes a set of coordinates W with $|W| = k$ then Y_W is the same distribution $Y_{[k]}$.*

Note: This lemma essentially says that due to the random permutation the adversary observing a constant fraction of the secret cannot learn anything about the secret.

Utilizing the above-mentioned lemmas we have the following theorem estimating the parameters in our case.

Theorem 6. *Let $n, m \in \mathbb{N}$, with $m \leq n$, $\epsilon, \eta \in [0; 1]$ and constant $a \geq 1, \alpha \in (0; 1]$. Suppose we have an explicit $(n' = O(n^a logn); (1 - \alpha)n')$ secret sharing scheme computable in AC^0 with share alphabet $\Sigma \times [n']$, message alphabet Σ_0, message length $\Omega(mn^{a-1})$, adaptive privacy error $O(n^{a-1})(\epsilon + 2^{-\Omega(k)}))$ and reconstruction error $O(n^{a-1}\eta)$, then, assuming a predefined order on the participants and a small storage to keep the information of the order of the participants, an explicit $(n' + O(log^3 n); (1 - \alpha)n')$ dynamic secret sharing scheme with privacy error $O(n^{a-1})(\epsilon + 2^{-\Omega(k)}))$ (adaptive) and error of reconstruction $O(n^{a-1}\eta)$ can be constructed.*

References

1. Akavia, A., Bogdanov, A., Guo, S., Kamath, A., Rosen, A.: Candidate weak pseudorandom functions in ac0 mod2. In: Proceedings of the 5th Conference on Innovations in Theoretical Computer Science. pp. 251–260 (2014)
2. Applebaum, B., Ishai, Y., Kushilevitz, E.: Cryptography in nc^0. SIAM J. Comput. **36**(4), 845–888 (2006). https://doi.org/10.1137/S0097539705446950
3. Applebaum, B., Ishai, Y., Kushilevitz, E.: Cryptography with constant input locality. J. Cryptology **22**(4), 429–469 (2009). https://doi.org/10.1007/s00145-009-9039-0
4. Ball, M., Rosen, A., Sabin, M., Vasudevan, P.N.: Average-case fine-grained hardness. Electronic Colloquium on Computational Complexity (ECCC) 24, 39 (2017), https://eccc.weizmann.ac.il/report/2017/039
5. Beimel, A.: Secret-sharing schemes: A survey. In: Coding and Cryptology - Third International Workshop, IWCC 2011, Qingdao, China, May 30-June 3, 2011. pp. 11–46 (2011). https://doi.org/10.1007/978-3-642-20901-7_2
6. Beimel, A., Othman, H.: Evolving ramp secret-sharing schemes. In: Catalano, D., De Prisco, R. (eds.) SCN 2018. LNCS, vol. 11035, pp. 313–332. Springer, Cham (2018). https://doi.org/10.1007/978-3-319-98113-0_17
7. Blakley, G.R.: Safeguarding cryptographic keys. In: IEEE Computer Society Managing Requirements Knowledge, International Workshop on. p. 313. Los Alamitos, CA, USA (1979). https://doi.org/10.1109/AFIPS.1979.98
8. Bogdanov, A., Ishai, Y., Viola, E., Williamson, C.: Bounded indistinguishability and the complexity of recovering secrets. In: Robshaw, M., Katz, J. (eds.) CRYPTO 2016. LNCS, vol. 9816, pp. 593–618. Springer, Heidelberg (2016). https://doi.org/10.1007/978-3-662-53015-3_21
9. Chen, L., Gollmann, D., Mitchell, C.J.: Key escrow in mutually mistrusting domains. In: Lomas, M. (ed.) Security Protocols 1996. LNCS, vol. 1189, pp. 139–153. Springer, Heidelberg (1997). https://doi.org/10.1007/3-540-62494-5_14
10. Cheng, K., Ishai, Y., Li, X.: Near-optimal secret sharing and error correcting codes in ac0. In: Kalai, Y., Reyzin, L. (eds.) Theory of Cryptography, pp. 424–458. Springer International Publishing, Cham (2017)
11. Cheraghchi, M.: Nearly optimal robust secret sharing. Designs, Codes and Cryptography **87**(8), 1777–1796 (Aug 2019). https://doi.org/10.1007/s10623-018-0578-y
12. Desmedt, Y., Jajodia, S.: Redistributing secret shares to new access structures and its applications. In: George Mason University, Technical Report ISSE-TR-97-01, July (1997)

13. Desmedt, Y., Morozov, K.: Parity check based redistribution of secret shares. In: 2015 IEEE International Symposium on Information Theory (ISIT). pp. 959–963 (2015). https://doi.org/10.1109/ISIT.2015.7282597
14. Frankel, Y., Gemmell, P., MacKenzie, P.D., Moti Yung: Optimal-resilience proactive public-key cryptosystems. In: Proceedings 38th Annual Symposium on Foundations of Computer Science. pp. 384–393 (1997). https://doi.org/10.1109/SFCS.1997.646127
15. Guruswami, V., Smith, A.D.: Optimal rate code constructions for computationally simple channels. J. ACM **63**(4), 35:1–35:37 (2016). https://doi.org/10.1145/2936015
16. Ito, M., Saito, A., Nishizeki, T.: Multiple assignment scheme for sharing secret. J. Cryptology **6**(1), 15–20 (1993). https://doi.org/10.1007/BF02620229
17. Komargodski, I., Naor, M., Yogev, E.: How to share a secret, infinitely. In: Hirt, M., Smith, A. (eds.) TCC 2016. LNCS, vol. 9986, pp. 485–514. Springer, Heidelberg (2016). https://doi.org/10.1007/978-3-662-53644-5_19
18. Komargodski, I., Paskin-Cherniavsky, A.: Evolving secret sharing: dynamic thresholds and robustness. In: Kalai, Y., Reyzin, L. (eds.) TCC 2017. LNCS, vol. 10678, pp. 379–393. Springer, Cham (2017). https://doi.org/10.1007/978-3-319-70503-3_12
19. Minsky, M., Papert, S.: Perceptrons. MIT Press (1969)
20. Naor, M., Shamir, A.: Visual cryptography. In: De Santis, A. (ed.) EUROCRYPT 1994. LNCS, vol. 950, pp. 1–12. Springer, Heidelberg (1995). https://doi.org/10.1007/BFb0053419
21. Nojoumian, M., Stinson, D.R.: On dealer-free dynamic threshold schemes. Adv. in Math. of Comm. **7**(1), 39–56 (2013). https://doi.org/10.3934/amc.2013.7.39
22. Shamir, A.: How to share a secret. Commun. ACM **22**(11), 612–613 (1979). https://doi.org/10.1145/359168.359176
23. Stinson, D.R., Wei, R.: Unconditionally secure proactive secret sharing scheme with combinatorial structures. In: Heys, H., Adams, C. (eds.) SAC 1999. LNCS, vol. 1758, pp. 200–214. Springer, Heidelberg (2000). https://doi.org/10.1007/3-540-46513-8_15

Short Papers

Multiply, Divide, and Conquer – Making Fully Decentralised Access Control a Reality

Bernd Prünster[1,2](✉) , Dominik Ziegler[3] , and Gerald Palfinger[1,2]

[1] A-SIT Secure Information Technology Center Austria, Graz, Austria
{bernd.pruenster,gerald.palfinger}@a-sit.at
[2] Institute of Applied Information Processing and Communications (IAIK),
Graz University of Technology, Graz, Austria
[3] Know-Center GmbH, Graz, Austria
dominik.ziegler@tugraz.at
https://www.a-sit.at, https://www.iaik.tugraz.at

Abstract. This paper tackles the issue of access control in fully decentralised systems. Previously, access control always fell back to some degree of centralisation. Our work approaches this problem by outsourcing access policy evaluation to the millions of trusted computing bases already deployed in the form of current Android devices. This assures correct policy evaluation to both data owners and those seeking data access. In essence, our solution encrypts to-be-shared data, splits and wraps the encryption key, and cryptographically binds it to an access policy. Policies are evaluated by freely selectable evaluators, that do not need to be enrolled beforehand. Evaluators then interface with attribute providers during policy evaluation. Each evaluator independently reaches a conclusion about whether or not to grant access, leading to a decision by majority vote. We designed this system with practicality and real-world applicability in mind, meaning that it can be deployed and used today. We achieve this by relying on efficient primitives and foregoing expensive cryptographic constructions, making it possible to define even highly complex access policies. Overall, this presents a clear advantage over previous concepts.

Keywords: Decentralised access control · Trusted computing · Peer-to-peer

1 Introduction

In the past years, decentralisation has been gaining momentum, with cryptocurrencies pushing decentralised payment systems, and projects like *IPFS*[1] advocating decentralised applications. When hosting some service with or without the help of such frameworks, enforcing access policies is trivial, as every access is handled by the entity providing the service. New, previously hardly addressed issues arise, however, when the entity owning some to-be-protected data might not be

---

[1] https://ipfs.io/.

© Springer Nature Switzerland AG 2020
M. Kutyłowski et al. (Eds.): NSS 2020, LNCS 12570, pp. 311–326, 2020.
https://doi.org/10.1007/978-3-030-65745-1_18

available when this data is to be accessed. Most importantly, when advocating the advantages of decentralised systems, falling back to centralised approaches diminishes some (if not all) of the inherent advantages of this paradigm. We therefore firmly believe that fine-grained access control needs to be made available in a decentralised manner.

We strive for attribute-based access control (ABAC) in this context because this flexible approach can emulate all other access control schemes. Recent advancements in implementing and deploying trusted computing at large have put the realisation of fully decentralised ABAC into reach. The key distinction of our approach compared to previously theorised concepts is its feasibility under real-world conditions.

Contribution: We propose *Multiply, Divide, and Conquer* to enable data owners to outsource data protected by access policies without the need to be involved in the data access and policy evaluation process. Since an open, fully decentralised context without any form of common governance implies mutually distrusting parties, we explicitly target this setting. We cater to this scenario by delegating policy evaluation to trusted computing devices. Our design targets practical applicability in the real world and does not represent a purely academic scheme. To accomplish this, we propose to utilise recent Android devices, equipped with trusted hardware modules, capable of extensive remote attestation capabilities for the policy evaluation process. As we will argue, it is feasible to delegate policy enforcement to current Android devices outside a data owner's control and guarantee correct policy enforcement both to the data owner as well as to the party seeking to access the policy-protected data. As we aim for practicality, our scheme is designed to remain efficient even when using complex policies. We have implemented a prototype and evaluated its performance to show that this goal was reached in practice.

Our design combines established ABAC frameworks with the trusted computing capabilities of modern Android devices and linear secret sharing. The decentralisation aspect is upheld by letting data owners freely select instances for policy evaluation as well as arbitrary attribute providers. In addition, relying on trusted computing for policy evaluation assures all parties that policies are evaluated correctly and honestly.

To securely share some data, the data owner defines an access policy and attribute providers. Data is encrypted, the encryption key is split, and each share is encrypted for a single policy evaluator selected by the data owner. Data, policy, and encrypted key shares can then be published. Upon data access, policy evaluators interface with attribute providers for policy evaluation. Each evaluator decides individually whether or not to grant access by divulging its respective key share to the accessing entity. In essence, if evaluators agree [2] to grant access, the data encryption key can be recovered and data access is thereby granted.

---

[2] No coordination between evaluators is needed.

2 Background

Multiply, Divide, and Conquer implements fully decentralised ABAC based on trusted computing and secret sharing. This section therefore provides the necessary background on these topics, with a focus on trusted computing on mobile devices.

2.1 Secret Sharing

The idea behind generic (k, n) threshold secret sharing is to split up a secret D among n parties, such that D can be efficiently reconstructed from k shares, while "knowledge of any $k - 1$ or fewer D_i pieces leaves D completely undetermined" [14]. More precisely, we rely on Shamir's secret sharing, since it (1) scales well (with the total size of all shares being $k \cdot \texttt{sizeof}(D)$), (2) can be implemented efficiently, and (3) reconstruction does not involve the dealer (who created the shares). As we will argue in Sect. 4, our design requires no verifiability with respect to the secret sharing scheme.

2.2 Attribute-Based Access Control

Attribute-based access control (ABAC) [4] provides authorisation mechanisms at a granular level. It achieves access authorisation by evaluating user-, global environment-, resource- as well as action-attributes to reach a decision. A widely used industrial standard is the eXtensible Access Control Markup Language (XACML; [8]), which is one of the most frequently referenced works of generic ABAC models. It does not, however, provide a standardised way to ensure data confidentiality. Attribute-based encryption (ABE), on the other hand, cryptographically enforces access control. Some ABE concepts offer properties similar to our proposal as outlined in Sect. 6.

2.3 Mobile Trusted Computing

Fides [10] is a scheme to verify the integrity of a remote application using the attestation capabilities of Android. It requires an Android device with trusted cryptographic hardware and remote attestation capabilities as supported by devices launched with Android 8.0 or later. The application attempting to prove its integrity first requests the creation of a public/private keypair from the hardware-based keystore and an attestation certificate. This certificate contains hardware-enforced information about the verified boot state and the lock state of the bootloader, certifying OS integrity and verified boot state. In addition, the hardware-enforced values include the OS version and its patch level, which makes it possible to lock out vulnerable smartphones. Furthermore, the attestation certificate contains information about the application requesting the attestation. By validating the signature certificate of the application, Fides can thus verify that the examined application has not been tampered with.

Prünster et al. [9] show that it is possible to utilise the aforementioned concept in a fully decentralised peer-to-peer (P2P) context to thwart Sybil attacks. The approach takes advantage of the fact that Android's remote attestation can be verified completely offline, by checking against Googles hardware attestation root certificate[3]. Although access to device identifiers as proposed by Prünster et al. [9] has been restricted in recent Android versions[4], it is still possible to impose a limit of running only a single instance of an application per device: App developers can enforce that only the so-called *system user* is able to use their app[5].

3   Multiply, Divide, and Conquer

Multiply, Divide, and Conquer requires no set of predefined entities for evaluating and enforcing access policies and no trusted setup phase. Instead, policy evaluation and enforcement needs to be delegated to trusted devices.

We define a current Android smartphone as described in Sect. 2.3 as *sufficiently trusted*: It is possible to remotely verify a device's integrity using key attestation, when not considering root exploits. Actually compromising an Android device using an exploit takes considerable effort even for device owners. For example, basic local privilege escalation exploits are priced at USD $> 100.000^6$ as of June 2020. To further raise the bar for attackers, we also introduce basic multi-party computation (MPC) to the policy evaluation process by letting multiple devices evaluate the same policy. The overall evaluation result is then reached by majority vote.

3.1   Architecture

Multiply, Divide, and Conquer is underpinned by a decentralised P2P network where every participant is equal. It employs attestation-based identifiers as discussed in Sect. 2.3. Our system defines the following actors to enable data sharing with outsourced policy enforcement:

Data Owner. The *data owner* seeks to publish data and protects it using an access policy. Every data owner is identified using a public-private key pair.
Attribute Provider. *Attribute providers* are used to attest that a user holds some set of attributes. We assume honest but curious attribute providers. Attribute providers are identified by a certificate.
Storage Provider. Any *storage provider* of choice may be used to host data. The only requirement towards the storage provider is availability.

---

[3] https://developer.android.com/training/articles/security-key-attestation#root_certificate.
[4] https://developer.android.com/about/versions/10/privacy/.
[5] https://developer.android.com/reference/android/os/UserManager#isSystemUser().
[6] https://zerodium.com/program.html.

Evaluator. Policy *evaluators* are responsible for evaluating and enforcing access policies. Data owners choose a subset of all *reasonably trusted* devices known at policy creation time. This set is composed of Android smartphones whose integrity can be remotely verified using key attestation (see Sect. 2.3). Consequently, each evaluator's identity is derived from a certificate chain whose leaf is an attestation certificate bound to a public-private key pair and a hardware identifier (see [9]).

Accessor. The set of *accessors* encompasses everyone who wants to access data published within Multiply, Divide, and Conquer. Each accessor is identified by a public-private key pair.

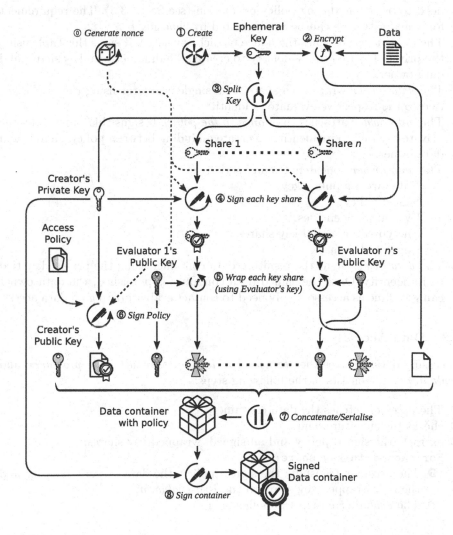

Fig. 1. Encryption process – all components are cryptographically linked.

3.2   Data Publishing

This section presents the general idea behind data encryption, with a detailed process description provided below in accordance with Fig. 1. This process focuses on the cryptographic operations and therefore assumes some data to be protected by an already defined policy at hand:

- ⓪ The *data owner* creates a nonce.
- ① The *data owner* creates an ephemeral bulk encryption key and
- ② encrypts some data using this key.
- ③ The *data owner* splits the key using a (k, n) threshold secret sharing scheme into n shares. Depending on the choice of k and n, more or less *evaluators* need to be online during policy evaluation (see Sect. 3.3). The requirement for a majority vote can be implemented by choosing $k > n/2$.
- ④ The *data owner* attaches the nonce to each key share. It signs this tuple using the private key tied to its identity to create a binding between key shares and data owner.
- ⑤ The *data owner* wraps each share for a single evaluator using the public key tied to the respective evaluator's identity.
- ⑥ The *data owner* attaches the *nonce to the policy*. It signs this tuple using the private key tied to its identity to create a binding between policy, shares, and data owner.
- ⑦ The *data owner* concatenates and serialises:
  - Data owner's public key
  - Signed policy
  - Evaluator's identities
  - Encrypted, wrapped key shares
  - Encrypted data
- ⑧ The *data owner* signs the resulting data container using the private key tied to its identity. Once the signed data container is published, the data owner can go offline as accessors only need to contact evaluators to gain data access.

3.3   Data Access

Accessing data involves the *storage provider*, *accessor*, *attribute providers*, and *evaluators* and consists of the following steps:

- ① The *accessor* fetches the data container,
- ② checks the signature, and
- ③ extracts the signed policy and all signed, wrapped key shares.
  For each i-th key share:
  - ❶ The *accessor* transmits the signed policy, the data owner's identity and the i-th wrapped key share to the i-th *evaluator*.
  - ❷ The *evaluator* checks the policy signature,

❸ evaluates the policy, and requests any information (such as user attributes) from the *accessor* that may be required to reach a verdict about whether access should be granted. This step usually involves one or more *attribute providers*, which is omitted from the process description for the sake of clarity.

❹ In case access should be granted, the *i*-th *evaluator* unwraps the *i*-th key share and checks its signature.

❺ The *evaluator* checks whether the received share and the policy belong to each other by comparing the nonce values and whether both items were signed by the same data owner.

❻ If so, the *evaluator* signs the unwrapped share, and

❼ transmits it to the *accessor*.

❽ The *accessor* checks both unwrapped key's signatures (the original one created by the *data owner*, and the one created by the *i*-th *evaluator*).

④ The *accessor* recovers the bulk encryption key from all received shares, and

⑤ finally decrypts the data.

As can be observed, no actor needs to perform computationally expensive operations. Policy evaluation itself is implemented using XACML, which has been shown to perform well, even on lower-end hardware [15]. A thorough performance analysis is provided in Sect. 5, which supports the claims of efficiency and real-world applicability.

4   Security Characteristics

This section argues how Multiply, Divide, and Conquer achieves fully decentralised, practically secure, and correct access control based on the data access process described in Sect. 3.3. Consequently, the security properties of each step are discussed below. Afterwards, general security properties, benefits over the current state-of-the-art, and a sketch of an adversary model are provided.

According to Sect. 3.3, the *accessor* ① initially fetches an encrypted data container and ② checks its signature using the included public key. Since the *data owner* created this container, we can assume that their correct public key was included. As a consequence, the *accessor* can unconditionally verify the data container's integrity without the need for verifiable secret sharing.

After ③ taking apart the data container and ❶ distributing the signed policy (including the nonce), data owner identity, and wrapped, signed key shares to *evaluators*, ❷ each *evaluator* can validate integrity and origin of the policy by means of a simple signature check.

Assuming policy evaluation (❸) results in the *accessor* being granted access—a conclusion each *evaluator* reaches independently of others—each *evaluator* can then ❹ unwrap their key share to recover the nonce and the signed, plain key share.

By ❺ verifying the share's signature against the previously received *data owner* identity, each *evaluator* can validate the received key share's integrity and origin. By also comparing the nonce attached to the signed policy with the nonce attached to the key share, the *evaluator* can verify that the key share actually belongs to the policy and has not been replaced with another policy signed by the same evaluator[7].

After ❻ signing and ❼ transmitting their share to the *accessor*, the evaluator is not involved anymore.

The *accessor* ❽ checks both signatures of the received shares (one initially created by the *data owner*, and one created by the *evaluator*). The original signature serves the purpose of enabling the *accessor* to verify the integrity of the received share. Thus no verifiable secret sharing scheme is required. The second signature serves accountability, in the unlikely event that of an evaluator being compromised using a root exploit and not producing the correct key share. Once all this has been done, the *accessor* can ④ recover the bulk encryption key and ⑤ finally recover the data. Appendix A provides more details on the adversary model and discusses the system's general security properties in detail.

While outsourcing a sensitive task like access control to essentially unknown entities may seem irresponsible, in this case it actually provides advantages even compared to traditional client-sever setups. As subsumed in Sect. 2.3, it is indeed possible to deploy code to current Android devices and remotely verify that it will be executed without modifications and that no sensitive data can be extracted. This effectively reduces the attack surface to highly targeted attacks, which we consider out of scope. In addition, it assures *data owners* and *accessors*, that access policies are indeed correctly evaluated.

5   Implementation and Performance

Multiply, Divide, and Conquer has been implemented in Kotlin, for easy bench-marking on the desktop and on Android. To obtain meaningful results regarding our system's performance, we only evaluated *scheme-specific* operations and do not consider *generic* operations that would be required for any form of confidential data exchange. Bulk encryption, for example, is considered a generic operation and has thus not been benchmarked.

5.1   Implementation Details and General System Characteristics

Multiply, Divide, and Conquer uses SHA3-256 and the Elliptic Curve Digital Signature Algorithm (ECDSA) (curve: *secp256k1*) as signature algorithm. Our system heavily relies on cryptographic signatures, which has two implications: (1) asymmetric operations (and hashing) will account for the bulk of performance overhead and (2) no verifiable secret sharing scheme is required. Instead, an implementation of Shamir's secret sharing[8] is used. Wrapping (encrypting) shares for evaluators relies on the Elliptic Curve Integrated Encryption Scheme (ECIES).

---

[7] Technically, this could also be accomplished by incorporating the random value used for secret sharing into the policy.

[8] https://github.com/codahale/shamir.

Creation and verification of signatures, participating in the secret sharing scheme, and policy evaluation are considered scheme-specific operations. These operations are not independent, however. Most prominently, the chosen number of evaluators directly impacts performance on all levels:

- Complexity of the secret sharing scheme increases.
- As each share needs to be signed, more shares result in more signature and verification operations.
- As each shares need to be wrapped, more shares result in more hybrid encryption operations.
- The number of shares increases the overall container size, which results in more hashing operations being performed as part of container signing/verifying.

The remaining factors impacting overall performance are payload and policy size as this affects the number of hashing operations during creating/verifying the policy's signature. Consequently, this also has a bearing on the number of hashing operations required for creating/verifying the overall container signature. Naturally, policy complexity has a direct impact on policy evaluation performance. We therefore used fixed container and policy sizes, as well as a fixed policy complexity.

5.2   Benchmarks

We have split our benchmarks into three groups to reflect the operations carried out by each actor and organised this section accordingly. To provide a constant container and policy size, we used a fixed 1kB policy and a 10MB payload. Policy evaluation was benchmarked against the IID302 policy from the XACML 3.0 conformance test suite provided by AT&T[9]. This policy was modified to grant access instead of denying it.

Setup: The primary device used for testing was a *bq Aquaris X*. All benchmarks were run single-threaded, as this reflects assigning only limited resources (i.e. a single CPU core) to Multiply, Divide, and Conquer running in the background. The remainder of this sections discusses the obtained results.

Data Publishing (Container Creation): This task is performed by the *data owner* and has been described in Sect. 3.2. The following operations as shown in Fig. 1 have been benchmarked:

- Splitting the bulk encryption key among evaluators (Step ③)
- Signing (Step ④) each key share and wrapping (Step ⑤) each share for it's designated evaluator
- Signing an access policy (Step ⑥) and signing the overall data container (Step ⑧)

---

[9] https://lists.oasis-open.org/archives/xacml-comment/201404/msg00001.html.

The results shown in Fig. 2a confirm the intuitive notion that asymmetric operations are the dominating factor with respect to the overall performance of data container creation. However, at less than 0.1 s for realistic secret sharing parameters, overall performance remains satisfactory.

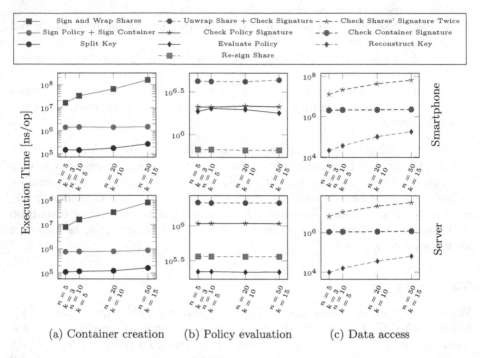

(a) Container creation   (b) Policy evaluation   (c) Data access

Fig. 2. Execution times: Each operation was carried out 100 times (excluding warmup runs). Server hardware: Intel *Xeon E5-2699 v4* @ 2.20 GHz. Smartphone hardware: Qualcomm *Snapdragon™ 626* octa core platform @ 2.20 GHz.

Policy Evaluation: This task has been benchmarked from a single *evaluator*'s point of view, since it scales linearly with the number of evaluators. However, this usually happens in parallel from the *accessor*'s point-of-view, which means the figures plotted below can be factored into the overall performance as-is. The following scheme-specific operations as defined in Sect. 3.3 have been benchmarked:

- Checking a policy's signature (Step ❷)
- Policy evaluation (Step ❸)
- Unwrapping the evaluator's share and verifying its signature (Steps ❹ and ❺)
- Re-signing the decrypted share using the evaluator's key (Step ❻)

Figure 2b clearly shows that the operations carried out by *evaluators* perform well, taking only few milliseconds even on less-than-current smartphone hardware.

Data Access: The following scheme-specific operations as shown in Sect. 3.3 were benchmarked from the *accessor*'s point of view:

- Check container signature (Step ②)
- Checking a share's original signature as well as checking the signature produced by the evaluator (Step ❸). These two operations are carried out k times each (since k out of n shares are required to reconstruct the secret)
- Reconstructing the bulk encryption key from k shares (Step ④)

Figure 2c displaying the *accessor*'s performance clearly correlates with Fig. 2a, since the operations related to secret sharing are again the dominating factor. Given that all scheme-specific operations total to less than half a second even when having to combine 15 shares to recover the key, interacting with *attribute providers* and network latency will have the most impact on the overall round-trip time. In summary, the benchmark figures obtained clearly show that Multiply, Divide, and Conquer performs well and does not strain the targeted smartphone hardware.

6   Related Work

On the surface, Multiply, Divide, and Conquer provides a similar feature set to some ABE schemes. Even though trusted computing has been proposed for access control before, no decentralised approach has so far been brought forward. We therefore refrain from discussing proposals that rely on a central trusted computing instance. Instead, this section focuses on summarising the major contributions in the field of ABE and compares them to our work.

Attribute-based encryption (ABE), in contrast to attribute-based access control (see Sect. 2), ensures fine-grained access control on a cryptographic level. It defines the recipients of a message as a set of attributes. Access rights are determined based on access structures, either embedded in the key (Key-Policy Attribute-Based Encryption (KP-ABE; [3]) or the ciphertext (Ciphertext-Policy Attribute-Based Encryption (CP-ABE; [1])). Users can only decrypt a ciphertext if their attributes match the embedded policy.

Since its introduction, subsequent work has improved ABE in terms of performance or functionality. The area most similar to our work is multi-authority ABE. First described by Chase [2], multi-authority ABE schemes allow for any party in the system to become an attribute authority. It is collusion-resistant, when assuming a trusted authority in place. Whenever new attribute authorities join, the system key needs to be modified and propagated to all users. Our scheme, on the other hand, imposes no limitation whatsoever on attribute providers, both in overall number and dynamics over time.

Another approach to decentralise ABE was proposed by Müller et al. [7]. They present a distributed ABE scheme, where an arbitrary number of parties can maintain attributes and secret keys. The scheme eliminates the need for a central attribute authority, but requires a trusted *master* to distributes secret keys. Policies are restricted to boolean formulas in in disjunctive normal form

(DNF) over attributes and their values. We, however, rely on a combination of secret sharing to distribute keys and trusted computing to enforce policies. Thus, our scheme does not rely on a central authority and can also enforce considerably more expressive policies.

Lewko and Waters [6] proposed a similar system to ours. In their scheme, any party, too, can become an attribute authority. Like our work, the proposed scheme does not require any central authority. However, the system has several limitations which impact usability in resource-constrained environments. First, the system is designed around composite order bilinear groups. As was shown by Kiraz and Uzunkol [5], this decision influences key size and thus performance. To maintain a desired security level, key sizes need to be increased. Secondly, the scheme requires a trusted global setup phase. In contrast, our scheme supports environments with mutually distrusting parties and needs no global setup phase.

Summarising, multi-authority ABE offers a cryptographic solution to provide fine-grained access control in distributed environments. More recent variants of multi-authority ABE improve existing schemes by adding support for, e.g., arbitrary large attribute strings [12], revocation [11], hidden policies [16] or tackling efficiency in resource-constrained environments [13]. What almost all variants of multi-authority ABE schemes have in common, though, is that they rely on expensive bilinear pairing operations or on one or more central entities.

7   Conclusions

This paper presented Multiply, Divide, and Conquer, a system to enforce access control in fully decentralised environments based on secret sharing and the trusted computing capabilities of current Android devices. Compared to previously proposed concepts, it relies on fast primitives and traditional trusted computing concepts, thus allowing for complex access policies, while remaining efficient, compared to attribute-based encryption. At its core, it utilises the fact that it is possible to remotely attest the integrity of current Android devices running in unmanaged environments and deploy software to these devices, such that the software cannot be tampered with in an undetectable manner. At no point does our system require any central instance. As such, our solution can be deployed to fully decentralised P2P networks without falling back to centralisation. Previously, this has not been possible. Most importantly, our system has been designed with practicality in mind, meaning that it is usable in the real world and does not remain a purely academic experiment. Its security parameters can be tweaked to suit different needs, all while keeping real-world applicability in mind.

A   Security Model

This appendix discusses the security properties of Multiply, Divide, and Conquer. First, assets to be protected are identified and characterised based on the system description provided in Sect. 3. Next, security services that need to pe provided are derived. Afterwards we define each actor and an according adversary model. Finally, this is mapped against our design's characteristics to show which properties and strategies ensure that each security service can be provided. We assume that all cryptographic primitives perform as expected and consider implementations flaws and targeted attacks out of scope.

A.1   Assets

The assets identified below are directly derived from Multiply, Divide, and Conquer's goals and the workflows described in Sect. 3.

Payload should only be revealed to those parties, who are rightfully allowed to access it according to the access policy. Every payload is encrypted, signed and cryptographically linked to an associated access policy.

Access policy defines which parties are authorised to access the payload. Access policies are public, must not be manipulated, and are cryptographically signed.

Key shares must only be revealed to authorised parties (according to the access policy) such that those parties are able to decrypt the payload.

Attributes are used to describe any party seeking to access some encrypted payload as inputs for policy evaluation.

A.2   Security Services and Goals

Based on our scheme's goals for fully decentralised access control to securely share data, the following security services need to be provided.

Confidentiality. Assets: *payload, key shares*: A payload shall only be disclosed to accessors who fulfil the access policy associated with a payload. As the payload is encrypted and the encryption key is split, key shares must also be kept confidential and only be revealed to authorised accessors.

Integrity. Assets: *payload, key shares, policy, attributes*: Information must remain intact; modifications must be detected. This excludes manipulated information that remains intelligible (see unforgeability).

Authenticity. Assets: *payload, key shares, policy, attributes*: It must be possible to verify the origin and integrity of any asset, thus authenticating all data.

Accountability. Assets: *payload, key shares, policy, attributes*: Following authenticity, the origin of every asset must be traceable such that the actor can be held accountable. This includes any (legitimate) manipulations of an asset, such as the decryption of key shares by evaluators.

Non-repudiation. Assets: *payload, key shares, policy, attributes*: Following accountability, no actor must be able to unrightfully disclaim authorship (or legitimate manipulation) of any asset.

Unforgeability. Assets: *payload, key shares, policy, attributes*: Forging a policy, payload, or key shares would mean that an attacker could replace assets with a modified, still intelligible version and integrity and signature checks, as well as authenticated encryption schemes would still produce valid outputs.

Availability. Assets: *payload, key shares, policy, attributes*: All information (and the actors required to process it) must be available when needed.

A.3 Actor and Adversary Model

This section briefly formalises Multiply, Divide, and Conquer's actor and adversary model and illustrates how an adversary may try to weaken its security properties by trying to compromise one of is security services. Due to the definition of system actors, attackers inherently assume the role of an adversarial actor. For example, a third party seeking to gain unauthorised access to protected data is considered to be an adversarial accessor.

Data owners seek to publish some data and protect it using an access policy.

Adversarial data owners may produce data that either overburdens *evaluators* with complex policies, or may occupy all other actors with a policy that requires long-running interactions between *accessors*, *attribute providers*, and *evaluators* while consuming *storage providers'* space. In general, limiting policy complexity and introducing timeouts are apt measures to combat adversarial *data owners*. We therefore consider this issue out of scope.

Attribute providers are used to attest that an *accessor* holds some set of attributes—assumed to be chosen such that they behave honestly but curious.

Adversarial attribute providers may, in theory, misbehave by inspecting an access policy to produce attributes accordingly in order to tilt the policy evaluation result towards denial or access. This targets confidentiality or availability. In established schemes like *OpenID Connect*[10], the service provider is free to choose identity providers (IdPs) they trust. Our design takes up on this idea and lets *data owners* freely choose *attribute providers* they trust, without any form of central governance. This strategy is therefore no worse than the current state-of-the-art. As a consequence, an adversarial attribute provider is degraded to an honest, but curious one, if we consider that trusted *attribute providers* behave honestly. The specific trust model to be used can be chosen based on the deployment scenario.

Storage providers are used to host data and are chosen by *data owners*.

Adversarial storage providers may try to gain access to the payload (targeting confidentiality), modify it (targeting integrity, authenticity, unforgeability), replace access policies (targeting integrity, authenticity, unforgeability, accountability). In addition, adversarial storage providers may simply delete data they are supposed to store, thus targeting availability.

Evaluators are responsible for evaluating and enforcing access policies. The evaluation process is carried out inside a trusted computing base. Our security model assumes that this secure execution environment can only be compromised by a powerful attacker (see Sect. 4), which we consider out of scope.

Adversarial evaluators may go offline at any point in time, based on realistic user behaviour. Thus, only availability concerns remain.

Accessors want to access data published within Multiply, Divide, and Conquer.

Adversarial accessors may seek to gain unauthorised access encrypted payloads, thus targeting confidentiality.

---

[10] https://openid.net/connect/.

A.4   System Properties Providing Security Services

Property 1 (Confidentiality). Assets : *payload, key shares.*
Since means for transport security like Transport Layer Security (TLS) are available, we assume authenticated, encrypted communication channels between all actors. This protects attributes and key shares in transit. The payload is encrypted prior to publishing and the randomly generated bulk encryption key is split and wrapped for evaluators, making these two assets initially confidential. Colluding evaluators could recover the key. However, this would violate the postulated trusted computing properties.

Property 2 (Integrity, Authenticity, Accountability, Non-repudiation). Assets : *payload, key shares, policy, attributes*
Considering honest, but curious attribute providers and TLS-secured connections, provided attributes are authentic. This implies that their source can be verified. As our system employs ECIES, and key shares are signed by the data owner and (after policy evaluation) also by evaluators, their authenticity can be verified. Authenticated encryption is used to encrypt the payload, and polices are signed and cryptographically linked to key shares and payload, the integrity and authenticity of these assets can also be verified at any given point. The use of cryptographic signatures and cryptographic linking using a nonce directly implies accountability and provides non-repudiation.

Property 3 (Unforgeability). Assets : *payload, key shares, policy, attributes*
Assuming all cryptographic primitives perform as expected, forging any asset is infeasible. Considering honest but curious attribute providers and providers and TLS, attributes cannot be tampered with. We assume a state-of-the-art protocol towards attribute providers that ensures freshness of all produced data.

Property 4 (Availability). Assets : *payload, key shares, policy, attributes*
Cheap (and even free), cloud-based storage is abundant. Since payload, key shares, and policy are stored together, this applies to all three of these assets. Defining multiple attribute providers (catering towards redundancy) is possible. In addition, secret sharing parameters can be tweaked to account for *evaluators* going offline to ensure availability.

Assuming the postulated trusted computing guarantees are upheld and attribute providers behave in an honest but curious manner, our design delivers on its promises.

References

1. Bethencourt, J., Sahai, A., Waters, B.: Ciphertext-policy attribute-based encryption. In: 2007 IEEE Symposium on Security and Privacy (SP 2007), pp. 321–334 (2007). https://doi.org/10.1109/SP.2007.11
2. Chase, M.: Multi-authority attribute based encryption. In: Vadhan, S.P. (ed.) TCC 2007. LNCS, vol. 4392, pp. 515–534. Springer, Heidelberg (2007). https://doi.org/10.1007/978-3-540-70936-7_28

3. Goyal, V., Pandey, O., Sahai, A., Waters, B.: Attribute-based encryption for fine-grained access control of encrypted data. In: ACM CCS, pp. 89–98, ACM, New York, USA (2006). https://doi.org/10.1145/1180405.1180418
4. Hu, V.C., et al.: Guide to Attribute Based Access Control (ABAC) Definition and Considerations. Technical reports, National Institute of Standards and Technology, Gaithersburg, MD (2014). https://doi.org/10.6028/NIST.SP.800-162
5. Kiraz, M.S., Uzunkol, O.: Still Wrong Use of Pairings in Cryptography. CoRR (2016). http://arxiv.org/abs/1603.02826
6. Lewko, A., Waters, B.: Decentralizing attribute-based encryption. In: Paterson, K.G. (ed.) EUROCRYPT 2011. LNCS, vol. 6632, pp. 568–588. Springer, Heidelberg (2011). https://doi.org/10.1007/978-3-642-20465-4_31
7. Müller, S., Katzenbeisser, S., Eckert, C.: Distributed attribute-based encryption. In: Lee, P.J., Cheon, J.H. (eds.) ICISC 2008. LNCS, vol. 5461, pp. 20–36. Springer, Heidelberg (2009). https://doi.org/10.1007/978-3-642-00730-9_2
8. OASIS Standard: eXtensible Access Control Markup Language (XACML) Version 3.0. Technical reports (2013). http://docs.oasis-open.org/xacml/3.0/xacml-3.0-core-spec-os-en.html
9. Prünster, B., Fasllija, E., Mocher, D.: Master of puppets: trusting silicon in the fight for practical security in fully decentralised peer-to-peer networks. In: ICETE 2019 - SECRYPT, vol. 2, pp. 252–259 (2019)
10. Prünster, B., Palfinger, G., Kollmann, C.: Fides: Unleashing the full potential of remote attestation. In: ICETE 2019 - SECRYPT, vol. 2, pp. 314–321 (2019)
11. Qian, H., Li, J., Zhang, Y., Han, J.: Privacy-preserving personal health record using multi-authority attribute-based encryption with revocation. Int. J. Inf. Secur. 14(6), 487–497 (2014). https://doi.org/10.1007/s10207-014-0270-9
12. Rouselakis, Y., Waters, B.: Efficient statically-secure large-universe multi-authority attribute-based encryption. In: Böhme, R., Okamoto, T. (eds.) FC 2015. LNCS, vol. 8975, pp. 315–332. Springer, Heidelberg (2015). https://doi.org/10.1007/978-3-662-47854-7_19
13. Sandor, V.K.A., Lin, Y., Li, X., Lin, F., Zhang, S.: Efficient decentralized multi-authority attribute based encryption for mobile cloud data storage. J. Netwk. Comput. Appl. 129, 25–36 (2019). https://doi.org/10.1016/j.jnca.2019.01.003
14. Shamir, A.: How to share a secret. Commun. ACM 22(11), 612–613 (1979). https://doi.org/10.1145/359168.359176
15. Suzic, B., Prünster, B., Ziegler, D., Marsalek, A., Reiter, A.: Balancing utility and security: securing cloud federations of public entities. In: Debruyne, C., et al. (eds.) OTM 2016. LNCS, vol. 10033, pp. 943–961. Springer, Cham (2016). https://doi.org/10.1007/978-3-319-48472-3_60
16. Zhong, H., Zhu, W., Xu, Y., Cui, J.: Multi-authority attribute-based encryption access control scheme with policy hidden for cloud storage. Soft. Comput. 22(1), 243–251 (2016). https://doi.org/10.1007/s00500-016-2330-8

A Model Specification Implementation for Trust Negotiation

Martin Kolar[1(✉)], Carmen Fernandez Gago[2], and Javier Lopez[1]

[1] Department of Computer Science, University of Malaga, 29071 Malaga, Spain
{kolar,jlm}@lcc.uma.es
[2] Department of Applied Mathematics, University of Malaga, 29071 Malaga, Spain
mcgago@lcc.uma.es

Abstract. Trust negotiation represents a suitable approach for building trust in online environments, where the interacting entities are anonymous. It covers important criteria on security and privacy. In this work, we propose a method for implementing our model specification that handles trust negotiation. We define the structure of the trust negotiation module that is a standalone unit capable of negotiating on its own. It may be included to any software by its defined interfaces. We realise our method with a ride-sharing scenario and four trust negotiation strategies that we apply in order to validate our design and implementation. We propose a solution that is fully customisable based on different requirements. The proposal provides guidelines for developers in the process of including trust negotiation into their software.

1 Introduction

The present world offers many opportunities and challenges. People need to exchange resources, such as information, services and products. They require trust for cooperation, which may be handled by trust negotiation *(TN)*. This is a suitable approach for online environments, where unknown entities interact together. Trust is built by a mutual exchange of credentials. In this work, we propose a method for implementing TN. Since the Software Development Life Cycle *(SDLC)* does not include trust by default, we provide it for all of its phases. We analyse our TN model specification [15] from the implementation-specific point of view and integrate it into a software product. We follow the Object-oriented programming *(OOP)* and propose a trust negotiation module *(TNM)* that is an autonomous unit capable of TN on its own. It connects to other modules by defined interfaces and its logical separation makes the implementation more secure. Developers will be guided through the whole process, which may spare their time and costs when developing their own TN model.

The rest of this paper is organised as follows. Section 2 deals with the previous work on TN and the SDLC. Section 3 presents the proposal of the TNM structure, whereas its implementation is done in Sect. 4. Section 5 defines a TN ride-sharing scenario that is applied in Sect. 6 and that validates the TNM. Finally, Sect. 7 concludes this paper and outlines the future work.

© Springer Nature Switzerland AG 2020
M. Kutyłowski et al. (Eds.): NSS 2020, LNCS 12570, pp. 327–341, 2020.
https://doi.org/10.1007/978-3-030-65745-1_19

2   Related Work

Trust is important for Computer Science. Gambetta [1] defines it as a probability, by which an entity expects another one to perform an action, on which its welfare depends. Jøsang [2] defines two categories: the reliability trust is based on the reliability of an entity, whereas the decision trust is based on a decision to be dependent. Winsborough [3] recognises two approaches for authentication: identity-based and capability-based. Another approach is suitable for online environments: trust is built by TN, i.e., a sequential exchange of credentials [4]. TN requires a set of criteria [5], a protocol and a strategy [6]. The dynamics of trust is managed by trust models. Moyano [7] classifies them into the decision and evaluation ones. The former include TN models and TrustBuilder [8] was the first one. Some TN models implement security agents that build trust on behalf of entities [3,9]. Hess et al. [10] propose a model that provides a run-time privacy protection. This approach is suitable for dynamically-generated contents. Guo and Jiang [11] propose a TN framework with an adaptive negotiation strategy that ensures a balance between building trust and privacy protection. Seamons et al. [12] examine privacy issues in online TN and propose methods for their elimination or minimisation. Our goal is to create a general TN framework for developers. Development issues were analysed in approaches, such as the SDLC that divides the development into phases. Ruparelia [13] summarises SDLC models, such as waterfall, spiral and incremental. Driver et al. [14] include digital trust into the SDLC and integrate third-party components. Kolar et al. [15] present a model specification that guides developers in the process of including TN into software. We follow up this work for the implementation phase of the SDLC. Bresciani et al. [16] present a development of agent-oriented software systems. Casey and Richardson [17] deal with the effective globally distributed software development. Ilieva et al. [18] deal with agile methodologies that are suitable for variable requirements. We will follow the implementation phase of the SDLC and extend it by the TN capabilities. To the best of our knowledge, there is no other work following this approach. We will follow the OOP in order to make a scalable implementation. Our framework is unique since it guides developers in the process of including TN into their software.

3   Specification of the Trust Negotiation Module

In this section, we present an implementation of the general TN functionality. Our approach is to develop the TNM that covers all aspects of TN [15]. We provide a general methodology of its design and internal composition. The TNM is a self-contained unit capable of performing TN on behalf of entities. It is connected to the other modules that participate in the initial set up of TN. We will analyse its structure and functionality:

- The TNM is generally designed in order to support any topology of software modules. They are connected by four interfaces.

- A database is required for accessing user data, such as credentials and policies. This data is accessed during trust negotiation on the fly.
- Two modes of operation are possible: either a complete control over TN, for which each step is supervised, or an automated process, when the TNM is initially configured and then performs TN on its own.
- A trusted authority is supported in order to validate credentials.

The TNM is depicted in Fig. 1. Its interfaces are as follows:

1) This interface connects to another TNM, with whom will be carried out TN. Both must use the same interface and negotiation protocol.
2) The control interface connects to the control module that manages the TN operations. It transfers all requests and returns responses.
3) This interface connects to a database. The compliance checker uses it for requesting credentials and policies based on the actual needs.
4) The last one optionally connects to a trusted authority. The compliance checker may need to verify and validate the incoming credentials.

The following sub-modules ensure the functionality of the TNM:

- **Negotiator** represents the entity that wants to build trust.
- **Compliance Checker** performs disclosure decisions for the negotiator and enforces preserving its privacy.
- **Trust** represents the currently established trust used by the negotiator.
- **Exposure** represents the current privacy exposure level.
- **Strategy** and **Protocol** represent the chosen negotiation strategy and the communication protocol used by the negotiators, respectively.

We proposed the TNM and its main components in compliance with our defined requirements for TN [5]. The next section introduces a deeper analysis and aims to the implementation in a programming language.

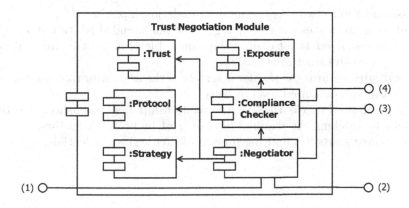

Fig. 1. The Inner Structure of the Trust Negotiation Module

4 Implementation of the Trust Negotiation Module

In this section, we decompose the TNM into the particular classes. We define attributes and methods in order to specify their features and behaviour. Figure 2 depicts the class diagram that is the core of our implementation. It depicts the design and topology of all classes.

4.1 The Core of Trust Negotiation

The *Negotiator* class is principal since it represents its owning entity that wants to build trust with another one. The negotiator carries out TN on behalf of the entity. When it is demanded for disclosing a credential, the compliance checker validates the request. Two negotiators have to use the same protocol (*protocol* attribute) that defines the exact content and order of the exchanged messages. The following methods are implemented for handling the incoming and outgoing credentials:

- **Provide** discloses the specified credential to the other negotiator if the compliance checker approves it.
- **Demand** requests the specified credential from the other negotiator.
- **Is_negotiating** returns the willingness of the negotiator to continue with TN. For example, *false* is returned in case of privacy violation.

The *TrustRelationship* class represents the trust relationship between two negotiators (*negotiator1*, *negotiator2* attribute). Their common goal (*goal* attribute) defines the purpose for building trust. The *trust* attribute specifies the actual trust level that has been built and is measured on a 7-degree scale. During TN, this level increases and once it is equal or higher than the required one (*req_trust* attribute), the negotiator is satisfied. When this happens for both negotiators, TN is successfully terminated. The TrustRelationship class implements the following methods:

- **Associate** links two negotiators into a relationship.
- **Define_goal** defines the common goal for the intended relationship.
- **Define_required_trust** defines the required level of trust in order to establish a successful trust relationship.
- **Is_satisfied** returns the satisfaction state of the negotiator that is determined by reaching its required level of trust.
- **Is_established** checks whether the relationship was established. It is determined by reaching the required level of trust by both negotiators.
- **Negotiate** starts TN and the process of exchanging credentials.

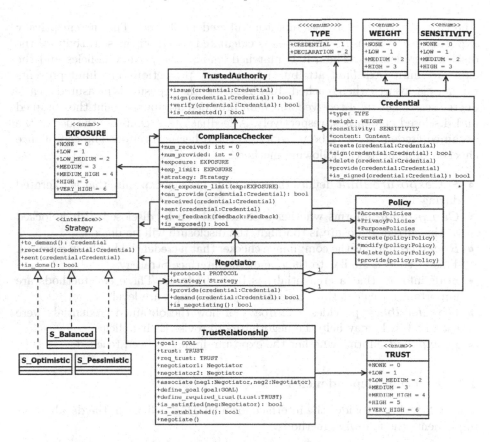

Fig. 2. The Class Diagram of the Trust Negotiation Module

4.2 Processing Trust Negotiation

Each negotiator must specify its own negotiation strategy. The interface *Strategy* defines the methods used by the classes implementing a specific strategy. We propose the *S_Optimistic*, *S_Pessimistic* and *S_Balanced* classes that represent an optimistic, pessimistic and balanced strategy, respectively. An instantiated class represents the active strategy. Each class determines the credentials to be disclosed, by which order and also reacts to the incoming ones. The following methods are defined:

- **To_demand** determines the credential to be requested, if any.
- **Received** is called by the negotiator and informs the strategy class about the incoming credentials. It is used for planning next disclosures.
- **Sent** is a similar method that informs about the disclosed credentials.
- **Is_done** returns the information, whether all the required credentials have been obtained or there are more to be requested.

The *ComplianceChecker* class monitors all credentials flow. The current privacy exposure level (*exposure* attribute) is calculated based on the sensitivity of the disclosed credentials. Then, it is matched against the privacy policies and the exposure limit (*exp_limit* attribute) for privacy protection. The limit prevents further disclosures when reached. Just like trust, the exposure is measured on a 7-degree scale. The *num_received* and *num_provided* attributes count the obtained and disclosed credentials, respectively. A feedback that confirms the use of the obtained credentials may be provided to the other negotiator. The compliance checker implements the following methods:

- **Set_exposure_limit** defines the maximum privacy exposure that is tolerated during TN.
- **Can_provide** informs whether a credential can be disclosed. If it is locked or the current exposure is too high, the disclosure will be denied.
- **Received** informs the compliance checker that a credential has been received. This method is similar to the one of the interface Strategy.
- **Sent** informs that a credential has been disclosed. These two methods are important for calculating the current privacy exposure level.
- **Give_feedback** provides a feedback of how the obtained credentials were used in TN. It may help the negotiators to revise their policies.
- **Is_exposed** informs whether the exposure limit has been reached.

4.3   External Dependencies

The *Policy* class provides the interface for managing policies in the database. It implements the following methods:

- **Create** defines a new policy and then adds it to the database.
- **Delete** erases the specified policy from the database.
- **Modify** updates a policy, e.g., based on the received feedback.
- **Provide** reads a policy and delivers it to the compliance checker.

The *Credential* class provides the interface for accessing credentials in the database. The type of a credential (*type* attribute) is either *CREDENTIAL* or *DECLARATION*. The former is signed, whereas the latter is not. The *weight* and *sensitivity* attributes specify its importance for building trust and its confidentiality level, respectively. They are measured on a 4-degree scale. The *content* attribute is the actual information of the credential. The following methods are implemented:

- **Create** adds a new unsigned credential of type DECLARATION.
- **Sign** serves for signing a credential, but requires a trusted authority. Its type is changed from DECLARATION to CREDENTIAL.
- **Delete** erases a credential. It is used for the no longer valid ones.
- **Provide** ensures the access to the credentials during TN.
- **Is_signed** informs whether a credential is signed.

The *TrustedAuthority* class represents the optional interface for connecting to a trusted authority. Its purpose is to issue and verify credentials, so that they may be more valuable for TN. These methods are implemented:

- *Issue* issues a new credential of type CREDENTIAL by default.
- *Sign* inputs an existing credential of type DECLARATION and signs it. In case of success, its type will change to CREDENTIAL.
- *Verify* inputs a signed credential by this authority and verifies its authenticity. This is intended for unknown or untrusted credentials.
- *Is_connected* informs whether the authority is connected.

5 Trust Negotiation Ride-Sharing Scenario

In this section, we propose a TN ride-sharing scenario implemented by using the TNM. Later, we will use it for validating the TNM. This demonstrative scenario is easy to follow: the web portal is a popular service that enables its users to share a ride. The drivers offer rides to the passengers that pay for it. Two of them want to travel to the same destination, which is their common goal. They have to establish a trust relationship and especially the passenger has to be confident that the driver is experienced and responsible. Their TN is as follows:

1. The passenger sends a message to the driver by the web portal. He requests a contact information.
2. The driver replies by providing his e-mail address and telephone number. Then, he asks for a contact information in return.
3. The passenger only discloses his telephone number as other information is too sensitive. He requests the driving experience and price.
4. The driver discloses the history of his rides and his price list.
5. Now, the passenger is more confident in the driving experience of the driver. He also demands a detailed information about the latest ride.
6. The driver discloses the exact route information and his usual speed. Then, he asks the passenger for the luggage he wants to carry.
7. The passenger is satisfied and acquires a sufficient confidence. He responds that the luggage is large and asks whether it is a problem.
8. The driver responds that he has a space. The passenger agrees with the offered price and decides to book the ride.

We implement this scenario by following our proposal and using the OOP paradigm. We specify modules that are depicted in Fig. 3. The TNM is the core unit that is connected to the following entities:

1. The other TNM. Two such modules are connected by a communication channel. They act on behalf of the driver and the passenger.
2. The control module managing TN and processing its results.
3. The data storage unit containing credentials and policies.
4. The web portal providing the online service for ride-sharing.

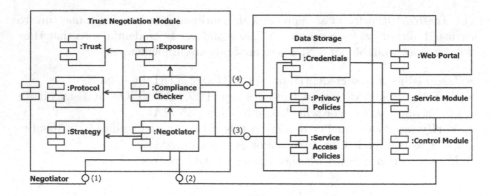

Fig. 3. The Ride-sharing Scenario Implementation

Both users have their own instances of the TNM, the control module, the service one and the data storage unit. They perform the following actions:

- **The service module** manages data for its user, such as updating the credentials and policies in the data storage unit. The module has full access. Then, it configures system variables, e.g., encryption keys.
- **The control module** manages the TNM. It initiates TN, supervises the exchange process and obtains its result. The module is acknowledged from the service one when all data is configured for TN.
- **The trust negotiation module** carries out TN. Both users request the TNM to build trust for them. Their credentials are exchanged based on the defined policies and the chosen negotiation strategy. Finally, TN is evaluated and the users are informed about its result.

This ride-sharing scenario has shown the method for implementing TN using the proposed specification. It has explained the purpose of the specific modules and their cooperation in the process of building trust.

6   Validation of the Trust Negotiation Module

In this section, we validate our proposal. We create four variations based on the scenario while each implements a different negotiation strategy. We compare their attributes for building trust. We assemble three equal devices with different roles: two negotiators and a trusted authority. They are made of the following components:

- **Arduino Nano** is a single-board electronics platform using the 8-bit ATmega328 microcontroller with 32 KB flash memory and 2 KB RAM. It performs the deployed TN scenario and drives the other components.
- **ESP8266** is a Wi-Fi microcontroller with the full TCP/IP stack ability. We use it for interconnecting the devices by a wireless network.

- **ST7735** is a small colour TFT display. It is not required for TN, however, we use it for outputting messages of its progress to the user.

We defined a general TN algorithm (*Negotiate* function) that is shown in Algorithm 1. TN is performed until both negotiators are willing to do so: the negotiator (1) checks his actual trust level and if it is lower than required, he demands a credential from the negotiator (2). Then, (2) checks whether he may disclose it. This depends on his privacy exposure level that, increased by the sensitivity of the credential, must be lower than his exposure limit. If it was disclosed, (1) increases his trust level by his defined weight of the credential and (2) increases his exposure level by the defined sensitivity. Otherwise, (1) demands another credential. The negotiators change their roles after each step so that trust is built evenly. TN continues until both establish the required trust and while their privacy is preserved. TN fails if the policies are improperly specified, the available credentials are not sufficient or privacy would be violated.

Algorithm 1. Trust negotiation

1: **function** NEGOTIATE(*negotiator1, negotiator2*)
2:      **while** *negotiator1* **is** *negotiating* **and** *negotiator2* **is** *negotiating* **do**
3:          **if** *negotiator1.current_trust < negotiator1.required_trust* **then**
4:              *negotiator1* **demands** *credential* from *negotiator2*
5:              **if** *negotiator2* **discloses** *credential* **then**
6:                  **increase** *negotiator1.current_trust* **about** *credential.weight*
7:                  **increase** *negotiator2.current_exposure* **about** *credential.sensitivity*
8:          **if** *negotiator2.current_trust < negotiator2.required_trust* **then**
9:              *negotiator2* **demands** *credential* from *negotiator1*
10:             **if** *negotiator1* **discloses** *credential* **then**
11:                 **increase** *negotiator2.current_trust* **about** *credential.weight*
12:                 **increase** *negotiator1.current_exposure* **about** *credential.sensitivity*
13:         **if** *negotiator1.current_exposure > negotiator1.exposure_limit* **or**
                negotiator2.current_exposure > negotiator2.exposure_limit **then**
14:             **return** failure
15:         **if** *negotiator1.current_trust >= negotiator1.required_trust* **and**
                negotiator2.current_trust >= negotiator2.required_trust **then**
16:             **return** success
17:     **return** failure

The algorithm is applied in four trust negotiation strategies. Each strategy extends it by specific features. We have implemented the following ones:

- **Optimistic strategy** basically follows the algorithm. The negotiators define their required trust and exposure limit. This strategy is marked as optimistic since credentials may be freely exchanged. It is fast, efficient for building trust and not demanding for computing resources.
- **Pessimistic strategy** is more restrictive. The unbalance level and limit are implemented: the former is a difference between the current exposure

and established trust. The latter defines its maximum value that changes as trust increases. Then, credentials use a locking mechanism. These features ensure a balance in exchanging credentials. The strategy preserves privacy well, however, is less efficient.

- **Balanced strategy** measures trust by the couple (t, c), for which t is the trust value and c is the confidence value [19]. This metrics provides a certainty to the established trust in TN. A trusted authority is used and the signed credentials are assigned high confidence levels. The strategy represents a good compromise in efficiency, so we mark it as balanced.
- **Improved balanced strategy** uses trust intervals *(TI)* [7], where the trust value lies on $<t_a, t_b>$. TI is a more intuitive alternative for (t, c) and the confidence value is hidden from the negotiator. Credentials are assigned the confidence levels as previously and the resulting trust value is computed as the arithmetic mean of TI.

All strategies successfully established trust for both negotiators. The TN process is depicted in appendices. Our approach provides a suitable procedure for implementing TN that a developer may utilise for his own TN scenario. It may significantly save his time and costs.

7   Conclusion

In this work, we have proposed a method for implementing our TN model specification. We have specified the TNM that is capable of automated TN. The TNM isolates the TN functionality, which increases security. Other software modules are connected by controlled interfaces. This versatile concept facilitates adding and removing modules based on requirements. We have provided a detailed TNM implementation by specifying its classes and their topology. Then, we have defined a ride-sharing scenario that is a practical use-case for TN. We have specified a general algorithm for TN that cares about privacy and that is used in four TN strategies. We have deployed the scenario for validating the TNM. We demonstrated how to implement a given TN scenario using the proposed TNM, connect it to the other entities and finally create a functional model.

In the future work, the proposed model specification will become a part of a TN framework and will be fully integrated into all phases of the SDLC. It will form a complete guide for the developers that want to include TN into their systems from the early phases of development to the successful end.

Acknowledgements. This research has been partially supported by the Spanish Ministry of Science and Innovation through the project SecurEdge (PID2019-110565RB-I00) and by the European Commission through the project EU H2020-SU-ICT-03–2018 Project No. 830929 CyberSec4Europe (cybersec4europe.eu).

Appendix A   Optimistic Strategy

	Driver		Trust Negotiation	Passenger	
	Required trust: 6			Required trust: 12	
	Exposure limit: 10			Exposure limit: 8	
Step	Trust	Exposure		Trust	Exposure
1	0	0	←— request: phone number ←—	0	0
2	0	1	—→ disclosure: phone number —→	3	0
3	0	1	—→ request: phone number —→	3	0
4	2	1	←— disclosure: phone number ←—	3	3
5	2	1	←— request: price list ←—	3	3
6	2	2	—→ disclosure: price list —→	5	3
7	2	2	—→ request: address —→	5	3
8	5	2	←— disclosure: address ←—	5	6
9	5	2	←— request: driving history ←—	5	6
10	5	6	—→ disclosure: driving history —→	8	6
11	5	6	—→ request: luggage info —→	8	6
12	6	6	←— disclosure: luggage info ←—	8	7
13	6	6	←— request: space info ←—	8	7
14	6	7	—→ disclosure: space info —→	10	7
15	6	7	←— request: address ←—	10	7
16	6	7	—→ **disclosure denied** —→	10	7
17	6	7	←— request: latest ride ←—	10	7
18	6	8	—→ disclosure: latest ride —→	12	7
19	6	8	←— **successful termination** —→	12	7

Appendix B   Pessimistic Strategy

	Driver				Trust Negotiation	Passenger			
	Required trust: 6					Required trust: 12			
	Exposure limit: 10					Exposure limit: 9			
Step	Trust	Exp	Unb.Level	Unb.Limit		Trust	Exp	Unb.Level	Unb.Limit
1	0	0	0	2	←— request: phone number ←—	0	0	0	0
2	0	1	1	2	—→ disclosure: phone number —→	2	0	-2	0
3	0	1	1	2	—→ request: phone number —→	2	0	-2	0
4	0	1	1	2	←— **disclosure denied** ←—	2	0	-2	0
5	0	1	1	2	—→ request: e-mail —→	2	0	-2	0
6	1	1	0	2	←— disclosure: e-mail ←—	2	2	0	0
7	1	1	0	2	←— request: price list ←—	2	2	0	0
8	1	2	1	2	—→ disclosure: price list —→	4	2	-2	2
9	1	2	1	2	—→ request: address —→	4	2	-2	2
10	1	2	1	2	←— **disclosure denied** ←—	4	2	-2	2
11	1	2	1	2	—→ request: phone number —→	4	2	-2	2
12	3	2	-1	2	←— disclosure: phone number ←—	4	5	1	2
13	3	2	-1	2	←— request: driving history ←—	4	5	1	2
14	3	2	-1	2	—→ **disclosure denied** —→	4	5	1	2
15	3	2	-1	2	←— request: space info ←—	4	5	1	2
16	3	3	0	2	—→ disclosure: space info —→	6	5	-1	2
17	3	3	0	2	—→ request: address —→	6	5	-1	2
18	3	3	0	2	←— **disclosure denied** ←—	6	5	-1	2
19	3	3	0	2	—→ request: luggage info —→	6	5	-1	2
20	4	3	-1	4	←— disclosure: luggage info ←—	6	6	0	2
21	4	3	-1	4	←— request: latest ride ←—	6	6	0	2
22	4	4	0	4	—→ disclosure: latest ride —→	8	6	-2	4
23	4	4	0	4	—→ request: address —→	8	6	-2	4
24	7	4	-3	5	←— disclosure: address ←—	8	9	1	4
25	7	4	-3	5	←— request: driving history ←—	8	9	1	4
26	7	8	1	5	—→ disclosure: driving history —→	11	9	-2	4
27	7	8	1	5	←— request: address ←—	11	9	-2	4
28	7	10	3	5	—→ disclosure: address —→	13	9	-4	4
29	7	10	3	5	←— **successful termination** —→	13	9	-4	4

Appendix C   Balanced Strategy

	Driver			Trust Negotiation		Passenger		
	Required trust: 6					Required trust: 12		
	Exposure limit: 10					Exposure limit: 8		
	Required conf.: 0.8					Required conf.: 0.6		
Step	Trust	Exp	Conf			Trust	Exp	Conf.
1	0	0	0	⟵ request: phone number ⟵		0	0	0
2	0	1	0	⟶ disclosure: phone number ⟶		3	0	0.6
3	0	1	0	⟶ request: phone number ⟶		3	0	0.6
4	2	1	0.7	⟵ disclosure: phone number ⟵		3	3	0.6
5	2	1	0.7	⟵ request: price list ⟵		3	3	0.6
6	2	2	0.7	⟶ disclosure: price list ⟶		5	3	0.6
7	2	2	0.7	⟶ request: address ⟶		5	3	0.6
8	5	2	0.88	⟵ disclosure: address ⟵		5	6	0.6
9	5	2	0.88	⟷ **authority: confirmed**		5	6	0.6
10	5	2	0.88	⟵ request: driving history ⟵		5	6	0.6
11	5	6	0.88	⟶ disclosure: driving history ⟶		8	6	0.75
12	5	6	0.88	**authority: confirmed** ⟷		8	6	0.75
13	5	6	0.88	⟶ request: luggage info ⟶		8	6	0.75
14	6	6	0.85	⟵ disclosure: luggage info ⟵		8	7	0.75
15	6	6	0.85	⟵ request: space info ⟵		8	7	0.75
16	6	7	0.85	⟶ disclosure: space info ⟶		10	7	0.72
17	6	7	0.85	⟵ request: address ⟵		10	7	0.72
18	6	9	0.85	⟶ disclosure: address ⟶		12	7	0.77
19	6	9	0.85	**authority: confirmed** ⟷		12	7	0.77
20	6	9	0.85	⟵ **successful termination** ⟶		12	7	0.77

Appendix D   Improved Balanced Strategy

	Driver				Trust Negotiation		Passenger			
	Required trust: 0.6						Required trust: 0.75			
	Exposure limit: 0.8						Exposure limit: 0.55			
St	Trust	Exp	Conf	TI			Trust	Exp	Conf	TI
1	0	0	0	$< 0, 1 >$	← req: phone number ←		0	0	0	$< 0, 1 >$
2	0	0.05	0	$< 0, 1 >$	⟶ dis: phone number ⟶		0.15	0	0.6	$< 0.09, 0.49 >$
3	0	0.05	0	$< 0, 1 >$	⟶ req: phone number ⟶		0.15	0	0.6	$< 0.09, 0.49 >$
4	0.20	0.05	0.7	$< 0.14, 0.44 >$	← dis: phone number ←		0.15	0.15	0.6	$< 0.09, 0.49 >$
5	0.20	0.05	0.7	$< 0.14, 0.44 >$	← req: price list ←		0.15	0.15	0.6	$< 0.09, 0.49 >$
6	0.20	0.15	0.7	$< 0.14, 0.44 >$	⟶ dis: price list ⟶		0.30	0.15	0.6	$< 0.18, 0.58 >$
7	0.20	0.15	0.7	$< 0.14, 0.44 >$	⟶ req: address ⟶		0.30	0.15	0.6	$< 0.18, 0.58 >$
8	0.50	0.15	0.88	$< 0.44, 0.56 >$	← dis: address ←		0.30	0.30	0.6	$< 0.18, 0.58 >$
9	0.50	0.15	0.88	$< 0.44, 0.56 >$	⟷ auth: confirmed		0.30	0.30	0.6	$< 0.18, 0.58 >$
10	0.50	0.15	0.88	$< 0.44, 0.56 >$	← req: driving history ←		0.30	0.30	0.6	$< 0.18, 0.58 >$
11	0.50	0.35	0.88	$< 0.44, 0.56 >$	⟶ dis: driving history ⟶		0.55	0.30	0.78	$< 0.43, 0.65 >$
12	0.50	0.35	0.88	$< 0.44, 0.56 >$	auth: confirmed ⟷		0.55	0.30	0.78	$< 0.43, 0.65 >$
13	0.50	0.35	0.88	$< 0.44, 0.56 >$	⟶ req: luggage info ⟶		0.55	0.30	0.78	$< 0.43, 0.65 >$
14	0.60	0.35	0.85	$< 0.51, 0.66 >$	← dis: luggage info ←		0.55	0.35	0.78	$< 0.43, 0.65 >$
15	0.60	0.35	0.85	$< 0.51, 0.66 >$	← req: space info ←		0.55	0.35	0.78	$< 0.43, 0.65 >$
16	0.60	0.45	0.85	$< 0.51, 0.66 >$	⟶ dis: space info ⟶		0.65	0.35	0.75	$< 0.49, 0.74 >$
17	0.60	0.45	0.85	$< 0.51, 0.66 >$	⟶ req: e-mail ⟶		0.65	0.35	0.75	$< 0.49, 0.74 >$
18	0.70	0.45	0.83	$< 0.58, 0.75 >$	← dis: e-mail ←		0.65	0.45	0.75	$< 0.49, 0.74 >$
19	0.70	0.45	0.83	$< 0.58, 0.75 >$	← req: address ←		0.65	0.45	0.75	$< 0.49, 0.74 >$
20	0.70	0.65	0.83	$< 0.58, 0.75 >$	⟶ dis: address ⟶		0.85	0.45	0.81	$< 0.69, 0.88 >$
21	0.70	0.65	0.83	$< 0.58, 0.75 >$	auth: confirmed ⟷		0.85	0.45	0.81	$< 0.69, 0.88 >$
22	0.70	0.65	0.83	$< 0.58, 0.75 >$	← success ⟶		0.85	0.45	0.81	$< 0.69, 0.88 >$

References

1. Gambetta, D.: Can we trust trust? Trust: Making Breaking Coop. Relat. **13**, 213–238 (1990)
2. Jøsang, A., Ismail, R., Boyd, C.: A survey of trust and reputation systems for online service provision. Decis. Support Syst. **43**, 618–644 (2007)
3. Winsborough, W.H., Seamons, K.E., Jones, V.E.: Automated trust negotiation. DARPA Information Survivability Conference and Exposition. In: DISCEX '00 Proceedings, vol. 1, pp. 88–102 (2000)
4. Winsborough, W.H., Li, N.: Towards practical automated trust negotiation. In: Proceedings Third International Workshop on Policies for Distributed Systems and Networks, pp. 92–103, IEEE (2002)
5. Kolar, M., Fernandez-Gago, C., Lopez, J.: Policy languages and their suitability for trust negotiation. In: Kerschbaum, F., Paraboschi, S. (eds.) DBSec 2018. LNCS, vol. 10980, pp. 69–84. Springer, Cham (2018). https://doi.org/10.1007/978-3-319-95729-6_5
6. Yu, T., Winslett, M., Seamons, K.E.: Interoperable strategies in automated trust negotiation. In: Proceedings of the 8th ACM Conference on Computer and Communications Security, pp. 146–155 (2001)
7. Moyano, F.: Trust engineering framework for software services. Universidad de Málaga, Lenguajes y Ciencias de la Computación. PhD thesis (2015)
8. Winslett, M., et al.: Negotiating trust in the web. IEEE Internet Comput. **6**(6), 30–37 (2002)
9. Bonatti, P., De Coi, J.L., Olmedilla, D., Sauro, L.: A rule-based trust negotiation system. IEEE Trans. Knowl. Data Eng. **22**(11), 1507–1520 (2010)
10. Hess, A., Holt, J., Jacobson, J., Seamons, K.E.: Content-triggered trust negotiation. ACM Trans. Inf. Syst. Secur. **7**(3), 428–456 (2004)
11. Guo, S., Jiang, W.: An adaptive automated trust negotiation model and algorithm. In: International Conference on Communications and Intelligence Information Security, Nanning, pp. 130–134. IEEE (2010)
12. Seamons, K.E., Winslett, M., Yu, T., Yu, L., Jarvis, R.: Protecting privacy during on-line trust negotiation. In: Dingledine, R., Syverson, P. (eds.) PET 2002. LNCS, vol. 2482, pp. 129–143. Springer, Heidelberg (2003). https://doi.org/10.1007/3-540-36467-6_10
13. Ruparelia, N.B.: Software development lifecycle models. ACM SIGSOFT Softw. Eng. Notes **35**(3), 8–13 (2010)
14. Driver, M., Gaehtgens, F., O'Neill, M.: Managing digital trust in the software development life cycle. ID G00326944, Gartner (2017)
15. Kolar, M., Fernandez-Gago, C., Lopez, J.: A model specification for the design of trust negotiations. Comput. Secur. **84**, 288–300 (2019)
16. Bresciani, P., Perini, A., Giorgini, P., Giunchiglia, F., Mylopoulos, J.: TROPOS: an agent-oriented software development methodology. Auton. Agent Multi-Agent Syst. **8**(3), 203–236 (2004). https://doi.org/10.1023/B:AGNT.0000018806.20944.ef
17. Casey, V., Richardson, I.: Implementation of global software development: a structured approach. Softw. Process: Improv. Pract. **14**(5), 247–262 (2009)
18. Ilieva, S., Ivanov, P., Stefanova, E.: Analyses of an agile methodology implementation. In: Proceedings of the 30th Euromicro Conference, pp. 326–333. IEEE (2004)
19. Theodorakopoulos, G., Baras, J.S.: Trust evaluation in Ad-Hoc networks. In: Proceedings of the 3rd ACM Workshop on Wireless Security (WiSe '04), New York, USA, pp. 1–10. ACM (2004)

Privacy and Utility Trade-Off for Textual Analysis via Calibrated Multivariate Perturbations

Jingye Tang[1], Tianqing Zhu[1(✉)], Ping Xiong[2], Yu Wang[3], and Wei Ren[1,4,5]

[1] School of Computer Science, China University of Geosciences,
Wuhan, People's Republic of China
tianqing.e.zhu@gmail.com, weirencs@cug.edu.cn
[2] Zhongnan University of Economics and Law, Wuhan, China
pingxiong@zuel.edu.cn
[3] Institute of Artificial Intelligence and Blockchain, Guangzhou University,
China-Singapore Guangzhou Knowledge City, Huangpu District, Guangzhou, China
yuwang@gzhu.edu.cn
[4] Guangxi Key Laboratory of Cryptography and Information Security,
Guilin 541004, People's Republic of China
[5] Key Laboratory of Network Assessment Technology,
CAS Institute of Information Engineering, Chinese Academy of Sciences,
Beijing 100093, People's Republic of China

Abstract. In recent years, the problem of data leakage often appears in our lives. As of today, a number of enterprises have been fined heavily for the leakage of user data, including Facebook, Uber and Equifax. This paper makes deep research on the privacy protection of the text. We proposed a three-layer privacy protection mechanism for carrying out privacy-preserving text perturbation. This approach allows different levels of privacy protection for different parts of the text, thereby increasing the level of privacy protection without reducing utility. Extensive experiments prove that the proposed method not only provides fine-grained control over the level of privacy in that data but also improves performance.

Keywords: Privacy preservation · Natural language processing · Differential privacy · Local differential privacy.

1 Introduction

With the development of big data analytics, there has been an ever-growing need to collect statistical data and obtain valuable information from organized user data [10]. However, the more valuable the information, the more sensitive it is to the user. Therefore, research institutions or enterprises need to provide users with strong privacy protection when collecting data, otherwise, users will face the risk of privacy leakage. However, the problem of data leakage often appears

© Springer Nature Switzerland AG 2020
M. Kutyłowski et al. (Eds.): NSS 2020, LNCS 12570, pp. 342–353, 2020.
https://doi.org/10.1007/978-3-030-65745-1_20

in our lives. As of today, a number of enterprises have been fined heavily for the leakage of user data, including Facebook, Uber, and Equifax [7]. Therefore, the calculation of sensitive data is an important research direction in recent years.

In this context, we define privacy breaches as a privacy breach that is unintended or unauthorized data disclosure during the intended system uses [2]. At present, the main ideas of privacy-preserving include Generalization, Anonymous, Encryption, and Perturbation. Generalization refers to reducing the details so that they contain less information. Anonymity is the first privacy protection technology proposed by hiding the identity attribute in the published data. Among them, k-anonymization [8], which is widely used, is an effective method of data publishing to protect private information.

When evaluating the published information, we need to consider two aspects: privacy and utility. However, Differential Privacy considered how to prevent data reconstruction and protect against any potential side knowledge. Differential privacy is an essential and prevalent privacy model that has been widely explored in recent decades [13].

The first challenge is how to improve utility while preserving privacy. Adding noise to the text is crucial for preserving tasks downstream of NLP. To preserve privacy in NLP tasks, Oluwaseyi. F et al. [5] applies a $d_\mathcal{X}$-privacy mechanism $\hat{x} = M(x)$ to obtain a replacement for the given word x. However, $d_\mathcal{X}$-privacy preserved every word in the text indiscriminately, which would reduce too much utility. Given this phenomenon, we propose a more targeted method that classifies the vector of words into three levels based on different privacy requirements and then adds perturbations to each level of word vectors respectively.

The second challenge is preserving text privacy better while guaranteeing the utility of the task. In this paper, we define two statistics to measure the privacy-preserving of words by a choice of privacy parameters, and the distance parameter. The mechanism will not be used to achieve privacy protection at the cost of more utility.

Overall, this paper makes the following contributions: (1) In order to implement text perturbation to protect privacy, we propose a three-layer privacy protection mechanism. This approach allows different levels of privacy protection for different parts of the text. Compared to a baseline, it increases the level of privacy protection without compromising usability. (2) Compared with the baseline method, extensive experiments prove that the proposed method provides more efficient privacy by adjusting privacy parameters with the same utility of text processing.

2 Preliminary

2.1 Centralized Privacy Protection Model

ε-differential privacy [4] is a privacy protection method under the centralized privacy protection model. The definition of ε-differential privacy is described below:

344   J. Tang et al.

Definition 1 (ε-Differential Privacy). *A randomized function $\mathcal{K}$ gives ε-differential privacy if for all data sets D_1 and D_2 differing on at most one element, and all $S \subseteq Range(\mathcal{K})$,*

$$e^{-\varepsilon} \leq \frac{Pr[\mathcal{K}(D_1) \in S]}{Pr[\mathcal{K}(D_2) \in S]} \leq e^{\varepsilon} \tag{1}$$

2.2 Local Privacy Protection Model

The biggest problem of the centralized privacy model is that all users still need to trust a central authority, the database maintainer, to protect their privacy.

We will use the definition of local differential privacy (LDP) given by:

Definition 2 (ε-Local Differential Privacy [12]). *A randomized algorithm $\mathcal{A}$ satisfies ε-Local Differential Privacy if for all parts of client's values v_1 and v_2 and for all $Q \subseteq Range(A)$ and for ($\varepsilon \geq 0$), Eq. (2) holds. Range(A) is the set of all possible outputs of the randomized algorithm A*

$$e^{-\varepsilon} \leq \frac{Pr[A(v_1) \in Q]}{Pr[A(v_2) \in Q]} \leq e^{\varepsilon} \tag{2}$$

For ε-Local differential privacy, the parameter ε determines the loss of privacy. When $\varepsilon = 0$, privacy protection is perfect, and there is almost no privacy loss. As $\varepsilon = \infty$, there is no guarantee of privacy. The $d_{\mathcal{X}}$-privacy, introduced below, is more flexible because it is based on LDP and liberates restrictions. $d_{\mathcal{X}}$-privacy was originally developed to address the trade-off between privacy and utility.

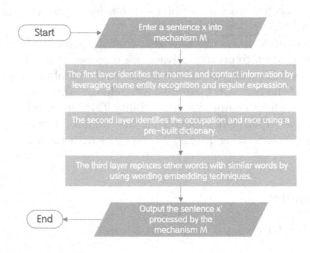

Fig. 1. A flowchart of our privacy-preserving mechanism.

2.3 $d_{\mathcal{X}}$-privacy: Improved LDP

The disadvantage of LDP is that it undermines the utility of data in order to protect privacy [1].

We say that a obfuscation mechanism $M : \mathcal{X} \to \mathcal{Y}$ satisfies $\varepsilon d_{\mathcal{X}}$-privacy if privacy parameter $\varepsilon > 0$ and for any $x, x' \in \mathcal{X}$ the distributions over outputs of $M(x)$ and $M(x')$ satisfy the following bound: for all $y \in \mathcal{Y}$, we have

$$e^{-\varepsilon \cdot d(x,x')} \leq \frac{Pr[M(x) = y]}{Pr[M(x') = y]} \leq e^{\varepsilon \cdot d(x,x')} \tag{3}$$

All output value $y \in \mathcal{Y}$ can be found its corresponding input x and x' in set $\mathcal{X}$ that is satisfied (1), and the log-likelihood ratio of the outputs y is bounded by $\varepsilon d(x, x')$. The above situation indicates that LDP is more indistinguishable than $d_{\mathcal{X}}$-privacy, which is less restrictive and has more flexible parameters and allowing the unsolvability of the output distribution to scale according to the distance between the respective inputs.

3 Privacy Preserving Mechanism

3.1 Notataions and Problem Definition

Notations. Let $\mathcal{W}$ donate a dictionary of strings. A string $x = w_1 w_2 ... w_l$ is the input text. Given a string x, privacy parameter $\varepsilon_1, \varepsilon_2$ and distance parameter θ, then the privacy-protected string x' can be derived from the privacy preserving machanism. Table 1 gives the description of all notations.

Table 1. Notations

Parameter	Description
M_i	Privacy preserving mechanism
S_l	The set of words
x	Input string
w_i	A word
$N(\varepsilon_i)$	The noise with ε_i as parameter
ϕ	Word embedding model
$\hat{\phi}$	Perturbed embedding
$d(w_i, w_i')$	The distance between w_i and w_i'
$d(x, x')$	The distance between x and x'

3.2   Mechanism Overview

Our goal is to design a three-tier ideal model that builds on the quantifiable privacy guarantees of the local privacy protection model. As shown in Fig. 1, the basic idea of private data release is that the privacy protection of each word is partitioned into different levels and a noisy vector sampled from the noise distribution p_N is added to the vector of certain words to achieve a privacy guarantee. For example, when we input the sentence "The European Union's decision to hold entry talks with Turkey receives a widespread welcome." into the privacy protection mechanism, the output is the sentence "in Cuba community's determination in save access speech behind Finland take to generalized popular."

Algorithm 1: Privacy Preserving Mechanism

Input: string $x=w_1w_2...w_l$, privacy parameter $\varepsilon_1, \varepsilon_2 > 0$

for $i \in \{1, 2, ..., l\}$ do

  if $w_i \in S_1$ then

    | $w_i' = M_1(w_i)$;

  else

    | $w_i' = w_i$;

  end

end

for $i \in \{1, 2, ..., l\}$ do

  Compute embedding $\phi(w_i')$;

  if $w_i' \in S_2$ then

    Perturb embedding to obtain $\hat{\phi}_i = \phi(w_i') + N(\varepsilon_1)$ with noise density $p_N(z) \propto exp(-\varepsilon_1||z||)$;

    Obtain perturbed word $w_i'' = argmin_{u \in W}|||\phi(u) - \hat{\phi}_i)|| - \theta|$;

  else

    | $w_i'' = w_i'$

  end

end

for $i \in \{1, 2, ..., l\}$ do

  String $x' = w_1''w_2''...w_l''$;

  if $(w_i'' \notin S_1)$ && $(w_i'' \notin S_2)$ then

    Perturb embedding to obtain $\hat{\phi}_i = \phi(w_i'') + N(\varepsilon_2)$ with noise density $p_N(z) \propto exp(-\varepsilon_2||z||)$;

    Obtain perturbed word $w_i''' = argmin_{u \in W}||\phi(u) - \hat{\phi}_i||$;

  else

    | $w_i''' = w_i''$

  end

  Insert w_i''' in ith position of x' ;

end

Output: x'

3.3 Method Details

In this part, we will introduce the type of text targeted by each layer and the corresponding algorithm in the three-layer privacy-preserving mechanism.

The first layer of the privacy protection mechanism protects six types of content in the text: the personal name, place name, organization name, email, fax, telephone number, and other information. These six categories of words are all included in the data set S_1. We used Named Entity Recognition (NER) and regular expressions to recognize these six types of words in the text, and randomly replace them with similar words from S_1. As described in algorithm 1, when any word in S_1 appears in the text, such as $w_i \in S_1$, the same type of word in S_1 is randomly selected to replace the original word w_i, so as to obtain $w_i' = M_1(w_i)$.

The second layer of privacy protection mechanism is mainly used to protect the identity (e.g., manager, lawyer, mother, grandfather, etc.) and race/ethnicity (e.g., Yellow, Germanic, etc.) information in the text. Set S_2 contains the two types of data sets mentioned above: the identity data set and the racial/ethnic data set. After we traverse all the words w_i and find the w_i that satisfies the S_2 set of the dataset, we complete the following steps: First, Compute the word embedding vector $\phi(w_i')$ of w_i'. In this part we compute the embedding word vector $\phi(w_i')$ if word $w_i' \in S_2$, and then the noise with ε_1 as privacy parameter is added to the embedding word vector $\phi(w_i')$ to obtain the corresponding perturbation embedding vector $\hat{\phi}_i = \phi(w_i') + N(\varepsilon_1)$. The noise $N(\varepsilon_1)$ is sampled from an n-dimensional distribution with density $p_N(z) \propto exp(-\varepsilon_1||z||)$, and then replacing the word w_i with perturbed word w_i'' whose embedding is at least θ away from the perturbed embedding of w_i'.

After the text has been protected by the first two layers of privacy protection, the remaining words belong to neither S_1 nor S_2. For this class of words, we have designed a third layer of privacy-preserving mechanism for them. We add noise $N(\varepsilon_2)$ with ε_2 as a parameter to obtain perturbation embedding $\hat{\phi}_i$ of w_i''. And then replacing the word w_i'' with the word w_i''' whose embedding is closest to $\hat{\phi}_i$. Finally, insert w_i''' in ith position of x'.

The metric between words or strings that in this paper is derived from a *word embedding model* $\phi : \mathcal{W} \rightarrow \mathbb{R}^n$ as follows: given $x, x' \in \mathcal{W}^l$, we let $d(w_i, w_i') = ||\phi(w_i) - \phi(w_i')||$, $d(x, x') = \sum_{i=1}^{l} ||\phi(w_i) - \phi(w_i')||$. The parameter θ determines the Euclidean distance between perturb embedding words. All the metrics described in this work are Euclidean.

The pseudo-code provides more details in our Privacy Preserving Mechanism and Sect. 3.4 presents how to sample noise from the multivariate distribution p_N for different values of ε.

3.4 Sampling from the Noise Distribution

To preserve privacy, noise derived from a differential privacy mechanism can be added to the learning model. The basic idea of private data release is that we take advantage of a vector-valued random variable $\mathbf{v} = [v_1...v_n]$ sampled from a multivariate normal distribution and a magnitude l sampled from Gamma distribution to determine the noisy vector at the privacy parameter ε. More details on the approach can be found in [11].

4 Statistics for Privacy Calibration

There are two important standards when calibrating privacy parameters $(\varepsilon_1, \varepsilon_2)$ and distance parameter (θ) of our Privacy-preserving mechanism based on the word embedding ϕ.

The following two statistics (N_w and S_w) will be used to observe the privacy protection of the text in the experimental analysis. The first statistics N_w [5] satisfied (4) is the probability of not modifying the input word w.

$$N_w = Pr[M(w) = w] \tag{4}$$

The second statistics S_w [5] satisfied (5) is an distribution of possible output words for an input w. It's worth noting that probability parameter η plays an important role in the definition of S_w. The definition of S_w can also be written as $S_w = min|\{S \subseteq \mathcal{X} : Pr[M(w) \in S] > 1 - \eta\}|$. As $\eta \to 0$, we have almost $\forall w \in W$ in $M(w)$ satisfies $Pr[M(w) \in S]$. Obviously, the S_w that corresponds to $\eta \to 0$ satisfies the condition for $S_w = \mathcal{X}$. In contrast, as $\eta \to 1$ we have $S_w = min|\{S \subseteq \mathcal{X} : Pr[M(w) \in S] > 0\}|$. S_w is the minimum that satisfies the equation above, therefore, we have $S_w = \varnothing$.

$$S_w = min|\{S \subseteq \mathcal{X} : Pr[M(w) \notin S] \le \eta\}|, (\eta > 0) \tag{5}$$

5 Experiment Evaluation

5.1 Experiment Setup

In the experiment, the datasets we used were AG_NEWS and IMDb movie reviews. AG is a collection of more than 1 million news articles collected from 2,000 news sources. The IMDb movie reviews contain 50,000 highly polarized comments from the Internet. And all layers in our experiments use $50d$ GloVe embeddings.

5.2 Experiment Results

We compared the utility and privacy of the baseline and our methods in the multiple classification and binary classification experiments, and the results showed that our mechanism can have better privacy protection and utility than the baseline by adjusting parameters.

Performance By Varying ε_1 and θ. The F_1 value of ε_1 and θ is described in Table 2. Table 2 describes the F_1 values of parameter ε_1 and parameter θ when parameter $\varepsilon_2 = 0$. For the distance parameter θ, Euclidean distance is chosen as

Table 2. The utility of text analysis tasks increases as ε_1 increases and θ declines.

	$\theta = 0$	$\theta = 5$	$\theta = 10$	$\theta = 20$	$\theta = 30$	$\theta = 40$
$\varepsilon_1 = 3$	0.8547	0.8625	0.8151	0.7931	0.8273	0.7808
$\varepsilon_1 = 4$	0.8642	0.8553	0.7908	0.8107	0.8035	0.8319
$\varepsilon_1 = 5$	0.8377	0.8749	0.8184	0.7952	0.8533	0.8269
$\varepsilon_1 = 6$	0.8922	0.8856	0.8440	0.8694	0.8146	0.7858
$\varepsilon_1 = 7$	0.8972	0.8604	0.8399	0.8549	0.8386	0.8119
$\varepsilon_1 = 8$	0.8733	0.9065	0.8710	0.8595	0.8450	0.8384

the metric. We can verify the following conclusions: (a) When ε_1 increases, the privacy loss is large and the utility is high; (b) When ε_1 decreases, the privacy loss is small and the utility is low. (c) When the words with a large distance from the original word are chosen as the replacement words, the loss of privacy is small and the utility is low; (d) When the words with a small distance from the original word are chosen as the replacement words, the loss of privacy is large and the utility is high.

Performance By Varying ε_2. Table 3 describes the precision, recall, accuracy and F_1 value corresponding to different ε_2 values. We explore the effect of ε_2 on utility if ε_1 and θ are fixed. (ε_1=5, θ=10) As can be seen from Table 3, if ε_1 and θ are fixed, the utility increases with the increase of ε_2.

Empirical S_w and N_w. S_w and N_w are the two statistics we described separately in Sect. 4.2. Under different privacy parameters of the GLOVE model, we ran the $d_{\mathcal{X}}$-privacy mechanism and our privacy mechanism for each word 500 times respectively to calculate the plausible deniability statistics S_w and N_w.

As shown in Fig. 2, the red figure represents the distribution of S_w under different privacy parameter ε values of baseline. As fewer privacy words need to be replaced in the first two layers of the text analyzed in Fig. 2, there is no significant statistical difference in privacy between the original method and the new method. The blue graph in Fig. 2 shows the distribution of S_w under different privacy parameters ε_2 when $\varepsilon_1 = 5$, $\theta = 10$ after using our privacy mechanism. Since the privacy words related to the first layer and the second layer in AG_NEWS and IMDb data sets account for less than 10% of the text, we fixed ε_1 and θ in Fig. 2, and only explored the privacy leakage that caused the change of S_w distribution response due to the change of ε_2.

In contrast, as shown in Fig. 3, the red figure represents the distribution of N_w under different privacy parameter ε values of baseline. As for the blue figure (corresponds to our new method), after the privacy parameter ε_1 and distance parameter θ are fixed, the influence of the change of parameter ε_2 on the N_w distribution is depicted.

The results presented in Fig. 2 and 3 provide a visual way to select appropriate values of ε_2 by knowing the worst that could happen, then observing the extreme values of the histograms for S_w and N_w. For example, at $\varepsilon_2 = 3$, each

Table 3. The utility of the text analysis task increases as ε_2 grows.

	$\varepsilon_2 = 10$	$\varepsilon_2 = 20$	$\varepsilon_2 = 30$	$\varepsilon_2 = 40$	$\varepsilon_2 = 50$	$\varepsilon_2 = 60$
Precision	83.7%	80.5%	84.8%	84.9%	85.4%	86.0%
Recall	78.6%	75.8%	82.1%	82.5%	83.6%	84.6%
Accuracy	78.6%	75.8%	82.1%	82.5%	83.7%	84.6%
F_1	81.1%	78.1%	83.4%	83.6%	84.5%	85.3%

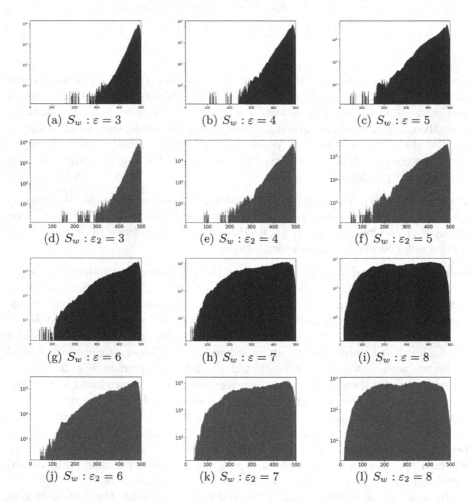

(a) $S_w : \varepsilon = 3$ (b) $S_w : \varepsilon = 4$ (c) $S_w : \varepsilon = 5$

(d) $S_w : \varepsilon_2 = 3$ (e) $S_w : \varepsilon_2 = 4$ (f) $S_w : \varepsilon_2 = 5$

(g) $S_w : \varepsilon = 6$ (h) $S_w : \varepsilon = 7$ (i) $S_w : \varepsilon = 8$

(j) $S_w : \varepsilon_2 = 6$ (k) $S_w : \varepsilon_2 = 7$ (l) $S_w : \varepsilon_2 = 8$

Fig. 2. The law of change in statistic S_w

word was typed into the privacy mechanism 500 times and produced at least 150 different new words (Fig. 2d). As for N_w, no word is returned more than 230 times even in the worst case (Fig. 3d).

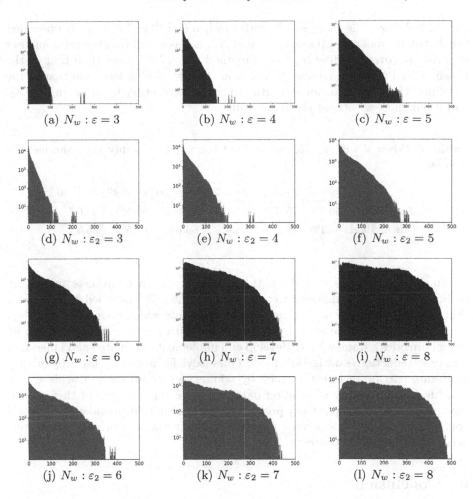

Fig. 3. The law of change in statistic N_w

Through repeated experiments, it is found that the parameter values in this paper have a great relationship with the distribution of privacy words in the text. The privacy words in the IMDb movie review dataset and AG_news dataset currently used the account for 8.96% and 7.47% of the whole text respectively. As a result, the privacy parameter ε_1 and distance parameter θ cannot have a significant impact on the classification results. However, in our mechanism, the first two layers of privacy protection content are the most vulnerable to disclosure. Therefore, the method proposed by us is targeted to protect the text privacy content while minimizing the impact on the classification results. Table 3 describes the baseline and comparison data for our proposed mechanism.

To compare with the baseline method, we made $\varepsilon_2 = \varepsilon$ and adjusted ε_1 and θ so that the average F_1 value of our method and the baseline method on the two text analysis tasks was not less than –0.5%.

Table 4 shows the change in F_1 with ε_2 when $\theta = 10$ and $\varepsilon_1 = 5$. By observing the distribution of corresponding S_w and N_w, it was found that the total number of words in corresponding S_w in our method was 2.54% more than that in the baseline, and the total number of words in N_w was 7.69% less than that in the baseline. Therefore, we can strengthen privacy protection by adjusting ε_1, ε_2, and θ parameters without changing utility.

Table 4. When $\theta = 10$, $\varepsilon_1 = 5$, our method has a higher utility than the baseline method.

	$\varepsilon_2 = 3$	$\varepsilon_2 = 10$	$\varepsilon_2 = 20$	$\varepsilon_2 = 30$	$\varepsilon_2 = 40$	$\varepsilon_2 = 50$
d_χ-privacy	56.1%	75.3%	82.1%	84.5%	85.5%	84.6%
Our method	65.1%	78.1%	83.4%	83.6%	84.5%	85.3%

Similarly, for plain text data, the following approach protects privacy in plain text data from different perspectives. Cumby [3] described a framework that quantifies the privacy leakage of text data sets which giving the user fine-grained control over the level of privacy needed. Furthermore, Sánchez, David [9] model provides a framework to develop and implement automated and inherently semantic redaction/sanitization tools. Oluwaseyi Feyisetan [6] uses d_χ-privacy mechanism to protect text privacy by adding perturbations and achieve geographic indiscernibility of location data. We have taken a step further on this basis and we designed a privacy protection mechanism that provides fine-grained control over the level of privacy for users and sets different privacy parameters according to different contents.

6   Conclusion

In this paper, we presented a three-layer privacy protection mechanism for carrying out privacy-preserving text perturbation. This approach allows different levels of privacy protection for different parts of the text, thereby increasing the level of privacy protection without reducing utility. Because this method can set different parameters for different content in the text, it applies to transactional data as well as plain text data. We evaluated the performance through extensive experiments, and the results prove that the proposed method provides a better tradeoff between task utility and privacy guarantee.

References

1. Alvim, M.S., Chatzikokolakis, K., Palamidessi, C., Pazii, A.: Invited paper: Local differential privacy on metric spaces: Optimizing the trade-off with utility. In: 31st IEEE Computer Security Foundations Symposium, CSF 2018, Oxford, United Kingdom, July 9–12, 2018. pp. 262–267. IEEE Computer Society (2018). https://doi.org/10.1109/CSF.2018.00026
2. Bambauer, D.E.: Privacy versus security. J. Criminal Law & Criminol. **103**, 667 (2013)
3. Cumby, C., Ghani, R.: Inference control to protect sensitive information in text documents. In: ACM SIGKDD Workshop on Intelligence & Security Informatics. pp. 1–7 (2010)
4. Dwork, C.: Dierential privacy. In: Proceedings of the 33rd International Conference on Automata, Languages and Programming - Volume Part II (2006)
5. Feyisetan, O., Balle, B., Drake, T., Diethe, T.: Privacy- and utility-preserving textual analysis via calibrated multivariate perturbations (2019)
6. Feyisetan, O., Balle, B., Drake, T., Diethe, T.: Privacy- and utility-preserving textual analysis via calibrated multivariate perturbations. In: WSDM 2020: The Thirteenth ACM International Conference on Web Search and Data Mining (2020)
7. Pang, H.H., Ding, X., Xiao, X.: Embellishing text search queries to protect user privacy. Proc. VLDB Endowment **3**(1), 598–607 (2010)
8. Samarati, P., Sweeney, L.: Generalizing data to provide anonymity when disclosing information (abstract). In: Mendelzon, A.O., Paredaens, J. (eds.) Proceedings of the Seventeenth ACM SIGACT-SIGMOD-SIGART Symposium on Principles of Database Systems, June 1–3, 1998, Seattle, Washington, USA. p. 188. ACM Press (1998). https://doi.org/10.1145/275487.275508
9. Sanchez, D., Batet, M.: C-sanitized: a privacy model for document redaction and sanitization. J. Assoc. Inf. Sci. Technol. **67**(1), 148–163 (2016)
10. Sanchez, D., Castella-Roca, J., Viejo, A.: Knowledge-based scheme to create privacy-preserving but semantically-related queries for web search engines. Inf. Sci. **218**(1), 17–30 (2013)
11. Wu, X., Li, F., Kumar, A., Chaudhuri, K., Jha, S., Naughton, J.F.: Bolt-on differential privacy for scalable stochastic gradient descent-based analytics (2016)
12. Xiang, Z., Ding, B., He, X., Zhou, J.: Linear and range counting under metric-based local diffcrential privacy (2019)
13. Zhu, T., Li, G., Zhou, W., Yu, P.S.: Differentially private data publishing and analysis: a survey. IEEE Trans. Knowl. Data Eng. **29**(8), 1619–1638 (2017)

PowerKey: Generating Secret Keys from Power Line Electromagnetic Interferences

Fangfang Yang[1], Mohammad A. Islam[2], and Shaolei Ren[1($\boxtimes$)]

[1] University of California, Riverside, USA
sren@ece.ucr.edu
[2] University of Texas at Arlington, Arlington, USA

Abstract. With the increasing adoption of Internet-of-Things devices, autonomously securing device-to-device communications with minimal human efforts has become mandated. While recent studies have leveraged ambient signals (i.e., amplitude of voltage harmonics) in a building's power networks to secure plugged IoT devices, a key limitation is that the exploited signals are consistent only among nearby outlets, thus resulting in a low key matching rate when devices are far from each other. In this paper, we propose PowerKey to generate secret keys for multiple plugged IoT devices in an electrical domain (e.g., a lab or an office suite). Concretely, PowerKey taps into ambient power line electromagnetic interferences (EMI): there exist multiple spatially unique EMI spikes whose frequencies vary randomly but also remain consistent at participating power outlets to which IoT devices are connected. We propose K-means clustering to locate common EMI spikes offline at participating outlets and then dynamically extract secret keys at runtime. For evaluation, we conduct experiments in two different locations—one research lab and one suite with multiple rooms. We show that with PowerKey, multiple devices can successfully obtain symmetric secret keys in a robust and reasonably fast manner (i.e., 100% successful at a bit generation rate of up to 52.7 bits/sec).

1 Introduction

The fast growing adoption of inter-connected Internet-of-Things (IoT) devices, such as smart thermostats, WiFi access points and smart power sockets, has been dramatically changing the way we interact with our daily work and living environments. Meanwhile, demand for security as well as usability is also soaring. In particular, a crucial concern is how to quickly establish a shared secret key among various co-located IoT devices without users' manual efforts.

Today, authentication and security for many IoT devices are often delegated to mobile-based apps rather than performed on their own in an autonomous manner. This usually needs to be done for each IoT device through a separate mobile app, since IoT devices may not be using a unified interface provided by

This work was supported in part by the NSF under grant ECCS-1610471.

M. Kutyłowski et al. (Eds.): NSS 2020, LNCS 12570, pp. 354–370, 2020.
https://doi.org/10.1007/978-3-030-65745-1_21

third-party vendors. Moreover, the current way to establish secure connections is often *one-time* (during the initial setup) and the secret keys typically remain unchanged for a long time, which poses hidden security threats.

In recent years, exploiting ambient contexts to generate dynamically shared or symmetric secret keys has been emerging as a promising solution to device authentication [1–8]. The key idea is that two or more physically co-located devices can sense similar *ambient* signals, which can serve as a proof of device authenticity. For example, the prior literature has extensively exploited radio frequency signals such as WiFi [2,3,5,9], acoustic signals [10–12], body electric/movement signals (for wearable devices) [1,6,13,14], among many others. However, a major limitation of these techniques is that they are mainly suitable for devices that are very close to each other. For example, to leverage ambient WiFi signals (e.g., amplitude and phase) for key generation, two devices must be placed within half a wavelength (i.e., a few centimeters), since otherwise the WiFi signal's attributes can be dramatically different between the devices [3,5]. While key generation based on wireless channel reciprocity (i.e., two communicating devices will experience similar channel conditions) can apply for a longer distance [15–17], channel reciprocity is limited to two participating devices. Moreover, it contains little entropy in the generated keys if the two devices are relatively stationary (which is the case for indoor plugged-in IoT devices) [8,17].

More recently, [7,8] have considered securing IoT devices within an authenticated electrical domain (e.g., a residential house, or a company's office suite) and proposed to exploit the amplitudes of voltage harmonics in the power network for symmetric key generation. Nonetheless, as amplitudes of voltage harmonics are subject to wiring topologies and hence consistent only among nearby outlets, the key matching rate can decrease significantly (to below 90%) when the devices are a few meters away from each other. Thus, this cannot continuously secure IoT devices with a high successful rate.

Contributions. We address the limitation of unreliable key generation under the same setting considered in [8], and present PowerKey, which exploits the consistency of electromagnetic interference (EMI) spike frequencies among outlets within an authenticated electrical domain to secure plugged-in IoT devices. Concretely, multiple devices, even in different rooms connected within a shared electrical domain, can see *similar* EMIs generated by switching mode power supplies (SMPS). These power supplies are used by many electronic devices such as computers, printers and TVs, and create prominent frequency spikes in the 40 ∼ 150 kHz range because of high-frequency switching operation [18–20]. Importantly, the frequencies of the EMI spikes vary randomly and, if detectable at participating outlets, will be the same at these outlets. Thus, they can be used as a *reliable* common source of randomness for symmetric key generation.

A key challenge is that most EMI spikes are limited to a small area due to very weak strengths and only a few spikes are detectable as common signals at participating outlets for legitimate devices. Thus, we propose K-means clustering as offline pre-processing to locate the frequency windows over which these common EMI spikes exist at participating outlets. At runtime, legitimate devices can extract secret key information from the selected EMI spikes.

To evaluate PowerKey, we conduct experiments in two locations—an office suite with multiple rooms and a research lab. We show that with PowerKey, devices can successfully generate symmetric secret keys in a robust and reasonably fast manner (i.e., 100% successful at a bit generation rate of up to 52.7 bits/sec). Moreover, even considering a strong attacker that knows all the details of PowerKey but collects voltage signals from an outside outlet, we show that the chance of an attacker obtaining the secret key is practically zero.

2   Preliminaries on Power Line EMI

Overview of EMR/EMI. Electromagnetic radiation (EMR) is generated when electromagnetic fields drive the movement of atomic particles, such as an electron. Another associated concept is electromagnetic interference (EMI), which occurs whenever electromagnetic fields are disturbed by an external source through induction, electrostatic coupling, or conduction [21]. EMI can be broadly classified as *radiated* EMI and *conducted* EMI: radiated EMI (typically > 300 MHz) propagates in radio frequencies over the air, whereas conducted EMI (< 300 MHz) traverses through power lines [22].

Existing Research on Exploiting EMR/EMI. EMR signals are good indicators of the system power consumption for power attacks [23]. Electronic devices plugged into power outlets also generate noises (i.e., conducted EMI) propagating through power lines [22,24]. The prior literature has tapped into power line EMI for simple gesture recognition by sensing its EMI-induced electrical potential [25]. Also, conducted EMI strengths can be extracted to infer a television's content [26] and stealthy data exfiltration from computers [27]. Other studies include exploiting power line EMI for detecting appliance on/off activities in a smart home [22,28], for estimating data center-level power usage information to launch load injection attacks [29], among others. In addition, the consistent deviation in power grid's nominal 50/60 Hz frequency has also been leveraged for wide-area (e.g., city-scale) clock synchronization [30,31]. By contrast, we exploit switching-induced EMI spikes in 40 ~ 150 kHz for a new and important purpose—key generation to secure IoT device communications.[1]

---

[1] Given a power network and a time window, the frequencies of switching-induced EMI spikes are unique (i.e., spatial-temporal uniqueness) and hence can be exploited for purposes other than key generation. For example, *proof of location*: when a computer is stolen and used elsewhere, the frequency statistics/patterns of EMI spikes will differ, which can prompt additional security measures such as passwords.

3   Problem and Threat Model

3.1   Problem Statement

Considering the same setting as in [7,8], multiple IoT devices are plugged into a power network (e.g., smart thermostats and wireless access points) and need to agree on symmetric secret keys for authenticated communications.

Trust Domain. In [7,8], the concept of authenticated electrical domain is introduced, which is also referred to as a *trust domain* and can be a small single-tenant commercial building or a tenant in a large commercial building with restricted physical accesses. Figure 1 illustrates a building's power network with a standard

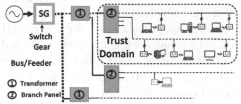

Fig. 1. Overview of a trust domain (i.e., authenticated electrical domain in [8]).

design [32]. Each panel box delivers electricity to multiple nearby rooms/outlets through parallel branch circuits protected by individual circuit breakers. In reality, each panel box often serves a small commercial building, a residential house, or a tenant (i.e., company) in an office complex, which is an authenticated electrical domain [8].

Legitimate Devices. A legitimate device can be any plugged-in device, such as smart light bulb and WiFi access point, that is physically located within a trust domain. Thus, the same as in [8], being physically in a trust domain also equals to authenticity. Legitimate devices are synchronized with a granularity of 100ms, which is not restrictive since device-to-device (wireless) communications require even better synchronization [33]. All legitimate devices can sample the voltage signals from the outlets they are plugged in [8].

3.2   Threat Model

Following the threat model in [3,8,11,12], attackers cannot forcibly enter the trust domain to acquire the voltage signals or obtain secret keys. The attacker is able to decode all message exchanged between any parties during key generation process. Thus, it knows all the details of PowerKey. The attacker can plug a voltage sensor into a power outlet to directly detect EMI spike frequencies. But, it can only do so outside the trust domain.

4   An In-Depth Look at High-Frequency EMI Spikes

All power outlets over a large area beyond a single trust domain share the same fundamental frequency as well as harmonics (i.e., multiples of 50/60 Hz) [30]. Thus, the low frequency information does not meet confidentiality requirement for key generation, motivating us to explore high-frequency EMI spikes.

358 F. Yang et al.

Sources for High-Frequency EMI Spikes. Many electronic appliances (e.g., computers, televisions, compact fluorescent lights) employ switching-mode power supplies (SMPS), a crucial part of which is the high-frequency switching circuit. Moreover, a power factor correction (PFC) circuit is mandated by international regulations to improve power quality for devices with a rating of more than 75 W, which applies to all desktop computers (including certain laptops) and many other appliances [18]. The core of a PFC circuit also relies on the high-frequency switching operation (typically between 40 ∼ 150 kHz) [18]. Consequently, the rapid switching operation in PFC and SMPS produces high-frequency conducted EMI, which has been extensively reported by prior studies [22, 28].

To demonstrate EMI spikes, we show in Fig. 2(a) the power spectral density (PSD) of voltage signals collected from a power outlet in our lab. Then, we turn on an additional desktop computer and show the new PSD in Fig. 2(b), which clearly demonstrates the creation of two new EMI spikes (as well as a few weaker spikes) centered around 67.2 kHz.

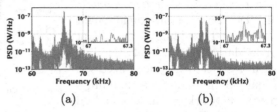

(a)   (b)

Fig. 2. Frequency analysis of voltage signals. (a) Without the additional computer; (b) With the additional computer.

Characteristics of EMI Spikes. While the amplitudes of EMI spikes can vary significantly depending on the measurement point [8], their frequencies exhibit the following characteristics: they vary rapidly over time, and some of them can remain consistent among multiple power outlets within a trust domain. We perform fast Fourier transform (FFT) on voltage signals to examine the frequency characteristics (detailed experiment setup in Sect. 6).

Varying Randomly. The switching frequency of each SMPS unit can vary randomly within a certain range, depending on the instantaneous load and random drifting [18]. Figure 9 in the appendix presents the probability distributions of eight EMI frequencies. Note that, due to frequency orthogonality, power line communication does not interfere with switching-induced EMI spikes [34].

Some EMI Spikes are Consistent for Nearby Power Outlets. While most EMI spikes have weak strengths, we see in Figs. 3(a) and 3(b) that two different outlets in our lab still have consistent EMI spikes around 67.2 kHz. The consistent EMI spikes depend on the locations of the outlets: when the set of outlets changes, the set of common EMI spikes also change.

Undetectable from Outside the Trust Domain. Most EMI spikes are localized to nearby outlets due to, e.g., fading over long wires. Moreover, because of physical isolation in different panel boxes, EMI spikes generated within a trusted domain typically vanish and become undetectable from outside the trusted domain. To see this, we collect voltage signals simultaneously both from outlets in our lab and from an outlet in a different electrical domain next to

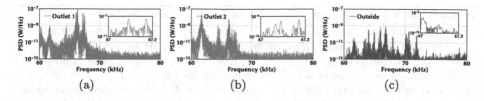

Fig. 3. PSD of voltage signals. (a) Outlet 1 in the lab. (b) Outlet 2 in the lab. (c) Outside the lab (i.e., outside trusted rooms).

our lab. From Fig. 3(c), we see that the outside outlet has dramatically different frequency patterns than the outlets in our lab. Actually, even for two outlets both in our lab, their voltage signals' frequency patterns shown in Figs. 3(a) and 3(b) are different, despite the similarity over certain frequency bands.

Even though a strong attacker outside the trust domain might detect some leaked EMI spikes from within the trust domain, it is very unlikely that the attacker can detect *all* the common EMI spikes used by legitimate devices for key generation because of the spatial uniqueness of conducted EMI signals [8].

5   The Design of PowerKey

PowerKey is built inside the power supply unit of plugged-in IoT devices. It consists of a high-pass filter (to filter out the dominant 50/60 Hz component), an analog-to-digital circuit (ADC), a data communication interface, plus a microcontroller unit. PowerKey is mainly responsible for sending digitized voltage signals to the IoT device, which runs our algorithms. The total hardware cost at scale is below US$5 [8]. Note that sampling voltage signals with 300 kHz or higher (to recover signals of up to 150 kHz) is not restrictive, as a simple SMPS is already controlled to sample and quantize the voltage signals at a high frequency. We refer to [7] for the detailed implementation. The key difference between PowerKey and VoltKey in [8] is that PowerKey runs FFT, whereas VoltKey leverages the amplitudes of voltages harmonics. Next, we describe PowerKey in detail.

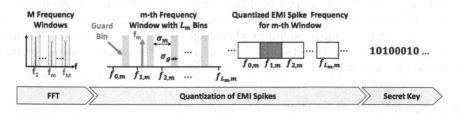

Fig. 4. The design overview of PowerKey.

Algorithm 1 Identify Freq. Windows for Common EMI Spikes

1: Collect voltage signals from devices' outlets for T seconds and divide their own signals into $N = \frac{T}{\Delta t}$ segments each with a duration of Δt seconds.

2: For the i-th segment $(i = 1, 2, \cdots, N)$, compare the voltage signals of all devices and find the set of common EMI spike frequencies $\{f_1^i, f_2^i \cdots f_{M_i}^i\}$.

3: Based on the common EMI spike frequencies, run K-means clustering [35] to find $K = \max\{M_1, M_2, \cdots M_N\}$ clusters, each corresponding to one EMI spike.

4: Calculate the correlation coefficient matrix of the EMI spike frequencies. Only one EMI spike is kept if multiple spikes have strongly correlated frequencies.

5: Return M frequency windows $[f_{m,L}, f_{m,R}]$ for $m = 1, 2, \cdots M$

5.1   Offline Pre-processing

Among numerous (mostly weak) spikes, PowerKey first identifies a set of EMI spikes, whose frequencies vary independently from each other (for more entropy) and are detectable among the participating devices.

● **Step 1.** Each device collects voltage signals for T seconds synchronously as training data and then divides the signal into $N = \frac{T}{\Delta t}$ non-overlapping segments with equal duration Δt.

● **Step 2.** The devices perform FFT analysis on each segment of their own collected voltage signals and pick up EMI spikes over the $40 \sim 150 \, \text{kHz}$ band. For the i-th segment, the devices exchange the frequencies of their own EMI spikes (i.e., local maxima of frequencies) and find the common ones, denoted by the set $\{f_1^i, f_2^i \cdots f_{M_i}^i\}$. Repeat this operation for all the N segments. Here, if the frequencies of an EMI spike at two devices have a difference no more than a threshold η, the two devices are said to have a common EMI spike.

● **Step 3.** Based on N sets of common EMI spikes, we run K-means clustering [35] to find frequency clusters. Then, we perform correlation analysis to remove strongly-correlated EMI spikes and find EMI spikes with little correlation. For each of the remaining M common EMI spikes, we identify its frequency window $[f_{m,L}, f_{m,R}]$, where $f_{m,L}$ and $f_{m,R}$ represent the lower and upper bounds of the m-th EMI spike frequency window. Later, the devices use the detected frequency windows to find EMI spike frequencies at runtime.

The pseudo code is described in Algorithm 1. The K-means algorithm and correlation analysis can be run by a leading device, which then sends back the results to other devices. Re-execution of Algorithm 1 is needed only when the power network environment significantly changes (e.g., some common EMI spikes disappear). Note that the actual EMI frequency, not the range identified offline, is needed to extract keys at runtime.

5.2   Quantize Frequencies of EMI Spikes

At runtime, within a certain frequency window, the common EMI spike can result in slightly different frequencies at different devices due to measurement errors. Thus, we quantize EMI spike frequencies into discrete bins. In this paper, if the frequency difference is no more than σ Hz for 80% of the time, then σ is chosen as the default quantization step size. To further mitigate the frequency discrepancies, we insert a guard frequency band of size σ_g between two valid quantized frequency bins. Figure 4 provides an illustration of the frequency quantization. For example, a device detects a EMI spike frequency of f within a frequency window $[f_L, f_R]$ and the chosen quantization step size is σ. Then, the frequency is quantized into a bin with index of $\lfloor \frac{f-f_L}{\sigma+\sigma_g} \rfloor$.

5.3   Extract Secret Keys

For key generation, participating devices convert indexes of valid EMI frequencies into binary bits using, e.g., Grey codes. Then, the devices shall exchange the information to remove invalid EMI spikes whose frequencies fall into guard bins. Finally, they perform reconciliation and privacy amplification.

Converting Frequency Index into Binary Bits. If the EMI spike frequency at any participating device falls into an invalid frequency guard band, then it becomes less certain to decide its corresponding frequency bin. Thus, the corresponding EMI spike window is discarded to avoid secret key discrepancies. The devices first find their own invalid windows (if any) and exchange this information with other participating devices. For the remaining valid EMI spike windows, the indexes of their frequency bins will be converted into binary bits.

Reconciliation. For better presentation, we focus on two legitimate devices, i.e., Alice and Bob, while it can also be extended to more than two devices [7,11]. Based on the valid EMI spike frequency windows and indexes, Alice and Bob each end up with a n-bit sequence, denoted by $\widetilde{K}_a$ and $\widetilde{K}_b$, respectively. While it is rare to have different $\widetilde{K}_a$ and $\widetilde{K}_b$, it can still occur in practice.

To improve the key matching rate between Alice and Bob, we apply a crucial step—reconciliation process [4,6], which uses error correction coding to fix the bit differences/errors at the expense of slowing down bit generation rate. Specifically, the key idea is that both Alice's n-bit sequence $\widetilde{K}_a$ and Bob's n-bit sequence $\widetilde{K}_b$ can actually be viewed as error-corrupted versions of a shared symmetric key, and errors can be fixable using error correction coding. Consider an (n, k, r) error correction code scheme $\mathcal{C}$, which maps any k-bit sequence into a n-bit codewords $(n > k)$ through a one-to-one encoding function and can correct up to r error bits. Meanwhile, there exists a many-to-one decoding function that maps any n-bit string into one of the 2^k valid codewords. Let $g_e(\cdot)$ and $g_d(\cdot)$ be the encoding and decoding functions of $\mathcal{C}$, respectively. First, Alice can first decode its n-bit string $\widetilde{K}_a$ and then produces the codeword $g_e(g_d(\widetilde{K}_a))$ that is the closest to $\widetilde{K}_a$. Then, Alice computes the bit-wise error string $\Delta\widetilde{K} = \widetilde{K}_a - g_e(g_d(\widetilde{K}_a))$ and sends it to Bob, which can be in cleartext without encryption. Then, if the bit error rate is roughly estimated and the number of error bits is no more than r, Bob can obtain Alice's n-bit sequence $\widetilde{K}_a$ with a high probability based on $\Delta\widetilde{K} + g_e(g_d(\widetilde{K}_b - \Delta\widetilde{K}))$.

To sum up, if $\widetilde{K}_a$ and $\widetilde{K}_b$ generated from Alice's and Bob's respective quantized EMI spike frequencies differ in no more than r bits, the reconciliation process using the coding scheme $\mathcal{C}$ can ensure that both Alice and Bob eventually possess the same n-bit string.

Privacy Amplification. During the reconciliation process, Alice's bit-wise error string $\Delta\widetilde{K} = \widetilde{K}_a - g_e(g_d(\widetilde{K}_a))$, which contains partial information of its n-bit string $\widetilde{K}_a$, is communicated to Bob and meanwhile also possibly leaked to attackers. To address the leakage of partial information about the keys, privacy amplification can be applied: instead of using all the n-bit strings to generate their keys, Alice and Bob can shrink their n-bit strings by $(n-k)$ bits to properly create k-bit strings, thus preventing attackers from acquiring partial information about the k-bit strings [4,6].

Table 1. Frequency Quantization Schemes.

Quantization Scheme	Q1	Q2	Q3	Q4	Q5
Valid Frequency Bin Size (Hz)	σ	σ	σ	$\sigma+1$	$\sigma+1$
Guard Bin Size (Hz)	0	$\sigma-1$	σ	$\sigma-1$	σ

6   Evaluation Methodology

Experiment Setup. We conduct experiments in two different trust domains—an office suite with multiple individual rooms and a research lab, as shown in the appendix. The office suite is shared by multiple faculty members while the lab has more than 20 workstations. We use the office suite as our default location with multiple faculty offices accessible through a corridor.

   Voltage signal collection and processing. For proof of concept, we use a Rigol 1074Z oscilloscope as a proxy ADC to collect voltage signals from the power outlets that are then transferred to a laptop for processing, while one can also follow the design in [7,8] and insert an additional FFT module.

   Error correction coding. We use the following commonly-used error correction coding (ECC) schemes with varying degrees of error tolerance [36]. (i) *Hamming Code*, a linear perfect error correction scheme that encodes every 4 bits of data with 3 parity bits and can withstand 1-bit error in the data. (ii) *Golay Code*, another linear code which encodes 12 bits data into 23 bits and can correct up to 3 error bits. (iii) *Reed-Solomon Code (RS)*, a non-linear cyclic code that can detect and correct multiple errors: an $RS(n,k)$ encoding can correct up to $\lfloor\frac{n-k}{2}\rfloor$ bit errors. In our evaluation, we use three variations of the RS code—$RS(7,3)$, $RS(15,5)$, and $RS(15,3)$.

   Frequency quantization and guard bin size. We set σ as the step size if the frequency difference between any two outlets is no greater than σ for 80% of the time. As shown in Table 1, we test five different quantization schemes with varying step sizes and guard bands, denoted as $Q1, Q2 \cdots, Q5$.

Experiment Durations. We first collect 500 s of voltage data simultaneously from the chosen power outlets to identify the common EMI spike windows offline (Sect. 5.1), and determine the quantization scheme. We use $\Delta t = 100$ ms as the length of each voltage signal segment. For online evaluation, we use the same segment length and run the experiments for 60 min.

Evaluation Metrics. We consider the following standard metrics.

• **Bit Generation Rate.** It is the number of secret bits generated per unit time. Consider a segment size of Δt seconds and M common EMI spikes with frequency windows $[f_{m,L}, f_{m,R}]$, quantization step size σ_m and frequency guard band size $\sigma_{g,m}$, for $m = 1, 2, \cdots M$. The bit generation rate (BGR) in bits per second with ECC $\mathcal{C}(n, k, r)$ is given by BGR $= \frac{k}{n} \cdot \frac{1}{\Delta t} \sum_{m=1}^{M} \log_2 \lfloor \frac{f_{m,R} - f_{m,L}}{\sigma_m + \sigma_{g,m}} \rfloor$.

• **Bit Error Rate.** It indicates the probability of differences between secret keys extracted by two or more devices. A low bit error rate (BER) is desirable.

• **Key Matching Rate.** This indicates, on average, the percentage of keys generated by PowerKey can be used as a valid shared secret key. We use the standard AES 128-bit key as the length requirement [37].

In addition, we also consider *Entropy* and *Mutual Information*. Entropy measures the amount of information contained in the random variable we generate from the EMI spike frequencies. Mutual information quantifies the amount of dependency between two random variables and we use this to measure the information possibly obtained by an attacker.

7 Evaluation Results

In this section, we present our evaluation results in the office suite, while the results in the lab are deferred to the appendix. Our results demonstrate that with the design of PowerKey, multiple devices can successfully generate symmetric secret keys in a robust and fast manner (i.e., with a 100% key matching rate at a bit generation rate of 52.7 bits/sec).

Analysis of EMI Spike Frequencies. By pre-processing the voltage signals in the office suite, we identify a total of 17 common EMI spikes out of hundreds of spikes. As shown in Fig. 5(a), only 8 of the 17 spikes are uncorrelated, while the remaining spikes are redundant and need to be removed. We also show the histograms of the 8 independent EMI spike frequencies and

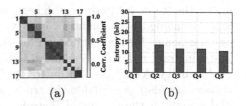

(a)   (b)

Fig. 5. (a) Correlation coefficients of EMI spike frequencies in the office. (b) Entropy with different quantizations.

the frequency differences at the two outlets in Fig. 9 and Fig. 10 in the appendix, respectively. It can be seen that each of the 8 EMI spike frequencies varies within a narrow window. We also run randomness test on frequencies of the 8 EMI spikes in Matlab using runstest($\cdot$). The results are all positive, verifying the randomness of EMI spike frequencies with a 95% significance level [38].

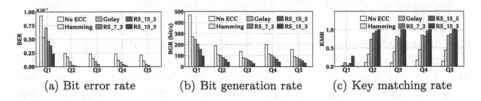

(a) Bit error rate   (b) Bit generation rate   (c) Key matching rate

Fig. 6. Performance of PowerKey in the office suite.

Performance of PowerKey. We now examine the performance of PowerKey.

Entropy of EMI Spike Frequencies. Figure 5(b) shows the impact of our quantization configurations on the overall entropy of the 8 EMI spike frequencies. Naturally, when the EMI spike frequency is mapped to fewer bins, the amount of entropy also decreases but still is better than some of the existing literature whose ambient signals can only have $1 \sim 2$bits [4,6].

Bit Error Rate. We now look at the bit error rate under different quantization and ECC schemes and show the results in Fig. 6(a). We see that either quantizations or ECC alone cannot achieve a low bit error rate. By combining quantization with an appropriate ECC scheme (e.g., $RS(15,5)$ or $RS(15,3)$), PowerKey essentially achieves a zero bit error rate in practice.

Bit Generation Rate. We show the bit generation rate in Fig. 6(b). As in the prior literature [4,6], the bit generation rate only considers how many secret key bits Alice and Bob can generate, without accounting for possible errors. Clearly, both quantization and ECC reduce the bit generation rate, but they are needed to achieve a high key matching rate as we show next.

Key Matching Rate. Next, we show the key matching rate (KMR) between Alice and Bob in Fig. 6(c) for the standard AES 128-bit key [37]. We see that ECC plays a vital role to correct mismatched bits between Alice and Bob. Specifically, the RS codes perform the best, achieving nearly 100% key matching rate when combined with quantization. By contrast, when using amplitudes of voltage harmonics for key generation for devices 18m (approx. 60 ft) away, the key matching rate reduces to below 90% [8].

Security Analysis of PowerKey. We consider an attacker that can collect voltage signals from outside the trust domain, be synchronized with Alice/Bob, and knows all the details of PowerKey (including the common EMI spike frequency windows located offline). In our experiment, we choose an outlet next to the entrance to our office suite. We assume that the attacker uses its most prominent EMI spikes, or estimates the EMI spike frequencies based on their probability distribution, within each valid EMI frequency window. Thus, the attacker is assumed to follow the same procedure as a legitimate device, except for that it extracts EMI spike frequencies from outside the trust domain.

We first calculate the mutual information between two parties in Fig. 7(a). We see that the mutual information between the attacker and Alice/Bob is much lower compared to that between Alice and Bob, thus showing that the attacker's signal contains little information about Alice's/Bob's. Next, we show the bit error rate in Fig. 7(b) for quantization scheme Q4 (Table 1) and see that, under various strategies, the attacker's bit error rate is significantly higher than that of Alice/Bob, resulting in almost random bits. Further, it achieves a practically zero key matching rate, and hence we omit the result. The reason that the attacker is not able to acquire the secret key is that the common EMI spikes located offline are spatially unique to the power outlets to which legitimate devices are connected.

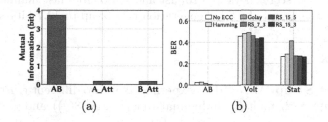

(a)   (b)

Fig. 7. (a) Mutual information: "AB" (Alice-Bob), "A-Att" (Alice-Attacker), and "B-Att" (Bob-Attacker). (b) Bit error rate. "AB" means Alice/Bob; "Volt" means the attacker uses the highest EMI spike for each window from its collected signals; "Stat" means estimating the EMI spike frequencies based on their probability distributions.

8   Related Works

For key generation, the prior research has exploited radio frequency signals such as WiFi [2,3,5,9], acoustic signals [10–12,15], body electric/movement signals (for wearable devices) [1,6,13,14], among many others. Nonetheless, the existing approaches can suffer from a limited distance [2,3,5,9], low key matching rate [6], and/or low bit generation rate [4,5,9]. While key generation based on wireless channel reciprocity can apply for a longer distance [15–17], channel reciprocity often needs time-division multiplexing and is limited to two participating devices each time. Moreover, it contains little entropy in the generated keys if the two devices are relatively stationary [17]. Other studies [11,12] look at secret key generation within a *single* room by utilizing ambient acoustic/luminous characteristics, but they require long-term statistics of the ambient signals and hence take several minutes or even longer to produce a valid key.

The recent study [8] considers key generation for plugged-in IoT devices under the same setting as ours, but it leverages amplitudes of voltage harmonics that are consistent only among nearby outlets. Thus, when the inter-device distance increases (e.g., 10 m), the key matching rate can significantly decrease.

Finally, our work is also relevant to studies that exploit conducted EMI for side channel inference/attacks [26,27,39]. Nonetheless, PowerKey is novel in that it exploits EMI spike frequencies for an orthogonal and important goal—secret key generation.

9   Conclusion

In this paper, we proposed a novel key generation approach, called PowerKey, based on EMI spikes in an authenticated electrical domain. PowerKey includes an offline pre-processing stage to identify common EMI spikes as well as run-time extraction of EMI spike frequency for key generation. For evaluation, we conducted real experiments in two different locations—one research lab and one suite with multiple offices. Our results demonstrated that PowerKey can successfully generate secret keys in a robust and reasonably fast manner (i.e., with 100% key matching rate at a bit generation rate of up to 52.7 bits/sec).

Appendix

Experiment Setup. We conduct experiments in two different trust domains—an office suite with multiple individual rooms (Fig. 8(a)) and a research lab (Fig. 8(b)).

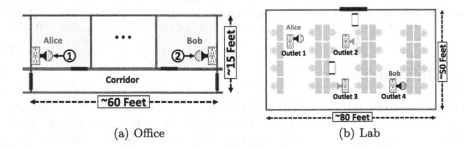

(a) Office   (b) Lab

Fig. 8. (a) Layout of the office. (b) Layout of the lab.

Analysis of EMI Spike Frequencies in the Office Suite. We show the histograms of the 8 independent EMI spike frequencies and the frequency differences at two outlets in Fig. 9 and Fig. 10, respectively. We see that the two outlets share certain time-varying EMI spike frequencies with only minor differences.

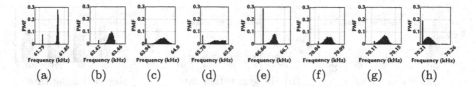

Fig. 9. Histogram of 8 different EMI spike frequencies in the office suite.

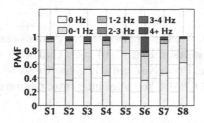

Fig. 10. Distribution of frequency differences between two outlets for 8 different EMI spike frequencies in the office suite. "S-n" means the n-the EMI spike. $\sigma = 1, 1, 1, 1, 1, 4, 1, 1$ Hz for the 8 EMI spike windows, respectively.

Results for Key Generation in the Lab. We now run experiments in a lab with 20+ desktops shown in Fig. 8(b).

Analysis of EMI Spike Frequencies. After offline pre-processing, PowerKey identifies a total of 11 EMI spikes for the lab. Then, as shown in correlation analysis in Fig. 11(a), 8 of the 11 spikes are uncorrelated, while the remaining ones are redundant and need to be removed.

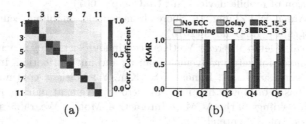

Fig. 11. (a) Correlation coefficients of EMI spike frequencies in the lab. (b) Key matching rate for four devices in the lab.

Key Generation Performance. We show the key generation performance for the lab. The main results are deferred to Fig. 12. We can see that in terms of all the evaluation metrics, the performance of PowerKey is consistent with that in the office setting. Likewise, the attacker can barely obtain secret keys successfully, with a high bit error rate and practically zero key matching rate.

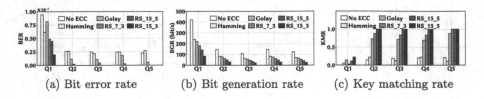

(a) Bit error rate   (b) Bit generation rate   (c) Key matching rate

Fig. 12. Performance of PowerKey in the lab.

Multiple Devices. Next, we consider four devices associated with four outlets in Fig. 8(b). Our results in Fig. 11(b) show that with an appropriate quantization and ECC scheme, PowerKey can still generate secret keys with a negligible bit error rate and almost 100% key matching rate, demonstrating its reliable key generation.

References

1. Yan, Z., Song, Q., Tan, R., Li, Y., Kong, A.W.K.: Towards touch-to-access device authentication using induced body electric potentials. In: MobiCom (2019)
2. Jana, S., Premnath, S.N., Clark, M., Kasera, S.K., Patwari, N., Krishnamurthy, S.V.: On the effectiveness of secret key extraction from wireless signal strength in real environments. In: MobiCom (2009)
3. Xi, W., et al.: Instant and robust authentication and key agreement among mobile devices. In: CCS (2016)
4. Mathur, S., Miller, R., Varshavsky, A., Trappe, W., Mandayam, N.: Proximate: proximity-based secure pairing using ambient wireless signals. In: MobiSys (2011)
5. Varshavsky, A., Scannell, A., LaMarca, A., de Lara, E.: Amigo: proximity-based authentication of mobile devices. In: UbiComp (2007)
6. Yang, L., Wang, W., Zhang, Q.: Secret from muscle: enabling secure pairing with electromyography. In: SenSys (2016)
7. West, J., et al.: Demo abstract: VoltKey: continuous secret key generation based on power line noise for zero-involvement pairing and authentication. In: IPSN (2019)
8. Lee, K., Klingensmith, N., Banerjee, S., Kim, Y.: Voltkey: continuous secret key generation based on power line noise for zero-involvement pairing and authentication. In: Proceedings of the ACM on Interactive, Mobile, Wearable and Ubiquitous Technologies, vol. 3, September 2019
9. Mathur, S., Trappe, W., Mandayam, N., Ye, C., Reznik, A.: Radio-telepathy: extracting a secret key from an unauthenticated wireless channel. In: MobiCom (2008)
10. Xie, P., Feng, J., Cao, Z., Wang, J.: Genewave: fast authentication and key agreement on commodity mobile devices. IEEE/ACM Trans. Netw. **26**, 1688–1700 (2018)
11. Miettinen, M., Asokan, N., Nguyen, T.D., Sadeghi, A.-R., Sobhani, M.: Context-based zero-interaction pairing and key evolution for advanced personal devices. In: CCS (2014)
12. Miettinen, M., Nguyen, T.D., Sadeghi, A.-R., Asokan, N.: Revisiting context-based authentication in IoT. In: DAC (2018)

13. Wang, W., Yang, L., Zhang, Q., Jiang, T.: Securing on-body IoT devices by exploiting creeping wave propagation. IEEE J. Selected Areas Commun. **36**, 696–703 (2018)
14. Luo, Z., Wang, W., Xiao, J., Huang, Q., Jiang, T., Zhang, Q.: Authenticating on-body backscatter by exploiting propagation signatures. In: Proceedings of the ACM on Interactive, Mobile, Wearable and Ubiquitous Technologies, vol. 2, pp. 123:1–123:22, September 2018
15. Lu, Y., Wu, F., Tang, S., Kong, L., Chen, G.: Free: a fast and robust key extraction mechanism via inaudible acoustic signal. In: MobiHoc (2019)
16. Zhang, J., Duong, T.Q., Marshall, A., Woods, R.: Key generation from wireless channels: a review. IEEE Access **4**, 614–626 (2016)
17. Wan, J., Lopez, A.B., Al Faruque, M.A.: Exploiting wireless channel randomness to generate keys for automotive cyber-physical system security. In: ICCPS (2016)
18. On Semiconductor, "Power factor correction (PFC) handbook". http://www.onsemi.com/pub/Collateral/HBD853-D.PDF
19. On Semiconductor, "Switch-mode power supply reference manual." https://www.onsemi.com/pub/Collateral/SMPSRM-D.PDF
20. Pressman, A.: Switching Power Supply Design. McGraw-Hill Inc, 2 ed. (1998)
21. Wikipedia, "Electromagnetic interference." https://en.wikipedia.org/wiki/Electromagnetic_interference
22. Gulati, M., Ram, S.S., Singh, A.: An in depth study into using EMI signatures for appliance identification. In: BuildSys (2014)
23. Callan, R., Zajić, A., Prvulovic, M.: A practical methodology for measuring the side-channel signal available to the attacker for instruction-level events. In: MICRO (2014)
24. Electronic Code of U.S. Federal Regulations, "Unintentional radiators, section 15.107 – conducted limits' (2018)
25. Cohn, G., Morris, D., Patel, S.N., Tan, D.S.: Your noise is my command: Sensing gestures using the body as an antenna. In: CHI (2011)
26. Enev, M., Gupta, S., Kohno, T., Patel, S.N.: Televisions, video privacy, and powerline electromagnetic interference. In: CCS (2011)
27. Shao, Z., Islam, M.A., Ren, S.: Your noise, my signal: exploiting switching noise for stealthy data exfiltration from desktop computers. In: Proc. ACM Meas. Anal. Comput. Syst., vol. 4, May 2020
28. Gupta, S., Reynolds, M.S., Patel, S.N.: Electrisense: single-point sensing using EMI for electrical event detection and classification in the home. In: UbiComp (2010)
29. Islam, M.A., Ren, S.: Ohm's law in data centers: a voltage side channel for timing power attacks. In: CCS (2018)
30. Viswanathan, S., Tan, R., Yau, D.K.Y.: Exploiting electrical grid for accurate and secure clock synchronization. ACM Trans. Sen. Netw. **14**, 12:1–12:32 (2018)
31. Li, Y., Tan, R., Yau, D.K.Y.: Natural timestamps in powerline electromagnetic radiation. ACM Trans. Sen. Netw. **14**, 13:1–13:30 (2018)
32. Arch Toolbox, "Electrical power systems in buildings." https://www.archtoolbox.com/materials-systems/electrical/electrical-power-systems.html
33. Goldsmith, A.: Wireless Communications. Cambridge University Press, Cambridge (2005)
34. IEEE Standards Association, "IEEE draft standard for broadband over power line networks: Medium access control and physical layer specifications amendment: Enhancement for internet of things applications" (2018). https://standards.ieee.org/project/1901a.html

35. Kanungo, T., Mount, D.M., Netanyahu, N.S., Piatko, C.D., Silverman, R., Wu, A.Y.: An efficient k-means clustering algorithm: analysis and implementation. IEEE Trans. Pattern Anal. Mach. Intell. **24**, 881–892 (2002)
36. Clark, G.C., Cain, J.B.: Error-Correction Coding for Digital Communications, 1st edn. Springer Publishing Company Incorporated, New York (2013). https://doi.org/10.1007/978-1-4899-2174-1
37. Wikipedia, "Advanced encryption standard." https://en.wikipedia.org/wiki/Advanced_Encryption_Standard
38. MathWorks, "Run test for randomness." https://www.mathworks.com/help/stats/runstest.html
39. Pu, Q., Gupta, S., Gollakota, S., Patel, S.: Whole-home gesture recognition using wireless signals. In: MobiCom (2013)

On the Vulnerability of Hyperdimensional Computing-Based Classifiers to Adversarial Attacks

Fangfang Yang and Shaolei Ren[✉]

University of California, Riverside, USA
sren@ece.ucr.edu

Abstract. Hyperdimensional computing (HDC) has been emerging as a brain-inspired in-memory computing architecture, exhibiting ultra energy efficiency, low latency and strong robustness against hardware-induced bit errors. Nonetheless, state-of-the-art designs for HDC classifiers are mostly security-oblivious, raising concerns with their safety and immunity to adversarial inputs. In this paper, we study for the first time adversarial attacks on HDC classifiers and highlight that HDC classifiers can be vulnerable to even minimally-perturbed adversarial samples. Specifically, using handwritten digit classification as an example, we construct a HDC classifier and formulate a grey-box attack problem, where an attacker's goal is to mislead the target HDC classifier to produce erroneous prediction labels while keeping the amount of added perturbation noise as little as possible. Then, we propose a modified genetic algorithm to generate adversarial samples within a reasonably small number of queries, and further apply critical gene crossover and perturbation adjustment to limit the amount of perturbation noise. Our results show that adversarial images can successfully mislead the HDC classifier to produce wrong prediction labels with a high probability (i.e., 78% when the HDC classifier uses a fixed majority rule for decision).

1 Introduction

Brain-inspired hyperdimensional computing (HDC) has emerged as an ultra-lightweight *classification* framework and architecture [1–3]. Specifically, HDC exploits the key principle that human brain "computes" based on certain patterns formed by a large number of neurons, without being directly associated with numbers [3]. Instead of computing with numbers like in today's deep neural networks (DNNs), a HDC classifier mimics the way brain cognition works by representing information using a hypervector with binary elements in a very high-dimensional space (e.g., with a dimensionality of $D = 10^4$ or more) [2].

HDC is inherently "in-memory" due to their binarized hypervectors and can be performed using basic logical operations like XOR without the need of sophisticated computation [3]. As a result, HDC classifiers offer several key advantages over conventional DNN-based classifiers, including extremely high energy efficiency, low latency, and strong robustness against hardware-induced component failures

© Springer Nature Switzerland AG 2020
M. Kutyłowski et al. (Eds.): NSS 2020, LNCS 12570, pp. 371–387, 2020.
https://doi.org/10.1007/978-3-030-65745-1_22

[2,3]. For example, recent studies have shown that the energy consumption and inference latency of HDC classifiers are lower by orders of magnitude than their DNN counterparts, yet achieving a reasonable inference accuracy [4–6].

HDC classifiers have been increasingly recognized as an alternative to or even replacement of DNNs for classification on edge devices with stringent resource constraints [2,3,7]. The quickly expanding list of applications building on HDC classifiers have already included language classification [8], image classification [1,9], emotion recognition based on physiological signals [10], distributed fault isolation in power plants [11], gesture recognition for wearable devices [6], and seizure onset detection and identification of ictogenic brain regions [12]. Nonetheless, the security aspect of HDC classifiers remains under-explored. This can raise serious concerns with the safety of HDC classifiers and limit their wider adoption, especially in mission-critical applications such as robot navigation and health monitoring [12,13].

Contribution. In this paper, we make a first-of-its-kind effort to investigate the potential vulnerability of emerging HDC classifiers. More concretely, we consider a threat model in which an attacker can launch grey-box attacks by repeatedly sending perturbed images to the HDC classifier and receiving the Hamming distance output as well as the prediction label from the classifier. We propose a modified genetic algorithm, called Genetic Algorithm with Critical Gene Crossover and Perturbation Adjustment (GA-CGC-PA). GA-CGC-PA only modifies critical genes (i.e., selected important pixels) and iteratively searches for the best candidate adversarial image. GA-CGC-PA also applies perturbation adjustment to further reduce the amount of perturbation noise added to the original benign image. Our evaluation results on handwritten digit classification demonstrate that, for most benign images, the attacker can add a reasonably small amount of perturbation noise and create adversarial images within a limited number of iterations, successfully misleading the target HDC classifier to a wrong prediction label.

2   Preliminaries on HDC Classifiers

In HDC, each hypervector is a pseudorandom D-dimensional vector taken by default from $\{-1, 1\}^D$ [1]. Given two hypervectors, Hamming distance (i.e., the number of distinct binary elements) is commonly used as a distance metric to measure their similarity. For the convenience of presentation, Hamming distance is often normalized with respect to the dimensionality D. Thus, two orthogonal hypervectors have a (normalized) Hamming distance of 0.5.

2.1   Random Indexing

A HDC classifier projects data onto a hyperdimensional space via random indexing. The almost-certain orthogonality due to the large dimensionality of D demonstrates that any two randomly chosen hypervectors are orthogonal or quasi-orthogonal with an extremely high likelihood [1–3]. In a hyperdimensional space, there are enormous hypervectors that are orthogonal to each other. Such uncorrelated hypervectors can be used to represent various types of information or features of an object, such as 26 letters in the alphabet set. The hypervectors representing the basic features are called *basis* hypervectors, which remain unchanged in an application once randomly chosen.

2.2 Multiply-Add-Permute Operation

The most widely-used HDC operation is Multiply-Add-Permute (MAP).

Binding (Multiplication). Given hypervectors HV_1 and HV_2, binding operation performs element-wise multiplication, denoted as $HV_1 \otimes HV_2$. The operation is used to represent the association of related hypervectors. The resulting hypervector of binding is orthogonal to both of its constituents [3].

Superposition (Addition). Superposition of $HV_1, \cdots, HV_M$ is an element-wise addition of hypervectors denoted as $HV_1 \oplus \cdots \oplus HV_M$. Superposition aims to generate a sum hypervector HV', which can represent a set of operand hypervectors and aggregate information conveyed by them. According to Hebbian Learning, after superposition, any of the constituents is more similar to HV' than a randomly generated hypervector [14,15].

If the component value of the resultant after addition is positive (i.e., there are more 1s than -1 s in superposition), it is converted to 1 and otherwise -1. In the even that the component value of the resultant is zero, it is randomly encoded to 1 or -1 with equal probabilities, which we also refer to as the random majority rule (RMR) [16]. Alternatively, we can always assign 1 or -1 to the component value in such cases (i.e., fix majority rule, or FMR).

Permutation. The permutation operation generates a dissimilar hypervector by shuffling coordinates of the original hypervector in a pseudo-random manner. A hypervector HV permuted n times is denoted as $\rho^n(HV)$. Permutation is used to store and differentiate the sequence of elements. For example, the letter sequence *abc* can be distinguished from *bac* by permutation.

3 A HDC Classifier on MNIST Dataset

As a proof of concept, we construct a HDC classifier on the MNIST dataset [17] for digit recognition, while noting that designing HDC classifiers for more complex tasks is still an active research direction [1].

3.1 Mapping

Considering that there are $28 \times 28 = 784$ pixels in an image in MNIST, we employ orthogonal distributed mapping to encode the position information of each pixel. Concretely, we assign a random hypervector to each position (called *position* hypervector), which automatically ensures that the 784 position hypervectors are distinct and quasi-orthogonal to each other due to the hyperdimensionality. We store these position hypervectors in a look-up table, which is referred to as position memory. Next, we map pixel values to hypervectors, which are called

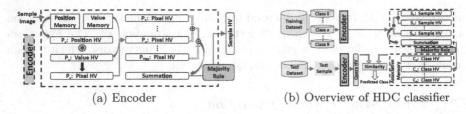

(a) Encoder   (b) Overview of HDC classifier

Fig. 1. (a) The encoder in our HDC classifier encodes a digital image (called sample image) to a sample hypervector. (b) The overview of the HDC classifier. An associative memory storing class hypervectors is generated using the training dataset. Then, a test sample can be classified based on its similarity to class hypervectors.

value hypervectors. Clearly, different pixel values are correlated. To preserve similarity of pixel values, we adopt the distance preserving mapping technique and create linearly similar value hypervectors to represent 256 pixel levels, since each pixel value in the MNIST dataset is stored as a 8-bit integer. Typically, the value hypervectors associated with the minimum and maximum pixel values are orthogonal. To do so, we initially pick a random hypervector to represent the minimal pixel value of 0. Then, starting from the initial value hypervector associated with the minimum pixel value, we generate a new value hypervector for the next pixel value by randomly flipping $\frac{D}{2 \times 255}$ elements of the preceding value hypervector each time. By doing so, we get 256 value hypervectors, including two orthogonal value hypervectors that represent the maximum and minimum pixel values. The 256 value hypervectors are stored in a value memory.

3.2 HDC Classifier

Like in conventional classification models [18], a HDC classifier also consists of a training stage and a testing/inference stage, as illustrated in Fig. 1(b).

Training. Figure 1(a) illustrates our HDC encoder. Specifically, for each pixel, a pixel hypervector is computed by multiplying the corresponding position hypervector and value hypervector. Next, we add up all the 784 pixel hypervectors and binarize the resulting hypervector using the majority rule, thus generating a sample hypervector that represents the sample image in a hyperdimensional space. To generate a class hypervector, we encode all the sample images in this class into the corresponding sample hypervectors, which are then combined using the superposition/addition operation. Similarly, the majority rule is adopted to guarantee the class hypervector to be binary. Each class hypervector represents the "center" of all sample hypervectors in that class.

Testing/Inference. For testing or inference, using the same encoder as that in the training stage, each new image is first encoded into a query hypervector. Next, we compare the similarity of the query hypervector to each class hypervector in the associative memory in terms of the (normalized) Hamming distance. The HDC classifier will return the label of the class hypervector, which has the minimum Hamming distance to the query hypervector.

4   Threat Model

We focus on a grey-box scenario where the attacker can (repeatedly) send images to the target HDC classifier and obtain the corresponding prediction labels. In addition, for each image, the attacker is also able to receive the Hamming distances between the image's query hypervector and each class hypervector, which thus forms our grey-box model. Our assumption of the attacker's knowing the Hamming distances is the counterpart of knowing softmax probabilities for attacks on standard DNN classifiers.

In the MNIST dataset with $K = 10$ classes, we denote the pixel representation of an input image in a vector form as $X \in \mathbb{R}^{784}$. Then, given the target HDC classifier, we use $\mathbf{f}(X) = [f_1(X), \cdots, f_K(X)] \in [0,1]^K$ to represent the normalized Hamming distances between the input X's hypervector and the K class hypervectors. The prediction class label t_X is decided as the one with the minimum Hamming distance.

Given a benign image X with its true class label t_0, the attacker would like to create an adversarially perturbed image $\tilde{X} \in \mathbb{R}^{784}$ such that the predicted label $t_{\tilde{X}} = \arg\min_k\{\mathbf{f}(\tilde{X})\}$ for $\tilde{X}$ differs from the true label t_0. Formally, we can define the objective function as

$$g(\tilde{X}, t_0) = \max\{\min_{k \neq t_0}[\mathbf{f}(\tilde{X})] - f_{t_0}(\tilde{X}), -\epsilon\}, \tag{1}$$

where $\min_{k \neq t_0}[\mathbf{f}(\tilde{X})]$ is the minimum Hamming distance of the perturbed image to any of the class hypervectors with wrong labels, $f_{t_0}(\tilde{X})$ is the Hamming distance of the perturbed image to the true class hypervector, and a small constant $\epsilon > 0$ indicates that the attacker does not need to add further perturbation if its attack is already successful (i.e., $\min_{k \neq t_0}[\mathbf{f}(\tilde{X})] - f_{t_0}(\tilde{X})$ is already less than $-\epsilon$). Thus, by minimizing $g(\tilde{X}, t_0)$, the attacker can effectively increase the Hamming distance of the perturbed image to the true class hypervector, misleading the HDC classifier to a wrong prediction label.

Meanwhile, the attacker also needs to keep its perturbation to the original image X as minimum as possible. Concretely, the attacker obtains $\tilde{X}$ by minimizing the following regularized objective function:

$$\min_{\tilde{X}} \left\{ g(\tilde{X}, t_0) + c \cdot \|\tilde{X} - X\| \right\}, \tag{2}$$

where $\|\tilde{X} - X\|$ is a certain norm that quantifies the difference between $\tilde{X}$ and X, and $c \geq 0$ adjusts the weight for regularization. We can also add multiple norms for regularization. For example, L_2 norm controls the squared difference between two images' pixel values, while L_∞ controls the maximum difference between two images' pixel values.

5   A Modified Genetic Algorithm

We first describe a basic genetic algorithm and then propose modifications so as to reduce the amount of perturbation introduced to the original benign input.

Algorithm 1. Modified Genetic Algorithm (GA-CGC-PA)

Input:
Original input X, true label t_0, population size N, maximum iteration $I_{\max}$
Output: adversarial sample $\tilde{X}$

  1   Create the initial generation P^0 from X.
  2   $G_{curr} \leftarrow P^0$
  3   **for** $ite = 1$ to $I_{\max}$ **do**
  4   Compute fitness score of each member in G_{curr}
  5   Find elite $Eli = \arg\max_{x \in G_{curr}} fitness(x)$
  6   Save Eli as a member of next generation G_{next}
  7   **if** $\arg\min_k(\mathbf{f}(Eli)) \neq t_0$ **then**
  8           $\tilde{X} \leftarrow Eli$
  9   **return** $\tilde{X}$
10   **break**
11   **endif**
12   Compute selection probability P_{sel} of G_{curr}
13   **for** $num{=}2$ to N **do**
14   Choose parents in G_{curr} according to P_{sel}
15   Apply Critical Gene Crossover (Algorithm 2)
16   Apply clipping and add clipped child to G_{next}
17   **endfor**
18       $G_{curr} \leftarrow G_{next}$
19   **endfor**
20   Apply Perturbation Adjustment (Algorithm 3)

5.1   Genetic Algorithm

The optimization problem in Eq. (2) involves non-convex integer programming, and $\mathbf{f}(\cdot)$ is non-differentiable and unknown to the attacker. Here, to solve Eq. (2), we propose a modified genetic algorithm, called Genetic Algorithm with Critical Gene Crossover and Perturbation Adjustment (GA-CGC-PA). Concretely, GA-CGC-PA described in Algorithm 1 takes an original input image as an ancestor, from which the first generation of population is generated by natural mutation. A basic genetic algorithm includes four main steps—population initialization, member selection, crossover, and mutation—as described in detail below.

Population Initialization. The first generation is initialized by applying uniformly distributed random noise in the allowed range $(-\sigma_{max}, \sigma_{max})$ to each gene of the ancestor X. For the MNIST dataset, each gene corresponds to one pixel. In total, there are $28 \times 28 = 784$ genes in each individual member, and the algorithm creates N members in each generation.

Member Selection. The quality of each population member is evaluated by computing a fitness score according to the fitness function (additive inverse of

Eq. 2). Population members with higher fitness scores are more likely to be selected to reproduce the next generation, whereas members with lower fitness scores are replaced with a higher probability. Towards this end, we compute the softmax of the fitness scores in one generation to obtain the selection probability distribution of the population. We then randomly choose pairs of parents to breed offsprings according to the softmax probability distribution. In order to save the member with the highest fitness score (called *elite* member) in one generation, an elitism technique [19] is employed, where the genes of the elite member are exactly cloned by a member in the next generation.

Crossover. Our algorithm makes use of uniform crossover to mate two parents. Each gene of an offspring is produced by combining genes of both parents, $Parent_1$ and $Parent_2$, according to the probability distribution $(p, 1 - p)$. We get p through dividing the fitness of the first parent P_1 by the sum fitness of both parents. Thus, the child's genes are given as follows:

$$child = p \times Parent_1 + (1 - p) \times Parent_2. \qquad (3)$$

Nonetheless, since it is required that the perturbation made to the original image be kept as minimum as possible, we reduce the number of perturbed genes (pixels) by using a modified version of uniform crossover, which we call critical gene crossover as described in Sect. 5.2.

Mutation. In order to promote diversity within a generation and improve the search power of the genetic algorithm, the child generated by crossover has to be mutated and clipped before becoming a member of the next generation. Like population initialization, random noise is sampled uniformly from a range $(-\sigma_{max}, \sigma_{max})$ and added to the chromosome of the child with a mutation probability ρ. Considering that a feasible solution has to possess a reasonable gene (e.g. pixel value for MNIST dataset), a mutated child is clipped to ensure that its genes are all within an allowable range.

5.2   Modification for Perturbation Reduction

While the basic genetic algorithm can generate an adversarial image to fool the HDC classifier, the amount of perturbation can be really significant (see Fig. 2(b) for an example), making the adversarial input more easily identified by human perception. Here, we propose to use *critical gene crossover* and *perturbation adjustment* to significantly reduce the amount of perturbation.

Critical Gene Crossover. The standard uniform crossover modifies each pixel of the original image, which unnecessarily introduces redundant perturbation. To reduce perturbation, we propose critical gene crossover to selectively cross the parents' most important genes. To do so, we first make a child by duplicating the parent with the higher fitness score and then select critical genes using the max

---

Algorithm 2. Critical Gene Crossover

Input:
$Parent_1$ and $Parent_2$, crossover probability $(p, 1 - p)$ of $Parent_1$ and $Parent_2$ with $p > 1 - p$, maximum L_∞ mutation distance σ_{max}, mutation probability ρ, critical threshold β

Output: $child$

1 $child \leftarrow Parent_1$.
2 Apply 2×2 max pooling: $child' = maxpooling(child)$
3 Up-sample $child'$ to the original dimension $28 \times 28 = 784$
4 Normalize values of $child'$: $child' = \frac{child' - min(child')}{max(child')}$
5 Find indexes of critical genes such that $child'[idx] > \beta$
6 Update critical genes of $child$
   $child[idx] = p \times Parent_1[idx] + (1 - p) \times Parent_2[idx]$
7 Mutate $child$
   $child[idx] = child[idx] + B(1, \rho) \times \mu(-\sigma_{max}, \sigma_{max})$
8 **return** $child$

Algorithm 3. Perturbation Adjustment

Input:
Original image X, true label t_0, adversarial image $\tilde{X}$

1   Find an index list $\mathcal{L}$ for pixels that differ in X and $\tilde{X}$
2   **for** p in $\mathcal{L}$ **do**
3       $v_{ori} \leftarrow X[p]$
4       $v_{adv} \leftarrow \tilde{X}[p]$
5   **for** $v = v_{ori}$ to v_{adv} **do**
6           $\tilde{X}[p] = v$
7   **if** $\arg\min_k(\mathbf{f}(\tilde{X})) \neq t_0$ **then**
8   **break**
9   **endif**
10   **endfor**
11 **endfor**

---

pooling operation. Next, we renew the critical genes by uniformly crossing those of the two parents. The detailed steps are described in Algorithm 2. We define critical genes as the ones that mostly differentiate images of different classes. For the example of the MNIST dataset, pixels that are close to and form the digit are more important than others that have lower pixel values and mostly form the background, and hence can be chosen as critical genes.

Perturbation Adjustment. Considering the fact that the genetic algorithm generates random mutation in each generation and thus can introduce unnecessary modification to the original image, we propose to further reduce the perturbation by using perturbation adjustment while still keeping the adversarial

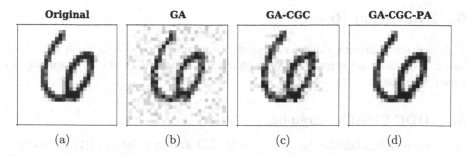

Fig. 2. Comparison of different adversarial attacks that mislead the HDC classifier to classify "6" as "2". (a) Original benign image. (b) Adversarial image by basic genetic algorithm (GA). (c) Adversarial image by genetic algorithm with critical gene crossover (GA-CGC). (d) Adversarial image by our proposed genetic algorithm with critical gene crossover and perturbation adjustment (GA-CGC-PA).

attack successful. Our perturbation adjustment technique is described in Algorithm 3. It starts by finding an index list $\mathcal{L}$ of modified pixels in the adversarial image compared to the original image. For each pixel in the list $\mathcal{L}$, its value is restored to the original value v_{ori}. Then, we gradually change the value towards the adversarial value v_{adv} and stop this process until the adversarial image can successfully mislead the HDC classifier to a wrong prediction.

5.3   Effect of Perturbation Reduction

We present an example of adversarial attacks on the digit "6" using three different algorithms in Fig. 2: standard genetic algorithm without modification (GA), modified genetic algorithm with only critical gene crossover (GA-CGC), and modified genetic algorithm with both critical gene crossover and perturbation adjustment (GA-CGC-PA). The HDC classifier is trained on the MNIST dataset as described in Sect. 6.1. In all the three attacks, the HDC classifier misclassifies the digit "6" as "2". Figure 2(a) shows the original benign image for digit "6" which can be correctly classified by the HDC classifier, while Fig. 2(b) shows the adversarial image using GA. We can clearly see that many pixels in the original image are modified and added with perturbation noise, making the adversarial image easily identifiable. Figure 2(c) shows the adversarial image generated by GA-CGC after using critical gene crossover. Compared with the result in Fig. 2(b), many background pixels in Fig. 2(c) are left unchanged and only pixels surrounding the digit are altered. By using GA-CGC-PA with further perturbation adjustment, the adversarial image is shown in Fig. 2(d), which looks very similar to the original benign image but is still misclassified by the HDC classifier as "2". The number of pixels modified is largely reduced from 438 (by GA)to 9 (by GA-CGC-PA). This shows the clear advantage of GA-CGC-PA over the basic genetic algorithm and only using critical gene crossover, in terms of reducing the amount of perturbation in adversarial images.

6   Evaluation Results

This section validates the effectiveness of our proposed GA-CGC-PA for adversarial attacks on a target HDC classifier using handwritten digit recognition for proof of concept.

6.1   HDC Classifier Training

We train a HDC classifier based on the MNIST training dataset [17] as an example. The dimensionality for each hypervector is $D = 10^4$. Then, as described in Sect. 3, we encode each training sample into a sample hypervector and obtain 10 class hypervectors based on the training dataset. Next, we project each test image into a query hypervector and compare it against class hypervectors. Recalling that in the hypervector encoding process, we use the majority rule for vector binarization. By using the random majority rule (RMR) that randomly assigns 1 or -1 in the rare event that the sum is zero after superposition operation, the HDC classifier may assign different labels in different inferences for the same input. To eliminate this uncertainty, we can also apply the fixed majority rule (FMR) that always assigns 1 or -1.

For the HDC classifier with RMR, we execute 1,000 rounds of classification for each test image to calculate the average accuracy, which we also refer to as *per-image* accuracy. Our HDC classifier can assign correct labels with 100% per-image accuracy for around 70% of the test images, while it behaves less confidently and sometimes yields misclassified results for the remaining images. Consequently, the test images that have 100% per-image accuracy are harder to attack (called *hard* cases) than those with a lower per-image accuracy (called *vulnerable* case). In other words, vulnerable images can be considered already "adversarial" to our HDC classifier to some extent. The overall accuracy of our HDC classifier is lower than that of DNNs [7], and can be improved by enlarging the MNIST dataset, which is beyond the scope of our work. We will show later, GA-CGC-PA can successfully mislead the HDC classifier with a high probability regardless of hard or vulnerable cases.

While the MNIST dataset is admittedly simple, we view it as an important proof of concept and starting point to study the vulnerability of emerging HDC classifiers. Importantly, our attack strategy based on genetic algorithms in Sect. 5 is general and applies to any HDC classifiers without being restricted to the MNIST example.

6.2   Attack on HDC Classifier with RMR

We first evaluate GA-CGC-PA with the random majority rule (RMR) for the HDC classifier. We use a population size $N = 6$, mutation probability $\rho = 0.05$, max pooling size 2×2, and critical threshold $\beta = 0$.

We focus on attacking the hard cases (i.e., those images with 100% per-image accuracy), while noting that the already-vulnerable images (i.e., those with less than 100% per-image accuracy) are even easier to attack. Figure 7 in

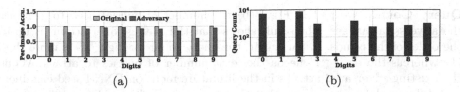

(a)   (b)

Fig. 3. (a) Per-image accuracies of benign/adversarial images shown in Fig. 7 (b) Query counts needed to generate adversarial images shown in Fig. 7.

Table 1. Perturbation for Images Shown in Fig. 7

Digit	0	1	2	3	4	5	6	7	8	9
# Modified Pixels	289	160	260	196	185	241	177	192	256	253
L_2-distance	4.626	5.073	3.02	3.703	1.37	3.028	2.58	4.017	2.029	1.537
L_∞-distance	0.867	0.968	0.643	0.956	0.276	0.653	0.737	0.92	0.401	0.271

the appendix visually illustrates the benign input images, adversarial perturbation noise, and the corresponding adversarial images. The adversarial images can significantly decrease the HDC classifier's performance, while they are still clearly recognizable by human eyes. Next, we show the corresponding per-image accuracies of both original images and adversarial ones in Fig. 3(a). It can be clearly seen that, with GA-CGC-PA, all the images become vulnerable with a per-accuracy lower than 100%. In particular, the sample images for digits "0" and "8" in Fig. 7 have the lowest accuracy after attacks and hence are easier to attack than others.

Amount of Perturbation. Next, we quantify the adversarial perturbation noise generated and added to the benign images. To have a successful attack, the adversarial images need to not only deceive the HDC classifier but also have as small perturbation as possible compared to benign ones. To this end, the amount of perturbation is an important metric to evaluate the attack algorithm. As in the prior studies on adversarial machine learning [20], we use L_0 norm, L_2 norm, and L_∞ norms to measure the amount of perturbation. Note that while L_0 is not a mathematical norm, it is commonly used to quantify the total number of modified pixels in our context. By definition, L_2 norm indicates the overall perturbation noise added to a benign image, while L_∞ norm measures the maximum per-pixel perturbation noise.

Table 1 shows the three norm distances for the perturbation noise added to the benign images shown in Fig. 7. It is worth noting that L_2 and L_∞ norms are calculated over the images with normalized pixel values in the range of $[0, 1]$. For all the adversarial images shown in Fig. 7, there are fewer than 300 modified pixels. While the L_∞ is large, the L_2 norm is reasonably small for most digits, indicating the overall perturbation added by GA-CGC-PA is not large, which can also be observed from Fig. 7.

Query Count. We plot in Fig. 3(b) the number of queries used to generate the adversarial images. The result shows that the average query count is up to the order of thousands. In particular, the query count for digit "2" is more than 7k, whereas the digit "4" needs the least number of queries to attack. While the existing adversarial attacks in the literature focus on DNN-based classifiers and different datasets, we note that they typically need an order of 10k or more queries to successfully attack an image [21,22].

6.3   Attack on HDC Classifier with FMR

We now turn to the fixed majority rule (FMR) such that the prediction label for a given image is fixed without uncertainties. The hyperparameters for GA-CGC-PA are the same as in Sect. 6.2.

Attack Success Rate. With FMR, the per-image accuracy is either 0 or 1. Thus, we randomly pick 200 correctly classified images for each digit from "0" to "9" from the MNIST dataset. For each image, we apply GA-CGC-PA to generate the corresponding adversarial image subject to a maximum query count of 10^5 (i.e., $I_{max} = 10^5$ in Algorithm 1). If an adversarial image is successfully generated to fool the HDC classifier within the query limit, it is regarded as a successful attack, and a failed attack otherwise.

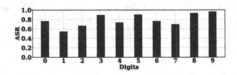

Fig. 4. ASR of digits 0–9 for HDC classifier with FMR.

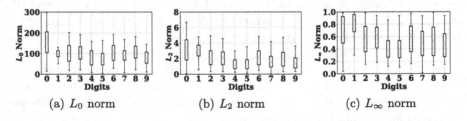

(a) L_0 norm   (b) L_2 norm   (c) L_∞ norm

Fig. 5. Box plot of perturbation noise added by GA-CGC-PA for the HDC classifier with FMR. Each box plot shows the values for the maximum/minimum/median/75th percentile/25th percentile, excluding outliers.

We compute the ASR over 200 images for each digit and present the results in Fig. 4. It can be seen that GA-CGC-PA is successful for all the digits in most cases, with digits "3", "5", "8" and "9" having the highest ASR. Considering the 10 digits altogether, we obtain an average ASR of 0.78.

Amount of Perturbation. We provide the bar plot of perturbation amount in terms of L_0, L_2 and L_∞ norms in Fig. 5. As one can see from the figure, the median number of modified pixels for most adversarial images is around 100. The L_2 norm for the majority of perturbation noise is between 2 and 4, whereas the L_∞ norm lies mostly between 0.3 and 0.8 for most images.

Additional results, i.e., query count and adversarial examples, are deferred to the appendix.

7 Related Works

Adversarial attacks on DNNs can be categorized into white-box attacks, black-box attacks, and grey-box attacks [20]. In a white-box attack, an attacker is assumed to know complete details about the target DNNs [23,24]. By contrast, in a black-box attack, only benign inputs and the corresponding prediction label (plus additional information such as softmax probabilities in a grey-box setting) are available to the attacker [22,25]. More recent studies on black-box or grey-box attacks have proposed to use gradient estimations to generate adversarial samples [26,27]. Nonetheless, these approaches are generally limited to differentiable objective functions, which is not the case in HDC classifiers that use MAP operation in a hyperdimensional space without differentiable objective functions.

Boundary attack is a gradient-free black-box attack, which uses an already-available adversarial sample as a reference [28,29]. Nonetheless, an adversarial sample is needed at the first place. Genetic algorithm is another effective approach to attacks on DNNs [21,22,30]. We leverage a genetic algorithm, but also modify it to reduce perturbation (see Fig. 2). Most importantly, we propose a new Hamming distance-based objective function that is tailored to the emerging HDC classifiers.

The existing studies on HDC classifiers have been predominantly focused on improving the energy efficiency, inference latency, privacy preservation, or architecture design [4–6,31–36]. Nonetheless, adversarial attacks on HDC classifiers have been neglected, raising serious concerns with their safety as they are being adopted in increasingly more applications including mission-critical scenarios [1,11–13]. Our study bridges the gap and demonstrates that, like their DNN counterparts, HDC classifiers can be vulnerable to adversarial inputs and hence need to be better safeguarded.

8 Conclusion

In this paper, we study adversarial attacks on HDC classifiers which are emerging for edge inference. We propose a modified genetic algorithm (GA-CGC-PA) to generate adversarial images with a reasonably small number of queries. Our results show that slightly-perturbed adversarial images generated by GA-CGC-PA can successfully mislead the HDC classifier to wrong prediction labels with a large probability. Future research includes more sophisticated attacks on HDC classifiers and, most importantly, effective *defense mechanisms*.

Appendix: Additional Results

Query Count for Attacks on HDC Classifier with FMR. We calculate the query counts for the successfully attacked images and show the results in a box plot in Fig. 6. We can notice that the median query count of all digits is less than 5,000, which is a reasonably good query efficiency for black-/grey-box attacks [21].

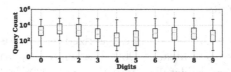

Fig. 6. Box plot of query count needed by GA-CGC-PA for the HDC classifier with FMR. Each box plot shows the values for the maximum/minimum/median/75th percentile/25th percentile, excluding outliers.

Table 2. Perturbation for Images Shown in Fig. 8 and Fig. 9. The values for Fig. 9 are shown in parentheses.

Digit	0	1	2	3	4	5	6	7	8	9
L_0	301(22)	123(82)	95(21)	104(107)	72(42)	117(34)	113(9)	74(86)	114(68)	97(45)
L_2	6.73(0.36)	4.48(0.95)	2.20(0.45)	0.82(0.65)	1.54(0.44)	0.69(0.66)	0.76(0.18)	1.90(1.12)	0.64(0.73)	0.72(0.49)
L_∞	0.92(0.21)	0.96(0.24)	0.69(0.21)	0.21(0.15)	0.53(0.13)	0.19(0.21)	0.23(0.16)	0.56(0.37)	0.18(0.25)	0.20(0.19)

Adversarial Examples. Finally, we visually show some adversarial examples for the HDC classifier with FMR. In the hard case, benign images would have a 100% per-image accuracy had the HDC classifier use RMR. In the vulnerable case, benign images are correctly classified by the HDC classifier with FMR, but would have less than 100% per-image accuracy had the classifier use RMR. That is, the vulnerable images are those borderline images that are already hard to be correctly classified by the HDC classifier.

The benign images, perturbation noise, and adversarial images for hard and vulnerable cases are shown in Fig. 8 and Fig. 9, respectively. Also, we give the amount of perturbation noises for the two cases in Table 2.

It is more difficult to launch successful attacks in the hard case than in the vulnerable case. Thus, as expected, the perturbation noise added by GA-CGC-PA in the hard case is generally more than in the vulnerable case. In particular, in the vulnerable case, the adversarial image is almost identical to the corresponding benign image by human perception. This can also be reflected from the perturbation noise figures and Table 2.

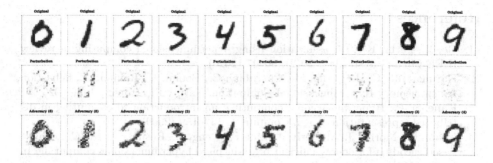

Fig. 7. Attacks on the HDC classifier with RMR. The first row shows the original images. The second row shows the perturbation noise added by the attacker. The third row shows the adversarial images, and the corresponding misclassified labels are given at the top of each image.

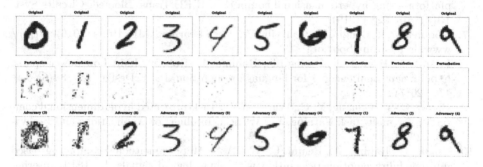

Fig. 8. Attacks on the HDC classifier with FMR (hard). The first row shows the original images. The second row shows the perturbation noise added by the attacker. The third row shows the adversarial images, and the corresponding misclassified labels are given at the top of each image.

Fig. 9. Attacks on the HDC classifier with FMR (vulnerable). The first row shows the original images. The second row shows the perturbation noise added by the attacker. The third row shows the adversarial images, and the corresponding misclassified labels are given at the top of each image.

References

1. Ge, L., Parhi, K.K.: Classification using hyperdimensional computing: a review. IEEE Circuits Syst. Mag. **20**(2), 30–47 (2020)
2. Karunaratne, G., Le Gallo, M., Cherubini, G., Benini, L., Rahimi, A., Sebastian, A.: In-memory Hyperdimensional Computing, Nature Electronics, June 2020
3. Kanerva, P.: Hyperdimensional computing: an introduction to computing in distributed representation. Cogn. Comput. **1**, 139–159 (2009)
4. Imani, M., Morris, J., Messerly, J., Shu, H., Deng, Y., Rosing, T.: BRIC: Locality-based encoding for energy-efficient brain-inspired hyperdimensional computing. In: DAC (2019)
5. Imani, M., Huang, C., Kong, D., Rosing, T.: Hierarchical hyperdimensional computing for energy efficient classification. In: DAC (2018)
6. Benatti, S., Montagna, F., Kartsch, V., Rahimi, A., Rossi, D., Benini, L.: Online learning and classification of EMG-based gestures on a parallel ultra-low power platform using hyperdimensional computing. IEEE Trans. Biomed. Circuits Syst. **13**(3), 516–528 (2019)
7. Goodfellow, I., Bengio, Y., Courville, A.: Deep Learning. MIT Press (2016). http://www.deeplearningbook.org
8. Imani, M., Hwang, J., Rosing, T., Rahimi, A., Rabaey, J.M.: Low-power sparse hyperdimensional encoder for language recognition. IEEE Design Test **34**(6), 94–101 (2017)
9. Chang, C.-Y., Chuang, Y.-C., Wu, A.-Y.A.: Task-projected hyperdimensional computing for multi-task learning. In: Artificial Intelligence Applications and Innovations (2020)
10. Chang, E., Rahimi, A., Benini, L., Wu, A.A.: Hyperdimensional computing-based multimodality emotion recognition with physiological signals. In: IEEE International Conference on Artificial Intelligence Circuits and Systems (2019)
11. Kleyko, D., Osipov, E., Papakonstantinou, N., Vyatkin, V.: Hyperdimensional computing in industrial systems: the use-case of distributed fault isolation in a power plant. IEEE Access **6**, 30766–30777 (2018)
12. Burrello, A., Schindler, K., Benini, L., Rahimi, A.: Hyperdimensional computing with local binary patterns: one-shot learning of seizure onset and identification of ictogenic brain regions using short-time ieeg recordings. IEEE Trans. Biomed. Eng. **67**(2), 601–613 (2020)
13. Mitrokhin, A., Sutor, P., Fermüller, C., Aloimonos, Y.: Learning sensorimotor control with neuromorphic sensors: toward hyperdimensional active perception. Sci. Robotics **4**(30), 1–10 (2019)
14. Plate, T.A.: Holographic reduced representations. IEEE Trans. Neural Networks **6**(3), 623–641 (1995)
15. Frady, E.P., Kleyko, D., Sommer, F.T.: A theory of sequence indexing and working memory in recurrent neural networks. Neural Comput. **30**(6), 1449–1513 (2018)
16. Kleyko, D., Rahimi, A., Rachkovskij, D., Osipov, E., Rabaey, J.: Classification and recall with binary hyperdimensional computing: tradeoffs in choice of density and mapping characteristics. IEEE Trans. Neural Netw. Learn. Syst. **29**, 1–19 (2018)
17. LeCun, Y., Cortes, C., Burges, C.J.C.: The MNIST database of handwritten digits. http://yann.lecun.com/exdb/mnist/
18. Mohri, M., Rostamizadeh, A., Talwalkar, A.: Foundations of Machine Learning. MIT press (2018)

19. Bhandari, D., Murthy, C., Pal, S.K.: Genetic algorithm with elitist model and its convergence. Int. J. Pattern Recognit. Artif. Intell. **10**(06), 731–747 (1996)
20. Ren, K., Zheng, T., Qin, Z., Liu, X.: Adversarial attacks and defenses in deep learning. Elsevier Eng. **6**(3), 346–360 (2020)
21. Alzantot, M., Sharma, Y., Chakraborty, S., Zhang, H., Hsieh, C.-J., Srivastava, M.B.: GenAttack: practical black-box attacks with gradient-free optimization. In: Genetic and Evolutionary Computation Conference (2019)
22. Liu, X., Luo, Y., Zhang, X., Zhu, Q.: A black-box attack on neural networks based on swarm evolutionary algorithm. Elsevier Comput. Secur. **85**, 89–106 (2019)
23. Akhtar, N., Mian, A.: Threat of adversarial attacks on deep learning in computer vision: a survey. IEEE Access **6**, 14410–14430 (2018)
24. Carlini, N., Wagner, D.: Towards evaluating the robustness of neural networks. In: S&P (2017)
25. Papernot, N., McDaniel, P., Goodfellow, I., Jha, S., Celik, Z.B., Swami, A.: Practical black-box attacks against machine learning. In: AsiaCCS (2017)
26. Chen, P.-Y., Zhang, H., Sharma, Y., Yi, J., Hsieh, C.-J.: Zoo: zeroth order optimization based black-box attacks to deep neural networks without training substitute models. In: AISec (2017)
27. Tu, C.-C., et al.: AutoZoom: autoencoder-based zeroth order optimization method for attacking black-box neural networks. In: AAAI (2019)
28. Brendel, W., Rauber, J., Bethge, M.: Decision-based adversarial attacks: reliable attacks against black-box machine learning models. In: ICLR (2018)
29. Narodytska, N., Kasiviswanathan, S.: Simple black-box adversarial attacks on deep neural networks. In: CVPR Workshops (2017)
30. Xu, W., Qi, Y., Evans, D.: Automatically evading classifiers: a case study on PDF malware classifiers. In: NDSS (2016)
31. Khaleghi, B., Imani, M., Rosing, T.: Prive-HD: privacy-preserved hyperdimensional computing. In: DAC (2020)
32. Imani, M., et al.: SemiHD: semi-supervised learning using hyperdimensional computing. In: ICCAD (2019)
33. Imani, M., Messerly, J., Wu, F., Pi, W., Rosing, T.: A binary learning framework for hyperdimensional computing. In: DATE (2019)
34. Imani, M., Rahimi, A., Kong, D., Rosing, T., Rabaey, J.M.: Exploring hyperdimensional associative memory. In: HPCA (2017)
35. Imani, M., Salamat, S., Gupta, S., Huang, J., Rosing, T.: Fach: FPGA-based acceleration of hyperdimensional computing by reducing computational complexity. In: ASPDAC (2019)
36. Salamat, S., Imani, M., Khaleghi, B., Rosing, T.: F5-HD: fast flexible FPGA-based framework for refreshing hyperdimensional computing. In: FPGA (2019)

ESCAPADE:
Encryption-Type-Ransomware: System Call Based Pattern Detection

Christopher Jun-Wen Chew[1] ⓘ, Vimal Kumar[1](✉) ⓘ, Panos Patros[2] ⓘ,
and Robi Malik[2]

[1] Department of Computer Science, University of Waikato, Hamilton, New Zealand
cc246@students.waikato.ac.nz, vimal.kumar@waikato.ac.nz
[2] Department of Software Engineering, University of Waikato,
Hamilton, New Zealand
{panos.patros,robi}@waikato.ac.nz

Abstract. Encryption-type ransomware has risen in prominence lately as the go-to malware for threat actors aiming to compromise Android devices. In this paper, we present a ransomware detection technique based on behaviours observed in the system calls performed by the malware. We identify and present some common high-level system call behavioural patterns targeted at encryption-type ransomware and evaluate these patterns. We further present our repeatable and extensible methodology for extracting the system call log and patterns.

Keywords: Android · Behaviour · Patterns · Encryption-ransomware

1 Introduction

As mobile phones become more pervasive and entangled in our lives, we amass more and more private information on them, such as personal photos, credit card information, contacts, and private messages. As a result of this, mobile phones have become more or less a portable identification card in the modern day. This obviously makes them a target of malware attacks.

One of the more frequent types of attacks on mobile are ransomware attacks. As noted by SecureList's 2019 *Mobile malware evolution report* [6], there were a total of 60,176 installed ransomware packages on mobile devices in 2018 and the number went up to 68,362 in 2019. Additionally, malware authors employ cunning techniques to adapt, evolve and take advantage of current events. For example, CovidLocker [23,40], a locker-type ransomware variant poses as a Covid tracking application to lure people into downloading and installing it. At times, the evolution results into completely different types of malware. For example, Black Rose Lucy [17,30] which was originally an information-stealing malware distributed as a Service (MaaS) has now evolved to a encryption-type ransomware variant due to its encryption capabilities.

© Springer Nature Switzerland AG 2020
M. Kutyłowski et al. (Eds.): NSS 2020, LNCS 12570, pp. 388–407, 2020.
https://doi.org/10.1007/978-3-030-65745-1_23

The effects of ransomware are widespread, posing a threat to both consumers and organisations. In June 2019, there were 1,625,351 consumers targeted by ransomware [29]. For businesses, ransomware is even more destructive. According to Sophos *The State of Ransomware 2020* report [43], 82% of the organisations surveyed in India were affected by ransomware in 2019. Ransomware heavily impacts businesses monetarily. The report [43] further stated that an average of $761,106 USD, globally was required to remediate the effects of an attack for an organisation. In July, 2020, Garmin suffered a ransomware attack [1] and paid an undisclosed ransom amount after being asked for $10 million. In another recent ransomware attack, Blackbaud [39] also paid an undisclosed amount to secure their data from being made public. This clearly shows that current defences are insufficient and there is a need for better protection of users from ransomware attacks, especially as mobile devices continue to grow in popularity.

In recent years, researchers have looked at system calls for dynamically analysing malware as it offers a balance between user-level and kernel-level analysis. User-level analysis is often unable to capture the behaviour of more sophisticated malware variants. Kernel-level offers more depth and resilience, however, the devised approaches can often lead to a complex design, thus leading to an over-fitted solution. Hence, our decision to focus on system calls. By using system call-level dynamic analysis, we aim to address the following research objectives:

– **RO1: Identify system call level behavioural patterns for encryption -type ransomware.** While there have been recent works on pattern detection on system call logs [19,26], none has focused on patterns produced by specific malware types. In this paper we aim to discover a set of common behavioural patterns for encryption-type ransomware, such as file encryption and tampering with user files through the reliance on the system call logs.
– **RO2: Evaluate the effectiveness of the behavioural patterns.** We also evaluated the viability and efficacy of these patterns at detecting encryption-type ransomware behaviours from different families, to discover the shared common behaviour among encryption-type ransomware.
– **RO3: Create and make available, a dataset of system call logs of malware activity.** We believe behaviour detection using system calls can be a useful technique for malware detection and analysis therefore we have made our dataset available for researchers to utilise in malware research.

2   Background and Related Work

In this section, we detail the evolution and improvements of Android security and its current state; following with an overview of different types of ransomware, and conclude with the different types of malware analysis techniques used throughout the years, and how our proposed approach can contribute to the existing area.

2.1   Android Security History

Since the introduction of Android—a mobile operating system—in 2008, there have been many updates and improvements to its security. In 2012, Bouncer was released in an effort to deter the upsurge of Android malware in the preceding year [31]. Bouncer targeted pre-existing applications as well as new applications. The approach that Bouncer took was sandboxing [28], where applications were executed, and scanned for malware in an isolated environment on a cloud infrastructure; this was devoid of any access to the users' real data.

However, individuals quickly detected the vulnerabilities of Bouncer. Oliva Hou from Trend Micro [18] noted that researchers were able to acquire specific details of the runtime environment, such as the duration of Bouncer's testing phase (which was five minutes), and the phone contents used in the simulated environment (two photos, one contact and the Google account). These details could easily be exploited by attackers through the use of simple obfuscation techniques to avoid detection by Bouncer.

Bouncer was, therefore, not a sustainable security mechanism. A few years later in May 2017, a more robust approach known as Play Protect was introduced. In addition to the introduction of Play Protect, a security Application Programming Interface (API) called SafetyNet Verify Apps was introduced in September of the same year. This API aimed to address three key ideas: to help further protect users from malicious applications, determine if a user's device is protected by Play Protect, and prompt users to enable Play Protect if it is disabled.

2.2 Ransomware

Ransomware, a type of malware that holds the users' data for ransom—often requesting monetary payment—has been one of the more prevalent malware types, with 61,132,338 ransomware related threats detected in 2019, which was a visible increase compared to 55,470,005 in 2018 [32]. In addition to its prevalence, newer variants and iterations have appeared throughout the years adopting more sophisticated techniques, such as self-propagation, stronger encryption, and alternative infection vectors [36, 37].

With the growing numbers of mobile devices, ransomware, such as WannaLocker, SimpleLocker, Filecoder, and Black Rose Lucy [17, 30], have found their way into the mobile ecosystem. Ransomware are generally of two types: locker ransomware and encryption ransomware [33]. Locker-type ransomware traditionally displays a persistent screen that prevents the user from interacting with the rest of the system. This screen will often display the ransom note demanding monetary payment. On mobile devices, specifically Android, locker-type ransomware makes the application persistent by displaying a perpetual alert dialog or activity, or disabling interactions with the navigation bar [3]. Another technique used is altering users' lock screens, thus preventing access to their devices [2, 20].

Encryption-type ransomware are more destructive where the user's files are encrypted to prevent the user from accessing any of their data [2, 21]. Similar to locker-type ransomware, a ransom note is often displayed after the encryption phase has been completed. Typically for encryption-type ransomware, the process begins by scanning the user's personal directories, such as *Documents*, and *Pictures* for files. Once the scanning phase has completed, the ransomware often identifies files containing specific extensions, such as, *.docx*, *.png*, and *.jpg* to encrypt. This method is normally used to speed up the encryption process, and efficiently determine the important user files to encrypt (i.e., the files most important to a user) [13]. For the encryption process, the data of the identified files are read, and written to a new encrypted file with an unknown file extension. The original file is then removed or overwritten [7].

2.3 Static Analysis

In static analysis, a malware analyst, observes the code of the given application and tries to determine if it is malicious or benign, and gains insight on its functionality without the necessity of executing the application. Static Analysis, however, has limited effectiveness when more sophisticated malware utilises advanced techniques, such as binary/code/control flow obfuscation, and polymorphic coding [9,12,34] to avoid detection.

AndroSimilar [10] and DroidMoss [47] adopted the idea of fuzzy hashing which compared similarities between the signatures generated. This produced a percentage of similarity with 100% being an exact match. This approach aimed to counteract the issue of code obfuscation and application repacking. However, AndroSimilar [10] produced high false negative rates (28%) when detecting unknown malware and considerably higher false negatives for the various methods of code obfuscation which consisted of method renaming (45%), junk method insertion (44%), goto obfuscation (43%), and string encryption (24%). DroidMoss's false negative rates were lower (10.7%). All the tested applications however, came from third-party app stores, whereas AndroSimiliar focused on both official Play store and third-party app stores.

2.4 Dynamic Analysis

In dynamic analysis, rather than observing the code, malicious applications are directly executed in an isolated environment and observed over time for malicious behaviour. This mitigates the core limitations of static analysis. Obfuscation is not an issue as dynamic analysis only observes the behaviour of the application at run-time. As a result of this, dynamic analysis is also capable of discovering new malware.

One of the dynamic analysis technique used is taint analysis, a method of observing data flow and tainting sensitive data paths that could potentially be used maliciously. TaintDroid [8] utilised this approach along with variable-level tracking of native methods within the Dalvik VM interpreter, which contained taint markings in a taint map. These taint markings were propagated through the Android Inter-Process Communication Binder, based on the defined data flow rules on how the application used the tainted data, to the untrusted application's taint map. If the untrusted application made a library call deemed as a taint sink (e.g., *network send*), then the application was marked as malicious.

In contrast, under our method of detection, we observe high-level behavioural patterns at a system call-level with each pattern classified in different levels of severity. This allows for more precise details regarding an application's behaviour and more flexibility with our detection model.

One of the dynamic technique is pattern detection at a system call level, which has often been used for kernel-level malware analysis. Works in [19, 26, 44] apply system call analysis on mobile operating systems such as Android. This approach is useful because system calls are able to determine the precise operations that occurred during the execution of an application/program, which can help identify malicious activities or behaviours.

One drawback, however, with system call monitoring is the size of the log files generated. Due to background processes—such as `clock_gettime()` that periodically record the system clock time—occurring in parallel with the core operations, the raw log size created from monitoring an application, is large.

Isohara et al. [19] addressed this issue by filtering out unnecessary system calls. They achieved this by grouping system calls into specific categories and filtered processes unrelated to the application through the use of a process tree. For their detection phase, Isohara et.al. created 16 different patterns represented as regular expressions. These regular expressions utilised assistant keywords, which relate to specific strings such as, file paths or commands such as `su`.

The work of Isohara provides a good insight into pattern detection in system call logs using regular expressions. Our proposed approach improves on this notion by introducing a formalised and reproducible methodology for safely collecting and extracting system call logs from Android applications. This methodology allows us to create a comprehensive dataset that will enable researchers to better analyse encryption-type ransomware, devise new behavioural patterns, and evaluate the efficacy of their own approaches. Furthermore, our approach focuses on the concept of extensibility where we adopt a customisable multi-level filtering process to allow the abstraction of information within the system call logs. This creates a more human readable log thus making it easier for analyses. In addition to the multi-level filtering, we utilise a token-based approach for our patterns where each token is represented as a smaller sub-pattern.

SCSDroid [26] is a thread-grained behavioural pattern detection method on the system call level leveraging the Longest Common Subsequence (LCS) algorithm to extract potentially malicious patterns from system calls. The Bayes theorem is then utilised with these patterns to determine if an application was a Maliciously Repackaged Application (MRA) or a benign application.

The proposed approach of SCSDroid gives a good perspective of the viability of pattern detection used in malware detection. However, as noted in their conclusion, one of the limitations is its inability to detect unknown families that have not been acquired (i.e., trained). In comparison, in our approach, we develop behavioural patterns to match high-level common behaviour based on a range of ransomware families. This allows us to capture a broader range of behavioural patterns as opposed to family-specific patterns. Furthermore, we demonstrate a reproducible experimental testbed for identify malicious patterns on Android applications.

3 Methodology

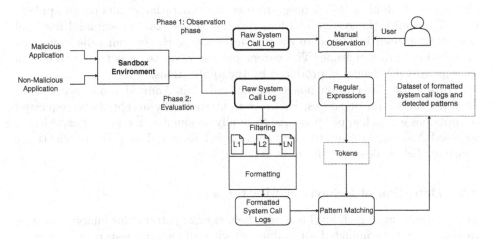

Fig. 1. Methodology process overview

Figure 1 provides an overview of the process followed in this work. The sandbox environment component is our run-time environment where applications are examined; this environment is described in more detail in Sect. 3.1. The output of the sandbox environment splits into two phases. The first phase is the observation phase where applications are observed for their behaviour during runtime. After which, regular expressions are created based on the benign and malicious behaviours observed during that phase. These regular expressions are then converted into our token representation for pattern matching.

These tokens are used in our second phase, labelled as *Evaluation*. This phase starts with the extraction of the raw system call logs (similar to the observation phase), then applies multiple layers of filtering to abstract and remove repetitive or unrelated system calls. After which, the filtered log is formatted for pattern matching using our created tokens. This process is repeated for all unique variants containing a unique hash—also known as a sample—resulting into the final dataset, which contains the formatted system call logs and detected patterns.

The following subsections extensively describe our methodology of collecting and formatting system call logs for detection of malware in more detail. The methodology proposed enables researchers to utilise a streamlined and reproducible approach to safely extract system call logs for effective pattern-based malware detection.

3.1   System Call Log Collection

The first part of our approach is the collection of system call logs. To achieve this, we devised an automatic process of installing applications and tracing system call logs. The environment we used was a Google Pixel 2 emulator running API level 24, created from Android Studio. To automate the process of installing applications and starting applications, we used Android Debug Bridge [15] (ADB) and Android Monkey [16], a program used for generating events on an application. To acquire the system call logs, we ran Strace [25], a command line tool originally utilised in Linux, to extract and capture the system calls from each application during runtime. The parent process (`Zygote`) was traced to ensure we capture all behaviours produced by the applications.

During the observation phase, we noticed that Android ransomware often prompts for admin privileges. Hence, we automatically accepted the requested permissions for each application. Additionally, to simulate a real-user experience, we used Android Monkey to insert events periodically during the application's runtime. This is described in more detail in Sect. 3.2.

3.2   Detection of Behavioural Patterns

To acquire a set of high-level common behavioural patterns for encryption-type ransomware, we conducted an evaluation with 10 encryption-type ransomware samples from five families obtained from CICAndMal2017 [24] and Koodous [22]. Each application was executed 10 times and manually observed during runtime to comprehensively acquire their malicious behaviour. Additionally, 10 benign samples were also analysed to observe the differences in behaviour.

The five ransomware families used for our pattern observation phase consisted of: WannaLocker, DoubleLocker, SimpleLocker, Filecoder, and Wipelocker. All samples were evaluated from each of these families to acquire our common high-level behaviours. The samples used within our pattern observations phase are excluded from our dataset of malicious applications to avoid any potential bias within our evaluation phase in Sect. 4. During the observation phase, we were able to discover 12 behavioural patterns. We classified the behavioural patterns in three categories, five of these patterns are classified as *Malicious*, four are classified as *Suspicious*, and three are *General* behavioural patterns.

Table 3 in the appendix shows the 12 patterns we identified and created. Within this table, the use of > is to concatenate each token. Additionally, Table 2 in the appendix provides each token's objective.

3.3   Pattern Acquisition and Classification

Our method of acquiring the patterns was based on our deduction in the observation phase. This was achieved by going through each application and identifying malicious (or potentially malicious) behaviour and its respective high-level system call counterpart via the captured log. For example, if an application encrypted the user's files then the high-level behaviour at a system call level would translate to `openat` - open user file, one or multiple `read` system calls, `openat` - create new encrypted file, one or multiple `write` system calls.

We aim to observe common high-level behavioural patterns specifically focusing on encryption-type ransomware. However, not all captured behavioural patterns correlate to malicious behaviour.

For example, consider the creation of a socket to connect to an external URL to transfer specific resources. This type of behaviour occurs in both benign and malicious applications. However, the usage will differ. A malicious application often uses that connection to contact a Command and Control (C&C) server [38] to download the payload, whereas a benign application would use the connection to download resources; often occurring in applications requiring frequent updates, such as online mobile games, or linking accounts such as social media accounts. Therefore, to aid in distinguishing the behaviour of patterns, we created a classification to better represent the patterns detected.

Patterns in the *Malicious* category are explicitly classified as malicious behaviours. Applications that contain *Malicious* patterns contain malicious segments that resemble behaviour of encryption-type ransomware.

Behavioural patterns classified in the *Suspicious* category are deemed as potentially malicious. These types of patterns can lead to malicious behaviour. However, the behaviour by itself does not indicate any malice.

Patterns in the *General* category are common benign behaviours that exist in malicious and benign applications with low indication of malicious behaviour.

Note: *Suspicious* and *General* patterns are not used in our evaluations for this paper. These patterns were primarily identified and created to aid future detection systems that utilise common high-level behaviour. Furthermore, encryption-type ransomware exhibits distinct malicious behavioural patterns unlike other types of malware, such as Adware and Trojans, where the malicious behaviours are not always immediately evident. The inclusion of these two pattern categories will be more beneficial in those types of malware.

Malicious Patterns. Our first malicious pattern observed from the logs was related to file renaming and unlinking within the user's main directory (*Rename & Unlink File*). This behaviour was observed in the WannaLocker/Slocker sample, which renamed the initial encrypted file using an unknown file extension. Once the file extension has changed, the ransomware proceeded to unlink the user's original file that was related to the encrypted file. We only looked for this pattern in files within the user directory or external directory (SDcard) as these directories are the points of interest for encryption-type ransomware due to the importance of the files residing within them (often important to the users, such as photos, notes, and other important documents, but not required for the system to work) [41]. Additionally, during our observation phase, the folder *Android* was also within the user directory. Hence, we added an additional condition to exclude that specific directory. The main system call sequences observed, began with `renameat`, followed by an `fstat`, which always occurred before an `unlinkat` operation.

The next malicious pattern from our observations was unlinking of users' files. From our analysis, we were able to find consistent occurrences of this pattern in the ransomware samples and there were no traces of this pattern occurring in the 10 benign samples during our observation phase. The sequence for this pattern began with an `unlinkat` system call followed by the location of the user directory, and the type of file removed.

Another malicious behavioural pattern discovered was the creation of files with unknown file extensions within the user's main directory (*Unknown File Ext Created*). From the different samples observed, this was a prevalent behaviour for encryption-type ransomware where a new file was created to hold the encrypted data of the original user's file. This encrypted file was in a nonstandard file extension and the file name consisted of the original file's name including its original file extension. The main sequence of tokens for this pattern started with an `openat` system call followed by the user directory token, then searched for any files created not matching a regular file extension type.

The last two common malicious patterns discovered were reading of user files and writing to a file with an unknown file extension. These two behavioural patterns represented the encryption segment of a encryption-type ransomware. This was a common behaviour that occurred in all of our ransomware logs.

The first pattern that represents the encryption component is *Read User File*. This pattern focuses on capturing the behaviour of applications reading three times from a file within the user directory. From our observation phase, some of the malicious variants observed read the contents of files within the user directory over multiple `read` operations in a specific block size, unlike the benign samples, which read the file contents in one single block. Hence, the inclusion of three read operations; this is to filter out apparent benign applications. The sequence of this pattern begins with an `openat` system call followed by the location of the user directory then three `read` operations.

The second pattern of the encryption component is *Write File Unknown Extension*. This pattern observed the behaviour of applications writing data to a newly created file with an unknown file extension. This pattern, together with *Read User File*, represented the encryption behaviour seen from the various encryption-type ransomware in our observation phase. The sequence of tokens for this pattern starts with an `openat` system call with the user directory specified, followed by a file created with an unknown file extension and a `write` operation.

Suspicious Patterns. The first suspicious pattern we noted was applications making connections to an external IPv4 address. This could mean the malicious app making connection to a C&C server, however, this can also just be a non-malicious app connecting to the outside internet. We, therefore classified as suspicious but not malicious. The sequence of this pattern observes any `connect` system call followed by an IPv4 address.

Another suspicious behavioural pattern was directory searching. This behaviour is traditionally exhibited by encryption-type ransomware, which searches for user files within the device to encrypt. However, this behaviour does not inherently signify malicious behaviour as there are benign applications that can exhibit the same behaviour, such as cache-cleaning applications. The sequence consists of an `openat` system call and a directory name, then a sequence of `getdents64` (system call for getting directory entries), ending with a `close`.

The next notable suspicious pattern discovered in some ransomware samples, was the creation of an obfuscated file. This file had no file extension and the content contained an external URL. Similar to the first suspicious pattern, we were unable to validate the legitimacy of the URL address. However, many of the ransomware logs observed, contained URL addresses that were related to C&C servers. The sequence of tokens for this pattern comprised an `openat` system call, then any obfuscated file name with no file extension, followed by a `pwrite64` operation with the contents matching any URL address.

The last suspicious pattern was the acquisition of network information via `getaddrinfo`. From our observations, the majority of the ransomware logs attempted to acquire network information, such as socket addresses, and socket types from unknown domains via `getaddrinfo`. However, this does not necessarily indicate malice as we discovered legitimate trusted domains in benign applications such as, `googleadservices`. This pattern began by matching a `socket` system call followed by the subsequent sequence of system calls: `setsockopt`, `connect`, `fnctl64`, `fstat64`, and concluding with a match for a URL address.

General Patterns. There are three patterns in the *General* category. These patterns consist of simple file I/O operations, read and write file behaviour, and generic file unlinking (targets known file extensions in any directory location), such as temporary files (`.tmp`, `_tmp`), backup files (`.bak`), or File locks (`.flock`).

The patterns in the *General* category aim to provide more detailed information regarding an application's behaviour regardless of whether the application is malicious or benign.

For *File Read*, and *File Write*, the sequence started with an `openat` system call, then a read/write operation. The last pattern *Generic File Unlink* matches any *unlinkat* system call with any file matching *.flock*, *.xml*, *.bak*, or *.db-wal*.

Our first research objective was to identify common high-level behavioural patterns for encryption-type ransomware at a system call level. To satisfy this requirement, we identified 12 different behavioural patterns, represented as tokens, and categorised them into different severity levels based on our observations. By utilising these patterns with our methodology for collecting and extracting system calls, we were able to devise a novel meta language for detecting malicious encryption-type ransomware behavioural patterns. This approach presents an easily reproducible testbed for researchers to evaluate potentially malicious applications, and create behavioural patterns based on system call logs.

4   Evaluation

This section details the method of evaluation used for our proposed method, which includes our testing environment, dataset acquisition, evaluation method, evaluation of detected patterns identified in a set of encryption-type ransomware and benign applications. These evaluations are conducted to identify shared commonalities that exists between different encryption-type ransomware families as well as assessing the viability against a benign set of applications. Thus, validating our second research objective.

4.1   Dataset Acquisition

To acquire our dataset of encryption-type ransomware samples, we retrieved the hash or package name publicised from established anti-virus vendors, such as Avast [5] and ESET [46], and relevant search tags, such as family name from Koodous [22]; then we manually verified each malicious application against VirusTotal [42] before downloading the APK from Koodous [22].

As our focus was encryption-type Android ransomware, it was difficult to acquire a large sample size due to the distinctive category. However, we managed to acquire 500 distinct samples to assess our behavioural patterns. Out of that sample size, 213 applications exhibited encryption-type ransomware behaviours. Applications that did not encrypt our files were manually re-evaluated to thoroughly examine the potential cause of failure. From the re-evaluation, we discovered 18 samples that required manual interaction to enable the encryption component. These 18 samples were included in the 213 malicious samples.

From our observations via manual reevaluation, we noticed several factors that caused the failure of encryption. This was likely due to some of the samples requiring a connection to a C&C server that was no longer active. Additionally, some of the applications were installed and crashed upon start-up; thus, preventing the malicious code from executing. Furthermore, there were applications that failed to install on the emulator due to issues, such as a missing manifest file.

As part of our contribution in this paper, we produced a dataset of system call logs collected from our evaluation of 213 encryption-type ransomware and made it publicly available online[1]. This can also enable other works surrounding system call pattern detection to evaluate their own approaches, or expand and develop new behavioural patterns from their own observations.

Alongside our malicious dataset of encryption-type ransomware, we acquired 502 benign applications from APKPure [4] to evaluate the efficacy of our approach. Two of these samples were cache cleaning applications. These two special samples were included as these types of applications closely resembled the high-level behaviours of encryption-type ransomware, specifically the behaviour of removing user files. These two applications were tested separately with manual interaction to ensure we captured the cleaning process.

4.2   Evaluation Method

We ran each application for two minutes using our automation script. Once all the system calls were extracted, we put them through our detection program, and calculated the number of all detected patterns for the different severity levels.

---

[1] https://crow.org.nz/tools/ransomwaresystemcalldataset.

For our ransomware dataset, we identified different malicious patterns for all six ransomware families. Any application whose log contained a match for at least one malicious pattern was classified as malicious. Any falsely identified malicious patterns were noted within this evaluation.

4.3 Detected Patterns

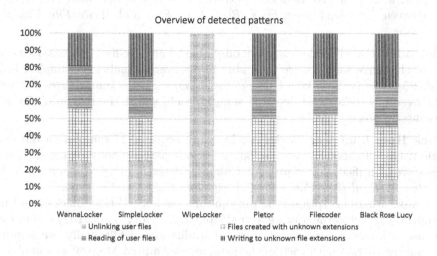

Fig. 2. Overall results of each detected pattern

This section details our evaluation of the six different encryption-type ransomware families. Figure 2 illustrates the results of our evaluation for the malicious dataset. The following paragraphs provides a thorough elaboration of each family and their discovered patterns.

WannaLocker: For WannaLocker we acquired 51 samples; from these 51 samples, we detected 850 malicious patterns. *Unlinking User Files* and *Read User File* were detected 211 times each, *Write File Unknown Extension* was detected 162 times, and 266 patterns were *Unknown File Ext Created*.

SimpleLocker: We acquired 64 encryption-type ransomware samples of SimpleLocker, and out of these 64 samples, we were able to discover 1280 malicious patterns. Within the 1280, we detected an even split of 320 *Unlinking User Files*, *Unknown File Ext Created*, *Read User File*, and *Write File Unknown Extension*. However, we were unable to detect any *Rename & Unlink File* as this behaviour did not occur in any of the samples.

WipeLocker: For WipeLocker, 70 samples were acquired for evaluation. All 70 samples detected 5 *Unlinking User Files* with no other malicious patterns detected. This led to a total of 350 malicious patterns detected. Although

WipeLocker did not indicate any behaviour of file encryption (even after re-evaluating the applications manually), the attributes this family exhibited were similar to encryption-type ransomware such as, the detected pattern of unlinking user files, and directory searching (a suspicious pattern, which we were able to detect a total of 733 occurrences); hence, the inclusion of this family within our evaluation.

Pletor: We were able to acquire six samples from Pletor and from those six samples, a total of 120 malicious patterns were discovered; with even split of 30 between *Unlinking User Files*, *Read User File*, and *Write File Unknown Extension*.

FileCoder: For Filecoder, we were only able to acquire five samples. However, out of these five samples, we were able to discover 95 malicious samples. From those 95 patterns, *Unlinking User Files* and *Write File Unknown Extension* were split evenly with 25 total detected samples each, whilst the remaining 20 were classified as *Read User File*.

Black Rose Lucy: For Black Rose Lucy, we acquired 17 samples for our evaluation. Out of these 17 samples, 307 malicious patterns were detected. Out of these, we identified 45 instances of *Unlinking User Files*, 95 *Unknown File Ext Created*, 72 *Read User File*, and 95 *Write File Unknown Extension*.

Unlike other encryption-type ransomware, we noticed that Black Rose Lucy specifically targeted the user's external storage directory (`/sdcard/`) rather than the user's internal directory during our evaluation. Additionally, we required manual interaction with each of the samples as Android Monkey was unable to detect the package name of the application.

One of the research objective was to evaluate the viability of the devised patterns for behavioural pattern detection against a set of encryption-type ransomware. Within our evaluation we were unable to discover any patterns for *Rename & Unlink File* as this behaviour was likely tied to a specific variant of WannaLocker or SimpleLocker. However, from the overall results of our evaluation, seen in Fig. 2, there is clear indication of shared common behaviour among encryption-type ransomware regardless of the family, with the only exception of WipeLocker, which is known to only remove user files. Through the patterns detected and shared commonalities identified, we have validated the viability of these common high-level behavioural patterns for detection of encryption-type ransomware. This further reinforces the conclusion of the first research objective.

4.4   Benign Applications Results

Table 1 contains a summary of our results where we evaluated the efficacy of our patterns on our benign dataset. The *Percentage* column provides the percentages of true negatives and false positives detected for all benign samples evaluated. The *Sample Size* column denotes the numerical value of true negatives and false positive samples detected.

To evaluate the efficacy and viability of our patterns, we tested our approach on a dataset consisting of 502 benign applications. Two of those are

Table 1. Summary of all benign applications evaluated

Benign samples	Percentage	Sample size
True negative	98.6%	495
False positive	1.4%	7

the cache-cleaning applications discussed separately below. Out of the other 500 benign applications, we encountered six falsely classified applications. This was due to a mismatch of four different patterns, specifically, *Unlinking User Files*, *Read User File*, *Unknown File Ext Created*, and *Write File Unknown Extension*.

For our pattern matching results, two applications incorrectly matched *Read User File*; this was due to the applications creating and reading application related files within the user directory, such as `dslv_state.txt`. To mitigate this issue, `openat` system calls with the flag `O_CREAT` could be excluded. This would ensure that only user created files were captured within this pattern.

The third benign application that was falsely classified incorrectly matched the patterns *Unlinking User Files* and *Read User File*, due to the application creating and utilising temporary files within the user directory. This was one of the drawbacks of capturing high-level behaviour. For most cases, these patterns would capture unlinking of user created files and existing user file access and reads, which is a behaviour often exhibited by encryption-type ransomware as part of the file encryption process. However, in the case of an application creating and utilising a file within the user directory, it would be classified as a false positive. A potential solution is to exclude files created by the application within the user directory, as previously suggested, or reduce and combine the behavioural patterns related to file encryption.

The last three benign applications falsely classified were incorrectly matching two behavioural patterns: *Unknown File Ext Created* and *Write File Unknown Extension*. These patterns were falsely classified due to the applications creating an application folder within the user directory and a file with an unknown file extension within the application folder.

Similar to the proposed solution for the aforementioned third application, combining behavioural patterns related to file encryption could provide a more accurate representation. Alternatively, the pattern could be altered to only check for primary directories (i.e., directories not created by the application), such as *Photos*, *Documents*, and *Downloads*.

Cache Cleaning Applications. For the two cache cleaning applications, one of them resulted in a false positive. There were four total malicious patterns matched and all four of those patterns were linked to *Read User File*.

From the examination of the patterns file and system call log file, these four patterns were deemed as irregular behaviour as it was unusual for a benign application to be reading the contents of user created files (i.e., pre-existing files, not created by the application).

5   Conclusions

In this paper, we identified and explored three core research objectives. The first research objective was to identify system call level behavioural patterns for encryption-type ransomware. To achieve this, we presented an extensive methodology for collecting and identifying behavioural patterns at a system call level. Using this methodology, we were able to discover a set of common high-level behavioural patterns at a system call level.

Our second research objective evaluates the effectiveness of the behavioural patterns identified. This was achieved by creating 12 behavioural patterns for detecting encryption-type ransomware. Consequently, we were able to evaluate these patterns against a set of encryption-type ransomware to identify shared commonalities between different families using pattern matching.

By utilising our methodology and behavioural patterns, we developed a publicly available dataset of formatted system call logs of encryption-type ransomware, which satisfied our third research objective. This dataset was created to contribute to the area of system call pattern detection that can be utilised in the future for purposes, such as evaluation or discovery of additional patterns.

5.1   Discussion and Future Work

There are limitations to the work presented in this paper. One of the limitations relates to the generation of regular expressions. Currently, we require manual observation and interaction to create regular expressions. This process can often be tedious and difficult. As we continue to develop our approach, we intend to automate this process.

Another limitation is our approach of identifying behavioural patterns. The patterns identified were based on our own observations from various applications. As a result of this, there may have been some behaviours that were not captured. In future, we would like to introduce a more formalised and robust methodology of identifying behavioural patterns at a system call level ensuring that all behaviours are captured without any uncertainty.

Additionally, we intend to introduce more behavioural patterns capable of detecting other types of malware, such as Backdoors and Trojans, which were identified as two of the most prominent types of infections for third-party apps [14]. This enables us to expand our dataset and evaluate the efficacy of our methodology on a larger sample size consisting of different types of malware.

Similar to static analysis, dynamic analysis suffers in keeping up with malware developers' avoidance techniques. Dynamic analysis generally relies on an isolated environment, most commonly through the use of Virtual Machines (VMs) to observe malicious applications. However, more sophisticated malware have processes in place to detect virtual environments [11,45]. There are several tests that a malware may perform to check if the environment is emulated. One of which is registry checks; whenever a virtual machine is spawned in, a new registry entry is inserted. Another possible way how malware can detect virtual environments is by checking the MAC address as certain virtual environment software, like VMware produces distinct MAC address prefixes for the VM. Specifically, for VMware, the following MAC address prefix can be 00-05-69, 00-0c-29, 00-1c-14 or 00-50-56 [35]. In practice, this holds true as the authors of ANDRUBIS [27] identified this as one of their limitations. Similarly, Copper-Droid [44] also noted in their related works section that DroidBox, a malware detection tool using taint analysis, also suffers from the same issue.

The aforementioned issue highlights the inadequacy of heavily relying on conventional VM-based dynamic analysis. Thus, to prevent this issue we adopted a deeper level of analysis through the utilisation of system call log data to identify malicious behaviour. Although we evaluated our approach on an emulated environment, our approach is still applicable as long as the system call log is producible. As part of our future work, we are working on a system that enables efficient capturing of system calls in real time on a real user device utilising the technique shown in this paper. This alleviates the reliance of a virtualised environment, which most dynamic analysis techniques utilise.

As previously mentioned in Sect. 3.3, *Suspicious* and *General* patterns were not utilised in our evaluations. However, these patterns were still identified and created to lead into future work. These patterns can be expanded to create a more robust real-time malware detection model for Android devices or aid current and future anti-malware applications in detecting and deterring malware.

Appendix

Listing 1.1. Filecoder match for Write To File Unknown Extension

```
4179;23:18:22;openat;(AT_FDCWD, "U_DIR/large_text.txt.seven",
    O_WRONLY|O_CREAT|O_TRUNC|O_LARGEFILE, 0666 <unfinished ...>
4179;23:18:22;openat;( ) = 36
4179;23:18:22;fstat64;(36, <unfinished ...>
4179;23:18:22;fstat64;( {st_mode=0, st_size=1, ...}) = 0
4179;23:18:22;write;(36,"\10\261{H|\254\226\32\202\342\322\222\230
    \376c\256h\347\253\347v\271\"\303\265W\203\"\203\244\265T"...,
    148720 <unfinished ...>
```

Listing 1.2. Benign cache-cleaning application pattern mismatch for Read User File

```
4436;21:30:03;openat;(AT_FDCWD, "U_DIR/large_image.jpg",
    O_RDONLY|O_LARGEFILE) = 119
4436;21:30:03;fstat64;(119, {st_mode=0, st_size=1, ...}) = 0
4436;21:30:03;read;(119, <unfinished ...>
4436;21:30:03;read;( "\377\330\377\340\0\20JFIF\0\1\1\1\0d\0d\0\0
    \377\376\0LFile sou"..., 8192) pow2
4436;21:30:03;read;(119, "\344\6Q,\24\266\325j\333\244\312N\371#
    \2\247\236*\244\363Bx\2\356\f\235\205(\266\360.\7"
    ..., 8192) pow2
4436;21:30:03;read;(119, <unfinished ...>
4436;21:30:03;read;( "l\214\254\223\10\250\222H\356\304\366\2\275\
    r-\251S\342\273t\357\177\336\306\376\33G\315\225p
    \272\276"..., 8192) pow2
```

Table 2. List of token names and their respective pattern

Token	Pattern purpose
OP	System call operation
AL	All including newline
UD	User directory
N	Newline
ON	Optional match newline
A	Match all
UFC	Unknown file creations
DQ	Dotted quad formats (i.e. IPv4)
AD	URL address
OF	Obfuscated file
SF	Socket flags
GA	Get address info
MD	Match directory
MF	Match file (regular file with one extension)

Table 3. List of common behavioural patterns discovered and their token representation

Pattern name	Pattern combination
Rename & Unlink File	OP(renameat)>UD>\\(?!Android)>N>ON >OP(fstatat64) >N>ON>OP(unlinkat)>UD>A
Unlinking User Files	OP(unlinkat)>UD>MF
Unknown File Ext Created	OP(openat)>UD>UFC>A
Read User File	OP(openat)>UD>MF>(>AL>OP(read)>N>){3}
Write File Unknown Extension	OP(openat)>UD>UFC>AL>OP(write)>A
IPv4 Connections	OP(connect)>DQ
Directory Search	OP(openat)>MD>N>N>(>OP(getdents64)>N>)* >OP(close)>A
URL to Obfuscated Filename	OP(openat)>OF>(>OP(openat>)?>AL >OP(pwrite64)>AD
Socket Create and Connect	OP(socket)>SF>N>(>OP(socket)>N>)?>A >OP(setsockopt) >N>(>OP(setsockopt) >N>)>?>OP(connect) >N>(>OP(connect) >N>)>?>OP(fcntl64) >N>(>OP(fcntl64)>N>) >?>OP(fstat64) >N>(>OP(fstat64)>N>) >?>OP(write)>GA
File Write	OP(openat)>AL>OP(write)>A
File Read	OP(openat)>AL>OP(read)>A
Generic File Unlink	OP(unlinkat) (.*?(.(\w+)(\bflock|xml|bak|db-wal\b)\").+)

Note: Some sub-patterns were retained as a regular expression as certain parts are too specific to be represented as tokens.

References

1. Abrams, L.: Confirmed: garmin received decryptor for WastedLocker ransomware (2020). https://www.bleepingcomputer.com/news/security/confirmed-garmin-received-decryptor-for-wastedlocker-ransomware/
2. Al-rimy, B.A.S., Maarof, M.A., Shaid, S.Z.M.: Ransomware threat success factors, taxonomy, and countermeasures: a survey and research directions. Comput. Secur. **74**, 144–166 (2018)
3. Andronio, N., Zanero, S., Maggi, F.: HELDROID: dissecting and detecting mobile ransomware. In: Bos, H., Monrose, F., Blanc, G. (eds.) RAID 2015. LNCS, vol. 9404, pp. 382–404. Springer, Cham (2015). https://doi.org/10.1007/978-3-319-26362-5_18
4. APKPure: Benign dataset (nd). https://apkpure.com/
5. Avast: Avast blog (2020). https://blog.avast.com/
6. Chebyshev, V.: Mobile malware evolution 2018. SecureList, 16 March 2019. https://securelist.com/mobile-malware-evolution-2018/89689/statistics
7. Chen, J., Wang, C., Zhao, Z., Chen, K., Du, R., Ahn, G.J.: Uncovering the face of Android ransomware: characterization and real-time detection. IEEE Trans. Inf. Forensics Secur. **13**(5), 1286–1300 (2017)
8. Enck, W., et al.: TaintDroid: an information-flow tracking system for realtime privacy monitoring on smartphones. ACM Trans. Comput. Syst. (TOCS) **32**(2), 5 (2014)
9. Faruki, P., et al.: Android security: a survey of issues, malware penetration, and defenses. IEEE Commun. Surv. Tutor. **17**(2), 998–1022 (2014)
10. Faruki, P., Laxmi, V., Bharmal, A., Gaur, M.S., Ganmoor, V.: AndroSimilar: robust signature for detecting variants of Android malware. J. Inf. Secur. Appl. **22**, 66–80 (2015)
11. Gadhiya, S., Bhavsar, K.: Techniques for malware analysis. Int. J. Adv. Res. Comput. Sci. Softw. Eng. **3**(4), 2277–3128 (2013)
12. Gandotra, E., Bansal, D., Sofat, S.: Malware analysis and classification: a survey. J. Inf. Secur. **5**(02), 56 (2014)
13. Gazet, A.: Comparative analysis of various ransomware virii. J. Comput. Virol. **6**(1), 77–90 (2010). https://doi.org/10.1007/s11416-008-0092-2
14. Google: Android security 2018 year in review (2019). https://source.android.com/security/reports/Google_Android_Security2018_Report_Final.pdf
15. Google: Android Debug Bridge (adb) (2020). https://developer.android.com/studio/command-line/adb
16. Google: UI/application exerciser monkey (2020). https://developer.android.com/studio/test/monkey
17. Goud, N., et al.: Black Rose Lucy ransomware attack on Android devices, April 2020. https://www.cybersecurity-insiders.com/black-rose-lucy-ransomware-attack-on-android-devices/
18. Hou, O.: A look at Google Bouncer [blog post], 20 July 2012. https://blog.trendmicro.com/trendlabs-security-intelligence/a-look-at-google-bouncer/
19. Isohara, T., Takemori, K., Kubota, A.: Kernel-based behavior analysis for Android malware detection. In: 2011 Seventh International Conference on Computational Intelligence and Security, pp. 1011–1015. IEEE (2011)
20. Kanwal, M., Thakur, S.: An app based on static analysis for Android ransomware. In: 2017 International Conference on Computing, Communication and Automation (ICCCA), pp. 813–818. IEEE (2017)

21. Kok, S., Abdullah, A., Jhanjhi, N., Supramaniam, M.: Ransomware, threat and detection techniques: a review. Int. J. Comput. Sci. Netw. Secur. **19**(2), 136 (2019)

22. Koodous: Malicious dataset (nd). https://koodous.com/

23. Lance, W.: CovidLock ransomware exploits coronavirus with malicious Android app. TechRepublic, 17 March 2020. https://www.techrepublic.com/article/covidlock-ransomware-exploits-coronavirus-with-malicious-android-app/

24. Lashkari, A.H., Kadir, A.F.A., Taheri, L., Ghorbani, A.A.: Toward developing a systematic approach to generate benchmark Android malware datasets and classification. In: 2018 International Carnahan Conference on Security Technology (ICCST), pp. 1–7. IEEE (2018)

25. Levin, D.V.: Strace (2020). https://strace.io/

26. Lin, Y.D., Lai, Y.C., Chen, C.H., Tsai, H.C.: Identifying Android malicious repackaged applications by thread-grained system call sequences. Comput. Secur. **39**, 340–350 (2013)

27. Lindorfer, M., Neugschwandtner, M., Weichselbaum, L., Fratantonio, Y., Van Der Veen, V., Platzer, C.: Andrubis-1,000,000 apps later: a view on current Android malware behaviors. In: 2014 Third International Workshop on Building Analysis Datasets and Gathering Experience Returns for Security (BADGERS), pp. 3–17. IEEE (2014)

28. Lockheimer, H.: Android and security [blog post], 2 February 2012. https://googlemobile.blogspot.com/2012/02/android-and-security.html

29. Malwarebytes: CTNT report cybercrime tactics and techniques: Ransomware retrospective (2020). https://resources.malwarebytes.com/files/2019/08/CTNT-2019-Ransomware_August_FINAL.pdf

30. Mana, O., Hazum, A., Melnykov, B., Kuperman, L.: Lucy's back: ransomware goes mobile, April 2020. https://research.checkpoint.com/2020/lucys-back-ransomware-goes-mobile/

31. Micro, T.: Behind the Android menace: Malicious apps–TrendLabs security intelligence blog. https://blog.trendmicro.com/trendlabs-security-intelligence/infographic-behind-the-android-menace-malicious-apps

32. Micro, T.: The sprawling reach of complex threats (2020). https://www.trendmicro.com/vinfo/us/security/research-and-analysis/threat-reports/roundup/the-sprawling-reach-of-complex-threats

33. Mohammad, A.H.: Ransomware evolution, growth and recommendation for detection. Modern Appl. Sci. **14**(3), (2020)

34. Moser, A., Kruegel, C., Kirda, E.: Limits of static analysis for malware detection. In: Twenty-Third Annual Computer Security Applications Conference (ACSAC 2007), pp. 421–430. IEEE (2007)

35. Ninja, S.: How malware detects virtualized environment (and its countermeasures) (2016). https://resources.infosecinstitute.com/how-malware-detects-virtualized-environment

36. O'Kane, P., Sezer, S., Carlin, D.: Evolution of ransomware. IET Netw. **7**(5), 321–327 (2018)

37. Richardson, R., North, M.M.: Ransomware: evolution, mitigation and prevention. Int. Manag. Rev. **13**(1), 10 (2017)

38. Lipovský, R., Lukáš Štefanko, G.B.: Labour party is latest victim of Blackbaud ransomware attack (2016). https://www.welivesecurity.com/wp-content/uploads/2016/02/Rise_of_Android_Ransomware.pdf

39. Scroxton, A.: Labour party is latest victim of Blackbaud ransomware attack (2020). https://www.computerweekly.com/news/252487002/Labour-Party-is-latest-victim-of-Blackbaud-ransomware-attack

40. Shivang, D.: CovidLock: Android ransomware walkthrough and unlocking routine, 16 March 2020. https://www.zscaler.com/blogs/research/covidlock-android-ransomware-walkthrough-and-unlocking-routine
41. Song, S., Kim, B., Lee, S.: The effective ransomware prevention technique using process monitoring on Android platform. Mob. Inf. Syst. **2016** (2016)
42. Sood, G.: virustotal: R Client for the virustotal API (2017). r package version 0.2.1
43. Sophos: The state of ransomware 2020 (2020). https://www.sophos.com/en-us/medialibrary/Gated-Assets/white-papers/sophos-the-state-of-ransomware-2020-wp.pdf
44. Tam, K., Khan, S.J., Fattori, A., Cavallaro, L.: CopperDroid: automatic reconstruction of Android malware behaviors. In: NDSS (2015)
45. Uppal, D., Mehra, V., Verma, V.: Basic survey on malware analysis, tools and techniques. Int. J. Comput. Sci. Appl. (IJCSA) **4**(1), 103 (2014)
46. WeLiveSecurity: WeLiveSecurity (2020). https://www.welivesecurity.com/
47. Zhou, W., Zhou, Y., Jiang, X., Ning, P.: Detecting repackaged smartphone applications in third-party Android marketplaces. In: Proceedings of the Second ACM Conference on Data and Application Security and Privacy, pp. 317–326. ACM (2012)

A Privacy Preserving Aggregation Scheme for Fog-Based Recommender System

Xiaodong Wang[1], Bruce Gu[3], Youyang Qu[1], Yongli Ren[2], Yong Xiang[1],
and Longxiang Gao[1(✉)]

[1] School of Information Technology, Deakin University,
Melbourne, VIC 3125, Australia
{xdwang,y.qu,yong.xiang,longxiang.gao}@deakin.edu.au
[2] School of Science, Computer Science and IT, RMIT University,
Melbourne, VIC 3000, Australia
yongli.ren@rmit.edu.au
[3] Discipline of IT, College of Engineering and Science, Victoria University,
Footscray, VIC 3000, Australia
bgu@deakin.edu.au

Abstract. With the rapid growth in the number of smart devices and explosive data generated every day by the mobile users, cloud computing comes to the bottleneck due to the far-off transmission and bandwidth limitation. Fog computing has been introduced as one of the promising solutions to meet the requirements under Internet of Things (IoT) scenarios such as location awareness and real-time services. The study of fog-based applications has become an attractive and important potential trend. The existing research about fog-based recommender systems focus on providing personalized and localized services to users while serving as a fog computing optimization tool in the system. However, there is little research about how to preserve user privacy in fog-based recommender systems. In this paper, we propose a novel privacy preserving aggregation scheme to handle the privacy issue for fog-based recommender systems.

Keywords: Fog computing · Recommender system · Location awareness · Differential privacy

1 Introduction

According to Cisco Visual networking index [9], more than 12.3 billion mobile devices and 50 billion connected things will be there by the end of year 2020. The emerging IoT services and personalized mobile applications put forward higher demands on low latency performance, uninterrupted service, real-time response, location awareness service and time-sensitive service [2,4]. While Cloud computing has been well developed and widely used in practice, it cannot meet the aforementioned requirements in IoT scenarios due to far-off data transmission

M. Kutyłowski et al. (Eds.): NSS 2020, LNCS 12570, pp. 408–418, 2020.
https://doi.org/10.1007/978-3-030-65745-1_24

and bandwidth limitation. Fog computing has been considered as one of the promising solutions to match these requirements [5]. Specifically, fog computing is dedicated to serving mobile users and IoT things by offloading computing to the fog nodes [23], to complementing conventional cloud computing by introducing an intermediate layer between mobile users and the cloud servers [4,5].

The research of fog-based application and scenarios has drawn a great deal of attention [15,24]. We have proposed a fog-based recommender system in our previous research work [22], which can provide personalized and localized recommendations to users, meanwhile, it also serves as a fog computing optimization tool as it can provide optimization recommendations. The system has been proved as practical and feasible. However, there are still some prospective issues has not been discussed, precisely speaking, the privacy issue in fog-based recommender system is one of them.

The motivation of this paper is to solve the privacy-preserving issue in fog based recommender system. Namely, while making reasonable recommendations, we aim to make sure that data sharing and publishing based on the location of fog are under privacy protection. We propose a privacy-preserving aggregation scheme for fog-based recommender systems. The proposed scheme is based on the location between two fog nodes in a fog network. By build a weighted fog network graph, we map the location level l_h to the privacy protection level ϵ. Through customizing the privacy protection levels, the proposed scheme provides flexible privacy protection based on location of fog nodes.

We propose two customized similarity functions based on the location of fog nodes with injected Laplace noise. The Laplace noise follows Laplace distribution which satisfy differential privacy protection requirements. We proposed a differential privacy topN (DP-topN) aggregation function to generate ratings based on the location parameter ω_h. Meanwhile, we also make sure that the parameter ω_o maximize the ϵ-differential privacy, thus, our proposed scheme ensures that the operation of inserting or deleting a record in the data set does not substantially affect the prediction in the fog-based recommender system.

We have conducted a set of experiments to evaluate the performance of our proposed privacy-preserving aggregation scheme. The experiments show that the privacy level remains low and increase slowly which indicate the adversaries can not easily gain more sensitive data even the adversaries might have obtained some background knowledge before. We have made corresponding improvements to ensure that the entire proposal meets the definition of differential privacy.

The rest of this paper is organized as follows. Section 2 discusses the background and related studies of fog computing and privacy issue in recommender systems. Section 3 describes the privacy-preserving aggregation scheme modeling. In Sect. 4, we describe the system implementation and present experimental results. Finally, Sect. 5 concludes the paper and presents future work.

2   Related Work

Fog computing is a relatively new networking paradigm and first introduced in 2012 by Cisco [4]. The purpose of fog computing is trying to solve some challenges in existing cloud computing which no longer meet the requirement of modern IoT scenario [10,11]. Fog computing bringing services formerly provided by the cloud much closer to end-users with uninterrupted and low-latency services. Fog computing dedicate to filling the technology gap between the cloud and end-users, it could also be seen as a complement to the cloud model in the IoT context [3,5]. By introducing an intermediate layer, the distance between users and services is much closer in fog computing [6,13,14,20].

In our previous study, we have proposed a fog-based recommender system which provides personalized and localized recommendation services to users [22]. However, as fog computing inherits many features from cloud computing, it is inevitable that many challenges such as privacy leakage issue has been introduced to fog computing paradigm [1,12,21]. Gu et al. [10] provides an overview of existing personalized privacy concerns in fog computing, particularly for the issues in trust, authentication, secure communications in fog computing, end user's privacy and malicious attacks [17,18].

Privacy-preserving data analysis can be considered as techniques dedicated to statistical disclosure control, reasoning control, privacy protection data mining and private data analysis [7,16,19]. Differential privacy is a method that publicly shares dataset information by describing group patterns in the dataset while preserving personal information in the dataset [7]. Differential privacy ensures that deleting or adding a single database item will not have a significant impact on any analysis results. Therefore, joining the database does not bring any risk, and provides a mathematically rigorous method to deal with the fact that the distributed information potentially be disclosive [8].

3   Privacy Preserving Aggregation Scheme Modelling

In this section, we present our privacy-preserving aggregation scheme based on a recommender system which can provide personalized and localized suggestions. We assume that the user-item preference information needs to be shared between different fog nodes as the fog-based recommender system is deployed on a group of collaboratively operating fog nodes. Because we can not guarantee which fog node is trustworthy, any fog node can be comprised as a potential adversary. In order to protect user-specific rating data from being leaked, we perform noise preprocessing on the original user-item rating data based on location informa-tion. By injecting the Laplace noise to the user-item preference, it can reduce the risk of privacy leakage caused by correlation analysis. We calculate the similar-ity based on generated new information between users, and predicts the target user's interest in the list of candidate items, and finally apply an aggregation function to generate aggregates of ratings of the most similar user for items.

3.1   Data Preprocessing

In the recommender system, user historical behavior data could extract for a user behaviour pattern, which is needed to provide suggestions or predict the rating. To make a suggestion or predict the rating of items in an item-based collaborative filtering algorithm, we need to compute the similarity of items first. We use a set of four quantities (user U, item I, location (corresponding fog node) L, rating of item R) to represent the user and item's preference based on different location. R denote a $|U| \times |I|$ user-item matrix, R_L is the rating preference based on location information.

Assume that user u is characterized by a fog location data L. Let $l_h \in L$, the fog location L corresponds to a value h that indicates the level of the location. For example, as Fig. 1 shows, a user location level is defined, going from large to small scale: city campus (level 1), building x (level 2), floor y (level 3), room z (level 4); thus, the location level is $h = 4$, ω_h also indicate the distance between source and destination fog nodes.

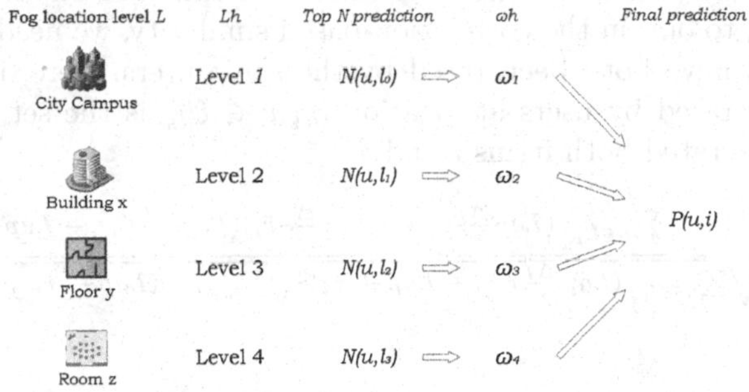

Fig. 1. Linear aggregation based on location level

ϵ-**Differential Privacy.** As Eq. 1 shows, two rating preference $r = r_{ulh}$ and $r = r_{u'lh}$ are two adjacent data set for user u and u', while M is a randomized mechanism which provides ϵ- differential privacy. Here, probability density function $Pr[M(r_{ulh}) \in R_L]$ denotes the probability of Laplace Mechanism $Lap(\Delta f)$.

$$Pr[M(r_{ulh}) \in R_L] \leq exp(\epsilon) \cdot Pr[M(r_{u'lh}) \in R_L] \tag{1}$$

The Composition Mechanism of Differential Privacy. The sequential composition mechanism provides differential privacy jointly work together and guarantees $\sum_i^m \epsilon_i$ composed. M is a ϵ-deferentially private mechanism under adjacency relation, a set of randomized mechanisms $M = \{M_1, M_2...M_m\}$ guarantee that corresponding privacy $\epsilon_1, \epsilon_2...\epsilon_m$ respectively. Each M_i provides ϵ-differential privacy and the sequential composition mechanism $M = \{M_1, M_2...M_m\}$ is $\sum_i^m \epsilon_i$- differentially private. The summation of total privacy protection level ϵ_i is determined by composition nechanism $\sum_i^m \epsilon_i$.

Injecting Laplace Noise. One of the most popular ways to differential privacy when calculating numeral measurements is to inject Laplace noise to the measurement. By adds controlled noise from Laplace distribution, the differential private protection requirements can be met. As Eq. 2 shows, we injecting the noise $Lap\frac{\Delta f}{\epsilon}$ to the numeral measurements by employed the Laplace mechanism M to implement ϵ-differential privacy.

$$M(S) = f(S) + Lap\frac{\Delta f}{\epsilon} \tag{2}$$

Pearson Correlation Similarity with Injected Noise. To make suggestions to users or predict the rating of items, we need to calculate the similarity of items first. There are different approaches to calculate the similarity, Pearson correlation similarity is one of the way to calculate the similarity between items. As Eq. 3 shows, to obtain the correlation-based similarity, we need to find some peer items that have both been rated by the same users. Here, items i and j have both been rated by users at location l_h, $u \in U_{l_h}$ is the set of users u at level h who have rated both items i and j.

$$DP_{sim}(i,j,l_h) = \frac{\sum_{u \in U_{l_h}}(Lap\frac{\Delta f}{\epsilon}r_{u,i} - Lap\frac{\Delta f}{\epsilon}\bar{r}_i)(Lap\frac{\Delta f}{\epsilon}r_{u,j} - Lap\frac{\Delta f}{\epsilon}\bar{r}_j)}{\sqrt{\sum_{u \in U_{l_h}}(Lap\frac{\Delta f}{\epsilon}r_{u,i} - Lap\frac{\Delta f}{\epsilon}\bar{r}_i)^2}\sqrt{\sum_{u \in U_{l_h}}(Lap\frac{\Delta f}{\epsilon}r_{u,j} - Lap\frac{\Delta f}{\epsilon}\bar{r}_j)^2}} \tag{3}$$

Cosine Similarity with Injected Noise. Another approach to calculate similarity is Cosine similarity, Here items i and j are considered as two vectors, the similarity between i and j is measured by compute the angle between two nonzero vectors. Cosine similarity does not regarded the scale of ratings assigned by different users, By subtracting average ratings, this shortcoming can be solved and this is also know as adjusted cosine similarity approach.

$$DP_{cos}(i,j,l_h) = \frac{(Lap\frac{\Delta f}{\epsilon}i \cap l_h \cdot Lap\frac{\Delta f}{\epsilon}j \cap l_h)}{||Lap\frac{\Delta f}{\epsilon}i \cap l_h||_2 ||Lap\frac{\Delta f}{\epsilon}j \cap l_h||_2} \tag{4}$$

The ideas of Pearson correlation similarity and adjusted cosine similarity are both deduct the mean and the respective mathematical formulae are quite similar. The difference between adjusted cosine similarity and correlation-based similarity is that the Pearson correlation-based similarity considers the average rating of each item i. while adjusted cosine similarity considers the average rating of each user who has rated item i.

3.2 DP-TopN Aggregation Function

In this section, we use an aggregation function to generate aggregates of ratings of most similar users for item i. Here, $r_{ulh} = \varnothing$ indicates that item i has not been rated by user u. $\hat{U}$ denotes the set of N users u' that are most similar to user u

who have rated item i that has not been rated by user u. Multiplier η is a normalizing factor defined by $\bar{r}_u = (1/|S_u|) \sum_{i \in S_u} r_{u,i}$, where $S_u = \{i | r_{ulh} \neq \varnothing\}$. As Fig. 1 shows, each level h of location generates top N predictions $N(u, l_h)$, using a linear additive weights ω_h to generate the final prediction $P(u, i)$.

$$p_{(u,i,l_h)} = Lap\frac{\Delta f}{\epsilon}\bar{r}_{i,l_h} + \eta \sum_{u' \in \hat{U}} DP_{sim}(u, u') \times (Lap\frac{\Delta f}{\epsilon}r_{u',i} - Lap\frac{\Delta f}{\epsilon}r_{u',l_h}) \quad (5)$$

Maximize ϵ_i- differential privacy, define $M(X)$ to be $f(X) + Lap(0, \rho)$;

$$\rho \geq \frac{\max}{r_{ulh} \approx r_{u'lh}} \|f(r_{ulh}) - f(r_{u'lh})| \, 1/\epsilon \quad (6)$$

$Lap\frac{\Delta f}{\epsilon}\bar{r}_{u',l_h})$ must contain in $[q_{min}, q_{max}]$.

where $Lap\frac{\Delta f}{\epsilon}\bar{r}_{i,l_h}$ is the average rating of item i given by all users at level h with injected noise.

$$Lap\frac{\Delta f}{\epsilon}\bar{r}_{i,l_h}, Lap\frac{\Delta f}{\epsilon}r_{u',i} \quad (7)$$

$$P(u, i) = \sum p(u, i, l_h) * \omega_h \quad (8)$$

Here, weights ω_h are used to compute a linear combination of predicted ratings at different location levels $p(u, i, l_h)$ to obtain the final prediction $P(u, i)$ of user u's rating for item $i.\omega_h$ is the weight at level h that controls prediction at each location level and affects the final prediction.

The weights satisfy the following constraints:

$$\omega_h \in [0, 1] \quad (9)$$

$$\omega_1 + \omega_2 + \cdots + \omega_h = 1 \quad (10)$$

For $i = 1$, and $\omega_h = \omega_1, \omega_2, \cdots \omega_o$, the ω_o is the optimal weight parameter, we are interested in how the value of location parameter ω_o and location parameter ω_h will change our prediction accuracy and also data utility in the experiment. The mapping function of location parameter ω_o maximize the ϵ - differential privacy is as follows:

$$M(\epsilon_i) = \frac{exp(\omega_i^t x)}{\sum_{o=1}^{h} exp^{\omega_o}} \quad (11)$$

4 Evaluation and Analysis

In this section, we evaluated the performance of our proposed Privacy Preserving Aggregation Scheme. By adjusting the parameters of controlled noise and location weigh, we demonstrated that our proposed scheme is feasible and effective. We performance a set of experiment based on a real-world dataset GBCA dataset which is collected from Global Business College of Australia located in Melbourne CBD. We depoly 7 fog servers on the city campus, 3 fog server on first floor, two fog servers on the second floor and two fog server on third floor. We use different platforms to simulate fog servers, typical platform is Windows10 OS with Intel Core i7 CPU@2.7 GHz and 16 GB memory. The experiments has been conducted by implementing algorithms on Matlab R2017a.

We collected 178790 records of different users interacting with different items in GBCA city Campus all data are obtained from the deployed seven simulated fog servers. Due to the small amount of data set, we use all the data and split data into 80% for training purpose, 20% as test data set.

4.1 Data Utility vs RMSE and MAE

We use two popular evaluation methods for recommendation, mean absolute error (MAE) and root-mean-square error (RMSE), to test our quality of the prediction. We also use the expected squared error to evaluate our data utility before making any recommendations. Both RMSE and MAE are used to measure the prediction accuracy. RMSE penalizes large errors by amplifying the differences between the predicted and the real preference of items:

$$RMSE = \sqrt{\frac{\sum(D_{test} - D_{result})^2}{|D_{test}|}} \tag{12}$$

MAE is the average absolute deviation of the predicted ratings from real rating of items:

$$MAE = \frac{\sum|D_{test} - D_{result}|}{|D_{test}|} \tag{13}$$

We set up a decay factor for the weight parameter ω_h to observe its impact to the prediction accuracy and data utility, here the decay factor has been set up as $(\frac{\omega_h}{n})$ for present location, the weight of the second level of location is $(\frac{\omega_h}{n})^2$. In Fig. 2, ω_h is fixed as 0.7, n varies from 1 to 5, this value also been mapped to the amount of privacy levels, thus there are 5 privacy levels from $\epsilon \in (0, \infty)$

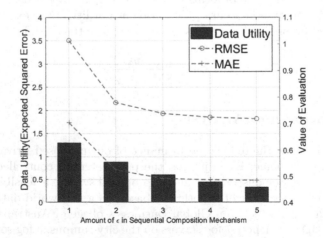

Fig. 2. Data utility vs RMSE and MAE

based on location. In Fig. 2, we observe that all three measurements shows the similar trend, the value of data utility decrease from 1.3 to 0.4, the RMSE and MAE value both decreased, RMSE decreased from 3.5 to 0.75, MAE decreased from 1.75 to 0.5. All three measurements deceased trend become weaker.

4.2   Privacy Level vs RMSE and MAE

In term of privacy level and the quality of the predictions, similarly, we setup a decay factor to observe the impact of parameters weight of location and number of ϵ in sequential composition mechanism which is mapped, the ω_h is fixed as 0.5. As Fig. 3 shows, both RMSE and MAE decreased while the value of privacy level are increased. The lowest value indicate to highest quality privacy protection which means the closest location to present location provides not only the best privacy protection but also the best prediction accuracy.

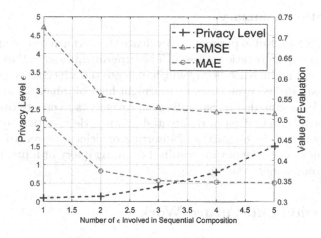

Fig. 3. Privacy level vs RMSE and MAE

4.3   Privacy Preserving vs Non Privacy Preserving

As Fig. 4 shows, we compare the RMSE and MAE under privacy preserving and without privacy preserving, the scale of location weight parameter ω_h has been set between 0 to 1, the step size of ω_h is 0.005. The smallest value of ω_h indicate traditional recommendation algorithm without consider any location information, the largest value of ω_h indicate use the data only in a specific location. In Fig. 4, both evaluation method perform better when location weight ω_h is close to 0.96. The prediction result under privacy preserving is very close to the performance of prediction output without privacy preserving and they show very similar movement trend as ω_h value change.

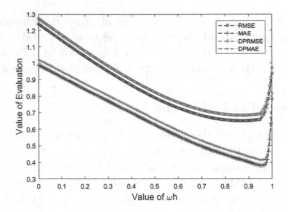

Fig. 4. Privacy preserving vs non privacy preserving

4.4   Evaluation Summary

We have conduct a set of experiment to evaluate the performance of our proposed privacy preserving aggregation scheme. The experiments shows that the privacy level remain low and increase slowly which indicate the adversaries can not easily gain more sensitive data even the attacker might have obtained some background knowledge. We have made corresponding improvements to ensure that the entire proposal meets the definition of differential privacy. Besides that, our proposed scheme ensures that the operation of inserting or deleting a record in a certain data set will not affect the output result of counting query or a prediction in the fog-based recommender system;

5   Conclusion and Future Work

In this paper, we propose a privacy-preserving aggregation scheme for fog-based recommender system, the proposed practical system make sure that privacy is under protection by implementing the ϵ differential privacy, while the fog-based recommender system still able to provide accurate predictions.

In future research, we intend to explore our research to the filed of more fog-based application and scenarios, we will identify certain attack technique against fog computing and try to find proper solutions.

References

1. Alrawais, A., Alhothaily, A., Chunqiang, H., Cheng, X.: Fog computing for the internet of things: security and privacy issues. IEEE Internet Comput. **21**(2), 34–42 (2017)
2. Bell, R.M., Koren, Y., Volinsky, C.: The bellkor solution to the netflix prize. Kor-Bell Team's Report to Netflix (2007)

3. Bonomi, F., Milito, R., Natarajan, P., Zhu, J.: Fog computing: a platform for internet of things and analytics. In: Big Data and Internet of Things: A Roadmap for Smart Environments, pp. 169–186 (2014)
4. Bonomi, F., Milito, R., Zhu, J., Addepalli, S.: Fog computing and its role in the internet of things. In: Proceedings of the First Edition of the MCC Workshop on Mobile Cloud Computing, pp. 13–16. ACM (2012)
5. Chiang, M., Zhang, T.: Fog and IoT: an overview of research opportunities. IEEE Internet of Things J. 3(6), 854–864 (2016)
6. Dastjerdi, A.V., Gupta, H., Calheiros, R.N., Ghosh, S.K., Buyya, R.: Fog computing: principles, architectures, and applications. In: Internet of Things: Principles and Paradigms, pp. 61–75 (2016)
7. Dwork, C.: Differential privacy: a survey of results. In: Agrawal, M., Du, D., Duan, Z., Li, A. (eds.) TAMC 2008. LNCS, vol. 4978, pp. 1–19. Springer, Heidelberg (2008). https://doi.org/10.1007/978-3-540-79228-4_1
8. Dwork, C., Roth, A., et al.: The algorithmic foundations of differential privacy. Found. Trends Theor. Comput. Sci. 9(3–4), 211–407 (2014)
9. Global Mobile Data Traffic Forecast: Cisco visual networking index: global mobile data traffic forecast update, 2017–2022. Update 2017, 2022 (2019)
10. Gu, B.S., Gao, L., Wang, X., Qu, Y., Jin, J., Yu, S.: Privacy on the edge: customizable privacy-preserving context sharing in hierarchical edge computing. IEEE Trans. Netw. Sci. Eng. (2019)
11. Mouradian, C., Naboulsi, D., Yangui, S., Glitho, R.H., Morrow, M.J., Polakos, P.A.: A comprehensive survey on fog computing: state-of-the-art and research challenges. IEEE Commun. Surv. Tutor. 20(1), 416–464 (2018)
12. Mukherjee, M., et al.: Security and privacy in fog computing: challenges. IEEE Access 5, 19293–19304 (2017)
13. Naha, R.K., et al.: Fog computing: survey of trends, architectures, requirements, and research directions. IEEE Access 6, 47980–48009 (2018)
14. OpenFog Consortium Architecture Working Group. OpenFog Reference Architecture for Fog Computing. OpenFogConsortium, (February), 1–162 (2017)
15. Qu, Y., Nosouhi, M.R., Cui, L., Yu, S.: Privacy preservation in smart cities. In: Smart Cities Cybersecurity and Privacy, pp. 75–88 (2019)
16. Qu, Y., Pokhrel, S.R., Garg, S., Gao, L., Xiang, Y.: A blockchained federated learning framework for cognitive computing in industry 4.0 networks. IEEE Trans. Ind. Inf. (2020)
17. Qu, Y., Yu, S., Gao, L., Niu, J.: Big data set privacy preserving through sensitive attribute-based grouping. In: 2017 IEEE International Conference on Communications (ICC), pp. 1–6. IEEE (2017)
18. Qu, Y., Shui, Yu., Gao, L., Zhou, W., Peng, S.: A hybrid privacy protection scheme in cyber-physical social networks. IEEE Trans. Comput. Soc. Syst. 5(3), 773–784 (2018)
19. Qu, Y., Yu, S., Zhou, W., Tian, Y.: Gan-driven personalized spatial-temporal private data sharing in cyber-physical social systems. IEEE Trans. Netw. Sci. Eng. (2020)
20. The OpenFog Consortium. OpenFog Architecture Overview. OpenFogConsortium, (February), 1–35 (2016)
21. Wang, X., Gu, B., Qu, Y., Ren, Y., Xiang, Y., Gao, L.: Reliable customized privacy-preserving in fog computing. In: ICC 2020–2020 IEEE International Conference on Communications (ICC), pp. 1–6. IEEE (2020)

22. Wang, X., et al.: A fog-based recommender system. IEEE Internet of Things J. **7**(2), 1048–1060 (2019)
23. Yousefpour, A., Ishigaki, G., Gour, R., Jue, J.P.: On reducing IoT service delay via fog offloading. IEEE Internet of Things J. **5**(2), 998–1010 (2018)
24. Zeng, X., et al.: IOTSim: a simulator for analysing IoT applications. J. Syst. Architect. **72**, 93–107 (2017)

The Impact of Differential Privacy on Model Fairness in Federated Learning

Xiuting Gu[1], Tianqing Zhu[1(✉)], Jie Li[1], Tao Zhang[2], and Wei Ren[1]

[1] China University of Geosciences, Wuhan, People's Republic of China
`tianqing.e.zhu@gmail.com`
[2] School of Computer Science with the Centre for Cyber Security and Privacy,
University of Technology Sydney, Sydney, Australia

Abstract. Federated learning is a machine learning framework where many clients (e.g. mobile devices or whole organizations) collaboratively train a model under the orchestration of a central server (e.g. service provider), while keeping the training data decentralized. Naively minimizing an aggregate loss function in such a network may disproportionately advantage or disadvantage some of the clients. Thus, federated learning could raise "unfairness" according to some fairness metrics. Differential privacy is a privacy model used to protect privacy in federated learning with bounded leakage about the presence of a specific point in the training data. Previous work showed that a reduction in accuracy induced by deep private models disproportionately impacts underrepresented groups. This motivates us to analyze the impact of differential privacy on model fairness in federated learning. In this work, we conduct extensive experiments to evaluate the impact of differential privacy on model fairness in federated learning. Experiments show that, with a proper choice of parameters, differential privacy might improve fairness with an ignoble reduction on accuracy.

Keywords: Federated learning · Differential privacy · Fairness

1 Introduction

In Federated learning (FL) [19], a model is learned by multiple clients in a decentralized model. Since the number of clients is generally large, naively minimizing the average loss in such a massive network may disproportionately advantage or disadvantage model performance on some devices. Indeed, although the accuracy may be high on average, there is no accuracy guarantee for the individual's client in the network, which leads to bias.

Previous work leave the investigation of how practical differential privacy (DP) interacts with other forms of (un)fairness to future work, noting that fairness definitions (such as equal opportunity) that treat a particular outcome as "advantaged" are not applicable to the tasks considered in federated learning.

© Springer Nature Switzerland AG 2020
M. Kutyłowski et al. (Eds.): NSS 2020, LNCS 12570, pp. 419–430, 2020.
https://doi.org/10.1007/978-3-030-65745-1_25

In this work, our goal is to analyze what is the impact of DP [9] on model fairness in federated learning. We train federated learning neural networks separately using two models with DP: local model and trusted curator model. We further compare these two cases with the baseline (federated learning without differential privacy) quantified by three fairness metrics.

In this paper, we show that noise addition and gradient clipping, the core techniques of differentially private stochastic gradient descent (DP-SGD) [1], affect the distance of different subgroups divided by the sensitive attribute of a dataset in the federated learning model. In the case of adding local differential privacy or adding global differential privacy, when noise scale and gradient clipping are properly chosen, the DP model may reduce the bias comparing with the non-DP model. The cost of differential privacy is an ignoble reduction in model accuracy.

Contributions. First, we evaluated the impact of differential privacy on model fairness in federated learning with three datasets over three fairness metrics. Second, we measured the effects of different hyperparameters on model fairness in federated learning. Finally, through extensive experiments on three real-world datasets we conclude that DP might improve fairness with a little sacrifice of accuracy with apposite parameters.

2   Related Work

2.1   Fairness in Federated Learning

In classical centralized machine learning setting, a substantial amount of advancement has been made in the past decade to train fair classifiers, such as constrained optimization, post-shifting approaches, and distributionally-robust optimization [4]. [3] demonstrates that, in the neural networks, the cost of training using differentially private stochastic gradient descent (DP-SGD) is not borne equally: accuracy of DP models drops much more for the underrepresented classes and subgroups, did not solve the bias in the training data listed in [14] which will result unfair. In [16] define the desired fairness criteria for federated learning, equivalent to the Distributed learning of deep neural network [12], which define fairness as the variance of the accuracy distribution across devices in federated learning. It has been observed that the bias in the data-generating process can also drive unfairness in the resulting models learned from data [10]. Research [21] explicates the various choices and assumptions made–often implicitly–to justify the use of prediction based decisions that can raise concerns about fairness.

3 Preliminaries

3.1 Differential Privacy

Basic Concepts of Differential Privacy. We use the standard definitions [7,9]. A randomized mechanism M : $D \leftarrow R$ with a domain D and range R satisfies (ϵ, δ)-differential privacy if for any two adjacent datasets d, d'$\in D$ and for any subset of outputs $S \subseteq R$, $\Pr[M(d) \in S] \leq e^{\epsilon} \Pr[M(d') \in S] + \delta$.

Local and Central DP Model. Differential privacy [8] can be achieved with applying differentially private stochastic gradient descent (DP-SGD) to a mechanism that processes a single user's local dataset, with the guarantee holding with respect to any possible other local datasets d'. This model is referred to as the local model of differential privacy (LDP) [15,17,23] which has been deployed effectively by Google, Apple and Microsoft [14,22]. Global differentially private algorithms developed to date operated in the trusted curator model: all users' data is collected by the curator before privatization techniques are applied to it. This model is referred to as the Trusted curator model of differential privacy (TDP) [2]. DP federated learning bounds the influence of any participant on the model using the DP-FedAvg algorithm [20], which clips the norm for each update vector and adds Gaussian noise N $(0, \sigma^2)$ to the sum.

3.2 Fairness Metrics

Fairness Criteria in Supervised Learning. In large part, the literature has focused on formalizing fairness into quantitative definitions and using them to solve a discrimination problem in a certain dataset [18]. We use these fairness definitions which as fairness metrics.

Definition 1 *(Equal opportunity) [13]. We say that a binary predictor Y' satisfies equal opportunity with respect to A (protected attribute) and Y (outcome) if,*

$$\Pr\{Y' = 1 \mid A = 0, Y = 1\} = Pr\{Y' = 1 \mid A = 1, Y = 1\} \tag{1}$$

Equal opportunity (EOP) consider non-discrimination from the perspective of supervised learning, where the goal is to predict a true outcome Y from features X based on labeled training data while ensuring the prediction is "non-discriminatory" with respect to a specified protected attribute A. That is, to samples from the joint distribution of (X, A, Y). This data is used to construct a (possibly randomized) predictor $Y(\hat{X})$ or $Y(\hat{X}, A)$, and we also use such labeled data to test for non-discriminatory.

Definition 2 *(Equalized odds) [13]. We say that a predictor Y' satisfies equalized odds with respect to protected attribute A and outcome Y, if Y' and A are independent conditional on Y.*

$$Pr\{Y' = 1 \mid A = 0, Y = y\} = Pr\{Y' = 1 \mid A = 1, Y = y\}, y \in \{0, 1\} \tag{2}$$

Equalized odds (EOD) is a strictly stronger fairness condition than EOP [13].

Definition 3 *(Demographic parity). It ensures that the positive outcome is given to the two groups at the same rate.*

$$Pr\{Y' = 1 \mid A = 0\} = Pr\{Y' = 1 \mid A = 1\} \tag{3}$$

Demographic parity (DEP) is a common conception of non-discrimination which requires that a decision independent of the protect attribute. However, the usefulness of demographic parity can be limited if the base rates of the two groups differ, i.e. if Pr(Y=1 | A=0)!=Pr(Y=1 | A=1).

Definition 4 *(Discrimination level). It contains three variants of exact fairness metrics.*

$$\alpha = Pr\{Y' = 1 \mid A = 0, Y = 1\} - Pr\{Y' = 1 \mid A = 1, Y = 1\} \tag{4}$$

$$\beta = Pr\{Y' = 1 \mid A = 0, Y = y\} - Pr\{Y' = 1 \mid A = 1, Y = y\}, y \in \{0, 1\} \tag{5}$$

$$\theta = Pr\{Y' = 1 \mid A = 0\} - Pr\{Y' = 1 \mid A = 1\} \tag{6}$$

In [6], the authors define equal opportunity as exact fairness. For ease of notation, they define subgroups in the database based upon group membership and true labeling the paper use A-discrimination as the notion of approximate fairness, which requires that group-conditional true positive rates are not different by more than A. In our work, we use the A-discrimination as fairness metric-approximate fairness. For three fairness metrics, we get three results (α, β, θ) to express the fairness utility.

4   Evaluation and Analysis

In this section, we first describe the implementation of LDP, GDP and aggregation of LDP and GDP. Then, we evaluate our method on three real-world datasets under the fairness metric of demographic parity, equal opportunity, and equal odds. Finally, we analyze the impact of parameters, including training epochs and noise scale. The aim of our experiments is to assess: the impact of differential privacy on model fairness in the federated learning setting.

4.1   Experimental Setup

We use a recent federated learning benchmark LEAF [5] to implement differential privacy, federated learning models. We use three fairness metrics which all get a result representing the difference between groups with the sensitive attribute as 0 or 1. When the result is smaller, fairness is better. Due to the limit of data rows, we use 5 participants per round. Dataset is split into five parts randomly.

Implement LDP. To add local differential privacy, we use local differential privacy to perform a few pieces of training on a set of hyperparameters: LR, clipping bound, and noise scale. LR is the global learning rate of federated learning models, clipping bound is to bound gradients on the update vector of every client before sending to the server, noise scale is the scale of Gaussian noise on update vector after gradient clipping of differential privacy in DP-SGD.

Implement GDP. To implement global differential privacy, we use the DP-FedAvg algorithm to perform the training on a set of hyperparameters: LR and σ. LR is the global learning rate of the federated learning model, σ is the differential privacy Gaussian noise parameter on the sum of the update vector after gradient clipping added on server aggregation. The norm of gradient clipping is decided by a model [11] using update vectors which can be found in our code. In this work, we do not set the global clip norms as a parameter.

Implement LDP and GDP. The third model type Both-DP: Simultaneously add global and local differential privacy.

4.2 Classification of the Adult Dataset

Dataset. UCI Adult dataset[1] contains over 40,000 rows of information describing adults from the 1994 US Census. We aim to predict each person's income category (either greater or less than 50K/year). We take the sensitive attribute to be gender, which is listed as Male or Female.

Model. Every participant in our federated learning uses a linear regression model, stochastic gradient descent optimization algorithm, 0.01 learning rate, and batch size 10. We run 300 epochs of training to get non-DP (non - differential privacy) the result with hyperparameter values: learning rate (LR) = 0.01 as baseline contains model accuracy and fairness.

Results. Fairness result and accuracy of different privacy models in federated learning see Fig. 1 and 2. Figure 1(a) shows that when the noise is on a good value, the local-DP model reduces the fairness metrics compare to the non-DP model, which means bias between different groups of the sensitive attribute is optimized. Figure 1(b) shows that when the global-DP noise is bigger, the fairness metrics is on a bigger value, which means bias is aggravated. When adding global-DP on the local-DP model to get both-DP model, the bias jump to a huge value. We believe that this is because the differential privacy noise is not properly chosen. Figure 1(a) shows that the DP models almost matches the accuracy of the non-DP model.

---

[1] https://archive.ics.uci.edu/ml/datasets/adult.

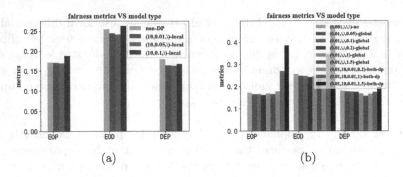

Fig. 1. The fairness metrics result of the adult dataset.

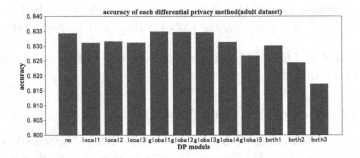

Fig. 2. The accuracy comparison of the adult dataset.

4.3 Classification of Bank Data

Dataset. UCI Bank Marketing dataset[2] is related to direct marketing campaigns (phone calls) of a Portuguese banking institution. The classification goal is to predict if the client will subscribe a term deposit (variable y). The dataset contains over 45000 rows of information describing clients' information. We take the sensitive attribute as whether a client has a personal loan.

Model. Every participant in our federated learning use a two hidden layer Neural Networks model, stochastic gradient descent optimization algorithm, 0.0001 learning rate, and batch size 10. We run 300 epochs of training to get non-DP results as baseline contains model accuracy and fairness. We calculate group distance of different sensitive group.

Result. Fairness metrics result and accuracy of different privacy models in federated learning see Figs. 3 and 4. Figure 4(a) shows that when the noise is on a good value, the local-DP model reduces the fairness metrics compare to the non-DP model, which means bias between different groups of a sensitive attribute is

---

[2] https://archive.ics.uci.edu/ml/datasets/Bank+Marketing.

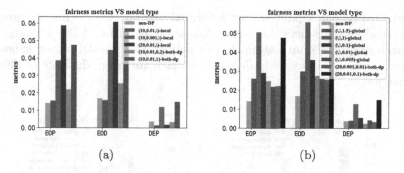

(a)   (b)

Fig. 3. The fairness metrics result of the bank dataset.

optimized. Figure 4(b) shows that when the global-DP noise is bigger, the fairness metrics is on a bigger value, which means bias is aggravated. Figure 4(b) shows that When adding global-DP on the local-DP model to get both-DP model, the bias jump to a huge value. We believe that this is because the differential privacy noise is not properly chosen. The differential privacy noise of both-DP model is the collective effect of local noise and global noise. Figure 4 shows that the DP model almost matches the accuracy of the non-DP model.

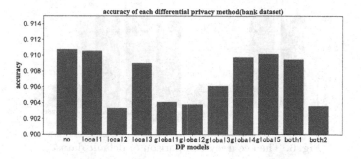

Fig. 4. The accuracy comparison of the bank dataset.

4.4 Classification of Clients' Default

Dataset. UCI default of credit card clients Dataset[3] aims at the case of customers default payments in Taiwan and compares the predictive accuracy of probability of default among six data mining methods. The classification goal is to predict accurately estimate the real probability of default. The dataset contains over 30000 rows of information. We take the sensitive attribute to be gender, which lists as Male or Female.

---

[3] https://archive.ics.uci.edu/ml/datasets/default+of+credit+card+clients.

Model. Every participant in our federated learning uses a linear regression model, stochastic gradient descent optimization algorithm, 0.001 learning rate, and batch size 10. We run 300 epochs of training to get non-DP result as baseline contains model accuracy and fairness. We calculate group distance of different sensitive group.

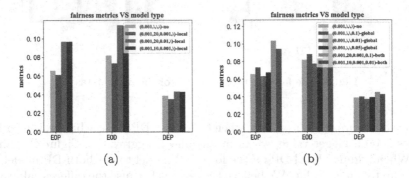

Fig. 5. The fairness metric result of the default dataset.

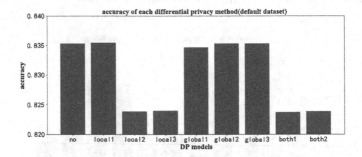

Fig. 6. The accuracy comparison of default dataset

Result. Fairness metrics result and accuracy of different privacy models in federated learning see Figs. 5 and 6. Figure 5(a) shows that when the noise is on a good value, the local-DP model reduces the fairness metrics result compare to the non-DP model, which means bias between different groups divided by sensitive attribute is optimized. Figure 5(b) shows that when the noise is on a good value, the global-DP model reduces the fairness metrics compare to the non-DP model, which means bias between different groups of a sensitive attribute is optimized. When adding global-DP on the local-DP model to get both-DP model, the bias jump to a huge value. We believe that this is because the differential privacy noise is not properly chosen. Figure 6 shows that the DP model almost matches the accuracy of the non-DP model.

4.5 Impact of Parameters

Different configurations is chosen for local-DP and global-DP with different hyperparameters basis on a good accuracy to achieve a good fair result. In Sect. 4.2, 4.3, We train the model without differential privacy to achieve good accuracy and determine hyperparameters that are not related to dp first. Then add local and global dp respectively and use several sets of different LDP and GDP hyperparameters based on training without dp to achieve fairness metric.

To know why local-DP and global-DP perform good in some settings while perform bad in other settings, we measure the effects of different hyperparameters, we use a bank dataset based on a federated learning model without differential privacy. We calculate group distance between the different sensitive group. We compare three fairness metrics as a result of model fairness.

Impact of Training Epochs. Every participant in our federated learning use a two hidden layer Neural Networks model, stochastic gradient descent optimization algorithm, 0.001 learning rate, and batch size 10, no gradient clipping.

Training a model for longer in every client may produce higher accuracy and higher fairness as Fig. 7 shows. However, that longer training can still saturate the accuracy of the DP model without matching the accuracy of the non-DP model in federated learning. Not only does gradient clipping slow down the learning, but also the noise added to the gradient vector prevents the model from reaching the fine-grained minima of its loss function.

Impact of Noise Scale. DP-SGD computes a separate gradient for each training example and add random noise before averages them per class on each batch. To understand how the noise behaves, we first run DP-SGD without clipping or noise. As Fig. 7 shows, accuracy and fairness metrics can get a good result after training. We run DP-SGD but clip gradients without adding noise. After 90 epochs, the fairness metrics and accuracy didn't change. Next, we run DP-SGD but adding noise with clip gradients as a hyperparameters 10. As Fig. 8 shows, training a model for a larger noise within a certain range in every client may

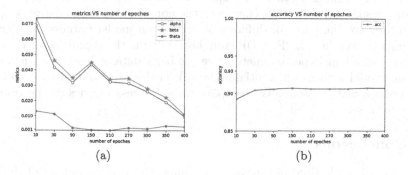

(a)   (b)

Fig. 7. Effect of epochs for fairness

produce limited higher accuracy and loss of fairness. However, a larger noise can still saturate the accuracy of the DP model without matching the accuracy of the non-DP model in federated learning.

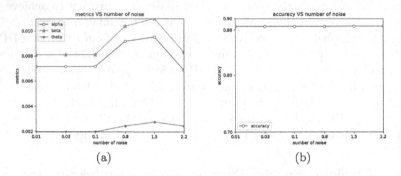

(a)   (b)

Fig. 8. Effect of noise for fairness

Discussion and Summary. As intuitively expected, noise scale and gradient clipping in DP-SGD have a major impact on the achieved model performance. A proper value of noise added by LDP or σ added by GDP, model accuracy does not reduce much, and the discrimination level stays significantly better than the non-DP. We conjecture that, with a fixed clipping bound, noise may result in a disparate accuracy drop because noise can affect the direction of gradient updates, especially when the noise scale is large enough. Clipping and noise are (separately) standard regularization techniques but their combination in DP-SGD disproportionately impacts underrepresented classes. With the datasets containing bias, we guess that noise with a fixed clipping results in a better fairness performance because noise addition and gradient clipping degrades model accuracy. In binary classification, it is believed that fairness is at the cost of accuracy. Here, we also believe that DP may improve model fairness in federated learning with the cost of model accuracy. Differential privacy can decrease the distance between sensitive groups. The fairness performance may be the opposite result if the datasets change to the non-discrimination datasets.

To measure the effect of differential privacy on model fairness in federated learning, we conduct LDP, GDP and both-DP on three real-world datasets. We study different hyperparameters, we use bank dataset based on a federated learning model without differential privacy. We calculate group distance between a different sensitive group. We compare three fairness metrics as the result of model fairness.

5   Conclusions

Random noise addition and gradient clipping, the core technique of differential privacy affect the distance of different subgroups divided by the sensitive attribute of three real-world datasets. In the condition of adding local differential privacy or adding global differential privacy, when the noise is on a good value with a stable clipping bound, the DP model reduces the fairness metrics of the non-DP model, which means bias between different groups of the sensitive attributes is optimized. When the noise is bigger than a good value with a stable clipping bound, the fairness metrics is on a bigger value, which means bias is aggravated. The cost of differential privacy is an ignoble reduction in the model's accuracy in the case of the limited noise adding and gradient clipping. DP model almost matches the accuracy of the original, non-DP model. We demonstrate this effect for three classification tasks with real-world datasets and hope that our results motivate further research on combining fairness and privacy in practical federated learning models. We not identify whether fairness performance will be the opposite result if the datasets change to the non-discrimination datasets and hope that our results motivate further research on the fairness performance of non-discrimination datasets in DP federated learning.

Acknowledgement. The research was financially supported by National Natural Science Foundation of China (No.61972366), the Foundation of Key Laboratory of Network Assessment Technology, Chinese Academy of Sciences (No. KFKT2019-003), the Foundation of Guangxi Key Laboratory of Cryptography and Information Security (No. GCIS201913), and the Foundation of Guizhou Provincial Key Laboratory of Public Big Data (No. 2018BDKFJJ009, No. 2019BDKFJJ003, No. 2019BDKFJJ011).

References

1. Abadi, M., et al.: Deep learning with differential privacy. In: Proceedings of the 2016 ACM SIGSAC Conference on Computer and Communications Security, pp. 308–318 (2016)
2. Avent, B., Korolova, A., Zeber, D., Hovden, T., Livshits, B.: Blender: enabling local search with a hybrid differential privacy model. J. Priv. Confidentiality **9**(2), 747–764 (2017)
3. Bagdasaryan, E., Shmatikov, V.: Differential privacy has disparate impact on model accuracy. In: Advances in Neural Information Processing Systems, pp. 15479–15488 (2019)
4. Bilal Zafar, M., Valera, I., Gomez Rodriguez, M., Gummadi, K.P.: Fairness constraints: mechanisms for fair classification. In: Artificial Intelligence and Statistics, pp. 962–970 (2015)
5. Caldas, S., et al.: Leaf: A benchmark for federated settings. arXiv preprint arXiv:1812.01097 (2018)
6. Cummings, R., Gupta, V., Kimpara, D., Morgenstern, J.: On the compatibility of privacy and fairness. In: Adjunct Publication of the 27th Conference on User Modeling, Adaptation and Personalization, pp. 309–315 (2019)
7. Dwork, C.: A firm foundation for private data analysis. Commun. ACM **54**(1), 86–95 (2011)
8. Dwork, C., McSherry, F., Nissim, K., Smith, A.: Calibrating noise to sensitivity in private data analysis. In: Halevi, S., Rabin, T. (eds.) TCC 2006. LNCS, vol. 3876, pp. 265–284. Springer, Heidelberg (2006). https://doi.org/10.1007/11681878_14

9. Dwork, C., Roth, A.: The algorithmic foundations of differential privacy. Found. Trends Theor. Comput. Sci. **9**(3–4), 211–407 (2014)
10. Eckhouse, L., Lum, K., Conti-Cook, C., Ciccolini, J.: Layers of bias: a unified approach for understanding problems with risk assessment. Crim. Justice Behav. **46**(2), 185–209 (2018)
11. Geyer, R.C., Klein, T., Nabi, M.: Differentially private federated learning: a client level perspective. arXiv preprint arXiv:1712.07557 (2017)
12. Gupta, O., Raskar, R.: Distributed learning of deep neural network over multiple agents. J. Netw. Comput. Appl. **116**, 1–8 (2018)
13. Hardt, M., Price, E., Srebro, N.: Equality of opportunity in supervised learning. Adv. Neural Inf. Process. Syst. **29**, 3315–3323 (2016)
14. Kairouz, P., et al.: Advances and open problems in federated learning. arXiv: Learning (2019)
15. Kasiviswanathan, S.P., Lee, H.K., Nissim, K., Raskhodnikova, S., Smith, A.: What can we learn privately? In: Proceedings of the 54th Annual Symposium on Foundations of Computer Science, pp. 531–540 (2008)
16. Li, T., Sanjabi, M., Smith, V.: Fair resource allocation in federated learning. arXiv: Learning (2019)
17. Madden, M., Rainie, L., Project, P.I.: Americans' attitudes about privacy, security and surveillance
18. Madras, D., Creager, E., Pitassi, T., Zemel, R.: Learning adversarially fair and transferable representations. arXiv preprint arXiv:1802.06309 (2018)
19. Mcmahan, H.B., Moore, E., Ramage, D., Hampson, S., Arcas, B.A.Y.: Communication-efficient learning of deep networks from decentralized data. In: Artificial Intelligence and Statistics, pp. 1273–1282 (2016)
20. Mcmahan, H.B., Ramage, D., Talwar, K., Zhang, L.: Learning differentially private recurrent language models. arXiv preprint arXiv:1710.06963 (2017)
21. Mitchell, S., Potash, E., Barocas, S., D'Amour, A., Lum, K.: Prediction-based decisions and fairness: a catalogue of choices, assumptions, and definitions. arXiv preprint arXiv:1811.07867 (2018)
22. Tran, B., Li, J., Madry, A.: Spectral signatures in backdoor attacks. In: Advances in Neural Information Processing Systems, pp. 8000–8010 (2018)
23. Warner, S.L.: Randomized response: a survey technique for eliminating evasive answer bias. J. Am. Stat. Assoc. **60**(309), 63–69 (1965)

Evading Stepping-Stone Detection with Enough Chaff

Henry Clausen[1(✉)], Michael S. Gibson[2], and David Aspinall[1,3]

[1] University of Edinburgh, Edinburgh, UK
{henry.clausen,david.aspinall}@ed.ac.uk
[2] BT Applied Research, Ipswich, UK
michael.s.gibson@bt.com
[3] The Alan Turing Institute, London, UK

Abstract. Stepping-stones are used extensively by attackers to hide their identity and access restricted targets. Many methods have been proposed to detect stepping-stones and resist evasive behaviour, but so far no benchmark dataset exists to provide a fair comparison of detection rates. We propose a comprehensive framework to simulate realistic stepping-stone behaviour that includes effective evasion tools, and release a large dataset, which we use to evaluate detection rates for eight state-of-the-art methods. Our results show that detection results for several methods fall behind the claimed detection rates, even without the presence of evasion tactics. Furthermore, currently no method is capable to reliably detect stepping-stone when the attacker inserts suitable chaff perturbations, disproving several robustness claims and indicating that further improvements of existing detection models are necessary.

1 Introduction

The problem of stepping-stones detection (SSD) has been studied for over 20 years, yet the body of literature fails at providing an informative overview of the detection capabilities of current methods. In this paper, we set out to do just that by evaluating and comparing a number of selected state-of-the-art approaches on a new and independently generated dataset.

In a stepping-stone attack, malicious commands are relayed via a chain of compromised hosts, called stepping-stones, in order to access restricted resources and reduce the chance of being traced back. Real-world attacks using stepping-stone chains include Operation Aurora [19], Operation Night Dragon [1], the Black Energy [13] attack on the Ukrainian powergrid, and the MEDJACK [3] attack where medical devices were used as stepping-stones. The European Union Agency for Cybersecurity currently classifies stepping-stone attacks as one of the top ten threats to IoT-devices [8].

The detection of interactive stepping-stones is challenging due to various reasons. Attackers are not constrained to specific proxy techniques and can obfuscate relayed traffic with evasive tactics. Packet-based methods are computationally expensive while false-positives can render a method unusable. Like many

© Springer Nature Switzerland AG 2020
M. Kutyłowski et al. (Eds.): NSS 2020, LNCS 12570, pp. 431–446, 2020.
https://doi.org/10.1007/978-3-030-65745-1_26

intrusion attacks, stepping-stones are rare and there exist no public datasets, leading researchers to evaluate their methods on self-provided private data, which makes a direct comparison of the achieved results impossible.

In this work, we provide the following contributions:

1. We describe a framework to generate data that represents realistic stepping-stone data without bias to particular detection mechanisms. Our framework is scalable and capable of generating sufficient variety in terms of network settings and conducted activity.
2. We release a large and comprehensive dataset suitable for the training of machine-learning-based methods and in-depth performance evaluation. To our knowledge, this is the first public SSD dataset.
3. We re-implemented eight SSD methods that represent the current state-of-the-art and provide a fair evaluation of their capabilities in a number of settings.
4. Our evaluation shows that while most methods can accurately detect command propagation, detection rates plummet when appropriate chaff is inserted. This result disproves the claims made for multiple methods that their detection rates are robust against chaff perturbations.

The rest of the paper is organised as following: Sect. 1 provides an introduction and background to the problem of stepping-stone detection. Section 2 discusses the particular design of the data generation framework. Section 3 presents the dataset arrangement in terms of background and attack data and discusses evaluation methods. Section 4 discusses the selection process, properties, and implementation of the eight SSD methods that we implemented for evaluation. Section 5 discusses the results achieved by the implemented methods on the given data. Section 6 discusses related work.

1.1   Background

Stepping-stones were first conceptualised by Staniford-Chen and Heberlein in 1995 [18]. In an interactive stepping-stone attack, an attacker located at the origin host, called *host O*, sends commands to and awaits their response from a target, *host T*. The commands and responses are proxied via a chain of one or more intermediary stepping-stone hosts, called *host* S_1, ..., S_N, such as depicted in Fig. 1. Once a host S_i is brought under control, it can be turned into a stepping-stone with simple tools and steps. Some of the most common set-ups are port forwarding via SSH-tunnels, setting up a backpipe with NetCat, or using metasploit to set up a SOCKS proxy [9].

Stepping-stone detection (SSD) is a process of observing all incoming and outgoing connections on a particular host h_i and determining whether it is used to relay commands. This is generally done with no prior information about any other stepping-stone hosts $S_1, \ldots S_N$ or the endpoints O and T. A popular approach to SSD is to compare connections pairwise to identify whether they carry the same information. To avoid detection, several evasive flow transformation

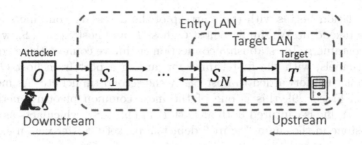

Fig. 1. Depiction of an exemplary stepping-stone chain.

techniques exist that aim at decreasing observable correlation between two connections in a chain.

- **Packet transfer delays/drops**: An attacker can choose to apply artificial delays to forwarded packets, or drop certain packets to cause retransmission, in order to create temporal disparity between connections. Researchers often assume the existence of a maximum tolerable delay [7].
- **Chaff perturbations**: Chaff packets do not contain meaningful content and are added to individual connections in a chain without being forwarded. Adding chaff perturbations can be used to shape the connection profile towards other traffic types.
- **Repacketisation**: Repacketisation is the practice of combining closely adjacent packets into a larger packet, splitting a packet into multiple smaller packets, or altering the packet content to change observed packet sizes and numbers.

In our evaluation, we set out to understand the effect of different evasive methods on detection rates.

2 Data Generation Setting

2.1 Containerisation

To ensure reproducibility, we rely on containerisation. A container is a standard unit of software that runs standalone in an isolated user space in order to remove platform dependencies and ensure repeatability. The use of containerisation for this project follows a traffic generation paradigm designed for machine learning, introduced by Clausen et al. [4].

2.2 Simulating Stepping Stones with SSH-Tunnels and Docker

We want to capture data not only from one interaction in a fixed stepping-stone chain, but from many interactions and chains with different settings. For that, we run multiple simulations, with each simulation establishing a stepping-stone chain and controlling the interactions between host O and host T.

A simulation begins with the start-up of the necessary containers and ends with their takedown. We simulate host O, host T, and host $S_1, \ldots, S_n$ with SSH-daemon containers. To establish a connection chain, we connect these containers via SSH-tunnels, with the first tunnel forwarding a port from host O to host S_1, which is then forwarded to host S_2 by the second tunnel etc. As mentioned by Gordon Fraser [9], this is one of the most common pivoting methods for attackers. Traffic is captured both at host T and host S_n, which acts as the final stepping-stone in the chain. Figure 2 depicts a packet transfer via an exemplary chain.

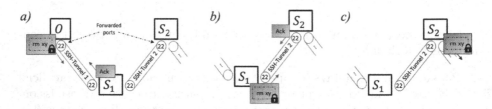

Fig. 2. Depiction of the way a command is packetised, encrypted, and travels through the different stages of the stepping-stone chain via SSH-tunnels.

Simulating Interactive SSH-traffic. In order to generate enough data instances representing interactive stepping stone behaviour, we automatised the communication between host O and host T. For each simulation, we generate a script which passes SSH-commands from host O to host T.

To mimic a user's actions, we compiled a command database which consists of common commands and their usage frequency, similar to [24]. Commands are drawn randomly according to their usage frequency and concatenated to a script. Commands can either be atomic, such as "ls-la" or "pwd", or compound commands such as inputting text to a file. Command inputs are randomized appropriately when a compound command is drawn. A scripts ends once the *End*-command is drawn at random from the command catalogue.

To simulate human behaviour that is reacting to the response from host T, all commands are separated by *sleep*-commands for time t, which is drawn from a truncated Pareto-distribution. Paxson et al. [16] have shown that interpacket spacings corresponding to typing and "think time" pauses are well described by Pareto distributions with a shape parameter $\alpha \approx 1.0$.

Simulating Different Network Settings. Hosts in a stepping-stone chains can be separated by varying distances. Some may sit in the same LAN, while others may communicate via the Internet from distant geographical locations, which influences the round-trip-time, bandwidth, and network reliability.

To retard the quality of the Docker network to realistic levels, we rely on the emulation tool NetEm, which allows users to artificially simulate network conditions such as high latency, low bandwidth, or packet corruption/drop [10]. We set the network settings and bandwidth limit for each host container individually before each simulation to allow hosts to experience different settings.

2.3 Evasive Tactics

Adding Transfer Delays. To simulate evasive behaviour, we add transfer delays to forwarded packets. This method, often called *jittering*, can destroy time-based watermarks in packet flows and help decrease observable correlation between two connections. The delays are added using NetEm. We draw delays from a uniform distribution, covering the interval $[0, \delta_D]$. This particular choice has been suggested by Padhye et al. [15] in order to mimic the interarrival distributions of streaming services. The value of δ_D is fixed before each simulation and can be varied to allow for different degrees of packet jittering. We explore values for δ_D up to 1500 ms, with values above leading to unstable communication. Results in Sect. 5 show that this is enough to render watermarking methods and most flow correlation methods obsolete.

Adding Chaff Perturbation. We insert chaff packets without actual information to individual connections in the chain using a Netcat client. To add and filter packets in a connection, we open additional ports in each SSH-tunnel that are however not forwarded through the entire chain. Padhye et al. [15] suggest to generate chaff that mimics the flow characteristics of streaming services to both spread the added perturbations evenly across the connection and increase the difficulty of detecting the perturbation itself. For this, packet sizes are drawn from a truncated Lognormal-distribution with mean μ_C, while transmission intervals are drawn from a uniform distribution that covers the interval $[\delta_C/2, \delta_C]$ to mimic a constant packet flow. By adjusting δ_C, we can control the amount of chaff sent.

Repacketisation. By design, SSH-tunnels perform repacketisation along with re-encryption and independent packet confirmations.

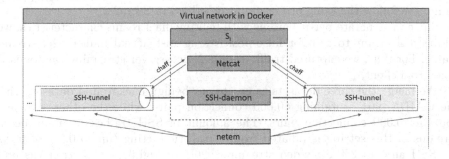

Fig. 3. Depiction the simulation setup for each host in the chain.

3   Evaluation Data

We want to look at a variety of attack scenarios to highlight the strengths and weaknesses of different SSD approaches. We created three main attack datasets that contain different forms and amounts of evasive behaviour, and a smaller dataset to highlight the influence of different chain lengths.

To present a valuable false positive test, we provide three datasets with benign background traffic. The first contains general real-world traffic, while the second and third contain benign data that bears similar traffic characteristics as the generated attack data.

3.1   Stepping-Stone Data

We create our main datasets using a chain of four stepping-stones S_1, S_2, S_3, and S_4. We subdivide into three datasets: We first capture data without transfer delays and chaff perturbations in **dataset BA** (baseline attack). We then capture data once with added transfer delays with varying δ_D to control delays in **dataset DA** (delay attack), and once with added chaff perturbations of varying δ_C in **dataset CA** (chaff attack). Each dataset contains 30.000 connection pairs. We furthermore create a smaller **dataset CL** (chain length) with differing numbers of stepping-stones (1,3,5, and 8 jumps) without transfer delays and chaff perturbations.

3.2   Benign Data

We include real-world traffic traces, taken from the **CAIDA** *2018 Anonymized Internet Traces* dataset [2], as overall background traffic. This data contains traces collected from high-speed monitors on a commercial backbone link, and is often used for research on the characteristics of Internet traffic.

To sufficiently test for false-positive, we also need to include benign traffic that has similar characteristics to the attack traffic and was generated in a similar network environment. We created a set of interactive SSH-connections that communicate directly between the client and the server without a stepping-stone. We follow the same procedure as described in Sect. 2.2.

Since we generate perturbations with multimedia streams characteristics, we additionally want to test for false-positives against actual multimedia stream traffic. For that, we captured traffic from a Nginx-server streaming randomised video to a client.

We merge the three datasets to create our benign background dataset, with the CAIDA part containing 60.000 connection pairs, while the other two each contain 20.000 connection pairs. The amount of SSH traffic and multimedia streams in this setting is inflated from a realistic setting (up to 0.2% of flows for SSH and up 3% for video streaming [20]) to highlight the strengths and drawbacks of SSD methods, which we consider in the evaluation. In Sect. A, we analyze false-positives for each dataset individually. Table 1 summarizes the different parts in our evaluation data.

Table 1. Summary of different components in our evaluation data.

	Label	Nr. of conn.	Purpose
Attack data	Set BA	30.000	Baseline attack data without evasion tactics
	Set DA	30.000	Inclusion of delays with varying δ_D
	Set CA	30.000	Inclusion of chaff with varying δ_C
	Set CL	40.000	Data from chains of different lengths, no evasion tactics
Background data	CAIDA	60.000	General background data
	SSH	20.000	Background data similar to attack commands
	Multim.	20.000	Background data similar to chaff perturbations

3.3 Evaluation Methodology

To create a fair playing field for the selected SSD methods, we only look at connections that exchange more than 1500 packets and exclude shorter connections from both the data. The number of packets necessary for detection should ideally be a low possible to enable early detection. The chosen number of 1500 packets seems like a suitable minimal limit since all of the selected methods are designed to make successful detection with 300–1500 packets. Furthermore, there were no connections with less packets in the stepping-stone dataset.

True stepping stone connections are rare compared to benign ones, making their detection an imbalanced classification problem. An appropriate evaluation measure for imbalanced data are false positive and false negative rates as well as the *Area-under-ROC-curve* (AUC) for threshold-based methods.

4 Selected SSD Methods and Implementation

A range of underlying techniques exist for SSD, and we try to include approaches from every area to create an informative overview and highlight strengths and weaknesses. We surveyed publications to create a collection of SSD methods. We started with the publications from surveys [17, 21], and then added impactful recent publications found via Google Scholar[1]. From here, we selected approaches based on the following criteria:

1. The achieved detection and false positive rates claimed by the authors,
2. and whether the model design shows robustness against any evasion tactics as claimed by the authors.
3. We always selected the latest versions if a method has been improved by the authors.

Table 2 contains a summary of the included methods. Especially for traditional packet-correlation as well as robust watermarking and anomaly-based methods, there has been little developments since the early 2010s. We labelled each method to make referring to it in the evaluation easier.

---

[1] Keywords "connection", "correlation" "stepping-stone", "detection", "attack", "chaff perturbation".

Table 2. Summary of included SSD-methods along with the claimed true positive and false positive rates and evasion robustness by the corresponding authors. We added labels to each method for later reference.

Category	Approach	TP	FP	Robustness	Label
Packet-corr	Yang, 2011 [26]	100%	0%	Jitter/< 80% chaff	PContext
Neural networks	Nasr, 2018 [14]	90%	0.0002%	Small jitter	DeepCorr
	Wu, 2010 [23]	100%	0%	-	WuNeur
RTT-based	Yang, 2015 [27]	Not provided		50% chaff	RWalk
	Huang, 2016 [12]	85%	5%	-	Crossover
Anomaly-based	Crescenzo, 2011 [5]	99%	1%	Jitter/chaff	Ano1
	Huang, 2011 [6,11]	95%	0%	> 25% chaff/ > 0.2 s jitter	Ano2
Watermarking	Wang, 2011 [22]	100%	0.5%	< 1.4 s jitter	WM

PContext, 2011. Yang et al. [26] compare sequences of interarrival times in connection pairs to detect potential stepping-stone behaviour. For that, the contextual distance of a packet is defined as the packet interarrival times around that packet. The authors focus on *Echo*-packets instead of *Send*-packets to resist evasion tactics. The authors evaluate their results with up to 100% chaff ratio with 100% detection rate.

WuNeur, 2010. Wu et al. [23] propose a neural network model based on sequences of RTTs , which are fed into a feed-forward network to predict the downstream length of the chain. The network itself only contains one hidden layer and achieves good results only if RTTs are small, i.e., when the stepping-stone chain is completely contained within one LAN-network.

DeepCorr, 2018. Nasr et al. [14] train a deep convolutional neural network to identify connection correlation from the interarrival times and packet sizes in each connection. The trained network is large with over 200 input filters, and consists of three convolutional and three feed-forward layers. On stepping-stones, the authors achieve a 90% detection rate with 0.02% false positives.

RWalk, 2015. Yang et al. [27] combine packet-counting methods and RTT mining methods to improve detection results from [25]. The model resists chaff perturbation by estimating the number of round-trips in a connection via packet-matching and clustering to determine if the connection is being relayed.

C-Over, 2016. Huang et al. [12] use the fact that in long connection chain, the round-trip-time of a packet may be longer than the intervals between two consecutive keystrokes. This will result in cross-overs between request and response, which causes the curve of sorted upstream RTTs to rise more steeply than in a regular connection.

Ano1, 2011. Crescenzo et al. [5] have proposed an anomaly-based methods to detect time delays and chaff perturbations in a selected connection. Packet time-delays are detected if RTTs exceed a threshold, while chaff detection compares the similarity of downstream with upstream sequences. The authors claim detection for chaff ratios 25% or more, and for delays introduced to up to 70% of all packets.

Ano2, 2011/2013. Huang et al. [6,11] proposed an anomaly-based method to detect chaff and delay perturbations since interarrival times in regular connections tend to follow a Pareto or Lognormal distribution, which chaffed connections supposedly do not. The authors state 95% detection rate at 50% chaff ratio and more while retaining zero false positives using a small set of interactive SSH stepping-stone connections.

WM, 2010. Watermarking typically yields very low false-positives for connection correlation. Wang et al. [22] provide an approach that offers at least some resistance against timing perturbations. The authors assume some limits to an adversary's timing perturbations, such as a bound on the delays. The authors state 100% TP with 0.5% FP with resistance against timing perturbations of up to 1.4 s.

5 Results

5.1 Data Without Evasion Tactics

First, we look at the detection rates for traffic from stepping-stones that did not use any evasive tactics, i.e. $S_1, \ldots, S_4$ are only forwarding commands and responses. The successful detection of this activity with low false-positives should be the minimum requirement for any SSD method. Since anomaly-based approaches aim to only detect evasive behaviour, we exclude them from this analysis.

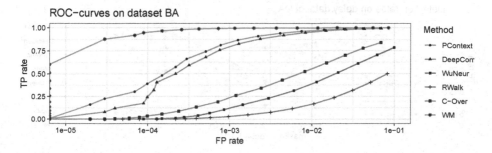

Fig. 4. ROC-curves for different SSD methods on dataset BA (no evasive tactics). Anomaly-based methods are excluded.

Table 3. AUC-scores for different methods on stepping-stone data without evasive tactics.

	PContext	DeepCorr	WuNeur	RWalk	C-Over	WM
AUC	0.998	0.997	0.938	0.853	0.965	0.9998

Figure 4 depicts the calculated ROC-curves, which plot the true positive rate against the false positive rate for varying detection thresholds. Table 3 depicts the overall AUC-scores.

Unsurprisingly, the watermarking method achieves high detection results with very low false-positives. Both the PContext and DeepCorr models start to yield good detection results of around 80% at a FP rate lower than 0.1%, with the PContext method slightly outpacing the DeepCorr method. RTT-based methods seem to not perform as well compared to the other included methods. Overall, the observed ROC curves seem to be in agreement with the stated detection rates of the selected methods except for RWalk.

5.2 Delays

We now consider the effect of transfer delays added by the attacker to packets on the detection rates. For that, we pick detection thresholds for each SSD methods corresponding to a FP rate of 0.4% as most methods are able to achieve at least moderate detection results at this rate. We look at delays added to only to outgoing packets on S_4, the last stepping stone in the chain. Figure 5 depicts evolution of detection rates in dependence of the maximum delay δ_D.

As visible, both anomaly-based methods are capable of detecting added delays relatively reliably above a certain threshold. Furthermore, both the detection rates of DeepCorr and the RTT-based C-Over only decrease slightly under the influence of delays. Detection rates for all other methods decrease significantly to the point where no meaningful predictions can be made. This is also reflected by the AUC-scores for traffic with $\delta_D = 1000$ ms, given in Table 4.

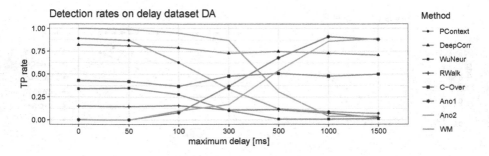

Fig. 5. Detection rates in dependence of δ_D for different methods on dataset DA with a fixed FP rate of 0.4%.

While the WM method is robust against transfer delays up to $\delta_D = 500$ ms, this value is smaller than the one claimed by the authors. This might however be a result of the slightly smaller quantisation step size that we used. It is surprising that the PContext method shows only little robustness against transfer delays, which contradicts the authors claims, potentially due to the incorrect assumption that relying on *Echo*-packets are not subject to transfer delays.

Table 4. AUC-scores for SSD methods with added transfer delays at $\delta_D = 1000$ ms.

	PContext	DeepCorr	WuNeur	RWalk	C-Over	Ano1	Ano2	WM
AUC	0.638	0.995	0.613	0.641	0.952	0.997	0.996	0.562

5.3 Chaff

We now consider the effect of chaff perturbations added by the attacker to individual connections on the detection rates. Again we pick detection thresholds for each SSD methods corresponding to a FP rate of 0.4%.

Chaff packets are added to both the connection between S_3 and S_4 as well as between S_4 and host T as described in Sect. 2.3. Figure 6 depicts evolution of detection rates in dependence of the ratio of number of chaff packets to packets from the actual interaction.

As visible, all methods struggle to detect stepping stones once the chaff packets become the majority of the transferred traffic. This is also evident from the AUC-scores given in Table 5. Several approaches claimed to be resistent to chaff perturbations, however prior evaluations were limited chaff ratios below 100% without obvious reason.

It is surprising that the anomaly detection methods do not perform better at detecting chaff perturbations. Chaff in both approaches was however evaluated

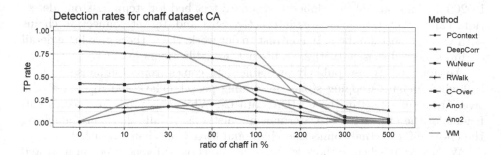

Fig. 6. Detection rates in dependence of δ_C for different methods on dataset CA with a fixed FP rate of 0.4%

with different traffic generation distribution and not compared against a background of traffic following a similar generation distribution, which could explain the disagreement between the results we are finding here.

Overall, these results are in disagreement with the "robustness" claims made for four of the selected approaches, namely PContext, RWalk, Ano1, and Ano2.

Table 5. AUC-scores for SSD methods with added chaff at 300% ratio.

	PContext	DeepCorr	WuNeur	RWalk	C-Over	Ano1	Ano2	WM
AUC	0.639	0.886	0.615	0.641	0.589	0.782	0.738	0.839

5.4 Summary

Overall, detection rates on dataset BA are mostly in line with the claimed capabilities except for RWalk, although detection rates are slightly lower than stated by most authors. Delay perturbation increases detection difficulty for most methods, except for Ano1, Ano2, and DeepCorr, which contradicts robustness claims for PContext and to some extend WM. Our inserted chaff perturbations however render detection impossible for all methods examined, which contradicts robustness claims for PContext, Ano1, Ano2, and RWalk, even though the claims were based on lower chaff levels.

As discussed in Sect. B and C, longer chains yield higher detection rates for RTT-based methods while Different network transmission settings seem to have overall little influence on detection rates.

6   Related Work

6.1   Testbeds and Data

In 2006, Xin et al. [24] developed a standard test bed for stepping-stone detection, called *SST* that generates interactive SSH and TelNet connection chains with variable host numbers. In contrast to our work, the authors give little detail on implemented evasive tactics, and is not available anymore.

An approach to use publicly available data comes from Houmansadr et al. [14],who simulate stepping stones by adding packet delays and drops retroactively to connections in the CAIDA data [2]. While this procedure seems sufficient for the evaluation of watermarking methods, it falls short on simulating the effects of an actual connection chain and leaves out chaff perturbations.

We find that when authors evaluate methods on self-generated data, tested evasive behaviours are often lacking analytical discussion and their implementations are too simplistic, leading to increased detection rates. An example of this can be seen in the evaluation of Ano1 [5], where a standard option in netcat is used to generate chaff perturbations for evaluation, or for PContext [27] where simulated chaff is added randomly after the traffic collection. Furthermore, often a relatively low limit on the amount of inserted chaff perturbations is assumed without obvious reason, thus avoiding evaluation at higher ratios.

7 Conclusion

In this work, we set out to evaluate the state-of-the-art of SSD methods using a comprehensive data generation framework. Our framework simulates realistic stepping-stone behaviour with SSH-tunnels in different settings and varying amounts of evasive perturbation tactics. We will release a large dataset that highlights multiple aspects in SSD, and is suitable to train ML-based methods.

Overall, our results show that attackers can reliably evade detection by using the right type and amount of chaff perturbation, which disproves several claims made about the robustness against this evasive tactic. Although to a lesser degree, our implemented delay perturbations still affect detection rates for most methods.

Currently, it seems that watermarking methods are most suited to reliably detect simple stepping-stones in real-life deployment. The performance of Deep-Corr indicates that deep neural networks show the most potential at detecting attacks that use chaff or delay perturbations if they are trained on suitable data. We find that detection and false-positive rates for RTT-based methods are significantly lower than for other methods.

Acknowledgments. We are grateful to BT Group PLC who are supporting the PhD research of the first author in the UK EPSRC CASE scheme, giving invaluable guidance on the needs and possibilities of intelligent security tools and their evaluation. The third author was supported by The Alan Turing Institute under the EPSRC grant EP/N510129/1 and the Office of Naval Research ONR NICOP award N62909-17-1-2065.

A   False Positives

Table 6 depicts the relative contribution[2] at $FP = 0.4\%$ of each of the three benign data types to the overall false positive rate. Most methods have more problems with the heterogeneous nature the CAIDA traces, with only PContext and DeepCorr seeing most false positives in the SSH traffic.

The multimedia traffic is causing most problems for the anomaly-based methods, persumably because it follows a similar distribution as the generated chaff perturbations.

---

[2] After adjusting for their weight.

Table 6. Relative contribution in % of different benign data to the FP rate.

	PContext	DeepCorr	WuNeur	RWalk	C-Over	Ano1	Ano2	WM
CAIDA	0.36	0.46	0.47	0.67	0.53	0.48	0.35	0.81
SSH	0.53	0.46	0.21	0.28	0.27	0.05	0.02	0.08
Multimedia	0.11	0.08	0.32	0.04	0.20	0.47	0.63	0.11

B   Influence of Chain Length

In this section, we look at the effect of differing chain lengths on the detection rates. We only focus on RTT-based methods here since the other methods should and do not see a significant effect from varying chain lengths[3]. Since RTT-based methods aim to measure the effect of packets travelling via multiple hosts, it is unsurprising that they perform better at detecting longer chains.

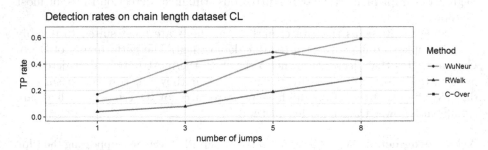

Fig. 7. Detection rates in dependence of chain length for different methods on dataset CL with a fixed FP rate of 0.4%

Of the RTT-based methods, only C-Over was able to yield consistent detection rates under transfer delays. Interestingly, if the C-Over method is applied to

Table 7. Influence of network congestion on detection rates at a fixed FP rate of 0.4%. The given percentages are describing the change of the detection rate under the given congestion setting when compared to the overall average.

	Value	TP deviation from average				
		DeepCorr	WuNeur	RWalk	C-Over	WM
RTT	5 ms	−0.2%	+41.3%	−42.3%	−36%	+0.03%
	70 ms	−5.6%	−5.8%	+35.1%	+51%	−2.2%
Packet loss	0%	+1.2%	+1.3%	+2.1%	+4.3%	+0.02%
	7%	−9.1%	−1.1%	−3.1%	−7.3%	−9.7%

---

[3] For non-RTT-methods, the detection rate error (2.6%–6.5%) for each length was larger than the detection rate differences (0.2%–3.7%) across different lengths.

connections between S_3 and S_4 instead of between S_4 and the target, detection rates decrease in the same manner as for other RTT-based methods. This is not surprising as the underlying assumption for robustness for this approach relies on Echo-packets not being delayed.

C   Influence of Network Settings

Finally, we look at the effect of different nework settings. We only show methods that show significant effects and omitted bandwidth from the evaluation as different values do not seem to have any effect on detection rates[4].

As visible in Table 7, the three RTT-based methods show different responses to small/large average round-trip-times. While WuNeur, as expected from prior results, performs better in LAN settings, detection rates of the RWalk and C-Over methods are boosted by larger RTTs. All methods profit from lower packet losses.

References

1. Mcafee technical report on night dragon operation. Technical report (2015)
2. The CAIDA UCSD Anonymized Internet Traces 2018 (2018). Accessed 10 Feb 2020
3. Ayala, L.: Active medical device cyber-attacks. Cybersecurity for Hospitals and Healthcare Facilities, pp. 19–37. Apress, Berkeley, CA (2016). https://doi.org/10.1007/978-1-4842-2155-6_3
4. Clausen, H., Flood, R., Aspinall, D.: Traffic generation using containerization for machine learning. In: Proceedings of the Dynamic and Novel Advances in Machine Learning and Intelligent Cyber Security Workshop. ACM (2019)
5. Di Crescenzo, G., Ghosh, A., Kampasi, A., Talpade, R., Zhang, Y.: Detecting anomalies in active insider stepping stone attacks. JoWUA **2**(1), 103–120 (2011)
6. Ding, W., Le, K., Huang, S.-H.S.: Detecting stepping-stones under the influence of packet jittering. In: 2013 9th International Conference on Information Assurance and Security (IAS), pp. 31–36. IEEE (2013)
7. Donoho, D.L., Flesia, A.G., Shankar, U., Paxson, V., Coit, J., Staniford, S.: Multiscale stepping-stone detection: detecting pairs of jittered interactive streams by exploiting maximum tolerable delay. In: Wespi, A., Vigna, G., Deri, L. (eds.) RAID 2002. LNCS, vol. 2516, pp. 17–35. Springer, Heidelberg (2002). https://doi.org/10.1007/3-540-36084-0_2
8. EU ENISA. Baseline security recommendations for IoT in the context of critical information infrastructures (2017)
9. Fraser, G.: Tunneling, pivoting, and web application penetration testing. Technical report, SANS (2015)
10. Hemminger, S., et al.: Network emulation with netem. In: Linux Conference au, pp. 18–23 (2005)

---

[4] For all methods, the detection rate differences (0.7%–6.2%) were smaller across bandwidths than the overall detection rate errors (2.6%–6.5%).

11. Huang, S.-H.S., Kuo, Y.-W.: Detecting chaff perturbation on stepping-stone connection. In: 2011 IEEE 17th International Conference on Parallel and Distributed Systems, pp. 660–667. IEEE (2011)

12. Huang, S.-H.S., Zhang, H., Phay, M.: Detecting stepping-stone intruders by identifying crossover packets in SSH connections. In: 2016 IEEE 30th International Conference on Advanced Information Networking and Applications (AINA), pp. 1043–1050. IEEE (2016)

13. Lee, R.M., Assante, M.J., Conway, T.: Analysis of the cyber attack onthe ukrainian power grid. Technical report, E-ISAC (2016)

14. Nasr, M., Bahramali, A., Houmansadr, A.: Deepcorr: strong flow correlation attacks on tor using deep learning. In: Proceedings of the 2018 ACM SIGSAC Conference on Computer and Communications Security, pp. 1962–1976 (2018)

15. Padhye, J.D., Kothari, K., Venkateshaiah, M., Wright, M.: Evading stepping-stone detection under the cloak of streaming media with sneak. Comput. Networks 54(13), 2310–2325 (2010)

16. Paxson, V., Floyd, S.: Wide area traffic: the failure of Poisson modeling. IEEE/ACM Trans. Networking 3(3), 226–244 (1995)

17. Shullich, R., Chu, J., Ji, P., Chen, W.: A survey of research in stepping-stone detection. Int. J. Electron. Commer. Stud. 2(2), 103–126 (2011)

18. Staniford-Chen, S., Heberlein, L.T.: Holding intruders accountable on the internet. In: Proceedings 1995 IEEE Symposium on Security and Privacy, pp. 39–49. IEEE (1995)

19. Tankard, C.: Advanced persistent threats and how to monitor and deter them. Network Secur. 2011(8), 16–19 (2011)

20. Velan, P., Medková, J., Jirsík, T., Čeleda, P.: Network traffic characterisation using flow-based statistics. In: NOMS 2016 2016 IEEE/IFIP Network Operations and Management Symposium, pp. 907–912. IEEE (2016)

21. Wang, L., Yang, J.: A research survey in stepping-stone intrusion detection. EURASIP J. Wirel. Commun. Networking 2018(1), 1–15 (2018). https://doi.org/10.1186/s13638-018-1303-2

22. Wang, X., Reeves, D.: Robust correlation of encrypted attack traffic through stepping stones by flow watermarking. IEEE Trans. Dependable Secure Comput. 8(3), 434–449 (2010)

23. Wu, H.-C., Huang, S.-H.S.: Neural networks-based detection of stepping-stone intrusion. Expert Syst. Appl. 37(2), 1431–1437 (2010)

24. Xin, J., Zhang, L., Aswegan, B., Dickerson, J., Daniels, T., Guan, Y.: A testbed for evaluation and analysis of stepping stone attack attribution techniques. In: 2nd International Conference on Testbeds and Research Infrastructures for the Development of Networks and Communities. TRIDENTCOM 2006, p. 9. IEEE (2006)

25. Yang, J., Huang, S.-H.S.: Mining TCP/IP packets to detect stepping-stone intrusion. Comput. Secur. 26(7–8), 479–484 (2007)

26. Yang, J., Woolbright, D.: Correlating TCP/IP packet contexts to detect stepping-stone intrusion. Comput. Secur. 30(6–7), 538–546 (2011)

27. Yang, J., Zhang, Y.: RTT-based random walk approach to detect stepping-stone intrusion. In: 2015 IEEE 29th International Conference on Advanced Information Networking and Applications, pp. 558–563. IEEE (2015)

Author Index

Printed in the United States
By Bookmasters